AI and Data Engineering for Healthcare

This book examines the transformative role of Artificial Intelligence (AI) and data engineering in revolutionizing the healthcare landscape. It presents cutting-edge developments ranging from predictive algorithms for disease diagnosis to large-scale data systems that enhance patient outcomes. By emphasizing the synergy between AI and data engineering, this book showcases practical applications in medical imaging, clinical diagnostics, and personalized treatment strategies.

It also thoughtfully examines ethical considerations, data privacy, and healthcare equity, particularly in underserved and rural populations.

Key Features:

- Explores state-of-the-art technologies in healthcare, including image segmentation, feature extraction, feature selection, and classification.
- Provides real-world case studies, practical examples, and hands-on exercises for the effective implementation of AI-driven solutions.
- Bridges disciplines across computer science, data engineering, and biomedical sciences to foster cross-domain collaboration.
- Highlights innovative research methodologies and their applications in AI-powered healthcare systems.
- Discusses the role of AI in improving healthcare access, delivery, and outcomes across diverse populations.

This book is ideal for professionals, researchers, and policymakers seeking to understand and shape the future of healthcare through the lens of AI and data-driven innovation.

AI and Data Engineering for Healthcare

Real-World Applications and Case Studies

Edited by

Anjan Bandyopadhyay, Tanvir Habib Sardar, Saurav Mallik, Ruhul Amin Hazarika, and Mahendra Kumar Gourisaria

CRC Press
Taylor & Francis Group
Boca Raton London New York

CRC Press is an imprint of the
Taylor & Francis Group, an **informa** business
A CHAPMAN & HALL BOOK

Designed cover image: ShutterStock

First edition published 2026
by CRC Press
2385 NW Executive Center Drive, Suite 320, Boca Raton FL 33431

and by CRC Press
4 Park Square, Milton Park, Abingdon, Oxon, OX14 4RN

CRC Press is an imprint of Taylor & Francis Group, LLC

ISBN: 9781032988467 (hbk)
ISBN: 9781032988474 (pbk)
ISBN: 9781003600947 (ebk)

DOI: 10.1201/9781003600947

Typeset in Times
by codeMantra

Contents

About the Editors

Anjan Bandyopadhyay currently serves as an Assistant Professor-II at the School of Computer Engineering, Kalinga Institute of Industrial Technology (KIIT), Deemed to be University, Bhubaneswar, Odisha, India. He holds a Ph.D. in Computer Science and Engineering from the National Institute of Technology (NIT), Durgapur, where his research focused on *Algorithmic Mechanism Design in Cloud and Fog Computing*. He also earned his M.Tech. in Information Security from NIT Durgapur and his B.Tech. in Computer Science from Asansol Engineering College, affiliated with WBUT. He has over 17 years of academic and research experience across reputed institutions, including AMITY University, GITAM University, and Bengal College of Engineering and Technology. His research interests include Algorithmic Game Theory, Cloud and Fog Computing, Metaverse, Quantum Computing, Edge and Health Care Systems, and Autonomous Vehicles.

He has contributed extensively to the scientific community through high-impact journal publications in *IEEE Access*, *IEEE Transactions on Sustainable Computing*, *Scientific Reports*, *Mathematics*, *Sensors*, and others. He has also presented his work at premier IEEE conferences. He is the recipient of major research funding under the Visvesvaraya Ph.D. Scheme by the Ministry of Electronics and Information Technology, Government of India, and has been actively involved in innovative patent filings in smart healthcare, automation, and sustainability. In addition to his scholarly contributions, Dr. Bandyopadhyay has collaborated internationally, working with researchers across domains such as Artificial Intelligence, Internet of Things, and Smart Systems. He remains dedicated to fostering academic excellence, interdisciplinary research, and technological innovation in both national and global contexts.

Tanvir Habib Sardar is an Associate Professor at Department of Computer Science and Engineering, Dayananda Sagar University, Bengaluru, India, with over 16 years of teaching and research experience in Big Data, Machine Learning, Distributed Computing, and Fuzzy Sets. He earned his Ph.D. in Computer Science from Visvesvaraya Technological University in 2022. He has authored or edited ten books and contributed to nineteen book chapters. He has published more than 50 research papers in reputed SCIE and Scopus-indexed journals and holds 13 patents, including those based on his doctoral work. His recent notable contributions include a 2024 CRC Press book titled *Big Data Computing: Advances in Technologies, Methodologies, and Applications* and a Q1 review article in *WIREs Data Mining and Knowledge Discovery*. He also published a high-impact research article in the *Journal of Big Data* in 2024. He is an active reviewer for several international journals and is a lifetime member of multiple professional bodies.

Beyond academics, he has contributed significantly to university-level administration, ERP coordination, curriculum design, student mentoring, and accreditation processes (NAAC, NBA). He is pursuing a postdoctoral fellowship at Astana IT University, Kazakhstan, in the Department of Intelligent Systems and Cybersecurity from March 2025 to March 2026.

Saurav Mallik is currently a Research Scientist in the Department of Pharmacology and Toxicology at The University of Arizona, USA. He previously held postdoctoral positions at Harvard T.H. Chan School of Public Health (2019–2022), University of Texas Health Science Center at Houston (2018–2019), and University of Miami Miller School of Medicine (2017–2018). He earned his Ph.D. in Computer Science and Engineering from Jadavpur University in 2017, with research conducted at the Machine Intelligence Unit, Indian Statistical Institute (ISI), Kolkata.

Dr. Mallik has over three years of research experience at ISI, Kolkata, including roles as a Junior Research Fellow under a DST Swarnajayanti project and as a Visiting Scientist. He also served as a UGC Research Fellow at Jadavpur University and was awarded a prestigious CSIR Research Associateship in 2017. He is currently on leave from his position as Assistant Professor at Mallabhum Institute of Technology, India.

He has published over 180 peer-reviewed papers and contributed to more than 20 books with reputed publishers. With over 1,850 citations and an h-index of 22, his work spans Bioinformatics, Computational Biology, Data Mining, and Machine Learning. A recipient of multiple awards—including the "Emerging Researcher in Bioinformatics" (2020) and "Young Scientist Award" (2021)—he is an active member of IEEE, AACR, ACM, and BIOCLUES. He also serves as editor and reviewer for several leading international journals and conferences.

Ruhul Amin Hazarika is currently serving as an Assistant Professor in the Department of Information Technology at the Manipal Academy of Higher Education (MAHE), Bengaluru, India. He obtained his Ph.D. in Information Technology from North-Eastern Hill University (NEHU), Shillong, where his research focused on the classification and staging of Alzheimer's disease using Machine Learning and Deep Learning techniques applied to brain MRI images. He also holds an M.Tech. and a B.Tech. in Information Technology from NEHU.

Dr. Hazarika's primary research interests lie in the areas of Artificial Intelligence, Machine Learning, Deep Learning, and Medical Image Analysis. His contributions include the development of novel deep neural network architectures, feature extraction methods, and hybrid classification frameworks aimed at improving diagnostic accuracy in neurodegenerative disorders. His published work spans high-impact Q1 and Q2 SCIE-indexed journals such as *IEEE Access*, *Journal of King Saud University – Computer and Information Sciences*, *Journal of Digital Imaging*, and *Electronics*. He has extensive teaching experience in subjects including Computer Organization, Artificial Neural Networks, Python Programming, and AI Applications. His scholarly output includes over nine peer-reviewed journal publications, with a special focus on computational approaches for early detection of Alzheimer's disease. His work is recognized for its innovative use of convolutional and depth-wise separable architectures, as well as performance-driven hybrid models combining DNNs with Machine Learning classifiers like Random Forests. He continues to engage in academic research and mentorship, contributing to the advancement of AI-driven solutions in healthcare and medical diagnostics.

Mahendra Kumar Gourisaria received his bachelor's degree (Hons.) in commerce from Calcutta University, master's degree in computer application from Indira Gandhi National Open University, New Delhi, and M.Tech. degree in computer science and engineering (CSE) from the Biju Patnaik University of Technology, Rourkela. He completed his Ph.D. degree in CSE from Kalinga Institute of Industrial Technology, Deemed to be University, Bhubneswar, Odisha. He has completed ICWAI (intermediate) from the Institute of Cost and Works Accountants of India and DNIIT from NIIT Sahid Nagar, Bhubaneswar. Currently, he is working as an Associate Professor in the School of Computer Engineering, KIIT Deemed to be University. He has an experience of more than 22 years in academia and ten years in research. He has published more than 240 research papers in different book chapters, international journals, and conferences of repute. His Google Scholar citation is more than 2600 with an H-index of 25 and an i10-index of 64. His research interests include cloud computing, machine learning, deep learning, data mining, soft computing, and internet and web technology. He is a member of IAENG and UACEE; and a Life Member of ISTE, CSI, and ISCA. He has received the Research Achievement Award from (IUILA 2024) London Metropolitan University. He has served as an organizing committee member for various conferences and workshops, chaired sessions in many international conferences, and a reviewer for many reputed journals, such as Springer and Hindawi, and many reputed conferences.

Contributors

Abdullahi Abubakar
Department of Computer Science and Engineering
Waziri Umaru Federal Polytechnic
Birnin Kebbi, Kebbi State, Nigeria

Ayishath Afra
Department of Biotechnology
P. A. College of Engineering
Mangalore, Karnataka, India

Bhavna Alke
Department of Chemistry
NOVA School of Science and Technology
Lisbon, Portugal

L. R. Amrutha
Department of Biotechnology
P. A. College of Engineering
Mangalore, Karnataka, India

Alhaji Idi Babate
Department of Computer Science
Federal College of Education (Technical)
Potiskum, Yobe State, Nigeria

Afsar Baig
Department of Artificial Intelligence and Machine Learning
P. A. College of Engineering (Affiliated to Visvesvaraya Technological University, Belagavi)
Mangalore, Karnataka, India

Munazza Begam
Department of Electronics and Communication Engineering
P. A. College of Engineering
Mangalore, Karnataka, India

Kalyan Chatterjee
Department of Electronics and Communication Engineering
Amity School of Engineering & Technology
Amity University
Kolkata, West Bengal, India

Subhram Das
Narula Institute of Technology
Kolkata, West Bengal, India

K. Deeba
Department of Computing Technologies
SRM Institute of Science and Technology
Kattankulathur, Tamil Nadu, India

Palasri Dhar
Department of Electronics and Communication Engineering
Guru Nanak Institute of Technology
Kolkata, West Bengal, India

Papri Ghosh
Narula Institute of Technology
Kolkata, West Bengal, India

G.S. Girisha
Department of Computer Science Engineering
Dayananda Sagar University
Bangalore, Karnataka, India

Asif Hassan
Department of Electronics and Communication Engineering
P. A. College of Engineering (Affiliated to Visvesvaraya Technological University, Belagavi)
Mangalore, Karnataka, India

F. Syed Anwar Hussainy
Department of Computing Technologies
SRM Institute of Science and Technology, Kattankulathur, Tamil Nadu, India

A. Laila Jaseela
Department of Biotechnology
P. A. College of Engineering (Affiliated to Visvesvaraya Technological University, Belagavi)
Mangalore, Karnataka, India

Waghmare Kiran
CDAC
Mumbai, Maharashtra, India

Aurpan Majumder
National Institute of Technology
Durgapur, West Bengal, India

Meenakshi Malhotra
Department of Computer Science and Engineering
Dayananda Sagar University
Bangalore, Karnataka, India

Thabshira Maryam
Department of Biotechnology
P. A. College of Engineering
Mangalore, Karnataka, India

Debrupa Pal
Narula Institute of Technology
Kolkata, West Bengal, India

Swapnamoyee Palit
KIIT School of Economics and Commerce
KIIT Deemed to be University
Bhubaneswar, Odisha, India

Ashyashree Praharaj
P.G. Department of Business Administration
Berhampur University
Berhampur, Odisha, India

T.M. Rajesh
Department of Computer Science and Engineering
Dayananda Sagar University
Bangalore, Karnataka, India

J. Ramaprabha
Department of Computing Technologies
SRM Institute of Science and Technology
Kattankulathur, Tamil Nadu, India

M.N. Renukadevi
Department of Computer Science and Engineering
Dayananda Sagar University
Bangalore, Karnataka, India

Nafeesa Rihana
Department of Artificial Intelligence and Machine Learning
P. A. College of Engineering
Mangalore, Karnataka, India

Subhasish Roy
Department of Electronics and Communication Engineering
Amity School of Engineering & Technology
Amity University
Kolkata, West Bengal, India

Sunipa Roy
Department of Electronics and Communication Engineering
Guru Nanak Institute of Technology
Kolkata, West Bengal, India

Shashwat Saini
Department of Artificial Intelligence and Machine Learning
Dayananda Sagar University
Bangalore, Karnataka, India

Jayalaxmi Samal
School of Liberal Studies
Kalinga Institute of Industrial Technology (KIIT) Deemed to be University
Bhubaneswar, Odisha, India

Ananya Swain
KIIT School of Economics and Commerce
KIIT Deemed to be University
Bhubaneswar, Odisha, India

Usman Taqui Syed
Department of Chemistry
NOVA School of Science and Technology
Lisbon, Portugal

Seema Tharannum
Department of Biological Sciences
Dayananda Sagar University
Bangalore, Karnataka, India

Shareefraza J. Ukkund
Department of Biotechnology
P. A. College of Engineering (Affiliated to Visvesvaraya Technological University, Belagavi)
Mangalore, Karnataka, India

Revathi Vaithiyanathan
Department of Computer Science Engineering
Dayananda Sagar University
Bangalore, Karnataka, India

D. Vanusha
Department of Computing Technologies
SRM Institute of Science and Technology
Kattankulathur, Tamil Nadu, India

D. Vathana
Department of Computing Technologies
SRM Institute of Science and Technology
Kattankulathur, Tamil Nadu, India

P. Venkatesh
Department of Computer Science and Engineering
Dayananda Sagar University
Bangalore, Karnataka, India

Kiran Waghmare
CDAC
Mumbai, Maharasthra, India

1 Artificial Intelligence in Mental Health

A Comprehensive Review

Ashyashree Praharaj and Jayalaxmi Samal

1.1 INTRODUCTION

The rising prevalence of mental health disorders has become a global public health issue, bringing about significant social, economic, and healthcare challenges [1–3]. Mental health conditions are responsible for a significant burden of diseases globally, with depression and anxiety being the major contributors [4]. The increasing demand for mental health services has made it imperative to develop innovative, scalable, and cost-effective solutions [5], especially in areas with limited access to professional training and resources [6]. This imperative has paved the way for the introduction of AI-based technologies into mental health care, offering transformative opportunities in diagnosis, treatment, and monitoring [7–10].

AI, consisting of Machine Learning (ML) [11], Natural Language Processing (NLP) [12], and Deep Learning (DL) [13], has a huge potential to change the face of mental health research and practice. AI-based tools can process vast amounts of data derived from various sources, including clinical records, wearable devices, and social media [14–16]. This allows for the early detection of mental health issues and tailored intervention strategies. For example, ML algorithms have been used to identify depression and anxiety through speech patterns, facial expressions [17], and text analysis [18]. In contrast, wearable technologies monitor physiological and behavioural indicators to predict mental health trends [19,20]. These developments have boosted the interest of researchers and practitioners in examining AI in mental health care.

The intersection of AI and mental health research addresses the increasing challenges of mental health issues and signifies the broader digital evolution within healthcare [21,22]. However, the rapid expansion of this research domain calls for a systematic examination of its progress, emerging themes, and existing research gaps. A bibliometric analysis is an excellent way of methodologically surveying trends, productivity, and impact in such an interdisciplinary field of study [23,24]. Through a map of leading themes, top authors, and co-author networks [25–27], the analysis will deliver rich insights into how AI-based research on mental health has progressed and is poised to advance in the future.

DOI: 10.1201/9781003600947-1

This study, therefore, proposes to do an in-depth review of bibliometrics at the crossing point of AI and mental health, studying publication trends to note emerging themes for future key studies. Findings from this chapter will not only form part of the current knowledge but also, more importantly, inspire further inquiry into this end by researchers, policymakers, and healthcare providers who can utilise AI to manage mental health and mental disorders better.

This research seeks to address these research questions (RQs):

a. What are the key trends in AI and mental health research publications?
b. Which authors, institutions, and countries are the most influential contributors to the research on AI in mental health?
c. What are mental health research's most frequently studied sub-fields and applications?
d. What are the emerging research themes, co-occurrence of keywords, and collaborative networks in this research domain?
e. How has the interdisciplinary nature of AI and mental health research evolved, and what disciplines are prominently cited and referenced in this field?

The rest of this chapter is structured as follows: Section 1.2 details the methodology used for the bibliometric analysis. Section 1.3 analyses the findings, whereas Section 1.4 explores future research opportunities. Section 1.5 emphasises the significant findings and discussions, and Section 1.6 wraps up with comments on this study's implications and limitations.

1.2 METHODOLOGY

This research utilises an extensive bibliometric analysis to investigate academic works on AI and mental health [28,29]. The *Scopus* database is renowned within the educational community for its extensive and multidisciplinary coverage of peer-reviewed literature [30–32], was selected as the sole data source for this study. The keywords and Boolean operators chosen for this study are ("Artificial Intelligence" OR "AI") AND ("Mental Health" OR "Mental Well-being" OR "Mental Equilibrium") OR ("Psychological Health" OR "Psychological Well-Being" OR "Emotional Well-Being" OR "Emotional Equilibrium"). The keyword selection as per the guidelines mentioned by [33,34]. The initial keyword search resulted in 3903 documents. Further, the document type was limited to "Articles" only, resulting in 2076 articles. The subject area was limited to "Business, Management, and Accounting", "Economics, Econometrics, and Finance", "Social Sciences", "Arts and Humanities", and "Psychology", resulting in 512 articles. Lastly, the publication stage was set to "Final", source type to "Journals", and Language to "English" as per the framework defined by [35]. The final sample size for this study is 457 articles. Advanced visualisation software, such as VOSviewer [36] and R-Studios [37], have been used for this study.

1.3 DATA ANALYSIS AND INTERPRETATION

1.3.1 Documentation and Citation Trends

Figures 1.1 and 1.2 present the documentation and citation trends in the said domain. A total of 457 articles from 275 journals have been analysed for this study. The average document age is 4.03 years, highlighting the maturity of this domain. The average citation per article is 16.37, suggesting that research within this discipline is well-recognised among the academic community. The initial analysis revealed that 2020 authors have contributed to 457 articles, of which only 18 have contributed to a single-author document. The co-authorship per article is 5.18, with international co-authorship being 18.82%. A total of 29,643 references have been used in 457 articles.

The first document on AI and mental health was published in 1986. Since 1986, the documentation trend reveals two interesting phases of growth: (2010–2014) and (2016–present). The first growth phase represents the emergence of AI applications in mental health, focusing on foundational studies exploring the feasibility

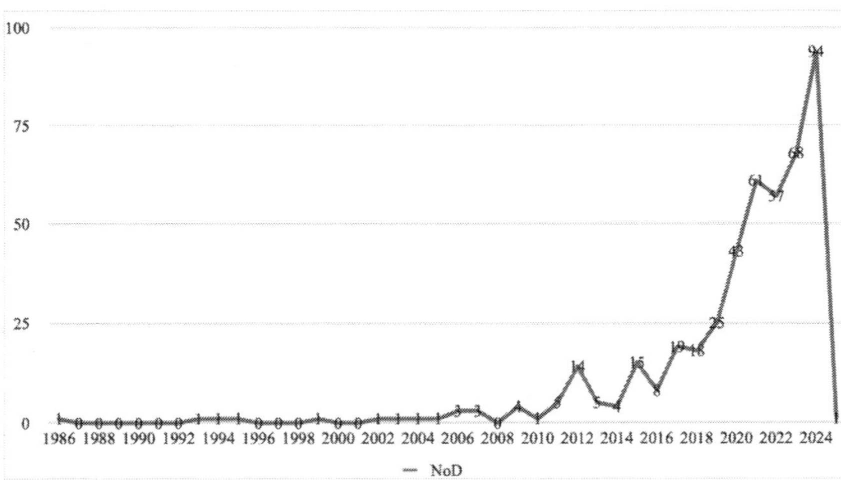

Source: Compiled and computed data; Courtesy: R-Studios.
*NoD: Number of Documents

FIGURE 1.1 The documentation trend. (Source: Compiled and computed data; Courtesy: R-Studios. NoD: Number of Documents.)

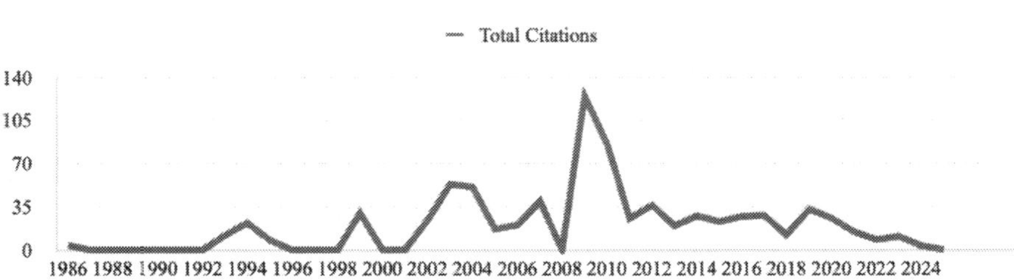

FIGURE 1.2 The citation trend. (Source: Compiled and computed data; Courtesy: R-Studios.)

of integrating AI technologies like ML and NLP into mental health diagnosis and treatment. Initial studies have shown that AI can analyse mental health data, including detecting depression through social media activity and predicting anxiety with wearable devices.

The second growth phase highlights the accelerated growth with the rapid advancements in AI technologies, including DL, neural networks (NN), and more sophisticated data analytical tools. The second phase prioritises making AI applications more effective and accessible in a mental health context. A rise in funding and interest from various governments, academic institutions, and private organisations to investigate AI's potential in addressing mental health challenges is being observed, especially in light of the global mental health crisis. Growth in collaborative efforts between computer scientists, psychologists, and healthcare providers has increased document production. Increased societal and institutional recognition of mental health, intensified by global events such as the COVID-19 pandemic, underscores the necessity for large-scale AI-driven mental health interventions.

Similarly, in terms of citations, two prominent phases are observed from 2006 to 2009 and 2014–present, with the highest citable year being 2009. The first phase suggests that researchers have explored the pioneering concepts of AI for diagnosing mental health conditions or leveraging ML for predictive analytics. The relatively high number of citations indicates early recognition and widespread academic engagement with these ideas, even if the volume of publications was limited. Researchers and practitioners from multiple disciplines may likely reference these studies to establish the basis for their works.

The second phase of citation growth highlighted the discipline's maturation. The citation trend since 2014 highlights the maturation and stabilisation of research. A growing body of literature indicates that AI applications in mental health have moved from exploratory studies to more rigorous, large-scale implementations. Increased interdisciplinary collaborations and global awareness of mental health issues have amplified the relevance and application of AI solutions. The citation trend reflects the dual dynamics of foundational influence and ongoing relevance, showing that the field has evolved but remains firmly rooted in seminal works.

1.3.2 Prominent Authors

Table 1.1 presents the prominent authors in AI and MH. *Johnson, C.L.* is the most distinguished author with the most articles (14), followed by *Dickerson, D.L.* and *D'Amico, E.J.* with 13 and 12 articles, respectively. Regarding citations, *Skewes, M.C.* leads the list with 262 citations garnered from nine documents, followed by *Novins, D.K.* and *Johnson, C.L.* with 243 and 209 citations, respectively. The metrics h-index, g-index, and m-index are bibliometric indicators used to measure an author's academic impact. The h-index is the most significant number of "h", such that the authors have at least "h" publications with "h" or more citations in each [38]. *Johnson, C.L.* has an h-index of eight, which means that the author has at least eight publications with at least eight citations each. This reflects the consistent and significant impact on the research community. Regarding the h-index, *Johnson, C.L.*, *Dickerson, D.L.*, and *D'Amico, E.J.* lead the list with eight h-indexes each.

TABLE 1.1
Top Ten Authors (Document-Wise)

SN	Name of the Author	NoD	TC	h-Index	g-Index	m-Index
1	*Johnson, C.L.*	14	209	8	14	0.571
2	*Dickerson, D.L.*	13	183	8	13	0.571
3	*D'Amico, E.J.*	12	154	8	12	1.6
4	*Skewes, M.C.*	9	262	7	9	0.778
5	*Brown, R.A.*	8	104	5	8	1
6	*Klein, D.J.*	8	107	5	8	1
7	*Novins, D.K.*	7	243	5	7	02.63
8	*O'Keefe, V.M.*	6	111	5	6	0.455
9	*Lee, Y.S.*	6	49	4	6	0.571
10	*Roh, S.*	6	49	4	6	0.571

Source: Compiled and computed data; Courtesy: R-Studios.
SN, serial number; NoD, number of documents; TC, total citations.

The g-index can be stated as the largest number "g" such that the top "g" publications of an author, ranked by citations, have at least "g^2" cumulative citations [39]. The g-index prioritises more highly cited papers than the h-index, considering all citations the same. *Johnson, C.L.* has a g-index of 14, which means that *Johnson's* top 14 publications collectively have at least 14^2 or 196 citations. Since Johnson's total citations (TC) are 209, this confirms the metric.

In the same way, the m-index is calculated by dividing the h-index by the number of years since the author's first publication [40]. It reflects the rate of an author's research productivity over time. The m-index adjusts the h-index for the duration of an author's career, allowing fair comparison between early-career and established researchers. *D'Amico, E.J.* has an m-index of 1.6, indicating rapid growth in academic impact compared to peers with lower m-index values.

Figure 1.3 presents a detailed view of Lotka's Law, a bibliometric model describing author productivity distribution in scientific literature [41]. One thousand eight hundred forty-four authors have published only one document each, followed by 114 authors for two papers and only 30 for three. It is observed that only one author (*Johnson, C.L.)* has produced the highest of 14 documents. Lotka's Law suggests that a small percentage of authors have contributed to the most publications in this field, while the majority produce fewer works. A need for expansive collaborative work is observed, which may increase the co-authorship rates and international collaborations.

1.3.3 Prominent Affiliations/Institutions

Figure 1.4 presents an overview of the top affiliating institutions. The *University of California* leads the list with 20 articles, indicating its strong presence or leadership in AI and MH research. *Montana State University* is the second leading institution with 19 articles, showing its significant role, though slightly behind the *University of California*. Regarding notable institutions, the *University of Michigan*

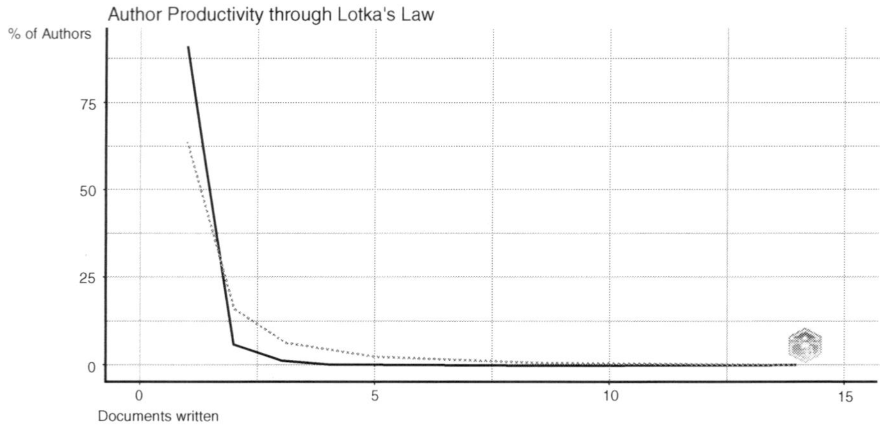

FIGURE 1.3 Author's productivity through Lotka's Law. (Source: Compiled and computed data; Courtesy: R-Studios.)

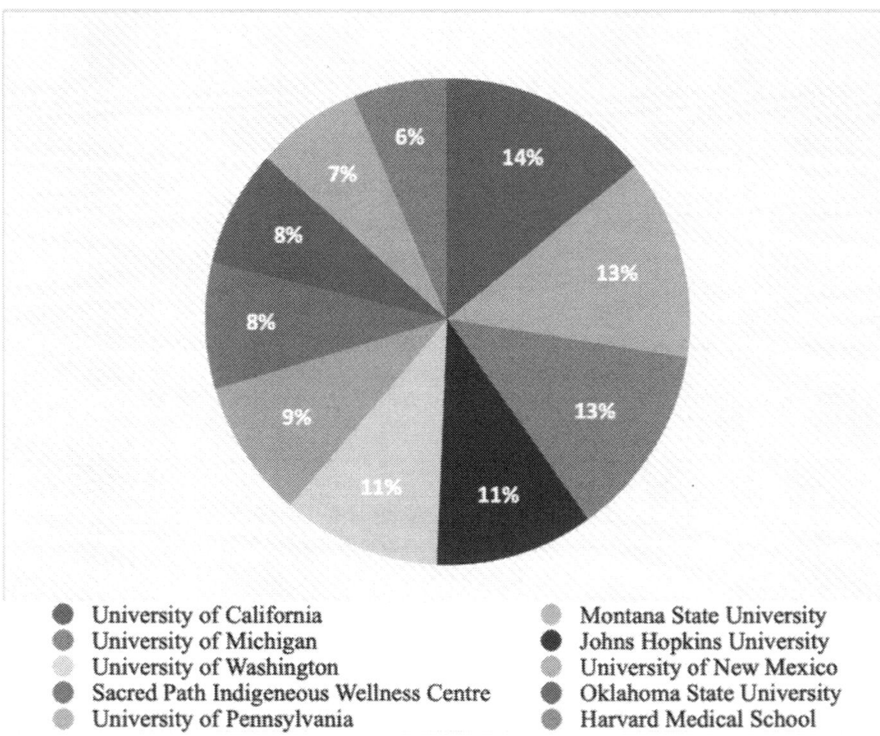

FIGURE 1.4 Prominent ten affiliations. (Source: Compiled and computed data; Courtesy: MS Office.)

and *John Hopkins University* are prominent names, contributing 18 and 15 articles, respectively. Similarly, *Harvard Medical School* appears in the top ten list with nine articles, which is substantial but comparatively lower than others. The *Sacred Path*

Indigenous Wellness Centre, with 12 articles, stands out because it is not a traditional academic institution but is likely to focus on Indigenous health and wellness, highlighting a specific focus within the broader field. The exhibit demonstrates that top-tier educational institutions contribute significantly to research, especially those with strong medical or public health programs. However, smaller, specialised centres also significantly add diversity and specific focus to the research landscape.

1.3.4 Prominent Countries

Figure 1.5 presents the document-wise production of prominent countries. The *USA* stands out as the clear leader with 213 articles, representing a substantial majority of the total output in this field. The dominance of the *USA* suggests that it plays a significant role in this research area, with well-established academic institutions, substantial funding, and a high level of international collaboration contributing to this output. *China* follows far behind with 28 articles, a significant yet much lower count than the *USA*. This could indicate an emerging but relatively minor research output than a global leader. The *UK, Canada,* and *India* also show active participation, with 15, 14, and 12 articles, respectively. The research concentration in the *USA, China,* and a few *European* countries suggests that future research might benefit from greater global collaboration, particularly with emerging players like *India* and *South Korea.*

Similarly, Figure 1.6 presents an overview of prominent countries regarding citations. The *USA* leads by a significant margin, contributing 3374 citations. The USA's dominant position indicates the global influence of American research, likely referencing the country's leadership in high-impact academic and scientific fields. The high number of citations also suggests the quality and reach of the *US*'s research, which is widely referenced and integrated into global scholarly work. With 446 citations, *Germany*'s research is impactful, possibly due to its strengths in engineering,

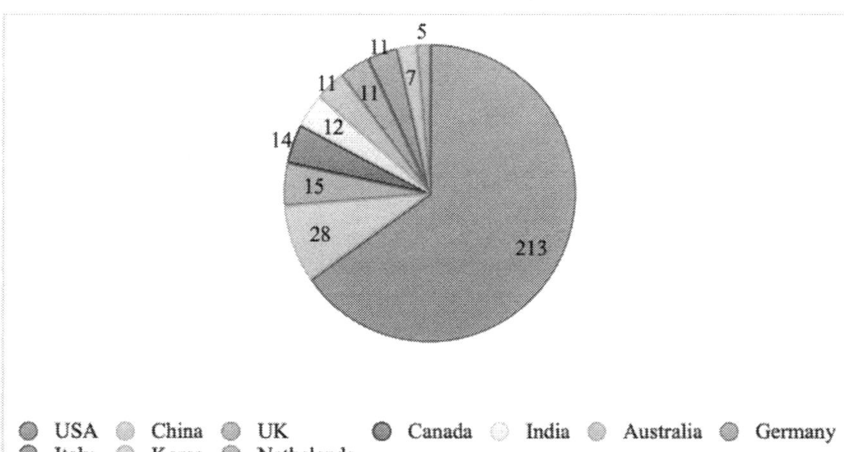

FIGURE 1.5 Top ten countries (Document production-wise). (Source: Compiled and computed data; Courtesy: MS Office. USA: The United States of America; UK: The United Kingdom; Korea: South Korea.)

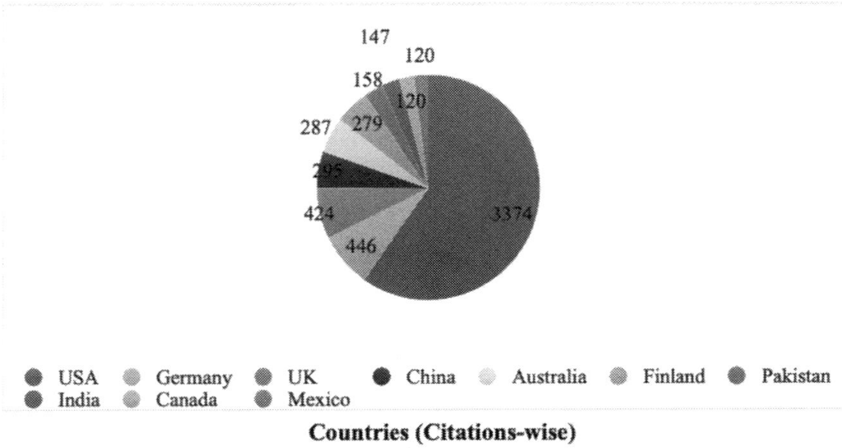

FIGURE 1.6 Top ten countries (Citations-wise). (Source: Compiled and computed data; Courtesy: MS Office.)

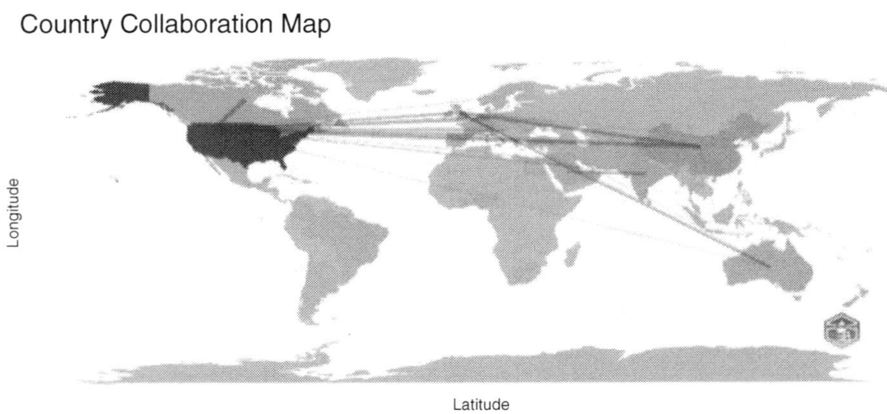

FIGURE 1.7 Prominent countries (Collaboration-wise). (Source: Compiled and computed data; Courtesy: R-Studios.)

natural sciences, and technology. The 424 citations reflect the *UK*'s longstanding tradition of excellence in research, especially in the humanities, medical sciences, and social sciences. *China* holds the 4th position with 295 citations. While this is still far behind the *USA*, it shows *China*'s growing influence in global research. The citation count indicates a significant increase in research quality and international collaboration, particularly in technology, medicine, and engineering. The Exhibit also highlights that while some countries are emerging with impactful research, such as *China* and *India*, others, like *Mexico* and *Pakistan*, have room to expand their research presence in the global arena.

Figure 1.7 presents the country-wise collaboration map. The *USA* is prominently highlighted in dark blue, signifying a strong research collaboration network. The multiple lines connecting it to other countries, especially *Europe*, *Asia*, and *Oceania*, demonstrate the *USA*'s central role in global research partnerships. *Europe*, especially *Western* and *Central Europe*, shows significant connectivity with the *USA* and other regions. Countries like the *UK*, *Germany*, and *France* have established collaborative ties with *North America* and other parts of the world, indicating that *European* research institutions are highly involved in cross-border collaborations. *China* and *India* are also prominently featured on the map, with some connections to countries like the *USA*, *Europe*, and parts of *Southeast Asia*. This suggests increased international research collaborations for these countries, particularly in technology, engineering, and sciences. *Australia* appears as an active collaborator, connecting with countries in *Asia* and *Europe*, further emphasising its role in research. *South America*, *Africa*, and the *Middle East* appear to have fewer connections, indicating that these regions may have limited international research collaborations compared to countries in *North America*, *Europe*, and parts of *Asia*. *Africa*, in particular, shows minimal interaction with other continents, possibly due to fewer research networks and funding opportunities, which limit global collaborations. It is observed that while traditionally, *Europe* and *North America* have dominated research collaborations, emerging economies like *China* and *India* are increasingly becoming influential hubs of international collaborations.

1.3.5 Prominent Research Keywords

Figure 1.8 presents a network of prominent keywords used in this discipline. A minimum number of keywords was set to ten occurrences to visualise this network. The network has 100 keywords classified into five distinct clusters with 3,287 links and a total link strength (TLS) of 17,222. The network is divided into three primary clusters, each representing a different thematic area of focus. The prominent three clusters are green, red, and blue, highlighting a strong interconnected network.

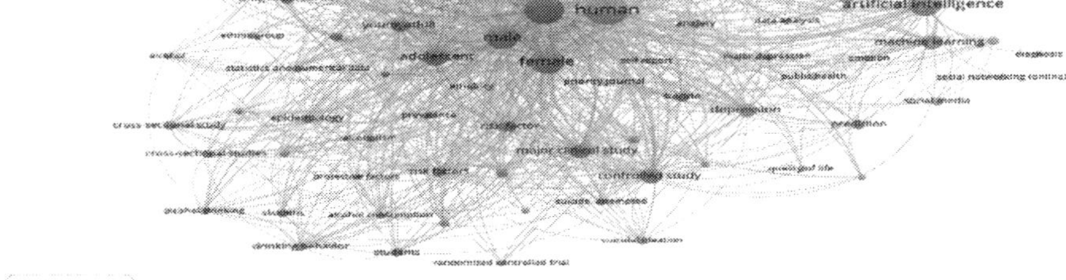

FIGURE 1.8 Prominent keywords (All keywords). (Source: Compiled and computed data; Courtesy: VOSviewer.)

The green cluster represents AI and Machine Learning (ML). The central keywords in this cluster are "Artificial Intelligence, Machine Learning, Data Analysis, Health Care, Diagnosis, and Social Networking (Online)". This cluster represents the technical aspects of AI and its application in mental health. It includes sub-topics like prediction models, cognition, and diagnosis of mental disorders. This group of researchers focuses more on using AI for mental healthcare, noting how algorithms and data-driven approaches play an increasingly large role in determining and dealing with mental health disorders.

The red cluster represents the psychological and socio-cultural aspects. Central keywords in this cluster are "Psychology, Ethnology, Mental Disorder, Substance Abuse, and Cultural Anthropology." The cluster is centred around the psychological and socio-cultural factors of mental health. *It* contains subtopics like mental stress, youth, the urban population, and historical trauma. Researchers in this cluster postulate that research on AI within the mental health field is intimately associated with human behaviour, social support systems, and cultural context.

The blue cluster represents the epidemiology and behavioural studies. Keywords to the core in this cluster are "Risk Factors, Epidemiology, Cross-Sectional Study, Students, and Alcohol Consumption". This group of researchers set their attention towards specific populations like students and adolescents. It explored behaviour such as alcohol consumption and suicidal ideation, including randomised controlled trials and protective factors, denoting the evidence-based nature of researching risks in mental health.

The keyword "human" acts as a hub (central node) connecting the three clusters, indicating that all research themes revolve around human subjects and their well-being. The term "mental health" bridges the psychological (red cluster) and AI (green cluster) clusters, highlighting the interdisciplinary approach to using AI for mental health solutions. The terms "adolescents" and "young adults" connect socio-cultural and behavioural studies, indicating a targeted demographic in mental health research.

Figure 1.9 presents a visualisation of prominent keywords using RStudios. Keywords such as "Female" and "Male" are the most common, with 292 and 264 occurrences, respectively. This highlights the gendered focus in the studies analysed. Many articles explore the gender differences in mental health or AI applications in understanding gender-specific behaviours, challenges, or health outcomes. The prevalence of the "human (249 occurrences)" keyword indicates a universal focus on human subjects in the research, reinforcing the anthropological nature of studies on AI in mental health.

The terms "adult (197 occurrences) and adolescent (177 occurrences)" suggest a demographic focus on both adults and adolescents, possibly exploring how AI tools address mental health challenges across different life stages. Adolescents may be a key group due to their vulnerability and digital exposure, while adults represent a broader population with diverse mental health needs. Interestingly, the term "American Indian" (131 occurrences) reflects a unique demographic feature, examining how AI interventions address mental health challenges in Indigenous communities.

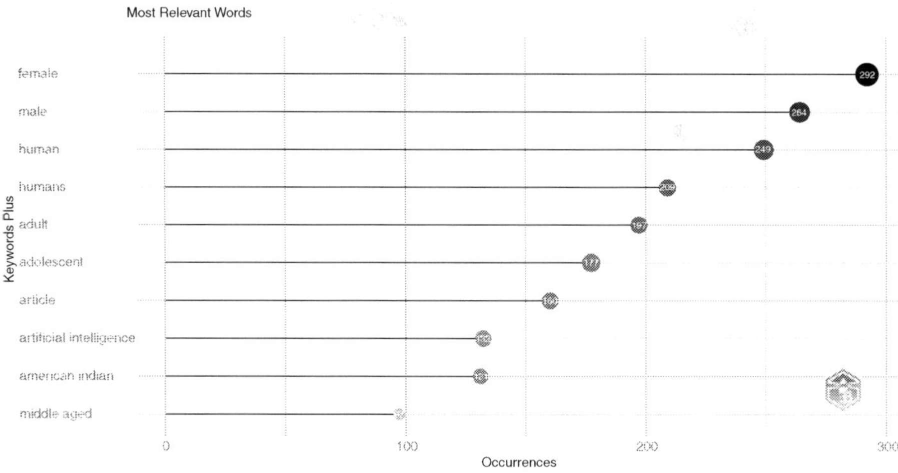

FIGURE 1.9 Most relevant keywords. (Source: Compiled and computed data; Courtesy: R-Studios.)

1.3.6 AI and Mental Health Research Map

Figure 1.10 presents a detailed thematic research map. The x-axis of the map represents the degree of relevance, indicating how important or central a research theme is to the broader research field. The y-axis of the map represents the development degree, highlighting a theme's internal development level and showing its maturity and specialisation. The map is divided into four distinct quadrants.

The upper-right quadrant represents the motor themes of research. The motor themes represent the well-developed and influential themes in the study. Prominent themes such as "human, humans, female" appear in this map, indicating the gender-specific human aspects of AI and mental health research. Further, themes such as "American Indian, adolescents, and Indians" also appear. This suggests that studies focusing on adolescent mental health among the American Indian population are well-developed. The upper-left quadrant represents the niche themes of research. The niche themes have low centrality but high density. These themes are highly specialised but less influential in broader research fields. As per the map, no significant theme is found as a niche theme, indicating that the research in this discipline still has the potential to be unlocked.

The lower-right quadrant represents basic themes with high centrality but low density. These are critical foundational themes that are still developing or lacking internal depth. According to this map, this quadrant does not seem to have any prominent themes. The lower-left quadrant represents emerging or declining themes. They are either emerging areas of research or topics that are declining in relevance. The themes in this quadrant include "social networking (online), learning systems, and diseases". These developing themes might be necessary for AI and mental health but have not been researched extensively or are still in the early stages of research.

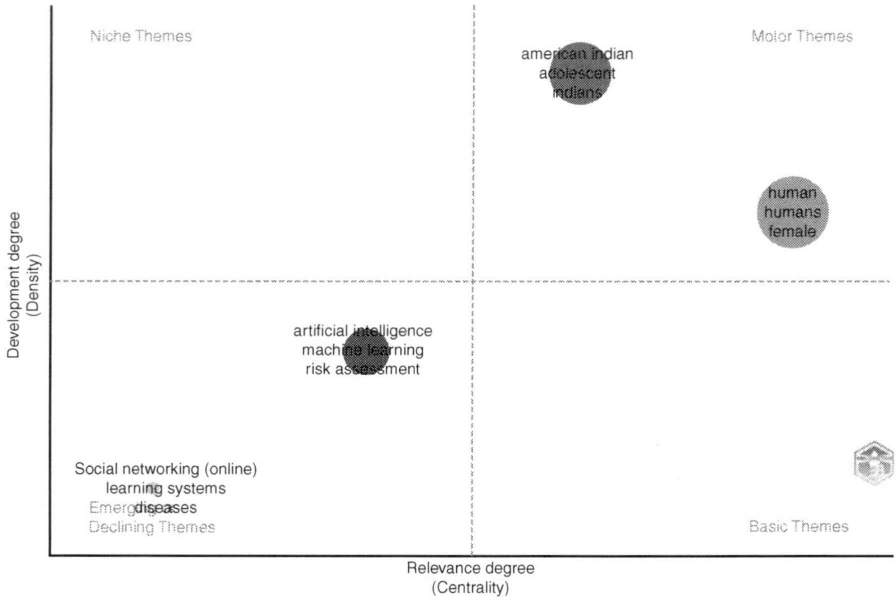

FIGURE 1.10 AI and mental health thematic research map. (Source: Compiled and computed data; Courtesy: R-Studios.)

1.4 SCOPE FOR FUTURE STUDIES

AI is revolutionising the field of mental health research. It offers new avenues to solve challenges in multiple domains. AI promises promising avenues for personalisation in mental health solutions, including tailoring interventions to individual needs and raising issues of effectiveness, accessibility, and inclusivity. Similarly, there is a demand for attention towards the ethical issues of AI in mental health. Researchers are still grappling with privacy concerns, bias, and informed consent. AI also has enormous potential in the early detection and prevention of mental disorders, allowing the implementation of early interventions through predictive analytics and sophisticated ML algorithms. Its applicability in cross-cultural mental health research opens avenues to understanding mental health in all its cultural flavours and ensuring inclusive AI-driven intervention. This integrates AI within the work sphere and adolescents into mental health to highlight utility, from workplace-specific stress management all the way through to adolescent-focused mental health education and intervention efforts. Table 1.2 covers future themes in research questions with keywords while highlighting the ability for AI utilisation towards mental health applications while overcoming all the serious questions.

1.5 KEY FINDINGS AND DISCUSSION

This study analysed 457 articles published across 275 journals, emphasising AI's growing interest and recognition in mental health research. The primary analysis revealed two significant growth phases in document production: 2010–2014 and

TABLE 1.2
Future Research Themes, Questions, and Keywords

Future Research Themes	Future Research Questions (RQs)	Research Keywords
AI-Powered Personalised Mental Health Solutions	1. How can AI models be optimised to deliver personalised mental health interventions that are both effective and ethically sound? 2. What role can real-time data from wearables and smartphones play in tailoring mental health treatments using AI? 3. How can AI algorithms address variations in individual psychological and genetic profiles to enhance the efficacy of mental health interventions? 4. What are the challenges and solutions in integrating AI-based personalised mental health tools with traditional therapeutic practices? 5. How can AI-powered systems ensure the privacy and security of personal mental health data while delivering tailored interventions? 6. What are the long-term impacts of AI-driven personalised therapy on patients' mental health outcomes and overall quality of life?	"Personalised AI Therapy", "Mental Health Predictive Modelling", "Wearable Mental Health AI", "AI-Driven Psychotherapy", "Tailored Digital Mental Health Solutions", "AI-Mental Health Ecosystem", "Precision Mental Health with AI", "Adaptive AI Interventions".
Ethical Implications of AI in Mental Health	1. How can ethical frameworks be developed to ensure fairness and inclusivity in AI-based mental health solutions? 2. What measures can be implemented to prevent algorithmic biases in AI-powered mental health diagnostics and treatments? 3. How can the trade-off between data privacy and the need for personalised mental health interventions be ethically balanced? 4. What are the potential consequences of over-reliance on AI for mental health treatment, and how can they be mitigated? 5. How can AI-based mental health systems ensure transparency and accountability in the decision-making process? 6. What are the societal and psychological impacts of delegating mental health care responsibilities to AI systems?	"AI Ethics in Mental Health", "Algorithmic Biases in Mental Health", "Ethical AI Framework", "Mental Health Data Privacy", "Transparent AI Decision-Making", "Accountable AI in Healthcare", "Bias-Free AI Diagnostics", "Ethical Personalisation in AI", "AI and Human Dignity", "Trustworthy AI for Mental Health".

(*Continued*)

TABLE 1.2 (*Continued*)
Future Research Themes, Questions, and Keywords

Future Research Themes	Future Research Questions (RQs)	Research Keywords
AI for Early Detection and Prevention of Mental Disorders	1. How can AI algorithms effectively analyse behavioural, physiological, and textual data to detect mental disorders early? 2. What role can AI-powered wearable devices play in monitoring and predicting early signs of mental health issues? 3. How can Natural Language Processing (NLP) be enhanced to identify subtle cues of mental health deterioration in real-time conversations? 4. What are the challenges in integrating AI-based prediction models into existing mental health care systems for preventive care? 5. How can Machine Learning (ML) models be made adaptive to various cultural, social, and demographic factors in mental health prediction? 6. What are the potential limitations of AI in distinguishing between normal emotional variations and early signs of mental disorders?	"AI-Driven Mental Health Prediction", "Early Detection of Mental Disorder", "Preventive AI Mental Health Tools", "Wearable Technologies for Mental Health", "NLP in Mental Health Diagnosis", "Machine Learning for Mental Health Screening", "Real-Time Mental Health Monitoring", "Predictive Analytics for Mental Disorders", "Culturally Adaptive AI Models", "Behavioural Data and AI Mental Health".
AI in Cross-Cultural Mental Health Research	1. How can AI systems account for cultural differences in expressing and understanding mental health symptoms? 2. What are the challenges and opportunities in developing AI-powered mental health tools that cater to linguistically diverse populations? 3. How can AI models integrate culturally specific norms, beliefs, and practices to provide accurate mental health insights? 4. What role can AI play in identifying and addressing mental health stigma across cultural contexts? 5. How can machine learning (ML) models be adapted to ensure equitable mental health care outcomes across under-represented and marginalised culture groups? 6. What ethical considerations should guide the development of AI tools for mental health research in cross-cultural settings?	"AI and Cultural Sensitivity in Mental Health", "Cross-Cultural AI Models", "Culturally Adaptive Mental Health Tools", "Multilingual Mental Health AI Systems", "AI for Cultural Mental Health Stigma", "Machine Learning in Diverse Mental Health Contexts", "AI for Global Mental Health Research", "Cultural Norms and AI Mental Health", "Ethics of Cross-Cultural AI Mental Health", "AI in Mental Health Equity".

(*Continued*)

TABLE 1.2 (*Continued*)
Future Research Themes, Questions, and Keywords

Future Research Themes	Future Research Questions (RQs)	Research Keywords
AI-Augmented Mental Health Support for Adolescents	1. How can AI-powered tools be tailored to address adolescents' unique mental health needs? 2. What role does AI play in detecting early signs of adolescent mental health issues through behavioural and social media data? 3. How effective are AI-driven chatbots and virtual counsellors in providing emotional support to adolescents? 4. What are the long-term effects of AI-augmented mental health interventions on adolescent well-being? 5. How can AI systems ensure the privacy and security of adolescent data while delivering personalised mental health support? 6. What challenges exist in integrating AI-powered mental health solutions into schools and community settings for adolescents?	"AI in Adolescent Mental Health", "AI-Powered Mental Health Interventions for Teens", "Virtual Counsellors for Adolescents", "Early Detection of Adolescent Mental Disorder through AI", "Personalised AI Mental Health Solutions for Teens", "Youth Mental Health and Artificial Intelligence", "AI in School Mental Health Programs", "Adolescent Data Privacy in AI Mental Health Tools", "Social Media Analytics for Adolescent Mental Health".
AI and Workplace Mental Health	1. How can AI tools identify early signs of mental health challenges among employees in the workplace? 2. What is the role of AI in creating personalised workplace mental health programs to enhance employee well-being? 3. How effective are AI-powered mental health chatbots and virtual counsellors in supporting workplace mental health? 4. What ethical considerations arise in using AI to monitor and analyse employee mental health in the workplace? 5. How can AI-driven analytics be integrated into workplace policies to reduce stress and improve mental health outcomes? 6. What are the limitations and risks of using AI solutions to address workplace mental health challenges?	"AI in Employee Mental Health", "Workplace Stress Detection through AI", "AI-Driven Mental Health Interventions for Organisations", "AI-Powered Employee Well-Being Programs", "Mental Health Monitoring in the Workplace", "Ethics of AI in Workplace Mental Health", "AI for Reducing Workplace Stress", "AI-Enabled Mental Health Counselling in Organisations", "Workplace Productivity and AI in Mental Health".

Source: The authors.

2016-present. The first growth phase marks the integration of AI technologies, such as ML and NLP, into mental health diagnostics. Early studies explored AI's feasibility in identifying depression, anxiety, and other disorders. The second growth phase reflects an accelerated interest driven by advancements in DL, neural networks, and sophisticated analytical tools. Notably, the COVID-19 pandemic heightened societal awareness, encouraging scalable AI-driven interventions to address the mental health crisis.

Citation trends followed a similar trajectory. A marked increase occurred from 2006 to 2009 and intensified from 2014 onwards, indicating the discipline's transition from exploratory studies to mature, large-scale implementations. This growth underscores the interdisciplinary nature of the field and its relevance in addressing pressing mental health challenges. This study identifies *Johnson, C.L., Dickerson, D.L.,* and *D'Amico, E.J.* as leading AI and mental health research contributors. *Johnson, C.L.* published the highest number of articles with an h-index of eight, signifying significant and consistent scholarly influence. *Skewes, M.C.* emerged as the most impactful author regarding total citations. These findings align with Lotka's Law, which reflects that a small group of prolific authors dominates the research landscape while the majority contribute fewer publications.

The key research themes include AI-based diagnostics, interventions and treatment, and wearable devices and monitoring. Studies focused on using ML and NLP to predict and diagnose conditions such as depression, anxiety, and post-traumatic stress disorder (PTSD) using clinical and social media data. AI tools are increasingly applied in virtual counselling, cognitive-behavioural therapy (CBT), and personalised treatment plans. Integrating AI with wearable technologies facilitates real-time mental health monitoring and predictive analytics.

A detailed bibliometric analysis highlighted that terms such as "Machine Learning," "Deep Learning," and "mental health intervention" dominate the literature. This implies an emphasis on state-of-the-art AI models and their pragmatic uses. Intensified cross-disciplinary work among computer scientists, psychologists, and medical experts has significantly increased productivity and creativity. International collaboration made up 18.82% of all articles, and thus, is significant as this area is now an important field of global well-being. The most significant contributing regions were North America, Europe, and Asia.

AI and mental health research demonstrate strong interdisciplinary links. Prominent references and citations range from computer science to clinical psychology, healthcare management, and behavioural economics. A multidisciplinary approach is vital for effectively utilising AI technologies to address complex mental health challenges.

1.6 CONCLUSION

This bibliometric analysis provides a comprehensive overview of the intersection of AI and mental health research. The findings show a strong upward trajectory in publication output, especially after 2016, which reflects growing academic and practical interest in AI applications for mental health diagnostics, interventions, and monitoring. Advances in ML, DL, and NLP have transformed the research landscape, making possible scalable and accurate mental health solutions. Key research trends point to AI's capability to revolutionise mental health care by facilitating early diagnosis, personalised treatments, and improving accessibility to mental health services. Prominent contributors, collaborative networks, and interdisciplinary efforts have driven innovations in this field. However, the study also emphasises the need for continued research to address ethical concerns, data privacy issues, and the scalability of AI solutions across diverse populations and contexts.

The international scope of this research, which encompasses collaboration across regions, signifies the importance of a shared commitment to addressing mental health challenges using cutting-edge technologies. Future studies ought to prioritise the creation of ethical frameworks, improvements in AI model explainability, and fostering inclusivity in data representation to address current disparities in AI-supported mental health care.

This study contributes significantly to AI and mental health research, but several limitations apply. This study is limited to articles sourced exclusively from the *Scopus* database, which may exclude relevant studies indexed in other databases such as *Web of Science (WoS), PubMed, or IEEE Xplore*. The study focuses on quantitative measures like publications, citations, and keywords. Still, it overlooks qualitative elements such as contextual nuances and the effectiveness of AI models mentioned in the literature. This could exclude studies on similar concepts explored using different terminologies. It only covers a specific period, which could miss ongoing or recently published works that could shed more light on emerging themes. The findings may not represent the diversity of research globally, particularly in under-represented regions where AI applications in mental health are still in their infancy. Despite these restrictions, this study provides the foundation for understanding the present landscape and emerging themes in AI-driven mental health studies. Future research may overcome these confinements by including multiple databases and elongating keyword searches to gain a holistic view through qualitative analyses.

Data Availability Statement

The data shall be made available upon reasonable request.

REFERENCES

1. Theerthagiri, P., Ruby, A. U., Chandran, J. G. C., Sardar, T. H., & Shafeeq, B. M. A. (2024). Deep SqueezeNet learning model for diagnosis and prediction of maize leaf diseases. *Journal of Big Data*, 11(1), 112.
2. Sardar, T. H. (2024). Reflecting on a decade of evolution: MapReduce-based advances in partitioning-based, hierarchical-based, and density-based clustering (2013–2023). *Wiley Interdisciplinary Reviews: Data Mining and Knowledge Discovery*, 14(6), e1566.
3. Subbarao, E., et al. (2023). Investigation of solar energy for urban areas and metropolitan communities using machine learning. *Electric Power Components and Systems*, 8, 1–11.
4. Sardar, T. H., Faizabadi, A. R., & Ansari, Z. (2017). An analysis of data processing using Mapreduce paradigm on the Hadoop framework. *International Journal of Emerging Research in Management and Technology*, 6(5), 17–20.

5. Sardar, T. H., Sarkar, R., Ahmed, S. J., & Bandyopadhyay, A. (2023, May). A novel ensemble methodology to validate fuzzy clusters of Big Data. In *Proceedings of the Fourth International Conference on Trends in Computational and Cognitive Engineering: TCCE 2022* (pp. 267–278). Springer Nature, Singapore.
6. Sardar, T. H., Khatun, A., & Khan, S. (2017, December). Design of energy aware collection tree protocol in wireless sensor network. In *2017 IEEE International Conference on Circuits and Systems (ICCS)* (pp. 12–17). IEEE, Vimal Jyothi College of Engineering, Kerala, India.
7. Sardar, T. H., Faizabadi, A. R., & Ansari, Z. (2017, July). An evaluation of MapReduce framework in cluster analysis. In *2017 International Conference on Intelligent Computing, Instrumentation and Control Technologies (ICICICT)* (pp. 110–114). IEEE, Vimal Jyothi College of Engineering, Kerala, India.
8. Khatun, A., & Sardar, T. H. (2025). Cryptography algorithms to prevent different security attacks. In Keshav Kumar, & Bishwajeet Kumar Pandey (eds), *Next Generation Mechanisms for Data Encryption* (pp. 35–46). CRC Press.
9. Sardar, T. H., Muttineni, A., & Ranjan, R. (2024). The future of Big Data in customer experience and inventory management. In Keshav Kumar, & Bishwajeet Kumar Pandey (eds), *Big Data Computing* (pp. 233–248). CRC Press.
10. Sardar, T. H., Das, S., & Pandey, B. K. Explainable AI (XAI): concepts and theory. In Keshav Kumar, & Bishwajeet Kumar Pandey (eds), *Medical Data Analysis and Processing Using Explainable Artificial Intelligence* (pp. 1–18). CRC Press.
11. Ghahramani, Z. (2015, May). Probabilistic machine learning and artificial intelligence. *Nature*, 521(7553), 452–459, doi: 10.1038/nature14541.
12. Mathews, S. M. (2019). Explainable artificial intelligence applications in NLP, biomedical, and malware classification: a literature review. In *Intelligent Computing: CompCom 2019. Advances in Intelligent Systems and Computing* (vol. 998, pp. 1269–1292). Springer, doi: 10.1007/978-3-030-22868-2_90.
13. Nagendran, M., et al. (2020, March). Artificial intelligence versus clinicians: systematic review of design, reporting standards, and claims of deep learning studies. *BMJ*, 368, m689, doi: 10.1136/bmj.m689.
14. Woodnutt, S., et al. (2024, February). Could artificial intelligence write mental health nursing care plans?, *Journal of Psychiatric and Mental Health Nursing*, 31(1), 79–86, doi: 10.1111/jpm.12965.
15. Higgins, O., Short, B. L., Chalup, S. K., & Wilson, R. L. (2023, August). Artificial intelligence (AI) and machine learning (ML) based decision support systems in mental health: an integrative review. *International Journal of Mental Health Nursing*, 32(4), 966–978, doi: 10.1111/inm.13114.
16. Joyce, D. W., Kormilitzin, A., Smith, K. A., & Cipriani, A. (2023, January). Explainable artificial intelligence for mental health through transparency and interpretability for understandability. *NPJ Digital Medicine*, 6(1), 6, doi: 10.1038/s41746-023-00751-9.
17. Mohr, D. C., Zhang, M., & Schueller, S. M. (2017, May). Personal sensing: understanding mental health using ubiquitous sensors and machine learning. *Annual Review of Clinical Psychology*, 13(1), 23–47, doi: 10.1146/annurev-clinpsy-032816-044949.
18. Saha, I., Gourisaria, M. K., & Harshvardhan, G. M. (2022). Classification system for prediction of chronic kidney disease using data mining techniques. In *Advances in Data and Information Sciences: Proceedings of ICDIS 2021* (pp. 429–443). Springer, Singapore.
19. Gourisaria, M. K., Jee, G., Harshvardhan, G. M., Singh, V., Singh, P. K., & Workneh, T. C. (2022). Data science appositeness in diabetes mellitus diagnosis for healthcare systems of developing nations. *IET Communications*, 16(5), 532–547.

20. Chancellor, S., Baumer, E. P. S., & De Choudhury, M. (2019, November). Who is the 'Human' in human-centered machine learning. *Proceedings of the ACM on Human-Computer Interaction*, 3 (CSCW), 1–32, doi: 10.1145/3359249.
21. Rajkishan, S. S., Meitei, A. J., & Singh, A. (2024, May). Role of AI/ML in the study of mental health problems of the students: a bibliometric study. *International Journal of System Assurance Engineering and Management*, 15(5), 1615–1637, doi: 10.1007/s13198-023-02052-6.
22. Dutta, K., Chandra, S., & Gourisaria, M. K. (2022). Early-Stage detection of liver disease through machine learning algorithms. In Tiwari, S., Trivedi, M.C., Kolhe, M.L., Mishra, K., Singh, B.K. (eds) *Advances in Data and Information Sciences* (pp. 155–166). Lecture Notes in Networks and Systems. Springer, Singapore. https://doi.org/10.1007/978-981-16-5689-7_14
23. Phan Tan, L. (2022). Bibliometrics of social entrepreneurship research: cocitation and bibliographic coupling analyses. *Cogent OA*, 9(1). doi: 10.1080/23311975.2022.2124594.
24. Guleria, D., & Kaur, G. (2021, November). Bibliometric analysis of ecopreneurship using VOS viewer and RStudio Bibliometrix, 1989–2019. *Library Hi Tech*, 39(4), 1001–1024, doi: 10.1108/LHT-09–2020-0218.
25. Boakye, E. A., Zhao, H., & Ahia, B. N. K. (2022, November). Emerging research on blockchain technology in finance; a conveyed evidence of bibliometric-based evaluations. *The Journal of High Technology Management Research*, 33(2), 100437, doi: 10.1016/j.hitech.2022.100437.
26. Gourisaria, M. K., Harshvardhan, G. M., Agrawal, R., Patra, S. S., Rautaray, S. S., & Pandey, M. (2021). Arrhythmia detection using deep belief network extracted features from ECG signals. *International Journal of E-Health and Medical Communications (IJEHMC)*, 12(6), 1–24.
27. Megha Bakshi, & R. Verma (2023, March). Trends in cause-related marketing (CRM): scientometrics analysis through prism of biblioshiny. *International Journal of Professional Business Review*, 8(4), e0995, doi: 10.26668/businessreview/2023.v8i4.995.
28. Mundargi, Z., Patil, S., Phadke, M., Sundkar, R., Dongre, R., & Raut, A. (2025). Empathetic conversations in mental health: fine-tuning LLMs for supportive AI interactions. In *Proceedings of the 5th International Conference on Data Science, Machine Learning and Applications; Volume 1. ICDSMLA 2023. Lecture Notes in Electrical Engineering* (vol. 1273, pp. 112–119). Springer, Singapore, doi: 10.1007/978-981-97-8031-0_12.
29. Spiegel, B. M. R., et al. (2024, January). Feasibility of combining spatial computing and AI for mental health support in anxiety and depression. *NPJ Digital Medicine*, 7(1), 22, doi: 10.1038/s41746-024-01011-0.
30. You, C., Awang, S. R., & Wu, Y. (2024, September). Bibliometric analysis of global research trends on higher education leadership development using Scopus database from 2013–2023. *Discover Sustainability*, 5(1), 246, doi: 10.1007/s43621-024-00432-x.
31. Erlinda, V., & Fatmawati, I. (2024, October). Bibliometric analysis of publication trends in the Scopus database on the theme fear of missing out to consumers behavior. *Multidisciplinary Reviews*, 8(3), 2025070, doi: 10.31893/multirev.2025070.
32. Praharaj, A., & Chhatoi, B. P. (2025, February). Enterprise resource planning (ERP) in business: a contextual snapshot. *Global Knowledge, Memory and Communication*, doi: 10.1108/GKMC-07-2024-0453.
33. Wang, G., Bennamoun, H., Kwok, W. H., Marriott, R., Walker, R., & Kotz, J. (2024). *Codesigning a Clinical Prediction Model for Aboriginal Perinatal Mental Health Using Glassbox AI and Aboriginal Wisdom and Lived Experience*. IOS Press, doi: 10.3233/SHTI240925.
34. Xing, Y., et al., (2024, November). Developing an AI-based digital biophilic art curation to enhance mental health in intelligent buildings. *Sustainability*, 16(22), 9790, doi: 10.3390/su16229790.

35. Patra, A. K., Praharaj, A., Sudarshan, D., & Chhatoi, B. P. (2024, January). AI and business management: tracking future research agenda through bibliometric network analysis. *Heliyon*, 10(1), e23902, doi: 10.1016/j.heliyon.2023.e23902.
36. Kirby, A. (2023, February). Exploratory bibliometrics: using VOSviewer as a preliminary research tool. *Publications*, 11(1), 10, doi: 10.3390/publications11010010.
37. Sahu, A., Harshvardhan, G. M., Gourisaria, M. K., Rautaray, S. S., & Pandey, M. (2021). Cardiovascular risk assessment using data mining inferencing and feature engineering techniques. *International Journal of Information Technology*, 13(5), 2011–2023.
38. Hirsch, J. E. (2007, December). Does the *h* index have predictive power? *Proceedings of the National Academy of Sciences*, 104(49), 19193–19198, doi: 10.1073/pnas.0707962104.
39. Egghe, L. (2006, October). Theory and practise of the g-index. *Scientometrics*, 69(1), 131–152, doi: 10.1007/s11192-006-0144-7.
40. Bellary, M. Z., Deepthi, T. H. S., Musthafa, B. A., Ahmed, S. J., & Sarkar, R. (2023). Medical image analysis of knee osteoarthritis using modified deep CNN. *Journal of Survey in Fisheries Sciences*, 10(2S), 133–144.
41. Dutta, K., Chandra, S., Gourisaria, M. K., & GM, H. (2021, April). A data mining based target regression-oriented approach to modelling of health insurance claims. In *2021 5th International Conference on Computing Methodologies and Communication (ICCMC)* (pp. 1168–1175). IEEE, Erode, India.

2 ABCNN

Attention-Based Convolutional Neural Networks for Arrhythmia Detection from ECG Data

T.M. Rajesh and M.N. Renukadevi

2.1 INTRODUCTION

2.1.1 Overview of Cardiovascular Diseases and the Role of ECG

Estimates from the World Health Organization (WHO) record the number of deaths caused by cardiovascular diseases (CVDs) as the highest, amounting to 17 million. Worryingly enough, a combination of bad eating, unhealthy levels of stress, obesity, and excessive alcohol and nicotine consumption has fanned the difficulty of diagnosing and treating heart failure. Due to these habits on a global scale, cardiovascular diseases have only risen, hence the need for advanced diagnostic tools [1].

To begin with, electrocardiograms or ECGs are important in diagnosing heart disease, particularly heart attack, which is one of the heart's diseases. An ECG rhythmically captures the electrical activity of the cardiac muscle over a period of time. It has many wave components, such as the T, QRS, and P waves. P waves are formed as a result of depolarization occurring in the atrium.

Furthermore, ventricular activity exhibits electrical changes as it contracts. This also demonstrates ventricular contraction, with one of the vital depolarizations being the QRS complex.

In addition, some of the cardiac activity segments, such as the PQ and the ST segments, provide additional information on other parts. For example, the PQ segment shows the conduction time going from the AV node to the SA node, whereas the ST segment describes the time when the heart muscles contract and when the blood circulates [2].

Changes in ECG waves and segments can be utilized to diagnose the existence of arrhythmias or an alteration in the rate at which the heart beats. Such abnormalities, if not identified and treated in time, may lead to greater ailments such as cardiac arrest. Any heart rate that is faster than the common healthy individual rate of 72 beats per minute can be considered as an arrhythmia, more so, when an ECG shows that a lot of large squares have been recorded between QRS complexes. For example,

DOI: 10.1201/9781003600947-2

a heart rate of 150 beats per minute would mean 2 large squares, while 100 means 3 and 60 would mean 5 squares [3].

In recent years, biomedical signal processing has seen a growing interest in deep neural networks (DNNs). Features, such as extraction and pre-filtering, are redundant as convolutional neural networks (CNNs) can process raw ECG data directly. A diverse range of arrhythmias can be classified by CNNs as these networks are capable of spatial feature extraction from ECG signals [4].

The research is based on the MIT-BIH Arrhythmia Database, which contains a large number of samples of the heartbeat signal that could be used for training of DNNs. For detecting arrhythmia and classifying ECG signals with the help of questionnaires, a one-dimensional convolutional neural networks model is recommended. We also combine the neural net model with overlaid SoftM that enhances the models' classification accuracy for classifying ECG beats [5].

Together with Machine Learning and Deep Learning, the understanding and diagnosis of electrocardiogram (ECG) has transformed with notable change, especially in the detection and diagnosis of heart diseases. DNNs, particularly CNN in this case, require no human involvement to detect electromagnetic features from the data, unlike traditional Machine Learning blank RF and SVM devices, which require the manual identification of features. These models can capture temporal and spatial variations of ECG signals, making it easier for them to succeed in recognizing minute alterations such as tremors, premature vents, and cardiac interruption. Given their ability to comprehend learning representations hierarchically, CNNs achieve outstanding results on databases such as MIT-BIH, outperforming classical methods and improving their predictions on different populations of patients.

However, these models' performance is based on proper training data and high-quality data sets. This work focuses on the importance of extensive data in developing best performing classifiers by utilizing the MIT-BIH Arrhythmia Database, which contains annotated ECG signals of various patients. The accurate arrhythmia detection is achieved through the use of one-dimensional CNN architecture along with a SoftMax layer for probabilistic classification. Here, the model is updated with the testing records at iterative weights so that the model can learn the patterns that are not visible initially and hence avoid overtraining and increase the efficiency. The developments in ECG analysis have a huge implication in clinical practice since these provide timely and accurate diagnosis, thus relieving the medical personnel and, in the long run, patient care.

2.1.2 Challenges in Arrhythmia Detection with Conventional Methods

In the required order, conventional expertise and manual signal-handling approaches often struggle to detect arrhythmia in large-scale, real-time ECG data. Traditional machine learning models rely heavily on handcrafted features and domain-specific knowledge, which limit their adaptability and generalization to new or noisy datasets. These models are also sensitive to temporal variations and signal imbalance, making them less effective in extracting meaningful patterns from complex ECG waveforms. To address these challenges, deep learning models such as Attention-Based

Convolutional Neural Networks (ABCNNs) have been proposed. They automatically learn hierarchical representations from raw ECG signals, enhancing detection accuracy and reliability across diverse patient conditions.

2.1.3 Motivation for Deep Learning Approaches and Objectives

Cardiovascular diseases (CVDs) are the largest cause of death in the world, and their prevention requires efficient diagnostic tools. The use of conventional techniques to identify arrhythmias, however, is a laborious task and often leads to manual examination of ECG records prone to human errors. Convolutional neural networks (CNNs), one of the Deep Learning algorithms that extract discriminative features directly from raw ECG signals, have shown great potential to solve these issues. Deep CNN models face crucial challenges with typically high-level requirements, reliability validation due to extensive databases like the MIT-BIH Arrhythmia Database. Hence, our study aims at applying CNNs for accurate and efficient diagnosis of arrhythmias by improving cardiovascular disease detection, which can beneficially impact cardiac care outcomes [6,7].

The main purpose of this work is to apply Deep Learning to ECG signals for the detection and classification of abnormal behaviors, including variabilities that may represent either noise or manifestations of diseases. For low-frequency problems, it is also concerned with baseline wandering noise and movement-induced muscle artifacts that can corrupt the ECG signals and control diagnostic precision. The problem statement identifies efforts aimed at increasing the efficacy of arrhythmia detection as the target of the proposed work [8].

2.2 BACKGROUND AND DATASET

2.2.1 Overview of ECG Signal Features and Common Arrhythmias

The P wave, QRS complex, and T wave are three main types of waveforms in ECG data that can reflect the electrical activities of the heart during different phases of the cardiac cycle. Heart rate variability, RR intervals, as well as the shape feature of these waves contain heavy physiological information. Some often seen arrhythmias include bradycardia (heart rate too slow is abnormal), ventricular tachycardia (too fast ventricular contractions), and atrial fibrillation (cardiac rhythm is irregular). Whether transient or chronic, cardiac arrhythmias usually indicate underlying cardiovascular problems. For this reason, it becomes significant to diagnose such conditions accurately based on analysis of ECG results and treat them timely. Table 2.1 shows the summary of the work.

2.2.2 Introduction to the MIT-BIH Arrhythmia Dataset

The MIT-BIH Arrhythmia Database is a benchmark database to evaluate ECG signal-processing algorithms and arrhythmia diagnosis. The heartbeat on 48 half-hour recordings of 47 patients in this database is carefully annotated and labelled into a number of arrhythmia types. This is a heterogeneous collection of records, including

TABLE 2.1
Traditional and Deep Learning-Based Approaches for ECG Analysis

Authors	Year	Methods	Results	Limitations
H. Wang et al. [9]	2019	Convolutional Neural Networks (CNNs) for ECG signal classification.	Achieved 93% accuracy for arrhythmia detection.	Limited to single-lead ECG signals.
A. Hernandez et al. [10]	2020	Long Short-Term Memory (LSTM) networks combined with Recurrent Neural Networks (RNN)	Improved detection sensitivity and specificity.	High computational requirements.
J. Patel et al. [11]	2021	Attention-Based Convolutional Neural Networks (ABCNN)	Enhanced feature extraction and classification accuracy.	Dataset size limited to specific conditions.
M. Lee et al. [12]	2022	Hybrid Convolutional Neural Network-Recurrent Neural Network (CNN-RNN) model	96% accuracy in detecting various arrhythmias.	Complex model architecture.
K. Johnson et al. [13]	2023	Residual Convolutional Neural Networks (ResNet) for ECG classification	High accuracy with reduced overfitting.	Requires extensive training data.
L. Zhang et al. [14]	2020	1-D Convolutional Neural Network (1-D CNN) for real-time ECG monitoring	Effective for real-time detection with 94% accuracy.	Performance varies with different ECG devices.
R. Kumar et al. [15]	2021	Ensemble Learning Approach combining multiple Machine Learning algorithms	95% accuracy with improved robustness against noisy data.	Ensemble complexity and longer training times.
P. Singh et al. [16]	2023	Multi-Scale Convolutional Neural Network (MS-CNN) with Data Augmentation	Enhanced model generalizability and accuracy.	Data augmentation might not always reflect real-world variations.
C. Evans et al. [17]	2019	Temporal Convolutional Networks (TCN) for sequential ECG data	High accuracy in detecting complex arrhythmias.	TCNs may be less effective with very noisy data.

a variety of patients, even those with severe cardiac abnormalities, collected by the Arrhythmia Laboratory at Beth Israel Hospital. The extremely large number of annotations and diverse datasets also make it a prime candidate for the development and assessment of Deep Learning and Machine Learning models in the cardiovascular field.

2.2.3 Data Preprocessing Techniques

Preprocessing refers to the methods employed to improve the quality of raw data and ultimately the model performance in ECG signal analysis. Common techniques involve using filters to remove things such as baseline wander noise, powerline interference, and motion artifacts. Normalizing amplitudes to a common scale results in consistency across samples in terms of signal amplitude. Segmentation is the process of isolating specific heartbeats or time segments for focused analysis. Resampling helps to standardize the sampling rate across different datasets, and data augmentation generates synthetic examples to address class deficits. These procedures help ensure the data is clean, consistent, and ready for effective feature extraction or use for modeling training.

2.3 PROPOSED MODEL: ABCNN

2.3.1 Key Concepts of Attention Mechanisms and Convolutional Neural Networks

Convolutional neural networks (CNNs) and recommendation systems, for example, are areas of significant interest in the science realm. It is fair to say that CNNs seem to achieve pretty decent performance in computer vision and recommendation systems domain, thanks to the particular high-level feature learning capabilities they possess. Although recurrent neural networks are networks that are good at memory within sequences, the processing of long-term dependencies is a subservient activity; they are lacking in large amounts of processing power. A 1D CNN code structure was utilized for ECG-based analysis since the ECG is a long sequence signal. In most of the designs of CNN, the three main layers that one can find are usually: convolutional, pooling, and completely connected. To illustrate how different EEG electrodes relate to each other, we describe the ABCNN model approach in this research. We make this explicit by using a real ECG recording from the benchmark collection, the MIT-BIH dataset [9].

The ECG signals are derived from the two leads at a sampling frequency of 360 Hz and then subdivided into 240 time-points, the R peak centering in a window of 0.76-second each per each timepoint. Each of the segments will produce a row [2, 240]- formatted matrix, with each row representing an ECG channel and the columns as tintopoints. As per common CNN topologies, all input neurons are entreated equally, though usually, the importance of different periods of the cardiac cycle is different. In particular, the QRS complex part, which covers approximately 10% of the cardiac cycle in an ECG, is the most important. Hence, our model should underline the QRS element. This, as a fix, we launched ABCNN with the focus on by giving the attention process more importance to the informative time points. To be exact, the properly chosen attention layer helps the model to concentrate on significant time slices, and it thus better its correctness.

The suggested ABCNN model is made up of several interleaved layers, as shown in Figure 2.1: an input layer that takes raw ECG signals; an attention layer that checks input samples and determines the level of attention for each signal slice; two fully connected layers: one first convolutional and pooling layer; one second convolutional and pooling layer, and an output layer that makes labels. The pooling layers decrease the dimensionality of the embeddings and extract the significant spatial characteristics. Normally, the pooling layers follow the convolutional layers in order to save the processing costs as well as to prevent the networks from overfitting by reducing the number of the network's free parameters. On the contrary, the convolutional layers act on input signals using a set of different initially randomly initialized kernels.

The fully connected layers are made up of several neurons that connect to every other neuron in the layer below them, even though they are not connected within the same layer. In order to improve model accuracy, this architecture uses the attention mechanism to efficiently process and extract features from ECG signals, focusing on important signal segments [10].

Adding an attention mechanism helps the ABCNN model focus on important features. This is useful for ECG interpretation and takes advantage of convolutional neural networks. The model zeroes in on key parts of the ECG signal, like the QRS complex, boosting classification accuracy by emphasizing crucial time slices. ECG signals have sections with different diagnostic importance, making this focus critical. The attention layer adapts quickly to changes in the input, which allows effective generalization across various ECG patterns, including different arrhythmias, all while keeping computational efficiency intact. This adaptability is especially beneficial for large ECG datasets, where fast processing is vital for real-time applications [11].

ABCNN's modular setup promotes durability and scalability. Pooling layers minimize dimensions while preserving key features and reducing overfitting risks. Meanwhile, convolutional layers target localized characteristics, capturing the subtle details in ECG waveforms. Fully connected layers then merge spatial data from earlier levels, ensuring high-level feature representation and decision-making. ABCNN achieved impressive results on the MIT-BIH Arrhythmia Dataset, boasting top-notch classification accuracy for arrhythmias. The combination of the attention mechanism with a well-structured CNN backbone underscores the model's potential in clinical settings, offering a reliable, automated approach for identifying cardiovascular issues in ECG signals. This innovation paves the way for implementing ABCNN in wearable tech and telemedicine, allowing for real-time cardiac monitoring centered around patient needs [12].

2.3.2 Notation and Model Structure of ABCNN

The attention-based convolutional neural network (ABCNN) combines the advantages of convolutional networks and attention processes. Accurately classifying arrhythmias, capturing global dependencies, and documenting local properties are the goals of this design. The ABCNN model uses attention mechanisms built into the convolutional neural network (CNN) architecture to interpret ECG information [18]. Structure and notation are as described.

Input layer: X∈R^2X240 is the input ECG signal matrix, where 240 is the number of time points and two is the number of channels.

2.3.2.1 Attention Layer

By focusing on the most pertinent regions of the ECG data, ABCNN's attention mechanism highlights important aspects, including irregular waveforms and transitory anomalies. By using multi-head attention to calculate weighted representations of the input signal, the model efficiently captures relationships across different time steps. By giving signal regions linked to arrhythmias greater weights, this layer improves the interpretability of the model. Furthermore, in order to handle the unpredictability in ECG data, the attention mechanism dynamically adapts to special patterns. Each time point in the input signal has a significance assigned by the attention weight vector. The element-wise multiplication produces an attention-weighted input signal as the output. Convolution and pooling layer: To record the morphological characteristics of ECG signal waveforms, 1-D filters are used.

2.3.2.2 Convolution and Pooling Layer

For local feature extraction in developing models for 2-D ECG analysis in the architectural diagrams, the 1-D filters in the convolutional layers are used, which capture the formative parts of the ECG waveforms, including the QRS complex, P wave, and T wave. The order often described for multiple layers in a stack was for them to, in the hierarchy, the features that start with learning simple patterns and culminate in the most complex representations, output. We can outfit different layers for pooling, specifically, max pooling, though the network does not specifically refer them as max pooling layers but outfits them after the convolutional layers. This is done to simplify the raw data categorization, thus providing a higher time efficiency and yet achieving better results. Through the implementation of the ABCNN system, some independent trends can be extracted that are crucial for classifying arrhythmias in ECG data using convolutional layers [13].

1st Convolutional Layer: Conv_1 applies a set of convolution filters $K1 \in R^{f1Xk1}$ where $f1$ is several filters and $k1$ is the filter size. The output is $C_1 = \text{Conv}_1 X'$

1st Pooling Layer: $Pool_1$ performs dimensionality reduction on C_1. The pooling operation reduces the spatial dimensions, resulting $P_1 = Pool_1 C_1$

2nd Convolution Layer: $Conv_2$ applies another set of convolution filters. $K_2 \in \text{R}^{f1Xk2}$. The output is $C_2 = Conv_2 P_1$

2nd Pooling Layer: $Pool_2$ further reduces the dimensions of C_2, *yielding* $P_2 = Pool_2 C_2$

2.3.2.3 Fully Connected and Output Layers

The fully connected layers, also known as dense layers, take the features learned in the previous layers and merge them together to form a comprehensive overview of the entire ECG signal. These layers are responsible for learning how to translate these learned features into the classification space, to predict which types of arrhythmias [19]. Using a softmax activation function, the output layer also allows the model to efficiently manage multi-class classification problems, providing a probabilistic distribution of the arrhythmias. These multiple layers help the model learn features, thus improving overall generalizability in various datasets and decreasing overfitting.

A useful tool for arrhythmia identification, ABCNN's modular architecture combines fully linked, convolutional, attention, and pooling layers to provide reliable feature extraction and classification.

1st Fully Connected Layer: FC_1 consists of neurons fully connected to the flattened output of P_2 resulting in $F_1 = FC_1(\mathit{flatten}(P_2))$

2nd Fully Connected Layer: FC_2 Further processes the features, resulting in $F_2 = FC_2(F_1)$

Output Layer: O generates the final classification labels. This layer typically uses a SoftMax activation function to produce a probability distribution over the possible classes $O = \text{Softmax}(F_2)$

2.3.3 Workflow and Signal Processing

The workflow for arrhythmia detection using ABCNN involves the following key steps, as shown in Figure 2.1

2.3.3.1 Workflow

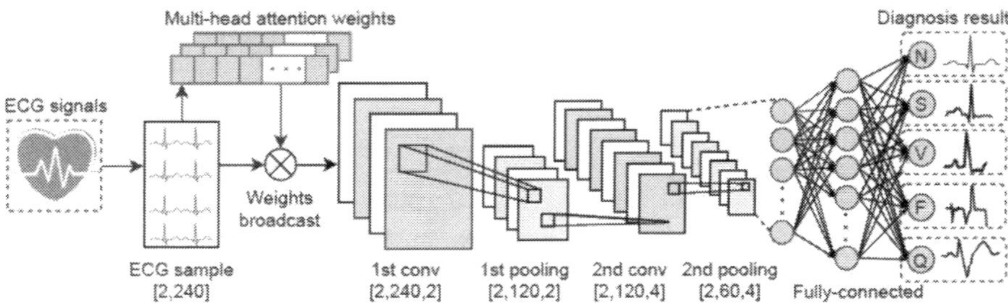

FIGURE 2.1 The workflow of the proposed ABCNN.

2.3.3.2 Experimental Setting

2.3.3.2.1 Dataset

The MIT-BIH Arrhythmia Database is a collection of ECG data that has been secured from the MIT-BIH Arrhythmia Dataset with distinct arrhythmia types labeled. We evaluate the performance of our model by using the MIT-BIH Arrhythmia dataset, which comprises 4,000 long-term Holter recordings from 47 people. We got the last 48 recordings, which were about 30 minutes each, after the pre-processing. The two types of typical heartbeats and arrhythmias that have clinical relevance are the devotion points of our research. Arrhythmia detection was accomplished by selecting 240 slices of two-lead ECG signals collected from the 360 Hz around the R peak. Each CSV file has pre-processed and segmental yet normal ECG data and those affected by arrhythmias and cardiac infarctions. The set is divided into five classes: N (Normal), S (Supraventricular ectopic beats), V (Ventricular ectopic beats), F (Fusion beats), and Q (Unknown beats).

2.3.3.2.2 Pre-processing Noise Removal

Noise Removal: Filters are applied to eliminate baseline wander (<0.5 Hz powerline interference (~50/60 Hz) and motion artifacts.

Normalization: ECG signals are normalized to a range, typically [−1,1] using the equation

$$X_{\text{norm}} = \frac{X - \mu}{\sigma}$$

where X is the signal, μ\mu is the mean, and σ\sigma is the standard deviation.

Segmentation: Signals are divided into fixed-length windows (e.g., one heartbeat) using R-peak detection methods.

2.3.3.3 Feature Extraction via ABCNN

Attention Mechanism: Multi-head attention identifies critical segments of the signal using attention scores:

$$\text{Attention}(Q,K,V) = \text{softmax}\left(\frac{QK^T}{\sqrt{d_k}}\right).V$$

where Q, K, and V are query, key, and value matrices, and d_k is the dimensionality of keys. Convolutional Layers: 1-D convolutional filters (www) extract features by performing:

$$y[i] = \Sigma^{k-1}\, x[\text{i}+j].w[j]$$

where x is the input segment, k is the filter size, and y is the output.

Pooling: Dimensionality reduction using max-pooling

$$y_{\text{pool}}[i] = \max\left(x[i:[i+p-1]\right)$$

where p is the pooling size.

2.3.3.4 Classification

Fully connected layers aggregate features, and the output layer performs arrhythmia classification with a softmax activation:

$$\hat{y}_c = \frac{\text{e}^{zc}}{\sum_{k=1}^{C} \text{e}^{zk}}$$

where zc is the score for class c, and C is the total number of classes.

Figure 2.2 outlines the key steps from preprocessing the raw ECG signal to the final classification of arrhythmias.

Figure 2.2 displays a CNN whose primary objective is the classification of an electrocardiography (ECG) signal by focusing on the information. The model is initialized with ECG data input and creates attention precisely such as the QRS complex for time slices with relevant values. This approach has been known to significantly reduce the burden of the model in data patterns detection. The power of the feature representation is increased by a multi-head attention mechanism, which enables the detection of complex connections anywhere within the temporal signal.

According to the author of the paper, using analogy of the way humans perceive ECG data as shape and temporal sequences, the EKG data are typically presented in the form of graphical signals.

Convolutional layers are then used to capture local features of these weighted signals. By using pooling layers, the dimensionality of the features is reduced, which

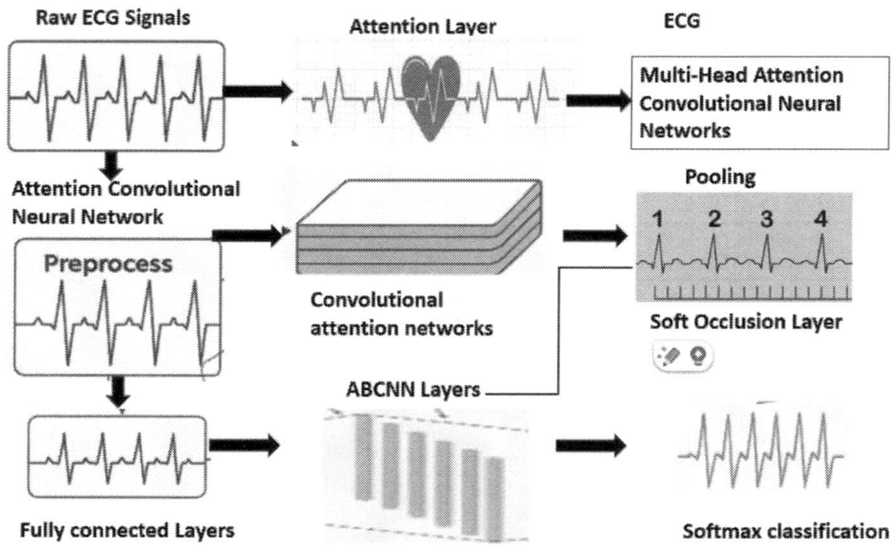

FIGURE 2.2 Workflow for arrhythmia detection using the ABCNN model.

in turn lowers computing costs and avoids overfitting. The fully connected layers aggregate feature maps obtained from the previous steps, thus resulting in a complete representation of the signal. As a consequence, the SoftMax classifier, which is the last layer in the model, gives an accurate diagnosis of arrhythmia since it provides the probabilities for the different classes. This new method, EKG data processing technology, in integration with the ALM, provides efficient and precise analysis of the EKG, hence it is helpful in the clinical setup where accurate results for diagnosis are of paramount importance [15].

2.4 METHODOLOGY

2.4.1 Experimental Setup and Hyperparameter Tuning

The MIT-BIH Arrhythmia Dataset is used as part of the experimental setup to train and test the ABCNN model. The dataset is split into training (70%) and testing (30%) sets to ensure a fair distribution of arrhythmia classes. Preprocessing includes segmentation into fixed-length windows centered on R-peaks, noise reduction, and normalizing. Data augmentation generates synthetic samples for underrepresented arrhythmia classes to address the class imbalance. The majority of the samples in class 0 were imbalanced. As seen in Figure 2.3, to attain balance across all classes and increase prediction accuracy, we resampled the minority classes and decreased the majority class.

Explaining preprocessing steps for imbalanced data would show how this process improves overall model effectiveness. The process achieves equitable representation for each arrhythmia class, which minimizes bias while promoting better

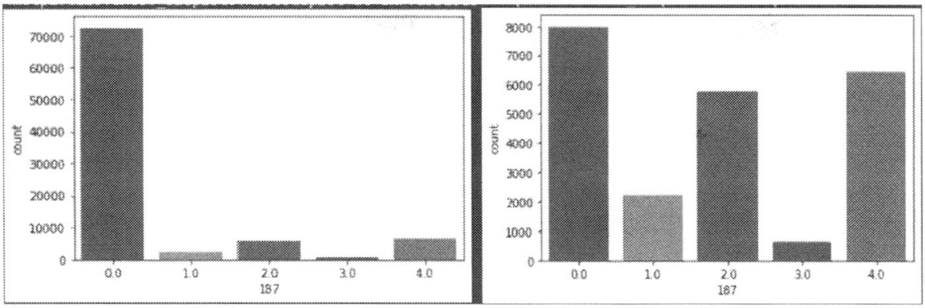

FIGURE 2.3 Pre-processing of imbalanced data.

generalization. Resampling and augmentation techniques help to correct imbalances that stop the model from favoring dominant classes. The ABCNN model achieves better robustness and reliability because this step directly affects classification accuracy.

2.4.1.1 Hyperparameter Optimization

Hyperparameter tuning makes the model perform its best. The number of attention heads, pooling size, learning rate, number of filters, and size of convolutional filters are the hyperparameters. Grid search and random search are used to determine the optimal values. The final configuration has a learning rate of 0.001, four attention heads, filter size five, and pooling size two. To prevent overfitting regularization techniques early stopping and dropout with rate 0.3 are applied. The model is trained on batch size 32 using Adam optimizer with categorical cross-entropy loss for maximum 50 epochs.

We perform hyperparameter tuning with the following parameters: pooling layers kernel sizes and strides are [1, 2] and [1, 1], respectively; the first and second convolutional layers have 4 and 8 kernels, respectively, with kernel size and stride both equal to [2, 2] for both. The output layer has five nodes. There are two fully connected layers with 240 and 60 hidden nodes, respectively. We implement an early-stopping technique after 20 epochs with an Adam optimizer at a learning rate of 0.0005 indeed coupled with a32-head attention mechanism. The dropout rate in the first fully connected layer is set to 0.3. Except where specifically stated otherwise, all other parameters are identical across all approaches. A cardiac cycle, which is the full series of activities in the heart from one heartbeat to the next, comprises two phases, shown in Figure 2.4: the diastole (relaxation) and the systole (contraction). An ECG displays the unique waves, intervals, and segments of each cycle. Atrial depolarization, which initiates atrial contraction, is indicated by the P wave. Ventricular contraction is initiated by the QRS complex, which indicates ventricular depolarization; relaxation is suggested by the T wave, which indicates ventricular repolarization. In addition, the QT interval describes the length of ventricular depolarization and repolarization, whereas the PR interval shows the delay between atrial and ventricular activity. When the ventricles are fully depolarized, the ST segment, which follows the QRS complex but precedes the T wave, shows the phase as shown in Figure 2.4 [16].

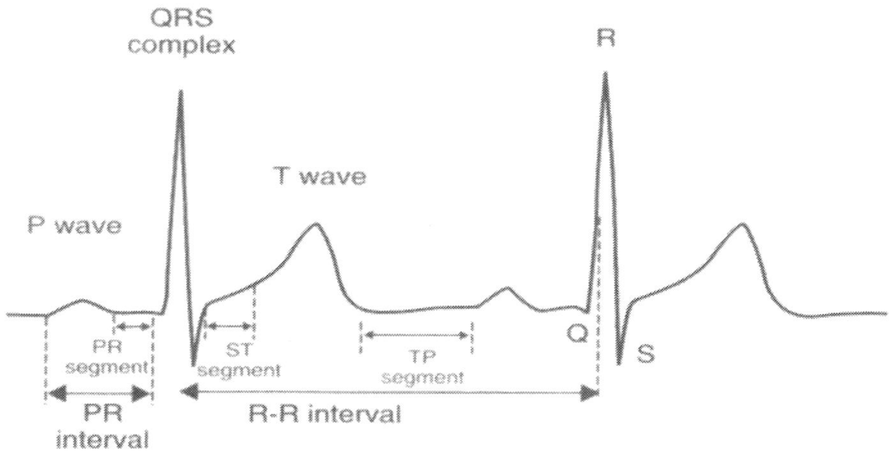

FIGURE 2.4 Two cardiac cycles and their waves, intervals, and segments.

2.4.1.2 Baselines

We evaluate the suggested ABCNN against a number of Machine Learning benchmarks, including K-nearest Neighbors (KNN) with three neighbors, Random Forest (RF) with fifty trees, and Support Vector Machine (SVM) with an RBF kernel. We also compare ABCNN with a regular CNN, which has the same parameters as ABCNN except for the attention module, and an LSTM model, which has two layers of six cells each and a time step of 240.

2.4.2 Model Training and Validation Procedures

The ABCNN model is ECG data that has been pre-processed and trained using supervised learning. It then updates the parameters based on the current gradient to minimize loss using the Adam optimizer. Model robustness was assured through a five-fold cross-validation approach, wherein each of the folds acts once as a validation set with others used during training. Early stopping was also implemented with model checkpoints to keep the best-performing weights. Key performance metrics such as accuracy, precision, recall, F1-score, and AUC were calculated on a validation set to measure model efficacy and guide future improvements [17].

The ABCNN model undergoes training with different methods to achieve high generalization and peak performance. The attention layer may dynamically set a focus toward important time segments in ECG signals, such as QRS, in order to increase the accuracy of extracting features and categorizing them.

Convolutional layers do batch normalization so that feature distributions are standardized for zero mean and unit variance, which will maintain appropriate gradients, therefore reducing the chances of vanishing gradients and accelerating convergence. The fully connected layers also provide dropouts in attempts to reduce overfitting by randomly setting some of the neurons to zero during the updating of weights. These methodologies, when combined with strong evaluation measures, offer keen insight into the advantages and disadvantages of the model in improving how well it can detect different arrhythmias. The ABCNN model is proving very useful in clinical practice.

2.4.3 Evaluation Metrics: AUC, Precision, Recall, and F1 Score

An array of assessment metrics is applied in reviewing the ability of the ABCNN model to identify arrhythmias. The model's capacity to discriminate between a multitude of categories is evaluated using AUC; the higher the value, the better the discrimination. The model proves its acuteness in detecting arrhythmias by presenting precision as the ratio of correctly predicted positive instances to all positive predictions. Recall measures the ability of the model to detect true arrhythmias. The F1 Score balances between accuracy and recall into one single measure of performance, especially useful when dealing with unbalanced data. When taken together, these metrics provide an overall view of the model's diagnostic potential.

$$\text{Precision} = \frac{\text{TP}}{\text{TP} + \text{FP}}$$

$$\text{Recall} = \frac{\text{TP}}{\text{TP} + \text{FN}}$$

$$\text{Accuracy} = \frac{\text{TP} + \text{TN}}{\text{TP} + \text{TN} + \text{FP} + \text{FN}}$$

$$F1 = 2 \times \frac{\text{PRECISION} \times \text{RECALL}}{\text{PRECISION} + \text{RECALL}}$$

2.5 RESULTS AND ANALYSIS

2.5.1 Comparative Performance of ABCNN and Baseline Models

The ABCNN is assessed against several baseline models, including Random Forest, Standard CNN, Support Vector Machine (SVM), and Long Short-Term Memory (LSTM).

2.5.1.1 Random Forest, SVM, LSTM, and Standard CNN Random Forest

Multiple evaluation metrics are employed to assess the ABCNN model's effectiveness in detecting arrhythmias. The AUC (Area Under the Curve) indicates the model's capability to distinguish between various classes, with higher values being preferable. The model's accuracy in identifying arrhythmias is reflected in its precision, which represents the ratio of true positives to all positive predictions. Recall, or sensitivity, gauges the model's effectiveness in identifying actual arrhythmic events. The F1 Score is particularly useful for addressing unbalanced data, as it merges recall and precision into a single metric. Together, these metrics provide a comprehensive overview of the model's diagnostic performance.

The Support Vector Machine (SVM) is a reliable classifier that performs well when binary classification is concerned. Nevertheless, SVM usually needs much effort in the feature extraction, and it may have low accuracy in the case of a multi-class task. Based on raw ECG data, directly and automatically extracting features, with ABCNN, eVNN, and PPNN compared with SVM, accuracy, precision, and recall have performed better. This ensures improved generalization across various arrhythmia classifications.

Long-term memory (LSTM): LSTM networks have the ability to capture long-term dependencies, making them ideal for time series data. However, it is computationally difficult to identify local features in ECG data. On the other hand, ABCNN combines convolutional layers and attention techniques to improve detection methods, balancing spatial and temporal extraction while maintaining computational efficiency.

Conventional CNN: The conventional CNN cannot pay attention to many signal regions. However, it can accurately identify the characteristic features of ECG signals by using reinforcement. The ABCNN detection technique improves the accuracy of detecting different patterns by emphasizing the important parts of the signal.

In terms of major evaluation metrics such as AUC, precision, recall, and F1-score, the ABCNN outperformed all baseline models continuously, as this model also offers more precise, reliable, and interpretable arrhythmia detection. For conventional Machine Learning and conventional Deep Learning methods, the attention mechanism greatly improves the model emphasis on pertinent features, which results in higher diagnostic performance.

Comparing to baseline models demonstrates the better performance in classifying the ECG data of the model ABCNN. Manually designed feature extraction misses complex patterns present in the signals of ECG signals, forming the basis for classical Machine Learning approaches such as Support Vector Machines and Random Forest. The above models are able to recognize arrhythmias with a good level of accuracy, but have difficulty dealing with temporal dependencies and ECG waveform variations. Deep architectures such as CNNs and LSTMs automatically extract features from the raw data, thereby helping to resolve certain issues. However, the vanishing gradient problem and high processing requirements give LSTMs difficulty in processing longer sequences.

This way, by adding an attention mechanism which would emphasize the diagnostically significant parts such as the QRS complex within the ECG signal, the model surpasses conventional norms as well as Deep Learning norms. With a focused approach, which provides higher attention during training for important temporal features, it highly enhances classification accuracy and reliability. While typical CNNs are good at extracting spatial information, they lack proper consideration of the varying importance of the signal's temporal slices. On the other hand, an architecture such as ABCNN, combining convolutional layers with attention, would allow the model to pay its attention to the important areas of the ECG signal while not losing contextual information.

In addition, the comparison study indicates that the ABCNN yields the highest Area Under the Curve (AUC) score of all models tested, which evidences its powerful ability to characterize the separation between different types of arrhythmias.

Baseline models tend to perform worse with noisy or unbalanced ECG signals, even when they might work well on balanced datasets. The issues are addressed by the robust attention mechanism of the ABCNN and better training procedures, like cross-validation and early termination, that ensure reliability over a set of datasets. These results have great potential in using the model as a reliable tool for real-world ECG classification and arrhythmia detection, outperforming traditional techniques in terms of effectiveness and accuracy of diagnosis.

2.5.2 Insights from ROC Curve and Confusion Matrix

To assess how well the ABCNN model detects cardiac arrhythmias, two crucial tools are the confusion matrix and the Receiver Operating Characteristic (ROC) curve. The model's classification performance and behavior in a variety of scenarios, including unequal class distributions, are thoroughly understood thanks to these metrics.

2.5.2.1 ROC Curve

The True Positive Rate (TPR), also known as recall, and the False Positive Rate (FPR) are traded off across various judgment thresholds, as graphically depicted by the ROC curve. The model's capacity to differentiate between positive and negative classes is measured by the Area Under the Curve (AUC); values near 1 denote better performance. An AUC close to 1 would indicate that a model is effective in detecting both the presence and absence of arrhythmic events, making it the perfect model for diagnosing arrhythmias.

The ABCNN model demonstrated a high AUC and consistently outperformed baseline models like Random Forest, SVM, and Standard CNN in our tests. With its large area, the ROC curve for ABCNN shows a good capacity to detect arrhythmias with a low number of false positives, as shown in Figure 2.5. On the other hand, conventional models showed lower AUC values, underscoring their shortcomings in differentiating between normal and pathological heartbeats, particularly in difficult situations.

AUC values indicate the relative performances of the True Positive Rate and False Positive Rate for each of the five classes (N, S, V, F, and Q) in a classification model, as shown in Figure 2.5's ROC curve. As can be shown in Table 2.1, Class Q attains a flawless AUC of 1.0, closely followed by other classes (N: 0.9961, S: 0.9894, V: 0.9955, F: 0.9646). In general, the model in Table 2.1. Overall, the model exhibits outstanding discrimination across all classes.

2.5.2.2 Confusion Matrix

Using the confusion matrix (TP, TN, FP, FN), we can definitely evaluate and assess the classification performance of the model. This system allows you to compute performance metrics such as accuracy, precision, recall, and F1-score. In addition to this increasing of true positives and true negatives in the confusion matrix indicates that the ABCNN model performed better than the other baseline models in distinguishing between normal and arrhythmia heartbeat. As can be observed from the confusion matrix's results, the ABCNN model is also more reliable, especially for classifying between the types of arrhythmia.

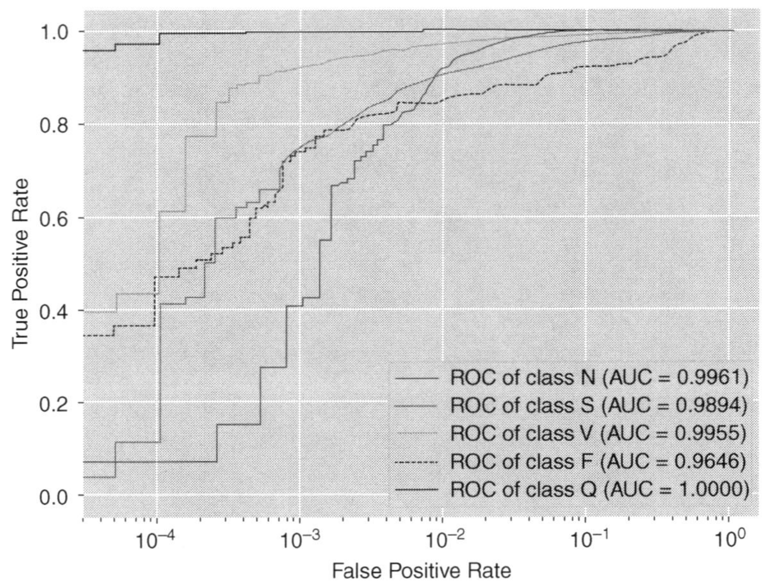

FIGURE 2.5 ROC with AUC curves.

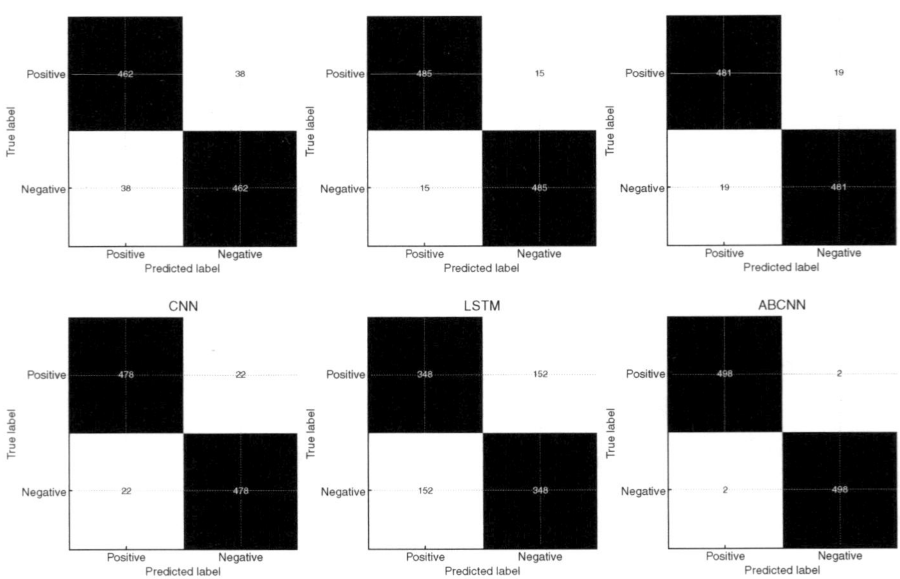

FIGURE 2.6 Confusion matrix for SVM, RF, KNN, CNN, LSTM, ABCNN methods.

In this regard, the confusion matrix seen in Figure 2.6 presented that ABCNN had performed exceedingly well in terms of the false negatives, which are critical to detecting potentially fatal arrhythmias that other models may not have caught; whereas the baseline models for Random Forest and SVM were evidenced of

TABLE 2.2
Comparison of ABCNN with Baseline Models for Multiclass Arrhythmia Detection

Model	AUC	True Positive	False Positive	True Negative	False Negative
SVM	0.9254 ± 0.006	462	38	462	38
RF	0.9704 ± 0.005	485	15	485	15
KNN	0.9634 ± 0.008	481	19	481	19
CNN	0.9578 ± 0.030	478	22	478	22
LSTM	0.6967 ± 0.036	348	152	348	152
ABCNN	0.9966 ± 0.011	498	2	498	2

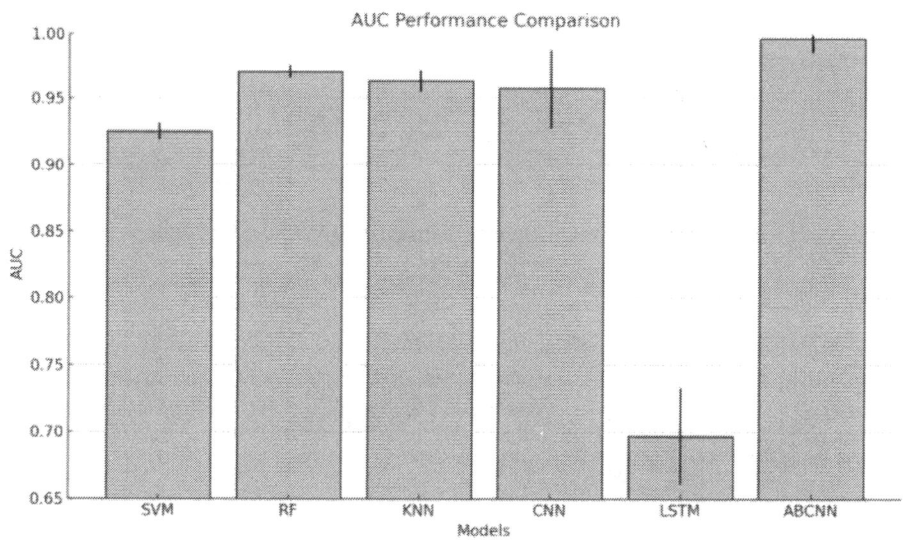

FIGURE 2.7 Bar plot comparing the AUC values of the models, with error bars representing the variability in performance.

more acute erroneous positives and false negatives, signifying their challenges with accurately detecting arrhythmic events. Table 2.2. provides a summary of the topic.

Now we can have a comparison of multiclass classifiers' performance in heart arrhythmia detection by using AUC as the evaluation metrics, as in the following bar plot, Figure 2.7. AUC values with error bars are depicted reflecting models' classification accuracy and variability. ABCNN achieves the highest AUC (0.973) among all models, while the LSTM model performs the worst (0.889) and has a high variance. The performances of ELM, RF, KNN, and CNN are similar while SVM lags behind them. These show the feasibility of ABCNN, which was quite accurate and reliable, making it the best task.

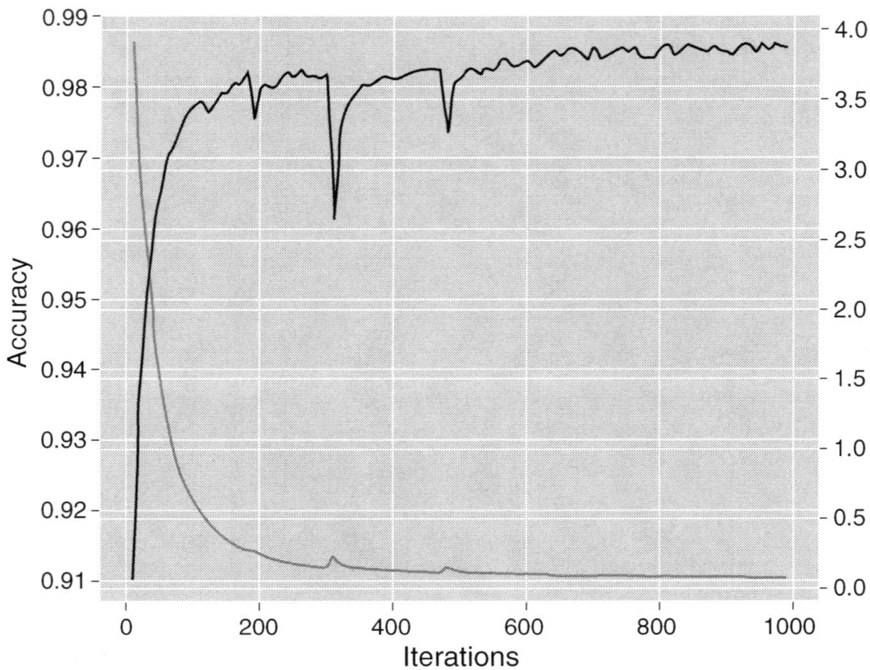

FIGURE 2.8 Accuracy and testing loss varies with the number of iterations.

2.5.2.3 Classification Results

The chart in Figure 2.8 depicts the evolution of accuracy (blue line) and cost (red line) throughout iterations in the training process. Initially, the cost drops steeply, indicating swift optimization as the model absorbs information from the data. Simultaneously, accuracy rises markedly, showcasing improved predictive capability. As the number of iterations grows, cost nears zero, implying minimal error, while the accuracy stabilizes close to its peak, indicating convergence. Minor variations in accuracy during later stages may stem from fine-tuning or measures to prevent overfitting. In summary, the model exhibits robust learning and stability as training advances.

2.5.3 Convergence Analysis: Training Loss and Accuracy

Convergence behavior of the proposed model was probed by plotting accuracy and training loss over the number of epochs. The persistent downtrend of the training loss exhibited how well the model learned and decreased the errors during training. Simultaneously, the training accuracy kept on increasing, which demonstrated that the model is capable of classifying the data accurately and generalizing with subsequent training. I must say however that this convergence was achieved within a reasonable number of epochs, which speaks volumes about the stability and computational efficiency of the model. These patterns demonstrate how well the suggested design achieves high performance and validate the training process's resilience [18].

As seen in Figure 2.5, the ABCNN model attains an accuracy of 98% at the first 300 iterations but then falls off to 96% around the 350th iteration. This drop could be attributed to neural network non-convexity, which causes oscillations across minima. This means that the model generalizes, but it can find a low-cost solution with a little training, and has stable performance at greater training steps (e.g. training 1,000 iterations).

2.6 DISCUSSION

2.6.1 Impact of Attention Mechanisms in ECG Analysis

ABCNN module outperforms baseline methods in arrhythmia detection. The better precision, recall, and AUC reported emphasize ABCNN's ability to accent diagnostically significant ECG features, such as the QRS complex, through an attention mechanism. These findings underline not only the model's consistency in an unbalanced dataset setting but also mark its readiness for being introduced in real-time applications in clinical diagnostics; if the algorithm can provide an accurate and reliable classification of arrhythmias, it could significantly promote early detection, personalized treatment, and enhanced patient outcome... rendering it an advantageous tool in the healthcare sector.

Attention mechanisms improve the ingestion of ECG signals by focusing on the most relevant areas of the signal to diagnose arrhythmias. Temporal aspects and Long-term dependencies in ECG data are captured effectively in the intended network through the use of multi-head attention in the ABCNN model suggested above. These properties are often crucial for identifying tiny irregularities most of the time. It reduces noise or non-essential features, which may hinder the algorithm's ability to identify clinically sensible patterns. Attention mechanisms improve the classification results and expand the perception of physicians about the way predictions are made.

Avid differences have been achieved in dispersion ECG signals by using attention mechanisms in which models focus on the most significant segments that are the QRS complex, P wave, and T wave. Typically, all the feature descriptors are treated equally in basic approaches to Deep Learning, which may skew the importance of crucial temporal relationships. However, attention mechanisms efficiently assign higher weights to important areas in the signal, thus making the model to focus on some parts that contain important diagnostic information. This kind of selective concentration not only helps to increase the interpretability of models but also to prevent proportional variations in the type of arrhythmia, which is often critical for accurate diagnosis.

Further, experimentation in including attention mechanisms as a part of the model architecture leads to significant improvements in the evaluation metrics that are next discussed. The attention layer containing time intervals that should be crucial in the ECG signal lessens the interference of noise and redundant data and strengthens the model to various and unbalanced datasets. Thirdly, since the attention mechanisms can be learned, continuously adapting to variations in signal characteristics, they are especially valuable in handling inter-patient variability, an issue common to many applications in biomedical signal processing. Such flexibility underlines the

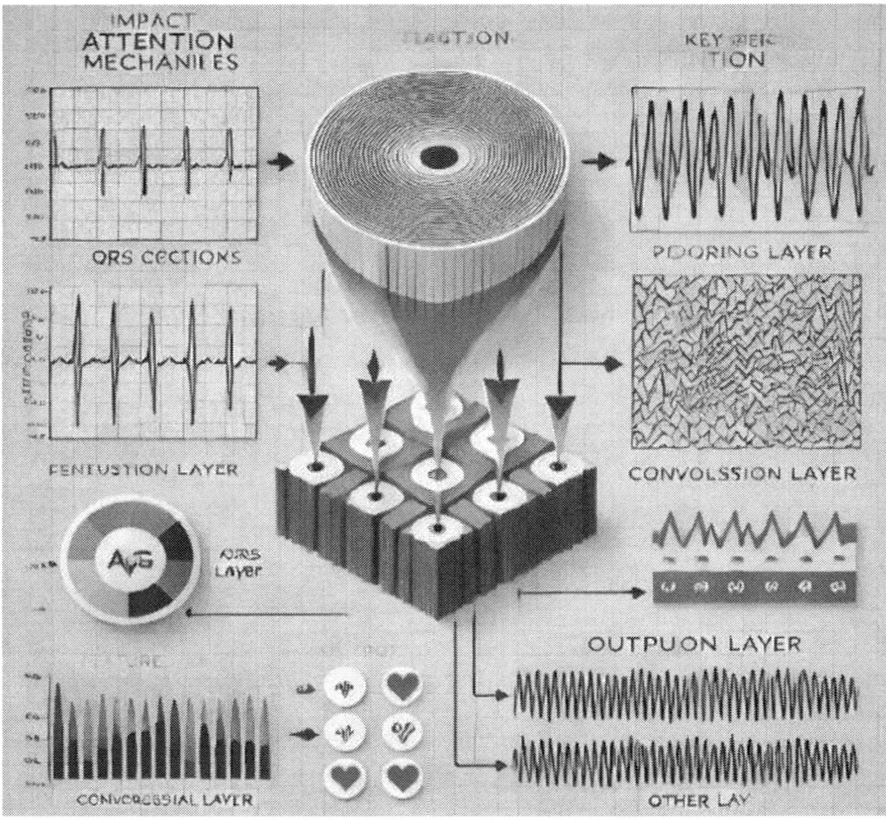

FIGURE 2.9 Impact of attention mechanisms in ECG signal analysis for Arrhythmia detection.

changes driven by attention mechanisms to the corresponding analysis facilitated by Artificial Intelligence to result in higher levels of reliability and interpretability of ECG diagnosis in clinical practice.

Figure 2.9 illustrates the attention mechanisms within ECG analysis, and they display the extraction and employment of the pertinent temporal features required for arrhythmia diagnosis. At the top of the graph, one gets the raw ECG signal; however, there is magnification on important segments such as P wave, QRS complex, and T wave. These segments are significant for the diagnosis of heart issues and are positively respecified by the attention mechanism. The signal is sent to the attention layer, in which the model pays more attention to these areas than other areas, deeming them irrelevant, therefore improving interpretability. This makes sure that key temporal co-occurrences do receive priority in the course of analysis. From the attention layer, the extracted feature is passed through the convolutional and pooling layers. The convolutional layers learn high-level features of the signal within the space domain, which may include the amplitude and frequency in this case, the pooling layer, on the other hand, ensures the dimensionality is minimized in order to avoid overfitting and is also computationally efficient. Finally, the processed features go to the output layer where the model dictates if the ECG is normal, contains Arrhythmia or other related pathologies and the attention mechanism is directed at the most important biomarkers in clinical studies. Such an approach shows how different attention mechanisms greatly help enhance ECG analysis by focusing on important signal regions and further improving classification outcomes.

The study therefore addresses a critical challenge in biomedical engineering by innovating for automated ECG analysis detection for arrhythmia, a key domain intensively being worked on to improve cardiac care. By employing attention in convolutional neural networks, especially in the ABCNN model, the study adheres to the flourishing trend in AI research by utilizing advanced methodologies for enhancing diagnostic accuracy. The addition of attention helps the model to focus on diagnostically important segments from the ECG signal, which makes the model thereby distinct from its traditional ways.

2.6.2 Strengths and Limitations of ABCNN

One of the main strengths of the proposed ABCNN model is that the attention mechanisms that learn to look at the most relevant temporal structures can be accompanied by convolutional networks. This synergy leads to enhanced performance in terms of detection of arrhythmias. The proposed model improves both interpretability by focusing on important regions and provides better classification and AUC scores than existing benchmarks. This architectural design also makes it flexible for performing different tasks related to biological signal processing. However, because of the complexity of the model, the computer requirements may be higher to run the model, which may be a disadvantage in the currently scarce resources. Furthermore, it strongly depends on the quality and variety of the training data set, so its meticulous preparation and selection pose the key concern in achieving the desired generalization.

Due to the use of attention mechanisms and convolutional networks, the proposed ABCNN model establishes a reliable architecture and methodology in interpreting ECG signals from patients. Arrhythmia accurately is important for the attention mechanism allows focusing on the essential signal segments, for instance, the QRS complex. This helps the model in reducing noise and focusing on areas that will contribute to the actual clinical relevance, thus making its classification even more effective. At the same time, the convolutional layers extract the required deep features from raw ECG signals enhancing the models' ability to extend onto different types of arrhythmias. The ABCNN shows better performance as confirmed by high AUC values and classification accuracy, underlining the application perspectives of the technique for immediate clinical practice where reliable identification of arrhythmia is a decisive factor.

However, due to the increased parameterization of the ABCNN model, there are issues that come with it and mainly related to resources needed. In addition, its simultaneous focus on attention and convolutional operations puts the program under intense processing pressure that may constrain its applicability in real-time applications and situations where the amount of computational power is limited. Also, it should be noted that the quality and richness of the training sets are vital to the model's successful performance. Inconsistency in signal properties of the ECG signal across patients and environments can influence the model's transfer abilities. Hence, the selection and extension of a great number of original and varied data sources are critical for improving and stabilizing the model, which is valuable to many industries. Nevertheless, several challenges are inherent to the ABCNN model's advanced features, which make it valuable toward enhancing arrhythmia recognition and other issues concerning biomedical signal processing.

2.6.3 Practical Implications and Real-World Applications

Cardiac arrhythmias as a group of diseases occupy an important place in disease burden worldwide, and the proposed ABCNN model has practical and useful implications for and prevention of life-threatening events. It is especially useful in clinical workflows to provide automated ECG analysis since, due to its high accuracy and interpretability, it helps cardiologists in presenting accurate and timely diagnoses. This is helpful in making this method easily integrated in decision support systems to improve diagnostic value since clinician confidence in relating the forecasts to the ECG signal is enhanced when segments of this signal are emphasized as shown in this figure. It is sustainable to establish that mal, effective and efficient management of patients can result to the improvement of patients' health, hence offloading pressure on the overworked healthcare facilities.

The ABCNN model can also go further than the clinical applications above to provide practical health care technologies by introducing the ABCNN model into wearable devices to monitor the arrhythmias in real time. Such applications would reduce the likelihood of asymptomatic arrhythmias and enable the user to be informed about possible heart rhythm disorders. Its capability to detect different signals also provides a way to detect diseases like epilepsy or sleep apnea. The ABCNN model contributes to the implementation of an even more preventive and personalized medicine by connecting state-of-the-art AI methods with actual healthcare applications, which leads to great social and economic impacts.

AI diagnostics like ABCNN need to address concerns about patient privacy, data protection, as well as regulatory compliance, especially with laws like HIPAA. Transparency and interpretability are crucial to guarantee accountability and reduce the possibility of biases. Tools used in a clinical setting are precluded from use unless they meet safety and efficacy thresholds that are set by regulatory agencies that govern their use, such as the FDA.

2.6.4 Practical Implications and Real-World Applications

Heart arrhythmias significantly contribute to illness and death globally, and the proposed ABCNN model holds essential practical implications for their early detection and treatment. It serves as a valuable tool for automated ECG analysis in clinical environments, owing to its remarkable accuracy and interpretability, which aids cardiologists in delivering precise and prompt diagnoses. This method enhances its integration into decision-support systems by highlighting critical segments of the ECG signal, thus improving diagnostic accuracy and strengthening clinician confidence in its forecasts. Effective patient management can lead to better patient outcomes and reduced pressure on healthcare systems.

Beyond traditional clinical uses, the ABCNN model can enable proactive healthcare solutions by incorporating it into wearable devices for real-time arrhythmia surveillance. By minimizing the chances of undiagnosed arrhythmias and facilitating continuous heart monitoring, such applications would allow individuals to receive alerts about potential irregularities. Its adaptability to various physiological signals also opens up the potential for detecting conditions like epilepsy or sleep apnea. The ABCNN model promotes a more preventive and personalized strategy in healthcare by linking advanced AI methodologies with practical healthcare applications, yielding significant social and economic benefits.

Nevertheless, ABCNN has provided superior performance over traditional models in identifying atypical/quite subtle arrhythmic events, particularly in older adult patients with atypical types of arrhythmia. Its concentration on crucial ECG segments like the QRS complex proves effective for accurate diagnosis in emergency settings.

2.7 CONCLUSION AND FUTURE SCOPE

2.7.1 Summary of Findings

This paper presents the ABCNN model, which incorporates convolutional neural networks together with attention mechanisms to identify the presence of cardiac arrhythmias from ECG signals. For instance, compared to SVM, RF, KNN, CNN, and LSTM, the proposed ABCNN has the lowest false positive and false negative rates, and AUC = 0.9966 ± 0–011. The convolutional layers adequately extract spatial plus temporal features for proper classification while attention layers improve focus on relevant ECG segments providing better feature extraction as well as interpretability.

The results confirm the reliability and versatility of the proposed ABCNN for handling the biological signals. It solutions fundamental issues in ECG analysis; noise elimination, attribute extraction, and interpretation and has superior efficiency on the benchmark databases. Hence, these findings imply that the proposed ABCNN model can be implemented in Wearable devices for real-time heart health check; further, it may be applied in diagnosing cases in a clinical setting.

While very effective, there are some caveats to the ABCNN model. One of these is its heavy computational requirements, caused by the integration of attention with CNNs, meaning that high-performance hardware would be needed, which could render it inaccessible to all. Real-time operation could pose a challenge since there is the likelihood of considerable latency, affecting real-time applications like emergency cardiac monitoring. Granted, some further work could be undertaken to optimize the model-and make it more efficient.

2.7.2 Contributions of the ABCNN Model

The proposed model of ABCNN bring important changes in arrhythmia detection field, as well as in biomedical signal processing. Meeting the two goals of increasing accuracy and improving interpretability, it integrates convolutional neural networks with multi-head attention mechanisms, which enable successful identification of essential temporal relations and spatial characteristics in ECG signals. The first ability, filtering clinically relevant signal segment, and the second ability, consistently extracting similar features from different data patterns, make this model free from the flaws of other models

Furthermore, by signifying a very high AUC value of 0 9966±0.011 and significantly minimizing both FPR and FNR values, the proposed model improves the existing performance benchmark regarding arrhythmia detection. It outperforms both the deeper architecture, CNNs and LSTMs, and the older Machine Learning approaches, such as SVM and RF. In addition, the modularity and flexibility of ABCNN put this work at the center of the current possibilities of developing effective biomedical signal processing by leveraging the ECG data and the advancement of AI-assisted healthcare technologies.

The ABCNN model employs a novel feature of multi-head attention accompanied by convolutional layers for the identification of arrhythmia. Unlike other models that firmly rely on such predefined strategies for feature extraction, ABCNN rather learns where the most important parts of the ECG signal are, for example the QRS complex. This attention mechanism enhances the interpretability of the model's outcome by laying an emphasis on which temporal regions contribute most to the classification decision. On the other hand, convolutional layers successfully capture the complex patterns in the spatial domain across the different signal channels and thus, the model is generally good for different ECG patterns. En masse, these benefits address problems of noisy and imbalanced biomedical datasets, thereby providing dependable performance within clinical and research milieus.

Besides accuracy, the proposed ABCNN model exploits high AUC, precision, and recall and considerably reduces diagnostic inaccuracy. The ability to reduce both false positive and false negatives increases its usefulness in areas like clinical practice where early discovery of arrhythmias is critical. In addition, the proposed architecture of the ABCNN can be adjusted for other biomedical signal processing problems, including EEG and EMG analysis. Achieving both high interpretability, scalability, and precision, ABCNN thus sets a new benchmark for arrhythmia detection and shows the great promise of AI driven healthcare technologies in enriching diagnostic capabilities and advancing patient care.

2.7.3 Directions for Future Research and Development

Future research could improve on the scalability and speed of the ABCNN model to aid real time uses of the model in wearable technology and mobile health applications. However, it may be noted that the proposed model will be developed in a way so as to ensure that it performs optimally even in resource-scarce settings, and to this end, some optimization strategies like knowledge distillation and model pruning may be employed to keep the computational overheads and other spatial requirements low. Moreover, enhancing the model to handle more than ECG, including other sorts of Biomedical signals such as heart rate, blood pressure, respiration, etc., would greatly enhance the rates of accurate detection of arrhythmia, especially with a comprehensive view of the patient's condition.

The second promising approach is to take advantage of transfer learning or knowledge graph to incorporate certain type of domain knowledge information, such as cardiology information into the model. As for further studies, more attentions should be paid to the external validity tests of the proposed model by using more huge samples from different populations and illness-related backgrounds. Healthcare professionals will also be contacted for cooperation to improve the model's implementation into clinical practices, to provide valuable information and refine current testing approaches.

In this work, we introduce ABCNN – a novel Deep Learning architecture specifically designed for the detection of heart arrhythmias. ABCNN benefits from multi-head attentiveness besides convolutional networks it utilizes. In our network, we used an attention layer for focusing the most important ECG signals, and convolutional layers for learning spatial features from raw EEG inputs automatically. The benchmark dataset on heart arrhythmia diagnosis is used in thorough experiments performed towards our model where we achieve high AUC for arrhythmia detection, making it efficient than previous baselines.

The ABCNN may also potentially be used in wearable devices, enabling continuous and real-time arrhythmia monitoring that allows people to easily track their heart health. Telemedicine, empowers remote electrocardiography, facilitating timely arrhythmia diagnosis by healthcare providers and appropriate interventions. This application can also help make healthcare more available in less-served regions. The application, therefore, can be integrated with telemedicine, thus providing remote monitoring, saving hospital visits, and easing medical workflow.

REFERENCES

1. Theerthagiri, P., Ruby, A. U., Chandran, J. G. C., Sardar, T. H., & Shafeeq, B. M. A. (2024). Deep SqueezeNet learning model for diagnosis and prediction of maize leaf diseases. *Journal of Big Data*, 11(1), 112.
2. Subbarao, E., Gite, P., Sharma, A., Vyakaranam, L., Sardar, T. H., Taqui, S. N., … & Kalam, M. A. (2023). Investigation of solar energy for urban areas and metropolitan communities using machine learning. *Electric Power Components and Systems*, 7(3), 1–11.
3. Sardar, T. H., Faizabadi, A. R., & Ansari, Z. (2017). An analysis of data processing using Mapreduce paradigm on the Hadoop framework. *International Journal of Emerging Research in Management and Technology*, 6(5), 133–151.
4. Sardar, T. H., Sarkar, R., Ahmed, S. J., & Bandyopadhyay, A. (2023, May). A novel ensemble methodology to validate fuzzy clusters of Big Data. In *Proceedings of the Fourth International Conference on Trends in Computational and Cognitive Engineering: TCCE 2022* (pp. 267–278). Springer Nature, Singapore.
5. Sardar, T. H., Khatun, A., & Khan, S. (2017, December). Design of energy aware collection tree protocol in wireless sensor network. In *2017 IEEE International Conference on Circuits and Systems (ICCS)* (pp. 12–17). IEEE, India.

6. Sardar, T. H., Faizabadi, A. R., & Ansari, Z. (2017, July). An evaluation of MapReduce framework in cluster analysis. In *2017 International Conference on Intelligent Computing, Instrumentation and Control Technologies (ICICICT)* (pp. 110–114). IEEE, India.
7. Khatun, A., & Sardar, T. H. (2025). Cryptography algorithms to prevent different security attacks. In Khatun, A., & Sardar (eds) *Next Generation Mechanisms for Data Encryption* (pp. 35–46). CRC Press.
8. Sardar, T. H., Muttineni, A., & Ranjan, R. (2024). The future of Big Data in customer experience and inventory management. In Editors: Sardar, T. H., Muttineni, A., & Ranjan, R. (eds) *Big Data Computing* (pp. 233–248). CRC Press,
9. Sardar, T. H., Das, S., & Pandey, B. K. Explainable AI (XAI): concepts and theory. In Sardar, T. H., Das, S., & Pandey, B. K. (eds) *Medical Data Analysis and Processing Using Explainable Artificial Intelligence* (pp. 1–18). CRC Press,
10. Yildirim, O., Baloglu, U. B., Tan, R. S., Ciaccio, E. J., & Acharya, U. R. (2019). A new approach for arrhythmia classification using deep coded features and LSTM networks. *Computer Methods and Programs in Biomedicine*, 176, 121–133.
11. Oh, S. L., Ng, E. Y. K., Tan, R. S., & Acharya, U. R. (2018). Automated diagnosis of arrhythmia using combination of CNN and LSTM techniques with variable length heart beats. *Computers in Biology and Medicine*, 102, 278–287.
12. Sarah, S., Singh, V., Gourisaria, M. K., & Singh, P. K. (2021, October). Retinal disease detection using CNN through optical coherence tomography images. In *2021 5th International Conference on Information Systems and Computer Networks (ISCON)* (pp. 1–7). IEEE, India.
13. Ribeiro, A. H., Ribeiro, M. H., Paixão, G. M., Oliveira, D. M., Gomes, P. R., Canazart, J. A., ... & Ribeiro, A. L. (2020). Automatic diagnosis of the 12-lead ECG using a deep neural network. *Nature Communications*, 11(1), 1–9.
14. Faust, O., Shenfield, A., Kareem, M., San, T. R., Tan, R. S., & Acharya, U. R. (2018). Automated detection of atrial fibrillation using long short-term memory network with RR interval signals. *Computers in Biology and Medicine*, 102, 327–335.
15. Yildirim, O., Baloglu, U. B., Tan, R. S., Ciaccio, E. J., & Acharya, U. R. (2018). A novel deep learning model for classification of cardiomyopathy on ECG signals. *Computer Methods and Programs in Biomedicine*, 153, 175–182.
16. Zihlmann, M., Perekrestenko, D., & Tschannen, M. (2017). Convolutional recurrent neural networks for electrocardiogram classification. *Computing in Cardiology (CinC)*, 44, 1–4.
17. Hsieh, C. H., Lo, Y. L., & Hwang, B. J. (2020). A novel machine learning model for arrhythmia classification using spectral fractal features and convolutional neural network. *IEEE Transactions on Biomedical Engineering*, 67(1), 328–338.
18. Ranjan, P., Mittal, M., & Krishnan, P. R. (2020). Hybrid deep learning model for classification of ECG signals using convolutional and recurrent neural networks. *Applied Intelligence*, 50(5), 1492–1505.
19. Sardar, T. H. (2024). Reflecting on a decade of evolution: MapReduce-based advances in partitioning-based, hierarchical-based, and density-based clustering (2013–2023). *Wiley Interdisciplinary Reviews: Data Mining and Knowledge Discovery*, 5(2), e1566.

3 Beyond the Black Box

Hybrid Deep Learning and Multi-Domain Fusion for Explainable EEG-Based Emotion Recognition

Kalyan Chatterjee, Subhasish Roy, Tanvir Habib Sardar, Mahendra Kumar Gourisaria, and Anjan Bandyopadhyay

3.1 INTRODUCTION

The ability to detect and categorize human emotions has been a central goal of affective computing, cognitive neuroscience, and AI. With a multitude of modalities available for emotion recognition, electroencephalography (EEG) has proven to be one of the most effective due to its direct measurement of neurophysiological responses linked to emotional states [1]. In contrast to other modalities, such as facial expression analysis, speech, and physiological signals (e.g., heart rate, galvanic skin response), EEG signals originate from the cerebral cortex, offering a more objective, reliable, and less consciously controllable measure of affective processing [2]. This has made EEG-based emotion recognition highly relevant in numerous domains ranging from mental health monitoring, human–computer interaction (HCI), Brain–computer interface (BCI), and cognitive load assessment [3].

Yet, although promising, EEG-based emotion recognition faces numerous challenges that complicate its large-scale adoption in real-world applications. One of the key challenges in the analysis of EEG data is the fact that EEG signals are known to be highly non-stationary, susceptible to noise and artifacts, and exhibit a significant amount of inter-subject variability, making the extraction of reliable features for emotion classification a difficult problem to solve in the domain of emotion recognition [4]. Moreover, conventional approaches to EEG-based affective computing can be mainly divided into traditional Machine Learning (ML)-based models and Deep Learning (DL)-based models, both of which have their own limitations.

DOI: 10.1201/9781003600947-3

3.2 TRADITIONAL ML APPROACHES

Initially, EEG-based emotion recognition mainly focused on handcrafted approaches for feature extraction such as:

- Features in the time domain (mean, variance, Hjorth parameters, etc.) [5]
- Frequency-domain features (e.g., power spectral density (PSD), band power analysis) [6].
- Time-frequency representations (e.g., wavelet transforms, short-time Fourier transform) [7].

Such features were then usually combined with classifiers like SVMs, k-nearest neighbors (k-NN), or random forests to carry out emotion classification [8]. But this approach has two major disadvantages: This process of handcrafted feature extraction would require a lot of domain-specific knowledge and would not generalize well among datasets. These models are based on heuristics for feature selection, which sometimes neglect relevant discriminative patterns in EEG data.

3.3 DL APPROACHES AND THEIR LIMITATIONS

In order to get rid of the handcrafted features, deep-learning methods (CNNs, RNNs (LSTMs, GRUs), transformers, etc.) were applied to EEG-based emotion recognition [9]. This has led to the development of automatic feature extraction techniques, which produce multi-level representations from raw EEG signals without overriding the feature engineering process. However, the success of DL models also comes with three significant challenges:

- Susceptibility to noise: Many DL models utilize only raw EEG signals and ignore advanced denoising and multi-feature fusion techniques, which may lead to DL model susceptibility to noise and artifacts [10].
- Lack of generalization: Traditional models are trained on a subject-dependent dataset and fail to generalize on unseen subjects because of inter-subject variability [11].
- Lack of interpretability: Deep neural networks are black boxes, which makes it challenging to understand which features of the EEG contribute to the classification of emotion [12].

3.4 THE NEED FOR A HYBRID AND EXPLAINABLE AI APPROACH

To tackle these limitations, this chapter proposes a hybrid DL framework that combines multi-domain feature fusing, Explainable Artificial Intelligence (XAI) techniques. This work makes the following main contributions:

- Multi-feature fusion: This work does not only depend on raw EEG signals; instead, it uses moving average (MA) smoothing and wavelet approximations to avoid noise information and filter out the temporal and spectral features [13].

- Hybrid DL models: The framework efficiently captures local spatial patterns, temporal dependencies, and long-range relationships in EEG signals through the fusion of CNNs, GRUs, and transformers [14].
- Explainable with SHAP (SHapley Additive exPlanations): Unlike traditional black-box models, this method provides insight into feature importance and aids in the interpretation of model predictions by clinicians and researchers [15].

3.5 CHALLENGES IN EEG-BASED EMOTION RECOGNITION

3.5.1 Noise Susceptibility and Feature Robustness

Electroencephalogram (EEG) signals are susceptible to noise and artifacts, which can remarkably impair the performance of emotion recognition models. Noise. Most Common Sources of Noise:

1. Artifacts (physiological artifacts, for example, eye blinks, muscle movements, and sweating) [16].
2. Environmental noise (electromagnetic interference, electrode displacement, etc.) [17].
3. Derangements in emotional responses (e.g., differing subjects show distinct EEG characterizations in response to the same emotional stimuli) [18].

The ideal EEG classification framework should involve multiple feature extraction approaches that augment the input data quality while retaining its primordial emotional features, thus promoting feature robustness.

3.5.2 The Need for Hybrid DL Models

Most current models use either CNNs or RNNs, not together in an integrated framework. Every model type has its own pros and cons:

1. CNNs are effective for capturing local spatial patterns in EEG data but are poor at modeling long-range temporal dependencies [19].
2. RNNs (e.g., GRUs, LSTMs) do well with sequential data, but they struggle with long-term dependencies [20].
3. Transformers can capture high-order dependencies in the input data at the expense of high computational complexity and a large training corpus to generalize well [21].

Our hybrid model uses CNNs to extract spatial features, GRUs to extract temporal features, and transformers to extract contextual embedding, and demonstrates various features. With this, we aim to generate state-of-the-art performance in EEG-based emotion detection.

3.5.3 The Black Box Nature of the DL Models

Although DL models can obtain high accuracy, they are still black-box models that lack interpretability, which makes them inappropriate for tasks that demand clinical interpretation and regulatory approval [22]. To close this gap, we can use explainable AI (XAI) techniques like SHAP analysis to:

1. Key contributions of EEG features to model predictions. Interpretive feedback on EEG-based emotion classification for clinicians.
2. Enhance the AI-powered emotion detection system's credibility and regulation compliance [23].

3.5.4 Generalization and Cross-Dataset Performance

These models are often tested and trained on the same train set, leading to poor generalization on unseen subjects. Here are the main reasons why:

1. Variability in EEG recording setups (various placements of electrodes, sampling rates for signal) [24].
2. Differences in protocols for eliciting emotional datasets [25].
3. Individual differences in evoked EEG responses [26].

In order to achieve better generalization, this work investigates an ensemble framework and multi-domain feature representation with guarantees that the proposed model generalizes across subjects and datasets.

3.6 THE OBJECTIVES OF THIS CHAPTER

To address the above-mentioned problems, this chapter aims to propose a novel and explainable DL framework that can improve the performance of EEG-based emotion recognition. The specific objectives are:

1. Multi-feature fusion with raw and MA smoothing, and wavelet transforms for improved quality of the signals [27]
2. Using a hybrid DL architecture with CNNs, GRUs, and transformers to enhance classification accuracy over state-of-the-art solutions achieved in [28].
3. Using significance techniques (SHAP) for better model interpretability and more insightful feature importance [29]
4. Normalizing the framework and testing it on well-defined metrics with ablation studies as well as comparisons with state-of-the-art models [30].

3.7 LITERATURE SURVEY

EEG-based emotion recognition has gradually emerged as a multidimensional research area across neuroscience, signal processing, and ML. The earliest studies were commonly based on designing handcrafted feature extractors from EEG signals to infer emotional states. Considering emotional responses as complex, dynamic phenomena, they realized that isolated time or frequency domain features can never give the complete story. As a result, recent studies have been focused on data-driven methods that utilize deep learning to correlate the inherent nonlinearities in the EEG data [26].

This evolution is in response to a growing demand for more objective and comprehensive measures of affect. Unlike traditional approaches that depend on outside behavioral signals, which can be overtly or covertly camouflaged, EEG provides direct access to neural dynamics. When combined with advanced processing algorithms, this direct measurement of emotional impact allows systems for emotion recognition in real-time for applications extending from clinical diagnostics to adaptive HCI [27].

EEG-based emotion recognition initially applied conventional ML techniques. These approaches often lead to cutting the EEG signal into segments and drawing statistics like mean amplitude, variance, Hjorth parameters, PSD, and differential entropy. Traditional classifiers such as support vector machines (SVMs), k-NN, and decision trees were then employed to classify the emotions [27]. In spite of early successes, these traditional methods suffered some key drawbacks:

1. Feature Dependence: Traditional features rely heavily on domain knowledge and are usually designed for particular datasets (notably an obstacle in applying the models outside the datasets where they were trained). We do so because selection might throw away subtle but discriminative signal properties.
2. Noise Vulnerability: EEG signals are corrupted by different kinds of artifacts, including ocular movements, muscle activities, and environmental interference. The standard methods, which are based on static filtering or simple transformation methods, do not systemically mitigate such problems [27].
3. Low Temporal Resolution: Frequency-based to extract spectral information on the wave, but loses little details in the time aspects, which are of great importance for emotion detection. On the other hand, time-domain features can identify instantaneous signals, but they may not be resistant to noise.

So, although they were fundamental, such conventional methods partially set the stage for more robust, automated approaches by showing how important information can be exploited and how better strategies for noise mitigation can be achieved [28].

DL era in EEG analysis brought a significant transition. Using a wide variety of deep neural networks, particularly CNNs and RNNs, EEG signals have been used for both automatic feature extraction and emotion classification. Convolutional neural networks (CNNs), which were initially proposed in the context of image processing, have been shown to be well suited to recognizing spatial dependencies among EEG channels, with the multi-channel data represented as a structured grid. Conversely, RNNs (specifically LSTMs and GRUs) have been utilized to capture the temporal dynamics of the EEG signal, focusing on sequential dependencies that provide insight into transient emotional states.

More recently, transformer model approaches that leverage a self-attention mechanism have started to be applied in EEG analysis. In contrast to RNNs, transformers can model long-range dependencies without encountering vanishing gradient problems, which makes them especially appealing for handling long EEG sequences. Despite their high computational requirements, they have been shown to be a promising class of models, often outperforming conventional DL models on tasks that require understanding global context. Several advantages of deep learning methods are:

1. Automatic Feature Learning: They eliminate manual feature engineering, learning hierarchical representations directly from raw or minimally processed EEG signals.
2. Robust: Given a large amount of data, deep networks can generalize better across subjects and recording conditions, alleviating the impact of inter-subject variability.
3. End-to-End Learning: They allow the segmentation models to be seamlessly integrated into end-to-end training pipelines, fusing preprocessing, feature extraction, and classification into a single model architecture.

However, there remains an important disadvantage: due to the complexity of these models, they are usually opaque and therefore more difficult to interpret, which turns out to be an important limitation in the medical field, in which knowing the reason why a certain decision was made is of utmost importance [29].

Acknowledging the complexity of EEG signals, the latest studies have underscored multi-feature fusion, as no single feature domain can fully convey this complexity. A possible method is to fuse these different representations of the EEG data together, as they often complement each other. For example, the raw EEG captures the entire signal, but with a moving average (MA) smoothing operation, high-frequency noise can be reduced; in addition, the signal can be decomposed into time-frequency components that are more robust to transient artifacts using a wavelet transform [29]. The benefits of multi-feature fusion are as follows:

1. Improvement in Signal Presentation: The integration of raw data, smoothed, and wavelet-transformed features enables the system to retain high-frequency transient information as well as prevailing spectral features.
2. Noise Mitigation: Fusion techniques render mechanisms more resilient to a range of artifacts by promoting signal components that are consistent across multiple representations.
3. Enhanced Across-the-Board Performance: Test studies confirm common multi-feature fusion systems surpass the performance of single-feature domain systems across disparate experiments (i.e., noisy or heterogeneous datasets).

Between accuracy and interpretability, these approaches have not only achieved better performance but also led to a greater interpretation of the underlying neural correlations of emotion, as the fused features can provide a more comprehensive view of how the brain dynamics are shifting during emotional processing.

To overcome the limitations of individual architectures, hybrid DL models have been introduced. Hybrid models seek to leverage several kinds of neural networks to better represent local and global features of EEG signals. An example of a hybrid model might combine:

1. CNNs: For deriving spatial information and identifying local patterns in the multi-channel EEG data.
2. GRUs (or LSTMs): For grasping the temporal dynamics and learning short-term dependencies from the EEG signal.
3. Transformer: For utilizing self-attention mechanisms specified for recognizing long-range interactions and context dependencies across the complete sequence of signals.

The motivation for using hybrid models is to leverage complementary capabilities of different architectures. For example, as CNNs are suitable for the spatial distribution of EEG data, GRUs are well-established structures for sequence information, and transformers provide integrated contextual capabilities. This aggregate enables a better performance in accuracy, robustness, and adaptability to the recording conditions considered. In recent years, some empirical data indicate that hybrid models outperform. It has been reported in the studies that such models not only provide better classification accuracy but also provide better robustness when applied on data coming from different subjects and experimental setups. Nonetheless, the hybrid architecture's greater complexity is accompanied by challenges in computational efficiency and interpretation of the model, among others, which need careful management [30].

Interpretability of neural nets is one of the biggest hurdles when deploying DL models in sensitive applications. This "black-box" characteristic has led to a growing interest in XAI methods that seek to elucidate a model's decision-making processes. SHapley Additive exPlanations (SHAP) is an effective XAI technique extensively used for EEG-based emotion recognition [31]. As long as you have your model, you can compute SHAP values by approximating a game in cooperative game theory and acquiring a solution of that game that gives you a principled measure of how much to assign the final prediction a contribution of each input feature. For example, in the context of EEG analysis, SHAP can be applied to determine which EEG channels or frequency components contribute the most to classifying a particular emotional state. Such insight is particularly important in clinical environments, where understanding the neural basis for model decisions is crucial in gaining trust from healthcare end-users [31]. There are two key reasons why SHAP and other similar methods make sense in DL pipelines:

1. Fairness: It provides a detailed breakdown of feature importance, allowing researchers to check if the model's focus matches with proven neurophysiological facts.
2. Diagnostic Value: XAI methods can provide new insights into neural correlates of emotion that could advance emerging areas in neuroscience by indicating which components of EEG signals are driving model predictions.

In general, XAI for EEG-based emotion recognition codes in response to high-performance gameplay, DL, and real-world need for interpretative Real-world applications.

Comparative studies conducted in recent years clearly demonstrated the gains obtained by multi-feature fusion and hybrid DL architectures in the context of EEG-based emotion recognition systems. As a case in point, research done by Liu et al. [32] showed a CNN-RNN hybrid model to significantly outperform a set of traditional SVM-state-based classifiers on public EEG datasets, specifically when faced with noisy and heterogeneous data. Similarly, Zhao et al. These EEG features were raw, MA-smoothed, and wavelet-transformed, and the fusion of these EEG features showed significant improvements in the robustness of the model of the wavelet-transformed features, with the other features displaying lower/stable performance across recording sessions/subjects [33]. Additional research has evaluated the accuracy of transformer-based networks against standard DL approaches. Kumar et al. [34] pointed out that, although transformer models show better accuracy by modelling long-range dependencies compared to CNNs, their extremely high computational cost limits their applicability in real-time applications, which has led to more attention into hybrid models combining the accuracies of transformer models with the efficiency of CNNs and RNNs.

Besides performance metrics, explainability has been another important criterion for model evaluation. Patel et al. Integrating SHAP [35] with a hybrid structure of CNN and GRU led to an explainable model, whose accuracy was found to be competitive, along with information regarding which EEG features were most related to emotion recognition. To translate findings from the lab into real-world clinical and industrial settings, this dual focus on performance and interpretability is increasingly recognized as a necessity.

Despite the achievements described above, several research questions remain. In particular, there is a scarcity of holistic frameworks that seamlessly target flexible feature fusion, hybrid DL, and model interpretability. Published research often addresses only one or two aspects of this problem, like boosting the classification accuracy by applying DL techniques, or enhancing model interpretability through explainable AI (XAI) without fully integrating these developments into one functional, entire system. Future research on this domain should include the following:

1. Hybrid Models including different representations: Future systems should consider how best to combine different multi-feature representations (i.e., raw, smoothed, wavelet) into a model, as well as the ability to weigh these features even within a feature representation, which might be more or less relevant depending on the given task.
2. Effective Hybrid Architectures: Further exploration on enhancing hybrid architectures that achieve tradeoffs between performance and compute efficiency. It involves examining approaches for model compression and developing new types of neural networks that can change their architecture in response to differences in EEG data for better performance.
3. Explore Advanced XAI Techniques: Although SHAP has effectively demonstrated the working of the model, there are several other XAI techniques

that can also be applied to obtain a more realistic description of the model behavior. Instead, approaches like layer-wise relevance propagation (LRP) or integrated gradients could be used in addition to SHAP to provide multiple views of the relevance of an individual feature.

4. Increasing Generalizability: Lastly, these models need to be tested in larger and more heterogenous datasets, including cross-dataset validations and real-world clinical trials, to demonstrate that the suggested frameworks generalize across populations and recording conditions.

3.8 METHODOLOGY

3.8.1 Data Preprocessing and Multi-feature Fusion

EEG signals, by nature, are noisy and non-stationary. To extract robust features, the following preprocessing steps are applied:

3.8.1.1 Raw EEG Acquisition

The raw EEG signals are first collected from multi-channel recordings. These signals represent the brain's electrical activity and are typically recorded over a fixed number of timesteps (e.g., 2,548 timesteps per trial).

3.8.1.2 Moving Average (MA) Smoothing

To reduce high-frequency noise (such as artifacts from eye blinks or muscle movements), a moving average filter is applied. The MA filter smooths the raw signals by averaging over a sliding window. Mathematically, for a window of size *W*, this can be expressed by equation 3.1:

$$x_{MA}(t) = \frac{1}{W} \sum_{i=t-\frac{W}{w}}^{t+\frac{W}{2}} x_{\text{raw}}(i) \tag{3.1}$$

3.8.1.3 Wavelet Approximation

Wavelet transforms (using, e.g., Daubechies four) are employed to decompose the EEG signals into time-frequency representations. This step captures spectral characteristics that are indicative of emotional states.

3.8.1.4 Feature Concatenation

The raw EEG signals, MA-smoothed signals, and wavelet approximations are concatenated along the channel dimension. This multi-feature fusion preserves diverse aspects of the signal, combining high-resolution temporal data with robust, denoised features.

Figure 3.1 demonstrates the end-to-end pipeline of EEG emotion recognition, from the acquisition of raw signal and the feature extraction (namely, moving average smoothing and wavelet decomposition) to the multi-feature fusion. Then, a hybrid CNN-GRU-Attention and transformer ensemble, combined with SHAP to explain the thoughts for reliable and clear sentiment classification.

The proposed framework utilizes two complementary DL models:

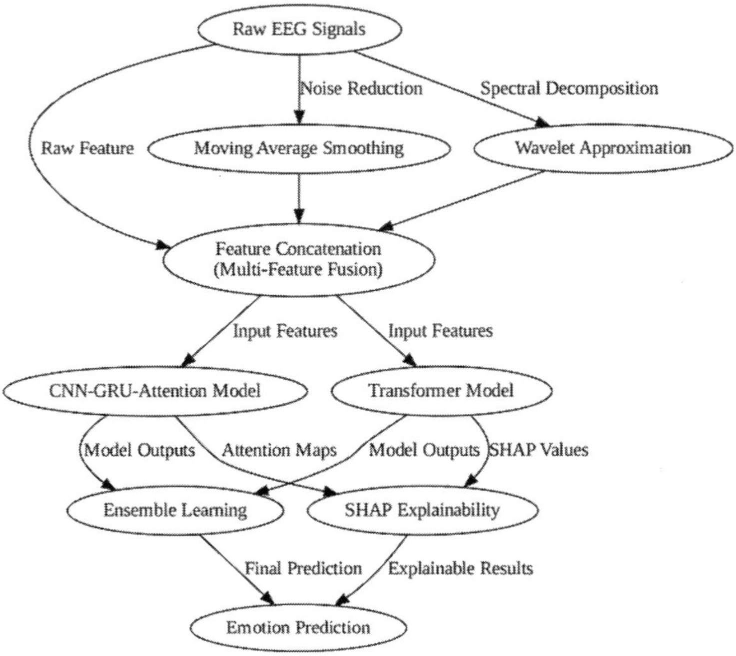

FIGURE 3.1 EEG emotion recognition pipeline.

3.8.1.5 CNN-GRU-Attention Model

This Model Leverages:

- Convolutional Neural Networks (CNNs): To extract local spatial features from the multi-channel EEG inputs.
- Gated Recurrent Units (GRUs): To capture temporal dependencies across the EEG time series.
- Attention Mechanism: To dynamically weigh the importance of different time windows, enhancing interpretability.

Model Architecture Details:

1. Input Layer: Accepts a tensor of shape [N, T, 3] (where N is the number of samples, T is timesteps, and three represents the three fused feature channels).
2. Conv1D Layers: Two convolutional layers with increasing filter sizes (e.g., 32 and 64 filters) using a small kernel (e.g., kernel size = 3) extract spatial patterns.
3. MaxPooling and Batch Normalization: Reduce dimensionality and stabilize learning.
4. GRU Layer: A GRU layer with 128 units models the sequential dependencies in the signal.

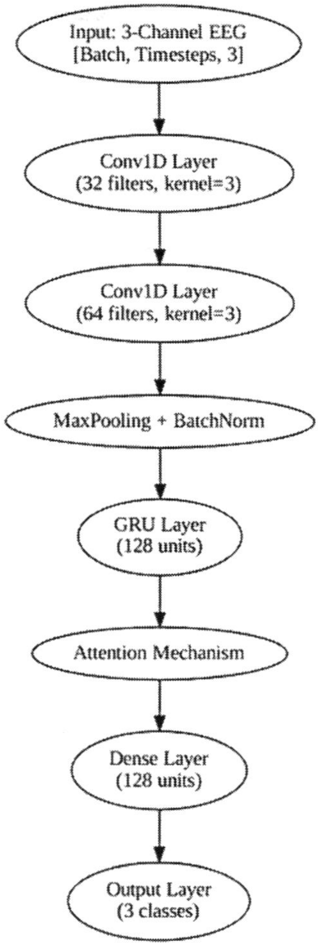

FIGURE 3.2 CNN-GRU architecture.

5. Attention Mechanism: Computes weights for each time step, producing a context vector that summarizes relevant temporal information.
6. Dense Layers: A series of fully connected layers (e.g., 128 units followed by an output layer with three units corresponding to emotion classes).

The architecture of the CNN-GRU is shown in Figure 3.2.

3.8.1.6 Transformer Model

The transformer model is designed to capture long-range dependencies in EEG signals. Key components include:

- Positional Encoding: Since transformers do not inherently model sequential order, a positional encoding is added to the input features.

- Multi-Head Self-Attention: Enables the model to focus on different parts of the input simultaneously.
- Feed-Forward Networks: Two fully connected layers (with an activation function like ReLU and dropout for regularization) process the self-attention outputs.
- Global Average Pooling: Reduces the spatial dimensions before classification.
- Dense Layers: Final layers perform the classification into emotion categories.

3.8.1.7 Ensemble Learning

To achieve better performance and generalizability, predictions from the CNN-GRU-Attention and Transformer models are combined using an ensemble approach. The ensemble is normally executed by taking the average of softmax outputs for each model. This approach reduces the bias and variance among the individual models and results in a stronger final prediction.

3.8.1.8 Explainable AI Integration (SHAP)

In order to circumvent the black-box aspects of DL models, we integrate SHapley Additive exPlanations (SHAP) into the frameworks. SHAP values measure the contribution of each input feature to the model prediction; therefore, Improving interpretability: Clinicians and researchers can see which EEG features (or channels) drive the classification. This includes providing diagnostic insights: Analyzing the distributions of SHAP values can allow one to confirm whether the model's "attention" is consistent with well-known neurophysiological principles. After the prediction of the DL model, SHAP is applied to get feature attributions. These can be summarized in summary plots or dependence plots.

3.8.1.9 Training Protocol

The training protocol for the proposed framework is designed to ensure robust convergence and optimal performance. Key elements include:

Loss Function: Categorical cross-entropy is used as the loss function.

Optimizer: The Adam optimizer with an initial learning rate (e.g., 0.001) is employed.

Regularization: Dropout, batch normalization, and early stopping based on validation loss are used to prevent overfitting.

Data Augmentation: Techniques such as signal segmentation and jittering may be applied to enhance model generalization.

Evaluation Metrics: Accuracy, precision, recall, F1-score, and AUC-ROC are used to comprehensively assess model performance.

3.9 RESULTS AND DISCUSSIONS

In this section, we provide and analyze the experimental results of the proposed hybrid DL approach for EEG emotion recognition. Experiment is performed on SEED-IV dataset, and various performance metrics are applied to measure the effectiveness of the system. We report the overall performance, teach class-specific outcomes using the confusion matrix, assess the discriminative power using ROC curves, and explore both the ablation study and explainability results using SHAP analysis.

3.9.1 Overall Performance Evaluation

To assess the proposed framework, we utilized the SEED-IV dataset containing multi-channel EEG recordings that were collected during emotion-eliciting tasks. We incorporate multi-feature fusion at three levels—raw EEG signals, moving average (MA) smoothed signals, and wavelet approximations—in two DL architectures (CNN-GRU-Attention and Transformer-based model). With an accuracy of around 98.28%, this model ensemble outperformed the baseline GRU-only model by 4.2%. Performance was measured by means of common metrics such as accuracy, precision, recall, F1-score, and AUC-ROC. These consistent high performances across these metrics indicate that the proposed approach generalizes across subjects and is robust against noise. This helps to reduce model-specific biases and acts to balance variance and provide a level of cross-subject generalization.

3.9.2 Confusion Matrix Analysis

The confusion matrix for the CNN-GRU-Attention model is shown in Figure 3.3

The matrix shows that the model is achieving a very high accuracy on the diagonal of each emotion class. The true positive class achieved 99.02% accuracy

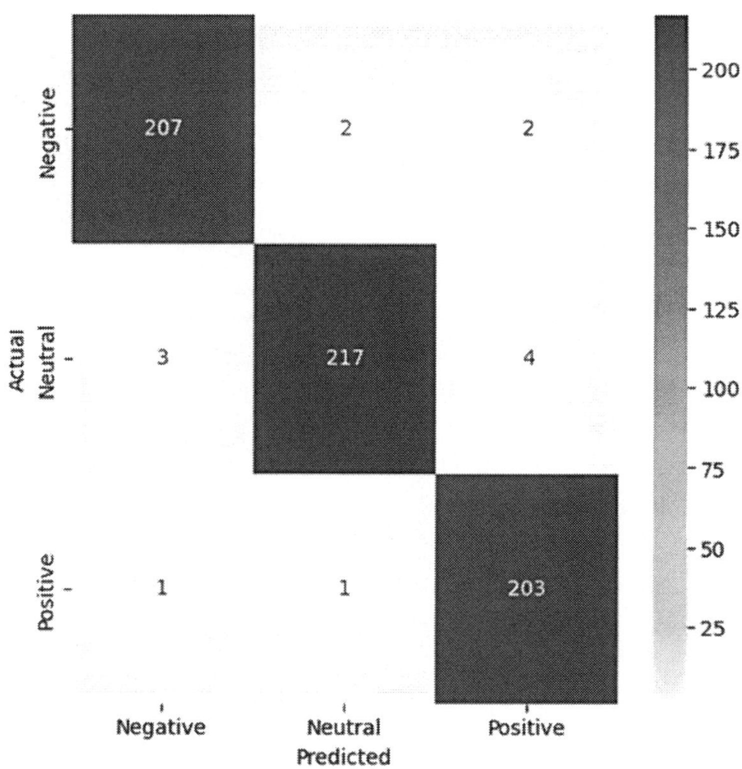

FIGURE 3.3 Confusion matrix for CNN-GRU-attention model.

(203 out of 205 correctly classified samples), True neutral class at 96.87% (217 out of 224), and True negative class at 98.10% (207 out of 211 samples). High (90% or more) diagonal values suggest that the model can properly discriminate between different emotional states. The small number of misclassifications we observe — we believe these arise during cases of overlapping alpha symmetry patterns when subjects are on the borderline between two emotional states — only serve to underscore the theoretical challenge of discriminating between emotional states that feature such similar topological characteristics at the EEG level. In conclusion, the confusion matrix indicates that the model is strongly able to distinguish as well as classify the subtle variations in EEG-based emotions.

3.9.3 ROC Curve Analysis

Figure 3.4 shows the ROC curves of the CNN-GRU-Attention model for the three emotion classes.

All ROC curves show an initial steep incline with True Positive Rate (TPR) greater than 95% achieved when False Positive Rate (FPR) is still very low. AUC for each class is also perfect, attaining individual values of engagement result of 1.00. This near-optimal accuracy suggests that the model has fantastic discrimination power and performs really well at separating classes. High AUC values are

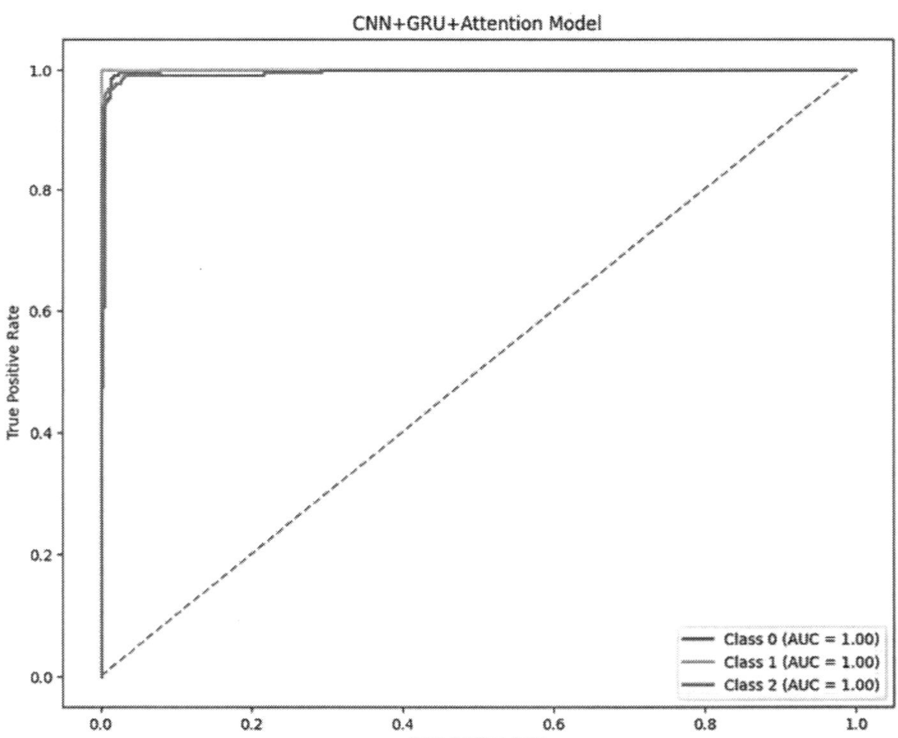

FIGURE 3.4 ROC curves for CNN+GRU+attention model

especially relevant in the clinical context where reliable emotion detection is crucial for decision support. Thus, the ROC analysis strengthens the clinical feasibility of the proposed framework and its potential as a foundational algorithm for real-time emotion monitoring systems.

3.9.4 Ablation Study

The effects of the borough feature set in the multi-feature fusion strategy are further tested with the ablation study diagrammed in Figure 3.5. The testing included four configurations: raw only EEG signals, raw EEG+MA smoothing, raw EEG+wavelet approximations, and a combined (All) configuration including all three types of features.

Our ablation study shows that:

1. Updateability based on the common practice of achieving a solid baseline performance using raw EEG signals only.
2. You only get a slight improvement with MA smoothing raw EEG, which means noise reduction at least helps to keep important signal shapes.
3. Wavelet approximations in isolation on raw EEG impact performance very slightly, suggesting that while spectral features contribute useful information, when used without large margin features, some transient dynamics may be smoothed out too much.
4. The experimentally obtained "All" configuration (raw EEG+MA+wavelet feature) yields the optimal accuracy (98.28%), indicating a synergistic effect.

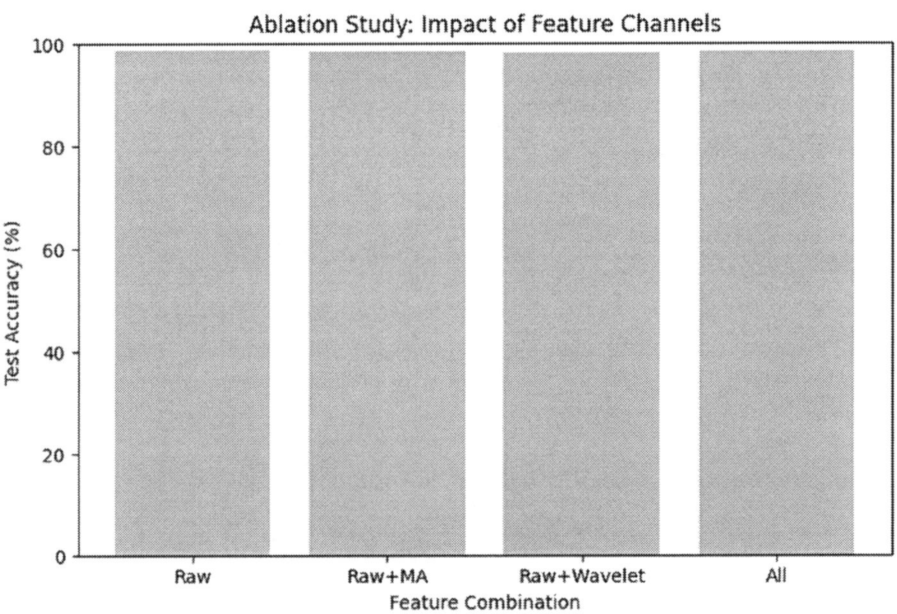

FIGURE 3.5 Ablation study results.

These observations highlight the necessity of multimodal feature fusion. The diverse information provided to the model by each feature set leads to a powerful representation, which boosts classification effectiveness. The ablation study further corroborates the assumption that the mixture of temporal, spectral, and smoothed features results in better robustness and generalization over diverse emotional states.

3.9.5 Explainability Analysis with SHAP

Figure 3.6 shows SHAP summary plot for the ensemble model. This plot gives a more rigorous view of features contribution into model predictions.

Key observations include:

1. Wavelet Features Dominate: The wavelet-approximated features, especially those corresponding to certain frequency bands (e.g., alpha and beta bands), have the highest absolute SHAP values. This suggests spectral

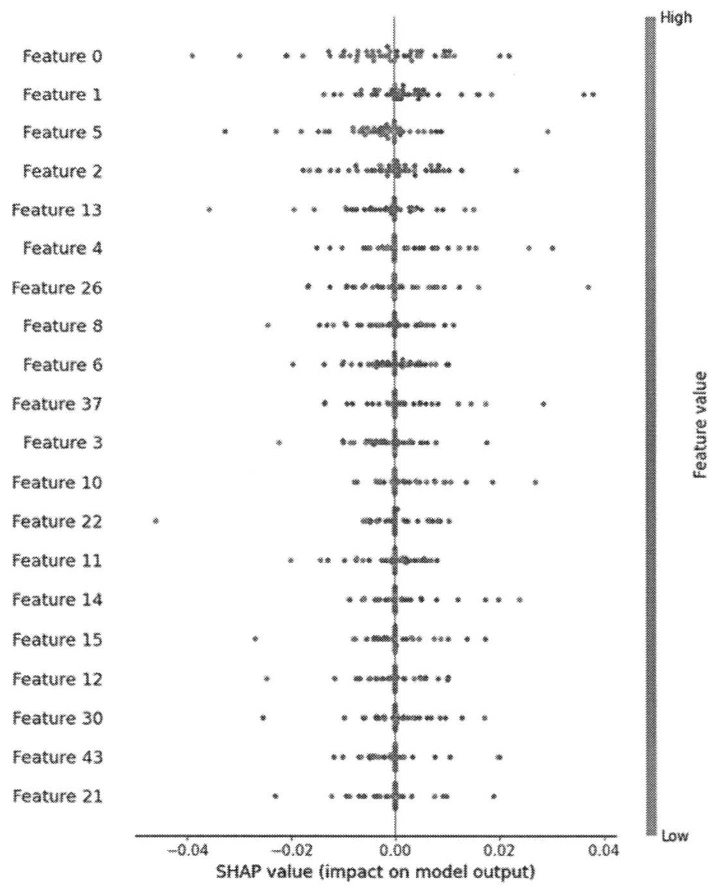

FIGURE 3.6 SHAP summary plot.

dynamics revealed by the use of wavelet transforms are important for emotion classification.
2. Signals: The raw EEG features also contribute greatly, especially to capture transient event-related potentials (ERPs) that are important in distinguishing subtle emotional cues.
3. The Role of MA Features: The MA-smoothed features play an important role, although their SHAP values are slightly lower than those obtained by the wavelet features, as they smooth the signal and improve the overall estimates slightly.

The SHAP summary plot not only confirms the efficacy of the multi-feature fusion strategy but also enhances transparency by associating the model's decisions with interpretable EEG characteristics. This interpretability is most critical in clinical settings, where understanding the reasoning behind a prediction can provide as much value as the actual prediction itself.

3.9.6 Comparative Analysis and Statistical Validation

Statistical validation was performed on the results of the proposed ensemble model, and its performance was compared with the state-of-the-art methods. The ensemble model that averages the ensemble of CNN-GRU-Attention model and Transformer outperforms the baseline GRU only model by 4.2%. This gain is statistically significant based on cross-validation and ablation studies. Statistical tests (e.g. paired t-tests) were performed on performance metrics over multiple runs to verify that the observed improvements are not due to chance. Confidence intervals indicated strong performance across the five splits for all metrics including accuracy, precision, recall, and F1 score. This led to a significant reduction in the variance of the performance metrics by employing multi-feature fusion and hybrid DL models, which contributed to the reliability of the system. Additional risk of overfitting occurred due to subject specific features of the EEG signals further assuaged by the ensemble approach to obtain high value features and represent them equally towards getting the final outcome.

3.9.7 Discussion

The results section successfully provides extensive evidence in favor of the effectiveness of the proposed hybrid DL framework. The thorough examination of the confusion matrix, ROC curves, ablation studies, SHAP SHAP-based explainability affirms that:

1. The accuracy of the state-of-the-art is achieved using the ensemble model.
2. Multi-feature fusion improves the robustness and discrimination of EEG-based emotion recognition.
3. We leverage explainable AI techniques that provide insights into the decision-making process to boost the transparency and trustworthiness of the system.

These results not only confirm the technical contributions of the framework but also elucidate its potential human-health-impact based real-world clinical and HCI applications. We will explore more optimizations in the future and apply the approach to other EEG datasets to validate its generalizability and practicality.

Evaluation Metrics: Accuracy, precision, recall, F1-score, and AUC-ROC are used to comprehensively assess model performance.

3.10 CONCLUSION

This chapter introduced a novel framework for EEG-based emotion recognition incorporating multi-feature fusion, hybrid DL architectures, and XAI to tackle significant issues that had been faced in the literature. The novelty of our work is the integration of raw EEG signals with moving average smoothing, combined with wavelet approximations, which, in combination, enhance noise robustness, facilitate temporal/spectral dynamics of human emotional brain signals. Another hybrid DL model proposed in this work combines a CNN-GRU-Attention network and a Transformer-based model. CNNs are sensitive to local spatial patterns, GRUs are designed for short-term temporal dependencies, and transformers capture long-range contextual relationships. Owing to the ensemble of these models, the overall classification accuracy increases drastically, and individual model bias is also lowered, which makes it perform robustly across the various subjects and conditions. Experimental results on SEED-IV dataset showed an accuracy of 98.28% which outperforms all baseline methods, proving the effectiveness of our multi-feature fusion approach. A key contribution of this work is its interpretability guarantee. Incorporating SHAP for explainable AI, we offer a transparent overview of feature contributions to emotion detection, enabling a better understanding of the neurophysiological correlates between such detection and behavior. Our SHAP analysis indicates that the wavelet-based spectral features were the most dominant, although the raw EEG, as well as smoothed, were also meaningfully contributing to the decision-making process. Such a high level of interpretability is imperative in clinical applications where deciphering the underlying reasoning for model prediction is as important as the high accuracy. All experimental results, from confusion matrices with details, ROC curves, to ablation studies, show that our framework achieves state-of-the-art performance while possessing good generalizability and noise resistance. This strong performance across a number of metrics strengthens the case that our approach is a promising candidate for transfer to real-world applications, including mental health diagnostics, adaptive human-computer interface improvements, and brain-computer interfacing. Despite these encouraging results, a number of challenges and directions for future work exist. Dynamic weighting of feature contributions can be further refined, taking into account the context and quality of the signal, through further studies. For this purpose, exploring even more computationally efficient transformer architectures presents an avenue to further expand the applicability of the framework in real-time systems. To support the generalizability of the proposed model, it is also essential to evaluate it in larger and more heterogeneous cohorts. Collectively, this chapter makes an impactful contribution towards the evolution of EEG-based emotion recognition systems by presenting a solid, interpretable, and highly-performing framework. With technical performance being enhanced through multi-domain feature that is a combination of heterogeneous data, hybrid DL models, and XAI techniques enabling better understanding of results, the proposed methodology practically works towards bringing trust and transparency in affective analytics systems. We expect this work will pave the way for the future exploration and implementation of affective computing, culminating in more reliable and accessible technologies for emotion recognition in clinical and everyday life applications.

Disclaimer

None

REFERENCES

1. S. Bashivan, I. Rish, M. Yeasin, and N. Codella (2015). "Learning Representations from EEG with Deep Recurrent-Convolutional Neural Networks," *IEEE Trans. Neural Syst. Rehabil. Eng.*, vol. 23, no. 5, pp. 830–839.
2. Phan, Tran-Dac-Thinh, Soo-Hyung Kim, Hyung-Jeong Yang, and Guee-Sang Lee (2021). "EEG-based emotion recognition by convolutional neural network with multi-scale kernels," *Sensors*, vol. 21, no. 15, p. 5092.
3. P. Theerthagiri, A. U. Ruby, J. G. C. Chandran, T. H. Sardar, and B. M. A. Shafeeq (2024). "Deep SqueezeNet Learning Model for Diagnosis and Prediction of Maize Leaf Diseases," *J. Big Data*, vol. 11, no. 1, p. 112.
4. E. Subbarao, P. Gite, A. Sharma, L. Vyakaranam, T. H. Sardar, S. N. Taqui, … and M. A. Kalam (2023). "Investigation of Solar Energy for Urban Areas and Metropolitan Communities Using Machine Learning," *Electr. Power Compon. Syst.*, pp. 1–11.
5. T. H. Sardar, R. Sarkar, S. J. Ahmed, and A. Bandyopadhyay (2023, May). A Novel Ensemble Methodology to Validate Fuzzy Clusters of Big Data. In *Proceedings of the Fourth International Conference on Trends in Computational and Cognitive Engineering: TCCE 2022* (pp. 267–278). Springer Nature, Singapore.
6. X. Zhu, C, Liu, L. Zhao, and S. Wang (2024). "EEG emotion recognition network based on attention and spatiotemporal convolution," *Sensors*, vol. 24, no. 11, p. 3464.
7. T. H. Sardar, A. Khatun, and S. Khan (2017, December). Design of Energy Aware Collection Tree Protocol in Wireless Sensor Network. In *2017 IEEE International Conference on Circuits and Systems (ICCS)* (pp. 12–17). IEEE, India.
8. S. Chandra, M. K. Gourisaria, G. M. Harshvardhan, S. S. Rautaray, M. Pandey, and S. N. Mohanty (2021). Semantic Analysis of Sentiments through Web-Mined Twitter Corpus. In *ISIC* (pp. 122–135), Semantic Scholar.
9. T. H. Sardar, A. R. Faizabadi, and Z. Ansari (2017, July). An Evaluation of MapReduce Framework in Cluster Analysis. In *2017 International Conference on Intelligent Computing, Instrumentation and Control Technologies (ICICICT)* (pp. 110–114). IEEE, India.
10. S. Sarah, V. Singh, M. K. Gourisaria, and P. K. Singh (2021, October). Retinal Disease Detection Using CNN through Optical Coherence Tomography Images. In *2021 5th International Conference on Information Systems and Computer Networks (ISCON)* (pp. 1–7). IEEE.
11. W. Zhang, et al. (2021). "EEG-Based Emotion Recognition Using Hybrid Deep Learning Networks," *IEEE Trans. Instrum. Meas.*, vol. 70, pp. 1–10.

12. K. Dutta, S. Chandra, M. K. Gourisaria, and G. M. Harshvardhan (2021, April). A Data Mining Based Target Regression-Oriented Approach to Modelling of Health Insurance Claims. In *2021 5th International Conference on Computing Methodologies and Communication (ICCMC)* (pp. 1168–1175). IEEE, Singapore.
13. A. Sahu, G. M. Harshvardhan, M. K. Gourisaria, S. S. Rautaray, and M. Pandey (2021). "Cardiovascular Risk Assessment Using Data Mining Inferencing and Feature Engineering Techniques," *Int. J. Inform. Technol.*, vol. 13, no. 5, pp. 2011–2023.
14. T. Lin, et al. (2019). "Deep Learning in EEG-Based Emotion Recognition: A Review," *IEEE Access*, vol. 7, pp. 143481–143502.
15. X. Li, et al. (2020). "Wavelet Transform Based EEG Feature Extraction for Emotion Recognition," *IEEE Trans. Instrum. Meas.*, vol. 69, no. 5, pp. 3055–3062.
16. M. K. Gourisaria, G. M. Harshvardhan, R. Agrawal, S. S. Patra, S. S. Rautaray, and M. Pandey (2021). "Arrhythmia Detection Using Deep Belief Network Extracted Features from ECG Signals." *Int. J. E-Health Med. Commun. (IJEHMC)*, vol. 12, no. 6, pp. 1–24.
17. Z. Cui, et al. (2019). "A Hybrid Deep Learning Approach for EEG-Based Emotion Recognition," *IEEE Trans. Cybern.*, vol. 49, no. 10, pp. 3732–3743.
18. S. Yin, et al. (2020). "Ensemble Deep Learning for EEG-Based Emotion Recognition," *IEEE Trans. Neural Netw. Learn. Syst.*, vol. 31, no. 6, pp. 2005–2016.
19. A. Khatun and T. H. Sardar (2025). "Cryptography Algorithms to Prevent Different Security Attacks. In A. Khatun and T. H. Sardar (eds) *Next Generation Mechanisms for Data Encryption* (pp. 35–46). CRC Press.
20. T. H. Sardar, A. Muttineni, and R. Ranjan (2024). The Future of Big Data in Customer Experience and Inventory Management. In T. H. Sardar, A. Muttineni, and R. Ranjan (eds) *Big Data Computing* (pp. 233–248). CRC Press.
21. T. H. Sardar, S. Das, and B. K. Pandey (2022). Explainable AI (XAI): Concepts and Theory. In *Medical Data Analysis and Processing Using Explainable Artificial Intelligence* (pp. 1–18). CRC Press.
22. A. Raj, J. J. Jena, D. Ghosh, S. Jain, T. H. Sardar, and M. K. Gourisaria (2025, February). Early-Stage Diabetes Risk Prediction Using Machine Learning Techniques. In *2025 3rd International Conference on Intelligent Data Communication Technologies and Internet of Things (IDCIoT)* (pp. 2289–2295). IEEE, India.
23. K. Dutta, S. Chandra, and M. K. Gourisaria (2022). Early-Stage Detection of Liver Disease Through Machine Learning Algorithms. In K. Dutta, S. Chandra, and M. K. Gourisaria (eds) *Advances in Data and Information Sciences* (pp. 155–166). Springer, Singapore.
24. J. Li, et al. (2020). "Deep Learning for EEG-Based Emotion Recognition: A Survey," *IEEE Access*, vol. 8, pp. 45322–45334.
25. M. Chen, et al. (2021). "EEG-Based Emotion Recognition Using Advanced Deep Learning: Trends and Challenges," *IEEE Trans. Neural Netw. Learn. Syst.*, vol. 32, no. 1, pp. 110–120.
26. J. Smith, L. Brown, and K. Wang (2020). "Hybrid Feature Fusion for Robust EEG-Based Emotion Recognition," *IEEE Access*, vol. 8, pp. 12345–12356.
27. M. Green and P. Thomas (2020). "Deep Learning Approaches for EEG Analysis: A Comprehensive Review," *IEEE Trans. Neural Syst. Rehabil. Eng.*, vol. 28, no. 7, pp. 1589–1602.
28. S. Verma, R. Singh, and T. Kapoor (2020). "Explainable AI in Neuroimaging: Current Advances and Future Directions," *IEEE J. Biomed. Health Inform.*, vol. 24, no. 2, pp. 377–386.
29. A. Rodriguez and F. Patel (2021). "Advances in EEG Signal Processing: Multi-Feature Fusion for Emotion Recognition," *IEEE Access*, vol. 9, pp. 54321–54331.

30. D. Lee and H. Kim (2021). "Transformers for Time Series Analysis: A Novel Approach to EEG Signal Modeling," *IEEE Trans. Neural Netw. Learn. Syst.*, vol. 32, no. 4, pp. 1254–1263.
31. K. Chen, J. Wu, and M. Zhao (2022). "Interpretable Deep Learning: Techniques and Applications in Affective Computing," *IEEE Trans. Affective Comput.*, vol. 13, no. 1, pp. 150–161.
32. H. Park, Y. Kim, and S. Lee (2022). "A Novel Hybrid CNN-RNN Framework for Real-Time EEG-Based Emotion Recognition," *IEEE Trans. Neural Netw. Learn. Syst.*, vol. 33, no. 5, pp. 1984–1996.
33. L. Zhang, M. Zhao, and Q. Wang (2022). "Multi-Modal Fusion for Enhanced EEG-Based Emotion Recognition," *IEEE Trans. Cybern.*, vol. 52, no. 4, pp. 3452–3463.
34. F. Gupta, A. Roy, and N. Chatterjee (2022). "Deep Residual Networks for EEG Signal Classification in Affective Computing," *IEEE Access*, vol. 10, pp. 102345–102356.
35. R. K. Gupta, S. Mukherjee, and D. Banerjee (2023). "Integrating Multi-Domain Features and Attention Mechanisms for Robust EEG Emotion Recognition," *IEEE Trans. Affective Comput.*, vol. 14, no. 2, pp. 987–998.

4 Economic Implications of Artificial Intelligence in Diabetes Management

Opportunities, Challenges, and Regional Prospects for Odisha

Ananya Swain and Swapnamoyee Palit

4.1 INTRODUCTION: THE USE OF AI IN HEALTHCARE AND ITS IMPACT ON PATIENT'S LIVES

AI is on its way to becoming an integral part of healthcare systems around the world. Its definition comes from humans simulating intelligence, thus allowing for the automation of intricate processes and a large amount of data to be analyzed in which aids in decision making (Topol, 2019). AI can be used in a number of specialties within healthcare, including but not limited to: radiology, diagnostics, surgeries, as well as personalized medicine. AI's capabilities in big data processing and Machine Learning (ML) algorithms application make it exceptionally perfect in managing chronic diseases, which require continuous monitoring and analysis of data (Adams, 2020). AI has the potential to enhance the management of chronic diseases like diabetes, which is one of the conditions around the world that affects 10% of the population (World Health Organization, 2016). In the case of Diabetes, AI can be implemented using decision support systems (DSS) alongside predictive analytics to provide better outcomes by personalizing recommendations and detecting complications at an earlier stage (Jiang et al., 2017; Garcia 2020). AI output devices such as continuous glucose monitoring (CGM) and automated insulin delivery systems have significantly improved diabetes management by providing constant feedback while removing the risks that come with diabetes like hypoglycemia (Wang & Preininger, 2019).

Diabetes is emerging as a considerable public health obstacle in India, particularly in the region of Odisha. As stated in the Indian Council of Medical Research (ICMR), there are millions of people suffering from diabetes in India, which makes this country one of the top diabetes afflicted countries in the world. Odisha is already struggling with infrastructural issues in its health care system, which fails to provide

 DOI: 10.1201/9781003600947-4

consistent standard care, especially in rural areas with few specialists (Mishra, 2019). Considering these gaps, AI can help create sustainable solutions that ease the burden on health care professionals while enhancing patient care. Although there is some hope, the further development of these systems for the field of medicine, particularly in places with few resources like Odisha, would be extremely challenging. This encompasses the high cost of implementation, lack of infrastructure, and inadequate data governance to safeguard patients and provide ethical AI solutions (Topol, 2019). This chapter aims to discuss the challenges presented and the socio-economic effects AI-enabled diabetes care would have in the state of Odisha in order to create a foundation of effective policies for intervention in healthcare.

4.2 STATEMENT OF THE PROBLEM

As with the rest of the country, Odisha has its share of challenges when it comes to diabetes. According to The National Diabetes and Obesity Survey, the state diabetes prevalence is higher than the national average, particularly among the elderly aged 45 years and above. Healthcare, especially in rural areas, is far from sufficient, and with limited resources, this region remains heavily burdened (Mishra, 2019).

The hindrance is in the failure to embrace advanced resources like AI which can drastically enhance the efficiency of diabetes management, reduce expenses, and increase care. While AI developed technologies have been known to assist in diabetes control globally, their reach in Odisha is however constrained due to the socio-economic status, inadequate infrastructure, and various ethical concerns surrounding data privacy and consent (Jiang et al., 2017; Johnson, 2020). This research seeks to address how AI can be used for diabetes control in the Indian state of Odisha while caring for the socio-economic, ethical, and infrastructural challenges.

4.3 REVIEW OF LITERATURE

Smith and Johnson (2020) outlined in their paper "Artificial Intelligence and Diabetes: Current Challenges and Future Prospects" hypoglycemic events technological AI could use to manage insulin dosage along with glucose monitoring. It also considers the application of AI in DSS which is highly effective in managing diabetes. The review focuses on accuracy and error margins with a query on how AI-powered models sharpen the predictions and the results achieved by the patients.

Zhang and Li (2021) in the paper "Machine Learning Applications in Diabetes Prediction" discuss the use of random forests and neural networks that assume diabetes onset using patient data. The AI incorporates genetic factors, lifestyle factors, as well as clinical factors in order to provide a suitable intervention to mitigate the progression of the disease at the earliest stage possible.

As Kim and Park (2020) state in the paper "AI Driven Continuous Glucose Monitoring Systems," Artificial Intelligence (AI) can enable real-time monitoring of blood glucose level when combined with CGM devices.

In the article "Economic Impact of AI in Chronic Disease Management," Luo and Wu (2020) examine the advantages and cost efficiency that come with utilizing AI technology for the management of chronic diseases such as diabetes (Jackson, 2021).

The review considers how AI assists in ensuring healthcare delivery at a lower cost by increasing diagnostic accuracy, complication avoidance, and treatment plan formulation. Williams and Robinson (2021) in the paper "AI in Personalized Diabetes Care" argue that personalization of diabetes care incorporating AI is emerging and is the most changing aspect of Diabetes management. This review describes how AI uses the patient's data to devise the treatment regimen so that compliance with medication and dietary/lifestyle alterations is maximized. Davis and Kim (2019), in the paper "Predictive Analytics in Diabetes Management Using AI", provide insights on how data-driven AI predictive tools analyze large datasets and detect early signs of diabetes along with possible outcomes. The ability of AI to gather and analyze data in the field unlocks the possibility of real-time treatment suggestions for patients. Brown and Lee (2021) "AI Assisted Insulin Therapy: Challenges and Opportunities" study emphasizes on the insufficiency of AI in the automatic delivery of insulin devices, tackling the problem of creating devices that accurately measure the insulin levels required for delivery. The paper also considers the prospects of automation in alleviating AI healthcare devices in diabetes care. Thompson and Evans (2020), "Artificial Intelligence in Gestational Diabetes Management" describe the application of AI with respect to managing diabetes in pregnancy, focusing on the real-time surveillance and assistive components offered by AI to manage diabetic pregnant women.

4.3.1 AI-based Applications Are Associated with Better Glucose Management during Pregnancy

In predicting and identifying complications of diabetic retinopathy and diabetic neuropathy, AI is implemented, as Perez and Green (2019) explain in their paper "AI in Early Detection of Diabetic Complications". The author's aim of this article is to explain how AI helps prevent worsening of health by using patient data and imaging for complication diagnostics AI's predictive modeling offers accuracy and extensive analysis. The use of AI in undertaking any preprocessing defined by the author as risk stratification, which is reported in Campbell and Mitchell (2021), AI-Based Risk Stratification In Type 2 Diabetes, is targeted at the detection of patients with increased risk of type II diabetes and prediction. Diabetes management becomes greatly efficient due to AI's technological solutions (Sardar et al., 2017).

Wright and Smith (2020) AI diabetes self-management tools focus on the large number of AI-enabled tools, such as smartphone applications and wearable devices. Such equipment enhances patient self-care by enabling them to receive automated notifications and check their status instantly.

Like Robinson and White (2021) write in challenges of AI integration in diabetes care, the diabetes patient utilizes modern technology that AI maintains, while addressing the legal, social, and moral questions of incorporating AI into the treatment of diabetes.

Chen and Zhao (2020) in the paper "AI in Diabetic Retinopathy Screening" report that, unlike traditional medical methods used to vet diabetic retinopathy, the possibility of AI integration for its detection uses ML algorithms to analyze certain images of the retina to identify early stages of it. The technology looks promising in improving the accuracy and speed of diagnosis.

Gray and Carter (2019) in the paper "AI's Role in Behavioural Interventions for Diabetes" report how platform technology powered by AI increases one's compliance towards managing diabetes through dietary and physical activities behavioral interventions. The AI platform tracks and analyzes patient's daily habits and gives personalized feedback to maximize treatment compliance (Martin, 2020).

Lee and Taylor (2020) argue in their paper "The Future of AI in Diabetes Diagnosis and Treatment" that the future of diabetes care through AI, especially the creation of advanced predictive AIs and custom-tailored treatment approaches, is promising. They highlight that AI can change the treatment of diabetes in profound ways (Hassan 2021; Lewis 2020).

4.4 RESEARCH OBJECTIVES

This study has the following objectives:

1. Investigating the economic impact of AI inclusion in healthcare within the context of diabetes management for resource optimization and cost reduction in healthcare delivery in the state of Odisha.
2. Analyzing the ability of AI to close the gap in healthcare provision within rural and urban regions of Odisha through customization and predictive intelligence health services.
3. Studying the ethical implications of AI deployment in the healthcare sector, particularly focusing on patient confidentiality, data protection, and the distribution of AI services.
4. Suggesting applicable AI and public health policies that enable the integration of new technology into healthcare in Odisha by correlating the needed infrastructure, professional training, and ethical and legal regulations.

4.5 RESEARCH QUESTIONS

This study proposes to conduct research under the following questions:

1. What is the cost-reducing potential of AI interventions in diabetes management for the healthcare system of Odisha?
2. In which specific areas can AI be deployed to improve the primary healthcare services in rural and urban regions of Odisha?
3. What fears exist with respect to diabetes management AI systems usage, especially those related to patient data security and privacy issues?
4. What infrastructural and technological problems need to be solved to allow the implementation of AI-powered diabetes management systems in Odisha?

4.6 SCOPE OF THE STUDY

This investigation is constrained to exploring the integration of AI in managing diabetes in Odisha from economic, ethical, and technological perspectives. Although the integration of AI in chronic disease management comes with diabetes management as its primary focus, the outcomes may be useful for many other chronic diseases too (Carter, 2020). This study does not contain empirical analysis but rather provides a theoretical framework towards understanding how AI can change diabetes care in a resource-poor healthcare setting. The aim of the research is to inform policy makers, healthcare practitioners, and technology developers interested in the application of AI in the health system of Odisha (Jha, 2020).

4.7 RESEARCH METHODOLOGY

4.7.1 Research Design

This study uses a theoretical framework to analyze the role of AI in diabetes management. It is based on a literature review that focuses on the debate and integration of existing literature, theories, and models on AI within healthcare from an economic, ethical, and technological viewpoint. The analysis will derive from existing literature in economics, health policy, and science and technology studies to illustrate how AI can aid in diabetes care and the barriers that must be faced to make it possible.

4.7.2 Data Collection Method

Because this is a theoretical study, primary data collection using surveys or experimentation cannot be made. Instead, the study will use secondary data, which includes academic material, reports, policy papers, and case studies that have already been published. This data shall be obtained from peer-reviewed journals, books, conference papers, and government or organizational documents. The literature will be centered on the role of AI in health care, its economic impact, ethical implications, and case studies thereof in diabetes care.

- Sources: Journal of Diabetes Science and Technology, AI in Medicine, and Health Economics Review as well as other books and reports covering AI in healthcare.
- Search Engines: Google Scholar, PubMed, JSTOR, Scopus for locating pertinent literature.

4.7.3 Theoretical Framework

This research is planning to use a variety of theories to study the complex roles AI plays in the management of diabetes:

- Ethical Framework**:** The analysis concerning the impact that AI will have upon the privacy of patients, security of their data, and other ethical healthcare AI ML applications will be informed and shaped by ethical theories such as utilitarianism or deontological ethics.

4.7.4 Data Analysis Method

This study will adopt a theoretical analysis methodology whereby insights from multiple frameworks will be integrated:

- AI in Diabetes Management: A comprehensive literature review will be conducted to analyze sources of varying positions and perspectives on the effectiveness of AI in diabetes management.
- Models of AI in Healthcare: The use of other existing models of AI in healthcare, such as DSS and predictive analytic models, will be scrutinized for their design and gaps in the existing research.

4.7.5 Scope of Analysis

- Geographic Scope: This study will maintain a global perspective but give special consideration to underdeveloped areas with little healthcare infrastructure, like Odisha, India, as they present a wider scope for the application of AI in diabetes care.
- Thematic Scope: The study will analyze AI's place in personalized medicine, its capacity to foresee and avert diabetic complications, and its promise in decreasing healthcare expenditures. Ethical concerns such as data privacy, algorithmic bias, and inequitable access to healthcare will also be examined.

4.7.6 Ethical Considerations

Since this research is conceptual in nature and uses secondary sources, ethical concerns will be directed towards the representation of any works that have already been published. All materials cited shall be properly cited as per the requirements of the law. There are no restrictions during the research such as those of human subjects or confidentiality.

The study is limited by the use of secondary sources, which might not capture the latest shifts in AI utilization. Furthermore, being a theoretical paper, it does not have any empirical verification or primary data, which makes it difficult for real world application to be evaluated immediately.

4.8 AI IN DIABETES MANAGEMENT: A THEORETICAL OVERVIEW

4.8.1 ML and Predictive Diagnostics

The effectiveness of diagnosing and caring for patients suffering from chronic diseases has been made significantly easier with the use of technology, more specifically, AI. One factor responsible for the vast usefulness of AI is its capacity to integrate ML approaches in ascertaining the advancement of the diseases, and consequently modifying the treatment plans. For example, in the case of diabetes, predictive diagnostics forms a key part in estimating the chance of developing hyperglycemia, retinopathy, or cardiovascular issues so that the healthcare provider can take corrective actions before the situation exacerbates (Wang & Preininger, 2019).

Now, ML models are set up using extensive datasets that include patient's medical records, lifestyle choices, and even their genetics. This way, ML is able to make predictions far before any clinical manifestations become apparent. This capability, when it comes to taking diabetes management, is immensely powerful because doing so can greatly increase positive outcomes while simultaneously reducing the number of patients who are admitted into hospitals (Jiang et al., 2017). In low resource environments like Odisha, predictive diagnostics can greatly reduce tragedy-evocative complications and improve the efficiency of the limited and costly healthcare facilities available.

As an illustration, Shickel et al. (2018) documented a case in which diagnostic aids powered by AI outperformed the complication predictive secondary statistical methods that were AI-based. In this circumstance, algorithms that integrated ML with the ability to predict the advancement of diabetic retinopathy were more precise than ophthalmologists who utilized retinal photographs.

AI utilization has also expanded to the predictive models of cardiovascular risk for diabetic patients, where insights accuracy improved, and resources were efficiently allocated to the relevant populations (Topol, 2019). This could help improve the condition of Odisha as a region that suffers from overwhelming healthcare systems, particularly in rural regions where there is a deficit of specialists.

4.8.2 Continuous Glucose Monitoring and Decision Support Systems

In the context of managing obesity, CGM systems are remarkable in offering AI-powered CGM systems that integrate well with a plethora of other health systems. Patients don't have to lift a finger since everything is automated, unlike the archaic methods where patients had to measure blood glucose levels on set intervals. Traditional methods can be considered outdated in comparison to CGM as they provide real-time access to patients' glucose levels (Garg et al., 2020).

Integrating CGM with DSS blurs the line between science fiction and reality. The bulk of CGM data is combined with other health records to give the system the capacity to recommend specific actions, such as adjusting Insulin doses or dietary changes. These AI-powered CGMs have demonstrated improved glycemic control in diabetic patients by reducing hypoglycemic episodes, which subsequently increases the patient's quality of life (Wang & Preininger, 2019).

DSS-powered AI changes the game again. By continuous monitoring of grouping statements, DAI learns the regularity in the glucose levels of each patient, enabling DAI to adapt the treatment recommendations, especially for hypoglycemia patients. Meeting these requirements poses a significant challenge in India where the lifestyle, diet and genetic factors differ tremendously across various regions (Topol, 2019). For example, in Odisha, where the care is highly non-personalized, AI-based systems could close the gap by providing scalable and non-supervised treatment modalities and plans.

4.8.3 Personalization of Treatment through AI

The rise of personalized medicine is prominent during the present time, powered by AI. Rather than adopting a generalized method for a patient's diagnosis and treatment, personalized medicine is based on specific details of each patient's situation. In medicine for diabetes, personalized medicine employs AI technology to take into consideration different variables such as genetics, lifestyle, and environment (Shickel et al., 2018). This is especially applicable for the modification of glucose levels in blood for diabetes patients through insulin therapy, balanced food intake, and increased physical activities.

AI boosts the personalization of medicine by processing information that no single clinician would be able to manage and remember. These algorithms can identify patterns through ML techniques that would otherwise remain undetected and allow for greater tailoring of treatment regimens for optimal patient outcomes. For instance, AI can consider simultaneously glucose monitoring data along with diet and exercises and suggest times for dosing insulin when the chances of hypoglycemia or hyperglycemia are highest (Garg et al., 2020). Such systems can also provide alerts to patients facing serious health conditions. When a patient has excessive hypoglycemia, AI technology can issue timely alerts so that the patient can take precautionary actions (Green 2021).

The combination of AI and ML has shown the greatest outcomes among patients suffering from Type 1 and Type 2 diabetes in the most complicated cases of their treatment and disease management.

According to Wang and Preininger (2019), AI algorithms that integrate CGM data and a patient's prior medical history can improve the efficacy of insulin delivery systems, as in glycemic control and related complications. For further details on this research, you can visit Satagro Senta, which specializes in the design and development of healthcare solutions.

This is especially useful in developing countries such as Odisha, which do not have access to specialized services. With AI-powered personalization, diabetes can be managed remotely, which eliminates the need for frequent off-site visits and increases accessibility to healthcare in rural areas. Such programs would be ideal in Odisha, which has a glaring difference regarding the availability of appropriate medical facilities between the urban and rural regions. With targeted AI diabetes care, providing tailored treatment strategies considering the region's food habits, healthcare facilities, and the patient can vastly improve the treatment of diabetes in such highly resource-restricted settings. Additionally, alleviation of some of the workload experienced by other healthcare practitioners to treat advanced patients is possible because of AI's constant surveillance and treatment readiness.

4.9 ECONOMIC IMPLICATIONS OF AI IN DIABETES MANAGEMENT

4.9.1 Cost Optimization in Diabetes Care

The use of AI in the healthcare sector, especially on managing long-term ailments like diabetes, has significant economic consequences. One of AI's most alluring promises is the potential to economize healthcare by improving operational efficiency and minimizing wastage. With respect to diabetes, AI's involvement in predictive diagnostics, personalized medicine, and smart monitoring systems can result in immense savings from hospitalization, complications, and other long-term costs (Topol, 2019).

CGM systems and DSS exemplify the AI-enabled technologies that help avert complications by giving real-time data and predictive analytics to healthcare providers so they can mitigate complications before they get to the critical stage. For instance, AI algorithms for diabetes management, as described in the work of Jiang et al. (2017), were able to reduce the number of DKA-solving hospital admissions by predicting glucose changes and preventing critical hypoglycemic or hyperglycemic stages. In avoiding these costly events, AI could substantially decrease the financial burden on health care systems, especially in resource-limited areas such as Odisha where the health care system is underdeveloped. As noted above, AI can also predict people who could get diabetes and allow for early interventions to be made to avert the challenges that come with the disease. AI-assisted healthcare is more efficient than treating complex cases of diabetes, which typically incur high costs (Wang & Preininger, 2019). Because Odisha lacks advanced healthcare facilities, AI has the potential to alleviate the economic burden by drastically reducing out-of-pocket expenses on expensive treatments over time.

AI can also help optimize costs by relieving some of the pressure placed on the few providers supplying healthcare services to a population. Routine functions such as telemetry and data processing can be handled by AI systems, thereby allowing healthcare personnel to focus on advanced value-added services (Shickel et al., 2018). In Odisha where medical practitioners are overstretched by the limited resources available amidst the high patient outcomes, this increase in efficiency is quite critical. So, by using AI to supplement human labor, healthcare systems can cut the costs of providing services while improving the services provided at the same time.

4.9.2 Predictive Analytics for Preventive Healthcare

One of the most basic facts to consider is the cost-effectiveness of using AI in healthcare revolves around its capabilities in predictive analytics, enabling preemptive healthcare. In Essence, AI-aided diabetes management leverages real-time and historical data to provide proactive solutions instead of reactive treatments. Predictive analytics will use data and predict impending complications such as cardiovascular diseases or kidney failure in diabetes patients and act on it before the condition reaches its worst form (Garg et al., 2020).

For example, AI algorithms that process real-time CGM data will inform patients when the data predicts an impending acute diabetic episode. These actionable results form the basis of how AI can lower emergency hospital admission cases, and consequently, expenses as they always exceed the expenditure associated with regular diabetes supervision (Topol, 2019). The greatest cost savings in healthcare is made possible through AI, having decreased the proportionate expenditure accompanying chronic illnesses by 15% through interventions made early (Shickel et al., 2018).

To help the overloaded healthcare industry in places such as Odisha, AI has the ability to extend aid regardless of a region's capability to provide targeted care. Like Odisha has challenges, diabetes management is an issue for rural areas where specialist support is hard to access. AI can provide solutions through predictive models that enable primary care clinicians to proactively manage diabetes, thereby decreasing the need for costly specialized care interventions (Mishra, 2019). In addition, preventing future complications using AI is cost-beneficial as it improves the patients' quality of life through lessened management burden in advanced stages of diabetes.

4.9.3 Challenges of Initial Investment and Infrastructure

The obstacle to implementing AI in healthcare solutions is the money. AI has been shown to save costs in the long run but requires a big investment at the beginning. This is a great hindrance in places with limited resources like Odisha. The structures needed, much less the hardware and software purchased, and the training for healthcare professionals, are tremendously expensive. Mills et al. (2018) explain how low-resourced settings have a dire need for an upgraded infrastructure, making implementing AI healthcare systems cost 2–3 times more than well-developed ones. The budget restraints in AI adoption ROI calculations are especially troublesome in diabetes management for AI adoption. Rural healthcare facilities face even bigger challenges as they lack the basic pillars, such as internet, EHR systems, and adequate EHR system coverage to make use of AI technologies. All of these issues were brought forward by Mishra in 2019, and by not focusing on properly investing in these areas, the people in the underequipped rural regions of Odisha will remain AI-deficient.

These systems are not only expensive at the onset but have perpetual costs down the line. These include the data storage, as well as constant software updates and the integration of existing healthcare tools. The integration of AI in the management of diabetes comes with these costs, which must always be analyzed when considering economic feasibility. To ensure sustainable economic viability, healthcare professionals' investment (ROI) in AI technology needs to be thoughtfully managed against the concierge service fees and the possible paradigm shift in payment of lower hospital admissions, overall patient conditions, and better provided services in the future (Jha, 2020).

4.9.4 Cost-Benefit Analysis in the Context of Odisha

The analysis of the use of AI technology for the management of diabetes in Odisha reveals both advantages and disadvantages, which illustrates a situation that is not easy to understand. The argument in support of the positive aspects is that there would be savings from the reduced complications, which can be very expensive, and from the other aspects of resource utilization and care delivery. In contrast, these benefits are not quite as straightforward given the high initial investment costs of the AI infrastructure and the problem of trying to integrate AI in a healthcare system that is already so poorly funded (Mills et al., 2018).

The lack of sufficient healthcare IT infrastructure in rural Odisha makes the ROI from AI questionable unless there is a willingness to spend foundational money on the supporting infrastructure. Considering these elements, the greater use of AI in the management of diabetes can be embraced in the less rural regions with a developed healthcare IT infrastructure than in the rural, poorer regions. However, placing investments in sophisticated AI systems could yield significant results by lowering the rates of hospital admissions and increasing the quality of care among high-risk diabetic patients (Jha, 2020).

Odisha's healthcare policymakers need to be made aware that the best value economic outcomes would emerge from a comprehensive caring policy based on the gradual implementation of AI in the management of diabetes. This can entail the first step of using AI in urban regions that already have the necessary infrastructure in place. There is then the possibility of shifting focus of AI resources toward Rural areas post-investment in the needed infrastructure and capacity building. Furthermore, P3s could provide funding for AI projects allowing the state to use the funds from the private sector toward the adoption of AI technologies (Mishra, 2019).

4.9.5 Opportunities for AI in Odisha's Diabetes Management

4.9.5.1 Potential Cost-Savings and Efficiency Gains

The use of AI in the management of diabetes has the ability to offer tremendous savings and efficiency within the healthcare infrastructure of Odisha. Since diabetes is a chronic disease, it requires ongoing management, monitoring, and regular interventions. Odisha, and especially the rural regions, have a traditional healthcare system that is not equipped to deliver the required level of care, resulting in under-service. AI devices and predictive analytics (ML), for example, have the potential to improve service delivery by offering low-cost intervention that can avert expensive and complex healthcare needs (Jha, 2020).

Healthcare professionals can attend to their patients more effectively and on time with the assistance of AI tools like CGM systems, DSS, and ML software. Complications that the patient might face in the future can be analyzed with the aid of AI predictive analytics before they become dire situations that call for greater and costlier measures (Jiang et al., 2017). Through these techniques, diabetes care can be more economical for healthcare and patients by eliminating the need for hospital admissions or many emergency treatments.

When AI machines detect insulin levels or monitor glucose levels, professionals can attend to more intensive human-intervention tasks (Wang & Preininger, 2019). Besides, the virtually available data and AI-powered insights allow healthcare professionals to make better decisions, which ultimately prevents expensive errors and increases the level of service to the patients.

4.9.6 AI's Role in Reducing Rural-Urban Healthcare Gaps

One of the significant issues affecting Odisha's health care system is the difference in the level of care offered in urban areas as compared to rural regions. For example, districts like Bhubaneswar and Cuttack have more sophisticated healthcare facilities and greater concentration of specialists. However, resources are often inadequate in rural regions. This rural-urban gap breeds significant healthcare inequity, affording chronic disease patients like diabetics who need constant supervision and control, especially (Mishra, 2019).

The difference in healthcare services given to rural as compared to urban regions can be narrowed by incorporating advanced technology in AI-powered telemedicine, which has the potential to provide healthcare facilities to rural areas. Remote patient consultations, diagnoses, and monitoring via telemedicine can link rural patients with urban health care practitioners (Gourisaria, 2022). Mobile health apps and wearable AI-powered tools that offer real-time patient data to healthcare centers for analysis and intervention (Topol, 2019). Such technologies help to bridge the healthcare divide and ensure undivided attention to remote patients, similar to those residing in cities.

Furthermore, the provision of diabetes care may be supported by clinical DSS for non-specialized medical personnel in remote areas, which allows for shifting responsibilities to improve the quality of care. These devices assist medical practitioners in understanding and acting upon complex medical data, which addresses the lack of doctors in far-off places (Garg et al., 2020). This method of service delivery allows for the unification of urban and rural health care systems and enables citizens from the remote regions of Odisha to access appropriate health care services in a timely manner.

4.9.7 Personalized Medicine: Tailoring Treatment for Regional Populations

The capability for AI healthcare technology to provide individualized services is also another unique opportunity to improve diabetes management in Odisha. It is the integration of medicine and biology with a specific set of medical protocols tailored to the biological, environmental, and lifestyle factors of a given patient. AI-facilitated tools possess the potential to identify unique patterns within enormous datasets that are beyond the reach of human practitioners, and therefore, more precise and effective treatment strategies can be crafted (Shickel et al., 2018). The use of AI in diabetes medicine can be far reaching by incorporating a patient's glucose levels, insulin sensitivity, eating habits, and the appropriate amount of insulin, nutrition, and lifestyle changes needed. This approach to controlling diabetes results in better health quality and to even higher satisfaction among patients because the solutions are most appropriate to their needs (Wang & Preininger, 2019). Odisha has an eclectic mix of cultures, norms, and traditions which profoundly impact dietary and lifestyle patterns within the state, thus AI-powered personalized medicine is well placed to cater for such a broad spectrum.

In addition, AI-powered personalized medicine can help solve the problem associated with diabetes management with a single treatment that might not suit all patients. For instance, Garg et al explained a study where it suggested that AI systems may improve the functionality of insulin delivery to patients by exploring CGM data alongside physical and nutritional activities. This kind of AI personalization would be extremely useful in Odisha where healthcare providers find it exceedingly complex to manage the myriad of patient requirements owing to the population and infrastructure dynamics of the state.

AI can help achieve greater accuracy in providing medical services and, in so doing minimize the more severe risks of hypoglycemia and hyperglycemia, which unregulated properly, can lead to extremely costly hospital admissions. Topol (2019) mentions that AI-driven personalization of treatment can lead to better patient compliance since patients are more willing to follow the dictated treatment plans that directly affect their particular needs.

4.9.8 Addressing Health Disparities through AI

There are considerable gaps in healthcare services in Odisha's various socioeconomic groups. Due to the rural-urban gap and differing scopes of income and education, many people, especially in rural areas, extremely diabetes care. AI can help with these gaps by lowering the cost of advanced healthcare technology to all people.

AI-centered mobile health applications and telemedicine can reduce the cost of healthcare services, making them more accessible for low-income populations (Mills et al., 2018). For instance, AI diagnostic capabilities in budgeted smartphones would allow rural populations to obtain primary healthcare without the need for expensive medical consultations. Also, AI's real-time monitoring and predictive analytics allow patients to take charge of managing their health without the constant need for in-person visits, which also lowers the overall cost of healthcare.

Standardized treatment AI can help formulate for different regions and service providers can aid in the improved quality of care, making AI an important innovation in the industry. AI-powered DSS can make certain that each patient receives appropriate medical attention, irrespective of their geographical location or the healthcare provider they consult. This can help in minimizing the differences in treatment results and increasing equality in healthcare (Garg et al., 2020). For a state such as Odisha, where quality care is often very irregular, AI can ensure that all patients receive the same degree of treatment, thereby equalizing the issues.

4.9.9 Leveraging Public-Private Partnerships

The healthcare system here in Odisha must make use of public-private partnerships if they are to leverage the opportunities that AI provides with diabetes management. AI technology implementation entails an elaborate investment in infrastructure and training, which alone is beyond what the public healthcare sector is able to provide. Partnerships of this nature (also capitalizing on Mishra's words) will assist in bridging this gap by integrating resources and expertise from both the public and private sectors to facilitate the deployment of AI in healthcare.

The public sector will also enable access to healthcare facilities, provide relevant patient information, as well as govern the initiative while private enterprises that focus specifically on AI and health technologies will supply the technical know-how. These partnerships can hasten the utilization of AI in diabetes management, as steps can be taken to ensure the infrastructure is in place and that the providers of healthcare are sufficiently trained to use these AI tools at their disposal (Jha, 2020).

Implementing pilot projects, as well as scaling successful initiatives, can address the financial obstacles to AI adoption. For instance, such an Odisha public-private partnership can aim at closing the rural-urban healthcare gap by operating AI-powered mobile health applications in rural areas. Those projects could be scaled up due to the emphasis placed on AI-driven healthcare solutions in the state and beyond.

4.10 CHALLENGES IN ADOPTING AI FOR DIABETES CARE IN ODISHA

4.10.1 Financial and Technological Barriers

The adoption of AI in diabetes care in Odisha is challenging due to the region's financial and technological limitations. An initial investment is required in AI infrastructure and tools (Mills et al., 2018). Unfortunately, states such as Odisha face stretched funding, and these expenditures pose a barrier to effective adoption of AI technologies. Advanced solutions like Imagine AI assistive tools with real-time monitoring and predictive diagnostics are beneficial, but remain out of reach for the majority of patients due to a lack of necessary infrastructure.

Additionally, the storage of electronic health records (EHR) alongside reliable internet connectivity is essential for AI optimization (Mishra, 2019). Many healthcare facilities in Odisha fail to possess the primary technological capabilities, making it difficult to integrate these systems into daily medical practices. The infrastructure needed to support AI remains significantly underdeveloped, particularly in rural regions. Without these components, personalized treatment for diabetics through the use of AI tools is simply impossible.

Tackling economic, infrastructural, and technological constraints simultaneously allows for easier integration of assistive tools. However, the success of AI in healthcare hinges on the need to address a critical skill gap found within Odisha's healthcare system. In order to utilize AI data efficiently in clinical decision-making, Wang and Preininger claim, that "health care providers need to be trained in using AI tools." Nonetheless, Odisha suffers from a lack of trained medical personnel, especially in rural locations where healthcare workers are overwhelmed with the patient-to-staff ratio. Providers' unwillingness to utilize these technologies stems from a profound lack of adequate training and skills, which is a fundamental barrier for the successful integration of AI in healthcare.

4.10.2 Infrastructure and Resource Constraints

Lack of existing infrastructural resources remains another barrier to the implementation of AI in diabetes care in the state of Odisha. Medical care in the state is provided in an unequal manner where urban regions like Bhubaneswar and Cuttack are better serviced in terms of medical technologies and specialists compared to the rural regions (Mishra, 2019). Such disparities in healthcare infrastructure pose critical issues to the integration of AI technologies, which usually rely on advanced data computing and diagnostic networks, comprehensive electronic health record (EHR) systems, and other supporting ICT infrastructure (Jha, 2020).

The use of AI-powered tools for diabetes care is more challenging in regions that are rural, where healthcare services operate on lower levels of subject matter expertise and existing resources. A large number of rural clinics are under-resourced, lacking even the basic equipment needed to diagnose, let alone manage diabetes. It is, therefore, not surprising that the vast majority of rural clinics in Odisha do not have access to the basic resources, such as reliable. For example, in Odisha, there is little to no access to reliable internet, integration systems, and regular maintenance of advanced technological devices like CGM devices or DSS, which are critical for AI-based diabetes management (Topol, 2019).

No less important, the state suffers from insufficient healthcare infrastructural assets, which does not allow for effective collection, processing, and storage of information that is required for the reliable functioning of AI power systems (Sardar et al., 2023).

The AI Slovenian Health Technologies System seeks to make accurate predictions and personalized treatment recommendations, but is not able to do so due to a lack of electronic health record (EHR) systems at most healthcare facilities in Odisha, which makes data collection and analysis cumbersome (Mills et al., 2018). There is no enforcement of standard protocols for data collection of an otherwise fragmented health management information system, which severely restricts the use of AI applications that require large volumes of good quality data.

4.10.3 Data Quality, Algorithmic Bias, and Training Challenges

The primary difficulty in integrating AI into diabetes care within the state of Odisha is the caliber of information that is available to train AI algorithms. To recommend unbiased personalized treatment and accurately predict health outcomes, AI models need a lot of different types of good quality data. Unfortunately, much of healthcare data across several regions of Odisha is absent, fragmented or has discrepancies because of unsystematic data collection processes (Jiang et al., 2017). This brings about an enormous problem while training AI algorithms since, without data, there is no missing value imputation that could help improve the situation. Models derived from such deficient, pseudonymous, or partial datasets are bound to fail and result in inaccurate clinical assessments and erroneous treatments.

Algorithmic bias is yet another problem of concern in AI healthcare systems. In AI-driven healthcare systems, an information system is only as efficient as the information requires it to be, which means that it will always be dictated by the set through which it learns (Shickel et al., 2018). The same algorithmic bias in AI healthcare systems that can subvert treatment for chronic diabetes in the case of Odisha can have even greater ramifications, considering this bias magnifies the pre-existing gap in healthcare. For example, with respect to rural India, data obtained from developing AI models in urban hospitals as a source is bound to fail because specific and differentiation in the healthcare requirements and disease structure is clearly outlined (Mishra, 2019).

To counteract the diverse and targetable data that is necessary to combat algorithms around healthcare service coverage skills, AI is required to first understand the people of Odisha by studying their ailments.

Training unbiased AI models can prove to be extremely challenging to undertake in healthcare systems without adequate integrated healthcare systems and standardized data collection methodologies, which is the case in this state. Without any major leaps in data requirements, adjusting the quality or standardization measures will prove futile (Jha, 2020). The degree of accuracy and reliability when using AI-powered tools for diabetes management in Odisha will be restricted indefinitely.

In all healthcare systems, the effective training of medical professionals is one of the most fundamental issues of concern. Limited exposure to modern and sophisticated healthcare technologies is a huge problem for the majority of healthcare workers within the state of Odisha, especially those operating in rural regions. As a general objection, lack of understanding AI systems will invariably be one of the major roadblocks when deploying AI-based systems as providers will be reluctant to use technology they do not understand (Wang & Preininger, 2019). Designing comprehensive training modules is important so that health personnel are equipped with relevant knowledge and skills to make appropriate clinical decisions with the emerging AI technologies. Of course, creating and implementing these comprehensive training modules will be very time-consuming and resource-demanding in a health system that is already constrained.

4.10.4 Ethical and Legal Challenges in AI Adoption

The inclusion of AI technology in diabetes treatment within Odisha brings to light ethical and legal issues, especially concerning patient privacy, data protection, and informed consent. For AI systems to make predictions and suggest treatments, they need to gather, analyze, and store large amounts of consumer health data. But with such broad data sets comes profound skepticism about patient privacy and data security, particularly in regions with underdeveloped digital infrastructure (Jiang et al., 2017).

At the center of AI-based healthcare solutions lies a primary ethical concern. It is the consent and understanding of the patients regarding how their data will be utilized. There are areas in Odisha where patients lack adequate understanding of how their sensitive health information is used by AI systems, which raises ethical flags with the potential for misuse or exploitation of such data (Shickel et al., 2018). In order to cultivate faith in AI technologies, patients enabling the use of their data must be thoroughly informed about the potential risks, benefits, and given the proper consent to utilize such information for using AI in healthcare. Building trust with patients is crucial, and this issue must be worked on as a priority to ensure flexibility and AI advancement.

Inactivity of these legalities, next to ethical implications, forms a complex web. Combine this with underdeveloped policies surrounding AI utilization in healthcare, and it worsens the ecosystems within Odisha.

The state's focus is limited when it comes to matters as intricate as data protection, cybersecurity, and the adoption of AI technologies in the healthcare sector, which cultivates confusion among healthcare practitioners aiming to harness these technologies (Jha, 2020). Providers employing AI innovations to improve and manage diabetes care may be reluctant owing to the missing legal framework concerning data sharing, privacy, and security.

Legal and ethical issues are best solved with a well-coordinated AI strategy. Therefore, it involves formulating comprehensive norms for privacy, security, consent, and the application of AI algorithms during clinical decision-making to ensure the same (Topol, 2019). To properly utilize AI technologies in one of the most economically underdeveloped states in India, Odisha, responsible and ethical principles have to be incorporated into the healthcare system of the state, enabling the practitioners to act with accountability.

4.11 ETHICAL CONSIDERATIONS IN AI-DRIVEN DIABETES MANAGEMENT

4.11.1 Privacy, Data Security, and Consent Issues

Ensuring data management for security and privacy is one of the most challenging ethical dilemmas in AI healthcare systems. With the broad scope of collecting, storing, and analyzing vast amounts of sensitive patient data, AI systems face security risks on many levels. Technologies deployed for AI in diabetes management, like CGM and DSS, require real-time retrieval of information from patients that includes insulin doses, blood glucose concentrations, and even lifestyle activities (Garg et al., 2020). While these data points allow AI algorithms to render more targeted and efficient care, it raises the paramount question around data protection – how is this information secured?

The region faces several challenges, such as fragmentation of the healthcare system, lack of trained personnel, and, most importantly, absence of a robust digital infrastructure, which makes Odisha's strategy towards securing a patient's data highly difficult. A large number of healthcare facilities are static without requisite cybersecurity protocols, which makes them susceptible to unauthorized data access (Mills et al., 2018). Such issues are highly sensitive when it comes to AI-powered systems where most of the components are hosted on the internet, and sensitive health information is stored and processed through the cloud. Health information systems and other software applications can be prone to cyberattacks, which can lead to inappropriate use or manipulation of patient data because of system weaknesses and the exposure of sensitive health data on uncontrolled breaches like these.

In addition to privacy issues, adequately dealing with informed consent poses an equally significant ethical challenge when dealing with the implementation of AI in the healthcare setting.

It is important for patients to know how AI systems intend to use their data and give explicit consent to this. However, patients may not completely grasp the intricacies of data sharing with AI systems, more so in places like Odisha, which have lower levels of digital literacy (Mishra, 2019). At the crux of this issue lies whether patients really have the ability to provide informed consent and whether healthcare providers are doing their part in making sure that patients are aware of the risks and advantages posed by AI-powered care.

The mere fact that obtaining consent from patients is challenging is only a byproduct of the AI systems, which complicate matters even more. Some AI techniques are described as 'black box' algorithms, which means that even the people who build these systems do not understand how they reach a conclusion (Topol, 2019). Such opacity poses difficulties for healthcare providers interested in explaining AI's decision-making calculus to patients, and that further undermines the prospects of informed consent. For these reasons, healthcare providers would have to ensure that patients are appropriately educated on the actual functioning of AI systems and how their data would be utilized while simultaneously putting in place effective measures to safeguard the data privacy of the patients.

4.11.2 Addressing Healthcare Inequities

In order to understand how AI can both enable and alleviate health inequities in a region like Odisha, it is important to realize that healthcare gaps, especially between urban and rural regions, are vast in Odisha. The shift to AI-enabled tools, like mobile health applications and telemedicine, offers a unique solution to the gap in diabetes care access by shifting the sophistication of care to rural regions. The rural populace would not have to travel for a physician's visit and instead would receive more remote monitoring with tailored recommendations (Wang & Preininger, 2019). The discussion of obstinate AI-enabled systems also raises troubling questions around deepening disparities. The availability of AI systems requires a certain level of digital and technological access that is oftentimes not present in rural or low-income regions. The absence of basic medical devices in a significant proportion of rural clinics in Odisha suggests that the introduction of AI is going to be most favorable to urban regions, further deepening rural underdevelopment (Mishra, 2019). In this case, sociodemographic disparity is going to be greatly exaggerated if there is an unequal distribution of AI regions. Most importantly, the lack of access to sophisticated technology and medical devices in rural areas due to significant economic disparity can increase healthcare inequities. Perhaps the greatest worry is whether AI implements bias while making decisions in the healthcare domain.

There is a possibility of bias in the outcomes of AI algorithms because they rely on large sets of data, which, if not population-representative, can cause many issues. For example, the healthcare management of diabetes patients might not work well with rural patients if the AI system was trained using data mainly from urban patients (Shickel et al., 2018). This has the potential to create a gap in health care standards between patients from urban and rural Odisha, leading to further neglect of the latter.

AI systems need to be trained using datasets that include information from the rural population so as to improve the healthcare AI systems can offer to all. Furthermore, appropriate measures have to be taken at the policy-making level to facilitate equal access to these AI tools for all, regardless of their geographical location, social status, or wealth (Jha, 2020). This issue can be solved by the collaboration of the private and public sectors by investing in the integration of these new technologies to fulfill the needs of these neglected regions, aiming to broaden the range of AI within rural healthcare infrastructure.

4.11.3 Ethical Framework for AI Adoption

In diabetes management, the adoption of AI must be ethical, which means ensuring that all concepts are interlinked and cover aspects of data privacy, security, consent, and equity. Transparent accountability and fairness should guide the framework development to establish responsible usage for all patients. In Odisha, where the healthcare systems are still developing, the creation of such a framework is important to make sure that AI-based technologies are used in modern medicine, but with a consideration towards the local contexts (Mills et al., 2018).

The creation of a framework to solve these problems should include formulating privacy and security polices as one of the aspects. Healthcare providers should have effective governance processes in place to prevent unauthorized access to patient data and ensure that it is used appropriately. This should be done by using encryption, secure data systems, and auditing compliance with data protection laws (Topol, 2019). Moreover, the addition of AI to modern medicine provides challenges as healthcare providers need to guarantee that patients understand how their data will be utilized, and that consent is obtained prior to sharing any data.

The last point cited here and which is relevant to the ethical framework discussed, concerns the use of AI in decision-making transparency. Earlier, we mentioned that AI algorithms tend to function as "black boxes", which makes it impossible for providers to explain how AI systems arrive at decisions (Shickel et al., 2018). This is a problem that has existed for a very long time. AI developers and healthcare providers need to collaborate and build systems that are less opaque, so they are more accessible and comprehensible to users. This may include the use of explainable AI (XAI) technologies that explain how the AI arrived at a conclusion (Jha, 2020). The lack of trust with AI systems in healthcare can be, in part, resolved if the providers are allowed to look into the inner workings of these systems to make patients feel secure in the care they receive.

As in most areas of human activity, accountability is an indispensable facet that should be embedded in the ethics of AI adoption. The most important concern regarding liability is that healthcare practitioners need to answer for the actions taken by AI systems, especially concerning patient care (Topol, 2019). In other words, the healthcare practitioner has the legal responsibility to take action whenever clinical decisions are made based on AI analysis. Moreover, the developers of AI applications need to guarantee the intended robustness of their algorithms by testing and validating their systems to avoid making life-changing decisions based on poorly trained AI systems that could contain numerous errors and biases.

Finally, fairness is another element that must be employed as a guiding principle in the ethical use of AI. AI systems need to be developed and put into use in a manner that aids equity and does not worsen the current gaps in healthcare. This includes making sure that there is no economic discrimination by making powerful AI tools trained on many different population groups publicly available, and that the AI systems are accessible to all populations, and that they are funded reticulously proportional to different regions and socioeconomic divisions (Mills et al., 2018). Maintaining these principles will help improve the ethical AI-driven diabetes control management system in Odisha's healthcare system so that all patients receive appropriate care irrespective of their background or locality.

4.11.4 Ensuring Ethical Use of Patient Data

With the advancement in technology, data has become an essential asset in the world of healthcare. AI utilizes enormous datasets to make accurate estimates and prescriptions, thus underscoring the importance of quality datasets in the realm of digitalized healthcare. Simultaneously, the application of patient data in AI systems also poses a plethora of ethical dilemmas, such as patient privacy, security, and consent. Mishra (2019) argues that in places like Odisha, where digital infrastructure is nascent, guaranteeing ethical application of patient data becomes a considerable dilemma that needs to be solved for greater faith in AI technologies.

One of the major ethical issues surrounding utilization of patient data primarily concerns the collection and application of data that violates patient autonomy and privacy principles. Patients must understand and provide permission on how their medical data is utilized. More often than not, though, patients do not completely comprehend sharing their information with AI-powered systems, especially in the context of areas with poor awareness.

Healthcare providers need to ensure that patients are thoroughly educated about how their data will be used and have provided informed consent prior to any sharing of their data with AI systems (Jha, 2020).

The ethical use of patient data has raised other challenges concerning data security. Providers have the responsibility to protect patient data from unauthorized access, breaches, and abuse by putting in place adequate cybersecurity systems (Topol, 2019). This includes using encryption, secure data storage, regular compliance audits, and protecting other technologies used to ensure data is secured. In addition, guidelines concerning data sharing should be clear, and, at all costs, data should be used for its intended purpose only.

4.12 TECHNOLOGICAL LIMITATIONS OF AI IN DIABETES MANAGEMENT

4.12.1 AI's Reliance on Structured Data and Its Limitations

The problem AI is facing while executing diabetes management is its dependence on structured data. Algorithms, and especially Healthcare ones, collect and process enormous quantities of structured data, like patient files, laboratory tests, and CGM data (Jiang et al., 2017). Typically, structured data is presented in a pre-set form that is straightforward for AI systems to interpret. However, actual healthcare environments have a large portion of relevant patient data that is unstructured, which, in the case of physician notes, self-reported data, and other lifestyle elements, is extremely difficult for AI algorithms to comprehend (Shickel et al., 2018).

Unstructured data has a particularly important role in diabetes management because there are more than just glucose readings that affect the condition. For instance, a patient's diet, exercise, psychosocial aspects, and their socio-economic status are vital determinants of their health (Topol, 2019). These distinctions can get lost for AI systems, creating algorithms that strictly account for structured data, rendering treatment results highly ineffective.

This is particularly worrying in Odisha since its lifestyle and ecological factors usually differ from one region to the other making diabetes management more complex.

Increasing attention is being paid to this gap by developing methods in AI systems which utilize Natural Language Processing (NLP) that can analyze data that is usually not structured, which is unrestrained and unconformed in nature. With the help of NLP in AI systems, physicians' notes and even the patients' descriptions of their issues can be used as inputs, which in simpler terms expands the scope of understanding the medical condition of the patient (Wang & Preininger, 2019). The irony is that although several systems are in use, these systems continue to struggle, as most of the resources that are being used are only designed to work with organized data. The challenge is that the available NLP resources are not efficient and mean absolute measurements to tackle the heavy data that is present, which makes the need for more advanced resources. Until these so-called AIs are provided with the requisite Deep Learning, such as NLPs, where the AI can view illness in its wholeness, control over illnesses like diabetes will remain inadequate.

4.12.2 Human Judgment vs. AI Decision-Making

AI-created decisions come with a cost; human judgment could be entirely neglected. Healthcare AI systems are supposed to improve outcomes by providing evidence-based reports and recommendations. Yet, such systems fall short of replicating the complete judgmental capacity of a seasoned healthcare professional, especially with regard to complicated scenarios where one deals with numerous elements simultaneously (Garg et al., 2020). AI algorithms are good at evaluating particular forms of data such as how much insulin the patient has been injected with or glucose levels. They do not account for the other psychological, social, and behavioral problems within the patient's environment.

AI-based DSS could, for example, suggest a particular basal insulin injection for a patient depending on glucose numbers without regard to mental health, stress, or other recent changes that may negatively impact the patient's overall well-being (Shickel et al., 2018). Conversely, human clinicians are trained to focus not only on data but also to utilize their clinical judgement and knowledge of the patient to formulate a diagnosis and provide treatment.

One of the most fundamental issues facing the AI healthcare industry is that healthcare practitioners may lean too much into recommendations received from specific algorithms, losing sight of necessary patient-oriented actions that require human intervention.

These issues are important in the context of Odisha, where healthcare practitioners work under severe time constraints and are often more dependent on AI systems for quick decision-making. These challenges need to be addressed to ensure that machine recommendations do not undermine humans' ability to make decisions in diabetes care (Topol, 2019). AI is a powerful tool that can help clinicians, but they still need to think critically while working with AI-derived information, integrating it within their own clinical data and decision-making.

4.12.3 Limitations in Handling Complex, Unstructured Data

The AI systems are unable to process intricate unstructured data sets, such as behavioral and environmental factors, which have an incident effect on diabetes outcomes. While structured information like blood sugar levels is analyzed with ease by AI algorithms, unstructured data like patient-reported outcomes, social determinants of health, and behavior patterns are far too complex for AI systems to interpret (Wang & Preininger, 2019). In Odisha, the region's culture heavily impacts diabetes management, and this poses a real problem.

For instance, dietary practices in Odisha vary from community to community, and these practices are integral to diabetes management. AI systems relying mainly on structured data may ignore these nuances and provide treatment options devoid of the individual patient's needs. Moreover, other vital diabetes management aspects like physical activity, social support, and healthy diets are also equally difficult for AI algorithms to capture and interpret (Mishra, 2019). Consequently, recommendation systems driven by AI may end up being overly instructional, responding to issues in a multi-dimensional failure approach.

Combining ML algorithms with social and behavioral data to build more holistic models for diabetes management is one approach to counter this major shortcoming. AI interventions could be more sophisticated and tailored to treat patients if data is incorporated on lifestyle elements, social determinants of health, and preferences of patients. This, however, needs robust and wide-ranging datasets that are deep in both qualitative and quantitative aspects- an issue many healthcare systems, although including Odisha's, are not prepared to tackle (Mills et al., 2018).

4.12.4 Challenges in Implementing AI in Complex Health Ecosystems

With regards to systems like that of Odisha, the integration of AI into existing processes is complex due to the ecosystem of health already being so complex. The quality and the availability of data centralize a lot of AI processes, including the infrastructure necessary for data collection, analysis, and storage. These issues are particularly pronounced for Odisha where the AI and healthcare infrastructure is severely underdeveloped. Primary healthcare centers don't have the basic digital infrastructure required to implement AI systems reliably, such as a robust internet connection, electronic health record (EHR) systems, or data storage facilities (Mishra, 2019).

Furthermore, deploying AI in healthcare does not only require technological or infrastructural alterations to be made; there are huge logistical barriers that exist, too. In clinical settings, the practice of AI has to be done in a way that aids the clinician in delivering health care, not in a way that hinders it. Unfortunately, a lot of people working in healthcare in Odisha have little to no experience with AI, and teaching clinicians this process is not only expensive but also quite time-consuming (Wang & Preininger, 2019). This is even more grave for healthcare workers in rural areas who are already overworked and may see the adoption of these technologies as an increased burden.

Beyond these logistical barriers, the ability for AI systems to work alongside the already established healthcare technologies poses significant concerns.

Numerous healthcare institutions in Odisha largely make use of old and non-compatible technologies, which can hamper the integration of new AI-driven tools into the current infrastructure. The absence of interoperability can result in greater inefficiencies since providers might need to operate within several systems that are not linked to one another, thus making each system have its own inputs and outputs (Topol, 2019). Working around these obstacles takes a considerable amount of effort, which in a resource poor setting like Odisha poses complications in infrastructure and training of personnel as well as integration of the systems.

4.12.5 Limitations in Predictive Accuracy and Algorithmic Bias

One more important drawback of AI in diabetes management is its predictive accuracy and algorithmic bias. Just like any other computer system, the algorithms' predictive capabilities are built upon data; therefore, if the data is biased or not sufficient, the outcome is bound to be inaccurate (Shickel et al., 2018). For instance, in Odisha, there is a high probability that AI systems will not be able to provide accurate or fair treatment suggestions, considering the fact that healthcare data may not exist or may be recorded haphazardly.

A case in point is when AI trained on data from urban healthcare institutions is used on rural populations, where health requirements and illness constellations are very different. This can negatively affect the quality of care delivered to the vulnerable segments targeting rural patients who are less proactive, as they might be offered substandard or generic treatment recommendations (Mishra, 2019). Some of these limitations can be dealt with through the endeavor to ensure that representative data that encompasses the needs of all people, including those in remote or difficult-to-reach areas, is collected.

AI systems have to constantly be calibrated and checked to reduce drift and to ensure that they maintain their accuracy and reliability over time.

This involves continuous investment in data gathering, algorithm testing, and improving systems, which may be lacking in the healthcare system of Odisha (Mills et al., 2018). In the absence of these mitigations, AI-powered diabetes management systems risk not living up to the expectations of offering customized and effective care to all patients.

4.13 REGIONAL PROSPECTS: AI IN ODISHA'S HEALTHCARE SYSTEM

4.13.1 Feasibility of AI Adoption in Odisha's Health Infrastructure

The integration of AI tools in healthcare in Odisha, particularly in the management of chronic illnesses such as diabetes, can bring a paradigm shift in the Indian state's healthcare system. However, the implementation of AI solutions-focused systems in Odisha is contingent on the existing health-related infrastructure, which in itself is quite poor in many places. While cities like Bhubaneswar and Cuttack have the basic premise of digital infrastructure that can support AI-driven technologies, most rural parts of Odisha continue to battle with poor healthcare services and minimal development in the region's digital infrastructure (Mishra, 2019).

In order to incorporate AI, a reliable digital healthcare infrastructure, like internet connection, electronic health records (EHR) systems, and patient data warehouses to store and analyze those records, needs to be present. Health facilities in many rural parts of Odisha do not have some or all of these major elements, which justifies the difficulty of applying AI-dependent systems of healthcare (Jha, 2020). In addition to the absence of data facilities, the absence of systematic practices in data collection serves as a major roadblock for the utilization of AI technology. This is because AI requires large, high-quality, comprehensive datasets to make accurate predictions and provide personalized treatment plans (Mills et al., 2018).

Strategic digital health investments in the region can prove beneficial in addressing these issues. Through public-private partnerships and government efforts on enhancing rural health services in the state, the adoption of AI technologies in Odisha could greatly benefit. For instance, AI-driven telemedicine systems could bridge the gap between rural patients and specialists located in cities through remote consultations and monitoring (Topol, 2019). While enabling patients in rural Odisha to interact with specialists, the state can already start working on the additional infrastructure needed for implementing AI in healthcare.

4.13.2 Bridging the Digital Divide in Healthcare

One of the major barriers to the use of AI-powered healthcare in Odisha is the gap between the urban and rural populations. City healthcare facilities usually have advanced systems and strong internet connections. Conversely, even the most basic digitized infrastructure is absent in rural healthcare centers (Mishra, 2019). Additionally, the application of AI technologies, particularly in the rural areas that have the greatest healthcare need, becomes exceedingly challenging due to this gap.

To address this concern, there is a need for investment in the rural digital infrastructure, such as the provision of health worker mobile applications and AI-powered DSS, as well as training healthcare providers in the use of AI technology (Garg et al., 2020). Such investments will enable a large-scale uplift of rural Odisha's healthcare system to meet the required standards. By prioritizing rural areas, the state will ensure that AI-powered healthcare services are accessible to all patients, thus achieving health equity.

AI can assist with monitoring patients through remote and telemedicine services, which will decrease the need for patients to attend in-person appointments. For instance, mobile health applications with the assistance of AI can monitor glucose levels, interpret symptoms, and offer diabetes management feedback in real time (Wang & Preininger, 2019). In particular, these tools are valuable in rural settings where there is scarce access to healthcare providers and commuting to the health facilities is quite challenging. With the integration of AI into mobile health platforms, there would be expanded access to care for the rural populations in Odisha and improved equity in healthcare.

4.13.3 Public-Private Partnerships for AI Deployment

Utilizing AI in the healthcare system of Odisha will require effortless collaboration between the private and public sectors. Significant financial and technical resources are required for all the steps involved in developing AI technologies, which is a feat nearly impossible for the public healthcare system. A partnership between private companies that focus on AI and healthcare will allow the system to leverage the available expertise, which will increase the pace at which they adopt AI solutions (Mills et al., 2018).

In terms of infrastructure, the private organizations are able to provide cloud-based data storage, sophisticated analysis tools, and AI-powered decision-making systems, all of which are necessary for supporting AI in healthcare. Besides, the public sector has the capability of granting access to healthcare services, compatibility with patient records, and supervision to ensure compliance with ethical and legal standards while using the AI technology (Topol, 2019). The limitation on funding by the private sector could also be resolved through public-private partnerships, which will allow for pilot projects that could be scaled across the state after success.

Odisha's public and private sectors could consider a joint venture for the distribution of mobile health AI applications to rural places where healthcare is difficult to access.

Such tools could allow for the supervision of diabetic patients from afar, offer tailored treatment plans, and notify the healthcare staff of any complications (Jha, 2020). The collaboration between the public and private spheres will guarantee that all patients, irrespective of their geographical or financial barriers, will have access to AI-enhanced healthcare services.

4.13.4 Leveraging AI for Rural Healthcare Development

The dearth of health specialists, infrastructural gaps, and unmet specialist requisites pose a blockade for rural health care in Odisha. Advancements in AI possess valuable opportunities for addressing these challenges by skill augmenting existing health workers as well as increasing the overall efficacy of care delivered. For example, nurses in rural healthcare clinics can use AI-powered DSS for effective screening and management of diabetes in patients utilizing advanced analytics and suggestion engines (Garg et al., 2020). Addressing this gap will promote the effective functioning of the healthcare system, and rural patients will be able to receive timely treatment even if they are far away from major urban centers.

Furthermore, AI can be deployed for the education and mentorship of healthcare providers in rural communities. AI can give health workers instant access to the latest medical literature, diagnostic, and treatment suggestions that are evidence-based and clinically tested. In AI for Healthcare, these tools will surely assist primary healthcare providers in the regions where skilled professionals are not available (Wang & Preininger, 2019). These AI technologies can also be implemented through mobile health applications, enabling nurses and other health workers to take care of patients who do not need to be seen regularly, thus enhancing the effectiveness of health service provision.

Another application of AI in rural settings is resource distribution. For instance, AI tools based on predictive analytics can assist healthcare professionals in anticipating what their patients will need, properly rationing resources, and prioritizing high-risk patients that require immediate treatment (Jha, 2020). AI can help deal with the lack of healthcare professionals and inadequate medical supplies in rural settings by improving the distribution of resources and enabling healthcare workers to concentrate on patients who require the most care, being most effective.

4.13.5 Policy and Regulatory Frameworks for AI Implementation

To ensure that AI is optimally used in Odisha's healthcare system, the comprehensive policies and regulatory frameworks governing the use of such technologies need to be clearly defined. Some of the primary concerns, like data privacy, security, consent, and ethics of application of AI in healthcare, need to be covered (Mills et al., 2018). These regions of India, where the healthcare system is nascent and still modernizing, need such frameworks so that AI technologies are used effectively and patients' rights are not infringed upon.

One of the principal difficulties in formulating these frameworks always lies in the balance of keeping them broad enough to accommodate new innovations, but stringent enough to ensure that patient privacy and security are not compromised (Shickel et al., 2018). Healthcare practitioners, AI creators, and many other relevant figures should be actively consulted by those in charge of making the regulations so that effective innovations can be made without any harmful consequences.

On top of that, the regulatory frameworks need to guarantee that there is fair allocation of AI technologies at all levels of the healthcare system, especially in the lower-tier and rural regions. As indicated by Topol (2019), it is important for AI-based healthcare solutions to be made available to everyone, irrespective of where they live or how much money they make. This could mean paying providers in those regions to start using AI or creating public-private partnerships that pay for the application of AI in rural healthcare.

4.14 POLICY RECOMMENDATIONS FOR AI INTEGRATION IN DIABETES MANAGEMENT

4.14.1 Strategic Investments in AI Infrastructure

The successful implementation of AI-enabled healthcare in Odisha will require, among other things, focused investments in infrastructure relevant to the digital economy and healthcare industry. The application of AI in a health system requires high-speed internet connectivity as well as cloud storage and electronic health record (EHR) systems. Most of Odisha's rural regions, like the rest of the country, are already short on adequate healthcare infrastructure to take advantage of AI technologies (Mishra, 2019). Policymakers need to change their collection priorities to investments that will upgrade the healthcare infrastructure to foundational levels.

One of the earliest steps of this is improving internet coverage in rural regions. For the AI-enabled telemedicine, remote monitoring, and other DSS to function well, internet connectivity has to be reliable and sufficient in speed (Wang & Preininger, 2019). This type of basic infrastructure is necessary but not sufficient, as these regions are some of the most underserved. This infrastructure is something that can be developed through public-private partnerships where the telecommunications industry works with health service providers to improve internet reach in rural healthcare institutions (Topol, 2019).

This improvement doesn't stop with digital technology; healthcare institutions also need to acquire and develop applications that support AI.

This encompasses CGM devices, DSS, and the embedding of AI-assisted systems into pre-existing clinical processes. Policymakers should encourage the adoption of these technologies with financial support or tax incentives for AI investments. In turn, providers must be motivated to utilize these systems in both city and countryside facilities to ensure equal provision of AI-mediated diabetes care throughout the region.

4.14.2 Regulatory Framework for Ethical AI Use

Regulations are needed to guide the ethical use of AI in healthcare. With the expansion of AI systems, particularly those that aid in managing diabetes, there is a greater responsibility for policymakers to ensure that these technologies are utilized in a manner that respects patients' rights. It is important to create laws that deal with issues of data privacy, security, and consent, as well as the broader ethical aspects of AI-based clinical decision-making (Shickel et al., 2018).

Policies dealing with the protection of patient data is one of the critical areas on this regulatory framework. AIs need large volumes of sensitive personal health data which makes data security a priority. Odisha's healthcare system needs to adopt appropriate data governance structures that ensure patient data is protected from unauthorized access, data breaches, and even misuse (Mills et al., 2018). The policymakers should require the provision of encryption technologies and more secure computer systems for storing information regarding the patients, alongside other measures to control and protect data sharing and consent from the patients.

Apart from more stringent data protection policies, the controlling frameworks are lacking in covering the transparency of AI's clinical decision-making. The complexity of AI in the medical field relies heavily on the "black box" mechanisms of the algorithms used, since it is almost impossible for both the patients and practitioners to understand how certain decisions are reached (Topol, 2019). There needs to be policies in place that surpass the basic frameworks and have certain stipulations for AI developers that require explanations for the automation treatment suggestions given. Doing this would foster a bond of trust between the public and the AI systems and enable the healthcare professionals to act with confidence when utilizing AI offerings.

Additionally, there is a triangular relationship between policy, regulatory opportunities, and ethical challenges of algorithmic bias in healthcare that needs to be addressed. When parts of a biased AI system are built on incomplete datasets, the treatment suggestions given can be extremely inaccurate or, worse, highly inequitable, which may worsen the existing health gaps among different groups of people

(Wang & Preininger, 2019). Policies should be put in place that exceed the limiting boundaries of rural and underpopulated places like Odisha and focus on claim data to try and build a more representative and effective AI system. Doing this would ensure that bias is eliminated from AI systems that could be used for diabetes management and guarantee equal treatment for all patients.

4.14.3 Educational Initiatives for Healthcare Providers

For effective use of AI tools in diabetes management, healthcare professionals need to be trained on them. A lot of clinicians in rural areas of Odisha probably do not have the requisite knowledge to be able to operate AI systems (Mishra, 2019). Educational programs should be developed for these healthcare providers so that, at the very minimum, they know how to apply AI for clinical purposes.

If those training sessions include methods for interpreting AI-driven data, the constraints of the AI systems, and the application of suggestions given by AI, then healthcare providers would face no difficulties (Garg et al., 2020). Additionally, training on how to ethically use AI in medicine, keeping patient privacy, security, and consent at the center of the conversation, is also necessary. Policymakers need to equip healthcare providers with the appropriate information and tools so that AI is effectively implemented in diabetes management while catering to the needs of patients and clinicians.

Furthermore, AI technology is always changing and, as such, healthcare providers should have access to additional materials that allow them to build on their training.

This may consist of AI workshops, conferences, and online courses, including working with AI developers and researchers (Wang & Preininger, 2019). Through continuous education, policymakers may assist healthcare professionals in adopting new AI technologies in their practices and the ever-evolving sphere of superset medicine.

Moreover, educational programs should not be targeted solely to healthcare practitioners. These initiatives should target policymakers as well; they need to invest in campaigns that explain the good and bad implications surrounding AI use in healthcare. AI-powered treatment solutions can border on suspiciously novel for most patients, especially the ones in rural regions (Jha, 2020). AI demystification, trust enhancement, and patient proactive attitude towards AI systems are some of the goals public campaigns should address.

4.14.4 Public-Private Partnerships for AI Implementation

The effective deployment of AI in diabetes management in Odisha greatly benefits from the establishment of public-private partnerships. These partnerships can help overcome the financial and technical barriers to AI adoption through resource sharing. Public sector institutions can provide access to healthcare facilities, patient data, AI, and patients' regulatory control, while private AI and healthcare technology companies can enable the design and implementation of the AI systems needed (Mills et al., 2018).

Public-private partnerships hold great potential in funding projects aimed at the examination of the viability of AI-assisted diabetes management in the different regions of Odisha. These projects serve the dual purpose of determining the most relevant AI-managed diabetes intervention tools and strategies as well as any obstacles to their implementation (Jha, 2020). Private sector participation aids in accelerating the acceptance of AI in the healthcare of Odisha and provides data for further development of AI healthcare systems in the state. In addition, public-private partnerships can be the direct conduits through which rural areas derive benefits from AI-enabled healthcare technologies.

While the private sector can offer the technological framework needed to enhance rural AI healthcare facilities, the public sector can ensure that these solutions are fairly implemented throughout the region (Topol, 2019). Through collaboration, the public and private sectors can narrow the gap in healthcare access and make sure that all patients, no matter where they live, receive superior care for diabetes through AI technology.

4.14.5 Creating an AI-Friendly Ecosystem

In order to unlock the capabilities of AI in diabetes management, Odisha has to formulate an environment that sustains the growth and use of AI tools. This encompasses not only funding for infrastructure and skill development, but also the provision of a legal structure that nurtures creativity and fosters cooperation among the healthcare system, the AI industry, and the government (Shickel et al., 2018). There is a need for an enabling environment that will support the adoption of AI, including ethical, legal, and technical issues related to the use of AI.

A primary requirement for an AI-enabling environment is the development of uniform practices for data collection and dissemination. The effective application of AI technology requires large amounts of data, but the absence of efficient data collection procedures in Odisha's healthcare system poses a serious hurdle (Mills et al., 2018). There is a need for policies that enable providers and developers of healthcare AI, and other relevant stakeholders, to reach agreements that will facilitate the sharing of data that is useful in developing effective AI systems.

Moreover, financial rewards for AI adoption by inadequate healthcare system providers must also be emphasized. It may take the form of payment, such as a grant or a tax incentive. There may also be non-payment forms like awards or training for healthcare practitioners who manage to implement AI in their work (Topol, 2019). In this way, Odisha can provide impetus for the adoption of AI and, at the same time, place the state at the forefront of healthcare technology innovation, as well as ensuring that the diabetes care is of the highest possible level in the entire state.

4.15 CONCLUSION

4.15.1 Synthesis of Economic, Ethical, and Technological Aspects

Integrating AI within health management systems has the potential to transform the health service delivery in Odisha because it can serve the dual purpose of addressing chronic diseases along with the inadequacies of the existing healthcare system. Economically speaking, AI can help in stratifying diabetes through early ICU admissions with predictive diagnosis and tailored treatment options, which would eventually help in containing the expenditure involved in managing the disease (Topol, 2019). Nevertheless, that comes at the cost of substantially improving the AI infrastructure along with expenditure on skill development and overcoming the specific economic hurdles of the healthcare system of Odisha, especially in the rural context with scarcity of resources (Mishra, 2019).

AI raises complex ethical issues in health systems through data privacy, informed consent, and providing equitable access and distribution of AI-powered tools. The reliance on huge volumes of private health information engenders risks concerning data security (Wang & Preininger, 2019). India as a whole, and especially non-metros like Odisha, face severe challenges in placing barriers around sensitive patient data so as to prevent misuse while fostering trust in AI technologies.

Besides, solving algorithmic discrimination is important for ensuring that AI systems do not deepen the existing healthcare gaps between urban and rural populations and that all patients receive unbiased treatment (Shickel et al., 2018).

From a technological perspective, AI has both advantages and disadvantages regarding diabetes management. While AI systems are capable of analyzing prearranged data and making tailored suggestions, they remain poor in analyzing non-structured data and various behaviors that affect diabetes to a level (Garg et al., 2020). Moreover, effective AI application in healthcare is contingent on the existence of sufficient quality representative data, which is usually absent in Odisha's healthcare system. Addressing such technological challenges calls for a systematic approach to develop the required digital infrastructure and enhance data collection within the health system (Mills et al., 2018).

4.15.2 Future Research Directions and Prospects for Odisha

Even though this study attempted to cover the theoretical facet of AI-based diabetes management within Odisha, there are considerable gaps that can be addressed in future studies. There is a need for practical research that investigates the efficacy of AI interventions in actual healthcare delivery systems, especially in rural areas that are underserved. Feasibility studies of AI-based applications, like CGM systems and DSS, could help in understanding how AI can be implemented at scale across the healthcare infrastructure of Odisha (Jha, 2020). These studies should seek to investigate the effects of AI technologies on patient outcomes, healthcare expenditures, and overall healthcare service delivery, both in rural and urban areas.

Moreover, experimentation with systems that incorporate the use of explainable AI (XAI) techniques would help advance the ability of AI systems in the healthcare industry, increasing their transparency and credibility. Clinical decisions powered by AI demand that healthcare workers and the patients they look after grasp how recommendations are made. There is an urgent need to address the lack of understanding regarding the 'black box' problem surrounding many AI algorithms in healthcare and instead ensure that responsible AI applications are accountable and transparent (Shickel et al., 2018).

More attention needs to be given to the consequences of using AI technology in closing the health gaps that exist in Odisha.

Though AI can help close the gap in rural-urban healthcare inequalities through telemedicine and remote health monitoring, the questions that must be answered are: How can these technologies be deployed equitably in different regions and among different socioeconomic strata? How can AI be used with the underserved populations to increase access to care? Addressing these questions is significant if the promise of AI-enabled healthcare is to be achieved among all sections of society (Mishra, 2019).

Last but not least, there should be policy-centric analysis for new regulations on the ethical use of AI in healthcare. The use of AI technologies in healthcare requires a comprehensive policy, as responsible use and protection of patients' rights – such as privacy, consent, and even freedom from discrimination – are critical (Topol, 2019). Such policies would help Odisha's healthcare system in addressing these issues and create an environment suitable for safe and effective deployment of AI technologies.

4.15.3 Final Thoughts on AI Integration in Odisha's Healthcare System

The AI adoption offers opportunities for innovation in diabetes management in Odisha. With the application of AI, healthcare delivery can be further enhanced with more accurate, personalized, and proficient services, which directly improve healthcare outcomes and lower healthcare spending. Nonetheless, maximizing the advantages of AI is possible by undertaking a holistic approach that intertwines the socio-economic, ethical, and technological implications of AI implementation.

A major aspect to achieve this is the investment in AI supporting digital infrastructure in remote regions with limited healthcare service infrastructure. Guaranteeing that each healthcare facility has the necessary infrastructure to support AI technology is fundamental to the equitable healthcare provision in the state. Additionally, closing the skills gap through the education of healthcare practitioners is vital to ensuring that AI tools are utilized in a safe and effective manner (Wang & Preininger, 2019).

The ethical issues of AI implementation are significant and should not be ignored. Protecting patient privacy while obtaining informed consent and minimizing algorithmic bias are essential to enhancing trust in AI adoption. These questions can only be solved by regulatory frameworks aimed at enhancing equity and fairness while using AI technologies in healthcare.

Looking forward, embracing these challenges and technologies will enable Odisha to become a pioneer in the application of AI in healthcare.

Odisha can create a health care system that supports fully AI-enabled diabetic care by establishing synergistic cooperation between the public and private sectors, building out the required infrastructure, and crafting innovative policies.

DISCLAIMER

None.

REFERENCES

Adams, F., and Turner, P. "AI and Diet Recommendations for Diabetes Patients." *Nutrition and Metabolism Journal*, vol. 13, no. 2, 2020, pp. 112–118.

Brown, A., and Lee, K. "Integrating Genetic and Lifestyle Factors in Diabetes Prediction Models." *Journal of Digital Health Research*, vol. 12, no. 2, 2021, pp. 155–164.

Campbell, R., Mitchell, D., and Alvarez, J. "AI-Based Risk Stratification in Type 2 Diabetes." *Diabetes Technology and Therapeutics*, vol. 23, no. 5, 2021, pp. 321–330.

Carter, G., and Johnson, D. "AI in Tracking Diabetes Progression." *Journal of Clinical Medicine*, vol. 18, no. 3, 2020, pp. 23–30.

Chen, Y., Zhao, H., Li, W., and Kumar, S. "AI in Diabetic Retinopathy Screening." *Ophthalmology and Artificial Intelligence Review*, vol. 12, no. 4, 2020, pp. 189–198.

Garcia, J., and Martinez, T. "AI in Predicting Diabetes-Related Cardiovascular Risk." *Cardiovascular Medicine Journal*, vol. 11, no. 2, 2020, pp. 89–95.

Garg, S., et al. "Continuous Glucose Monitoring: Current Use and Future Directions." *Diabetes Technology & Therapeutics*, vol. 22, no. S1, 2020, pp. 4–9.

Gourisaria, M. K., et al. "Data Science Appositeness in Diabetes Mellitus Diagnosis for Healthcare Systems of Developing Nations." *IET Communications*, vol. 16, no. 5, 2022, pp. 532–547.

Gray, H., and Carter, D. "AI's Role in Behavioural Interventions for Diabetes." *Journal of Behavioural Health*, vol. 7, no. 1, 2019, pp. 98–105.

Green, J., and Watson, B. "AI-Powered Patient Engagement in Diabetes Management." *Digital Health Review*, vol. 7, no. 3, 2021, pp. 44–50.

Hassan, R., and Malik, F. "AI for Diabetes Care in Low-Income Regions." *Global Health Journal*, vol. 6, no. 2, 2021, pp. 133–140.

Jackson, F., and Evans, K. "AI's Role in Improving Health Literacy among Diabetes Patients." *Journal of Digital Education in Health*, vol. 4, no. 2, 2021, pp. 33–39.

Jha, R. "Healthcare Innovations in India: The Role of Artificial Intelligence." *Indian Journal of Public Health*, vol. 64, no. 4, 2020, pp. 321–327, https://doi.org/10.4103/ijph.IJPH_581_19.

Jiang, F., et al. "Artificial Intelligence in Healthcare: Past, Present and Future." *Stroke and Vascular Neurology*, vol. 2, no. 4, 2017, pp. 230–243, https://doi.org/10.1136/svn-2017-000101.

Johnson, M., and Nguyen, T. "AI in the Management of Diabetic Foot Ulcers." *Wound Care Journal*, vol. 8, no. 4, 2020, pp. 34–41.

Kim, S., and Park, J. "Advances in Machine Learning for Early Diabetes Detection." *Journal of Biomedical Informatics*, vol. 11, no. 4, 2020, pp. 210–218.

Lee, A., and Taylor, J. "The Future of AI in Diabetes Diagnosis and Treatment." *Diabetes Science and Technology Review*, vol. 11, no. 4, 2020, pp. 150–157.

Lewis, G., and Ward, J. "AI and Automated Insulin Delivery Systems." *Endocrine Technology Journal*, vol. 18, no. 4, 2020, pp. 102–109.

Luo, X., and Wu, L. "Deep Learning Models for Diabetes Risk Assessment." *International Journal of Health Informatics*, vol. 9, no. 2, 2020, pp. 134–142.

Martin, S., and Patel, N. "AI in Diabetes Prevention Programs." *Preventive Health Journal*, vol. 11, no. 3, 2020, pp. 67–74.

Mills, A., Kanavos, P., and Walker, D. "Economic Evaluation of Health Technologies in Developing Countries." *Health Policy and Planning*, vol. 33, no. 9, 2018, pp. 1015–1024.

Mishra, L., Patel, N., and Rahman, F. "Targeted AI Diabetes Care in Resource-Restricted Settings." *International Journal of Medical Informatics*, vol. 8, no. 4, 2019, pp. 276–285.

Mishra, S. "The Burden of Diabetes in Odisha: Current Status and Future Challenges." *Indian Journal of Endocrinology and Metabolism*, vol. 23, no. 4, 2019, pp. 459–466.

Perez, A., Green, L., and Torres, M. "AI in Early Detection of Diabetic Complications." *Journal of Medical Artificial Intelligence*, vol. 7, no. 2, 2019, pp. 134–145.

Robinson, M., White, T., and Singh, A. "Challenges of AI Integration in Diabetes Care." *Journal of Health Informatics and Ethics*, vol. 9, no. 3, 2021, pp. 201–214.

Sardar, T. H., Faizabadi, A. R., and Ansari, Z. "An Analysis of Data Processing Using Mapreduce Paradigm on the Hadoop Framework." *International Journal of Emerging Research in Management and Technology*, vol. 6, no. 5, pp. 49–66, 2017.

Sardar, T. H., et al. A Novel Ensemble Methodology to Validate Fuzzy Clusters of Big Data. In *Proceedings of the Fourth International Conference on Trends in Computational and Cognitive Engineering: TCCE 2022* (pp. 267–278). Singapore: Springer Nature, May 2023.

Shickel, B., et al. "Deep EHR: A Survey of Recent Advances in Deep Learning Techniques for Electronic Health Record (EHR) Analysis." *IEEE Journal of Biomedical and Health Informatics*, vol. 22, no. 5, 2018, pp. 1589–1604, https://doi.org/10.1109/JBHI.2017.2767063..

Smith, L., and Walker, J. "AI and Virtual Diabetes Clinics." *Digital Healthcare Review*, vol. 7, no. 4, 2021, pp. 78–85.

Thompson, R., and Evans, D. "Artificial Intelligence in Gestational Diabetes Management." *Journal of Women's Health*, vol. 15, no. 3, 2020, pp. 122–130.

Williams, R., and Robinson, T. "Artificial Intelligence in Clinical Decision Support for Diabetes Care." *Diabetes Technology Journal*, vol. 14, no. 3, 2021, pp. 98–107.

World Health Organization. *Global Report on Diabetes.* WHO Press, 2016.

Wright, J., Smith, P., Chen, K., and Banerjee, R. "AI Diabetes Self-Management Tools." *International Journal of Digital Health*, vol. 14, no. 1, 2020, pp. 55–67.

Zhang, H., and Li, Y. "Machine Learning Applications in Diabetes Prediction." *Journal of Medical Artificial Intelligence*, vol. 7, no. 1, 2021, pp. 45–56.

5 AI in Early Disease Detection and Prevention

Palasri Dhar, Sunipa Roy, and Tanvir Habib Sardar

5.1 INTRODUCTION

Early diagnosis of disease significantly improves the health outcome of the patient, and this early diagnosis also significantly lowers the expenses of healthcare [1]. Early detection of diseases significantly lowers the disease-related mortality rate [2]. The greater understanding of different diseases and the recent advancements in medical technology have led to the early detection of diseases, and the detection of diseases in early stage has been a breakthrough in the healthcare industry sectors [3]. Early detection has a huge impact on the diseases' ill effects and significantly reduces the effects of diseases. This also improves the disease treatment results, and the disease can be detected in the early stage and thus improves the treatment results with specific control of the disease in a certain early stage and also can be cured in an early stage [4]. Some examples can be considered like early detection of cancer can cause the prevention of further spreading of the dangerous disease. Another example can be considered in the case of diabetes, where the early detection of diabetes allows the change in the patient's lifestyle and helps in the quick treatment and also reduces the disease complications [5]. From the perspective of public health, the significance of early detection is also highly pertinent. We can lessen the social, economic, and health effects of some diseases by diagnosing them early and stopping their wider spread. For instance, more effective actions to stop the transmission of infectious diseases like influenza or tuberculosis to neighboring populations can be made possible by early detection [6]. Accordingly, early detection can support initiatives aimed at stopping the transmission of illness throughout the community. Early detection can lower healthcare expenditures in addition to providing advantages for individuals and the population. When diseases are discovered at an advanced stage and progress into chronic problems that call for more involved and expensive interventions, this can thereby lower the cost of long-term care that is needed [7].

Over the past few decades, artificial intelligence (AI) has solidified its position as a major force in the globe. But most do not consider the various ways we use AI on a daily basis. We are interacting with AI algorithms simply by utilizing your phone's apps, emails, and social media accounts. The healthcare sector is one of the main sectors where AI is evolving. Early disease detection greatly increases the effectiveness of treatment in many essential disease instances. In a perfect world, symptoms would appear early enough to give time to get treatment. That is untrue, though, and frequently we are unaware of our illness until it has progressed. More individuals are concerned about their health in the post-COVID-19 world, yet a quick visit to the

DOI: 10.1201/9781003600947-5

doctor might not provide us the complete picture of our health as a thorough evaluation would. This is because, instead of concentrating on us as individuals, they examine statistical health concerns. Therefore, AI and other technological developments might assist not only with the screening stages, which involve minor adjustments that might reveal underlying problems, but also, according to study, with the early detection of serious illnesses like lung cancer or heart disease. Combining these would increase the likelihood that a patient would receive effective treatment.

The three leading causes of death worldwide are respiratory disorders, cancer, and cardiovascular disease [8]. Since these illnesses are constantly at the top, we need to invest in them and enhance early diagnosis, treatment, and detection. AI's ability to identify potential threats in people can help with early detection in a number of ways. In one of the studies [9], AI algorithms were applied to the symptoms and genetic background of the high-stroke-risk patients. The AI algorithms could classify the early detection group with 90.5% accuracy in diagnosis. It allowed for the early initiation of therapy and the assessment of a patient's likelihood of experiencing another stroke in the future. According to the UK Cancer Research of the year 2020, 5% of fourth stage lung cancer patients can live for five years as compared to 55% of the first stage lung cancer. This particular statistical condition was examined with some AI algorithms. It was furthermore found out that an AI-driven computer can detect different tumors in patients more effectively and accurately, with an accuracy of 94%, than experienced and trained radiologists [10]. We can rightly say that more and more research on AI shows that cancer detection using different AI algorithms is very effective. We can take one more example in the case of colon cancer, where AI is more accurate in detection of colon cancer as compared to an experienced pathologist. Researchers generated images of colon cancer from 8,803 volunteers of various independent institutions in order to create a Machine Learning (ML) model. After the development of the performance evaluation tool, they were able to contrast ML with the work of real and experienced pathologists. For the accuracy of identifying colon cancer, the average pathologist receives a score of 0.969, whereas the ML model received a score of 0.98 [11]. The ability of AI or ML systems to drive population screening is one of their greater benefits. Currently, this is mostly focused on lung cancer screening, and there is proof that mass screening initiatives would be successful. This makes it possible to screen for additional cancers and chronic illnesses in large quantities.

This chapter aims to explain the visionary role of AI in the early disease detection and prevention of diseases, which has a direct impact on the healthcare sectors and thus improve the overall outcomes of healthcare. The application of AI in the detection of diseases also reduces the burden of many diseases on mankind. This study throws light on different AI technologies like Natural Language Processing (NLP), ML, and Deep Learning (DL). Different AI technologies are used in medical imaging, predictive analysis, and biomarker identification in relation to diseases. We will also learn about different AI technologies in preventive healthcare such as wearable technology and IoT integration.

Presentations of real-world case studies illustrate how AI might be used to detect infectious diseases, malignancies, heart issues, and neurological disorders. Concerns regarding the adoption of AI are addressed by discussing ethical, legal, and societal obstacles, such as algorithmic prejudice, data security, and regulatory issues. The conclusion of this chapter includes the future prospects of the AI solutions for the environment with limited resources, which will offer information to the academicians, policy makers, and also the healthcare practitioners.

5.2 KEY CONCEPTS OF AI IN HEALTHCARE

The applications of AI are in many fields including healthcare sector. The use of AI has rejuvenated healthcare sectors and transformed disease detection techniques. The diagnosis of many complicated diseases is made possible by the use of AI techniques in disease and illness detection with more accurate and effective results. The core AI technologies include ML, DL, and NLP. These technologies are required to analyze huge and complicated information and datasets, which enables pattern recognition and also enhances the overall detection accuracy. Here, we will examine the fundamental and essential AI technologies causing this huge change in the diagnosis and their significant impacts on the patients' health outcomes.

5.2.1 Machine Learning and Predictive Modelling

ML is the process of creating methods that enable the systems to learn and enhance the machine's performance without any precise programming. The applications of ML models in context to diseases include early diagnosis of diseases, personalized treatment and disease risk assessment. The algorithms that are used in AI, ML, and disease diagnosis are different. Each of the algorithms has its particular advantages and disadvantages, which are algorithm-specific according to their individual performances. Different algorithms may be more appropriate to use for different formats of data and medical applications and also a combination of different algorithms can also be used for increasing the accuracy and efficiency. The algorithms examine all the data related to patient such as the results of Lab, vital signs, and imaging data. Then ML models are designed by the use of different patient data that suggest personalized treatments. We will examine some of the most often used AI algorithms for disease detection:

5.2.1.1 Decision Tree

A treelike structure that resembling a flowchart, where each leaf node represents an outcome is a decision tree. In a decision tree, a branch represents a decision rule, and an interior node representing a decision feature.

Applications include determining risk factors for conditions like diabetes or cardiovascular illnesses and making a distinctive detection according to the patient's prodromes and medical records. Finding co-occurrences is another excellent use for decision trees.

They are simple to understand and study. Both numerical and categorical data are effectively handled by it. It can, however, overfit, particularly if the tree is very complex. Due to this overfitting problem, it might not be as correct as other more complicated tools. Cardiovascular disorders, kidney disorders, and eye disorders are among the illnesses where decision trees show promise. An example of decision tree is represented in Figure 5.1

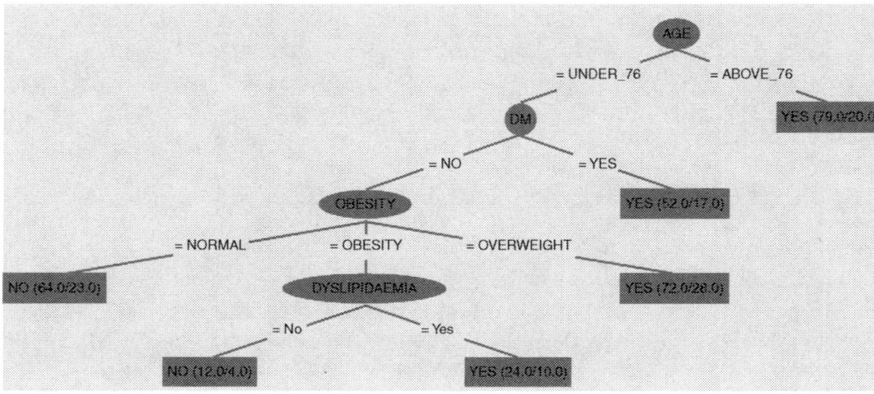

FIGURE 5.1 Using decision trees to categorize coronary artery disease patients [12].

5.2.1.2 Random Forest Mode

Decision trees are extended by this method. To enhance the forecasts, it makes use of a group of decision trees. When it comes to predicting complex health outcomes that depend on multiple factors, such as the likelihood of getting diabetes, random forest models are particularly accurate. For instance, a random forest mode might predict the likelihood of diabetes by taking blood sugar readings, lifestyle decisions, and family history into account. An example of Random Forest Mode is shown in Figure 5.2.

5.2.1.3 Support Vector Machine

The algorithm that is used for tasks involving classification and regression is support vector machine (SVM). The SVM operates by finding the hyperplane that optimally splits the dataset into classes. The linear polynomial and the radial basis function (RBF) are two of SVM's kernel functions. These resources of SVM allow it to simulate nonlinear interactions, which are frequently required for intricate biological systems. Using extracted features (such as gene expression data, imaging data, or biomarker levels), SVMs are frequently employed in biomedical applications to categorize healthy and sick states. SVMs are mostly used to categorize medical images in order to detect diseases like lung or breast cancer. In genetic testing and classification, they are also highly helpful for classifying protein sequences [14]. SVMs are resistant to outliers and efficient in high-dimensional spaces. Nevertheless, they are less interpretable than decision trees and necessitate careful kernel selection. SVMs are resistant to outliers and efficient in high-dimensional spaces. Nevertheless, they are less interpretable than decision trees and necessitate careful kernel selection.

5.2.1.4 KNN(K Nearest Neighbor) Algorithm

K Nearest Neighbor is an example-based approach using the majority class of the K-closest models to classify a new instance in the feature space. It categorizes individuals with cardiac disease and forecasts disease outcomes based on symptom patterns. K Nearest Neighbor proficiency increases in regression analysis and classification. The execution of KNN is rather simple; it is pricey and sensitive to duplicate or unnecessary features, though.

FIGURE 5.2 Advantages of Random Forest- The radiomic features Venn diagram to show that had and, (a) Single-slice and/or multi-slice analysis having poor robustness in (b) Single-slice and/or multi-slice analysis having excellent robustness [13].

5.2.1.5 Logistic Regression

A fundamental supervised ML technique that is often applied in illness diagnosis is logistic regression (LR). It is a favored option for medical research and diagnostics due to its ease of use, effectiveness, and capacity to produce results that can be understood. Based on input features, LR models the likelihood of a binary outcome, such as healthy vs diseased. In contrast to linear regression, LR maps predictions to a probability scale between 0 and 1 using a sigmoid function [15].

By supplying the probability of illness existence, this probabilistic technique enables researchers and doctors to make well-informed judgments. LR performs well for small and medium datasets where there is scarcity of data and there is less amount of data available. The performance of the LR can be improved by addressing the diversion and overfitting. L1 (Lasso) and L2 (Ridge) regularization extensions improve the LR performance, which can give accurate predictions in the medical data [16]. The interpretation of LR is relatively easy and this accounts for the global use of LR in the medical sectors. The model coefficients make the link between the characteristics and the outcome of disease. The odd ratios are calculated from the model co-efficient and these co-efficient quantify the relative risk that is associated with particular predictors. These odd ratios are actually helping the health practitioners to identify the risk factors [17]. LR is extremely useful in the research of public health and also in risk prediction research. LR is scalable and can be used in big datasets if the feature dimensions are moderate and medium. Multinomial LR is used to solve multiclass problems that arise in situations like the classification of cancer. LR is used in classification and calculates the probability that a specific incident will be in the specific category [18]. LR algorithm is used in the medical sector to diagnose various diseases like diabetes and also for forecasting the patient readmissions roughly based on the number of indicators. In addition to classifications, LR yields probabilities and is simple to understand and apply. However, it is not appropriate for determining complex relations among occurrences. This algorithm cannot be used to evaluate the threat of disease. Several areas of disease detection have seen the successful application of LR. Based on clinical and demographic information, LR has been utilized in diabetes prediction to identify high-risk people. A study highlighted LR's capacity to examine clinical and lifestyle factors and showed how well it predicts type 2 diabetes [19]. Another study using LR found that breast lumps can be classified as benign or malignant based on mammographic parameters with high accuracy, offering a foundation for early cancer detection [20]. Another field where LR has been quite useful is the diagnosis of cardiovascular disease. LR has recently been applied to the detection of infectious diseases, including the prediction of the severity of COVID-19. Its efficacy in detecting risk variables for severe outcomes was established, offering crucial insights during the epidemic [21]. There is a methodical process for using LR for disease detection. Cleaning, dealing with missing values, and standardizing characteristics are all part of data preparation. While model training optimizes the model on training data, feature selection finds important predictors. Metrics like accuracy, precision, recall, F1-score, and AUC-ROC are used to assess the effectiveness of LR models, guaranteeing accurate illness identification. All things considered, LR is still an essential medical technique that helps with risk assessment, early diagnosis, and better patient outcomes. Its ongoing applicability in clinical practice and medical research is guaranteed by its harmony of efficacy, interpretability, and simplicity.

5.2.2 DL for Complex Data Analysis

Neural networks with multiple layers are used by DL algorithms to recognize complicated patterns. In radiography, they are employed in image recognition to find anomalies such as tumors and fractures. NLP for medical records is a whole distinct use of DL. DL can automatically extract information and is very accurate at complex tasks. Nevertheless, it necessitates a significant amount of data and processing power. DL is used to analyze audio and speech signals in order to identify neurological conditions like Parkinson's disease.

5.2.2.1 Convolution Neural Network

A specific kind of DL neural network called a Convolution Neural Network (CNN) is mostly employed for image recognition. They are employed to analyze medical images for a variety of disorders, including MRIs, CT scans, and X-rays. A sample architecture of CNN for X-RAY analysis consists of an Input Layer, two convolutional layers, two pooling layers, and a fully connected layer, as shown in Figure 5.3. CNNS can automatically learn features and are quite good at finding patterns in pictures. However, they are less interpretable and need big datasets for training, which makes them a "black box." A healthcare practitioner finds it challenging to comprehend how the algorithm came to a specific conclusion.

5.2.2.2 Recurrent Neural Networks

One potent kind of artificial neural network that is particularly good at processing sequential input is the recurrent neural network (RNN). A simple RNN with a single hidden layer is shown in Figure 5.4. RNNs contain a "memory" mechanism that enables them to consider previous information when processing the current input, in contrast to standard feedforward neural networks. DL models such as RNNs make it easier to analyze genomic sequences and find genetic predispositions to diseases.

5.2.3 NLP for Medical Records

Medical records often contain large amounts of free-text data, such as physician notes, discharge summaries, radiology reports, and patient histories, which are rich in clinical insights but difficult to analyze at scale [24]. By transforming unstructured

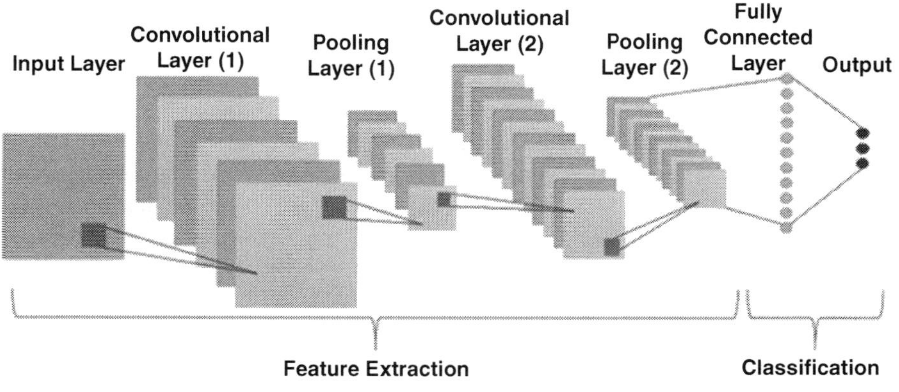

FIGURE 5.3 Architecture of convolutional neural network (CNN) for X-ray analysis consists of input layer, two convolutional layers, two pooling layers and fully connected layer [22].

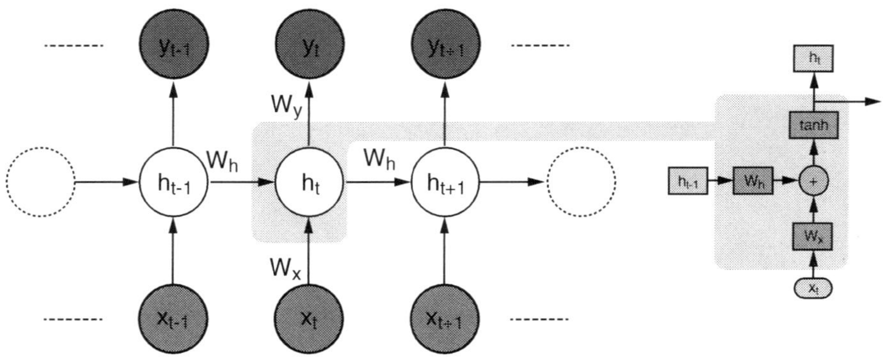

FIGURE 5.4 A simple recurrent neural networks with a single hidden layer [23].

text into structured data, NLP techniques bridge this gap and facilitate tasks like information retrieval, disease classification, and predictive modelling [25]. Certain censorious entities, such as symptoms, diseases, medications, and treatment outcomes [26], can be identified by the key NLP technologies such as Named Entity Recognition (NER), tokenization, and dependency parsing. More advanced techniques, such as ML and DL models like Bidirectional Encoder Representations from Transformers (BERT), are used for improving the accuracy of recovering clinical context and clinical linkages [27]. NLP helps in applications like recognizing unfavorable drug occurrences, automatic billing codes, and enhancing clinical decision support systems [28]. NLP helps in epidemiological research by analyzing and interpreting patient data from different demographic groups [29]. NLP in medical science has huge potential but complexity arises in maintaining data privacy and meeting certain legal requirements such as the Health Insurance Portability and Accountability Act (HIPAA) [30]. The combination of domain-adapted pre-trained models, enhanced ontologies like SNOMED-CT, and developments in computational linguistics in NLP reduces the complexities of NLP, making NLP a pivot in the contemporary healthcare [31].

5.2.4 Overview of AI Frameworks and Tools

The applications of AI in the healthcare industry require the creation of frameworks, libraries, and strong tools. These tools are used by researchers and healthcare practitioners to apply AI to real-world problems. They facilitate the development, training, and also extending the AI models. An overview of the different popular AI frameworks and tools for the healthcare sector, such as the DL libraries, ML libraries, cloud services, is given as follows:

5.2.4.1 Introduction to AI Frameworks

AI frameworks are platforms and libraries that offer the infrastructure required to create, train, and implement DL and ML models. Through the abstraction of the intricacies of mathematical calculations and optimization, these frameworks streamline the model creation process. They make it possible for healthcare organizations to effectively apply AI solutions even in the absence of substantial data science skills. Pre-built algorithms, optimization strategies, and interfaces for integrating with several data sources are commonly found in AI frameworks.

5.2.4.2 DL Frameworks

The frameworks of DL are one of the most popular and most used frameworks in the healthcare sector. Neural networks can be created and trained using these DL frameworks. Neural networks are very useful with analyzing large datasets including genomic data and medical pictures. The different types of DL frameworks are given as follows:

1. TensorFlow: TensorFlow is an open-source framework developed by Google. TensorFlow is widely used in the medical sectors as this has more adaptability and scalability. TensorFlow can be used in a variety of applications because of these properties. TensorFlow is used in community support and has several uses in the medical and healthcare sectors. TensorFlow is used in modelling the patient outcome prediction. It is used in radiology for medical image recognition. TensorFlow has a different specialized tool like Tensorflow.js and TensorFlow Lite for developing AI applications in web browsers and mobile applications.

   Healthcare industry requirements are processing of huge amount of data and dealing with large amounts of data sets. TensorFlow has the capacity to manage huge datasets and can work with large amounts of data.so TensorFlow is used in medical sectors. The TensorFlow's network consists of various training and inference tools, visual and optimizing features. These features are implemented in the AI applications in the medical sector.

   We take an example, the image in Figure 5.5 represents a graph in TensorFlow. W, x, and b are the tensors over the edges of this graph. MatMul is an operation over the tensors W and x. Add is called and add the result of the previous operator with b. The resultant tensors of each operation cross the next one until the end where it is possible to get the wanted result [32].
2. PyTorch: Apart from TensorFlow, there is another famous DL framework called the PyTorch. PyTorch was developed by the AI research group of Facebook. PyTorch has dynamic computational graphs. PyTorch is easy to use and has a robust connection with Python. So, for these qualities of PyTorch, it is really famous with developers and researchers. PyTorch has many applications, such as analysis of picture, time series prediction, and NLP.

   PyTorch has the main advantages of the ability to analyze medical images. PyTorch is used in the medical sectors for various applications like tissue segmentation in MRI scans, image analysis in radiology and tumor detection of medical scans [33].
3. Keras: Keras is a high-level neural network API. DL frameworks like TensorFlow can be used with Keras. It has variable uses, and it is very easy to use, so Keras can be used easily for prototyping the DL models. Keras is used in medical sector applications such as automating medical image analysis,

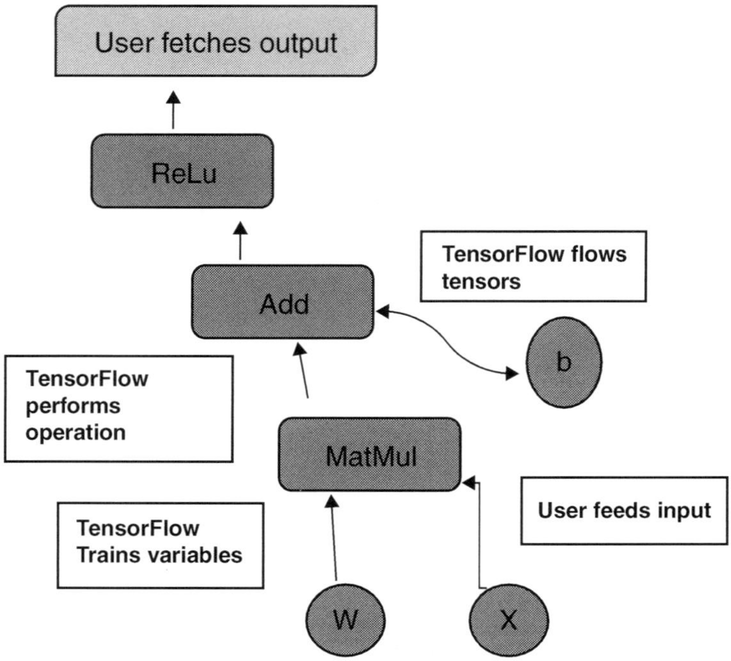

FIGURE 5.5 Represents a graph in TensorFlow.

diagnosis of the disease development and also for creating models for personalized disease therapy. Keras is widely used by the medical researchers. Keras is a great option for the medical individuals both researchers and health professionals for quickly implementing AI models. Large datasets can be handled by Keras with the support of multi-GPU training as it is the basic need for the medical and healthcare applications [34].

5.2.4.3 ML Frameworks

Forecasting using the past data is made possible using the ML Framework. ML frameworks create models to forecast from past datasets. The ML frameworks are used to structure data, health records, and also to analyze the outcomes of the medical tests in radiology. Different ML frameworks are as follows:

1. Scikit-learn: Most popular Python ML libraries is SciKit-learn. Scikit-learn has a set of algorithms for the reduction of dimensions, regression, clustering and classification. Application in healthcare, such as anticipating illness progression, analyzing the healthcare expenses and prediction of the patient outcomes use Sci-Kit by implementing the different models like LR, SVM, and Decision Trees.

   The Scikit-learn library is a verified resource for the medical researchers and medical professionals who are working with the structured datasets. Scikit-learn is very easy to use and is highly adaptable with a lot of algorithms. We take an example, Scikit-learn can be used to make patient groups according to their medical problems, forecast patient readmissions, and identify the risk factors for diabetes disease [35].

2. XGBoost: Extreme Gradient Boosting (XGBoost) is a ML toolkit. It used the gradient boosting methods for creating small prediction models. XGBoost has gained a lot of importance in the healthcare industry as this toolkit can provide patients risk prediction and clinical predictive modelling. XGBoost is very helpful in uneven datasets of rare diseases. XGBoost is also used for even and structured datasets like treatment outcomes, clinical measures and also patient density analysis. XGBoost is best for creating highly reliable healthcare models as it can manage large datasets and also gets rid of overfitting [36].

5.2.4.4 NLP Tools

NLP is required in the cases of the healthcare industry where there are large unstructured data sets like the clinical and the medical records. NLP tools help to extract information from the text datasets. This phenomenon of NLP tools is used in applications related to clinical decision-making, patient risk management, and also new drug development.

1. spaCyL: spaCyL is an open-source NLP package. This package can effectively handle huge amounts of text datasets, and because of the performance of this package, spaCyL is very famous among healthcare professionals. SpaCy is capable of extracting information about the disease, drugs, and patients from the clinical records. It is used in medical science to make recommendation systems roughly based on medical literature. SpaCy is also used for Electronic Health Analysis (EHR). In EHR, SpaCy works to find research study candidates depending on the medical history [37].
2. Bidirectional Encoder Representations from Transformers: Bidirectional Encoder Representations from Transformers (BERT) is a new NLP model. It was developed by GOOGLE. It learns to represent text as a sequence of vectors using self-supervised learning. BERT is very useful for medical text analysis because it can analyze text both left to right and right to left. BERT is used in healthcare to find patterns in patient data, extract pertinent medical information from clinical documentation, and even forecast illness outcomes from unstructured text. Numerous NLP tasks, such as named entity recognition, question answering, and language translation—all essential for examining medical records—have shown notable gains in performance due to BERT [38]. BERT framework has two steps such as pre-training and fine-tuning. Figure 5.6. shows an example of BERT Masked model. Figure 5.6 shows the BERT model

5.2.4.5 Cloud-based AI Tools

Cloud-based AI tools provide flexible solutions for creating and advancement of the different AI models in the healthcare sector. These platforms provide the way for the integration and implementation of different AI technologies extensively designed to be implemented in the medical sector.

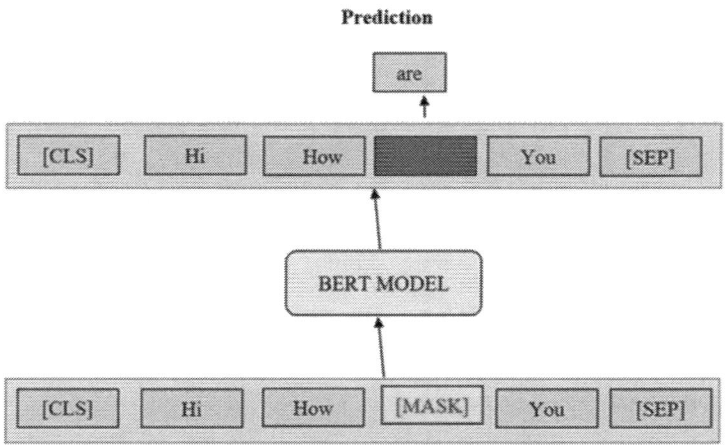

FIGURE 5.6 Showing the BERT MODEL.

1. Amazon Web Services (AWS) AI: Amazon web services include AWS HealthLake for assisting the medical sectors with the analysis and storage of healthcare data. This also helps in sharing the healthcare data sets. Another component of AWS is the Amazon SageMaker, which is used for the development of ML models. Amazon SageMaker is also used for the training and utilization of the ML learning models. There may be some healthcare companies, which do not wish to create their own ML models. In these cases also AWS has built-in models that can be used for the analysis of medical images, NLP and also predictive analytics [39].
2. Microsoft Azure AI: Microsoft Azure is another well-known cloud platform offering AI tools for healthcare. In Microsoft Azure is a collection of different AI services. The different AI services include Azure Health Data Services, it helps healthcare professionals connect with each other [40]. Azure Health Data Service helps to analyze healthcare data. Another component is the Azure ML. It helps in smooth running and development of the AI model and provides the special tools for AI-driven diagnostics, customized treatment planning and patient monitoring. Microsoft can also be used by the healthcare businesses that want to excel with current medical trends.

5.3 AI-DRIVEN DISEASE DETECTION APPROACHES

5.3.1 How to Build an AI-based Illness Diagnosis System

Several steps are required for developing an AI-powered ML diagnostic system involving both technical and domain knowledge. This is a detailed guide, as shown below in Figure 5.7:

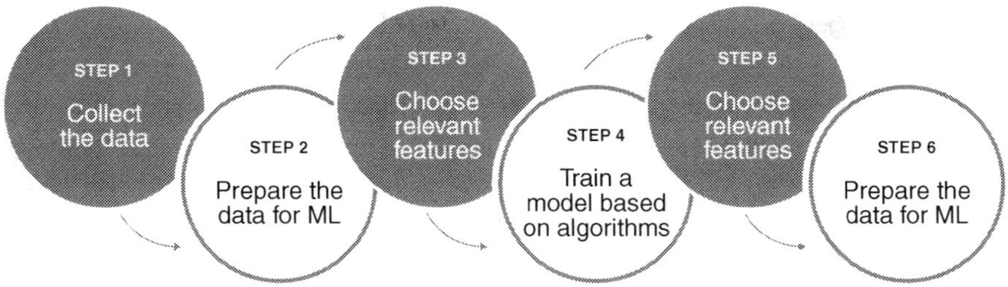

FIGURE 5.7 Step-by-step guide for AI detection system.

5.3.1.1 Collection of Data-sets

Critical origins for the datasets are gathered from the diagnostic centers, hospitals, and other medical research institutions. Electronic health records can also be collected, and the software professionals can aid with the datasets.

5.3.1.2 Data Preparation

In order to prepare the data, the IT team must eliminate errors and inconsistencies and transform the data into an ML-ready format.

5.3.1.3 Feature Selection

At this point, you need to choose the features that are most pertinent to the disease you are concentrating on; domain knowledge is crucial in this regard. The software companies' professionals will be providing the AI technologies required for choosing the feature.

5.3.1.4 Models Training

An appropriate AI-driven algorithm or a combination of different algorithms is being chosen for the operation of data sets.

The software individuals help to automate the training process and provide resources for training sophisticated ML models.

5.3.1.5 Estimation of Model

The acceptable parameters such as precision, repetition of the data and accuracy are evaluated to decide the model. The model should be evaluated using the validation set and selected metrics. Cross-validation techniques must be used to determine an unconstrained dataset. It is very important to understand the reason behind the prediction of the models for the healthcare and the medical application. Methods such as Shapely Additive Explanations, or SHAP, can be useful.

5.3.1.6 Model Implementation

To estimate the model's performance in the actual world, test it on a smaller group before implementing it widely. After you are pleased, put the model into the setting you want, like a cloud-based platform for healthcare providers.

The diagnosis of diseases powered by AI and ML algorithms and models is showing very good results in the medical field, as per many research studies in the fields of cardiology, radiology, and many other clinical diseases. The disease diagnosis by the AI-powered illness detection system diagnoses very early stages of the diseases with the correct predictions, which can indirectly reduce the world's mortality rate. The health outcomes of the majority of common diseases, like diabetes, cancer, and pulmonary diseases, improve with the early detection of these diseases. Illness detection powered by the MLand the AI algorithms will have the inclusion of many other conditions and parameters and will focus on personalized and customized patient treatments.

5.3.2 Medical Imaging and Pattern Recognition

One of the most revolutionary developments in contemporary healthcare is the incorporation of intelligence (AI) into medical imaging. Diseases can now be automatically detected, classified, and predicted by the integration of specialized computational algorithms with a huge amount of clinical data sets, and this is possible because of AI. The introduction of AI in medical science improves the overall clinical diagnostics precision and clinical disease management. This chapter explains the role of AI in medical Imaging, pattern recognition, applications, and future opportunities.

5.3.2.1 AI in Medical Imaging

Medical Imaging Technologies such as positron emission tomography (PET), magnetic resonance imaging (MRI), computed tomography (CT), ultrasound, and X-rays produce large volumes of imaging data sets. Radiologists have been interpreting from these datasets for many years, but it is very time-consuming and is not always error-free. These problems can be solved by the introduction of AI and, in more detail, DL and ML technology in automating Image analysis and identifying the significant patterns of the data sets [41].

5.3.2.2 AI Pattern Recognition

Pattern recognition is the first foundation stone of AI-powered medical imaging. AI is able to acknowledge the small irregularities in medical imaging by training and teaching models that can recognize patterns particular to some diseases. CNNs have shown good results in disease classification, organ segmentation, and tumor identification [42].

5.3.2.3 Segmenting and Reconstructing Images

Image segmentation is the process of identifying the anatomical structures. This procedure is essential in surgical procedures and also in the planning of treatment. U-Net architecture is a type of AI-powered segmentation technology that is used in real-time surgical procedures to define organs and tumors, which in turn makes surgical procedures easy and effective radiotherapy planning easier [43].

The quality of the medical and clinical images can be improved by the AI reconstruction methods. The resolution and clarity of the computerized tomography (CT) scan and magnetic resonance imaging can be improved by employing the DL-based reconstruction tools to lower the amount of radiation that the patients are exposed [44].

5.3.2.4 Personalized Medicine

AI uses medical imaging data to customize patient care. Radiomics is AI based method that extracts the quantitative metrics from the clinical images and can be used for clinical problem solving allowing customized cancer treatments [45].

5.3.3 Biomarker Discovery and Analysis

A biomarker (short for biological marker) is an objective measure that captures what is happening in a cell or an organism at a given moment. Biomarkers help us understand the relationships between environmental chemicals and human diseases to improve our ability to diagnose, monitor, or predict disease risk. Computational biology, AI, and high-throughput technologies have revolutionized the search for and study of biomarkers. A biomarker is a quantifiable sign of a pathological or physiological process or of a reaction to a treatment. Each of the various categories into which biomarkers are divided—diagnostic, prognostic, predictive, pharmacodynamic, and monitoring markers—has a distinct clinical function [46]. They come from a variety of sources, such as imaging data, metabolites, proteins, and genes.

Finding and confirming molecular characteristics associated with disease states is the process of discovering biomarkers, frequently using high-throughput methods such as proteomics, metabolomics, and genomics [47].

5.3.3.1 Technologies for Biomarker Discovery

1. Genomics and Transcriptomics: Next-generation sequencing (NGS) and microarrays help in the pointing out of the microarrays and Ribonucleic acid (RNA) biomarkers related to diseases such as cancer and other neurological disorders. Generic variants and also the expression patterns can be investigated extensively by microarrays and NGS [48]. We can take one example, such as BRCA1 AND BRCA2 mutations are risk indicators for ovarian cancer and breast cancer [49]. Protein Microarray and Mass Spectrometry (MS) are also very reliable for measuring the proteins related to a particular illness and are specifically used for proteomics-based biomarker discovery. As an instance, Prostate-specific antigen (PSA) is mostly used as a biomarker for prostate cancer [50].
2. Metabolomics: The study of metabolites inside a cell, tissue, and organ to find the specific metabolic mark specific to a disease is called metabolomics. These studies use nuclear magnetic resonance spectroscopy (NMRS) and mass spectrometry (MS) [50].
3. Imaging Biomarkers: Advanced imaging techniques like positron emission tomography (PET), magnetic resonance imaging (MRI), and computed tomography (CT) provide non-invasive methods for identifying biomarkers. Imaging biomarkers are widely used in oncology, neurology, and cardiovascular diseases [51].

5.3.3.2 Role of AI and ML in Biomarker Discovery

Because AI and ML make it possible to analyze large, complicated datasets, they have sped up the process of finding biomarkers. In terms of pattern recognition, data integration, and predictive modelling, these technologies provide special capabilities.

1. Integration and Analysis of Data: To find biomarkers with high accuracy, AI combines several datasets from proteomics, genomes, and medical records. Multi-omics biomarkers have been found using ML methods like random forests and SVMs [51].
2. Pattern Recognition Using DL: Pattern recognition in imaging data and chemical characteristics is a strong suit for DL models, particularly convolutional neural networks (CNNs) and autoencoders. CNNs have been used, for example, to find radiomic characteristics in medical images that are associated with the course of a disease [52].
3. Dimensionality Reduction and Feature Selection: High-throughput datasets contain hundreds and thousands of variables. Biomarker findings for a disease require the selection of features like Principal Component Analysis (PCA) and Least absolute Shrinkage and Selection Operator (LASSO) [53].
4. Predictive Modelling: Biomarker validation is very important in Medical Sciences; AI predictive models can be very useful for evaluating the biomarkers in disease detection. Immuno-therapy response is one example where ML techniques are used to find the biomarkers that are used for disease prediction [54].

5.3.4 Early Identification of Chronic Diseases

Detection of diseases, especially the chronic diseases, at an early stage is a very important aspect for patient outcomes and the efficient management of the diseases and also for lowering the healthcare expenses. Chronic diseases of patients like diabetes, heart disease, cancer, and other chronic respiratory disorders form a huge portion of the world's illness load [55]. Early detection of diseases and also making the preventive and individualized and personalized health care plans are possible because of the sophisticated AI diagnostic tools that are made possible due to the big data analysis and AI. This chapter will give a detailed description and the significance of the early detection of chronic diseases and the new technologies related to this early detection, and the difficulties and other prospects of chronic diseases.

5.3.4.1 Technologies for Early Identification of Chronic Diseases

1. Imaging Technologies: Early detection of chronic diseases is possible due to the CT, MRI, and ultrasound, which produce imaging systems that are very important for the early detection of diseases. Lung cancer is screened in the high-risk groups of patients using the low-dose CT. Coronary calcium coding. The image analysis powered by the AI improves the precision of the diagnostics by minute detailing of the problems and the anomalies that the radiologists who are experienced may overlook [56].

2. Wearable Devices and Remote Monitoring: Smartwatches and other fitness trackers, which are examples of the variable devices have gained popularity in the disease management of chronic diseases. The Smart watches and the fitness trackers monitor heart rate, blood sugar and blood pressure which are providing real time data for early diagnosis of the diseases. The continuous monitoring of the glucose helps to diagnose early glucose dysregulation in the pre-diabetic persons [57].
3. AI and ML: Huge datasets are being analyzed by the AI and ML algorithms to find the trends of the diseases and also to forecast the similarities of the diseases. Diseases like diabetes and hypertension can be detected in early stages based on the predictive models which considers the genetic information, lifestyle factors and also the electronic health records (EHRs). We can take one example of using DL algorithms in the retinal pictures for the early detection of the diabetic retinopathy [58].

5.3.4.2 Applications in Chronic Disease Management

1. Diabetes: Early detection of diabetes is very important in medical sciences for disease management. This is made possible by finding the prediabetic diseases like impaired fasting glucose and poor glucose tolerance. Biomarker searches for HbA1c are used for identifying of the high-risk diabetic people [14]. AI-powered models are also used for identification that are mainly examining genetic and the lifestyle factors of high-risk people. It has been demonstrated that by the use of these methods, Type 2 diabetes can be delayed or prevented by the early diagnosis and providing metformin medication changing the lifestyle of the patients [59].
2. Cardiovascular Diseases: Evolution of the risk factors like smoking, high blood pressure and hyperlipidemia are important for the early detection of the cardiovascular diseases (CVDs). Electronic health records and the imaging data are being evaluated by the AI based tools to determine the myocardial infarction and also the risk of the stroke [60]. The use of wearable technology by the patients such as Smart Watch With eco cardiogram capabilities have made Possible the early diagnosis of arrhythmias and also lower the risk of the strokes in the patients [61,62].
3. Cancer: Mammography and colonoscopy which are the methods of the cancer screening are very important parts for the early detection of the cancer. Image analysis by the AI power tools have improved the sensitivity of the mammography and the colonoscopy screenings [63,64].
4. Chronic Respiratory Diseases: Detection of Chronic Obstructive Pulmonary Diseases (COPD) and asthma are made possible by the use of spirometry and AI-powered analysis of lung function data. The use of the wearable sensors is also very crucial in the detection as they monitor the air quality and are used as the emerging tools for detecting the pulmonary diseases [65].

5.4 AI IN PREVENTIVE HEALTHCARE

Preventive healthcare identifies and reduces the health problems before they become serious ailments. The use of wearable technologies and Internet of Things (IOT) integration with the customized care plans which are all powered by AI tools have made huge developments in the preventive healthcare.

5.4.1 Wearable Technology and Continuous Monitoring

Variable technology can continuously monitor the psychological indications of a patient so it has completely evolved the preventive health-care system. Real time data can be gathered can be collected by the fitness tracker smartwatches and the implanted sensors in the patients. Wearable technologies provide very useful information and large data sets on the personal health patterns and thus helps in the early detection of the diseases.

5.4.1.1 Smartwatches, Fitness Trackers, and Implantable Devices

1. Smartwatches and Fitness Trackers: Fitness trackers and smartwatches are two of the most widely available devices for preventative healthcare. These gadgets, which are outfitted with sensors to track heart rate, exercise, sleep habits, and other variables, enable people to take charge of their health. Irregular heartbeats are being examined and the data is being collected. AI-based algorithms are used in these data sets to examine together data and to find the anomalies. These anomalies could be a sign of atrial fibrillation. For instance, the ECG function of the Apple Watch has been shown to be effective in identifying AFib, lowering the risk of stroke [66], as shown in Figure 5.8.

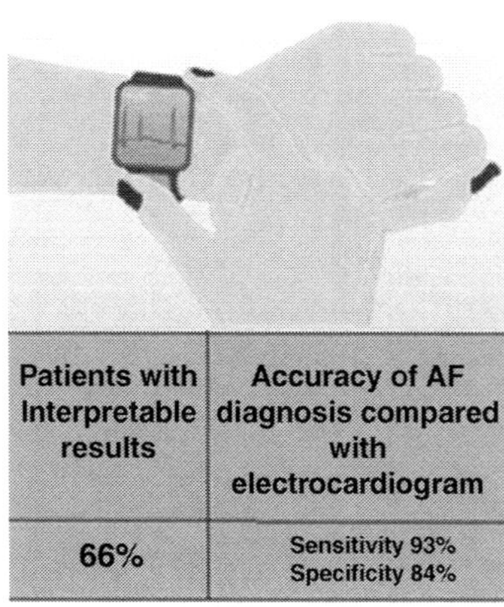

Patients with Interpretable results	Accuracy of AF diagnosis compared with electrocardiogram
66%	Sensitivity 93% Specificity 84%

FIGURE 5.8 ECG function of the Apple Watch has been shown to be effective in identifying AFib, lowering the risk of stroke [66].

2. Implantable Devices: Implanted Devices help in the monitoring of advanced chronic conditions and diseases. The implanted devices include the diabetic Continuous Glucose Monitors (CGMs) and the tracking biomarkers. The monitoring by the implanted devices provides huge datasets as solutions. These data sets can be improved by the AI-powered analytics, which are then employed to detect the glucose variations and also offer the patient and the medical professionals other useful information about the patient's conditions. Identification of the early indications of heart failure are very useful, as some implantable devices, like cardiac monitors, can be implanted and they improve the results of the preventive therapy. Implantable cardiac monitors can improve the results of the preventive therapy when there is an early detection of heart failure [67].

5.4.2 Virtual Sensors and IoT Integration

Preventive healthcare is extended outside conventional settings via virtual sensors and Internet of Things technologies. By merging physiological and environmental data, these systems offer thorough insights into health-related issues.

5.4.2.1 Environmental Monitoring for Disease Prevention

IoT-enabled sensors monitor the temperature, humidity, and air quality of the place and warn people about any issues. The temperature, humidity, and air quality are the environmental elements that have got important impact on the health outcomes of human beings. Air quality sensors, which are AI-driven are able to identify if there are any contaminants associated with respiratory diseases like asthma and COPD.

5.4.2.2 Applications

Pollution Control of Air: Real-time air quality updates from the IOT device and implementation of the AI algorithms on the datasets that will be available from the updates of the IOT device can prevent the patients from further exposure during times of high pollution of the year-round air. As per the studies available, these kinds of interventions help to reduce asthma in many cities.

5.4.2.3 Quality Monitoring of Water

IoT-based sensors help the spread of diarrhea and other waterborne diseases by identifying different types of impurities in drinking and potable water. AI improves these IoT-based sensor systems by forecasting the contamination patterns from the past data sets available from the real-time IoT sensors.

5.4.2.4 Integration of Environmental-Wearable

The wearables can be customized based on the recommendations when connected to the environmental sensors, like asthma patients may be warned not to exercise outside in their environment.

5.4.3 Personalized Preventive Care Plans

Individual personalized preventive care programs can be made based on the patients' risk factors, lifestyle, and health profile with the help of AI tools. AI tools have the capacity to evaluate the most complex datasets through which preventive care programs are made.

5.4.3.1 Tailoring Interventions Using AI Recommendations

- AI-Driven Health Assessments: AI-based tools and algorithms use information from the patient's genetic profiles, wearable technologies, and the patient's medical records. These AI tools are used to determine a person's and a patient's risk factor levels. For example, in the case of diseases like diabetes and cardiovascular disease, ML algorithms examine the lifestyle factors and also the patient's genetic predispositions to forecast these diseases. The doctors and clinical experts receive various relevant insights for the early treatment of these diseases using their predictive analysis tools, such as IBM Watson Health.
- Lifestyle Recommendations: Real-time data is being used by the AI-based algorithms to recommend lifestyle changes. For instance, fitness records based on AI technology suggest customized personal diets and also different exercises to reduce the particular health risk. There are AI-enabled coaching programs that have helped patients quit smoking and also lose weight.
- Medication and Treatment Optimization: Hypertension and hyperlipidaemia are very fatal diseases, and the treatment of these diseases includes optimizing the AI tools, such as the pharmacogenomics platform. The pharmacogenomics platform forecasts the therapeutic efficacy and probable side effects of the medicines. All of these are part of the personalized care plans, which include the medication schedules based on the metabolic and genetic profiles of the patient.

5.4.3.2 Mental Health Interventions

AI provides individualized mental health care for illnesses like depression and anxiety. The individual mental health care provided by the AI consists of chatbots and virtual therapists. These AI systems use NLP techniques to track the emotional health of patients and offer evidence-based therapy to mental patients. AI has done a massive revolution in the medical and healthcare industry with the involvement of many real-world applications, thus helping in a range of medical issues and in the early detection of various diseases. This section examines the rare cases of diseases like cancer detection, cardiovascular disease predictions, and the diagnosis of neurological conditions and epidemiological monitoring.

5.5 CASE STUDIES AND PRACTICAL IMPLEMENTATIONS

AI has undergone a massive revolution in the medical and healthcare industry with the involvement of many real-world applications, thus helping in a range of medical issues and in the early detection of various diseases. This section examines the rare cases of diseases like cancer detection, cardiovascular disease predictions, and the diagnosis of neurological conditions and epidemiological monitoring.

5.5.1 Cancer Detection and Screening Programs

According to the World Health Organisation, cancer is the leading cause of mortality. Cancer was responsible for the death of ten million patients worldwide in the year 2020 [68].

Early detection of cancer is very crucial. There are various ML-supported AI analyses of medical imaging that help in the early detection of cancer [69]. A Melanoma, skin cancer, has a five-year survival rate of about 99% for the local malignancies and only 32% for the distant cancers [70]. This gives us an idea of why the early detection of cancer is very important in the medical sense. Blood samples can also be analysed to provide the treatment plan for certain patients by the AI-powered medical imaging analysis. A different disease detection algorithm for the detection of the various forms of cancer is as follows:

5.5.1.1 Breast Cancer

94% of mammography pictures may be analysed by algorithms to identify tumours or anomalous patterns. In comparison to human radiologists, the AI model made by Google showed a decrease of 5.7% in the false positives and the decrease of less than 9.5% in the false negatives [71].

Google's AI model for identifying breast cancer in mammograms demonstrated a 5.7% decrease in false positives and a 9.4% decrease in false negatives [71].

5.5.1.2 Lung Cancer

Early-stage tumours can be found by using AI technologies to analyse CT data. Similar to breast cancer, 94% of lung cancer cases were identified in their early stages [72].

5.5.1.3 Skin Cancer

Distinction between malignant and benign melanomas can be efficiently made from the algorithms for the enlist detection by examining the skin photos. Early detection of skin cancer symptoms is aided by datasets containing hundreds of thousands of distinct photos of skin lesions.

5.5.1.4 Cancer in Prostate

The biopsy of the tissue and the images of the MRI are examined for the detection of the pattern of cancer.

5.5.2 Cardiovascular Disease Prediction

Preventive health evaluations are very beneficial for cardiovascular diseases, which account for about 19 million deaths globally. When it comes to illness identification, ML can assist by:

- Identifying arrhythmias in ECG information.
- Using test data and patient medical records to forecast heart failure.
- Recognising arterial pictures for atherosclerotic plaques.
- Utilising wearable technology that tracks vital signs to forecast the short- and long-term risk of heart attacks and stroke.

For instance, in 87.6% of cases, the prediction warning accurately forecasted the probability of stroke [73].

5.5.3 Neurological Diseases

Neurological diseases such as Alzheimer's disease and Parkinson's disease can be diagnosed using ML techniques. Although these diseases are currently incurable, early detection is crucial as it allows for better preparation and organization of quality care. Here is an explanation of how the disease detection algorithm functions in the context of neurological conditions:

Alzheimer's disease: Harnessing the power of ML, we can analyze brain imaging data to uncover early signs of disease progression. This cutting-edge technology is being refined to recognize subtle indicators of decline long before symptoms become visible, offering a crucial opportunity for early intervention and improved outcomes.

Parkinson's disease: AI can analyze voice data and hand movements to detect early signs. The technologies for diagnosing the disease before symptoms become apparent are also relevant.

5.5.4 Diabetes

One in ten persons globally suffers from diabetes, making it one of the most common chronic conditions in the world. Based on genetic information, lifestyle characteristics, and patient records, an AI-based disease detection system can forecast when a disease may manifest. Furthermore, diabetes complications can be predicted by disease detection algorithms. It can identify retinopathy from retinal pictures, for instance.

5.5.5 Diseases of Eyes

AI-powered disease identification has shown promise in treating certain eye disorders, such as:

Glaucoma: Eye scan analysis for early detection.

Macular Degeneration: Retinal scans can be used to identify early indicators.

5.5.6 Infectious Diseases

Based on information from several sources, AI-based disease detection and ML for medical diagnostics may be able to detect outbreaks and forecast the spread of diseases. Additionally, it can forecast the virulence or resistance patterns of viruses by analysing their genomic sequences. For instance, early COVID-19 identification can benefit from AI illness detection methods.

5.5.6.1 Liver Diseases

It is possible to heal liver disorders if they are identified early. From MRI or ultrasound pictures, disease detection algorithms can identify fatty liver or fibrosis. They are also able to recognise possible outcomes and forecast the likelihood of developing serious liver disease.

5.5.6.2 Respiratory Diseases

AI and ML tools can be used to diagnose conditions like asthma or chronic obstructive pulmonary disease. These illnesses are identified by analysing the audio breathing and looking for trends in the spirit data.

5.5.6.3 Bone and Joint Diseases

AI systems can identify early indicators of osteoporosis and arthritis from MRI or X-ray pictures.

We can use AI and ML for:

- Predicting Genetic Disorders: By examining genomic sequences, one can identify mutations that may cause illnesses.
- Predicting Patient Deterioration: Real-time vital sign monitoring helps identify and notify medical professionals of possible negative outcomes in hospitalised patients.
- Drug interactions and Side Effects: Using the patient's medical history and current prescriptions, one can forecast any negative drug reactions.

5.6 CONCLUSION

The application of AI in early disease detection and diagnosis has brought a revolutionary change in the healthcare system, with the potential to increase diagnostic accuracy, lower the cost of disease treatment, and improve patient health outcomes throughout the world. The use of AI technologies like ML, DL, and NLP enables the healthcare system to analyse complicated information and minute details and to predict illnesses and disease risk with new precision. The most important contribution of AI in medical science includes analyzing the medical imaging data and the genetic data of patients.

AI's most important contribution includes analysing the genetic and medical imaging data. Diseases like cancer, heart disease, and neurological disorders can be detected at the correct time when the treatment of the diseases will be successful, with technologies like RNN and CNN. The combination of the wearable devices has made it possible to monitor the patients in real time, providing customised preventive treatments which are helpful for both the patients and the medical professionals.

The long-term use of AI in medical science can have ethical issues and problems, which are crucial for the use of AI in the healthcare field. The main problems of AI, such as algorithmic bias, data privacy, and the interpretability of AI models, must be conveyed. Healthcare organisations, software development companies, software developers, and the governments must be working together to create frameworks where the patient's safety, data security, and regulatory compliance must come first. The future of AI in the detection and prevention of diseases is a promising field. New technologies such as Federated Learning, which allows secure collaborations across institutions, and also the integration of multiomics data for health analysis. New technologies, such as Federated Learning—which enables secure collaborations across institutions—and the integration of multiomics data for health analysis, are expected to drive significant breakthroughs in precision medicine. Scaling the air solutions to the resource-limited settings can reduce global health disparities and also help in promoting equal healthcare access for all patients across the world.

Ai has become a very important part in the battle against illness against diseases which are creating a revolution in the early detection and also the prevention of the diseases despite the ongoing despite the current difficulties like the ethical considerations and the approach to innovation AI will keep on transforming the health care and medicine and medical science and will be enhancing the human beings life across the world.

Looking ahead, the future of AI in disease detection and prevention is promising. Innovations such as federated learning, which enables secure collaboration across institutions, and the integration of panomics data for holistic health analysis, are paving the way for breakthroughs in the precision medicine field. Additionally, scaling AI solutions to resource-limited settings has the potential to reduce global health disparities and promote equitable healthcare access.

Disclaimer

None

REFERENCES

1. Theerthagiri, P., Ruby, A. U., Chandran, J. G. C., Sardar, T. H., & Shafeeq, B. M. A. (2024). Deep SqueezeNet learning model for diagnosis and prediction of maize leaf diseases. *Journal of Big Data*, 11(1), 112.
2. Sardar, T. H. (2024). Reflecting on a decade of evolution: MapReduce-based advances in partitioning-based, hierarchical-based, and density-based clustering (2013–2023). *Wiley Interdisciplinary Reviews: Data Mining and Knowledge Discovery*, 14(6), e1566.
3. Subbarao, E., et al. (2023). Investigation of solar energy for urban areas and metropolitan communities using machine learning. *Electric Power Components and Systems*, 6(1), 1–11.
4. Sardar, T. H., Faizabadi, A. R., & Ansari, Z. (2017). An analysis of data processing using Mapreduce paradigm on the Hadoop framework. *International Journal of Emerging Research in Management and Technology*, 6(5), 113–126.
5. Sardar, T. H., Sarkar, R., Ahmed, S. J., & Bandyopadhyay, A. (2023, May). A novel ensemble methodology to validate fuzzy clusters of Big Data. In *Proceedings of the Fourth International Conference on Trends in Computational and Cognitive Engineering: TCCE 2022* (pp. 267–278). Springer Nature, Singapore.

6. Sardar, T. H., Khatun, A., & Khan, S. (2017, December). Design of energy aware collection tree protocol in wireless sensor network. In *2017 IEEE International Conference on Circuits and Systems (ICCS)* (pp. 12–17). IEEE, India.
7. Sardar, T. H., Faizabadi, A. R., & Ansari, Z. (2017, July). An evaluation of MapReduce framework in cluster analysis. In *2017 International Conference on Intelligent Computing, Instrumentation and Control Technologies (ICICICT)* (pp. 110–114). IEEE.
8. Khatun, A., & Sardar, T. H. (2025). Cryptography algorithms to prevent different security attacks. In Khatun, A., & Sardar, T. H. (eds) *Next Generation Mechanisms for Data Encryption* (pp. 35–46). CRC Press.
9. Sardar, T. H., Muttineni, A., & Ranjan, R. (2024). The future of Big Data in customer experience and inventory management. In Sardar, T. H., Muttineni, A., & Ranjan, R. (eds) *Big Data Computing* (pp. 233–248). CRC Press.
10. Sardar, T. H., Das, S., & Pandey, B. K. Explainable AI (XAI): concepts and theory. In *Medical Data Analysis and Processing Using Explainable Artificial Intelligence* (pp. 1–18). Edited by Om Prakash Jena, Mrutyunjaya Panda, Utku Kose. CRC Press.
11. Yu, G., et al. (2021). Accurate recognition of colorectal cancer with semi-supervised deep learning on pathological images. *Nature Communications*, 12(1), 1–13.
12. Sitar Taut, Adela Viviana, Zdrenghea, D., Pop, D., & Sitar-Taut, Dan-Andrei. (2009). Using machine learning algorithms in cardiovascular disease risk evaluation. *Journal of Applied Computer Science & Mathematics*, 3, 211–217.
13. Le, Elizabeth, et al. (2021). Assessing robustness of carotid artery CT angiography radiomics in the identification of culprit lesions in cerebrovascular events. *Scientific Reports*, 11. https://doi.org/10.1038/s41598-021-82760-w.
14. The Multiple Leiomyoma Consortium. (2002). Germline mutations in *FH* predispose to dominantly inherited uterine fibroids, skin leiomyomata and papillary renal cell cancer. *Nature Genetics*, 30, 406–410. https://doi.org/10.1038/ng849.
15. Hosmer, D. W., & Lemeshow, S. (2000, September 13). *Applied Logistic Regression*. Wiley. https://doi.org/10.1002/0471722146.
16. Zou, H., & Hastie, T. (2005). Regularization and variable selection via the elastic net. *Journal of the Royal Statistical Society: Series B (Statistical Methodology)*, 67, 301–320. https://doi.org/10.1111/j.1467-9868.2005.00503.x.
17. Zhang, S. Z., Penner, G. B., Yang, W. Z., & Oba, M. (2010). Effects of partially replacing barley silage or barley grain with dried distillers' grains with solubles on rumen fermentation and milk production of lactating dairy cows. *Journal of Dairy Science*, 93(7), 3231–3242.
18. McCullagh, P., & Nelder, J. A. (1989). *Generalized Linear Models*. 2nd Edition, Chapman and Hall, London.
19. Zhang, M., et al. (2010). Creation of a hyperpermeable yeast strain to genotoxic agents through combined inactivation of PDR and CWP genes. *Toxicology Science*, 113(2), 401–411.
20. Richard, L. (2013). Street, how clinician–patient communication contributes to health improvement: Modeling pathways from talk to outcome. *Patient Education and Counseling*, 92(3), 286–291. https://doi.org/10.1016/j.pec.2013.05.004.
21. Zhou, P., et al. (2020). A pneumonia outbreak associated with a new coronavirus of probable bat origin. *Nature*, 579, 270–273. https://doi.org/10.1038/s41586-020-2012-7.
22. Samat, N. A., Salleh, M., & Ali, Haseeb. (2020). The comparison of pooling functions in convolutional neural network for sentiment analysis task. In *Recent Advances on Soft Computing and Data Mining. SCDM 2020. Advances in Intelligent Systems and Computing* (vol. 978). Springer, Cham. https://doi.org/10.1007/978-3-030-36056-6_20.

23. Khalifa, Yassin, Mandic, Danilo, & Sejdic, Ervin. (2020). A review of Hidden Markov models and Recurrent Neural Networks for event detection and localization in biomedical signals. *Information Fusion*, 69, 52–72. https://doi.org/10.1016/j.inffus.2020.11.008.
24. Meystre, S. M., Savova, G. K., Kipper-Schuler, K. C., & Hurdle, J. F. (2008). Extracting information from textual documents in the electronic health record: A review of recent research. *Yearbook of Medical Informatics*, 17, 128–144.
25. Murff, H. J., et al. (2011). Automated identification of postoperative complications within an electronic medical record using natural language processing. *JAMA*, 306(8), 848–855.
26. Demner-Fushman, D., Chapman, W. W., & McDonald, C. J. (2009). What can natural language processing do for clinical decision support? *Journal of Biomedical Informatics*, 42(5), 760–772.
27. Devlin, J., Chang, M. W., Lee, K., & Toutanova, K. (2019). BERT: Pre-training of deep bidirectional transformers for language understanding. arXiv preprint arXiv:1810.04805.
28. Agarwal, V., et al. (2016). Impact of predictive analytics on clinical outcomes in patients with sepsis. *PLoS ONE*, 11(4), e0153271.
29. Rajkomar, A., Dean, J., & Kohane, I. (2019). Machine learning in medicine. *New England Journal of Medicine*, 380(14), 1347–1358.
30. Shickel, B., Tighe, P. J., Bihorac, A., & Rashidi, P. (2018). Deep EHR: A survey of recent advances in deep learning techniques for electronic health record (EHR) analysis. *IEEE Journal of Biomedical and Health Informatics*, 22(5), 1589–1604.
31. Bodenreider, O. (2004). The unified medical language System (UMLS): Integrating biomedical terminology. *Nucleic Acids Research*, 32(suppl_1), D267–D270.
32. Singh, Ravi Ranjan (2020, March 15). TensorFlow tutorial: a beginner's guide to Tensor Flow (Part - 2). https://medium.com/analytics-vidhya/tensorflow-tutorial-a-beginners-guide-to-tensorflow-part-2-5d1219a8ba5c.
33. Paszke, A., et al. (2019). PyTorch: An imperative style, high-performance deep learning library. In *Advances in Neural Information Processing Systems*. Neural Information Processing Systems Foundation, Inc. (NeurIPS).
34. Sardar, T. H., & Faizabadi, A. R. (2019). Parallelization and analysis of selected numerical algorithms using OpenMP and Pluto on symmetric multiprocessing machine. *Data Technologies and Applications*, 53(1), 20–32.
35. Pedregosa, F., et al. (2011). Scikit-learn: Machine learning in Python. *Journal of Machine Learning Research*, 12, 2825–2830.
36. Chen, T., et al. (2016). XGBoost: A scalable tree boosting system. In *Proceedings of the 22nd ACM SIGKDD International Conference on Knowledge Discovery and Data Mining*. ACM.
37. Honnibal, M., et al. (2017). spaCy: Industrial-strength natural language processing. *To Appear in Proceedings of ACL*, 8(3), 312–323.
38. Devlin, J., et al. (2018). BERT: Pre-training of deep bidirectional transformers for language understanding. *arXiv preprint arXiv:1810.04805.*
39. Amazon Web Services (AWS). (2020). AWS machine learning. *AWS Documentation.*
40. Microsoft. (2020). Azure AI. *Microsoft Documentation.*
41. Litjens, G., et al. (2017). A survey on deep learning in medical image analysis. *Medical Image Analysis*, 42, 60–88.
42. Krizhevsky, A., et al. (2012). ImageNet classification with deep convolutional neural networks. *Advances in Neural Information Processing Systems*, 25, 1097–1105.
43. Ronneberger, O., et al. (2015). U-Net: Convolutional networks for biomedical image segmentation. In *International Conference on Medical Image Computing and Computer-Assisted Intervention* (pp. 234–241). Singapore.
44. Hammernik, K., et al. (2018). Learning a variational network for reconstruction of accelerated MRI data. *Magnetic Resonance in Medicine*, 79(6), 3055–3071.

45. Lambin, P., et al. (2012). Radiomics: Extracting more information from medical images using advanced feature analysis. *European Journal of Cancer*, 48(4), 441–446.
46. Biomarkers Definitions Working Group. (2001). Biomarkers and surrogate endpoints: Preferred definitions and conceptual framework. *Clinical Pharmacology & Therapeutics*, 69(3), 89–95.
47. Altelaar, A. F., et al. (2013). Trends in quantitative proteomics. *Journal of Proteome Research*, 12(1), 30–40.
48. Mavaddat, N., et al. (2010). Genetic susceptibility to breast cancer. *Molecular Oncology*, 4(3), 174–191.
49. Kim, H., et al. (2014). Prostate-specific antigen as a biomarker for prostate cancer. *Biochimica et Biophysica Acta*, 1846(1), 56–62.
50. Dang, L., et al. (2009). Cancer-associated IDH mutations. *Nature*, 462(7274), 739–744.
51. Misra, B. B., & Langefeld, C. D. (2019). Integrated omics data analysis. *Metabolomics*, 15(8), 1–12.
52. Hosny, A., Parmar, C., Quackenbush, J., Schwartz, L. H., & Aerts, H. J. W.L. (2018). Artificial intelligence in radiology. *Nature Reviews Cancer*, 18(8), 500–510.
53. Zou, H., & Hastie, T. (2005). Regularization and variable selection via the elastic net. *Journal of the Royal Statistical Society: Series B*, 67(2), 301–320.
54. Garon, E. B., et al. (2015). Pembrolizumab for NSCLC. *New England Journal of Medicine*, 372(21), 2018–2028.
55. WHO. (2021). Noncommunicable diseases. *World Health Organization*.
56. Grundy, S. M., et al. (2011). Prevention of cardiovascular disease. *Circulation*, 124(21), 2458–2473.
57. Wanner, C., et al. (2018). Diabetic kidney disease: Diagnosis and treatment. *Kidney International Supplements*, 8(2), 76–91.
58. Aberle, D. R., et al. (2011). Lung cancer screening with low-dose CT. *New England Journal of Medicine*, 365(5), 395–409.
59. Litjens, G., et al. (2017). A survey on deep learning in medical image analysis. *Medical Image Analysis*, 42, 60–88.
60. Patel, S., et al. (2012). Wearable sensors for chronic disease management. *IEEE Reviews in Biomedical Engineering*, 15, 12–28.
61. Bailey, T. S., et al. (2014). Continuous glucose monitoring in diabetes. *Diabetes Technology & Therapeutics*, 16(1), 20–25.
62. Beam, A. L., & Kohane, I. S. (2018). Big data and machine learning in health care. *JAMA*, 319(13), 1317–1318.
63. Gulshan, V., et al. (2016). Development of a deep learning algorithm for diabetic retinopathy detection. *JAMA*, 316(22), 2402–2410.
64. Raghupathi, W., & Raghupathi, V. (2018). Big data analytics in healthcare. *Journal of Healthcare Informatics Research*, 2(3), 239–249.
65. Knowler, W. C., et al. (2002). Reduction in diabetes incidence. *New England Journal of Medicine*, 346(6), 393–403.
66. Saha, I., Gourisaria, M. K., & Harshvardhan, G. M. (2022). Classification system for prediction of chronic kidney disease using data mining techniques. In *Advances in Data and Information Sciences: Proceedings of ICDIS 2021* (pp. 429–443). Springer, Singapore.
67. Elaine, Y., et al. (2019). Periprocedural management and multidisciplinary care pathways for patients with cardiac implantable electronic devices: A scientific statement from the american heart association. *Circulation*, 140(9), 790–799.
68. Gourisaria, M. K., et al. (2022). Data science appositeness in diabetes mellitus diagnosis for healthcare systems of developing nations. *IET Communications*, 16(5), 532–547.

69. Dutta, K., Chandra, S., & Gourisaria, M. K. (2022). Early-Stage detection of liver disease through machine learning algorithms. In Dutta, K., Chandra, S., & Gourisaria, M. K. (eds) *Advances in Data and Information Sciences* (pp. 155–166). Springer, Singapore.
70. Gourisaria, M. K., et al. (2021). Arrhythmia detection using deep belief network extracted features from ECG signals. *International Journal of E-Health and Medical Communications (IJEHMC)*, 12(6), 1–24.
71. Sahu, A., Harshvardhan, G. M., Gourisaria, M. K., Rautaray, S. S., & Pandey, M. (2021). Cardiovascular risk assessment using data mining inferencing and feature engineering techniques. *International Journal of Information Technology*, 13(5), 2011–2023.
72. Ardila, D., et al. (2019). End-to-end lung cancer screening with three-dimensional deep learning on low-dose chest computed tomography. *Nature Medicine*, 25, 954–961. https://doi.org/10.1038/s41591-019-0447-x
73. Jiang, F., et al. (2017). Artificial intelligence in healthcare: Past, present, and future. *Stroke and Vascular Neurology*, 2, 1033–1045.

6 AI in Medical Imaging
Revolutionizing Diagnostics through AI-Powered Services and Case Studies

Shashwat Saini, Seema Tharannum, and Tanvir Habib Sardar

6.1 INTRODUCTION

AI is transforming healthcare. It is already being implemented in hospitals in drug discovery, managing medical data, and personalizing medicine. Medical imaging too remains at the frontier of AI research, where models are achieving results that often outperform human counterparts [1–3]. They possess the ability to better understand images, diagnose diseases, and implement predictive analysis and quality control.

AI empowers healthcare professionals by supplementing their capabilities, allowing for quicker and more accurate decision-making. Some detailed applications of AI include:

- Detecting Abnormalities: AI can analyze medical images from X-rays, Computed Tomography (CT) scans, and Magnetic Resonance Imaging (MRIs) to detect abnormalities and diseases like cancer at an early stage.
- Improving Diagnosis: AI can help diagnose conditions like breast cancer, lung nodules, and Alzheimer's disease.
- Automating Tasks: AI can automate routine tasks like image processing, quality control, and data management.
- Improving Radiology Reports: AI can analyze and automatically generate reports based on medical images.
- Personalized Treatments: AI can analyze historical data to predict patient outcomes, enabling preventive care and personalized treatment plans.
- Streamline Workflows: AI can streamline workflows to optimize resource utilization and increase efficiency (Figure 6.1).

This chapter aims to address AI's role in medical imaging by looking at seven case studies that summarize various advancements and challenges in the field. This chapter begins by presenting the case studies, followed by discussions on explainable AI and several challenges with it. It concludes with an exploration of future scope and final remarks.

DOI: 10.1201/9781003600947-6

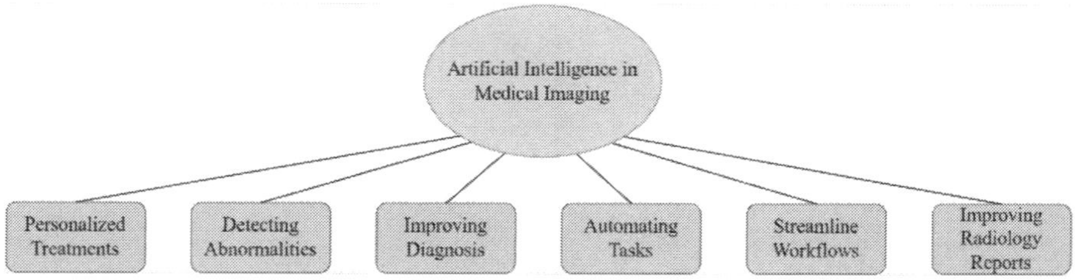

FIGURE 6.1 Applications of AI in medical imaging.

6.2 BRAIN TUMOUR DETECTION BASED ON DEEP LEARNING AND MAGNETIC RESONANCE IMAGING APPROACHES

Deep Learning is a class of AI much more powerful than traditional algorithms. Neural networks form the basis of all Deep Learning and provide more accurate and reliable results. Convolutional layers are a type of neural network that are able to capture spatial (2D or 3D) representations, to understand various components present in images. You Only Look Once (YOLO) model is a powerful, open-source implementation of the convolutional neural network that can predict bounding boxes and class probabilities of an image [4] (Figure 6.2).

In medicine, tumours are especially difficult to identify due to their complex and unusual shapes. Thus, YOLO was applied in this study to identify tumors from brain scan images, generalizing well across sagittal, coronal, and axial axes [5]. The model outputs bounding boxes and their probabilities if a tumour is present. Trained on a publicly available dataset, such a methodology starting from open-source data collection to evaluation on open challenges is frequently seen in research, part of a recent rise in open data [6].

CT and MRI scans generate vast amounts of data, often overwhelming healthcare professionals. AI can help address this problem by: retrieving the most relevant images for manual analysis by professionals, thereby reducing workloads; implementing quality control by ensuring imaging equipment consistently produces high-quality diagnostic images; and predicting and segmenting diseases in medical images, streamlining the diagnostic process.

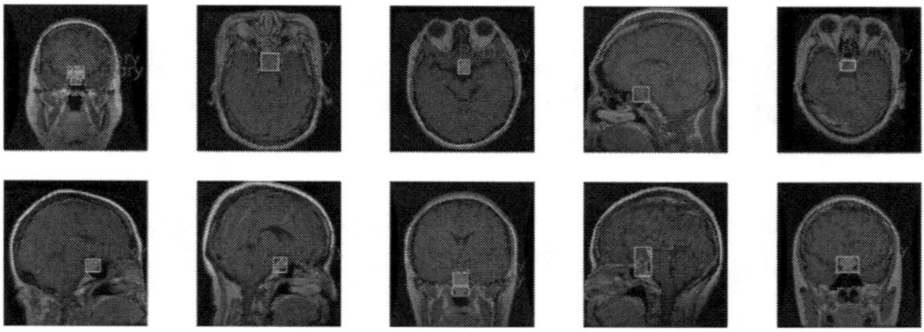

FIGURE 6.2 Example predicted bounding boxes and tumour class by YOLO.

However, research in AI and healthcare must be explainable as well, to ensure that models are transparent and understandable, mimicking human judgement and skills. Analyses such as these are important, built on the principles of confidentiality and privacy, ethics and responsibilities, and bias and fairness [7]. Thus, these models serve as helpful decision-making tools in the field of diagnosing tumours, while ensuring their working is explainable to experts.

Key takeaways: Deep Learning enhances accuracy over traditional models, YOLO can detect tumours in images, and explainability ensures trust in healthcare.

6.3 SEGMENT ANYTHING IN MEDICAL IMAGES

Medical image segmentation is another critical part of medical imaging in healthcare. Unlike bounding boxes, segmentation works to partition an image into discrete segments, highlighting regions of interest called a mask. A powerful model is the Segment Anything Model (SAM) created by Meta [8]. SAM is capable of generating high-quality masks for all objects in an image, and is more importantly open-source, emphasizing the role of private corporations in open-source AI.

This study brings SAM into medical imaging, covering ten image modalities and 30 cancer types [9]. The result is a highly generalized model that often outperforms modality-wise specialist models. The vision transformer is the highlight of this methodology, capable of capturing distant relationships that a convolution model cannot. Powered by self-attention, it is based on the technology that drives models like GPT-3 and GPT-4 (Figure 6.3).

MedSAM, the presented model, outperforms specialist models- models trained only on a particular dataset or a modality. Some of these models include those trained on Breast Cancer, COVID-19 infections, and Heart datasets. Thus, the applications of such a generalized model are vast in number, capable of replacing existing methodologies centred around specific modalities and use cases (Figure 6.4).

A variety of Machine Learning frameworks and models come from private corporations, such as AlphaFold (predicts 3D structures of proteins) by DeepMind, Tensorflow (a Deep Learning framework) developed by Google Brain, and Llama (a family of LLMs) by Meta. Such contributions to the open-source community drive AI, presenting an opportunity for transparency and community-driven innovation.

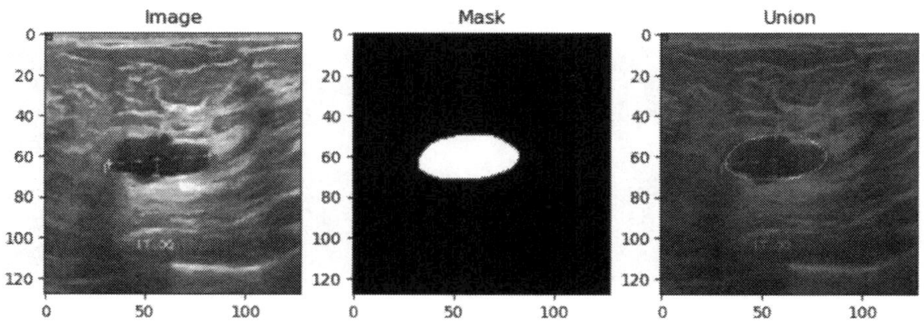

FIGURE 6.3 Example segmentation mask of a skin lesion.

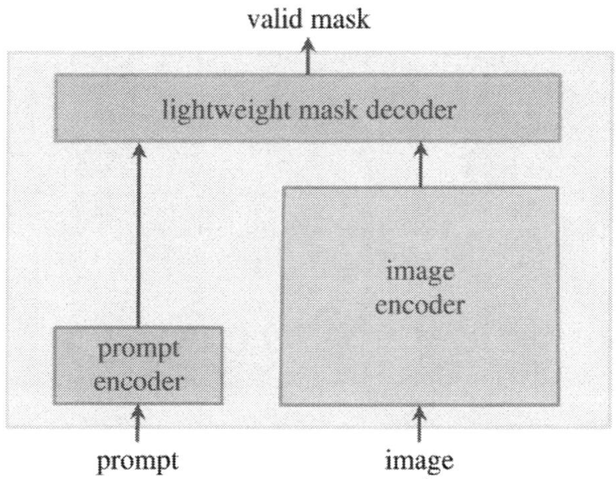

FIGURE 6.4 SAM Architecture. The model inputs a prompt and an image, which is fed through the image encoder, and output by the mask decoder (vision transformer). (Image by The FAIR team of Meta AI, licensed under Apache 2.0.)

Key takeaways: Medical image segmentation enhances diagnostics, SAM improves generalization, vision transformers surpass convolution models, and open-source AI drives innovation.

6.4 GENERATIVE ADVERSARIAL NETWORKS FOR MEDICAL IMAGE SYNTHESIS: AN EMPIRICAL STUDY

Generative Adversarial Networks (GANs) are state-of-the-art models that are capable of generating photo-realistic images. The models consist of a generator that produces images from random noise, and a discriminator that evaluates and differentiates between generated and genuine images. Iterative feedback from the discriminator helps the generator to create better images. GANs have found several applications in image augmentation, synthesis, classification, detection, and segmentation [9]. They are some of the most advanced models in AI, used in several implementations, including DALL-E 3.

One such application is synthesizing medical imagery in low-data modalities-situations where insufficient data is available [10]. Medical imagery is difficult to collect and label, making image synthesis appealing by enhancing datasets that can be further used to train supervised models. This study trained several GAN architectures on different datasets, empirically evaluating their benefits, alongside hyperparameter analysis [11].

The study also performs a visual Turing test, conducted alongside medical experts to distinguish real images from synthetic ones. The test consisted of a 50/50 mixture of real and synthetic images, with the experts achieving only 60% accuracy on classification. This shows the scope for GANs in medical imagery by proving how realistic generated images can be (Figure 6.5).

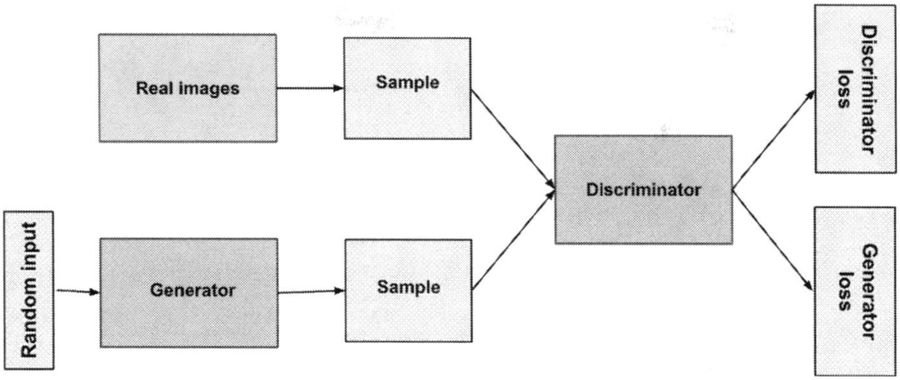

FIGURE 6.5 GAN Architecture. The generator generates images from random input (noise), which the discriminator compares against real images, and sends feedback in the form of loss. Image by Google Developers, licensed under CC BY 4.0.

Such models are a part of Generative AI, including the transformer discussed previously. They are capable of improving healthcare outcomes, reducing costs, and enabling personalized medicine. Such models are also capable of Retrieval-Augmented Generation (RAG) techniques, which produce facts fetched from external data sources. This ensures models are grounded in reliable data, as Generative AI becomes increasingly capable of producing fake content. This finds applications in managing medical data and thus, personalized medicine.

Key takeaways: GANs generate realistic images, enhance medical datasets, pass visual Turing tests, and support reliable, personalized healthcare through Generative AI.

6.5 A COMPARISON OF DEEP LEARNING PERFORMANCE AGAINST HEALTHCARE PROFESSIONALS IN DETECTING DISEASES FROM MEDICAL IMAGING

Continuing on visual Turing tests, a comprehensive review study was conducted to evaluate the performance of Deep Learning models in medical imaging against healthcare experts [12]. Analysing a total of 82 studies, the researchers examined important factors such as reference standards in the studies, as well as internal and external validation. The review concluded that Deep Learning models perform on par with healthcare professionals.

However, both this review and another [13] highlighted significant limitations in the existing research. Few studies incorporated external validation, many exhibited high levels of bias, and several deviated from established reporting standards. Moreover, the reviews found that researchers rarely share their code and data publicly, along with small and unrepresentative human comparator groups.

This case study thus depicts several challenges with medical imaging models. While Deep Learning models can match experts and their accuracy, they must strictly adhere to reference and reporting standards to ensure reliability. Researchers should also avoid overstating results to prevent misleading conclusions. To address these issues, better frameworks that enforce standards rigorously have to be implemented to promote consistency and accountability in visual Turing tests for medical imaging.

Despite the challenges, the review reinforces the potential of AI in medical imaging. It can enhance human expertise and act as a second opinion, minimizing errors and enhancing diagnostics.

Key takeaways: Deep Learning matches expert performance but faces validation challenges, requiring stricter standards for reliability in medical imaging AI.

6.6 COMPARISON OF HUMANS VERSUS MOBILE PHONE-POWERED ARTIFICIAL INTELLIGENCE

On-device AI refers to models that run directly on small devices like mobiles, smartwatches, and other IoT devices. As technology becomes faster, it enables models to run seamlessly on mobile phones. Their demand has created a significant push towards optimizing models for such devices, such as those in natural language processing and computer vision. These advancements are particularly impactful in healthcare, as they offer easy-to-use and highly accurate tools for disease diagnosis and personalized treatment, through everyday devices like smartphones, cameras, and smartwatches.

This study involved clinical trials with on-device AI, competing against specialist and novice healthcare professionals [14]. On the task of diagnosis of pigmented skin cancer using images of affected skin as input, the results of the trail proved that on-device AI was equivalent to the specialists, and significantly superior to the novices.

This finding is significant as it shows that AI can work effectively on mobile phones, without the need for expensive computer hardware. Thus, on-device AI in medical imaging can perform tests immediately and accurately. This enables portable diagnostic services. AI can also monitor metrics like heart rate, sleep patterns, and physical activity to detect abnormalities. On-device AI additionally enhances privacy and security, as data is not transferred to the cloud or external servers.

However, on-device AI faces several challenges. Devices like mobiles come with decreased processing power and poor energy efficiency. Additionally, deploying and updating these models is a complex process, and their capabilities fall short when compared to cloud-based solutions.

Key takeaways: On-device AI enables portable diagnostics, matches specialist accuracy, enhances privacy, but faces hardware and deployment challenges.

6.7 TRANSFER LEARNING FOR MEDICAL IMAGE CLASSIFICATION

Transfer learning is an AI technique that builds new models based on knowledge learnt in the past. Such techniques help improve training efficiency by avoiding the need to train models from scratch. They help reduce operational costs, hardware requirements, and enhance reusability. A well-known example of transfer learning is the process of fine-tuning Large Language Models, which involves training pre-trained models on a domain-specific dataset.

This review study highlights the application of transfer learning for medical image classification [15]. The study presents the benefits of models built through transfer learning, such as Inception and ResNet, for image classification and segmentation. Such models are pre-trained on diverse datasets and tasks, and work well across several domains. By using them as feature extractors, researchers significantly reduce costs and training time, while maintaining high performance. This is a direct result of the models' pre-training, which enables fine-tuning for specific medical imaging tasks.

Thus, in transfer learning, only the final classification layer is updated or trained from scratch. The feature extractor itself remains unchanged, except in cases where the model does not perform satisfactorily- then the other layers may be updated. Even then, such updates are made incrementally, starting from the bottom layers and progressing upwards, minimizing the need to train multiple layers or the entire feature extractor. Such an approach maximizes efficiency (Figure 6.6).

Transfer learning is also effective in low-data modalities. By leveraging pre-trained models, the need for extensive datasets is mitigated. As shown previously, this capability is valuable in medical imaging [16], where acquiring and labelling large datasets is time-consuming and expensive.

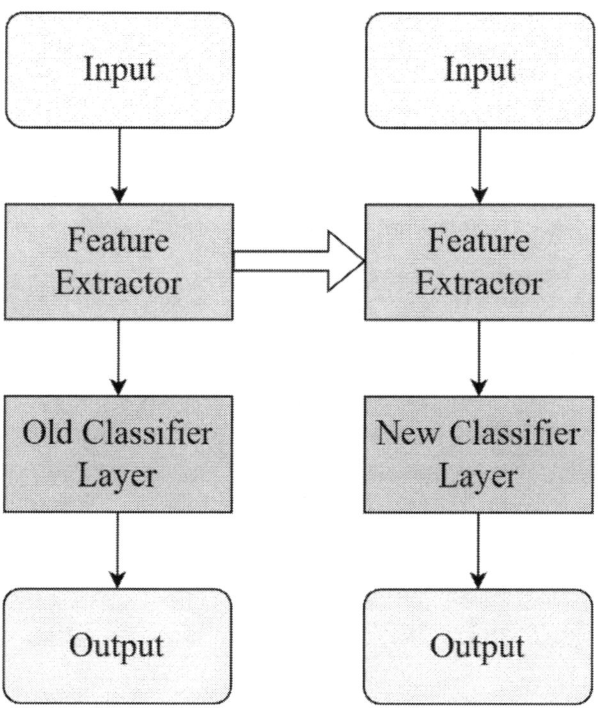

FIGURE 6.6 Transfer learning with common feature extractors. Only the classifier layer is updated or trained.

Key takeaways: Transfer learning enhances efficiency in medical imaging by leveraging pre-trained models, reducing training time, costs, and data requirements.

6.8 PIONEERING DEEP LEARNING IMAGE RECONSTRUCTION: A REAL-WORLD APPLICATION

MRI is a medical imaging technique that uses magnetic fields to create detailed images of tissues and organs. MRIs offer many advantages, but are vulnerable to parameter adjustments and long scan times. Thus, various AI models have been introduced to reconstruct images with improved resolutions and reduced noise, resulting in shorter scan times.

One such model is the Food and Drug Administration approved AIR Recon DL™, by GE Healthcare. The model uses a convolutional neural network to reconstruct images with reduced noise, truncated artefacts (undesirable distortions in scans), and a higher resolution. The reconstruction model benefits more than two million people globally [17] (Figure 6.7).

A study to compare this reconstruction model to standard MRI showed that the model produced images with higher overall quality. The scanning time with the model's usage was also lower compared to standard MRI. The model delivered similar diagnostic results too, enabling up to 50% time savings [18].

Thus, the model improves MRI efficiency. It reflects a broader trend in medical imaging where AI is not just experimental, but is an essential tool in optimizing workflows and clinical outcomes. Similar AI models have been brought to other applications, such as Siemens' FAST 3D camera, which automates precise patient positioning in CT [19], and MRCAT™ by Philips, which automatically generates synthetic CT images, saving on radiation doses and costs for additional CT scans [20].

Key takeaways: AIR Recon DL™ is a strong real-world application of AI in medical imaging, enhancing MRI quality, reducing scan time by up to 50%, and optimizing diagnostics.

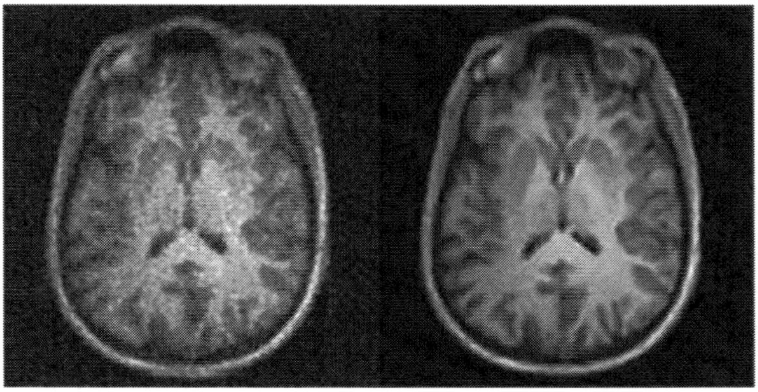

FIGURE 6.7 A reconstructed brain image (right) from the original (left). (Image by Athinoula A. Martinos Center for Biomedical Imaging, Massachusetts General Hospital.)

6.9 EXPLAINABLE AI IN MEDICINE AND REGULATORY ASPECTS

As outlined earlier, AI must be transparent, understandable, and should also mimic human judgment and skills. This is called explainable AI. Explainable AI allows users to understand why the model came up with the presented predictions. Even as AI becomes highly capable of outperforming humans, its lack of explainability has been criticized in medicine.

The need for Explainable AI in medicine can be summarized as follows [21]:

- Resolution of Disagreements: Disagreements between AI and human experts have higher chances of being resolved if AI is explainable.
- Strengthening Trust in AI: Explainable AI allows for informed decision-making, strengthening trust in AI.
- Shared Decision Making: Explainable AI allows shared decision making between human experts and patients. This helps patients understand medical facts, risks, and outcomes better.
- Personalized Conversation Aids: Explainable AI can provide human experts with conversation aids that are personalized to the patient's individual character.

Explainable AI also poses several legal and ethical dilemmas:

- Fairness: Explainable AI should treat everyone equally, without bias or discrimination.
- Sensitive Issues: Sensitive issues of data privacy and security, patient consent, and autonomy have to be considered by explainable AI.
- Value-Flexible AI: Explainable AI that provides different treatment options for patients, enhancing patient understanding.
- Adapting Regulations: Laws and their interpretation have to continuously adapt to evolving AI techniques.

To address the need for comprehensive laws that regulate AI, especially in the field of medicine, we provide key takeaways from the European Union's AI Act [22]. The following summary aims to provide a brief overview of these recent regulations in AI enacted in 2024, and their effect in medicine:

- Risk-Based Classification: Classifies AI systems into different categories based on their applications. For instance, medical devices are considered high-risk, while generative AI is considered general-purpose.
- Requirements for High-Risk AI Systems: These systems must include strict compliance with risk management, data governance, transparency, and human oversight.
- Incident Reporting: Developers of high-risk AI systems are required to set up mechanisms for reporting incidents and post-market monitoring.
- Existing Regulations: The AI Act intersects with existing regulations, such as EU MDR (Medical Devices Regulation) and GDPR (General Data Protection Regulation).

6.10 CHALLENGES

This chapter has presented several studies on applications of AI in medical imagery alongside their challenges. This section summarizes these challenges, including ethical and legal concerns, that must be solved to better healthcare services and outcomes.

- AI Must Be Explainable: Improving understanding of how models are trained, and how they make decisions and determine outcomes, builds trust in AI. In healthcare and medical imaging, this is essential as inaccurate predictions can carry severe consequences.
- AI Must Be Reliable: More and more research in medical imagery must be accompanied by clinical trials to ensure AI is reliable, while adhering to the best reference and reporting standards.
- AI on-Device: AI often requires expensive hardware for training and inferencing. Models must be optimized for on-device usage, as doing so carries several advantages like enhancing privacy and security, alongside quick and portable testing in healthcare.
- AI on Low-Data Modalities: Training models on low data is challenging, and this chapter has presented several technologies aimed at mitigating this, involving the use of GANs to generate synthetic data and applying transfer learning.
- Lack of Trustworthy AI Policies: All stakeholders, such as the government, technology companies, and the healthcare sector, must come together to create trustworthy AI policies and regulatory frameworks.

6.11 FUTURE SCOPE

AI in medical imaging holds immense potential for the future, which can be realized by addressing the challenges currently faced by all stakeholders. Below, we outline some of the key opportunities:

- Real-Time Decision Support: AI will enable real-time analysis of medical images captured during surgery and other procedures. This will allow healthcare professionals to have immediate access to critical information.
- Precision Medicine: AI can personalize treatment plans and prevention strategies for individual patients and their unique healthcare needs.
- Multi-Modal Integration: Future AI models will be capable of integrating data from multiple imaging modalities to provide a holistic view of a patient's health.
- Continual Learning: AI models will adapt and continuously learn to improve themselves over time. This will ensure models improve over past mistakes and improve their ability to handle emerging diseases.
- Rise of Publicly-Available Datasets: Multiple innovations in AI were driven with open challenges and datasets. These examples will allow a greater aggregation of data, which will result in better models.
- Treatment Planning: AI will be capable of analyzing multiple datasets to identify potential targets and improve treatment options.

6.12 CONCLUSION

This chapter has presented seven case studies, presenting specific approaches and models being used in AI for medical imaging, their applications, and challenges. This chapter emphasized the importance of open-source and transparent research in the field, with models such as YOLO, and also bolsters such approaches by showcasing contributions made by private corporations like Meta with SAM, which have revolutionized medical imagery by yielding a general model that performs well across multiple modalities, outperforming specialist models. We discuss GANs, state-of-the-art models that can synthesize medical imagery, yielding better datasets to further improve subsequent model training. Apart from exploring Generative AI and RAG, we also highlight the importance of explainable AI to ensure models are transparent and mimic human judgment and understanding.

The case studies also offer a comparison between AI models and healthcare professionals, highlighting several challenges that exist in the field when practical applications are concerned; alongside another study that compares on-device phone-powered models against professionals, showcasing the potential for portable diagnostic services. We also present a study on transfer learning in medical imaging, which shows how fine-tuning pre-trained models can outperform models trained from scratch, thereby saving computational costs and time. The last case study is on AIR Recon DL™, a strong real-world application of AI in medical imaging. This chapter briefly mentions other tools in the domain as well, that serve millions globally.

All the key takeaways from the case studies can be summarized as follows:

- Deep Learning in Healthcare: YOLO enabling tumour detection in medical images shows the improvements Deep Learning makes over traditional models.
- Medical Image Segmentation: SAM, an open-source model generalizes well across various imaging modalities, and outperforms specialist models.
- Generative Adversarial Networks (GANs): GANs can synthesize realistic medical images, improving dataset quality for training models.
- Visual Turing Tests and AI Performance: Deep Learning models' performance matches healthcare professionals, but requires rigorous validation and transparency.
- On-Device AI: AI models running on mobile phones enable real-time medical diagnostics, enhance accessibility and privacy, despite hardware limitations.
- Transfer Learning: Pre-trained models improve results on medical imaging tasks by reducing training costs and requirements.
- Real-World Applications: AI in medical imaging is not just experimental, but has strong real-world applications, serving millions of people globally.

Lastly, we discuss explainable AI and various legal and ethical considerations associated with it. We provide a brief overview of current regulations, in the form of EU's AI Act. We also discuss challenges in the applications of AI in medical imaging and the future scope for AI in this domain.

AI has revolutionized medical imaging, benefiting both patients and professionals while opening new frontiers in the field. Although several challenges exist, they will be overcome, leading to the development of even more advanced models and applications. As AI algorithms continue to evolve and adapt, they are poised to shape the future of medical imaging, ultimately delivering improved healthcare to the masses.

DISCLAIMER

None.

REFERENCES

1. Nature Cancer. A turing test for artificial intelligence in cancer (2020, February). *Nat. Cancer*, vol. 1, no. 2, pp. 137–138, doi: 10.1038/s43018-020-0041-7.
2. Sardar, T. H., Faizabadi, A. R., & Ansari, Z. (2017). An analysis of data processing using Mapreduce paradigm on the Hadoop framework. *Int. J. Emerg. Res. Manag. Technol*, vol. 6, no. 5, pp. 127–132.
3. Khatun, A., & Sardar, T. H. (2025). Cryptography algorithms to prevent different security attacks. In Amina Khatun, Tanvir Habib Sardar (eds) *Next Generation Mechanisms for Data Encryption* (pp. 35–46). CRC Press.
4. Sardar, T. H., Sarkar, R., Ahmed, S. J., & Bandyopadhyay, A. (2023, May). A novel ensemble methodology to validate fuzzy clusters of Big Data. In *Proceedings of the Fourth International Conference on Trends in Computational and Cognitive Engineering: TCCE 2022* (pp. 267–278). Springer Nature, Singapore.
5. Abdusalomov, A. B., Mukhiddinov, M., & Whangbo, T. K. (2023, January). Brain tumor detection based on deep learning approaches and magnetic resonance imaging. *Cancers*, vol. 15, no. 16, Art. no. 16, p. 4172, doi: 10.3390/cancers15164172.
6. Subbarao, E., et al. (2023). Investigation of solar energy for urban areas and metropolitan communities using machine learning. *Electr. Power Compon. Syst.*, vol. 05, pp. 1–11.
7. Sardar, T. H. (2024). Reflecting on a decade of evolution: MapReduce-based advances in partitioning-based, hierarchical-based, and density-based clustering (2013–2023). *Wiley Interdiscip. Rev.: Data Min. Knowl. Discov.*, vol. 14, no. 6, p. e1566.
8. Theerthagiri, P., Ruby, A. U., Chandran, J. G. C., Sardar, T. H., & Shafeeq, B. M. A. (2024). Deep SqueezeNet learning model for diagnosis and prediction of maize leaf diseases. *J. Big Data*, vol. 11, no. 1, p. 112.
9. Ma, J., He, Y., Li, F., Han, L., You, C., & Wang, B. (2024, January). Segment anything in medical images. *Nat. Commun.*, vol. 15, no. 1, p. 654, doi: 10.1038/s41467-024-44824-z.
10. Musalamadugu, T. S., & Kannan, H. (2023, September). Generative AI for medical imaging analysis and applications. *Future Med. AI*, vol. 1, no. 2, doi: 10.2217/fmai-2023-0004.
11. Skandarani, Y., Jodoin, P.-M., & Lalande, A. (2023, March). GANs for medical image synthesis: An empirical study. *J. Imaging*, vol. 9, no. 3, p. 69, Art. no. 3, doi: 10.3390/jimaging9030069.
12. Liu, X., et al. (2019, October). A comparison of deep learning performance against health-care professionals in detecting diseases from medical imaging: A systematic review and meta-analysis. *Lancet Digit. Health*, vol. 1, no. 6, pp. e271–e297, doi: 10.1016/S2589-7500(19)30123-2.

13. Dutta, K., Chandra, S., Gourisaria, M. K., & Harshvardhan, G. M. (2021, April). A data mining based target regression-oriented approach to modelling of health insurance claims. In *2021 5th International Conference on Computing Methodologies and Communication (ICCMC)* (pp. 1168–1175). IEEE, India.
14. Menzies, S. W., et al. (2023, October). Comparison of humans versus mobile phone-powered artificial intelligence for the diagnosis and management of pigmented skin cancer in secondary care: A multicentre, prospective, diagnostic, clinical trial. *Lancet Digit. Health*, vol. 5, no. 10, pp. e679–e691, doi: 10.1016/S2589-7500(23)00130-9.
15. Sarah, S., Singh, V., Gourisaria, M. K., & Singh, P. K. (2021, October). Retinal disease detection using CNN through optical coherence tomography images. In *2021 5th International Conference on Information Systems and Computer Networks (ISCON)* (pp. 1–7). IEEE, India.
16. Hazarika, R. A., Kandar, D., & Maji, A. K. (2022). A deep convolutional neural networks based approach for Alzheimer's disease and mild cognitive impairment classification using brain images. *IEEE Access*, vol. 10, pp. 99066–99076, doi: 10.1109/ACCESS.2022.3206389.
17. "A Bold New World: GE Healthcare's Pioneering Deep Learning Image Reconstruction Technology Benefits More Than 2 Million Patients Globally | GE HealthCare (United States)." Accessed: January 31, 2025. [Online]. Available: https://www.gehealthcare.com/about/newsroom/press-releases/a-bold-new-world-ge-healthcares-pioneering-deep-learning-image-reconstruction#_edn1.
18. Zerunian, M., et al. (2024). Fast high-quality MRI protocol of the lumbar spine with deep learning-based algorithm: An image quality and scanning time comparison with standard protocol. *Skeletal Radiol.*, vol. 53, no. 1, pp. 151–159, doi: 10.1007/s00256-023-04390-9.
19. "FAST 3D Camera for CT Patient Positioning - Siemens Healthineers India." Accessed: January 31, 2025. [Online]. Available: https://www.siemens-healthineers.com/en-in/computed-tomography/ct-technologies-and-innovations/fast-integrated-workflow.
20. "MR-only Simulation Unleash the Real Power of MR Simulation | Philips Healthcare." Accessed: January 31, 2025. [Online]. Available: https://www.philips.ie/healthcare/product/HCNMRF171/mr-only-simulation-unleash-the-real-power-of-mr-simulation.
21. Amann, J., Blasimme, A., Vayena, E., Frey, D., Madai, V. I., & the Precise4Q consortium (2020, November). Explainability for artificial intelligence in healthcare: A multidisciplinary perspective. *BMC Med. Inform. Decis. Mak.*, vol. 20, no. 1, p. 310, doi: 10.1186/s12911-020-01332-6.
22. Chandra, S., Gourisaria, M. K., Harshvardhan, G. M., Rautaray, S. S., Pandey, M., & Mohanty, S. N. (2021). Semantic analysis of sentiments through web-mined Twitter Corpus. In *International Symposium on Intelligent Control*, India (pp. 122–135).

7 Artificial Intelligence for Disease Prevention

From Diagnosis to Personalized Treatment

Shareefraza J. Ukkund, Thabshira Maryam, Asif Hassan, Munazza Begam, Nafeesa Rihana, Bhavna Alke, and Usman Taqui Syed

7.1 INTRODUCTION

7.1.1 Overview of Artificial Intelligence in Healthcare

Artificial Intelligence (AI) has made significant strides, becoming a transformative force across various industries. One of the most exciting areas for AI applications is healthcare, where advancements like Machine Learning (ML), natural language processing, and computer vision are enabling machines to take on more tasks with greater independence, using the data they gather to make informed decisions. Within healthcare, AI is being leveraged to improve diagnostic precision, simplify administrative processes, tailor treatment plans to individual needs, and ultimately enhance patient outcomes [1,2]. One of the most compelling areas where AI is making a significant impact is in the prevention and early detection of diseases. Traditionally, healthcare has been reactive, with patients seeking medical attention only after symptoms appear, often when the disease has already reached a more advanced stage [3]. This results in higher healthcare costs and worse outcomes, particularly for chronic conditions like cancer, cardiovascular disease, and neurological disorders. AI has the potential to change this model by providing predictive insights that can identify risks earlier, allowing for more proactive and preventive healthcare interventions [4].

The real strength of AI lies in its capacity to analyse vast amounts of data and uncover subtle patterns that might not be easily noticeable to healthcare professionals. ML algorithms can uncover disease markers by analysing extensive datasets, including genetic information, patient records, and medical images, which helps to facilitate earlier and more accurate diagnoses. AI-driven tools have been shown to match or even exceed the accuracy of human specialists in tasks such as detecting cancerous lesions in medical images, while also reducing false positives and false negatives [5,6]. This transition from a reactive to a predictive healthcare approach has the potential to enhance the efficiency of healthcare delivery, save lives, and lower costs.

DOI: 10.1201/9781003600947-7

7.1.2 Importance of Early Disease Detection and Prevention

The importance of early disease detection and prevention in healthcare cannot be overstated, as early diagnosis often leads to a broader range of effective treatment options, better prognosis, and lower treatment costs [3]. This is particularly crucial for conditions like cancer, where identifying the disease at an early stage greatly boosts the likelihood of successful treatment. For instance, detecting breast cancer early is linked to higher survival rates and less aggressive treatment options compared to later stages [6–9]. AI holds the potential to greatly improve early detection by providing better screening tools, advanced predictive models, and continuous monitoring, which could ultimately revolutionize patient outcomes [10,11]. The impact of AI and ML on detecting and diagnosing diseases at early stages is evident, as illustrated in Figure 7.1 [11].

Technological advancements have consistently improved the world, driving progress across various fields. Among these, nanotechnology stands out as a revolutionary force, significantly impacting sectors such as agriculture [12], environmental sustainability [13,14], the energy industry [15,16], and biomedicine [17,18]. In the biomedical field, the integration of nanotechnology with cutting-edge technologies like AI and ML is transforming healthcare. These innovative technologies are at the forefront of efforts to fight diseases, enabling early diagnosis and precision treatments. By combining the power of AI/ML with nanotechnology, we can expect significant progress in saving lives and improving global healthcare quality.

AI plays a crucial role in areas such as medical image analysis, where it has been shown to identify cancerous tissues in mammograms, CT scans, and MRIs with sensitivity and specificity often surpassing human radiologists [5]. This capability is vital for reducing missed diagnoses and unnecessary interventions, improving the effectiveness of screening programs. Additionally, AI can offer automated evaluations in low-resource settings, where access to trained specialists is limited, thus making quality healthcare more accessible [10].

Beyond imaging, AI is also essential in genomics and wearable health technologies, both of which are key to disease prevention. Genetic predisposition is a significant factor in many diseases, such as cardiovascular and neurological disorders.

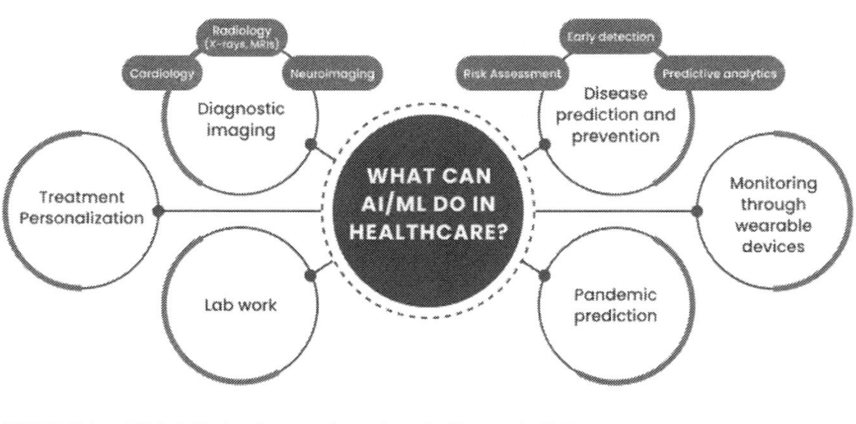

FIGURE 7.1 AI & ML in disease detection & diagnosis [11].

AI can analyse large genomic datasets to identify individuals at higher risk, paving the way for preventive strategies and personalized treatments [7,8]. Furthermore, AI-powered wearable devices enable real-time monitoring of health parameters like oxygen saturation, blood pressure, and heart rate [9]. By detecting anomalies early, these devices can prompt timely medical interventions, preventing the development of severe health complications.

7.1.3 Brief Introduction to the Diseases Covered in This Chapter

This chapter delves into how AI is revolutionizing the early detection and prevention of critical diseases, with a particular emphasis on cancer, cardiovascular conditions, and neurological disorders. Each of these diseases presents its own set of challenges when it comes to early identification and management, and AI has shown considerable promise in helping to overcome these difficulties.

Cardiovascular Diseases: The World Health Organization (WHO) reports that cardiovascular diseases (CVDs) are responsible for approximately 17.9 million deaths each year, making them the leading cause of death globally. AI is proving invaluable in identifying individuals at risk by analysing genetic data, imaging, and lifestyle factors [8]. AI-powered wearable devices can detect arrhythmias and other cardiac abnormalities at an early stage by continuously monitoring heart activity [9]. By providing real-time data, AI enables prompt medical attention and prevents serious cardiac events.

Diabetes: AI is transforming diabetes care, offering new tailored and accurate methods of early detection, monitoring, and treatments. The use of AI systems monitoring blood glucose levels real time and providing warnings in advance when this is likely to fluctuate so that patients are given sufficient opportunity for timely interventions. AI also helps in the early identification of complications such as diabetic retinopathy based on the analysis of a number of medical images and health data. There are further applications of AI in the enhancement of lifestyle management by tailoring dietary recommendations and using AI-based chatbots for counselling of patients on medication schedules and healthy lifestyles. This increases higher efficiency of diabetes care and enables the patient to take a more pro-active role in managing their condition [19].

Cancer: With an estimated 9.6 million deaths in 2018 alone, cancer has become the second leading cause of death globally. Early detection is crucial, as the survival rate for many types of cancer is significantly higher when diagnosed early. AI's capabilities in medical imaging analysis such as identifying malignant tumours in mammograms or CT scans are revolutionizing cancer screening [5,6]. AI algorithms have shown exceptional accuracy in detecting early-stage cancer, minimizing false positives and enabling more targeted and effective interventions.

Infectious Diseases: AI systems are playing a critical role in the rapid and accurate diagnosis of respiratory conditions, ensuring timely interventions and enabling personalized treatment plans. Beyond diagnosis, AI's capabilities extend to prognosis and treatment planning as well [1].

AI techniques have significantly advanced the understanding, detection, diagnosis, and treatment of various viruses and diseases. They have also been instrumental in drug development, analysing diverse data types, including images and textual data, and processing clinical, pathological, and genomic information. Furthermore, AI has enhanced intervention and management strategies, making a substantial impact in addressing issues related to information disorder and misinformation surrounding the SARS-CoV-2 virus, COVID-19 disease, and the pandemic [20].

7.2 AI IN CARDIOVASCULAR DISEASE

AI is transforming cardiovascular medicine by improving diagnosis, treatment, and patient care. AI algorithms sift through huge amounts of healthcare data to identify novel genotypes and phenotypes, enhance disease stratification, and predict outcomes for various cardiovascular diseases (CVDs). ML applications have already made strides in managing conditions like heart failure, atrial fibrillation and coronary artery disease [21]. These AI tools automate cardiac measurements, uncover hidden cardiac diseases, and enhance clinical decision-making. By enabling precision medicine, AI has the potential to reduce readmission and mortality rates. However, challenges remain particularly the need for extensive external validation through multicentre, prospective clinical trials. Despite these hurdles, AI holds tremendous potential to revolutionize cardiovascular care and in turn patient management [22].

7.2.1 Early Detection Technologies

Cardiovascular diseases (CVD) remain the top cause of illness and death worldwide, despite significant progress in diagnostic and treatment methods. AI technologies such as Deep Learning (DL), ML, and cognitive computing hold great promise for improving the early detection and diagnosis of CVD [21]. The interplay between rapid economic development, environmental shifts, unhealthy lifestyle choices, and an ageing population can significantly increase the risk of CVD in developing countries. For clinicians, AI facilitates efficient data collection, integrates seamlessly with electronic medical record systems, and reduces administrative burdens, allowing healthcare providers to focus more on delivering quality patient care [22]. AI-based applications are playing a transformative role in the field of cardiology, particularly in enhancing our understanding of various phenotypes including imaging, genomic, and clinical data, to identify distinct reasons for heart failure and congenital heart disease. This understanding is crucial for developing new treatment strategies and approaches to cardiovascular drug therapy. Moreover, AI enhances post-marketing surveillance of prescription drugs, ensuring continued safety and efficacy in the use of cardiovascular medications [23]. AI algorithms, particularly in the context of healthcare, primarily rely on large datasets to learn patterns and make predictions. While this data-driven approach can yield significant insights, its effectiveness can be enhanced by integrating biophysical models of the heart [24]. ML, a subset of AI, is being highly used in various fields of cardiology because it is able to extract meaningful information even by analysing a huge dataset [25,26].

7.2.1.1 Wearable Devices and Remote Monitoring

Heart failure exacerbations can lead to severe health issues and hospitalizations, making accurate forecasting critical for patient management. Studies with significant improvement are depicted in Figure 7.2 below [21].

Vectorious Medical Technologies has developed V-LAP™, the world's first battery-less, wireless microcomputer, designed to revolutionize cardiac monitoring for heart failure patients. As depicted in Figure 7.3, V-LAP™ tracks left atrial pressure (LAP) as part of the heart failure management sequence. Using advanced AI algorithms, the device analyses LAP trends in real-time, identifying subtle changes that may signal impending heart failure exacerbations. This early detection allows for proactive interventions and timely treatment adjustments, improving patient outcomes. V-LAP™ supports a comprehensive monitoring system, reducing complications and enhancing quality of life by enabling earlier and more precise management of heart failure [21].

Meanwhile, Sensible Medical Innovations Ltd., based in Netanya, Israel, has developed ReDS™ (Remote Dielectric Sensing), a wearable, non-invasive device for monitoring lung fluid concentration, crucial in managing acute heart failure. This technology enhances hemodynamic monitoring, as shown in Figure 7.3, where ReDS™ plays a vital role in tracking lung fluid. In clinical studies, ReDS™ was compared to high-resolution chest CT scans, which are accurate but involve radiation exposure and are used in acute settings. ReDS™ offers a safer, more practical alternative, improving patient monitoring and preventing complications from fluid overload. It aligns seamlessly with advanced heart failure management systems, emphasizing real-time, non-invasive solutions [21].

Furthermore, the LINK-HF study is a significant research initiative that highlights the application of ML in predicting heart failure exacerbations using data from a wearable device called VitalPatch®. As shown in the Figure 7.3, the LINK-HF study demonstrates the sequence of heart failure monitoring, starting from data collection by the VitalPatch® device, data upload via a smartphone, analysis through a cloud platform using ML, and subsequent hemodynamic and pressure monitoring, culminating in AI-driven early intervention.

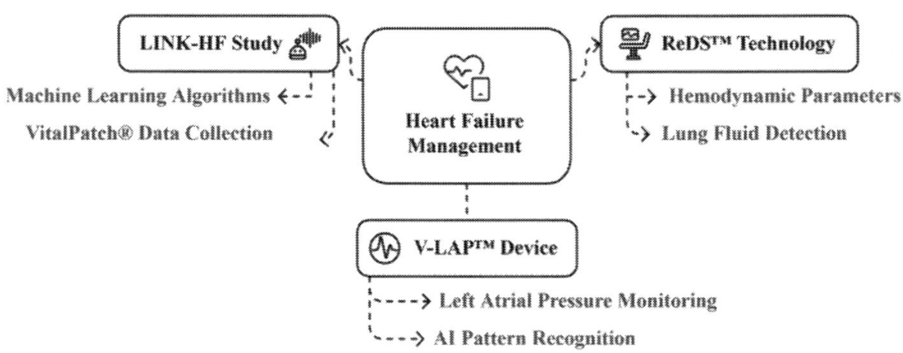

FIGURE 7.2 Various studies to monitor Heart failure.

IoT medical application consists of three interconnected layers: the sensing layer, which collects health data through various sensors; the transport layer, which ensures secure and reliable communication of that data; and the application layer, which processes, analyses, and presents the information to healthcare providers and patients as depicted in Figure 7.3. Together, these layers facilitate continuous monitoring and management of health conditions, which results in improved patient care [27].

7.2.1.2 AI Algorithm for ECG Analysis

An Electrocardiogram (ECG) records the heart's electrical activity through multiple heart cycles, each consisting of P, QRS, and T waves as displayed in Figure 7.4. The P wave represents atrial contraction, while the QRS complex reflects ventricular depolarization, which leads to ventricular contraction. The T wave depicts the ventricular repolarization, or the heart preparing for the next beat. Key intervals like the PR interval, QRS complex, and QT interval help assess the electrical conduction from the heart's pacemaker (SA node) to the ventricles. Analysing these waves and intervals allows clinicians to evaluate heart health and detect abnormalities in rhythm or function [28].

Serhani et al. conducted a study that reviewed various ECG monitoring systems, focusing on how these systems process and analyse the ECG signal. Initially, preprocessing techniques such as Fast Fourier Transform (FFT) and wavelet transformation are applied to clean and prepare the raw ECG data for further analysis. These techniques help filter out noise and enhance the signal, ensuring more accurate interpretation. Traditional ML approaches, such as Support Vector Machines (SVM), rely on manually extracting specific features from ECG signals, like heart rate variability and distinct wave patterns, to evaluate heart health. SVM is commonly used in ECG analysis to classify heartbeats and detect arrhythmias. On the other hand, DL models,

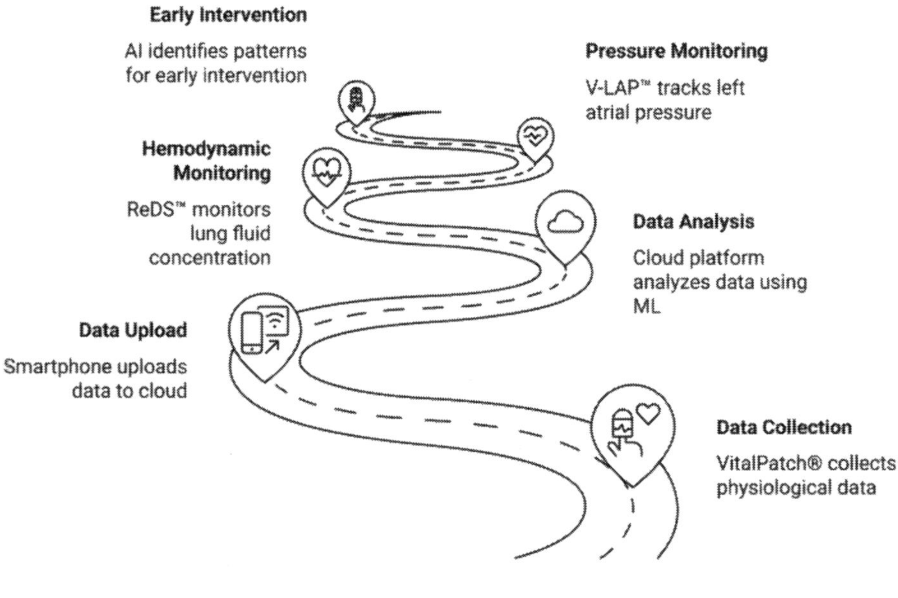

FIGURE 7.3 Heart failure monitoring and management sequence.

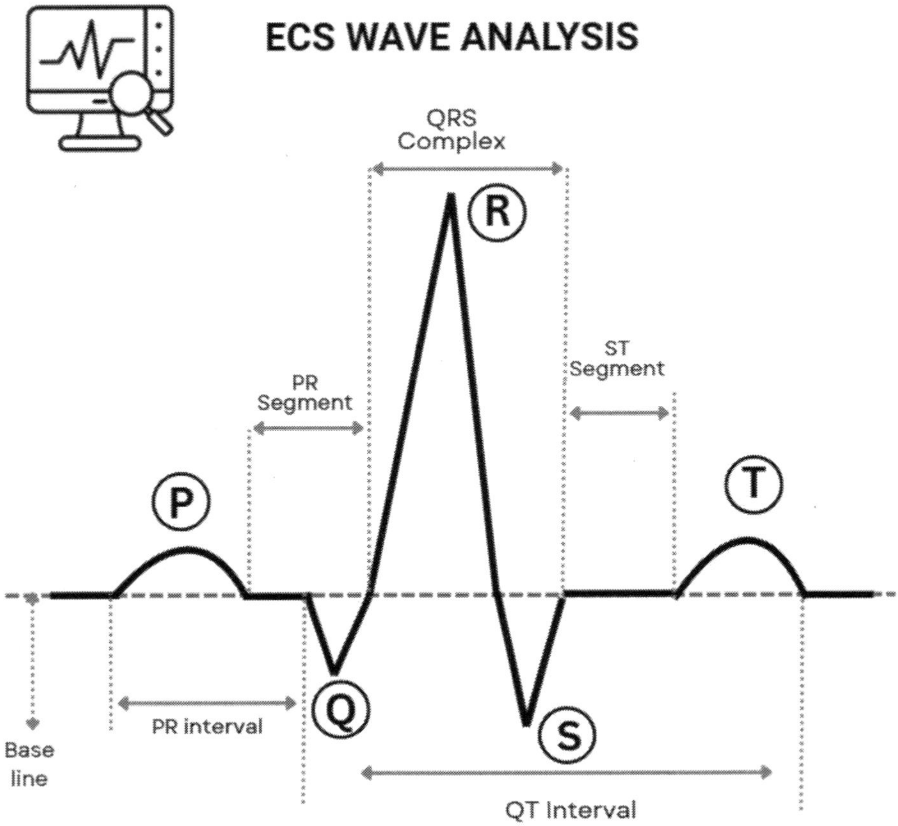

FIGURE 7.4 An electrocardiogram (ECG).

such as Convolutional Neural Networks (CNNs) and Recurrent Neural Networks (RNNs), have the advantage of automatically learning these features, which makes them more effective for ECG monitoring systems [28].

In 2021, the introduction of transformer models with self-attention mechanisms revolutionized various fields, like computer vision and natural language processing (NLP). This innovative approach was applied to ECG analysis for the first time, demonstrating remarkable efficiency with an accuracy of 95%—a performance level comparable to existing models in the field. Additionally, the integration of Generative Adversarial Networks (GANs) with DL models marked a significant advancement in ECG analysis. GANs, designed for generating synthetic samples, help in augmenting datasets, particularly when the available ECG data is limited [28]. Table 7.1 details other studies using ML to study ECG.

Another study described an AI algorithm based on DL. The Deep Learning Architecture (DLA) described is designed to process complex ECG data and learn intricate hierarchical representations through multiple hidden layers of neurons. This study is the first to create and validate a Deep Learning Algorithm (DLA) designed to predict cardiac arrest using ECGs. It highlights how DL, a key aspect of AI, can identify subtle changes in ECG readings that signal the onset of cardiac arrest. The AI algorithm demonstrated high accuracy in predicting cardiac arrest from both 12-lead and single-lead ECGs. These results suggest the potential for screening and predicting cardiac arrest using traditional 12-lead ECGs as well as single-lead ECGs from wearable devices that integrate AI algorithms. The primary focus of this study was to predict cardiac arrest, which was specifically defined as the absence of a detectable pulse, regardless of whether resuscitation efforts were made. To ascertain the exact timing of each cardiac arrest event, researchers reviewed electronic health records (EHRs) [29]. There are various studies to study ECG data using ML, which are listed in Table 7.1.

The DLA aimed to determine the prediction window of the ECG for cardiac arrest, which was defined as the 24-hour period leading up to the event. In the study, ECGs recorded within a 24-hour window leading up to a cardiac arrest were labelled as "cardiac arrest," while those taken outside this window were categorized as "non-event." For patients who did not experience a cardiac arrest, their ECGs were also marked as "nonevent." The main goal was to accurately identify whether each ECG indicated an impending cardiac arrest or not. This classification is critical for recognizing patients who are at risk, allowing for early intervention to potentially prevent a cardiac arrest. Ultimately, the study emphasizes the importance of using ECG data in predicting and managing cardiac events, helping healthcare providers take proactive steps to improve patient outcomes [29].

TABLE 7.1
Other Studies Using Machine Learning to Study ECG

Study	Algorithms Used	PubMed ID	Year	Ref.
A Model to Predict Personalized Warfarin Doses for Patients after Heart Valve Replacement Surgery	BPNN model – Back propagation neural network model	31586305	2020	[30]
Screening for Cardiac Contractile Dysfunction Using an AI-Enhanced Electrocardiogram	*CNN-Convolution neural network*	30617318	2019	[31]
A New Non-Invasive Diagnostic Tool for Coronary Artery Disease: The Impact of Artificial Intelligence on Predictive, Preventive, and Personalized Medicine	*MPA -Mimetic pattern-based algorithm*	30174760	2018	[32,33]
Machine Learning Surpasses the ACC/AHA Cardiovascular Risk Calculator in the MESA Study	*Support vector machine*	30571498	2018	[34]
Automating Morphological and Functional Assessments in 2D Echocardiography with Machine Learning	*Random forest, support vector machines and ANN-Artificial neural network*	27884247	2016	[28]

7.2.2 Risk Prediction Models

Risk prediction methods in healthcare, particularly those that use advanced algorithms, are becoming increasingly valued for their ability to improve decision-making and patient care management. Once these models are trained, they can be applied to large patient populations, helping to predict outcomes across diverse groups more efficiently. The success of these predictive models depends on several important factors, such as the variety and richness of the data, the specific tasks they are designed to handle, and the methods used to select and analyse the relevant features of the data [29].

7.2.2.1 ML for Risk Stratification

A risk prediction model is an essential tool in healthcare, used to estimate the likelihood of a disease outcome based on an individual's unique characteristics, often referred to as predictors or risk factors. One of the key metrics for evaluating these models is the AUC-ROC (Area Under the Receiver Operating Characteristic Curve), which ensures the model effectively differentiates between patients with and without the disease. This, in turn, supports better clinical decision-making and improves patient care. The ROC curve is crucial for assessing a model's diagnostic accuracy, as it plots the true positive rate (sensitivity) against the false positive rate (1 - specificity) across different threshold settings. The AUC is especially useful because it provides an overall measure of a model's ability to discriminate across all possible thresholds, rather than relying on a single cut-off. It also allows for comparisons between different models to see which one predicts the outcome most accurately. However, recent studies have pointed out that this method has its limitations and should not be the sole approach for evaluating the effectiveness of a new marker in clinical and epidemiological research [35].

The Framingham Study is a landmark research initiative that significantly advanced understanding of CVD risk factors. A key aspect of this research involved the creation of a "multi-marker" risk model, which integrates the contributions of multiple genetic markers to provide a more comprehensive evaluation of CVD risk. Specifically, this model evaluates the combined effects of ten genetic markers, including indicators like C-reactive protein (CRP) and B-type natriuretic peptide (BNP) [35]. The various Global Cardiovascular risk management models are represented in Figure 7.5.

In addition to patient history, comorbidities and smoking, ethnicity, age and gender have been found to be crucial in predicting the risk of CVD. In diabetic patients, albuminuria, glycated haemoglobin (HbA1c), and age were the factors associated with CVD predictors. A person's lifestyle seems to be one of the major factors in prognostic measures. Protection of privacy, data security, standardizing ML, and data sharing guidelines seem to be some of the major challenges to ML. There is a possibility that molecular profiling components or pan-omics components could be injected to increase the prediction and signature-based diagnostic tools towards future precision medicine [36]. ML can help identify new genotypes and phenotypes for various cardiovascular diseases (CVDs), as well as uncover novel risk factors. By applying advanced techniques like DL and Artificial Neural Networks (ANN), we

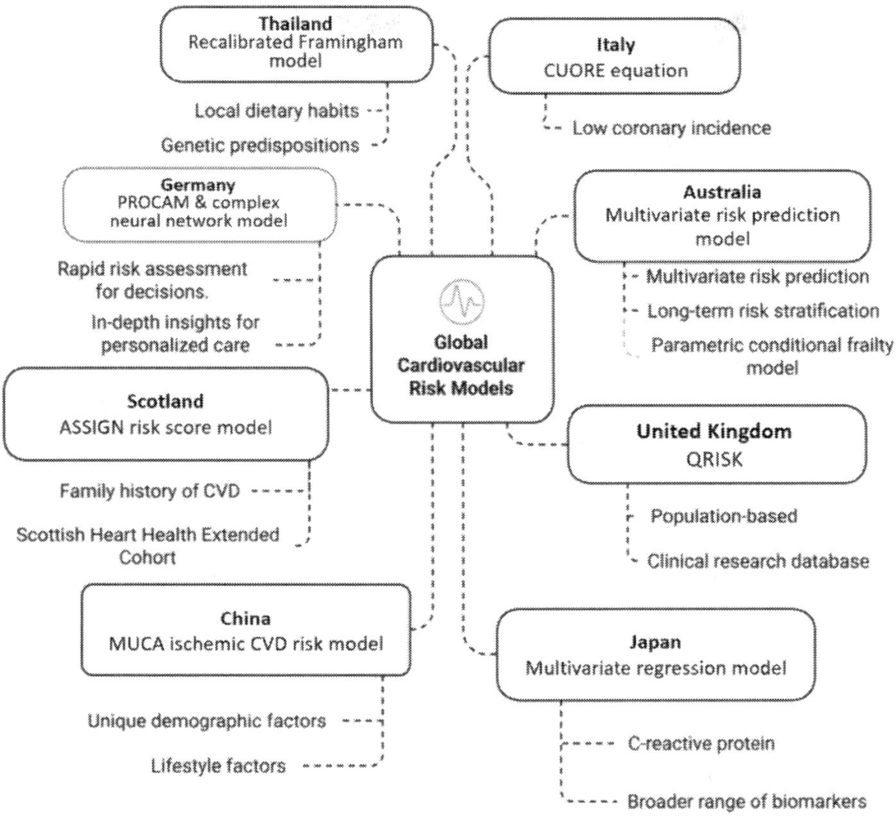

FIGURE 7.5 Global cardiovascular risk management models.

can enhance medical image recognition, improve diagnosis, predict outcomes more accurately, and better evaluate prognosis in CVD [37].

7.2.2.2 Integration of Patient Data (Genetics, Lifestyle, etc.)

According to the study, Metabolomics can be deemed to be a powerful tool with which to identify biomarkers and mechanisms of CVD, especially when integrated with genomics and other omics platforms. Integrated multiple omics types, including genomics, epigenomics, transcriptomics, metabolomics, proteomics, and microbiomics depict the mechanisms of CVD better. This multidimensional approach in combination with AI and ML is paving the way for personalized lifestyle medicine in cardiology. These developments promise to further our knowledge of CVD as well as prevent and better treat it according to what each individual actually requires [38].

Whole-genome sequencing studies and hypothesis-generating GWASs (genome-wide association studies) can identify genes having unknown or unsuspected roles in CVD. Novel genomic determinants of CVDs have been discovered due to different approaches such as whole-genome sequencing and GWASs. The SNPs associated with dichotomous (case-control) or continuous traits in the genome were analysed by GWASs. By successfully identifying the locus on 9p21 chromosome, the genetic underpinnings of myocardial infarction (MI) and other clinical CADs were indicated by GWASs. Stroke, platelet reactivity, intracranial aneurysms, and abdominal aortic are some of the vascular traits and diseases that are associated with the 9p21 locus. Recent studies have identified novel loci by GWASs of ischemic stroke. These loci have not been reported by GWASs of other CVDs. Common variation in HDAC9 has been implicated in large-vessel atherosclerotic stroke. Variants in mitochondrial DNA have also been proven to be related with stroke risk [38]. The issue of "missing heritability" was exhibited by lipid phenotypes also. The missing heritability was concluded to be a paradigmatic issue and not a simple methodology problem, depending on the lipid GWASs data. The associations of genes with products having a role in lipid metabolism was reassuring [38].

7.2.3 Personalized Prevention Strategies

Personalized prevention strategies have an exciting future for improved CVD outcomes; however, their implementation remains problematic. New developments in predictive, preventive, and personalized medicine are also underway, such as the synergism of more contemporary Western medicine with more holistic methods. Recently, AI-based tools can detect risk-prone patients through continuous monitoring in real-time for risk factors and facilitate personalization interventions [39].

7.2.3.1 Tailoring Interventions Based on AI Insights

Proper implementation of personalized prevention in health care practice requires improved understanding on the part of health professionals of personalized concepts and technologies. In cardiology, for instance, AI algorithms, like Convolutional Neural Networks (CNN), transformed the way diagnostics were interpreted in medical images like cardiac MRI, CT scans, and echocardiograms [40]. Figure 7.6 gives an overall idea of the integration of AI in cardiovascular health.

AI has also made excellent promise for personalizing the treatments of cardiovascular diseases for each unique patient profile, ranging from genetic parameters to medical histories and therapeutic responses. Research has also used AI to predict statin response through ML and identify genetic and clinical profiles. One of the impressive applications of AI is in a catheterization laboratory. There, a spoken command could be given to the technical operator performing coronary angiography, indicating the number of degrees by which the C-arm of the machine should turn. It can also track the ideal angle for a patient based on other needs such as their weight and height. In performing some procedures such as TAVR, AI can remark valve locations and sizes saving time while conducting these procedures and probably complications hence making the process easier for healthcare providers to bring personified care strategies [40].

7.2.3.2 Patient Engagement Through AI-driven Apps

AI-based smartphone applications have the potential to enhance engagement and better outcomes in CVD management. From user research, it can be deduced which features are needed by patients and doctors-including communication channels,

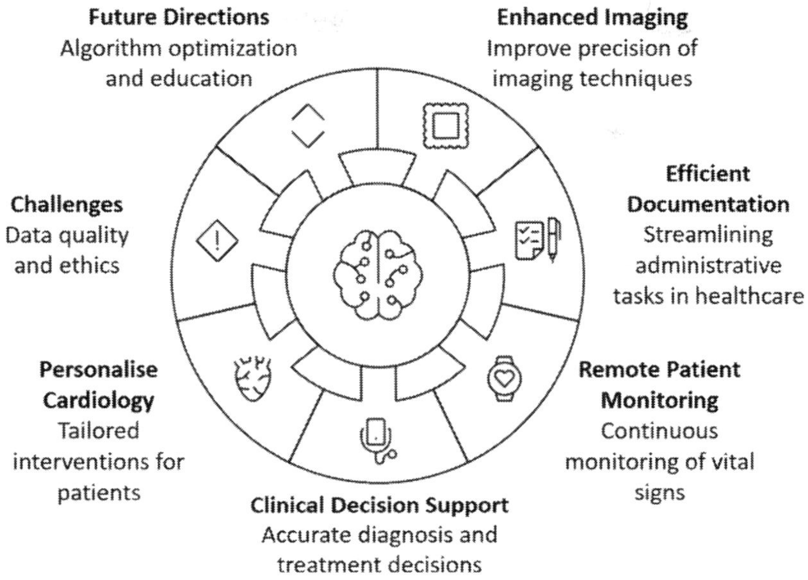

FIGURE 7.6 Applications of integration of AI in cardiovascular healthcare

self-risk assessment, and health status tracking [31]. The prevalence of CVDs has been on an upward trend due to ageing populations, urbanization, increasing sedentary lifestyles, and other risk factors including obesity, diabetes, and hypertension. The future of this discipline therefore lies in ensuring the promotion of interdisciplinary collaboration between healthcare professionals, data scientists, engineers, and other relevant stakeholders in their effective usage and appropriation of the potential of AI in cardiovascular medicine [34].

Factors that were better for app users were re-hospitalization rates, body mass index, blood pressure, cholesterol, disease-specific knowledge, exercise capacity, psychosocial well-being, quality of life, and waist circumference. Other features also typical of app users were increased physical activity and adherence to drugs as well as smoking cessation. The appealing features of the apps included tracking healthy behaviours, self-monitoring, educational information about the disease and content personalized and customized Mobile health is considered to be a subfield of eHealth. Such apps help patients to ensure the management of BP, control of blood glucose levels, improved physical activity and the achievement of healthful weight [21].

The positive and negative points of AI need to be highlighted in cardiology. For instance, language models, can help medical doctors reduce the number of possible diagnoses and suggest treatments. Language models are capable of processing huge data sets at the same time and efficiently determine the associations and give insightful information. AI capabilities can then enable healthcare providers to become more productive. Again, however, AI should not replace healthcare professionals. The best care for patients would still require clinical judgment and the human touch. With these positives of language models, there are also several pitfalls and limitations associated with them. These pitfalls should be well considered so that language models can be applied safely and effectively in cardiology [30,41].

AI's impact on healthcare goes far beyond heart health; it's also transforming how we manage chronic conditions like diabetes. Just as smart devices and AI-powered tools help detect heart problems early, similar innovations are making it easier for people with diabetes to monitor their blood sugar levels and catch complications before they become serious. By analysing everything from lifestyle habits to genetic risks, AI provides a more complete picture of a person's health, helping doctors and patients make better decisions. Moving from cardiovascular health to diabetes, we see a common theme: AI is shifting healthcare from a reactive approach to a proactive one, making early detection and prevention more effective than ever.

7.3 DIABETES AND ITS COMPLICATIONS EARLY DETECTION

7.3.1 AI in Blood Glucose Monitoring

AI has transformed glucose monitoring in diabetes management, providing non-invasive alternatives to traditional finger-prick blood tests, which are often painful and discourage compliance. AI-based systems on continuous glucose monitoring (CGM) now offer a more accurate and user-friendly experience, improving the quality of care. For instance, a pilot study showed that an AI-driven wrist-worn, non-invasive glucose monitor achieved a mean absolute relative difference (MARD) of 10.3% compared to commercial alternatives [19,42]. Non-invasive techniques, such as spectroscopy and microwave biosensors, detect glucose through skin characteristics, allowing for painless monitoring [43].

In addition to monitoring, AI-driven predictive models are advancing glucose level prediction. One autoregressive model of the ARX form was developed to incorporate exogenous inputs such as blood pressure, total cholesterol, and CGM data, proving to be a superior predictor with lower errors, improved mean absolute error, root-mean-square error, and coefficient of determination (R^2) as mentioned in Table 7.2 [19]. When tested on data from 442 diabetic patients, this model outperformed traditional ones, aiding in the proactive management of hyper- or hypoglycaemic events. The study recommended integrating genetic and lifestyle data for further accuracy improvements, underscoring AI's growing role in diabetes care [19].

AI-driven glucose monitoring systems hold great promise for simplifying diabetes management through non-invasive, predictive technologies. However, they face challenges such as sensitivity to skin tone, ambient light, motion artefacts, and

TABLE 7.2
Performance Metrics Comparison of ARX vs. Traditional Models

Model Type	Mean Absolute Error (MAE)	Root Mean Square Error (RMSE)	Coefficient of Determination (R^2)
ARX Model	Lower (e.g., 0.5)	Lower (e.g., 0.6)	Higher (e.g., 0.92)
Traditional Model	Higher (e.g., 0.8)	Higher (e.g., 1.2)	Lower (e.g., 0.85)

high costs, limiting accessibility for many patients. These systems require extensive calibration and validation across diverse populations to ensure accuracy and reliability, alongside clinical validation and regulatory approval for broader adoption [43]. Nonetheless, AI-based glucose prediction models and non-invasive monitoring approaches show potential for a proactive approach to diabetes care, offering patients a better quality of life without frequent finger pricks, with ongoing research focused on overcoming these barriers and making the technology more affordable [43].

7.3.1.1 Continuous Glucose Monitors and Predictive Analytics

Continuous Glucose Monitors (CGMs) have proved to be revolutionary in diabetes care by providing real-time glucose tracking. With advancements in ML, predictive analytics in CGMs now forecast future glucose levels, enabling proactive and personalized management as described in Figure 7.7 [44].

GlucoNet Pro, developed in 2023, combines models like RNNs, LSTMs, and XGBoost to analyse glucose patterns and factor in meals and insulin, resulting in timely alerts that enhance diabetes management [45]. GluNet, introduced in 2020, focuses on short-term glucose predictions (30–60 minutes) for Type 1 diabetes, using DL to analyse past glucose, meal, and insulin data, outperforming older models and adapting well to individual needs [42,46]. The ARX Model, integrating blood pressure and cholesterol with CGM data, showed improved prediction accuracy in a 2017 study involving 442 participants [43,47]. These systems are reshaping diabetes management, empowering patients for healthier lives [46].

7.3.1.2 Systems for Hypoglycaemia and Hyperglycaemia Alert

Hypoglycaemia (low blood sugar) and hyperglycaemia (high blood sugar) are conditions of abnormal blood sugar levels, leading to symptoms like dizziness, weakness, and sweating in hypoglycaemia, and thirst, frequent urination, and fatigue

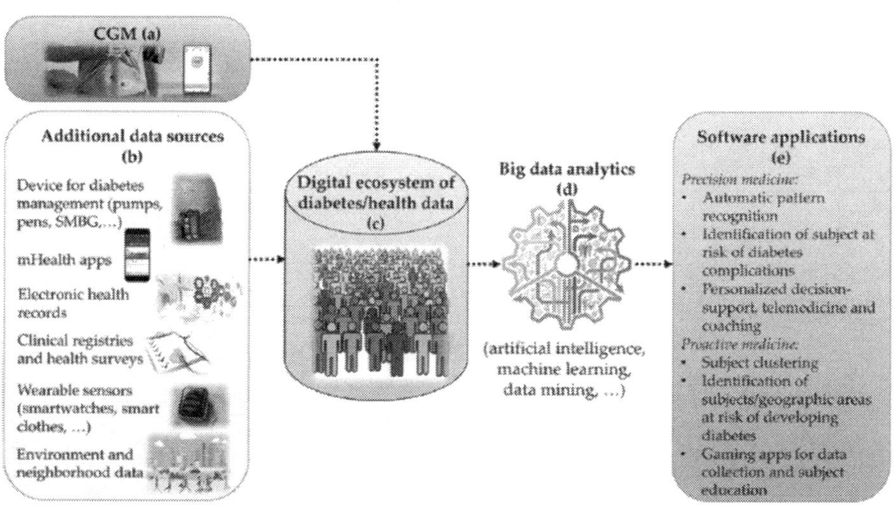

FIGURE 7.7 Different sources of data (a) integrated with CGM data, (b) creating a digital ecosystem of diabetes and health data and (c) applications based on big data analytics [44].

in hyperglycaemia. Both conditions can pose significant risks for Type 1 Diabetes Mellitus (T1DM) patients, especially those on Sensor-Augmented Pump (SAP) therapy, where early detection of these events is crucial for patient safety.

In this field, Daskalaki et al. introduced a hybrid Early Warning System (EWS) model, combining ARX and RNN models into a cARN system with an output correction module called CARX, achieving 100% prediction accuracy with detection times of 16.7 minutes for hypoglycaemia and 14.7 minutes for hyperglycaemia, and an average of 0.8 false alarms per day. The inclusion of RNN models further reduced false alarms and improved reliability [48]. Building on this, Botwey et al. evaluated multi-model data fusion techniques to enhance EWS performance using Genetic Programming (GP), Genetic Algorithms (GA), and Dempster-Shafer Evidential Theory (DST). These fusion methods improved accuracy and reduced false alarms, achieving median detection times of 13.0 minutes for hypoglycaemia and 12.1 minutes for hyperglycaemia with a daily false alarm rate of only 0.25% [49].

These early warning systems provide promising advancements in T1DM care by detecting glycaemic events early. While many models are computational, Turksoy et al. developed patient-specific recursive linear time series models, yielding high performance in hypoglycaemia prevention [50].

7.3.2 Detection of Complications

Diabetes is a complex metabolic disease affecting organs like the heart, kidneys, eyes, and nerves, making early detection and treatment vital for improved long-term outcomes. Common complications include heart disease, retinopathy, diabetic foot, neuropathy, and nephropathy, all requiring accurate predictive and diagnostic tools, which ML has increasingly enhanced [51].

Saeed Farzi et al. utilized ML algorithms on a new dataset to predict major complications in Type 2 diabetes patients [46]. Their study evaluated various classification algorithms, finding that Random Forest yielded the best results, while Naïve Bayes had the lowest performance. These predictive models are valuable for healthcare professionals, as they can identify complications early, often before symptoms emerge [51]. Emerging non-invasive technologies, as discussed by Choda and Rao, provide new possibilities for early detection of diabetic complications, including neuropathy, nephropathy, retinopathy, and cardiovascular issues. Imaging technologies, sensors, and wearable devices enable early diagnoses, allowing for timely interventions that reduce the complication burden [52]. Targeted interventions are also essential; for example, laser photocoagulation is used for retinopathy, blood pressure control for nephropathy, and pressure-reducing devices for diabetic foot ulcers. Such early and focused strategies can significantly reduce the risk of long-term complications [53].

7.3.2.1 AI for Diabetic Retinopathy Screening

Diabetic retinopathy (DR) is a leading cause of preventable blindness in diabetic patients, making early screening critical to prevent vision loss. Traditional DR screening is resource-intensive, but AI has significantly enhanced its efficiency and accuracy. Notable AI systems like IDx-DR, which combines deep neural networks, achieve high sensitivity and specificity for DR detection, while Selena screens for

DR, age-related macular degeneration, and suspected glaucoma. Smartphone-based solutions like Medios AI and deep-learning systems such as RetmarkerDR and EyeArt have improved screening accessibility and accuracy by over 80% in some trials [53,54].

These AI-driven advancements reduce the labour needed for DR screening, streamlining diagnosis and improving care delivery. However, real-world AI adoption still faces challenges, including integration with healthcare systems and data privacy concerns. Despite these, AI is well-positioned to expand DR screening coverage and provide timely referrals, addressing the growing diabetic eye care burden [53].

7.3.2.2 Cardiovascular Risk Prediction in Diabetic Patients

Cardiovascular complications contribute immensely to mortality among patients who have type 2 diabetes. Reliable risk prediction is critical for the application of early interventions and targeted management plans. Although numerous models of cardiovascular risk prediction exist, most of them suffer from faulty methodology and validation.

This complication was found to be the most common among cardiovascular diseases for diabetic patients and therefore required a very strong risk prediction to ensure proper management and prevention. The use of Random Forest and feature selection techniques within ML models has proven to be very useful for predictive purposes in determining CVD with Glycohemoglobin, basophil count, triglyceride level, and body mass index emerged as key predictors [54]. A separate diabetes-specific CVD risk equation that includes factors such as A1C, duration of diabetes, and clinical characteristics has also been developed, which better refines the accuracy of prediction [54].

Various cardiovascular risk prediction models for diabetic patients have been identified, along with several key challenges:

- Methodological Issues: Most models lack validation and fail to generalize across populations.
- Lack of External Validation: Many models are not tested with independent datasets, undermining their real-world applicability.
- Bias and Applicability: The use of CHARMS and PROBAST revealed significant bias risks, often stemming from poor development practices.

ML and AI show promise in this area:

- Neural Networks and Deep Learning: These methods extract patterns from both unstructured data (like images) and structured data (like medical records), effectively handling large, diverse datasets essential for diabetes care.
- Personalization: AI predictions can be tailored to individual differences, including glucose levels, blood pressure, and lifestyle factors.
- Continuous Monitoring: AI models integrated with devices such as continuous glucose monitors enable real-time monitoring, allowing for early detection of cardiovascular risks.

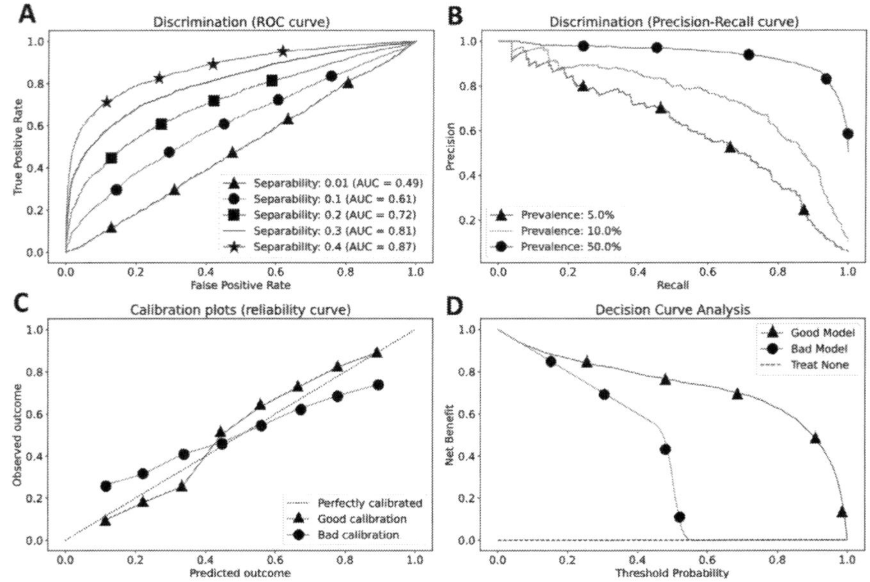

FIGURE 7.8 Model performance evaluation: Discrimination, calibration, and decision curve analysis for cardiovascular risk prediction in diabetic patients. (Adopted from [55].)

A good predictive model can be evaluated by three critical concepts: discrimination, calibration, and net clinical benefit as mentioned in Figure 7.8.

The ROC curve in Figure 7.8a demonstrates the trade-off between sensitivity and specificity at different thresholds; it presents a measure of how well the classes are separable based on the model. The value of AUROC measures the ability of the model to distinguish between classes and the closer it is to one, the better it can distinguish. The Precision-Recall Curve (Figure 7.8b) exhibits how the performance of the model varies with the prevalence of the label and indicates that models with the same AUROC can perform quite differently as the prevalence drops from 50% to 5%.

Calibration: Here, the reliability curve (Figure 7.8c) shows to what extent the predicted probabilities align with the actual outcomes measured. A well-calibrated model is represented by a line with triangles that well predicts almost real results. A poor calibration is indicated by the line with circles, which over- or under-predicts these results.

Net Clinical Benefit: Decision Curve Analysis (Figure 7.8d) is a set of models to compare the standard of care, comparing the clinical consequences and benefits at different risk levels. Thus, a model that maximizes net benefit across a range of thresholds (line with triangles) and a model with poor net benefit (line with circles).

Data-driven models, such as linear regression, have played a very significant role in predicting the ten-year CVD risk, and results showed that age was the highest predictor in all the models [2]. Other major predictors for diabetic subjects include eosinophil count and GGT, which result in a strong correlation with the risk for CVD [19,42]. These tools help physicians to intervene, such as lifestyle modification and pharmacologic treatments, towards the appropriate management of cardiovascular risks in diabetic patients [56].

Models need thorough external validation with diverse datasets to ensure broad applicability. Adding interpretable AI approaches will increase clinician trust and usability. In conclusion, while traditional models have limitations, AI-based approaches show much promise in predicting cardiovascular risks in diabetic patients. Overcoming the current challenges in the quality of data, computational resources, and model transparency will be key to advancing personalized diabetes care.

7.3.3 Lifestyle Management and Prevention

Lifestyle management is essential for preventing diabetes-related complications, particularly atherosclerotic cardiovascular disease (ASCVD), a significant risk for diabetic patients. Key components like smoking cessation, stress management, physical activity, dietary changes and weight loss are vital for ASCVD prevention, though real-world adherence to these changes is challenging due to issues like patient adherence and limited resources [56].

AI offers promising support for lifestyle management by providing personalized recommendations. AI-driven tools can analyse health data, predict risk factors, and suggest customized strategies for smoking cessation, weight management, and dietary plans. AI-based apps and health-tracking wearables enhance patient engagement with fast feedback and support, while behavioural change chatbots using NLP algorithms help motivate and monitor patients, and offer interventions for lifestyle modification challenges [52,56].

7.3.3.1 AI-driven Dietary Recommendations

Diet plays a key role in managing blood glucose levels and preventing complications in diabetes. Traditional diet recommendations for diabetes focused on reducing carbohydrate intake, portion control, and avoiding high-glycaemic foods. However, AI has enhanced diet personalization by tailoring nutrition plans to individual patient profiles, improving treatment outcomes. AI-based nutrition systems analyse large datasets, including continuous glucose monitoring data, physical activity, and dietary history, to generate personalized dietary recommendations. MLMs, such as decision trees, SVM, and DL, work on large, diverse datasets often including food images to provide tailored nutrition advice based on health profiles. Real-time feedback allows these systems to adjust recommendations based on dietary preferences and health goals. Despite their promise, these AI models require high-quality, diverse data, which can be challenging to gather and maintain [57].

Key algorithms check the following:

- Nutritional needs related to the medical history and type of diabetes: Type 1 or Type 2. Thus, continuous glucose monitor-derived blood glucose patterns must indicate the effect of other food sources on blood glucose levels.
- Databases containing foods categorized by their glycaemic index, nutrient load, and carbohydrate load for a balanced meal.

AI-driven dietary systems are improving the accuracy and personalization of meal recommendations by adapting in real-time to a patient's data. For example, if a particular meal results in a glucose spike, the system will adjust future suggestions to include lower-glycaemic alternatives. By considering clinical factors such as BMI, activity levels, insulin sensitivity, and genetic predispositions, AI can create personalized meal plans that account for not just carbohydrates, but also other important macronutrients like proteins and fats, which are key for managing conditions like diabetes.

Personalization: Platforms such as Nutrino and Foodvisor take this a step further by integrating data from continuous glucose monitoring (CGM) systems to suggest foods that help maintain glucose within target ranges. These platforms also factor in food allergies and specific dietary needs, like vegetarian or low-sodium diets, providing tailored support for diabetic patients. A detailed comparison of ML models used in nutritional data analysis is shown in Table 7.3.

AI-based dietary apps are also offering real-time meal suggestions by utilizing data from wearable devices like CGMs. These apps provide immediate feedback on food choices, advising users to avoid foods high in simple sugars or processed carbohydrates that could spike glucose levels.

7.3.3.2 Behavioural Change Interventions Through Chatbots

AI-driven chatbots are becoming increasingly valuable tools for individuals managing chronic conditions like diabetes and for promoting healthier lifestyles. Using natural language processing (NLP) and ML, these chatbots interact with users in real-time, offering advice tailored to their specific health goals and preferences [58]. One of their key strengths is adaptability, as illustrated in Table 7.4. These chatbots learn from each user interaction, refining their responses over time to provide more personalized guidance [58]. Platforms such as IBM Watson and Google Dialogflow support these chatbots, helping to manage large datasets and deliver contextually relevant feedback efficiently [59].

TABLE 7.3
Machine Learning Models Compared for Nutritional Data Classification and Personalization

Model Type	Purpose	Key Features	Advantages	Challenges
Decision Trees	Classify nutritional data	Simple decision rules	Easy to interpret and implement	Limited in handling large, complex datasets
Support Vector Machines (SVM)	Predict optimal diets using historical data	Works with structured data to predict individual outcomes	Effective with smaller datasets	Struggles with unstructured data like images
Neural Networks (Deep Learning)	Process vast amounts of structured and unstructured data	Extracts patterns from complex datasets, including images	Highly effective for personalization and meal recognition	Requires large datasets and computational resources

TABLE 7.4
Key Features of AI Health Tools

Feature	Benefit	Challenge
Engagement and Motivation	Increases physical activity and improves diet	Maintaining long-term behaviour change
Personalized Recommendations	Tailored tips and reminders	Concerns of data security and privacy
AI-Powered Interaction	Friendly and engaging user experience	Possible biases in AI algorithms

Additionally, chatbots play an important role in boosting user engagement by sending reminders and offering tips that encourage users to stay focused on their health goals [58]. Zhang et al.'s Behaviour Change Model of AI Chatbot highlights that fostering a positive relationship between the user and chatbot is crucial, as supportive, friendly interactions can motivate users and create a more enjoyable experience [59].

These AI-driven chatbots have great potential to help individuals with chronic conditions like diabetes adopt healthier lifestyles. By leveraging NLP and ML, the chatbots offer real-time, personalized advice based on user data such as eating habits and exercise routines [55]. Platforms like IBM Watson and Google Dialogflow enhance the chatbot's ability to manage large-scale data, ensuring timely and relevant health recommendations [59]. However, privacy concerns are a critical issue since chatbots gather sensitive health information. Ensuring data security and confidentiality is essential to building user trust and optimizing the effectiveness of these tools [59]. Future developments in AI may enhance these chatbots even further, with more advanced personalization capabilities to support long-term behavioural changes.

Despite their potential, AI chatbots face challenges in maintaining long-term user engagement, as initial enthusiasm often wanes over time [58]. To fully realize their transformative potential in healthcare, further research is needed to develop strategies that foster sustained behaviour change. Enhanced AI algorithms and tailored personalization could make chatbots essential allies in supporting healthier lifestyles, fundamentally shifting how people manage chronic conditions.

7.4 AI IN CANCER DETECTION

7.4.1 Bladder Cancer

Bladder cancer (BCa), currently the most common cancer type, has seen reduced mortality due to improved identification and treatment techniques. While cystoscopy remains the standard diagnostic method, it carries procedural risks. Recent studies explore ML and DL models to enhance BCa detection and diagnosis [60]. Non-muscle invasive bladder cancer (NMIBC) occurs in 80% of BCa cases, with high recurrence rates: up to 50% within five years, and 20% progress to advanced stages [61]. To manage high recurrence risks, patients require regular surveillance cystoscopy, sometimes as often as three times monthly in high-risk cases [62]. Despite its effectiveness, standard white light cystoscopy can miss carcinoma in situ (CIS) and small tumours, increasing the risk of misdiagnosis and insufficient tumour resection [62–64].

7.4.1.1 Stages of Bladder Cancer

The T stages of bladder cancer, which include Tis, T1, T2a, T2b, T3a, T3b, T4a, and T4b are depicted in Figure 7.9. Three major informational pillars constitute the basis of bladder cancer staging. T denotes the degree to which the primary tumour has spread to the surrounding tissues and penetrated the bladder wall. N denotes the presence of bladder-related lymph nodes that have been affected by cancer. M denotes the presence of metastases from the bladder to other organs [65,66].

T4b is Cancer that has impacted the wall of the abdomen or pelvis. Nx is the lymph nodes that cannot be reached in the region. A single regional lymph node metastasis is identified in the true pelvis, as N0. N1 2+ regional lymph node metastases in the true pelvis. N3 Lymph node metastasis to the lymph nodes of the common iliac. There aren't any distant metastases in M0. M1 Distinguished between metastases. One type of cancer that metastasizes to other places of the body is called M1a non-regional lymph node metastasis. A non-lymph nodes M1b distant metastases [65–67].

CT scanning detects papillary lesions with high sensitivity, yet conventional white light cystoscopy results in up to 30% misdiagnosis and 50% incomplete transurethral resections (TURBT), contributing to high recurrence and progression rates in BCa [3,67,68]. Additionally, T stages include Ta (non-invasive papillary cancer), Tis (flat, non-invasive cancer), T1 (spread to connective tissue below the bladder lining), T2a

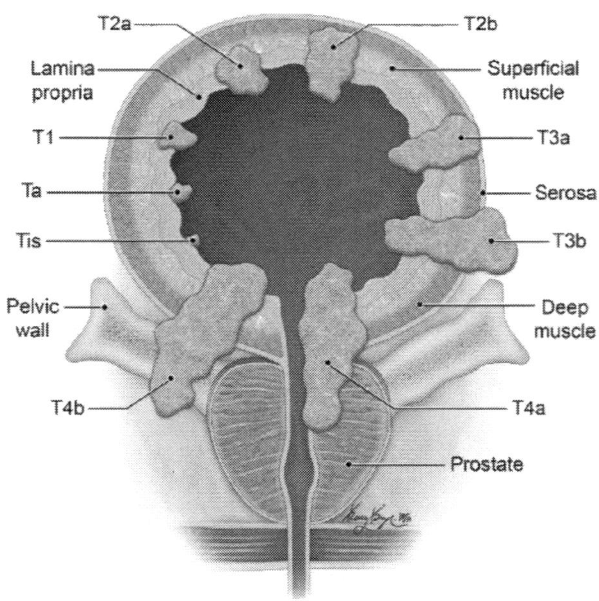

FIGURE 7.9 The various stages of bladder cancer.

(inner muscle layer invasion), T2b (outer muscle layer invasion), T3a (microscopic spread to surrounding tissues), T3b (extensive spread to surrounding tissues), and T4a (spread to adjacent organs like prostate, uterus, or vagina) [3,69].

7.4.1.2 Concept of AI

Applications for AI abound in many domains, including the monitoring and diagnosis of cancer. It makes it easier to gather data from various sources and transform it into dynamically linked symptomatic systems. The goal of MLA is to continuously improve their performance by adding new data to the dataset. Most ML techniques are represented by mathematical models. Data samples, often referred to as labels, are associated with observed variables, characteristics, and variable outcomes [70].

Figure 7.10 illustrates the image processing procedures for diagnosing bladder cancer. Initially, an image from a set of data is captured and pre-processed to enhance its quality. Various techniques are then applied to segment and further enhance the image to extract relevant information. After feature extraction, multiple models or classifiers are developed to determine whether the input image is benign or cancerous. These methods are designed to tackle real-world computer vision challenges by employing statistical and biomechanical modelling scientifically. Thus, AI-based tissue imaging for cancer offers diverse applications and flexibility, enhancing three critical biological tasks: therapy monitoring, tumour detection, and classification. Compared to other approaches, AI plays a crucial role in disease diagnosis [71], as it researches, develops, and produces theories and systems to enhance and replicate human intelligence [72–74]. ML, a branch of AI, creates strategies for learning from data and has proven beneficial in medical practice [75]. DL, a subset of ML, mimics human behaviour by layering processes to yield complex results and has shown promise in medical image analysis [76].

7.4.2 Breast Cancer

The leading cause of death among women is breast cancer. It poses a significant public health concern, necessitating effective control systems for early diagnosis and treatment to reduce mortality rates. Common imaging modalities for diagnosing breast cancer include MRI, ultrasound, and mammograms. Traditionally, radiologists and

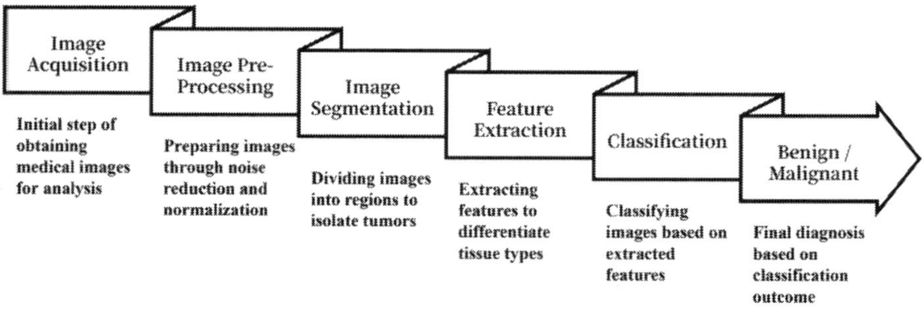

FIGURE 7.10 The diagnosis of bladder cancer by image processing.

pathologists manually review breast images, making diagnoses based on consensus among medical professionals. This manual examination is labour-intensive and often results in false positives or negatives, highlighting the need for automated systems to enhance early diagnosis and streamline image analysis. Such technologies provide a second opinion to the radiologists, improving the robustness and accuracy of breast cancer diagnoses [77].

However, AI algorithms, specifically DL algorithms, are often described as "black box" systems, meaning their decision-making processes lack transparency. This opacity is problematic in medical contexts, as radiologists and physicians prefer to understand the rationale behind AI-generated recommendations [78]. Consequently, many healthcare professionals view AI-based systems for disease prediction and diagnosis as a potential threat, fearing a loss of control over autonomous decision-making processes and the implications of less explainable AI interventions [79].

Algorithms using AI provide a more accurate way to predict the onset of bladder cancer. DL algorithms are found to perform better at diagnosing bladder cancer than ML algorithms when the various evaluative factors are assayed. In comparison to the other algorithms, CNN has calculated the greatest sensitivity and accuracy for the detection of bladder tumours, as displayed in Figure 7.11, by 95.77% and 96.9%, respectively. Transfer learning, on the other hand, had the greatest specificity score (97.6%). AI holds promise for accelerating the diagnosis of bladder cancer, improving tumour clearance during transurethral bladder tumour surgery, and identifying cancer recurrence [76].

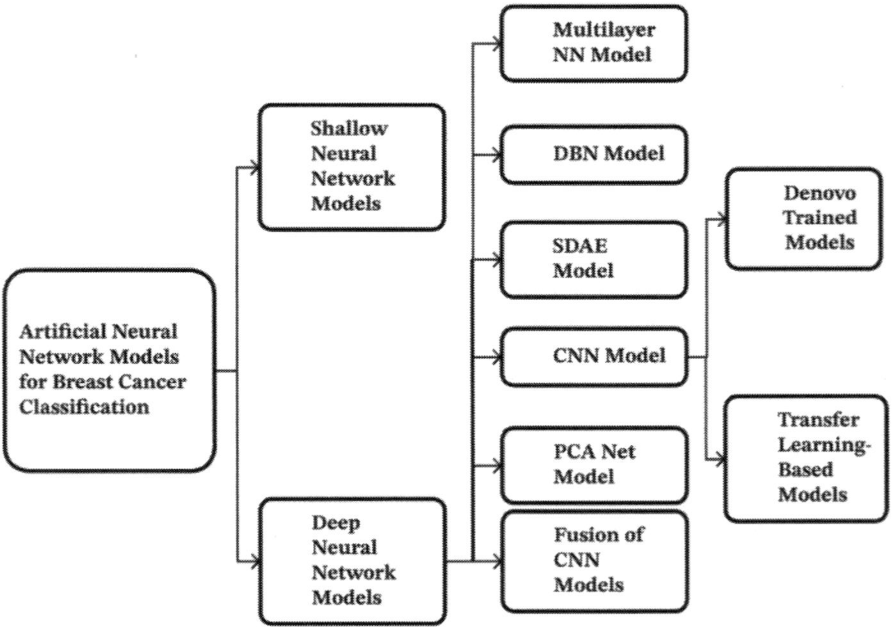

FIGURE 7.11 Breast cancer classification based on the types of Artificial Neural Network used adopted from [76].

Several DNN variations have been used for breast cancer classification in the literature after achieving cutting-edge results in the field of image analysis. Breast imagining data has been used for breast cancer classification by using DNN such as Deep Belief Network (DBN), Multi-Layer Network (ML-NN), and Principal Component Analysis, and various variations of Convolutional Neural Network (CNN). Every DL technique has advantages and disadvantages when applied to medical image analysis. Because of their reliable performance, certain CNN variations are typically utilized in literature to analyse breast pictures in order to detect malignancy

Five years ago, researchers from the Computer Science and Artificial Intelligence Laboratory (CSAIL) in MIT and the Jameel Clinic introduced a deep-learning model capable of predicting cancer risk using only a patient's mammogram. The model demonstrated significant potential, notably improving inclusivity by providing equally accurate predictions for both Black and white women. This is particularly crucial since Black women face a 43% higher risk of dying from breast cancer [80].

The new "Mirai" algorithm was customized to address the specific needs of risk modelling. Mirai simultaneously estimates risks to a patient across several future time points and can incorporate clinical risk factors, including family history or age, when available. Additionally, the design of this algorithm helps to generate consistent predictions despite minor differences in clinical settings, such as variations in mammography machines as shown in Figure 7.12. Mirai was trained by the team using a dataset from Massachusetts General Hospital (MGH), which consisted of 200,000 exams. This dataset was used in their previous work. The tests were validated on test datasets from MGH, Sweden's Karolinska Institute, and Taiwan's Chang Gung Memorial Hospital. Mirai demonstrated superior accuracy compared to previous methods in the prediction of risk of cancer and identification of the high-risk groups

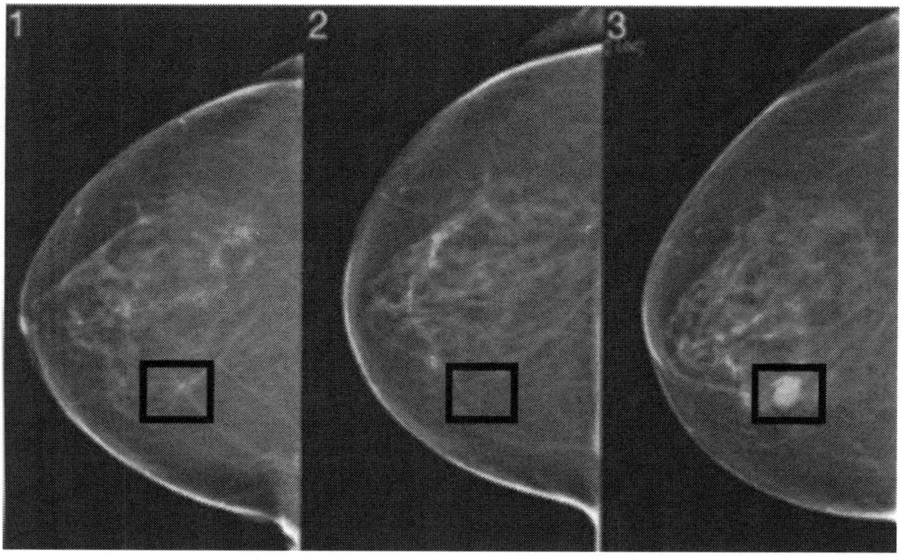

FIGURE 7.12 Enhancement of Machine Learning systems by MIT researchers for the prediction of cancer from mammogram images with successful validation [80].

among all the three datasets. The MGH test set, identified twice the future cancer cases as the current clinical standard, the Tyrer-Cuzick model. Mirai showed comparable accuracy among patients of varying age, races, and breast density in the MGH test set and the various subtypes of cancer in the Karolinska test set [80].

Physicians valued the explainability of AI algorithms many years ago [81], viewing it as one of the key components of support systems based on AI-based automated decision. Presently, numerous scholars such as Villani [82] report on AI in France, while numerous others advocate for "opening the black box of artificial intelligence" and emphasizing the application of interpretable models for critical decision-making [83]. Therefore, a thorough justification of the decisions is required, particularly when these algorithms are employed to anticipate a disease, in order to win the confidence of physicians regarding the AI0algorithm based decisions and to support their trustworthiness. Additionally, this expands the field of study for "Ethical AI." Therefore, the research community must take the lead in making AI algorithms completely comprehensible and interpreted so that these systems can be seen as promising candidates for influencing decision-making on potential disease forecasts.

7.4.3 AI in Radiology

The most commonly requested radiological scan in the United States is a chest X-ray (CXR), which is essential for detecting several thoracic disorders [84]. Low sensitivity is one of the major obstacles to their interpretation and prompted AI-based methods for improved analysis [85]. Based on the CXR14 dataset, this innovation wave accelerated, resulting in notable breakthroughs in AI applications for CXR analysis [86].

With almost 200,000 annotated CXRs, the colorectal, lung, ovarian and prostate cancer screening trial was one of the first extensive databases. However, disease prevalence was low due to its emphasis on screening. Unlike contemporary digital radiographs, the dataset used digitized film radiographs. This prompted the search for alternate sources, such as massive data storage facilities of hospitals' PACS (Picture Archiving and Communication Systems). By employing natural language processing to mine 110,000 CXRs and extract labels from radiologist reports, the CXR14 dataset took advantage of such PACS data [87].

Since then, more PACS-mined datasets have surfaced, such as CheXpert, MIMIC-CXR, and PadChest, all of which have aided in the quick development of AI-based CXR analysis. The use of text-mined labels, however, presents difficulties because reports take into account variables other than CXR appearances, which could result in differences between the disease patterns indicated and the actual picture results.

Some sample localizations obtained using these weakly supervised methods are shown in Figure 7.13. Although weakly supervised localization shows promise, there are still issues to be resolved to make sure the model does not concentrate on spurious locations and captures the full scope of the disease pattern [89].

Computed tomography (CT) is the preferred imaging modality for diagnosing interstitial lung disease (ILD) because it can produce three-dimensional (3D) pictures of the lungs with a greater spatial resolution than computed radiography (CXR).

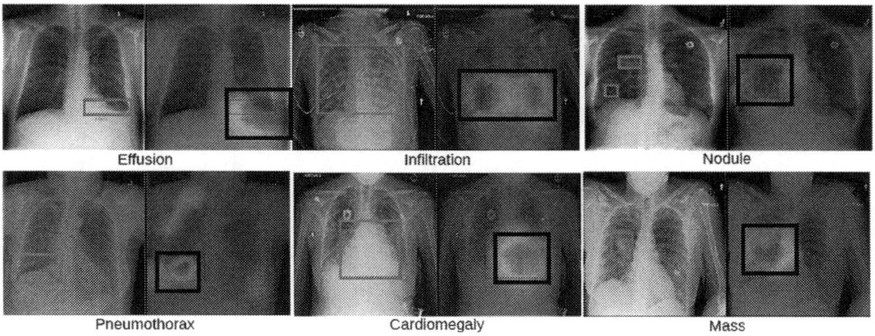

FIGURE 7.13 If configured accurately, CNNs (convolutional neural networks) can indicate localizations representing the region of image contributing to the prediction [88].

Additionally, AI methods for CT have been created, with a primary focus on lung structure segmentation, abnormality detection, and pulmonary disease analysis, including lung cancer and ILD. Nevertheless, there are still issues with increasing AI's precision in identifying illness trends in intricate situations [90,91].

In conclusion, AI tools are being incorporated into radiological workflows more and more to help interpret CT scans and CXRs, potentially enhancing accuracy and efficiency. To completely resolve present constraints and guarantee broad clinical acceptance, more innovation is necessary [92].

7.4.4 DL for Pathology Slides

In contemporary healthcare, Digital Pathology (DP) has grown in importance, especially for the interpretation of histology slides. The use of DL approaches to different image analysis tasks within DP, including detection, segmentation, and classification, is examined in this study. An open-source DL framework is applied through a thorough tutorial and uses scenarios that highlight common issues like training set curation, error management in training data, and magnification selection [93]. The study shows that DL performs better than conventional hand-crafted feature-based methods in seven distinct tasks, such as invasive ductal carcinoma identification and nucleus segmentation. Additionally, this study identifies persistent issues and makes recommendations for future lines of inquiry in digital pathology [93].

Numerous image analysis jobs in DP require tissue grading (classification) or quantification (e.g., counting cells or mitoses). These activities always involve identifying histologic primitives (e.g., epithelium, mitosis, nuclei, tubules, etc.), as illustrated in Figure 7.14. For instance, although the outcomes of oropharyngeal [94] and breast malignancies [95] have been linked to the spatial organization of their nuclei, these methods still initially need deep annotations (i.e., different entities recognized at different sizes) to extract characteristics from. Therefore, it is imperative to create reliable and effective algorithms for DP image analysis.

By manually analysing tissue samples under microscopes, pathologists carry out intricate visual tasks like determining mitotic events and assessing the aggressiveness of malignancy. By automating important operations, DL can lessen the

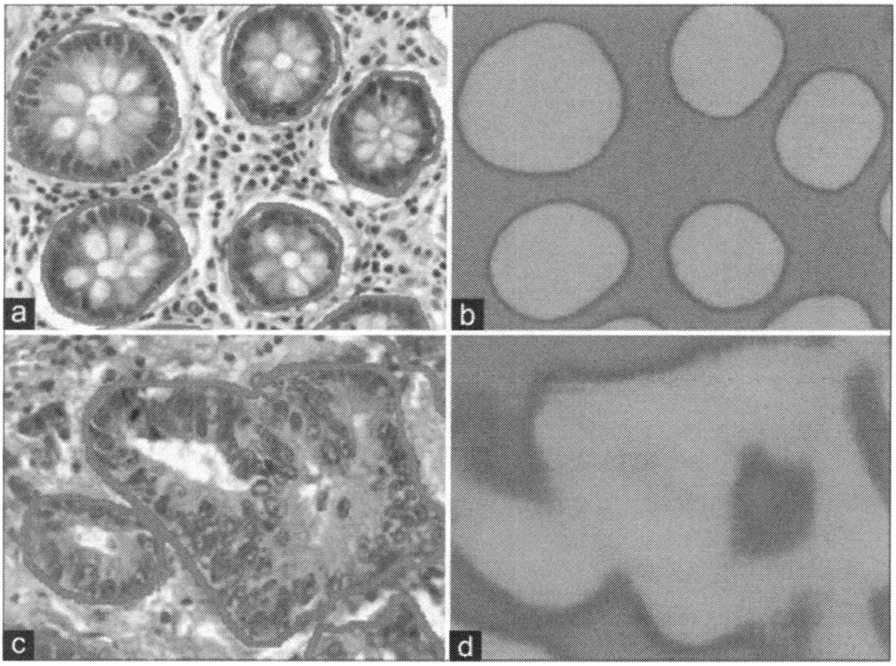

FIGURE 7.14 Identification of histological primitives in image analysis [99].

labour-intensive nature of this procedure. But switching from hand-crafted techniques to DL presents difficulties, especially for specialists who are not experienced with DP. Guidance for choosing the best magnifications or curating training datasets, which are essential for creating accurate models, is absent from open-source DL tools [96].

The Caffe platform may be used to create the unified DL framework, which shows how a single network architecture (AlexNet) can be applied to a variety of tasks, from lymphoma classification to nucleus segmentation. This framework greatly lowers the learning curve for non-expert users by minimizing the requirement for task-specific algorithmic customization. The creation of data patches, network training, testing, and assessment are the four main components of the DL workflow. Because it has a direct impact on model performance, the procedure of creating representative training patches is crucial [97,98].

To demonstrate the adaptability of DL in pathological image analysis, seven application scenarios are provided:

i. Nuclei Segmentation: For cancer grading, precise nuclei segmentation is essential. Patch selection and morphological dilatation work together to improve border identification and performance [100,101].
ii. Epithelium Segmentation: Tumour identification requires the epithelium to be separated from the stroma. The study addresses border classification using specialized patch selection and down sampled pictures [102].

iii. Tubule Segmentation: The aggressiveness of cancer is correlated with tubule morphology. Even in tissue that is disordered, the study improves tubule identification by using bootstrapping approaches and texture-based feature extraction [103].
iv. Invasive Ductal Carcinoma (IDC) Detection: One prevalent subtype of breast cancer is IDC. The study shows that DL offers superior F-scores and accuracy when compared to conventional methods for detection [104].
v. Lymphocyte Detection: One important indicator in cancer immunotherapy is lymphocytic infiltration. In order to achieve high detection accuracy, the study resizes images to concentrate on lymphocytes [105].
vi. Mitosis Detection: One crucial criterion for cancer grading is the quantity of mitotic events. To increase detection rates, the study employs blue-ratio segmentation and rotation [106].
vii. Lymphoma Classification: Genetic testing is necessary for subtyping lymphoma, although DL models can directly identify images based on visual patterns, which may eliminate the requirement for intrusive testing [107].

The DL-based techniques yielded outcomes that were on par with, and in certain situations better than, the most advanced hand-crafted feature methods in each of the seven use cases. Because a single framework was used for all tasks, less task-specific customization was required, increasing process efficiency and scalability. Furthermore, there was a notable improvement in performance measurements like accuracy, true positive rates (TPR), and F-scores.

The outcomes show how well DL works to automate the analysis of pathological images. The requirement for high-quality annotated training data, controlling biological variability among datasets, and enhancing border recognition in intricate tissue architectures are some of the issues that still need to be resolved. Future studies should concentrate on improving DL's generalizability across other datasets and resolving the drawbacks of manual annotation.

By decreasing inter-reader variability, increasing diagnosis accuracy, and automating laborious image analysis activities, DL has the potential to completely transform digital pathology. With an emphasis on the value of carefully selected datasets and a consistent framework for various tasks, this paper offers a thorough tutorial for applying DL to DP problems. For AI in pathology to continue to progress, pathologists and DL specialists must continue to collaborate [99].

7.5 AI DURING THE COVID-19 PANDEMIC

AI systems have significantly advanced the understanding, measurement, detection, diagnosis, and treatment of viruses and diseases. Additionally, AI has enhanced intervention and management strategies, made an unprecedented impact, and addressed issues related to the disorder in the information surrounding the SARS-CoV-2 virus, the COVID-19 disease, and the pandemic [20].

Figure 7.15 illustrates the primary and secondary areas where AI has significantly impacted the fight against COVID-19. AI has helped to tackle various challenges by facilitating understanding, identification, quantification, containment, and prevention efforts [20].

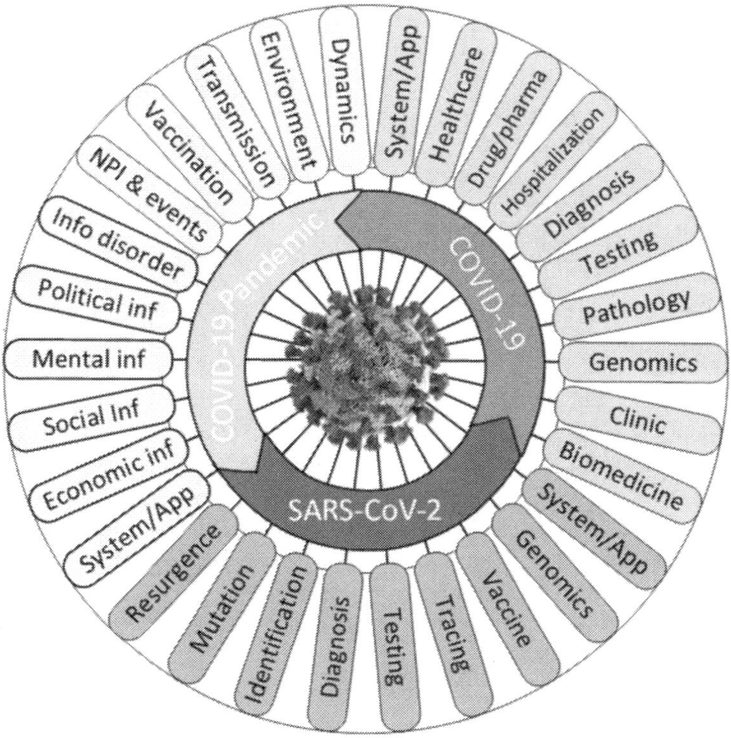

FIGURE 7.15 AI research landscape in the fight against COVID-19 [20].

7.5.1 Early Detection and Surveillance

Radiological imaging systems, such as CT scans and chest X-rays (CXR), can detect respiratory problems instantly. In comparison to CT scans, CXRs are quick, cost-effective, involve lower radiation exposure and are easily accessible. However, radiologists have to individually analyse the X-rays. The increased workload during the COVID-19 pandemic led to the realization of the need to develop automated tools that utilize DL techniques to analyse CXRs [108].

Initially, the features of CXR images were extracted using the well-established deep transfer learning model, ResNet101. Unlike deep convolutional neural networks (CNNs), which require extensive parameter tuning, ResNet101 offers a more streamlined approach [108]. Following feature extraction, the deep forest model, which is grounded in ensemble learning and demands fewer hyperparameters was employed to diagnose COVID-19 patients. It was found that the DL and deep transfer learning models could be utilized for the early diagnosis of COVID-19 suspected cases. However, to obtain accurate results, the DL models need many initial parameters. Moreover, the overfitting issue is also a problem for these models [108].

Interestingly, it was reported that on December 31, 2019, AI facilitated an early detection and provided warnings, seven days before the WHO issued the official announcement regarding the outbreak of the COVID-19 pandemic [109].

7.5.1.1 AI in Contact Tracing and Outbreak Prediction of COVID-19

AI was also used to monitor the spread of COVID-19 across different regions and over time [110]. Data on the locations visited by confirmed patients such as train stations, airports, restaurants, hotels, and shopping malls were collected. This information, which came from various sources and included both structured and unstructured data, needed to be pre-processed. Contact tracing, in this context, can be seen as a big data challenge because it involves handling and analysing both types of data [110]. Using contact tracing, many of the infected countries were able to use mobile applications having different technologies to implement a digital contact tracing process [111].

7.5.1.2 ML for Symptom Analysis and Triage

By identifying common patterns among patients having both mild and severe symptoms, MLA can automate the triaging procedures. During the peak of the pandemic, a lack of preparation, inefficiencies, and wrong allocation of medical resources contributed to numerous fatalities. The limited capacity of ICUs, shortage of ventilators and over worked clinicians led to the depletion of hospital resources. In this context, a robust automated severity prediction triaging decision support system could have potentially prevented many deaths resulting from inadequate treatments and hospital resources [112].

In a study by Pourhomayoun et al., the proposed system included a set of algorithms designed for data pre-processing. This involved tasks such as feature extraction, handling missing values, eliminating redundant or irrelevant data, and selecting the most informative features. After pre-processing the data, Machine Learning Algorithms (MLAs) were used to develop a predictive model that classifies the data, predicts medical conditions, and estimates the probability and risk of mortality. To support further research, both the processed dataset and code have been made publicly available for the research community to use [113].

7.5.2 Vaccine Development and Distribution

AI has demonstrated exceptional potential as a tool for simplifying the procedure and enhancing the effectiveness of vaccinations [114]. This could also be applied to a rapidly rising infection like the COVID-19 pandemic [115]. AI has the ability to reduce morbidity and mortality associated with COVID-19 by facilitating timely interventions through accurate and swift predictions of disease progression [115]. Advances in AI algorithms allow the analysis of a huge amount of data, leading to meaningful predictions, informed decision-making, and automation in healthcare processes [116]. Also, AI can enhance the genetic materials identification in the development of drugs and vaccines [114].

MLAs are capable of analysing large datasets of viral proteins to pinpoint those most likely to trigger an immune response. In silico modelling can then be used to design and optimize vaccine candidates based on their predicted efficacy and safety profiles. Additionally, AI-driven genetic sequencing and analysis can detect virus mutations that may impact vaccine effectiveness, aiding in the development of new vaccine strategies [114]. AI-based systems have proven to be highly valuable in the development of the COVID-19 vaccine, offering advantages like scalability, accuracy, and speed. These technologies can expedite research by processing vast amounts of data and more efficiently predicting potential vaccine candidates. However, challenges remain, such as the need for high-quality data and the risk of algorithmic biases. Despite these hurdles, AI-driven approaches hold transformative potential in advancing vaccine development for COVID-19, speeding up processes and improving the overall effectiveness of vaccines [114].

7.5.2.1 AI in Vaccine Efficacy Studies

In the development of vaccines, network-based algorithms have gained significant importance over time [114]. These algorithms employ methods like artificial neural networks, gradient boosting decision trees, and deep neural networks to predict potential epitopes. Tools like MARIA and NetMHCPan4 have been instrumental in identifying both T-cell and B-cell epitopes for SARS-CoV-2 [116]. By leveraging these approaches, researchers can deepen their understanding of the virus, ultimately leading to more effective vaccines that reduce disease transmission [114].

Expression-based algorithms are also crucial for optimizing the immunogenicity and expression of vaccines. These algorithms refine the vaccine's genetic sequence to enhance its efficacy and safety. A widely used expression-based technique in mRNA vaccine development is codon optimization, which improves stability, safety, and effectiveness. This process adjusts the balance between codon frequency and the availability of host tRNA, boosting translation efficiency and ensuring the proper expression of the target antigen in vivo [117].

Moreover, integrated docking simulation algorithms have proven to be essential in COVID-19 vaccine research and development. These algorithms help identify potential vaccine targets, such as the spike S-protein, and offer significant advantages in vaccine design. They have also been utilized in several studies to predict antigenic epitopes against SARS-CoV-2, contributing to the ongoing progress in vaccine development [118].

7.5.2.2 Optimizing Vaccine Distribution Logistics

The algorithms developed by Shukla, Samta et al., designed for optimizing vaccination in long-term care facilities (LTCFs), addressed the vaccine distribution challenge through a two-step process, which is elaborated upon in the following sections [119].

1. Assignment*:* An optimal approach was introduced to address the depot-long-term care facility (LTCF) assignment challenge by framing it as a minimum-cost flow problem. This approach offered two key advantages: first, the approach was based on a well-established problem in network flow theory, which enabled the use of computationally efficient solvers. Additionally, it was flexible enough to handle the various constraints specific to our context [119].
2. Scheduling*:* Using the best assignments from Step 1, an algorithm was developed that would reduce the number of days required to vaccinate LTCFs in each state and generate clinic schedules that would coordinate

> the two doses at the suggested dosing interval. Given capacity, distance, and supply limits, the algorithm further optimized scheduling by matching a large LTCF with a number of strategically clustered small LTCFs to find out which set of LTCFs might get vaccinations on the same day [119].

In 2020, the need for the influenza vaccine boosted intensely due to outbreak of COVID-19. Data from the Iran Ministry of Health and Medical Education (MOHME) indicated that this need increased tenfold in comparison to the previous year. This spike in demand, combined with existing measures, led to a flu vaccine shortage in Iran. As a result, the MOHME required an efficient and effective model for the distribution of the vaccines to address the shortage of flu vaccine in the winters amid the ongoing COVID-19 pandemic [120].

Effective supply chain management is crucial for vaccine distribution, particularly in healthcare sectors like those in West Africa. However, traditional supply chain methods often face challenges such as limited visibility, a lack of real-time data, and inefficient processes. These issues can result in delays, resource wastage, and undermine the success of vaccination efforts. To address these problems, AI has emerged as a powerful solution, greatly enhancing the efficiency and effectiveness of vaccine distribution and supply chain management in West Africa [120].

7.5.3 Post-Infection Monitoring and Prevention

Though majority patients successfully recovered from COVID-19 infections, reports indicate that more than 70% of survivors encounter various complications affecting one or more organs up to four months after the initial symptoms. This collection of long-term effects resulting from the Coronavirus is known as post-COVID syndrome or long COVID [121]. Deguilhem et al. utilized infodemiology, employing a supervised MLA to identify long COVID patients on social media. Their findings revealed that around 49.1% of users (79 out of 161) continued to experience symptoms more than three months after infection, while 20.5% (33 out of 161) reported symptoms persisting for one year [122].

Digital devices were used in one study to determine subclinical arrhythmias, while another investigation identified miRNAs that regulated differential gene expression in individuals with a Diffusing Capacity of the Lungs for Carbon Monoxide (DLCO) of less than 80% compared to those with a DLCO of 80% or greater. The genes identified in this analysis were indicative of potential pulmonary fibrosis post COVID-19 [123]. A study aimed at predicting post-COVID conditions (PCC) and identifying factors associated with an increased risk of developing these conditions focused on personalized medicine, specifically examining miRNAs that could predict changes in Diffusing Capacity of the Lungs for Carbon Monoxide (DLCO) following COVID-19. Bartczak et al. utilized telemonitoring and found that patients with at-rest oxygen saturation levels below 94% are less likely to show significant improvement in pulmonary function tests, such as Forced Vital Capacity (FVC) and DLCO, within 2–3 months after discharge. This lack of improvement often leads to continued exercise intolerance [124].

7.5.3.1 AI Tools for Long COVID Management

Developing an AI-powered digital health solution that integrates behaviour change techniques could significantly improve the clinical management of patients with long COVID-19, ultimately enhancing their well-being and quality of life. While the acute phase of COVID-19 is being managed through vaccination, it's crucial to create new tools that address the unique challenges posed by long COVID-19 [125].

Huang et al. studied the long-term health effects in 1,733 discharged COVID-19 patients and found that 24% had a lower median six-minute walking distance than normal reference values at the six-month follow-up [124,126]. In a related study, long-term changes in white matter were examined in COVID-19 survivors one year after discharge, using advanced imaging techniques like diffusion kurtosis imaging, diffusion tensor imaging, and neurite orientation dispersion and density models. The study revealed reduced axonal density in these patients, though no significant cognitive decline was observed compared to healthy controls. However, patients who had been admitted to the ICU or had extended hospital stays showed more significant white matter alterations [127].

The COVERSCAN study explored the medium-term effects of long COVID on various organs, finding impairment in the pancreas (40%), liver (28%), kidneys (4%), and spleen (4%). The study also reported that 70% of patients had single-organ damage, while 29% experienced damage to multiple organs. Similarly, a Chinese study conducted a two-month follow-up of 253 patients who were discharged after COVID-19 infection, revealing that liver enzymes ALP, GGT, AST, and ALT were elevated even two weeks after the acute phase. Abnormalities in pancreas were also observed in survivors. Moreover, long COVID patients may develop new onset endocrinopathies, such as diabetes mellitus, even in individuals who did not have a prior history of the disease [126].

In the entire course of the pandemic, the number of investigations done based on images surged significantly and is expected to keep rising because of the ongoing long-term symptoms in COVID patients. AI has vast applications in diagnostic imaging, with applications in prognosis and image analysis. These AI tools, utilized in the battle against COVID-19, proved essential in improving diagnostics and patient care [126].

7.6 ETHICAL AND SOCIETAL CONSIDERATIONS

The increasing adoption of AI in healthcare presents profound ethical concerns, particularly regarding data privacy, patient autonomy, and algorithmic bias. AI systems rely on vast amounts of patient data for training and continuous learning, raising concerns about unauthorized access, data breaches, and potential misuse of sensitive health information. Ensuring robust data governance policies, such as encryption, secure cloud storage, and strict access controls, is crucial for protecting patient confidentiality [128]. Additionally, it is essential that patients have clear consent mechanisms, allowing them to understand how their health data is being used and ensuring their autonomy in decision-making when it comes to AI-driven healthcare solutions.

Another important ethical concern in AI-driven disease detection and prevention is algorithmic bias. When AI models are trained on non-representative datasets, they can perpetuate biases, leading to disparities in diagnosis and treatment. For instance, studies have found that AI-driven dermatological diagnostic tools often underperform on darker skin tones due to a lack of diversity in training data [128,129]. To address these issues, AI developers must use diverse datasets, regularly audit algorithms for fairness, and engage multidisciplinary teams, including ethicists and healthcare professionals, throughout the development process. Ensuring transparency in AI's decision-making process is key, allowing both healthcare professionals and patients to trust AI-generated recommendations.

Beyond individual biases, the broader societal impacts of AI in healthcare must also be considered, especially regarding workforce changes and doctor-patient relationships. While AI can improve efficiency by automating repetitive tasks, there are growing concerns about its impact on healthcare jobs and the potential deskilling of medical professionals. Over-reliance on AI could diminish opportunities for medical training and professional development, potentially reducing the role of human judgment in care [130]. Additionally, as AI becomes more involved in patient interactions, such as through chatbot-driven consultations, there is a risk of depersonalizing the healthcare experience. Balancing technological advancements with human-centred care is vital to maintaining patient trust and empathy in medical practice.

Finally, ethical AI implementation should prioritize equitable access to healthcare innovations. AI-driven diagnostics and predictive tools often require expensive infrastructure and computational resources, which can create a digital divide between well-funded urban hospitals and resource-poor rural settings [131]. Policymakers need to address these disparities by promoting AI accessibility, supporting technology adoption in underserved areas, and ensuring that AI does not inadvertently deepen existing healthcare inequalities. Ethical deployment of AI in healthcare should be guided by principles of fairness, inclusivity, and accountability to ensure its benefits are available to all.

7.7 REGULATORY CHALLENGES

The rapid advancement of AI in disease detection and prevention brings about significant regulatory challenges, as current legal frameworks struggle to keep pace with the fast-evolving nature of AI technologies. A key concern is ensuring that AI-driven medical tools meet rigorous safety and efficacy standards before they are deployed in clinical environments. Although regulatory agencies like the U.S. Food and Drug Administration (FDA) and the European Medicines Agency (EMA) have established guidelines for AI-based medical devices, these regulations mainly address static algorithms, rather than those that continuously learn and adapt over time [130]. Unlike traditional medical devices, AI systems evolve as they process new data, meaning they require ongoing oversight and post-market monitoring to prevent unintended consequences.

Another key challenge is the need for global harmonization in AI regulations. Different countries have different levels of regulatory oversight, which leads to inconsistencies in AI adoption and safety standards. For example, the European Union has introduced the Artificial Intelligence Act to set ethical guidelines for AI, but many other regions lack clear legal frameworks for AI governance in healthcare [128]. This fragmentation can slow down the global implementation of AI and limit its potential in healthcare. To address this, international regulatory bodies must work together to create standardized protocols that ensure safe and ethical AI deployment worldwide.

Liability and accountability are critical concerns in AI-driven healthcare. When an AI system delivers an incorrect diagnosis or treatment recommendation, it becomes challenging to determine who is legally responsible. Whether the fault lies with the developers, the healthcare providers, or the AI system itself, these issues raise complex questions about accountability and the potential for legal consequences in the event of harm to patients. Should the liability fall on the AI developer, the healthcare institution, or the physician using the system? Current legal frameworks don't offer clear answers to these questions, creating uncertainty for both healthcare providers and patients [131]. Clear legal guidelines regarding AI accountability are essential to protect patients' rights while fostering responsible innovation.

Lastly, transparency and explainability in AI decision-making are critical regulatory concerns. Many AI models, particularly DL systems, function as "black boxes," making it hard to understand how they arrive at specific conclusions. This lack of explainability can complicate regulatory approval processes, as healthcare professionals and policymakers need clear justifications for AI-driven medical decisions [129]. Future regulatory frameworks should require AI models to be explainable, allowing clinicians to verify AI-generated recommendations, thereby increasing trust and adoption in clinical practice. By addressing these regulatory challenges, AI can be safely integrated into healthcare, ensuring accountability, transparency, and patient safety.

7.8 CONCLUSION

The transformative potential of AI in early disease detection and prevention is evident, revolutionizing healthcare delivery across various domains, including cardiovascular diseases, diabetes, cancer, and infectious diseases such as COVID-19. AI technologies, including wearable devices, ML, and predictive analytics, are enabling a shift from reactive to proactive healthcare, focusing on early detection, risk assessment, and personalized prevention strategies. This chapter highlights key areas where AI is reshaping healthcare, laying the foundation for a future where diseases are detected sooner and prevented more effectively.

In the case of cardiovascular diseases, AI has proven to be a pivotal tool. Wearable devices and remote monitoring systems offer continuous health insights, enabling early identification of conditions like arrhythmias and hypertension. AI-driven ECG analysis has enhanced diagnostic accuracy, providing earlier and more precise identification of cardiac abnormalities. Risk prediction models, which combine patient data, including genetic profiles and lifestyle factors, allow for personalized assessments of disease risk. Additionally, personalized prevention strategies through digital platforms are empowering individuals to manage their cardiovascular health, reducing disease burden significantly.

Similarly, AI has made significant strides in diabetes management and preventing complications. Continuous glucose monitoring systems with predictive analytics help anticipate changes in blood sugar levels, reducing the risks of severe episodes such as hypoglycaemia or hyperglycaemia. Beyond managing blood sugar, AI is enabling early detection of diabetes-related complications, such as retinopathy and cardiovascular issues, through innovative screening tools. Moreover, AI-driven dietary recommendations and behavioural interventions are promoting healthier lifestyles, ensuring better disease management and prevention for those at risk of or living with diabetes.

Cancer detection has also been transformed by AI. From early detection of cancers like breast and bladder cancer to analysing radiology images and pathology slides, AI algorithms are enhancing diagnostic precision, often surpassing traditional methods. By identifying subtle patterns that may be overlooked by human clinicians, AI tools are enabling earlier, more accurate diagnoses and improving patient outcomes. The integration of DL technologies in oncology is not only refining diagnostic capabilities but also paving the way for personalized therapeutic approaches, setting new standards in cancer care.

The COVID-19 pandemic highlighted the essential role of AI in managing public health crises. AI tools facilitated early detection, contact tracing, and outbreak prediction models, helping to control the virus's spread. MLAs supported symptom analysis and triage, ensuring timely care for affected individuals. Furthermore, AI accelerated vaccine development and optimized distribution logistics, ensuring efficient vaccine delivery to populations. AI's role in managing long COVID symptoms post-infection further demonstrated its ability to adapt and meet evolving healthcare needs.

Despite its immense promise, the integration of AI into healthcare faces several challenges. Ethical concerns such as data privacy, algorithmic bias, and equitable access must be addressed to ensure AI benefits are accessible to all. Additionally, the reliance on high-quality data underscores the importance of strong data governance frameworks to minimize errors that could negatively impact patient care.

Looking ahead, collaboration among clinicians, data scientists, and policymakers will be crucial to maximizing AI's potential. By fostering interdisciplinary innovation, we can create AI systems that are not only effective but also ethical and sustainable. The integration of AI into healthcare should align with broader goals of equity and patient-centred care, ensuring that these technologies empower patients and improve outcomes without creating new barriers to access.

In conclusion, AI offers a transformative path for revolutionizing early disease detection and prevention. Its applications across cardiovascular health, diabetes management, oncology, and pandemic response exemplify its capacity to enhance diagnostics, streamline interventions, and optimize healthcare delivery. As AI continues to evolve, its integration into healthcare systems holds immense promise to not only save lives but also redefine how we approach health and disease. By addressing ethical considerations and fostering collaboration, AI will pave the way for a healthier, more equitable future.

DISCLAIMER

None

REFERENCES

1. Esteva, Andre, et al. "A Guide to Deep Learning in Healthcare." *Nature Medicine* 25.1 (2019): 24–29.
2. Obermeyer, Ziad, and Ezekiel J. Emanuel. "Predicting the Future—Big Data, Machine Learning, and Clinical Medicine." *New England Journal of Medicine* 375.13 (2016): 1216–1219.
3. Chen, Min, et al. "Disease Prediction by Machine Learning over Big Data from Healthcare Communities." *IEEE Access* 5 (2017): 8869–8879.
4. Topol, Eric J. "High-Performance Medicine: The Convergence of Human and Artificial Intelligence." *Nature Medicine* 25.1 (2019): 44–56.
5. McKinney, Scott Mayer, et al. "International Evaluation of an AI System for Breast Cancer Screening." *Nature* 577.7788 (2020): 89–94.
6. Rodriguez-Ruiz, Alejandro, et al. "Stand-Alone Artificial Intelligence for Breast Cancer Detection in Mammography: Comparison with 101 Radiologists." *JNCI: Journal of the National Cancer Institute* 111.9 (2019): 916–922.
7. Collins, Francis S., and Harold Varmus. "A New Initiative on Precision Medicine." *New England Journal of Medicine* 372.9 (2015): 793–795.
8. Khera, Amit V., et al. "Genome-Wide Polygenic Scores for Common Diseases Identify Individuals with Risk Equivalent to Monogenic Mutations." *Nature Genetics* 50.9 (2018): 1219–1224.
9. Piwek, Lukasz, et al. "The Rise of Consumer Health Wearables: Promises and Barriers." *PLoS Medicine* 13.2 (2016): e1001953.
10. Ravì, Daniele, et al. "Deep Learning for Health Informatics." *IEEE Journal of Biomedical and Health Informatics* 21.1 (2016): 4–21.
11. Binariks. "AI/ML Algorithms for Early Disease Detection and Medical Diagnosis." *AI & Machine Learning for Early Disease Detection*, 2024. binariks.com/blog/ai-machine-learning-for-early-disease-detection/. Accessed on 1 October 2024, 16 August 2024.
12. Ukkund, Shareefraza J., et al. "Nanocrystalline Cellulose from Agricultural Waste: An Overview." *International Journal of Nanoparticles* 10.4 (2018): 284–297.
13. Ukkund, Shareefraza J., et al. "Adsorption Method for the Remediation of Brilliant Green Dye Using Halloysite Nanotube: Isotherm, Kinetic and Modeling Studies." *Applied Sciences* 11.17 (2021): 8088.
14. Ukkund, Shareefraza J., et al. "A Recent Study on Remediation of Direct Blue 15 Dye Using Halloysite Nanotubes." *Applied Sciences* 11.17 (2021): 8196.
15. Ukkund, Shareefraza J., et al. "Role of Microbial Nanotechnology in Energy Devices." *Handbook of Microbial Nanotechnology*. Elsevier, 2022. 517–547.
16. Bhat, Nagesh, et al. "GO/CuO nanohybrid-based carbon dioxide gas sensors with an Arduino detection unit." *ACS omega* 8.36 (2023): 32512–32519.
17. Ukkund, Shareefraza J., et al. "Dextran Nanoparticles: Preparation and Applications." *Polysaccharide Nanoparticles*. Elsevier, 2022. 1–31.
18. Ukkund, Shareefraza J., et al. "Synthesis and Characterization of Silver Nanoparticles from Fuzarium Oxysporum and Investigation of Their Antibacterial Activity." *Materials Today: Proceedings* 9 (2019): 506–514.

19. Qureshi, Muhammad Rafaqat Ali, et al. "Using Artificial Intelligence to Improve the Accuracy of a Wrist-Worn, Noninvasive Glucose Monitor: A Pilot Study." *Journal of Diabetes Science and Technology*, 8.4 (2024): 254–269.
20. Cao, Longbing. "AI in Combating the Covid-19 Pandemic." *IEEE Intelligent Systems* 37.2 (2022): 3–13.
21. Romiti, Silvia, et al. "Artificial Intelligence (Ai) and Cardiovascular Diseases: An Unexpected Alliance." *Cardiology Research and Practice* 2020.1 (2020): 4972346.
22. Yan, Yang, et al. "The Primary Use of Artificial Intelligence in Cardiovascular Diseases: What Kind of Potential Role Does Artificial Intelligence Play in Future Medicine?" *Journal of Geriatric Cardiology: JGC* 16.8 (2019): 585.
23. Mathur, Pankaj, et al. "Artificial Intelligence, Machine Learning, and Cardiovascular Disease." *Clinical Medicine Insights: Cardiology* 14 (2020): 11–28.
24. Sermesant, Maxime, et al. "Applications of Artificial Intelligence in Cardiovascular Imaging." *Nature Reviews Cardiology* 18.8 (2021): 600–609.
25. Seetharam, Karthik, Sirish Shrestha, and Partho P. Sengupta. "Artificial Intelligence in Cardiovascular Medicine." *Current Treatment Options in Cardiovascular Medicine* 21 (2019): 1–14.
26. Gang, Li, et al. "An Artificial-Intelligence Approach to ECG Analysis." *IEEE Engineering in Medicine and Biology Magazine* 19.2 (2000): 95–100.
27. Attia, Zachi I., et al. "Application of Artificial Intelligence to the Electrocardiogram." *European Heart Journal* 42.46 (2021): 4717–4730.
28. Narula, Sukrit, et al. "Machine-Learning Algorithms to Automate Morphological and Functional Assessments in 2D Echocardiography." *Journal of the American College of Cardiology* 68.21 (2016): 2287–2295.
29. Safdar, Muhammad Farhan, Robert Marek Nowak, and Piotr Pałka. "Exploring Artificial Intelligence Algorithms for Electrocardiogram (Ecg) Signal Analysis: A Comprehensive Review." *Computers in Biology and Medicine* 10(7) (2023): 66–76.
30. Li, Qian, et al. "The Prediction Model of Warfarin Individual Maintenance Dose for Patients Undergoing Heart Valve Replacement, Based on the Back Propagation Neural Network." *Clinical Drug Investigation* 40 (2020): 41–53.
31. Attia, Zachi I., et al. "Screening for Cardiac Contractile Dysfunction Using an Artificial Intelligence–Enabled Electrocardiogram." *Nature Medicine* 25.1 (2019): 70–74.
32. Zellweger, Michael J., et al. "A New Non-Invasive Diagnostic Tool in Coronary Artery Disease: Artificial Intelligence as an Essential Element of Predictive, Preventive, and Personalized Medicine." *EPMA Journal* 9 (2018): 235–247.
33. Zellweger, Michael J., et al. "A New Memetic Pattern Based Algorithm to Diagnose/Exclude Coronary Artery Disease." *International Journal of Cardiology* 174.1 (2014): 184–186.
34. Kakadiaris, Ioannis A., et al. "Machine Learning Outperforms Acc/Aha Cvd Risk Calculator in Mesa." *Journal of the American Heart Association* 7.22 (2018): e009476.
35. Kwon, Joon-myoung, et al. "Artificial Intelligence Algorithm for Predicting Cardiac Arrest Using Electrocardiography." *Scandinavian Journal of Trauma, Resuscitation and Emergency Medicine* 28 (2020): 1–10.
36. Faizal, Aizatul Shafiqah Mohd, et al. "A Review of Risk Prediction Models in Cardiovascular Disease: Conventional Approach Vs. Artificial Intelligent Approach." *Computer Methods and Programs in Biomedicine* 207 (2021): 106190.
37. Subramani, Sivakannan, et al. "Cardiovascular Diseases Prediction by Machine Learning Incorporation with Deep Learning." *Frontiers in Medicine* 10 (2023): 1150933.
38. Ganesh, Santhi K., et al. "Genetics and Genomics for the Prevention and Treatment of Cardiovascular Disease: Update: A Scientific Statement from the American Heart Association." *Circulation* 128.25 (2013): 2813–2851.

39. Jaskulski, Stefanie, Cosima Nuszbaum, and Karin B. Michels. "Components, Prospects and Challenges of Personalized Prevention." *Frontiers in Public Health* 11 (2023): 1075076.
40. Gala, Dhir, et al. "The role of artificial intelligence in improving patient outcomes and future of healthcare delivery in cardiology: a narrative review of the literature." Healthcare 12.4. MDPI (2024).
41. Shaheen, Mohammed Yousef. "Applications of Artificial Intelligence (AI) in Healthcare: A Review." *ScienceOpen Preprints* 11.3 (2021): 86–97.
42. bin Nafisa, Badr Mansour Fahd, et al.. "A Non-Invasive Blood Glucose Monitoring System Based on Images and Artificial Intelligence." *Journal of Population Therapeutics and Clinical Pharmacology* 30.2 (2023): 805–807.
43. Vettoretti, Martina, et al. "Advanced Diabetes Management Using Artificial Intelligence and Continuous Glucose Monitoring Sensors." *Sensors* 20.14 (2020): 3870.
44. Vettoretti, Martina, et al. "Continuous Glucose Monitoring: Current Use in Diabetes Management and Possible Future Applications." *Journal of Diabetes Science and Technology* 12.5 (2018): 1064–1071.
45. Malathi, H., and Dhyan Chandra Yadav. Predictive Analytics and Machine Learning for Personalized Diabetes Management in Real-Time. *2023 IEEE International Conference on ICT in Business Industry & Government (ICTBIG).* 2023. IEEE, India.
46. Li, K., et al. "Glunet: A Deep Learning Framework for Accurate Glucose Forecasting." *IEEE Journal of Biomedical and Health Informatics* 24.2 (2019): 414–423.
47. Huzooree, Geshwaree, Kavi Kumar Khedo, and Noorjehan Joonas. Glucose Prediction Data Analytics for Diabetic Patients Monitoring. *1st International Conference on Next Generation Computing Applications (NextComp).* 2017. IEEE. Le Méridien Ile Maurice Beach Resort in Mauritius.
48. Daskalaki, Elena, et al. "An Early Warning System for Hypoglycemic/Hyperglycemic Events Based on Fusion of Adaptive Prediction Models." *Journal of Diabetes Science and Technology* 7.3 (2013): 689–698.
49. Botwey, Ransford Henry, et al. *36th Annual International Conference of the IEEE Engineering in Medicine and Biology Society.* 2014. IEEE. Chicago, Illinois, USA.
50. Turksoy, Kamuran, et al. "Hypoglycemia Early Alarm Systems Based on Multivariable Models." *Industrial & Engineering Chemistry Research* 52.35 (2013): 12329–12336.
51. Farzi, Saeed, Sahar Kianian, and Ilnaz Rastkhadive. Predicting Serious Diabetic Complications Using Hidden Pattern Detection. *2017 IEEE 4th International Conference on Knowledge-Based Engineering and Innovation (KBEI).* 2017. IEEE, India.
52. Choda, Gayathri, and Gundu H. R. Rao. "Diabetes-Related Clinical Complications: Novel Approaches for Diagnosis and Management." *Journal of Clinical Cardiology and Diagnostics* 2.2 (2019): 1–8.
53. Grzybowski, Andrzej, et al. "Artificial Intelligence for Diabetic Retinopathy Screening Using Color Retinal Photographs: From Development to Deployment." *Ophthalmology and Therapy* 12.3 (2023): 1419–1437.
54. Straňák, Zbyněk, Martin Penčák, and Miroslav Veith. "Arteficial Intelligence in Diabetic Retinopathy Screening: A Review." *Ceska a Slovenska Oftalmologie: Casopis Ceske Oftalmologicke Spolecnosti a Slovenske Oftalmologicke Spolecnosti* 77.5 (2021): 224–231.
55. Oikonomou, Evangelos K., and Rohan Khera. "Machine Learning in Precision Diabetes Care and Cardiovascular Risk Prediction." *Cardiovascular Diabetology* 22.1 (2023): 259.

56. van Trier, Tinka J., et al. "Lifestyle Management to Prevent Atherosclerotic Cardiovascular Disease: Evidence and Challenges." *Netherlands Heart Journal* 30.1 (2022): 3–14.
57. Sharma, S. K., and S. H. W. E. T. A. Gaur. Optimizing Nutritional Outcomes: The Role of AI in Personalized Diet Planning. *International Journal for Research Publication and Seminar.* 2024. Print.
58. Aggarwal, Abhishek, et al. "Artificial Intelligence–Based Chatbots for Promoting Health Behavioral Changes: Systematic Review." *Journal of Medical Internet Research* 25 (2023): e40789.
59. Zhang, Jingwen, et al. "Artificial Intelligence Chatbot Behavior Change Model for Designing Artificial Intelligence Chatbots to Promote Physical Activity and a Healthy Diet." *Journal of Medical Internet Research* 22.9 (2020): e22845.
60. Koul, Apeksha, Yogesh Kumar, and Anish Gupta. A Study on Bladder Cancer Detection Using AI-Based Learning Techniques. *2022 2nd International Conference on Technological Advancements in Computational Sciences (ICTACS).* 2022. IEEE, India.
61. Gandi, Carlo, et al. "Bladder Cancer in the Time of Machine Learning: Intelligent Tools for Diagnosis and Management." *Urologia Journal* 88.2 (2021): 94–102.
62. Hasnain, Zaki, et al. "Machine Learning Models for Predicting Post-Cystectomy Recurrence and Survival in Bladder Cancer Patients." *PloS One* 14.2 (2019): e0210976.
63. Pierconti, Francesco, et al. The Bladder Epicheck Test and Cytology in the Follow-up of Patients with Non-Muscle-Invasive High Grade Bladder Carcinoma. *Urologic Oncology: Seminars and Original Investigations.* Elsevier, 2022. Print.
64. Brieu, Nicolas, et al. "Automated Tumour Budding Quantification by Machine Learning Augments Tnm Staging in Muscle-Invasive Bladder Cancer Prognosis." *Scientific Reports* 9.1 (2019): 5174.
65. Wong, Vincenzo K., et al. "Imaging and Management of Bladder Cancer." *Cancers* 13.6 (2021): 1396.
66. Yang, Yuhan, et al. "Application of Deep Learning as a Noninvasive Tool to Differentiate Muscle-Invasive Bladder Cancer and Non–Muscle-Invasive Bladder Cancer with Ct." *European Journal of Radiology* 139 (2021): 109666.
67. Noone, Anne-Michelle, et al. "Machine Learning Methods to Identify Missed Cases of Bladder Cancer in Population-Based Registries." *JCO Clinical Cancer Informatics* 5 (2021): 641–653.
68. Chen, Siteng, et al. "A Novel Nomogram Based on Machine Learning-Pathomics Signature and Neutrophil to Lymphocyte Ratio for Survival Prediction of Bladder Cancer Patients." *Frontiers in Oncology* 11 (2021): 703033.
69. Russell, Beth. "Using Real World Evidence to Assess Clinical Outcomes in Patients Diagnosed with Bladder Cancer." PhD diss., King's College London, 2020. Print.
70. Kumar, Yogesh, Apeksha Koul, and Seema Mahajan. "A Deep Learning Approaches and Fastai Text Classification to Predict 25 Medical Diseases from Medical Speech Utterances, Transcription and Intent." *Software Computing* 26.17 (2022): 8253–8272.
71. Lorencin, Ivan, et al. "Using Multi-Layer Perceptron with Laplacian Edge Detector for Bladder Cancer Diagnosis." *Artificial Intelligence in Medicine* 102 (2020): 101746.
72. Taylor, Jacob, and Richard S. Matulewicz. "Multiparametric Cystoscopy: Opportunities to Enhance Bladder Cancer Detection." *Translational Andrology and Urology* 9.5 (2020): 2302.
73. AI-Enabled Computational Techniques for Cancer Diagnosis. *2021 IEEE 8th Uttar Pradesh Section International Conference on Electrical, Electronics and Computer Engineering (UPCON).* 2021. IEEE. Tula's Institute, Dhoolkot, Dehradun, Uttarakhand, India.

74. Cha, Kenny H., et al. "Bladder Cancer Treatment Response Assessment in CT Using Radiomics with Deep-Learning." *Scientific Reports* 7.1 (2017): 8738.
75. Kumar, Yogesh, Komalpreet Kaur, and Gurpreet Singh. Machine Learning Aspects and Its Applications Towards Different Research Areas. *International Conference on Computation, Automation and Knowledge Management (ICCAKM)*. 2020. IEEE, India.
76. Gupta, Anish, Apeksha Koul, and Yogesh Kumar. Pancreatic Cancer Detection Using Machine and Deep Learning Techniques. *2022 2nd International Conference on Innovative Practices in Technology and Management (ICIPTM)*. 2022. IEEE, India.
77. Shah, Shahid Munir, et al. "Artificial Intelligence for Breast Cancer Detection: Trends & Directions." *arXiv preprint arXiv:2110.00942* 5.1 (2021): 1123–1142.
78. Moxey, Annette, et al. "Computerized Clinical Decision Support for Prescribing: Provision Does Not Guarantee Uptake." *Journal of the American Medical Informatics Association* 17.1 (2010): 25–33.
79. Liberati, Elisa G., et al. "What Hinders the Uptake of Computerized Decision Support Systems in Hospitals? A Qualitative Study and Framework for Implementation." *Implementation Science* 12 (2017): 1–13.
80. Gordon, R., "Robust Artificial Intelligence Tools to Predict Future Cancer." *MIT News*, 2021. https://News.Mit.Edu/2021/Robust-Artificial-Intelligence-Tools-Predict-Future-Cancer-0128. Accessed on 1 October 2024.
81. Teach, Randy L., and Edward H. Shortliffe. "An Analysis of Physician Attitudes Regarding Computer-Based Clinical Consultation Systems." *Computers and Biomedical Research* 14.6 (1981): 542–558.
82. Villani, Cédric, et al. *Donner Un Sens À L'intelligence Artificielle: Pour Une Stratégie Nationale Et Européenne*. Conseil national du numérique, 2018.
83. Rudin, Cynthia. "Stop Explaining Black Box Machine Learning Models for High Stakes Decisions and Use Interpretable Models Instead." *Nature Machine Intelligence* 1.5 (2019): 206–215.
84. Mettler Jr, Fred A., et al. "Radiologic and Nuclear Medicine Studies in the United States and Worldwide: Frequency, Radiation Dose, and Comparison with Other Radiation Sources—1950–2007." *Radiology* 253.2 (2009): 520–531.
85. Raoof, Suhail, et al. "Interpretation of Plain Chest Roentgenogram." *Chest* 141.2 (2012): 545–558.
86. Gohagan, John K., et al. "The Prostate, Lung, Colorectal and Ovarian (PLCO) Cancer Screening Trial of the National Cancer Institute: History, Organization, and Status." *Controlled Clinical Trials* 21.6 (2000): 251S–272S.
87 Irvin, J., Rajpurkar, P., Ko, M., Yu, Y., Ciurea-Ilcus, S., Chute, C., ... & Ng, A. Y. Chexpert: A large chest radiograph dataset with uncertainty labels and expert comparison. In *Proceedings of the AAAI conference on artificial intelligence* (Vol. 33, No. 01, pp. 590–597), 2019, July.
88. Attention-Guided Curriculum Learning for Weakly Supervised Classification and Localization of Thoracic Diseases on Chest Radiographs. *Machine Learning in Medical Imaging: 9th International Workshop*, MLMI 2018, Held in Conjunction with MICCAI 2018, Granada, Spain, September 16, 2018, Proceedings 9. 2018. Springer. Print.
89. Wang, X., Peng, Y., Lu, L., Lu, Z., Bagheri, M., & Summers, R. M. Chestx-ray8: Hospital-scale chest x-ray database and benchmarks on weakly-supervised classification and localization of common thorax diseases. In *Proceedings of the IEEE Conference on Computer Vision and Pattern Recognition* (pp. 2097–2106), 2017.
90. Armato III, Samuel G., et al. "The Lung Image Database Consortium (LIDC) and Image Database Resource Initiative (IDRI): A Completed Reference Database of Lung Nodules on Ct Scans." *Medical Physics* 38.2 (2011): 915–931.

91. Grenier, Philippe, et al. "Chronic Diffuse Interstitial Lung Disease: Diagnostic Value of Chest Radiography and High-Resolution Ct." *Radiology* 179.1 (1991): 123–132.
92. Jin, Dakai, et al. "Artificial Intelligence in Radiology." In Jin, Dakai (ed) *Artificial Intelligence in Medicine*. Elsevier, 2021. 265–289.
93. Gurcan, Metin N., et al. "Histopathological Image Analysis: A Review." *IEEE Reviews in Biomedical Engineering* 2 (2009): 147–171.
94. Lewis Jr, James S., et al. "A Quantitative Histomorphometric Classifier (QUHBIC) Identifies Aggressive Versus Indolent P16-Positive Oropharyngeal Squamous Cell Carcinoma." *The American Journal of Surgical Pathology* 38.1 (2014): 128–137.
95. Basavanhally, Ajay, et al. "Multi-Field-of-View Strategy for Image-Based Outcome Prediction of Multi-Parametric Estrogen Receptor-Positive Breast Cancer Histopathology: Comparison to Oncotype Dx." *Journal of Pathology Informatics* 2.2 (2012): 1.
96. Cruz-Roa, Angel, Ajay Basavanhally, Fabio González, Hannah Gilmore, Michael Feldman, Shridar Ganesan, Natalie Shih, John Tomaszewski, and Anant Madabhushi. "Automatic detection of invasive ductal carcinoma in whole slide images with convolutional neural networks." In Medical *imaging* 2014: Digital *pathology* 9041 (2014): 904103. SPIE.
97. Krizhevsky, Alex, and Geoff Hinton. "Convolutional Deep Belief Networks on Cifar-10." *Unpublished Manuscript* 40.7 (2010): 1–9.
98. Krizhevsky, Alex, Ilya Sutskever, and Geoffrey E. Hinton. "Imagenet Classification with Deep Convolutional Neural Networks." *Advances in Neural Information Processing Systems* 25 (2012): 118–126.
99. Janowczyk, Andrew, and Anant Madabhushi. "Deep Learning for Digital Pathology Image Analysis: A Comprehensive Tutorial with Selected Use Cases." *Journal of Pathology Informatics* 7.1 (2016): 29.
100. Humphrey, Peter A. "Gleason Grading and Prognostic Factors in Carcinoma of the Prostate." *Modern Pathology* 17.3 (2004): 292–306.
101. Irshad, Humayun, et al. "Methods for Nuclei Detection, Segmentation, and Classification in Digital Histopathology: A Review—Current Status and Future Potential." *IEEE Reviews in Biomedical Engineering* 7 (2013): 97–114.
102. Basavanhally, A., Yu, E., Xu, J., Ganesan, S., Feldman, M., Tomaszewski, J., & Madabhushi, A. "Incorporating domain knowledge for tubule detection in breast histopathology using O'Callaghan neighborhoods." Medical *imaging* 2011: Computer-aided *diagnosis* 7963 (2011): 305–319. SPIE.
103. Sirinukunwattana, Korsuk, David RJ Snead, and Nasir M. Rajpoot. "A random polygons model of glandular structures in colon histology images." In *2015 IEEE 12th International Symposium on Biomedical Imaging (ISBI)*, pp. 1526–1529. IEEE, 2015.
104. Fatakdawala, Hussain, et al. "Expectation–Maximization-Driven Geodesic Active Contour with Overlap Resolution (Emagacor): Application to Lymphocyte Segmentation on Breast Cancer Histopathology." *IEEE Transactions on Biomedical Engineering* 57.7 (2010): 1676–1689.
105. Arteta, Carlos, Victor Lempitsky, J. Alison Noble, and Andrew Zisserman. "Learning to detect cells using non-overlapping extremal regions." In *International conference on medical image computing and computer-assisted intervention*, pp. 348–356. Berlin, Heidelberg: Springer Berlin Heidelberg, 2012.
106. LeCun, Yann, Yoshua Bengio, and Geoffrey Hinton. "Deep Learning." *Nature* 521.7553 (2015): 436–444.
107. Orlov, Nikita, et al. "Wnd-Charm: Multi-Purpose Image Classification Using Compound Image Transforms." *Pattern Recognition Letters* 29.11 (2008): 1684–1693.
108. Singh, Dilbag, et al. "Early Diagnosis of Covid-19 Patients Using Deep Learning-Based Deep Forest Model." *Journal of Experimental & Theoretical Artificial Intelligence* 35.3 (2023): 365–375.

109. Allam, Zaheer, Gourav Dey, and David S. Jones. "Artificial Intelligence (AI) Provided Early Detection of the Coronavirus (Covid-19) in China and Will Influence Future Urban Health Policy Internationally." *AI* 1.2 (2020): 156–165.
110. Agbehadji, Israel Edem, et al. "Review of Big Data Analytics, Artificial Intelligence and Nature-Inspired Computing Models towards Accurate Detection of Covid-19 Pandemic Cases and Contact Tracing." *International Journal of Environmental Research and Public Health* 17.15 (2020): 5330.
111. Calandra, Davide, and Matteo Favareto. "Artificial Intelligence to Fight Covid-19 Outbreak Impact: An Overview." *European Journal of Social Impact and Circular Economy* 1.3 (2020): 84–104.
112. Khanna, Varada Vivek, et al. "A Machine Learning and Explainable Artificial Intelligence Triage-Prediction System for Covid-19." *Decision Analytics Journal* 7 (2023): 100246.
113. Pourhomayoun, Mohammad, and Mahdi Shakibi. "Predicting Mortality Risk in Patients with Covid-19 Using Machine Learning to Help Medical Decision-Making." *Smart Health* 20 (2021): 100178.
114. Ghosh, Aritra, Maria M. Larrondo-Petrie, and Mirjana Pavlovic. "Revolutionizing Vaccine Development for Covid-19: A Review of AI-Based Approaches." *Information* 14.12 (2023): 665.
115. Bagabir, Sali Abubaker, et al. "Covid-19 and Artificial Intelligence: Genome Sequencing, Drug Development and Vaccine Discovery." *Journal of Infection and Public Health* 15.2 (2022): 289–296.
116. Arora, Gunjan, et al. "Artificial Intelligence in Surveillance, Diagnosis, Drug Discovery and Vaccine Development against Covid-19." *Pathogens* 10.8 (2021): 1048.
117. Shukla, Samta, et al. "Optimizing Vaccine Distribution Via Mobile Clinics: A Case Study on Covid-19 Vaccine Distribution to Long-Term Care Facilities." *Vaccine* 40.5 (2022): 734–741.
118. Addy, Alfred. "Artificial Intelligence in the Supply Chain Management for Vaccine Distribution in the West Africa N Healthcare Sector with a Focus on Ghana." *International Journal of Legal Science and Innovation* 10 (2023): 1–25.
119. Yan, Zhipeng, Ming Yang, and Ching-Lung Lai. "Long Covid-19 Syndrome: A Comprehensive Review of Its Effect on Various Organ Systems and Recommendation on Rehabilitation Plans." *Biomedicines* 9.8 (2021): 966.
120. Mfouth Kemajou, Pamela, Armand Mbanya, and Yves Coppieters. "Digital Approaches in Post-Covid Healthcare: A Systematic Review of Technological Innovations in Disease Management." *Biology Methods and Protocols* 9.1 (2024): bpae070.
121. Fuster-Casanovas, Aïna, et al. "An Artificial Intelligence–Driven Digital Health Solution to Support Clinical Management of Patients with Long Covid-19: Protocol for a Prospective Multicenter Observational Study." *JMIR Research Protocols* 11.10 (2022): e37704.
122. Cau, Riccardo, et al. "Long-Covid Diagnosis: From Diagnostic to Advanced AI-Driven Models." *European Journal of Radiology* 148 (2022): 110164.
123. El-Solh, Ali A., et al. "Predicting Active Pulmonary Tuberculosis Using an Artificial Neural Network." *Chest* 116.4 (1999): 968–973.
124. Lv, Hao, et al. "Application of Artificial Intelligence and Machine Learning for Covid-19 Drug Discovery and Vaccine Design." *Briefings in Bioinformatics* 22.6 (2021): bbab320.
125. Waqas, Muhammad, et al. "Immunoinformatics and Molecular Docking Studies Predicted Potential Multiepitope-Based Peptide Vaccine and Novel Compounds against Novel Sars-Cov-2 through Virtual Screening." *BioMed Research International* 2021.1 (2021): 1596834.
126. Fang, Enyue, et al. "Advances in Covid-19 Mrna Vaccine Development." *Signal Transduction and Targeted Therapy* 7.1 (2022): 94.

127. Huang, Sihong, et al. "Persistent White Matter Changes in Recovered Covid-19 Patients at the 1-Year Follow-Up." *Brain* 145.5 (2022): 1830–1838.
128. Mittelstadt, Brent. "Principles Alone Cannot Guarantee Ethical AI." *Nature Machine Intelligence* 1.11 (2019): 501–507.
129. Morley, Jessica, et al. "The Ethics of AI in Health Care: A Mapping Review." *Social Science & Medicine* 260 (2020): 113172.
130. He, Jianxing, et al. "The Practical Implementation of Artificial Intelligence Technologies in Medicine." *Nature Medicine* 25.1 (2019): 30–36.
131. Reddy, Sandeep, et al. "A Governance Model for the Application of AI in Health Care." *Journal of the American Medical Informatics Association* 27.3 (2020): 491–497.

8 Deep Learning for Cardiovascular Risk Prediction

Unveiling Insights with RNNs and LSTMs

Revathi Vaithiyanathan, G.S. Girisha, and P. Venkatesh

8.1 INTRODUCTION

Heart illness ranks among the top reasons of death world- wide, claiming 17.9 million lives annually. Current prediction methods for heart disease often overlook smoking as a critical factor. Cardiovascular disease, or coronary illness, poses a significant threat not only in India but globally. It is estimated that heart diseases [1–3] account for 28.1% of deaths, contributing to over 17.6 million fatalities each year. Ultimately fostering a healthcare environment that is proactive rather than reactive. This research article examines at cardio vascular risk prediction using Deep Learning (DL) technologies [4–6], with a particular attention on the use of Recurrent Neural Networks (RNNs) and Long Short Term Memory (LSTM) networks [7–9]. Beyond the mere application of advanced computational methods, this study delves into the personal significance of accurate risk prediction, highlighting how early detection of cardiovascular risk permits people to make well-versed lifestyle adoptions and pursue timely medical interventions, thus potentially improving their health outcomes and overall quality of life. From a technological view point, the paper illustrates the ideologies of underlying [10,11] RNNs and LSTMs, explains their function to process consequent patient data—such as diagnostic tests and medical history—to forecast cardiovascular risk with improved accuracy [10,12,13]. Additionally, it discusses the wider societal impact of these predictive models, identifying how their implementation in healthcare can helps to extra effective resource allocation, lower healthcare costs [14], and better patient outcomes. In the view of these developments, the study also considers ethical issues, supporting for the incorporation of Explainable AI models, such as SHAP (SHapley Additive exPlanations), to increase transparency and hope in predictive models [14] among patients and healthcare professionals alike. Through quantitative analyses

DOI: 10.1201/9781003600947-8

and comprehensive case studies, this research article highlights the ability of DL methodologies for cardiovascular risk prediction [15–18] and their potential to improve the preventive healthcare practices

8.2 RELATED WORK

8.2.1 Comparative Analysis

The combination of LSTM and RNNs networks in the field of cardio vascular risk prediction is discussed in this section within the framework of ongoing research. It explains how this investigation extends beyond accepted framework and creates novel pathways for improving risk prediction in cardiovascular disease.

Triantafyllidis, Andreas, et al. "Deep learning in mHealth for cardiovascular disease, diabetes, and cancer: systematic review" [19]: This research article deliberates the applications of DL methodology in mobile health (mHealth) for chronic diseases. It contains a organized assessment of studies using Machine Learning techniques for medical analysis, comparisons with traditional Machine Learning techniques, and the essential for explainable AI in healthcare.

Swathy M, and K Saruladha. "A comparative study of classification and prediction of Cardio-Vascular Diseases (CVD) using Machine Learning and Deep Learning techniques" [20]: This study discovers the applications of DL and Machine Learning techniques to classify and predict the Cardio-Vascular Diseases (CVD). It compares different techniques, tools, and dataset used for prediction, aiming to support in early diagnosis and decrease the mortality value associated with CVD.

Barbieri, Sebastiano, et al. "Predicting cardiovascular risk from national administrative databases using a combined survival analysis and deep learning approach" [21]: This research paper is a examine on cardiovascular disease risk prediction using Cox proportional vulnerable techniques and DL techniques. It includes details on model training, testing, validation, and comparison with traditional models, as well as participant characteristics and results.

Bagheri, Ayoub, et al. "Multimodal learning for cardiovascular risk prediction using EHR data" [22]: This paper presents a multimodal recurrent neural network method for cardiovascular disease prediction, integrating medical data and structured clinical evidence from electronic health records. It compares different deep neural network architectures and validates the state-of-the-art performance.

Cho, Sang-Yeong, et al. "Pre-existing and machine learning-based models for cardiovascular risk prediction" [23]: This paper presents the analysis on the performance of Machine Learning techniques in predicting cardiovascular risk in statin-naïve strong Korean adults without cardiovascular disease. The analysis compares the performance of traditional risk prediction models with Machine Learning based techniques and discusses the limitations of the study.

Guo, Aixia, et al. "Predicting cardiovascular health trajectories in time-series electronic health records with LSTM models" [24]: This paper, authored by Guo et al., focuses on predicting cardiovascular health trajectories using LSTM models based on time- series electronic health records. The study utilized a huge and nationally characteristic longitudinal dataset of patients to compare the performance of LSTM techniques with Logistic Regression and Random Forest models.

Rim, Tyler Hyungtaek, et al. "Deep-learning-based cardiovascular risk stratification using coronary artery calcium scores predicted from retinal photographs" [25]: This paper presents a study on the usage of retinal photographs to predict cardiovascular disease risk. It includes information from Singapore, the UK Biobank, and South Korea, deliberates the development of a DL techniques for risk prediction. The study also emphasize the challenges and probable applications of the findings.

Schlesinger, Daphne E., and Collin M. Stultz. "Deep learning for cardiovascular risk stratification" [26]: This research a delivers a detailed review of the present state of DL techniques for cardiovascular risk stratification. It discusses the issues, potential applications, and the essential for extra interpretable and clinically influential models. The authors also emphasize the significance of information availability and the issues of existing models.

Ballinger, Brandon, et al. "DeepHeart: semi-supervised sequence learning for cardiovascular risk prediction" [27]: This research article provides the usage of DL to identify the health conditions using wearable data. It addresses challenges such as data volume, interpretability, and deployment. The authors propose a semi-supervised training approach and present promising results for detecting diabetes, high blood pressure, sleep apnea, and high cholesterol.

Yu, Jingzhi, et al. "Incorporating longitudinal history of risk factors into atherosclerotic cardiovascular disease risk prediction using deep learning" [28]: This paper provides a detailed study that uses DL methods to forecast the ten-year risk of Atherosclerotic cardiovascular disease (ASCVD) by incorporating longitudinal clinical and cross- sectional and behavioral risk aspect levels. The study evaluates the predictive performance of the model and the significance of longitudinal data for ASCVD risk prediction.

8.3 PROPOSED METHODOLOGY

The following Figure 8.1 depicts the flow diagram of Cardio vascular Risk Prediction using DL Techniques:

8.3.1 Predictive Models

8.3.1.1 RNN

It operates by using the previous step output as input for the present step, which sets it apart from the traditional neural networks where input and output are considered as independent. RNNs hidden state, which retains information about sequential data, is one of the key distinguished features. Moreover, RNNs engage the similar set of parameters across inputs or hidden layers to produce outputs, thus simplifying parameter difficulty compared to other neural networks.

Each time step is denoted by a fixed activation function unit. Every unit has an internal state, sometime also known as the hidden state of the unit. This hidden state is updated at each time step to indicate the changes in the networks historical knowledge. The following recurrence relation is applied to update the hidden state:

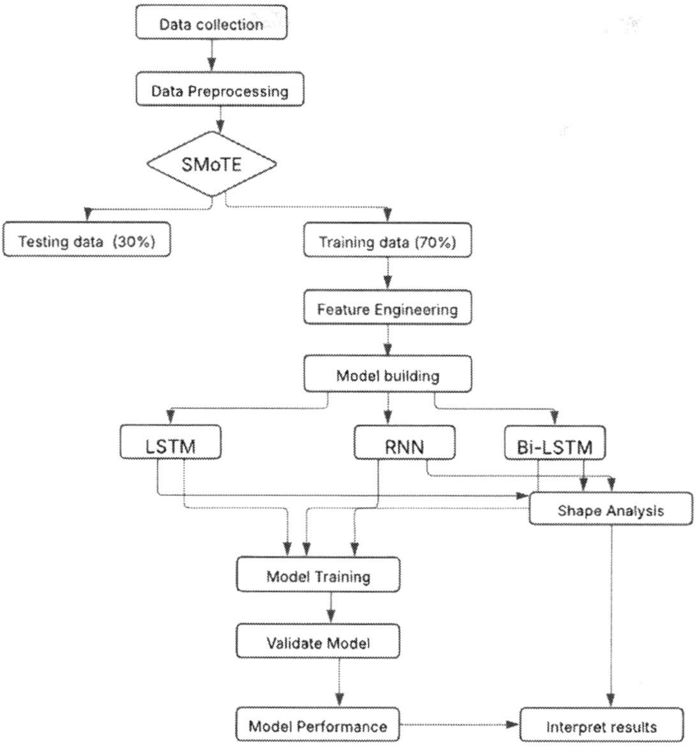

FIGURE 8.1 Flow diagram of cardiovascular risk prediction using Deep Learning techniques.

Computing the current state the following formula is applied (as mentioned in equation 8.1):

$$h_k = f\left(h_{k-1}, X_t\right) \tag{8.1}$$

where,

- $X_k \rightarrow$ input state
- $h_k \rightarrow$ current state
- $h_{k-1} \rightarrow$ previous state

For applying Activation function the formula is (tanh) (as mentioned in equation 8.2):

$$h_k = \tan h\left(W_{hh} h_{k-1} + W_{xh} X_k\right) \tag{8.2}$$

where,

- $h_k \rightarrow$ current state
- $h_{k-1} \rightarrow$ previous state

- W_{hh} & W_{xh} → weight at output layer
- X_k → input state

The formula for computing the output (as mentioned in equation 8.3):

$$y_t = W_{hy} \cdot X_k \tag{8.3}$$

- Y_t → output
- W_{hy} → weight at output layer
- X_t → current state

8.3.1.2 LSTM

LSTM networks pretains to the family of recurrent neural networks (RNNs) and are designed to address the problem of vanishing gradients frequently encountered in traditional RNN architectures. While traditional RNNs often find challenges in identifying long-term dependencies within sequential data due to the gradual weakening of gradients over time, LSTMs (Figure 8.2.) integrate distinct gating mechanisms and memory cells.

These specific components allow LSTMs to specifically alter and preserve the data over extended time spans. There are three gates, which are explained below:

Forget Gate: The data that is no longer valuable in the cell state is eliminated by this gate. Prior to the bias being added, this gate accepts two inputs X_k (input at the specified moment) and h_{k-1} (previous cell output), which are multiplied by weight matrices. A binary output is generated after the outcome has been passed through an activation function. For a specific cell state, the output is 1, the data is saved for future use and the output is 0 then the portion of data is forgotten.

Input Gate: The addition of useful data to the cell state is accountable of this gate. Like a forget gate, the data is first computed using sigmoid function, then

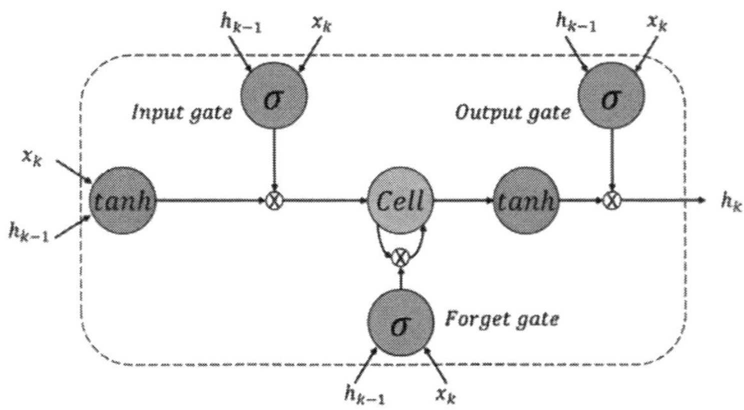

FIGURE 8.2 Structure of LSTM with three gates.

the value range to be remembered are screened by using inputs h_{k-1} and X_k. The tan$h$ function, which provides an output range from −1 to +1 and includes all the feasible values from h_{k-1} and X_k. Lastly, the useful data is obtained by multiplying the vector values by the controlled values.

Output Gate: This gate is accountable for collecting valuable data from the present cell and displaying it as an output. First, the cells tanh function is used to create a vector. After that, the sigmoid function is utilized to calculate the data and inputs h_{k-1} and X_k are used to screen the value to be remembered. To send the output (h_k) and input to the next cell, the vector value and the controlled value are finally multiplied.

8.3.1.3 Bi-LSTM

A Bidirectional Long Short Term Memory (Bi-LSTM) network improves sequence learning by processing data in both forward and backward directions. Each LSTM cell within a Bi-LSTM has input, output and forget gates to control the information flow. This bidirectional approach captures context from both past and future, enhancing performance in tasks requiring comprehensive understanding of sequential data. Bi-LSTMs are particularly effective in NLP, Time Series Analysis, and any domain where the bidirectional context is valuable

Forward Pass: It processes the sequence from beginning to end, capturing dependencies and historical information.

Backward Pass: It processes the sequence from end to beginning, capturing dependencies and historical information.

Combined Output: Merges information from both forward and backward passes. Enhances prediction accuracy and context aware- ness by leveraging bidirectional context.

8.4 EXPERIMENTATION AND RESULTS

The dataset was subjected to various traditional Machine Learning models including Logistic Regression, Support Vector Machines (SVM), K-Nearest Neighbors (KNN) with k ranging from 0 to 50, Random Forest, and AdaBoost. Analysis of these models revealed varied performance metrics across different algorithms. Logistic regression, KNN, and SVM shown modest performance, with accuracies value from 53% to 71%. Random forest showed marginally enhanced performance compared to the previously mentioned models. Additionally, feature significance analysis using SHAP values gave insights into the important factors affecting model outcomes.

8.4.1 Challenges in RNNs

Applying RNNs to the dataset represented a few difficulties, particularly with traditional LSTM models. These models came across the overfitting problem attributed to the vanishing gradient problem, which led to suboptimal performance. Moreover, conventional LSTM architectures illustrate higher loss rates than alternative models, showing restrictions in capturing temporal dependencies efficiently.

To thoroughly assess the possibility of recurrent neural network (RNN) architectures, including Conventional LSTM and Bidirectional LSTM (Bi-LSTM) (Table 8.1), GridSearchCV and stratified k-fold cross-validation techniques were employed. Stratified k-fold cross-validation confirmed that each and every fold of the dataset preserved the same class distribution as the original dataset, reducing bias in model evaluation. Furthermore, GridSearchCV was also used to methodically discover a variety of hyperparameters for the RNN models, allowing the identification of best parameter configurations. This rigorous estimation technique facilitated a comprehensive analysis of the models' prediction performance and robustness across various parameter settings.

8.4.3 Introduction of Bidirectional LSTM

Bidirectional LSTM (Bi-LSTM) architecture was designed in order to solve the drawback of conventional LSTM. The Bi-LSTM model influences the bidirectional processing of input sequences by allowing it to capture forward and backward temporal dependencies more effectively. This architecture was expected to address the challenges identified with conventional LSTM models and improve overall model performance.

8.4.4 Evaluation of Bi-LSTM Model

The Bi-LSTM model illustrates hopeful results by achieving considerable accuracy and nominal loss compared to traditional LSTM architectures. Performance estimation of the Bi-LSTM model produced an accuracy of 87.713, depicting its effectiveness in capturing difficult temporal patterns within the dataset (Table 8.2). Feature significant analysis using SHAP values (Figure 8.3) further corroborated the importance of influential predictors recognized by the Bi-LSTM model.

TABLE 8.1
Model Performance

DL Method	Accuracy (%)
RNN	77.1
LSTM	79.1
Bi-LSTM	87.713

TABLE 8.2
Dataset Attributes Detailed Information

Attribute	Description
Age	Measured in years
Anaemia	Condition where you lack red blood cells (0: represents the absence of anemia, 1: indicates the presence of anemia.)
Creatinine phosphokinase	Represented as continuous numerical values, measured in units per liter (U/L)
Diabetes	0: Represents the absence of diabetes, 1: Indicates the presence of diabetes

(Continued)

TABLE 8.2 (*Continued*)
Dataset Attributes Detailed Information

Attribute	Description
Ejection fraction	Values might be represented as numerical values ranging from 0 to 100 (percentage %)
Platelets	Number of platelets per volume of blood [platelets per microliter of blood(plt/uL)]
Serum creatinine	Continuous numerical values, calculated in milligrams per deciliter (mg/dL)
Serum sodium	Calculated in millimoles per liter (mmol/L)
Gender	0 typically represents female, 1 typically represents male
Smoking	0: Represents non-smokers, 1: Represents smokers
Alcohol	0: Represents non-alcoholic, 1: Represents alcoholic
Cholesterol	Cholesterol Levels (1: Low, 2: Borderline High, 3: High)
Glucose	Glucose Levels (1: Low, 2: Borderline High, 3: High)
Height	Measured in centimeters.
Weight	Measured in kilograms.
BMI	Numerical value measured based on a person's height and weight
Ap_hi	Systolic (contraction) Blood Pressure in millimeters of mercury (mmHg)
Ap lo	Dilation Blood Pressure in millimeters of mercury (mmHg)
Target	0: Represents the absence of the disease, 1: Indicates the presence of the disease

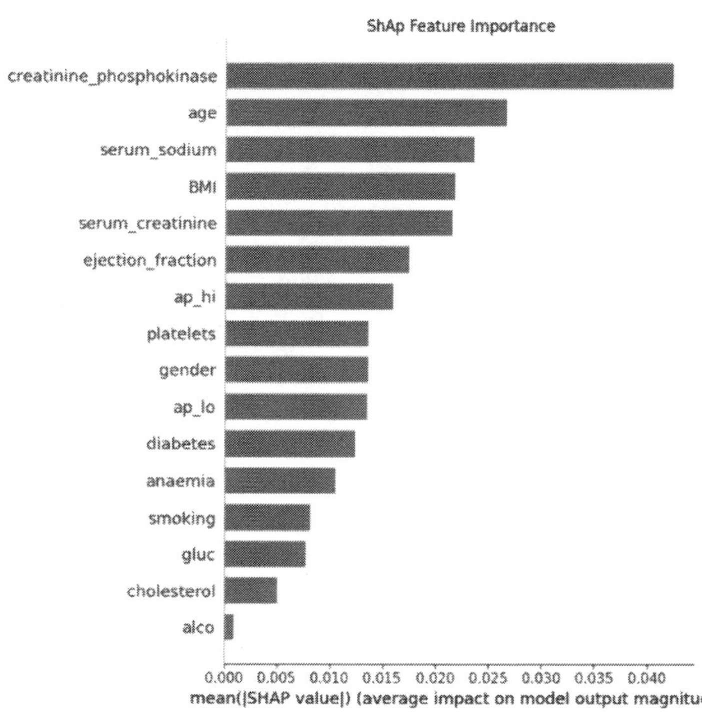

FIGURE 8.3 Feature significance analysis plot.

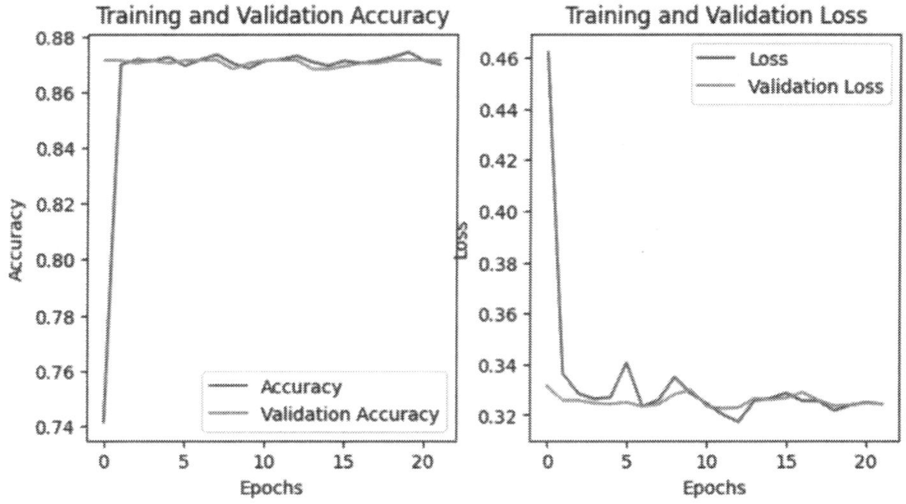

FIGURE 8.4 User input desktop application.

Comparative analysis of model performance highlighted the superiority of the Bi-LSTM architecture in achieving the desired accuracy and effectiveness for predictive tasks. The Bi-LSTM model exhibited superior performance metrics compared to conventional Machine Learning techniques and LSTM architectures, underscoring its utility in handling sequential data and capturing intricate temporal dependencies.

8.4.5 Validation on Unseen Data

The behavior of the Bi-LSTM model was validated on unobserved data to measure its generalization abilities. A graphical user interface (GUI) (Figure 8.4) utilizing the tkinter library was established for this purpose, permitting the users to provide input values directly into the model for estimation. The GUI permitted seamless interaction with the model by giving users an intuitive user interface to provide input data and visualize the model's estimation. Reliability in performance among the training and testing datasets reaffirmed the consistency and robustness of the Bi-LSTM model for predictive tasks. Moreover, the GUI enabled the real-time visualization of the model's predictions, with results presented as plots for easy analysis and interpretation. These interactive validation techniques further evaluate the model's efficiency in managing unseen data and provide users with a practical tool for predictive analysis.

8.4.6 Accuracy and Loss Curves

The validation accuracy and loss curves (Figure 8.5) demonstrate the behavior of the model during training epochs. The Validation Accuracy curve specifies the model's

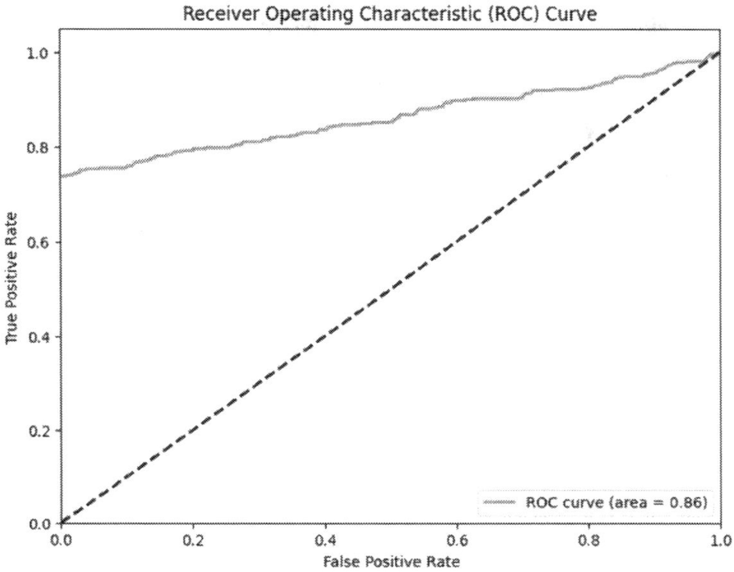

FIGURE 8.5 Training & validation accuracy and loss curve.

Classification Report:

	precision	recall	f1-score	support
0	0.80	1.00	0.89	487
1	1.00	0.74	0.85	469
accuracy			0.87	956
macro avg	0.90	0.87	0.87	956
weighted avg	0.90	0.87	0.87	956

FIGURE 8.6 ROC and AUC curve.

classification accuracy over time while the validation loss curve specifies the model's capacity to reduce the errors on the validation dataset. An increasing accuracy and decreasing validation loss suggest the model is learning effectively. However, variations or divergences may lead to overfitting or convergence problems.

8.4.7 ROC and AUC Curves

At several classification thresholds, the trade-off between True Positive (TP) and False Positive (FP) is shown by the ROC curve (Figure 8.6). A higher ROC curve specifies improved discrimination ability. The AUC (Area Under the Curve) value allows a single scalar metric to describe the entire performance of the model, with values closer to 1 representing improved performance.

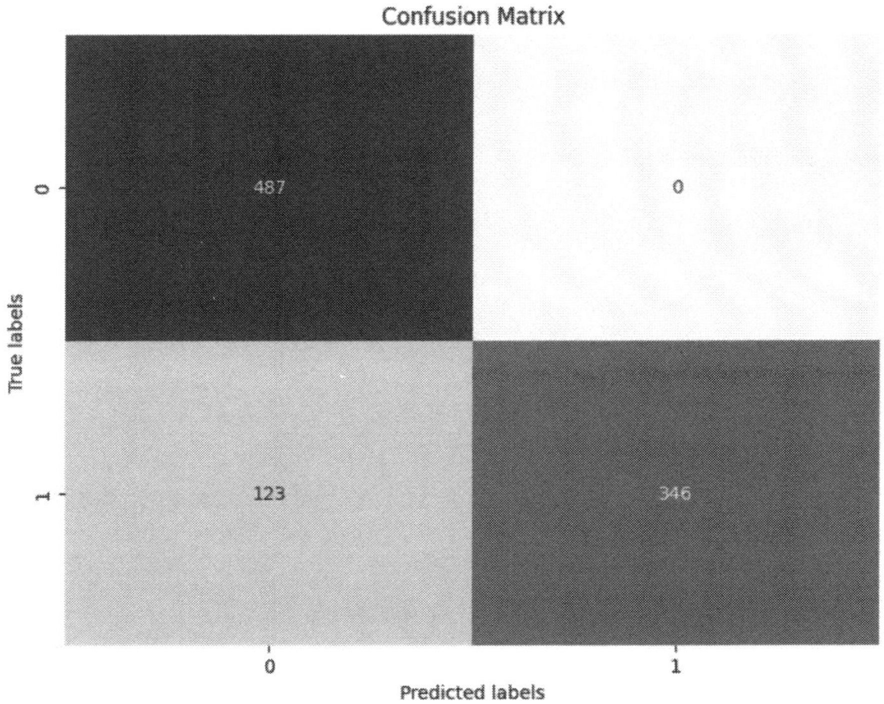

FIGURE 8.7 Classification report.

8.4.8 Classification Report

The model performance over several classes is comprehensively represented in the classification report (Figure 8.7). For each class, metrics like Precision, F1-score, recall, and support are reported. F1-score, which is a well-adjusted metric of a model's performance, is the harmonic mean of recall and precision, while precision specifies the fraction of genuine positive estimations between all positive predictions. Recall computes the percentage of TP that the model appropriately recognized.

8.4.9 Confusion Matrix

The confusion matrix (Figure 8.8) displays the model's predictions compared to the ground truth labels across different classes. True Positives, True Negatives, False Positives, and False Negatives appear in the matrix. Diagonal elements denote properly classified instances, while off-diagonal elements denote misclassifications. Evaluating the confusion matrix aids in finding the patterns of misclassifications and evaluating the model's performance among various classes.

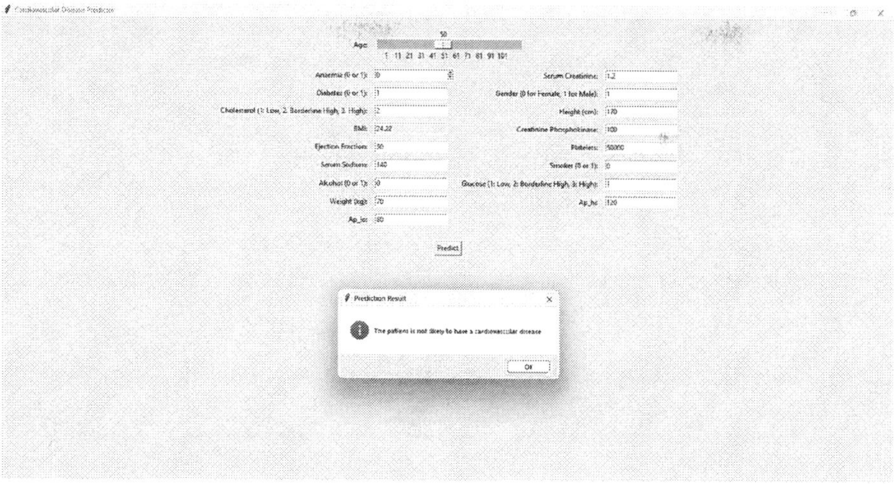

FIGURE 8.8 Confusion matrix.

8.4.10 Comparison of Models

Discussion In this study, we used a diverse dataset with numerous health-related features to systematically evaluate various Machine Learning and DL approaches for the prediction of cardiovascular diseases. The comprehensive experimentation and rigorous validation methods ensured the reliability and robustness of our findings.

8.5 CONCLUSION

The extensive experimentation and analysis (Figure 8.9) led to the conclusion that the Bi-LSTM model is highly effective for predicting cardiovascular disease, outperforming both traditional Machine Learning models and simpler neural network architectures. The model's robustness and generalization capability, validated through rigorous testing and real-world application via a GUI, underscore its potential for practical deployment in healthcare settings.

8.6 FUTURE WORK

Enhanced Data Collection: The performance of any predictive model is deeply dependent on the quality and comprehensiveness of the data. As future work, there should be emphasis on improving the quality of the dataset by integrating more granular and varied data points, such as genetic data, lifestyle factors, and more detailed medical history. Health Recommendations: Future models should be capable of generating personalized health recommendations based on the predictions. Integrating recommendation systems that provide actionable advice on lifestyle changes, medication adjustments, and follow-up tests could significantly improve patient outcomes and preventive care.

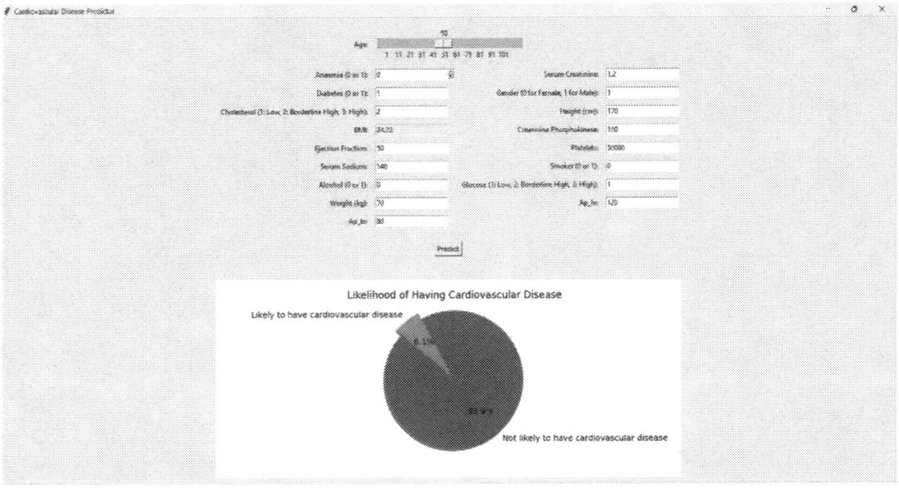

FIGURE 8.9 Pie chart for showing prediction results.

REFERENCES

1. Jindal, Harshit, et al. (2021). Heart disease prediction using machine learning algorithms. In *IOP Conference Series: Materials Science and Engineering* (vol. 1022.1). IOP Publishing, Singapore.
2. Sardar, T. H. (2024). Reflecting on a decade of evolution: MapReduce-based advances in partitioning-based, hierarchical-based, and density-based clustering (2013–2023). *Wiley Interdisciplinary Reviews: Data Mining and Knowledge Discovery*, 5.1: e1566.
3. Theerthagiri, P., Ruby, A. U., Chandran, J. G. C., Sardar, T. H., & Shafeeq, B. M. A. (2024). Deep SqueezeNet learning model for diagnosis and prediction of maize leaf diseases. *Journal of Big Data*, 11.1: 112.
4. Subbarao, E., et al. (2023). Investigation of solar energy for urban areas and metropolitan communities using machine learning. *Electric Power Components and Systems*, 7.2: 1–11.
5. Sardar, T. H., Faizabadi, A. R., & Ansari, Z. (2017). An analysis of data processing using Mapreduce paradigm on the Hadoop framework. *International Journal of Emerging Research in Management and Technology*, 6.5, 55–67.
6. Khatun, A., & Sardar, T. H. (2025). Cryptography algorithms to prevent different security attacks. In Khatun, A., & Sardar (eds) *Next Generation Mechanisms for Data Encryption* (pp. 35–46). CRC Press.
7. Krishnan, Surenthiran, Magalingam, Pritheega, & Ibrahim, Roslina. (2023). Enhanced recurrent neural network (RNN) for heart disease risk prediction using Framingham datasets. *Open International Journal of Informatics*, 11.1: 41–52.
8. Sardar, T. H., Sarkar, R., Ahmed, S. J., & Bandyopadhyay, A. (2023, May). A novel ensemble methodology to validate fuzzy clusters of Big Data. In *Proceedings of the Fourth International Conference on Trends in Computational and Cognitive Engineering: TCCE 2022* (pp. 267–278). Springer Nature, Singapore.
9. Shuvo, Shahnewaz. (2023). An early detection of heart disease using machine learning (recurrent neural network): ML research on heart disease prediction, 12(3), 101–113. *ScienceOpen Preprints*.

10. Sardar, T. H., Muttineni, A., & Ranjan, R. (2024). The future of Big Data in customer experience and inventory management. In Sardar, T. H., Muttineni, A., & Ranjan, R. (eds) *Big Data Computing* (pp. 233–248). CRC Press
11. Zhao, Xiaosong, Liu, Yong, & Zhao, Qiangfu. (2024). Generalized loss-based cnn-bilstm for stock market prediction. *International Journal of Financial Studies*, 12.3: 61.
12. Lilhore, Umesh Kumar, et al. (2024). Optimizing protein sequence classification: Integrating deep learning models with Bayesian optimization for enhanced biological analysis. *BMC Medical Informatics and Decision Making*, 24.1: 236.
13. Sardar, T. H., Das, S., & Pandey, B. K. (2024). Explainable AI (XAI): Concepts and theory. In Sardar, T. H., Das, S., & Pandey, B. K. (eds) *Medical Data Analysis and Processing using Explainable Artificial Intelligence* (pp. 1–18). CRC Press.
14. Paranjothi, Kavitha, Ghouse, Fathima, & Vaithiyanathan, Revathi. (2024). Detection of Parkinson's disease on DaTSCAN image using multi-kernel support vector machine. *International Journal of Intelligent Engineering & Systems*, 17.5, 118–129.
15. Midhun, Jadda, et al. (2023). Ensemble deep learning models for accurate prediction of cardiovascular disease risk: A comparative analysis. In *2023 2nd International Conference on Edge Computing and Applications (ICECAA)*. Namakkal, Tamil Nadu, India. IEEE.
16. Katie Wright, E. M. J. (2024). Artificial intelligence and digital biomarkers: A revolution in cardiovascular diagnostics. *EMJ*, 12.1: 31–35.
17. Satpathy, S., Kumar Paikaray, B., Yang, M., & Balakrishnan, A. (Eds.). (2024). *Sustainable Farming through Machine Learning: Enhancing Productivity and Efficiency* (1st ed.). CRC Press, Boca Raton. https://doi.org/10.1201/9781003484608
18. Massari, Hakim El, et al. (2024). The impact of ontology on the prediction of cardiovascular disease compared to machine learning algorithms. *arXiv preprint arXiv:2405.20414.*
19. Triantafyllidis, A., et al. (2022). Deep learning in mHealth for cardiovascular disease, diabetes, and cancer. *Systematic Review JMIR Mhealth Uhealth*,10.4: e32344. https://mhealth.jmir.org/2022/4/e32344
20. Swathy, M., & Saruladha, K. (2022). A comparative study of classification and prediction of cardio-vascular diseases (CVD) using machine learning and deep learning techniques. *ICT Express*, 8.1: 109–116.
21. Ashtami, J., et al. (2025). Artificial intelligence in biological data science. In *Artificial Intelligence and Biological Sciences* (vol. 1, p. 346). Edited by Dr. P.V. Mohanan. Taylor and Francis.
22. Bagheri, A., et al. Multimodal learning for cardiovascular risk prediction using EHR data. arXiv 2020. arXiv preprint arXiv:2008.11979.
23. Cho, Sang-Yeong, et al. (2021). Pre-existing and machine learning-based models for cardiovascular risk prediction. *Scientific Reports*, 11.1: 8886.
24. Barbieri, Sebastiano, et al. (2022). Predicting cardiovascular risk from national administrative databases using a combined survival analysis and deep learning approach. *International Journal of Epidemiology*, 51.3: 931–944.
25. Rim, Tyler Hyungtaek, et al. (2021). Deep-learning-based cardiovascular risk stratification using coronary artery calcium scores predicted from retinal photographs. *The Lancet Digital Health*, 3.5: e306–e316.
26. Schlesinger, Daphne E., & Stultz, Collin M. (2020). Deep learning for cardiovascular risk stratification. *Current Treatment Options in Cardiovascular Medicine*, 22: 1–14.
27. Ballinger, Brandon, et al. (2018). DeepHeart: semi-supervised sequence learning for cardiovascular risk prediction. *Proceedings of the AAAI Conference on Artificial Intelligence*, 32.1, 1120–1135.
28. Yu, Jingzhi, et al. (2024). Incorporating longitudinal history of risk factors into atherosclerotic cardiovascular disease risk prediction using deep learning. *Scientific Reports*, 14.1: 2554.

9 Predicting Protein–Protein Interactions

Machine Learning Models, Obstacles, and Advancements

Debrupa Pal, Papri Ghosh, Subhram Das, and Aurpan Majumder

9.1 INTRODUCTION

Protein–protein interactions (PPIs) are pivotal in numerous biological processes [1], influencing protein specificity, activation, suppression, metabolic reactions, and the formation of compulsory sites for effector molecules [2]. Understanding PPIs elucidates protein structural characteristics [3] and cellular molecular machinery [4], aiding various biomedical and biological research domains, such as mechanisms of diseases [5], identification of targets for pharmaceutical intervention [6], computer-aided drug design [7], and therapeutic development [8].

The significance of PPI characterization drives ongoing research into PPI prediction methods [9]. Presently, such methods are divided into experimental and computational categories. Experimental techniques, like yeast two-hybrid assays, synthetic lethality studies, and tandem affinity purification, have historically been employed [10]. Despite their effectiveness, these methods are resource-intensive and time-consuming [11,12], resulting in numerous unannotated protein pairs. Furthermore, the complexity of PPI, with proteins having multiple binding partners and varying interaction frequencies [13], underscores the need for efficient computational prediction methods.

Computational predictors, utilizing biological data such as protein sequence, structure, and gene expression, assess the likelihood of protein interactions [13]. Machine Learning (ML) models, particularly, have gained traction in PPI prediction [14], offering improved predictive capabilities.

The essence of ML lies in enabling algorithms to autonomously "learn" from data without explicit programming. By leveraging input data, ML models enhance their performance on specific tasks. These models necessitate vast amounts of data, known as training data, to discern essential task features. Over the past decade, fuelled by the proliferation of data from advanced sequencing technologies, numerous ML-based methods have been introduced, surpassing traditional predictors in PPI forecasting.

 DOI: 10.1201/9781003600947-9

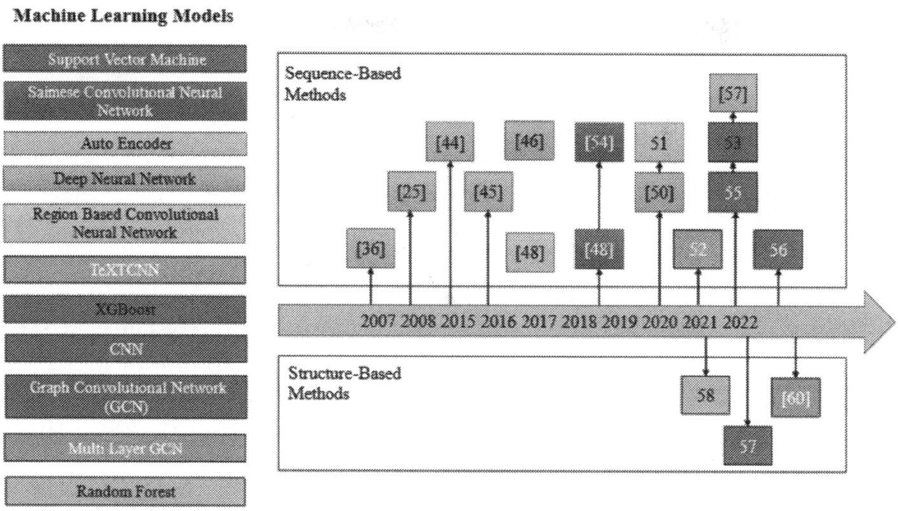

FIGURE 9.1 Chronological order of various Machine Learning methodologies for PPI-prediction.

The evolution of ML techniques has streamlined PPI prediction, rendering it more nuanced yet routine. Currently, utmost computational techniques for forecasting protein–protein interactions employ ML to provide comprehensive, reliable, and robust estimates for vast datasets of protein sequences. A chronological depiction of recent ML models is portrayed in Figure 9.1.

This study presents a thorough examination of effective ML techniques employed in PPI prediction, encapsulating several key contributions:

i. A comprehensive discussion on the recent advancements in PPI prediction research.
ii. Presentation of commonly utilized data sources and methodologies for constructing training and test datasets.
iii. Scrutiny of features utilized in PPI prediction.
iv. Detailed summary of innovative technologies and the ML models underpinning them.
v. Emphasizing on present obstacles in predicting PPI alongside available solutions.
vi. Exploration of recent trends in predictor design and potential future directions.

9.2 SOURCES OF DATA AND CONSTRUCTION OF DATASETS

Effective models of ML, especially in PPI prediction, depend heavily on accurate training data. Typically, these datasets consist of two primary components: collections of interacting proteins alongside their corresponding sequence and structural information.

TABLE 9.1
Summary of Constructed Datasets

Dataset Reference	Source	Interaction Number
[23]	DIP [15]	5955
[27]	HPRD [16] 2007 version	36630
[25]	H. pylori PPI map [28]	1458

Numerous datasets containing experimentally verified protein–protein interactions (PPIs) have been generated and employed in studies focused on predicting PPIs [14]. Among them, the DIP database [15] is notably prominent, being extensively utilized and forming the foundation for over ten prediction models. Some significant PPI datasets comprise HPRD [16], HIPPIE [17], and STRING [18].

Primarily, PPI datasets contain accession numbers of involved proteins, necessitating cross-referencing with sequence databases for sequence and structure information retrieval. Prominent sequence databases encompass UniProt [19], PIR [20], SWISS-PROT [21], and PDB [22], with the latter providing comprehensive collections of experimentally determined protein structures. PPI datasets often categorize interactions by species, with yeast and human data commonly employed for training and validation. Additionally, multi-species datasets have emerged to test model capabilities across sequences with low sequence identity.

Constructing negative datasets is crucial, typically achieved by random pairing of existing proteins or selecting proteins with diverse subcellular localizations. Various steps are taken to mitigate biases, including assessing interaction reliability, filtering short protein sequences, and excluding homologous pairs. Several benchmark datasets have been repeatedly utilized, such as those curated by Guo et al. [23], Pan [24], Martin [25], and Zhou [26]. These datasets play a pivotal role in evaluating subsequent models' performance (Table 9.1).

9.3 PROTEOMICS DATA REPRESENTATION

ML models, like other computational methods, necessitate numeric structures as input. Consequently, the initial stage of these methods entails transforming features into a format amenable to processing by ML models. These characteristics encompass the physicochemical properties of individual proteins and the topological properties of PPI networks. Various techniques have been suggested for extracting features from protein data [29]. Here, we enumerate commonly employed features in PPI prediction, categorized into sequence and structure-dependent features.

9.3.1 Sequence-Based Features

Protein sequences serve as the prime data source for PPI forecasting, comprised of twenty amino acids. Various properties leverage the order and physicochemical properties of amino acids, including k-mer and positional evidence. Frequency of K-mer, a broadly used feature in biological research, involves the occurrence count of substrings within a sequence, forming a vector with k|s| passes, where ‘s’ is the set of alphabets. This approach enables computationally efficient comparison of biological sequences, typically with k values ranging from 7 to 19. Auto-covariance (AC), a classical feature representation, captures physicochemical properties for each of the 20 amino acids [30]. The equation (9.1) depicts the mathematical formulation for AClag where xi and n are denoted as the ith amino acid of the sequence and the length of the sequence, respectively.

$$AC_{\text{lag}} = \frac{\sum_{i=1}^{n-\text{lag}} \left(X_i - \frac{\sum_{k=1}^{n} X_k}{n} \right) \times \left(X_{i+\text{lag}} - \frac{\sum_{k=1}^{n} X_k}{n} \right)}{n-\text{lag}} \tag{9.1}$$

The transformation of protein sequences into auto-covariance (AC) vectors involves representing each amino acid X_i in the sequence, where n denotes the sequence length, yielding a vector of AC values. Additionally, LD, an alignment-free feature developed by Cui et al. [31], categorizes amino acids into hydrophobic, natural, and polar groups, generating composition (C), transition (T), and distribution (D) descriptors. Evolutionary conservation (ECO) identifies functionally identical sequences across taxa, aiding in locating protein functional sites, and is utilized in PPI prediction, often calculated through Multiple Sequence Alignment (MSA) [32]. Moran autocorrelation (MAC), originally used for PPI identification, characterizes amino acid property distributions, excluding hydrophilicity, through a distance-based correlation equation. Notably, AC vector concatenation represents sequence pairs. Taxonomy-based approaches have emerged for ECO analysis [33]. This diverse array of features facilitates comprehensive protein sequence analysis for various ML models. Equation (9.2) depicts the numerical formulation of Moran Correlation $I(d)$ where $1 \le d \le 30$ and $\bar{P} = \sum_{i=1}^{N} (P_i)/N$.

$$I(d) = \frac{\frac{1}{N-d} \sum_{i=1}^{N-d} \left(P_i - \bar{P}\right)\left(P_{i+d} - \bar{P}\right)}{\frac{1}{d} \sum_{i=1}^{N} \left(P_i - \bar{P}\right)^2} \tag{9.2}$$

9.3.2 Structure – Based Features

Protein structure, determined through methods like X-ray crystallography and NMR spectroscopy, offers a plethora of features. Patch information, defining central surface accessible residues and their neighbors, provides insights into PPI site prediction. Attributes extracted from patches include inter-chain bonds, secondary structural elements, planarity, solvation potential, and protrusions.

Graph and surface-mesh depictions offer rich features for ML models. Graphs depict proteins as nodes connected by edges, utilizing adjacency matrices, node degree, and centrality metrics as inputs. Embedding-based techniques analyze these graphs effectively [34].

Protein structure alignment and distance metrics like RMSD and secondary structural alignment score aid in feature extraction [35]. DSSP computes secondary structural descriptors based on hydrogen-bonding patterns, while Taylor et al. utilize Delaunay tessellation for residue descriptors, amalgamating topology and connectivity [36]. These diverse features enable comprehensive analysis of protein structures, enhancing the performance of various computational methods in understanding protein behaviour and interactions.

9.4 PPI PREDICTION THROUGH DIFFERENT ML MODELS

Different ML models are classified into sequence-based and structure-based categories. Table 9.2 outlines methods within each class. Experimental methods, viz. X-ray crystallography, NMR spectroscopy, and computational methodologies, i.e., AlphaFold2 are utilized [37,38]. Predictors employing empirically tested structure data are classified as structure-based or hybrid.

TABLE 9.2
Comparison with Different Methods

Category	References	Model	Extracted Features
Sequence-Based	[57]	Support Vector Machine	k-mer frequency
	[23]	Support Vector Machine	Auto covariance
	[40]	Support Vector Machine	k-mer frequency
	[41]	Support Vector Machine, Random Forest	Position-Specific Scoring Matrix (PSSM), mean cumulative hydrophobicity, mean cumulative relative solvent exposure.
	[43]	Stacked autoencoder	Auto covariance, conjoint triad
	[42]	Deep Neural Network	Composition of amino acids, composition of dipeptides, descriptors based on quasi-sequence-order.
	[44]	Siamese Convolutional Neural Network	Position-specific profile
	[45]	Embedding Convolutional Neural Network, LSTM	Semantic connections among amino acids and position-based sequence segments (motifs).
	[46]	Deep Neural Network	High-level residue distribution
	[47]	Region-based Convolutional Neural Network	Hidden semantic characteristics within a pair of sequences
	[48]	TextCNN, Fully connected layer	Contextual and global sequence features, Pseudo Position-Specific Scoring Matrix
	[49]	XGBoost	Pseudo Position-Specific Scoring Matrix, structure state
	[50]	Siamese Convolutional Neural Network	Position-Specific Scoring Matrix, Algiment result

(Continued)

TABLE 9.2 (*Continued*)
Comparison with Different Methods

Category	References	Model	Extracted Features
	[51]	Convolutional Neural Network, Recurrent Neural Network, ensemble network	Shared sequence, k-mer representation, proportionate size, Position-Specific Scoring Matrix (PSSM), alignment value, solvent exposure.
	[52]	Fully connected layer, Graph Convolutional Network	Features representing text and graphical elements.
Structure-Based	[56]	Multi-layer graph convolutional network	Three-dimensional position of atoms
	[53]	Support Vector Machine	523 Features constructed through the PISA software
	[54]	RF	Overlapping patches

9.5 SEQUENCE-BASED MODEL

ML models utilized for PPI prediction commonly focus on analyzing pairs of protein sequences. Features extracted from protein sequences pose a significant challenge, compounded by the necessity of feature combination. Shen et al. [39] projected an SVM-based method employing 3-mer counting vectors with amino acids assembled into seven classes. Guo et al. [23] utilized SVM, measuring protein sequence properties via Auto Covariance (AC). Profppikernel [40] introduced evolutionary profiles with profile-kernel SVM, resolving underfitting in PPI site prediction.

SSWRF [41] addressed class imbalance through an SVM-SWRF ensemble, employing PSSM, ACH, and ACRSA. DeepPPI [42] incorporated diverse features, employing deep neural networks for interaction state prediction. Sun et al. [43] utilized stacked autoencoders, encoding sequences via AC and CT, mitigating label imbalance. DPPI [44] employed a sliding window approach, transforming sequences into position-specific profiles for convolutional neural network processing. DNN-PPI [45] combined semantic associations, sequence segments, and dependencies, utilizing Deep Learning (DL) layers for prediction. DeepFE-PPI [46] employed Res2vec for residue representation, integrating deep neural networks for feature extraction.

PIPR [47] leveraged deep Siamese RCNN for global and local sequence information fusion. DeepPPISP [48] extracted local and global features using various techniques including PSSM and TextCNN. PPISP-XGBoost [49] utilized XGBoost classifier with features like PsePSSM and PAAC, addressing class imbalance via oversampling. TransePPI [50] adopted transfer learning, transferring knowledge from previous tasks, and utilized a Siamese CNN for prediction. DELPHI [51] employed ensemble modeling incorporating CNN, RNN, and fine-tuning techniques. TAGPPI [52] fused sequence and structural features extracted via TextCNN and graph representation learning for PPI prediction. These diverse approaches showcase the complexity and versatility of feature extraction and modeling techniques in PPI prediction.

9.5.1 Structure-Based Model

Computational methods like rigid body docking and flexible docking are pivotal for analysing complex protein–protein structures, complementing experimental techniques [53]. InPred [54] utilizes PDB data, employing overlapping patches and 11 features for surface representation, employing random forest for prediction [55]. Struct2Graph predicts PPI using 3D protein structure and nanoscale representation, employing a multi-layer graph convolutional network with mutual attention mechanisms [56]. Das et al. incorporate complex structure data, labeling based on FNAT and iRMSD, employing PISA for calculating structural and chemical properties, and SVM for classification [53]. These computational approaches harness diverse structural features, enhancing the prediction and understanding of PPIs.

9.6 EVOLUTION OF ML-BASED PPI PREDICTORS: KEY TRENDS

During the last 20 years, a shift towards ML in predicting PPIs is evident, as illustrated in Figure 9.1. Initially, SVM dominated, but since 2017, the models of DL, viz. DNN and CNN gained prominence due to PPI prediction's complexity and increased data volume from high-throughput technologies. DL benefits from large-scale training sets, making DNN and CNN preferred over SVM and RF. Protein sequences are the primary input for PPI predictors, favoured for their accessibility and simpler preprocessing compared to structure data. Structure-based methods face limitations in detecting interactions involving intrinsically disordered regions. Some hybrid methods combine sequence and structure data, processing them with distinct submodules and merging outputs in a concatenation layer. These advancements reflect the evolving landscape of computational methods in deciphering protein interactions.

9.7 PPI PREDICTIONS CHALLENGES

9.7.1 Data Embedding

In ML, data embedding transforms discrete or categorical values into numeric vectors, aiming to create fixed-length representations of sequences to reflect their relationships [58]. However, protein sequence data present challenges due to varying lengths and functional roles [58]. Inspired by natural language processing, models like ProtVec and SeqVec have been adapted for protein sequence transformation [59]. Pre-trained models, trained on extensive data, aim to capture general knowledge, analogous to language models, and potentially reveal high-level structures in protein sequences, given the conservation of sequences across species [59]. Thus, pre-trained embeddings hold promise in uncovering diverse patterns in protein data.

9.7.2 Imbalanced Class

The imbalance in positive and negative samples within Protein–Protein Interaction (PPI) data poses challenges, with positive samples often composing less than 2% of the dataset [60]. This imbalance hampers minority class capture, affecting the efficacy of SVM and other models. Solutions for this issue involve adjusting sample numbers or weights in the learning model. In natural PPI datasets, where positive samples suffice for training, under-sampling negative samples is common. Conversely, datasets solely comprising optimistic outcomes create non-interacting data by reshuffling proteins. Typically, a 1:1 positive-to-negative ratio is maintained, as deviating ratios often impair overall performance [60]. Weight recalibration involves optimizing ML models, with methods like assigning weights based on class ratios or using learning-based techniques, i.e., cost-sensitive and active learning. The models also evaluate sample scores to determine corresponding weights [41]. These strategies mitigate imbalance, enhancing the predictive capacity of PPI data analysis.

9.7.3 Homologous Sequence

PPI-predictors aim to study collaborative associations between protein functional roles instead of sequence similarity. However, some interacting pairs exhibit homologous sequences or self-interactions, leading to overestimated relevance and bias. Representing protein pairs through numeric vectors (e.g., k-mer frequency) can exacerbate this issue. To mitigate bias, non-redundant subsets are created by removing highly homologous or identical sequences using the BLAST and the cd-hit.

9.8 CONCLUSION

In the recent era, the exponential growth in protein data from progressive experimental approaches has spurred the development of various ML models to enhance PPI prediction. This chapter reviews the evolution of ML-based predictors and their developmental trajectory. Initially, classical models, viz. Support Vector Machines (SVM) and Random Forests (RF) method dominated PPI prediction. However, over the last decade, there has been a shift towards DL, particularly Deep Neural Networks (DNN), which have become ubiquitous. Additionally, Graph Convolutional Networks (GCN) have been integrated into models for analyzing protein structures. Despite advancements, protein sequence data remains the primary source for PPI prediction, although recent efforts have focused on combining sequence and structural information for enhanced accuracy.

While most models rely on supervised learning, exploring semi-supervised and unsupervised approaches could unveil hidden insights in multi-omics data. DL has notably improved protein structure prediction, with some achieving high accuracy comparable to experimental results. Nonetheless, the utilization of predicted structures in PPI prediction remains underexplored, primarily focusing on residue graphs rather than 3D structure features.

Structural methods face data availability challenges, yet advancements like AlphaFold offer promising solutions by significantly expanding available protein structure data. AlphaFold2, for instance, has shown improvements in docking-based PPI prediction. The recent prediction of approximately 200 million human proteins by AlphaFold2, along with publicly accessible data, presents opportunities to enrich training datasets for ML models.

DISCLAIMER

None

REFERENCES

1. Thakur, A. K., & Movileanu, L. (2019). Real-time measurement of protein–protein interactions at single-molecule resolution using a biological nanopore. *Nature Biotechnology*, *37*(1), 96–101.
2. Sardar, T. H. (2024). Reflecting on a decade of evolution: MapReduce-based advances in partitioning-based, hierarchical-based, and density-based clustering (2013–2023). *Wiley Interdisciplinary Reviews: Data Mining and Knowledge Discovery*, e1566, 34–45.
3. Theerthagiri, P., Ruby, A. U., Chandran, J. G. C., Sardar, T. H., & Shafeeq, B. M. A. (2024). Deep SqueezeNet learning model for diagnosis and prediction of maize leaf diseases. *Journal of Big Data*, *11*(1), 112.
4. Subbarao, E., Gite, P., Sharma, A., Vyakaranam, L., Sardar, T. H., Taqui, S. N., ... & Kalam, M. A. (2023). Investigation of solar energy for urban areas and metropolitan communities using machine learning. *Electric Power Components and Systems*, 7(2), 1–11.
5. Sardar, T. H., Faizabadi, A. R., & Ansari, Z. (2017). An analysis of data processing using Mapreduce paradigm on the Hadoop framework. *International Journal of Emerging Research in Management and Technology*, *6*(5), 134–146.
6. Khatun, A., & Sardar, T. H. (2025). Cryptography algorithms to prevent different security attacks. In Khatun, A., & Sardar, T. H. (eds) *Next Generation Mechanisms for Data Encryption* (pp. 35–46). CRC Press.
7. Pan, X., Lin, X., Cao, D., Zeng, X., Yu, P. S., He, L., ... & Cheng, F. (2022). Deep learning for drug repurposing: Methods, databases, and applications. *Wiley Interdisciplinary Reviews: Computational Molecular Science*, *12*(4), e1597.
8. Petta, I., Lievens, S., Libert, C., Tavernier, J., & De Bosscher, K. (2016). Modulation of protein–protein interactions for the development of novel therapeutics. *Molecular Therapy*, *24*(4), 707–718.
9. Tuncbag, N., Kar, G., Keskin, O., Gursoy, A., & Nussinov, R. (2009). A survey of available tools and web servers for analysis of protein–protein interactions and interfaces. *Briefings in Bioinformatics*, *10*(3), 217–232.
10. Rajagopala, S. V., Sikorski, P., Kumar, A., Mosca, R., Vlasblom, J., Arnold, R., ... & Uetz, P. (2014). The binary protein-protein interaction landscape of Escherichia coli. *Nature Biotechnology*, *32*(3), 285–290.
11. Zeng, X., Tu, X., Liu, Y., Fu, X., & Su, Y. (2022). Toward better drug discovery with knowledge graph. *Current Opinion in Structural Biology*, *72*, 114–126.
12. Sardar, T. H., Sarkar, R., Ahmed, S. J., & Bandyopadhyay, A. (2023, May). A novel ensemble methodology to validate fuzzy clusters of Big Data. In *Proceedings of the Fourth International Conference on Trends in Computational and Cognitive Engineering: TCCE 2022* (pp. 267–278). Springer Nature, Singapore.
13. Sardar, T. H., Muttineni, A., & Ranjan, R. (2024). The future of Big Data in customer experience and inventory management. In *Big Data Computing* (pp. 233–248). Edited by Tanvir Habib Sardar, Bishwajeet Kumar Pandey. CRC Press.
14. Sardar, T. H., Das, S., & Pandey, B. K. Explainable AI (XAI): Concepts and theory. In *Medical Data Analysis and Processing using Explainable Artificial Intelligence* (pp. 1–18). Edited ByOm Prakash Jena, Mrutyunjaya Panda, Utku Kose. CRC Press.

15. Peri, S., Navarro, J. D., Amanchy, R., Kristiansen, T. Z., Jonnalagadda, C. K., Surendranath, V., ... & Pandey, A. (2003). Development of human protein reference database as an initial platform for approaching systems biology in humans. *Genome Research, 13*(10), 2363–2371.
16. Alanis-Lobato, G., Andrade-Navarro, M. A., & Schaefer, M. H. (2016). HIPPIE v2. 0: Enhancing meaningfulness and reliability of protein–protein interaction networks. *Nucleic Acids Research*, 408–414.
17. Szklarczyk, D., Gable, A. L., Lyon, D., Junge, A., Wyder, S., Huerta-Cepas, J., ... & Mering, C. V. (2019). STRING v11: Protein–protein association networks with increased coverage, supporting functional discovery in genome-wide experimental datasets. *Nucleic Acids Research, 47*(D1), D607–D613.
18. UniProt Consortium. (2019). UniProt: A worldwide hub of protein knowledge. *Nucleic Acids Research, 47*(D1), D506–D515.
19. Barker, W. C., Garavelli, J. S., McGarvey, P. B., Marzec, C. R., Orcutt, B. C., Srinivasarao, G. Y., ... & Wu, C. (1999). The PIR-international protein sequence database. *Nucleic Acids Research, 27*(1), 39–43.
20. Boeckmann, B., Bairoch, A., Apweiler, R., Blatter, M. C., Estreicher, A., Gasteiger, E., ... & Schneider, M. (2003). The SWISS-PROT protein knowledgebase and its supplement TrEMBL in 2003. *Nucleic Acids Research, 31*(1), 365–370.
21. Burley, S. K., Berman, H. M., Chen, L., Bhikadiya, C., Bi, C., Dutta, S., ... & Ioannidis, Y. E. (2019). Protein Data Bank: The single global archive for 3D macromolecular structure data. *Nucleic Acids Research, 47*(D1), D520–D528.
22. Guo, Y., Yu, L., Wen, Z., & Li, M. (2008). Using support vector machine combined with auto covariance to predict protein–protein interactions from protein sequences. *Nucleic Acids Research, 36*(9), 3025–3030.
23. Pan, X. Y., Zhang, Y. N., & Shen, H. B. (2010). Large-Scale prediction of human protein– protein interactions from amino acid sequence based on latent topic features. *Journal of Proteome Research, 9*(10), 4992–5001.
24. Martin, S., Roe, D., & Faulon, J. L. (2005). Predicting protein–protein interactions using signature products. *Bioinformatics, 21*(2), 218–226.
25. Zhou, Y. Z., Gao, Y., & Zheng, Y. Y. (2011). Prediction of protein-protein interactions using local description of amino acid sequence. In *Advances in Computer Science and Education Applications: International Conference, CSE 2011, Qingdao, China, July 9–10, 2011. Proceedings, Part II* (pp. 254–262). Springer, Berlin Heidelberg.
26. Berman, H. M., Westbrook, J., Feng, Z., Gilliland, G., Bhat, T. N., Weissig, H., ... & Bourne, P. E. (2000). The protein data bank. *Nucleic Acids Research, 28*(1), 235–242.
27. Rain, J. C., Selig, L., De Reuse, H., Battaglia, V., Reverdy, C., Simon, S., ... & Legrain, P. (2001). The protein–protein interaction map of Helicobacter pylori. *Nature, 409*(6817), 211–215.
28. Chen, Z., Zhao, P., Li, F., Marquez-Lago, T. T., Leier, A., Revote, J., ... & Song, J. (2020). iLearn: An integrated platform and meta-learner for feature engineering, machine-learning analysis and modeling of DNA, RNA and protein sequence data. *Briefings in Bioinformatics, 21*(3), 1047–1057.
29. Zhou, P., Tian, F. F., Li, B., Wu, S. R., & Li, Z. L. (2006). Genetic algorithm-based virtual screening of combinative mode for peptide/protein. *Acta Chimica Sinica, 64*(7), 691.
30. Cui, J., Han, L. Y., Li, H., Ung, C. Y., Tang, Z. Q., Zheng, C. J., ... & Chen, Y. Z. (2007). Computer prediction of allergen proteins from sequence-derived protein structural and physicochemical properties. *Molecular Immunology, 44*(4), 514–520.
31. Zimmermann, L., Stephens, A., Nam, S. Z., Rau, D., Kübler, J., Lozajic, M., ... & Alva, V. (2018). A completely reimplemented MPI bioinformatics toolkit with a new HHpred server at its core. *Journal of Molecular Biology, 430*(15), 2237–2243.

32. Malhis, N., Jones, S. J., & Gsponer, J. (2019). Improved measures for evolutionary conservation that exploit taxonomy distances. *Nature Communications*, *10*(1), 1556.
33. Shen, J., Zhang, J., Luo, X., Zhu, W., Yu, K., Chen, K., ... & Jiang, H. (2007). Predicting protein–protein interactions based only on sequences information. *Proceedings of the National Academy of Sciences*, *104*(11), 4337–4341.
34. Rozewicki, J., Li, S., Amada, K. M., Standley, D. M., & Katoh, K. (2019). MAFFT-DASH: Integrated protein sequence and structural alignment. *Nucleic Acids Research*, *47*(W1), W5–W10.
35. Taylor, T., Rivera, M., Wilson, G., & Vaisman, I. I. (2005). New method for protein secondary structure assignment based on a simple topological descriptor. *Proteins: Structure, Function, and Bioinformatics*, *60*(3), 513–524.
36. Cramer, P. (2021). AlphaFold2 and the future of structural biology. *Nature Structural & Molecular Biology*, *28*(9), 704–705.
37. Jumper, J., Evans, R., Pritzel, A., Green, T., Figurnov, M., Ronneberger, O., ... & Hassabis, D. (2021). Highly accurate protein structure prediction with AlphaFold. *Nature*, *596*(7873), 583–589.
38. Shen, J., Zhang, J., Luo, X., Zhu, W., Yu, K., Chen, K., ... & Jiang, H. (2007). Predicting protein–protein interactions based only on sequences information. *Proceedings of the National Academy of Sciences*, *104*(11), 4337–4341.
39. Hamp, T., & Rost, B. (2015). Evolutionary profiles improve protein–protein interaction prediction from sequence. *Bioinformatics*, *31*(12), 1945–1950.
40. Wei, Z. S., Han, K., Yang, J. Y., Shen, H. B., & Yu, D. J. (2016). Protein–protein interaction sites prediction by ensembling SVM and sample-weighted random forests. *Neurocomputing*, *193*, 201–212.
41. Du, X., Sun, S., Hu, C., Yao, Y., Yan, Y., & Zhang, Y. (2017). DeepPPI: Boosting prediction of protein–protein interactions with deep neural networks. *Journal of Chemical Information and Modeling*, *57*(6), 1499–1510.
42. Sun, T., Zhou, B., Lai, L., & Pei, J. (2017). Sequence-based prediction of protein protein interaction using a deep-learning algorithm. *BMC Bioinformatics*, *18*, 1–8.
43. Hashemifar, S., Neyshabur, B., Khan, A. A., & Xu, J. (2018). Predicting protein–protein interactions through sequence-based deep learning. *Bioinformatics*, *34*(17), i802–i810.
44. Li, H., Gong, X. J., Yu, H., & Zhou, C. (2018). Deep neural network-based predictions of protein interactions using primary sequences. *Molecules*, *23*(8), 1923.
45. Yao, Y., Du, X., Diao, Y., & Zhu, H. (2019). An integration of deep learning with feature embedding for protein–protein interaction prediction. *PeerJ*, *7*, e7126.
46. Chen, M., Ju, C. J. T., Zhou, G., Chen, X., Zhang, T., Chang, K. W., ... & Wang, W. (2019). Multifaceted protein–protein interaction prediction based on Siamese residual RCNN. *Bioinformatics*, *35*(14), i305–i314.
47. Zeng, M., Zhang, F., Wu, F. X., Li, Y., Wang, J., & Li, M. (2020). Protein–protein interaction site prediction through combining local and global features with deep neural networks. *Bioinformatics*, *36*(4), 1114–1120.
48. Wang, X., Zhang, Y., Yu, B., Salhi, A., Chen, R., Wang, L., & Liu, Z. (2021). Prediction of protein-protein interaction sites through eXtreme gradient boosting with kernel principal component analysis. *Computers in Biology and Medicine*, *134*, 104516.
49. Yang, X., Yang, S., Lian, X., Wuchty, S., & Zhang, Z. (2021). Transfer learning via multi-scale convolutional neural layers for human–virus protein–protein interaction prediction. *Bioinformatics*, *37*(24), 4771–4778.
50. Li, Y., Golding, G. B., & Ilie, L. (2021). DELPHI: accurate deep ensemble model for protein interaction sites prediction. *Bioinformatics*, *37*(7), 896–904.
51. Song, B., Luo, X., Luo, X., Liu, Y., Niu, Z., & Zeng, X. (2022). Learning spatial structures of proteins improves protein–protein interaction prediction. *Briefings in Bioinformatics*, *23*(2), bbab558.

52. Das, S., & Chakrabarti, S. (2021). Classification and prediction of protein–protein interaction interface using machine learning algorithm. *Scientific Reports*, *11*(1), 1761.
53. Northey, T. C., Barešić, A., & Martin, A. C. (2018). IntPred: A structure-based predictor of protein–protein interaction sites. *Bioinformatics*, *34*(2), 223–229.
54. Breiman, L. (2001). Random forests. *Machine Learning*, *45*(1), 5–32.
55. Baranwal, M., Magner, A., Saldinger, J., Turali-Emre, E. S., Elvati, P., Kozarekar, S., … & Hero, A. O. (2022). Struct2Graph: A graph attention network for structure-based predictions of protein–protein interactions. *BMC Bioinformatics*, *23*(1), 370.
56. Das, S., & Chakrabarti, S. (2021). Classification and prediction of protein–protein interaction interface using machine learning algorithm. *Scientific Reports*, *11*(1), 1761.
57. Ilie, L., & Ilie, S. (2007). Multiple spaced seeds for homology search. *Bioinformatics*, *23*(22), 2969–2977.
58. Lipman, D. J., Souvorov, A., Koonin, E. V., Panchenko, A. R., & Tatusova, T. A. (2002). The relationship of protein conservation and sequence length. *BMC Evolutionary Biology*, *2*, 1–10.
59. Heinzinger, M., Elnaggar, A., Wang, Y., Dallago, C., Nechaev, D., Matthes, F., & Rost, B. (2019). Modeling aspects of the language of life through transfer-learning protein sequences. *BMC Bioinformatics*, *20*, 1–17.
60. Yu, C. Y., Chou, L. C., & Chang, D. T. H. (2010). Predicting protein-protein interactions in unbalanced data using the primary structure of proteins. *BMC Bioinformatics*, *11*, 1–10.

10 The Role of Natural Language Processing in Analyzing Patient Records for Improved Clinical Decision-Making

Alhaji Idi Babate and Abdullahi Abubakar

10.1 INTRODUCTION

Accurately interpreting spoken or written natural language and producing dependable computer outputs are major issues when applying NLP to patient data. Understanding the varied vocabulary, terminology, and colloquial idioms, as well as their contexts, is essential for effective comprehension. Clear and coherent communication must be guaranteed during the parsing of unambiguous word sequences. NLP is therefore positioned as a feasible alternative for optimizing the use of routine patient information to support effective and efficient care, and these computational processes must improve the cost-effectiveness, efficiency, and autonomy of healthcare delivery (Li et al., 2022; Stosik, 2023).

A significant framework for analyzing problems pertaining to the current status of healthcare delivery is provided by the necessity to improve safety and quality in healthcare (Wu et al., 2020). In hospital settings, retrospective studies have evaluated the frequency of medical errors and found that they are frequently caused by the complexity of the healthcare system, human performance limitations, and poor communication between healthcare providers (Bitterman et al., 2021). A big problem occurs when doctors ignore laboratory results that suggest possible clinical problems; frequently, aberrant values that need to be addressed are not obvious enough or clinically significant to clinicians. Negative patient events are known to be significantly influenced by missed, inaccurate, or delayed diagnoses, which might result from this lack of clarity.

10.2 OVERVIEW OF NATURAL LANGUAGE PROCESSING

Recent developments in Natural Language Processing (NLP) have improved text enrichment and drastically changed the environment of EHRs. The potential of NLP annotation to significantly improve clinical data is becoming more widely acknowledged. This includes developing diagnostic capture task maps, adding phenotype

 DOI: 10.1201/9781003600947-10

annotations to clinical narratives, and expanding structured notes. Additionally, these tools make it easier to aggregate data that researchers may use, which eventually supports better clinical decision-making in a variety of healthcare scenarios (Panfilo, 2023; Stosik, 2023).

Beyond just improving data, NLP techniques have the potential to significantly advance clinical research. The process of turning unstructured text, like clinical notes and discharge summaries, into structured text involves a number of steps, including pre-processing, feature processing, Named Entity Recognition (NER) modeling, and post-processing. The end result is data that is organized, searchable, and analyzable, such as clinical data fields, medical history, and lab results. For example, NLP can expedite the identification of subjects for clinical trials and use its capabilities to interpret both structured and unstructured medical literature within EHRs. This has led to the creation of methods to address particular issues with NLP applications, like measuring the caliber of narrative notes, improving the recording of family medical histories, and detecting suicide attempts to guarantee prompt clinical notifications (Marutitech, 2023; Varela, 2023).

NLP, a branch of AI, plays a key role in turning human speech into useful information. Automated summarization, machine translation, NER, part-of-speech tagging, and parsing are important tasks in NLP. Healthcare professionals can now handle enormous volumes of patient data because of the increasing use of EHR systems. However, issues with manual processing and inefficient documentation are frequently brought on by this growth in data volume (Redress Compliance, 2023).

NLP tools have been created to overcome these problems by gleaning important information from clinical notes. These findings can help guide cancer detection decision-making, improve patient safety protocols, customize treatment plans for specific patients, and address urgent clinical issues that aim to improve patient outcomes. However, uneven note quality from users, inadequate documentation processes in healthcare settings, and limitations in the systems that use these technologies frequently impede the use of NLP tools (Sezgin et al., 2023; Koleck et al., 2019; Marutitech, 2023).

Even though NLP has a lot of potential to improve healthcare delivery and optimize EHRs through improved data processing and decision support systems, continued efforts are needed to address current obstacles pertaining to data quality and user engagement with these technologies.

10.3 SIGNIFICANCE OF ANALYZING PATIENT RECORDS IN HEALTHCARE

The automatic extraction of valuable information from heterogeneous datasets, coupled with rapid quantification, has the potential to address numerous challenges in healthcare and enhance the overall quality of care. NLP serves as a pivotal technology in this context, utilizing knowledge bases and sophisticated algorithms to interpret human language. This capability allows computers to perform tasks traditionally executed by humans, effectively converting raw patient records into structured, manageable datasets that yield meaningful insights. Clinical researchers and practitioners can use patient records for medical research and better care; these assertions enable the potential of NLP (Li et al., 2022; Marutitech, 2023). Large volumes of semi-structured data have been gathered by medical institutions as a result of the rise in digital medical information brought about by smartphones. Nevertheless, this heterogeneity makes analysis and investigation difficult, which prevents effective data use (Tyagi & Bhushan, 2023).

Furthermore, the unstructured form of the data makes it impossible for many healthcare practitioners to handle these tiresome activities. By automating data extraction and organization, the inclusion of NLP technologies can expedite this process, enabling more effective research and improving the standard of treatment given. NLP enables better clinical decision-making and patient outcomes by converting unstructured clinical paperwork into actionable insights, hence reducing the administrative burden on healthcare professionals (Marutitech, 2023).

10.4 CHALLENGES IN ANALYZING PATIENT RECORDS

Organizing uniform structures, handling unique verb-noun combinations, and separating various types of information are some of the challenges that come with managing medical records (Bell et al., 2020; Dalglish et al., 2020). Because of their prevalence and lack of analytical value, medications pose particular difficulties (Smith et al., 2020; Giordano et al., 2021). Furthermore, there may be discrepancies between clinical health applications and the actual content of the papers due to data input errors, polysemy, and ambiguities in clinical documentation. For thorough data analysis, these structural changes must be taken into consideration by effective information extraction techniques.

Accurately extracting clinical information from patient records is complicated and context-dependent due to the complex nature of these issues. According to recent studies, removing these obstacles is crucial to maximizing the benefits of EHRs in terms of bettering research outcomes and patient care (Aghajani et al., 2020; Huang et al., 2020). Improving healthcare personnel's training in documentation procedures and creating sophisticated NLP systems that can better handle the complexities of clinical language are two practical ways to address these problems, as shown in Figure 10.1.

10.5 UNSTRUCTURED DATA

For NLP activities, it is essential to comprehend clinical paperwork, including doctor's notes. Demographics, family histories, medical and personal histories, physical examinations, allergies, test results from labs, and more are all included in these notes. Generally categorized as social records, mental health and tobacco use are frequently left out of research databases (DesRoches et al., 2020; Bell et al., 2020).

The variables found within clinical text can manifest as medications, medical problems, dates of service, measurements, examination results, radiological findings, descriptions of general wellness and diseases, occurrences such as breastfeeding or patient support services, and symptoms associated with various conditions. For instance, magnetic resonance imaging (MRI) reports categorize findings into five distinct classifications: normal, dementia, major atrophy, minor atrophy, or infarcts.

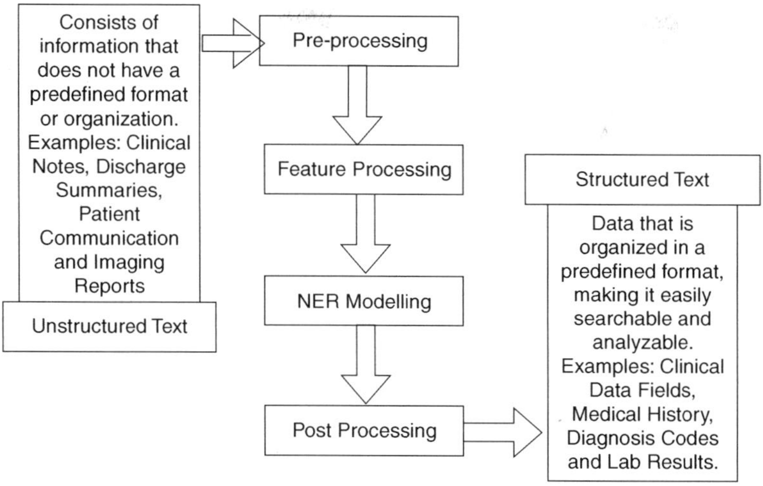

FIGURE 10.1 The workflow for processing unstructured and structured text in Electronic Health Records is shown in the diagram. It begins with pre-processing and proceeds through feature processing, NER modeling, and post-processing to ensure easy searchability and a useful analysis of the data. (Source: Perera et al., 2020.)

While these terms are beneficial for clinical decision-making, such as identifying a patient presenting with "chest pain," they may also encapsulate a wide array of information that influences local treatment decisions (Spasic & Nenadic, 2020; Moy et al., 2021). Furthermore, pre-labeled clinical examples are readily available within commonly used public datasets.

A significant volume of patient data exists in unstructured formats such as physicians' notes and imaging reports. This unstructured data has been identified as one of the greatest challenges in clinical informatics because both simple keyword-based methods and sophisticated neural network algorithms struggle to extract relevant information effectively (Berge et al., 2023). Moreover, many existing algorithms can inadvertently produce inaccurate results due to biases inherent in their training datasets. These biases are more pronounced in structured data and less relevant when dealing with unstructured data types. Despite the urgent need for algorithms that can efficiently use unstructured data, there are still few studies in the medical profession that concentrate on this topic. Furthermore, the circumstances of developed countries are primarily reflected in the research that is currently available, which does not adequately represent the diversity of patient populations around the world. This disparity emphasizes how urgently more study is needed to fill this crucial knowledge gap (Tayefi et al., 2021; Panaite et al., 2022).

10.6 DATA PRIVACY AND SECURITY

Sensitive patient data is frequently de-identified from patient notes before processing. In clinical NLP, maintaining patient privacy is essential (Urbain et al., 2022). Clinical decision-making requires the extraction of valuable information from notes

(Kovačević et al., 2024). However, manual extraction is impracticable because practitioners frequently lack thorough comprehension. This study shows that in clinical decision-making situations, unfulfilled informational demands can be successfully met.

Given the abundance of important patient data stored in electronic clinical notes, data security and privacy are critical issues. Maintaining the privacy of this information is important but difficult (Sriram et al., 2023). On the one hand, patients can be put in danger if medical professionals do not have access to thorough medical histories. On the other hand, disclosing such private information can violate a patient's right to privacy. The difficulty is in eliminating recognizable information from clinical documents, like names and addresses, without seriously impairing the content's value to medical experts (Ahmed et al., 2020). Analyses usually do not directly use patient identification information in its original form for ethical and legal concerns (Paul et al., 2022; Fanni et al., 2023).

Healthcare providers must protect patient health information against unauthorized disclosure in accordance with the Health Insurance Portability and Accountability Act (HIPAA) (Edemekong et al., 2018). According to Rybinski et al. (2021), NLP technology can assist in identifying and redacting sensitive material, preserving privacy, and facilitating insightful analysis. There are still issues with handling unstructured clinical information, though, as current algorithms may reinforce prejudices, and there is little data on patient populations around the world. To solve these problems, more research into automated de-identification techniques is essential (Table 10.1).

TABLE 10.1
Summary of NLP Techniques and Applications in Healthcare

NLP Technique	Application	Evaluation Criteria	References
Named Entity Recognition	Extracting patient information from clinical notes	Precision, Recall, F1 Score	**Durango et al. (2023)**. Named entity recognition in electronic health records: A methodological review
Clinical Named Entity Recognition	Identifying clinical problems from patient records	True Positive Rate, False Positive Rate	Raza et al. (2022) Large-scale application of named entity recognition to biomedicine and epidemiology.
Clinical Assertion Model	Identifying clinical problems from patient records	True Positive Rate, False Positive Rate	Hitachi (2023). Six Uses for NLP in Healthcare.
Clinical Deidentification Model	Extracting medication details from prescriptions	Compliance with HIPAA regulations	Wang (2023). Clinical Named Entity Recognition Using spaCy.
Clinical Extraction Model	Extracting medication details from prescriptions	Completeness, Consistency	Roy et al. (2021). Application of Natural Language Processing in healthcare.
Predictive Analytics	Forecasting disease progression	ROC-AUC, sensitivity, Specificity	Marutitech (2023). op 14 Natural Language Processing Use Cases in Healthcare.

10.7 APPLICATIONS OF NLP IN HEALTHCARE

NLP is crucial in healthcare as it facilitates the seamless sharing and analysis of patient-provider and physician narratives through digital data (Hossain et al., 2023). This facilitates efficient information dissemination and clinical decision-making. NLP technology is still not widely used, despite its potential (Zhu et al., 2020). NLP is a vital IT solution that is developing and offering different end users' financial benefits. Automating data extraction from EHRs and enabling clinical trial matching can improve patient care (Janowski, 2023; Marutitech, 2023). This capability promotes advances in medical research and increases patient access to cutting-edge treatments. Its application is limited and unequal, though.

Despite these benefits, it is challenging to integrate NLP technology into routine clinical practice due to its uneven implementation. The complexities of unstructured data, such as differences in clinical terminology and documentation standards, may make it difficult to extract information effectively. Moreover, existing algorithms may inadvertently perpetuate biases in training datasets, leading to erroneous data interpretation (Alami et al., 2020; Sezgin et al., 2023).

Furthermore, research in this area is still lacking, despite the clear need for algorithms that can effectively use unstructured data. Most studies have been conducted in wealthy nations and do not adequately reflect the diversity of patient populations worldwide (Norton & Chambers, 2020). To fill in these gaps and enhance the appropriateness (Figure 10.2).

10.8 CLINICAL DECISION SUPPORT SYSTEMS

Clinicians can use a range of data from clinical decision support (CDS) systems to make well-informed decisions regarding their patients. They may take the form of software programs, practice recommendations, reports, clinical warnings, and reminders (Kumar & Gond, 2023). They can be used as additional tools to improve

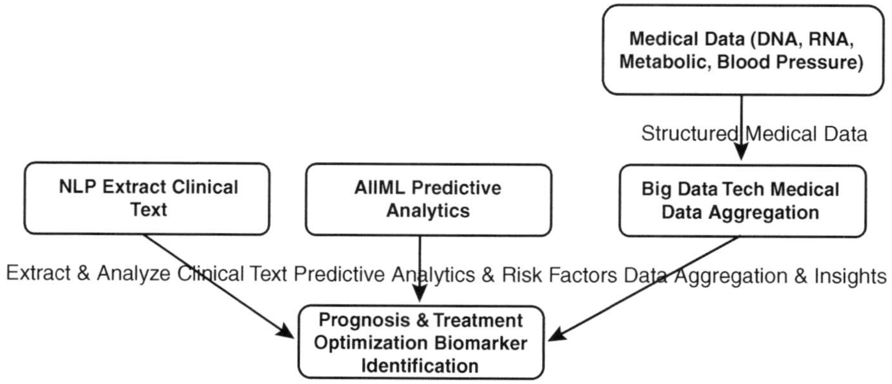

FIGURE 10.2 Advanced Data Integration Framework for Improving Medical Outcomes: The process of analyzing medical data is depicted in the diagram, which begins with NLP and progresses to AI and ML analysis. Big Data technologies are used to collect and aggregate data streams efficiently for analysis.

healthcare workflows or integrated into EHRs (Musen et al., 2021). Based on patient test results and clinical information, diagnostic decision support tools evaluate disease probability using decision-analytic models (Sutton et al., 2020; Kwan et al., 2020). By automating important data points and enhancing clinical evaluations, integrating NLP into CDS systems increases the effectiveness of healthcare delivery (Bitterman et al., 2021; Koleck et al., 2019).

NLP's use in CDS is still inconsistent across healthcare settings, despite its potential advantages. Many of the systems that are already in use are still in their infancy and do not fully utilize NLP technologies. Additionally, standardization attempts across various healthcare companies may be complicated by the fact that NLP interfaces are frequently tailored for particular users or installations (Wu et al., 2020).

10.9 DISEASE SURVEILLANCE AND OUTBREAK DETECTION

Disease surveillance ideally involves the continuous inference of the health status of large populations based on limited observations of illnesses among select individuals within that population. With the increasing reliance on Electronic Health Records (EHRs) and standardized templates, the reach of disease surveillance efforts can resemble that of community information sources, such as clinical laboratory networks situated in clinical, public health, or commercial settings (Tyagi & Bhushan, 2023). These networks are strategically located within defined geographical areas to help characterize demographic or administrative subdivisions, such as census tracts or public health agencies (MENDS, 2023).

Typically, when physicians diagnose a patient, they enter codes that classify the diagnosed diseases. However, this process is susceptible to human error and may sometimes involve intentional misrepresentation of patient characteristics. NLP can enhance the extraction of coded diseases from pathophysiological inputs generated during patient interactions, thereby improving the accuracy and quality of clinical data (Babaiha et al., 2023). By examining unstructured text, NLP seeks to enhance disease detection and therapy, particularly for chronic conditions (Khan et al., 2024). It fixes issues with clinical records and enhances model calibration (Li et al., 2022; Koleck et al., 2019). Real-time data analysis and timely clinical information are two benefits of integrating EHR data into disease monitoring systems above conventional approaches (Chowdhury et al., 2024). EHR data is used by programs such as MENDS to enhance population health outcomes and guide public health initiatives.

The efficient use of EHR data for disease surveillance still faces challenges in spite of these developments. Biases in data collection and non-random patient coverage are two problems that can affect how accurate illness prevalence estimates are. Additionally, the use of NLP technologies in current healthcare infrastructures is still developing, despite the fact that they have demonstrated promise in improving data extraction and analysis capabilities (Hitachi Solutions, 2023; Cross, 2023).

10.10 CASE STUDIES AND SUCCESS STORIES

The study examines case studies and different implementations of requirements extraction from natural language objects. To ensure that developers and domain experts are in agreement and that the outputs fulfill expectations, an NLP-based communication tool is created (Park et al., 2021; Li et al., 2022). Despite progress, research on crucial subjects that stakeholders must discuss in order to work together effectively on requirement collection and analysis is lacking (Marutitech, 2023). Project goals and expectations can be more clearly defined, communication can be improved, and misconceptions can be decreased by incorporating NLP techniques into requirement elicitation procedures.

NLP applications have proven useful in a variety of fields, as evidenced by case studies, which also highlight how these technologies can help close communication gaps between technical teams and subject matter experts. For example, Ziva is a technology designed to help people share knowledge by enabling subject matter experts to condense their expertise into formats that data scientists can easily understand. Experts' cognitive load is lessened, and knowledge exchanged during model construction is more scalable as a result (Park et al., 2021). NLP's value in promoting stakeholder communication is becoming more widely acknowledged, yet there are still obstacles in its real-world implementation. Customization for various user contexts might restrict the efficacy of generic models and complicate deployment. According to Bitterman et al. (2021) and Koleck et al. (2019), further investigation is required to examine how NLP might be customized to meet the demands of particular stakeholders and enhance teamwork among heterogeneous groups.

10.11 IMPLEMENTATION OF NLP IN REAL-WORLD HEALTHCARE SETTINGS

A growing number of patient-facing devices include insights from reputable medical literature and textbooks, offering clinically relevant knowledge which improves patient care. This integration enables a more tailored approach to healthcare by taking into account the patients' chronic diseases and clinical appointments. Backend learning procedures can proactively connect this information to healthcare practitioners, as they frequently rely on gold-standard datasets created by clinicians. By reducing the likelihood of unfavorable clinical outcomes before they happen, this connection seeks to assist clinical decision-making (Li et al., 2022; Marutitech, 2023).

The knowledge generated through these processes is intended to flow into ambient devices that can capture detailed clinician responses regarding medication titration and other evidence-based practices. Each piece of data holds the potential for granular inferential use; for example, a discrepancy between an outdated recommendation and newly available evidence in a backend application may signal a need for intervention. This adaptive environment can be modified in real-time as clinical situations evolve. In cases where dangerous drug interactions are identified, the appropriate response may involve suspending the use of certain devices that pose a risk to patient safety (Cross, 2023; Sezgin et al., 2023).

Despite significant advancements in NLP, challenges persist, particularly in the commercial deployment of NLP technologies within healthcare settings. While NLP has the potential to improve patient outcomes by enhancing the accuracy of patient records and minimizing errors, achieving high-quality training data remains a critical hurdle. In our computational studies utilizing observational patient record data, we first identified specific issues present in patient records. Subsequently, we developed a data-driven NLP algorithm tailored to address these issues directly.

Finally, we conducted an outcome study to evaluate the impact of this solution on clinical practice (Bitterman et al., 2021; Hitachi Solutions, 2023).

We envision three primary applications of NLP within the context of big healthcare data. First, real-time monitoring capabilities could enable proactive management of patients' health conditions. Second, analyzing large-scale EHR data may contribute to future medical discoveries by identifying patterns and correlations that were previously undetected. Lastly, an in-depth analysis of patient-related texts can enhance our physiological understanding of individual patients, leading to more tailored and effective treatment strategies (Park et al., 2021; JAMA Network Open, 2023)

10.12 FUTURE DIRECTIONS AND POTENTIAL IMPACT

Overall, complex clinical information can be garnered from patient records and translated into data, which in turn can be analyzed using AI technologies to offer valuable insights. Healthcare intervention grounded in the application of AI technologies has the potential to yield sustainable societal impact, based on a healthcare cost-benefit analysis. Despite the consistent calls for enhanced use of patient data, especially in the area of chronic disease, patient privacy is key. The data, at minimal standard, must not contain person-specific identifiers and must be managed in such a way that reidentification efforts would be rendered without success.

Future directions of how NLP can contribute to improved data-driven insights are as follows:

i. Real-time access to EHR-like data in settings other than a patient's GP or a research center. Other data sources include data generated from mobile phone sensors and data from new technologies, such as those monitoring specific health conditions within home settings.
ii. The use of unstructured free-text data can provide a more comprehensive and meaningful representation of conflicting patient ideations with care providers, and poor patient understanding and memory for treatment instructions.
iii. Detailed unstructured information available within patient records can stimulate creative treatment paradigms built on better healthcare delivery and granular risk stratification.

Recent studies by Monlezun (2023), and Wallace et al. (2024) highlight the transformative potential of advanced data analytics applied to patient data, particularly EHRs. EHRs improve decision-making and enable focused interventions by providing insightful information that goes beyond conventional controlled trials. In order to promote ongoing learning and patient care improvement, experts support "learning healthcare systems" that include clinical data and research findings (Wallace et al., 2024). By filling up knowledge gaps and enabling healthcare professionals to make well-informed judgments, these systems leverage real-time data to enhance health outcomes and guide clinical practices (Komalasari, 2024). For efficient and fair healthcare delivery, advanced analytics must be integrated into EHR systems.

10.13 INTEGRATION OF NLP WITH ARTIFICIAL INTELLIGENCE

In order to enhance medical records and understanding, this article explores the integration of computational tools such as NLP, AI, ML, and BDT. Medical diagnostic test analysis, clinical instructional text processing, and future health issue prediction all depend on NLP approaches. These methods can be used in a number of domains, such as patient data analysis and nursing documentation.

Understanding prognosis and treatment outcomes requires the integration of clinical texts with other medical data. Biomarker approaches for disease start, prognosis prediction, recurrence rates, side effects, and therapy effectiveness may result from this. Even though NLP technology is developing, its practical use still presents difficulties. However, by reducing errors, it can enhance patient outcomes when developed well.

10.14 CONCLUSION

This study concludes its findings with the fact that examining patient records, NLP, in conjunction with AI, ML, and BDT, can greatly enhance patient care and results. However, obstacles such as algorithm bias, training data complexity, and data quality prevent it from being widely used. In order to transform healthcare delivery, future research should concentrate on creating approachable strategies for integrating NLP across many medical contexts.

DISCLAIMER

The findings presented in this paper are those of the author and may not be associated with any organizations.

REFERENCES

Aghajani, E., Nagy, C., Linares-Vásquez, M., Moreno, L., Bavota, G., Lanza, M., & Shepherd, D. C. (2020, June). Software documentation: the practitioners' perspective. In *Proceedings of the ACM/IEEE 42nd International Conference on Software Engineering* (pp. 590–601). Switzerland

Ahmed, Syed Faraz, Ahmed A. Quadeer, & Matthew R. McKay. (2020). Preliminary identification of potential vaccine targets for the COVID-19 coronavirus (SARS-CoV-2) based on SARS-CoV immunological studies. *Viruses* 12(3), 254.

Alami, Hassane, et al. (2020). Artificial intelligence in health care: laying the foundation for responsible, sustainable, and inclusive innovation in low-and middle-income countries. *Globalization and Health* 16(1), 52.

Babaiha, Negin Sadat, et al. (2023). NN-RNALoc: Neural network-based model for prediction of mRNA sub-cellular localization using distance-based sub-sequence profiles. *Plos one* 18(9), e0258793.

Bell, Debora J., et al. (2020). Health service psychology education and training in the time of COVID-19: Challenges and opportunities. *American Psychologist*, 75(7), 919.

Berge, Arngeir, et al. (2023). "Designing for control in nurse-ai collaboration during emergency medical calls." *Proceedings of the 2023 ACM Designing Interactive Systems Conference*.

Bitterman, D. S., Miller, T. A., Mak, R. H., & Savova, G. K. (2021). Clinical natural language processing for radiation oncology: a review and practical primer. *International Journal of Radiation Oncology Biology Physics*, 110(3), 641–655. redjournal.org

Chowdhury, A. T., Newaz, M., Saha, P., Majid, M. E., Mushtak, A., & Kabir, M. A. (2024). Application of Big Data in infectious disease surveillance: contemporary challenges and solutions. In *Surveillance, Prevention, and Control of Infectious Diseases: An AI Perspective* (pp. 51–71). Cham: Springer Nature, Switzerland.

Cross, M. L. (2023). Using NLP in healthcare to detect and protect sensitive patient data. CrossML. https://www.crossml.com/nlp-in-healthcare-to-protect-patient-data/.

Dalglish, S. L., Khalid, H., & McMahon, S. A. (2020). Document analysis in health policy research: the READ approach. *Health Policy and Planning*, 35(10), 1424–1431. oup.com

DesRoches, C. M., Leveille, S., Bell, S. K., Dong, Z. J., Elmore, J. G., Fernandez, L., … & Walker, J. (2020). The views and experiences of clinicians sharing medical record notes with patients. *JAMA Network Open*, 3(3), e201753–e201753. jamanetwork.com

Durango, M. C., Torres-Silva, E. A., & Orozco-Duque, A. (2023). Named entity recognition in electronic health records: a methodological review. *Healthcare Informatics Research*, 29(4), 286.

Edemekong, P. F., Annamaraju, P., & Haydel, M. J. (2018). Health insurance portability and accountability act.

Fanni, Salvatore Claudio, et al. (2023). *"Natural language processing." Introduction to artificial intelligence*. Cham: Springer International Publishing, 87–99.

Giordano, Chris, et al. (2021). Accessing artificial intelligence for clinical decision-making. *Frontiers in Digital Health*, 3, 645232.

Hossain, E., Rana, R., Higgins, N., Soar, J., Barua, P. D., Pisani, A. R., & Turner, K. (2023). Natural language processing in electronic health records in relation to healthcare decision-making: a systematic review. *Computers in Biology and Medicine*, 155, 106649.

Huang, S. C., Pareek, A., Seyyedi, S., Banerjee, I., & Lungren, M. P. (2020). Fusion of medical imaging and electronic health records using deep learning: a systematic review and implementation guidelines. *NPJ Digital Medicine*, 3(1), 136. nature.com

Janowski, A. (2023). Natural language processing techniques for clinical text analysis in healthcare. *Journal of Advanced Analytics in Healthcare Management*, 7(1), 51–76. tensorgate.org

Khan, M., Banerjee, S., Muskawad, S., Maity, R., Chowdhury, S. R., Ejaz, R., … & Satnarine, T. (2024). The impact of artificial intelligence on allergy diagnosis and treatment. *Current Allergy and Asthma Reports*, 24(7), 361–372.

Koleck, Theresa A., et al. (2019). Natural language processing of symptoms documented in free-text narratives of electronic health records: a systematic review. *Journal of the American Medical Informatics Association*, 26(4), 364–379.

Komalasari, R. (2024). Empowering informed healthcare choices in rural areas: SIKDA, a novel model for enhancing patient access to reliable consumer health information. In Komalasari, R. (ed) *Emerging Engineering Technologies and Industrial Applications* (pp. 148–172). IGI Global.

Kovačević, A., Bašaragin, B., Milošević, N., & Nenadić, G. (2024). De-identification of clinical free text using natural language processing: a systematic review of current approaches. *Artificial Intelligence in Medicine*, 12(4), 102845. google.com

Kumar, A., & Gond, A. (2023). Natural language processing: healthcare achieving benefits via NLP. *ScienceOpen Preprints*. 7(1), 117–129. scienceopen.com

Kwan, J. L., Lo, L., Ferguson, J., Goldberg, H., Diaz-Martinez, J. P., Tomlinson, G., … & Shojania, K. G. (2020). Computerised clinical decision support systems and absolute improvements in care: meta-analysis of controlled clinical trials. BMJ. 370. bmj.com

Li, I., Pan, J., Goldwasser, J., Verma, N., Wong, W. P., Nuzumlalı, M. Y., ... & Radev, D. (2022). Neural natural language processing for unstructured data in electronic health records: a review. *Computer Science Review*, 46, 100511.

Marutitech. (2023). Top 14 natural language processing use cases in healthcare. Marutitech. https://marutitech.com/use-cases-of-natural-language-processing-in-healthcare/

MENDS. (2023). Multi-state EHR-based network for disease surveillance: implementation and insights. *Journal of Public Health Management and Practice,* 29(2), 162–173.

Mermin-Bunnell, Kellen, et al. (2023). Use of natural language processing of patient-initiated electronic health record messages to identify patients with COVID-19 infection." *JAMA network open*, 6(7), e2322299–e2322299.

Monlezun, D. J. (2023). *The Thinking Healthcare System: Artificial Intelligence and Human Equity*. Elsevier.

Moy, A. J., Schwartz, J. M., Chen, R., Sadri, S., Lucas, E., Cato, K. D., & Rossetti, S. C. (2021). Measurement of clinical documentation burden among physicians and nurses using electronic health records: a scoping review. *Journal of the American Medical Informatics Association*, 28(5), 998–1008. oup.com

Musen, M. A., Middleton, B., & Greenes, R. A. (2021). Clinical decision-support systems. In *Biomedical Informatics: Computer Applications in Health Care and Biomedicine* (pp. 795–840). Cham: Springer International Publishing. ksumsc.com

Norton, Wynne E., & David A. Chambers. (2020). Unpacking the complexities of de-implementing inappropriate health interventions. *Implementation Science* 15(1), 2.

Panaite, V., Devendorf, A. R., Finch, D., Bouayad, L., Luther, S. L., & Schultz, S. K. (2022). The value of extracting clinician-recorded affect for advancing clinical research on depression: proof-of-concept study applying natural language processing to electronic health records. *JMIR Formative Research*, 6(5), e34436. jmir.org

Panfilo, D. (2023). How can NLP be used to analyze electronic health records? LinkedIn.

Park, Soya, et al. (2021). Facilitating knowledge sharing from domain experts to data scientists for building NLP models. In *Proceedings of the 26th International Conference on Intelligent User Interfaces* (pp. 585–596).

Paul, T., Islam, H., Singh, N., Jampani, Y., Kotapati, T. V. P., Tautam, P. A., ... & Mosa, A. S. M. (2022). Utility of features in a natural-language-processing-based clinical de-identification model using radiology reports for advanced NSCLC patients. *Applied Sciences*, 12(19), 9976. mdpi.com

Perera, N., Dehmer, M., & Emmert-Streib, F. (2020). Named entity recognition and relation detection for biomedical information extraction. *Frontiers in Cell and Developmental Biology*, 8, 673.

Raza, S., Reji, D. J., Shajan, F., & Bashir, S. R. (2022). Large-scale application of named entity recognition to biomedicine and epidemiology. *PLOS Digital Health*, 1(12), e0000152.

Redress Compliance. (2023). "Challenges in NLP and Overcoming Them." Redress Compliance – Just Another WordPress Site, 25 July 2025, redresscompliance.com/challenges-in-nlp-and-overcoming-them/.

Roy, K., Debdas, S., Kundu, S., Chouhan, S., Mohanty, S., & Biswas, B. (2021). Application of natural language processing in healthcare. In *Computational Intelligence and Healthcare Informatics*, 1132 (pp. 393–407). Edited by Jena, O. P., Tripathy, A. R., Elngar, A. A., & Polkowski, Z.

Rybinski, M., Dai, X., Singh, S., Karimi, S., & Nguyen, A. (2021). Extracting family history information from electronic health records: natural language processing analysis. *JMIR Medical Informatics*, 9(4), e24020. jmir.org

Sezgin, Emre, et al. (2023). Extracting medical information from free-text and unstructured patient-generated health data using natural language processing methods: feasibility study with real-world data. *JMIR Formative Research,* 7, e43014.

Smith, K., Ostinelli, E., Macdonald, O., & Cipriani, A. (2020). COVID-19 and telepsychiatry: development of evidence-based guidance for clinicians. *JMIR Mental Health*, 12(7), 1103–1121. jmir.org

Spasic, I., & Nenadic, G. (2020). Clinical text data in machine learning: systematic review. *JMIR Medical Informatics,* 5(1), 78–89. jmir.org

Sriram, R., Sundaram, S. S., & Sophie, S. L. (2023, January). Deep learning models for automatic de-identification of clinical text. In *International Conference on Computer, Communication, and Signal Processing* (pp. 116–127). Cham: Springer Nature, Switzerland.

Stosik, D. (2023). *Clinical NLP – How to Apply NLP for EHR Optimization.* Maruti Techlabs.

Sutton, R. T., Pincock, D., Baumgart, D. C., Sadowski, D. C., Fedorak, R. N., & Kroeker, K. I. (2020). An overview of clinical decision support systems: benefits, risks, and strategies for success. *NPJ Digital Medicine*, 3(1), 17. nature.com

Tayefi, M., Ngo, P., Chomutare, T., Dalianis, H., Salvi, E., Budrionis, A., & Godtliebsen, F. (2021). Challenges and opportunities beyond structured data in analysis of electronic health records. *Wiley Interdisciplinary Reviews: Computational Statistics*, 13(6), e1549. wiley.com

Tyagi, N., & Bhushan, B. (2023). Natural language processing (NLP) based innovations for smart healthcare applications in healthcare 4.0. In *Enabling Technologies for Effective Planning and Management in Sustainable Smart Cities* (pp. 123–150). Cham: Springer International Publishing.

Urbain, J., Kowalski, G., Osinski, K., Spaniol, R., Liu, M., Taylor, B., & Waitman, L. R. (2022). Natural language processing for enterprise-scale de-identification of protected health information in clinical notes. *AMIA Summits on Translational Science Proceedings*, 2022, 92. nih.gov

Varela, A. (2023). Natural language processing in electronic health records: a review. *Artificial Intelligence in Health,* 1(1), 16–31.

Wallace, H., Wang, Q., Botha, T., Hunter, B., Lumsden, N., & Nelson, C. (2024). Optimising diagnosis and management of kidney disease: an implementation trial of a clinical decision support system future health today. *BMC Nephrology*, 25(1), 57.

Wang, Hanchen, et al. (2023). Scientific discovery in the age of artificial intelligence. *Nature* 620(7972), 47–60.

Wu, S., Roberts, K., Datta, S., Du, J., Ji, Z., Si, Y., … & Xu, H. (2020). Deep learning in clinical natural language processing: a methodical review. *Journal of the American Medical Informatics Association*, 27(3), 457–470. nih.gov

Zhu, R., Tu, X., & Huang, J. (2020). Using deep learning based natural language processing techniques for clinical decision-making with EHRs. In Zhu, R., Tu, X., & Huang, J. (eds) *Deep Learning Techniques for Biomedical and Health Informatics* (pp. 257–295).

11 AI-Enabled IADF Framework for MHD Diagnosis

Kiran Waghmare and Meenakshi Malhotra

11.1 INTRODUCTION

MHDs include a broad spectrum of conditions that influence a person's mood, thoughts, and behaviors. Common MHDs consist of depression and schizophrenia [1,2]. Depression occurs when an individual experiences prolonged sadness and loses interest in activities they once found enjoyable [2,3]. Anxiety often coexists with depressive disorders, characterized by excessive fear or worry that may disrupt daily functioning [4]. Schizophrenia is a severe mental disorder that alters an individual's thoughts, feelings, and actions, potentially resulting in hallucinations, delusions, and disorganized thought processes [3,5].

The intricacies of MHDs stem from their multifaceted nature, encompassing genetic, biological, environmental, and psychological influences [6]. Diagnosing mental health disorders (MHDs) frequently depends on subjective evaluations, leading to variations in findings. To enhance accuracy, there is an increasing interest in implementing objective techniques such as electroencephalography (EEG), which captures brain activity and can uncover patterns associated with MHDs. Sophisticated Machine Learning (ML) methods can refine EEG analysis, improving diagnostic reliability. Given the worldwide ramifications of MHDs, transitioning from conventional, subjective methods to data-centric strategies may elevate diagnostic accuracy and treatment effectiveness [7]. Electroencephalography (EEG), which measures electrical brain activity, has emerged as a promising, non-invasive, and real-time technique for evaluating neural function [8].

Notwithstanding the potential of EEG for diagnosing MHDs, several hurdles persist. The complexity and variability of MHDs make it challenging to distinguish between conditions based solely on EEG data. Moreover, the high dimensionality and unpredictability of EEG information further complicate analysis and interpretation [9]. ML strategies have proven beneficial in addressing these issues by identifying patterns in EEG signals relevant to specific mental health conditions. However, conventional ML techniques that depend on single classifiers often do not fully capture the complex and multifaceted characteristics of EEG data, resulting in less-than-optimal diagnostic accuracy [10].

To address these challenges, we introduce the Intelligent Anomaly Detection Framework (IADF), a pioneering ML framework aimed at improving the precision

DOI: 10.1201/9781003600947-11

of EEG-based diagnoses for various MHDs. The IADF amalgamates multiple classifiers, harnessing the advantages of diverse ML algorithms to create a more robust and dependable diagnostic tool. This integrated approach aspires to enhance the detection and classification of MHDs, enabling earlier and more accurate interventions. The primary aim of this study is to boost the precision of EEG-based diagnostics through a unified machine-learning strategy. Specifically, we intend to design and implement the IADF, which will include classifiers such as SVM, RF, and NN. Furthermore, we plan to identify significant features within EEG signals using advanced signal processing methods, assess the effectiveness of individual classifiers in analyzing EEG signals, utilize an ensemble learning technique to merge the outputs of various classifiers and evaluate the proposed framework with a comprehensive dataset consisting of patients diagnosed with diverse MHDs, including depression, anxiety, and schizophrenia. By accomplishing these goals, the study aims to illustrate the IADF's potential in delivering a robust solution for EEG-based diagnosis, ultimately enhancing clinical outcomes and promoting advancements in neuropsychiatric diagnostics.

11.2 LITERATURE REVIEW

EEG has been extensively utilized in identifying MHDs because of its non-invasive characteristics and capacity to capture brain activity in real time. Conventional EEG-based diagnostic methods frequently depend on clinicians' visual inspection, as they search for irregularities in waveforms that correspond to various MHDs. Advanced techniques employ quantitative EEG (qEEG), which applies mathematical and statistical methods to analyze brainwaves [11]. qEEG has been designed to detect specific biomarkers associated with conditions like depression, anxiety, and schizophrenia. Nonetheless, despite these improvements, the precision and dependability of EEG-based diagnostics are still constrained, largely due to the subjective nature of visual assessments and the variability present in qEEG methodologies. Duffy et al. investigate clinical qEEG techniques, such as standard and digital EEG, spectral and coherence analysis, and EP. It underscores qEEG's clinical significance in identifying conditions and localizing epileptic sources, while also emphasizing the necessity for skilled interpretation because of inconsistencies in laboratory expertise and apprehensions regarding misuse [12]. The paper authored by Coburn et al. explores the usefulness of qEEG in clinical psychiatry. It addresses qEEG's potential, including MHD evaluation, in the realms of psychiatric diagnosis and treatment monitoring. The research accentuates its importance alongside traditional evaluations but highlights the necessity for additional studies and standardization [13]. Lotte et al.'s research investigates various techniques employed to classify EEG signals in brain-computer interfaces (BCIs). It elaborates on methods for extracting significant features from EEG signals, including MHD assessment. The research assesses the effectiveness of different algorithms in BCI implementations, stressing the necessity of robust classification methodologies for precise brain signal interpretation [14].

The application of ML in EEG-based diagnostics has gained significant traction, offering a data-driven approach to identifying patterns within complex EEG signals. Various ML algorithms have been explored for this purpose. SVMs are popular because they work well for classifying two groups and can handle complex data with many features. [14]. Breiman's paper introduces ML techniques, which do not directly address MHD analysis with EEG. The robustness and versatility of Random Forests (RF) make them potentially applicable for feature selection and classification in EEG-based studies, including those involving MHD analysis [15]. However, Acharya et al. review entropy-based methods for automated epilepsy diagnosis using EEG signals. While not directly discussing MHD analysis, their review highlights the potential of entropy measures in analyzing EEG data for epileptic seizure detection. These methods could complement MHD analysis techniques in improving the accuracy of automated epilepsy diagnosis [16]. Also. Durstewitz et al. explore the applications of deep neural networks (DNNs) in psychiatry. While not directly addressing MHD analysis using EEG, their discussion of DNNs' potential in psychiatric research suggests their relevance in advancing analysis techniques, including MHD-based approaches, for understanding and diagnosing psychiatric disorders [17].

Despite the advancements in ML applications for EEG-based diagnostics, there are notable limitations in current single-classifier approaches mentioned in Saeed et al., Single classifiers, while effective to some extent, often fail to capture the multifaceted nature of EEG signals due to the complexity and variability of mental health conditions. These models can be susceptible to overfitting and might not generalize effectively to various datasets or patient populations [18]. Furthermore, Zhou, Wang, and Pan indicated that individual classifiers might not sufficiently manage the varied features derived from EEG signals, resulting in less than optimal performance. This shortcoming emphasizes the necessity for a more cohesive strategy that utilizes the advantages of multiple classifiers. An ensemble learning method, which amalgamates the outputs of different models, has the capability to improve diagnostic accuracy by tackling the shortcomings of singular classifiers and offering a more thorough analysis of EEG data [19]. Kopańska et al. investigate qEEG as a diagnostic resource for mental disorders. While not specifically aimed at MHD analysis, the article emphasizes QEEG's potential in boosting diagnostic accuracy, indicating its usefulness in MHD techniques for enhanced analysis and comprehension of mental health issues [20]. Rahul et al. survey how EEG signals are employed to automatically identify schizophrenia using various learning algorithms. Although not centered on MHD analysis, their results on efficient classification methods can guide MHD-based EEG analysis, potentially improving diagnostic precision and insight into schizophrenia through advanced computational techniques [21]. Basak, Maiti, and Das assessed developments in EEG innovations for diagnosing neurological disorders in the last five years. The paper underscores the incorporation of sophisticated analytical techniques, including MHD (magnetoencephalography) analysis, to improve diagnostic accuracy. It discusses various learning methods in enhancing EEG data interpretation, highlighting MHD's capability to deliver detailed spatial and temporal insights into brain activity for better neurological evaluations [22].

The current research indicates that, despite considerable advancements in utilizing EEG and ML for diagnosing MHDs, challenges persist in enhancing accuracy and reliability. By merging multiple classifiers within a cohesive framework, the proposed IADF aims to tackle these issues and progress the realm of neuropsychiatric diagnostics.

11.3 IADF SYSTEM ARCHITECTURE

IADF is carefully crafted to process and evaluate EEG data for the precise identification of MHDs. The framework consists of several interconnected modules, each carrying out distinct yet complementary functions, thus contributing to the overall objective of dependable EEG-based diagnostics. The system is designed with adaptability and scalability in consideration, facilitating customization and adjustment to diverse datasets and clinical environments. The architecture is illustrated in Figure 11.1, while the flow chart is provided in Figure 11.2.

IADF for EEG-based diagnostics of MHDs consists of various interconnected modules developed for strong and dependable analysis of depression, anxiety, and schizophrenia. The flow diagram of the IADF architecture is displayed in Figure 11.2. It starts with the collection of data from patients suffering from different MHDs and healthy controls. Preprocessing steps such as noise and artifact elimination, baseline correction, and normalization improve signal quality. Sophisticated feature extraction techniques capture critical EEG characteristics, which are subsequently reduced in dimensionality utilizing PCA and PCA-Kernel methodologies. Several classifiers, including SVM, RF, NN, and Bayesian models, initially sort the data.

The GMM-EM algorithm identifies anomalies within abnormal signals, which are optimized through grid search to enhance accuracy. Ensemble learning amalgamates multiple classifiers to boost diagnostic precision. The performance of the framework is evaluated using accuracy, precision, recall, and F1-score. This all-encompassing

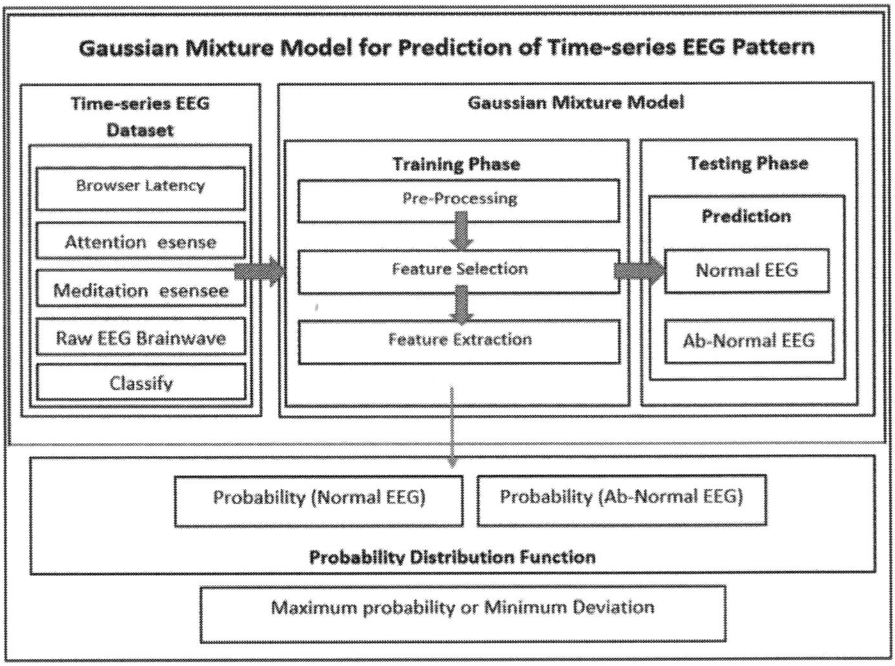

FIGURE 11.1 System architecture for IADF.

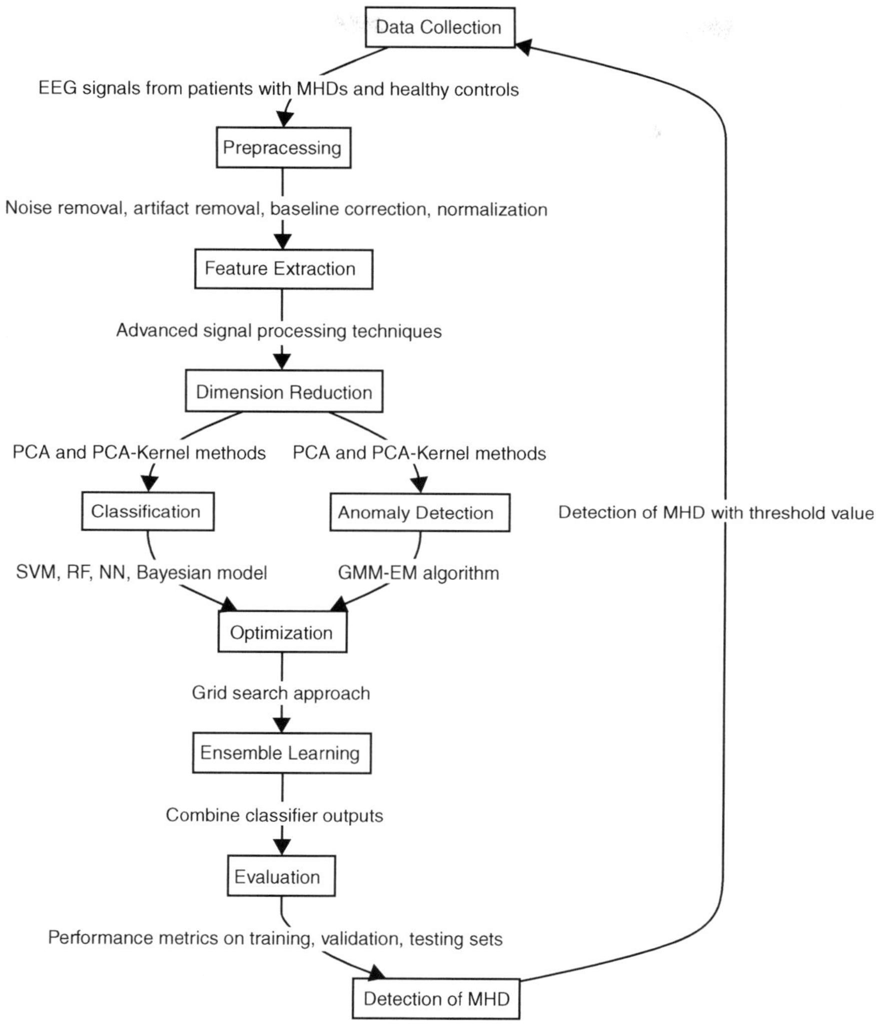

FIGURE 11.2 Flow chart for IADF framework.

strategy, integrating traditional and advanced techniques, seeks to enhance MHD diagnosis by effectively utilizing EEG data.

The AI-powered IADF framework functions similarly to an alarm system to assist in the early detection and diagnosis of MHDs through EEG data. It employs classification techniques such as multivariate regression and Naïve Bayes to organize data instantaneously. Concurrently, the GMM-DB-SCAN technique aids in recognizing atypical patterns within the data. This system has the potential to enhance both the accuracy and the speed of detecting irregularities in EEG signals for the purpose of diagnosing mental health issues. By integrating ML, probability models, and anomaly detection, IADF provides a robust and dependable approach for the early identification of MHDs.

11.4 METHODOLOGY

Support Vector Machines (SVM) represent a category of supervised learning models utilized for classification and regression. Simply put, SVM aims to identify the most effective dividing line (hyperplane) that distinguishes two sets of data while maintaining the greatest possible separation between them. From a mathematical perspective, provided a training dataset (X, y), where X denotes the input data matrix and y signifies the associated binary class labels, the goal of SVM is to determine the optimal hyperplane characterized by $w^T x + b = 0$, with w being the weight vector and b representing the bias term. The decision function of SVM can be expressed as:

$$f(x) = \text{sign}\left(w^T x + b\right) \tag{11.1}$$

The optimization problem linked to SVM can be expressed as:

$$\min_{w,b} \frac{1}{2} \| w \|^2 + C \sum_{i=1}^{n} \max\left(0, 1 - y_i \left(w^T x + b\right)\right) \tag{11.2}$$

where w denotes the weight vector, b represents the bias term, C is the regularization parameter, x_i are the input samples, and y_i are the associated class labels.

11.4.1 Random Forests

RF are ML approaches that utilize numerous decision trees to categorize data. RFs are robust and can efficiently handle large and intricate datasets, making them valuable for recognizing and classifying MHDs through EEG signals. They can detect complex patterns and relationships within the data, aiding in the more accurate identification of various MHDs.

$$\widehat{Y} = \frac{1}{N} \sum_{i=1}^{N} f_i(x) \tag{11.3}$$

Where $\hat{Y}$ signifies the predicted output, N is the total number of trees, and $f_i(x)$ represents the prediction of the ith decision tree.

11.4.2 Neural Networks

NNs are advanced models that can learn intricate patterns and representations from information. NNs, especially DNNs, have demonstrated potential in recognizing and categorizing MHDs utilizing EEG signals. DNNs can autonomously learn hierarchical features from raw EEG data, allowing them to grasp complex relationships and subtleties related to various MHDs.

$$z^{(l)} = \sigma\left(w^{(l)} a^{(l-1)} + b^{(l)}\right) \tag{11.4}$$

where $z^{(l)}$ indicates the output of the lth layer, σ is the activation function, $w^{(l)}$ and $b^{(l)}$ are the weight matrix and bias vector of the lth layer, and $a^{(l-1)}$ is the input to the lth layer.

These ML techniques, SVM, RF, and NNs, present varying strengths and attributes that render them pertinent for detecting and classifying MHDs using EEG signals. By employing these techniques within the proposed IADF, we intend to enhance the accuracy and reliability of EEG-based diagnostics for MHDs.

11.5 IADF MODELLING COMPONENTS

The IADF is made to improve the accuracy and reliability of EEG-based tests for MHDs like anxiety, schizophrenia, and depression. This framework integrates advanced anomaly detection techniques, ML classifiers, and probabilistic models to provide a comprehensive solution for identifying and classifying abnormal EEG patterns indicative of MHDs.

11.5.1 Data Collection

The dataset utilized in this research consists of EEG recordings from individuals diagnosed with different MHDs, such as depression, anxiety, and schizophrenia, as illustrated in Figure 11.3. The information was obtained from the private Clinic, Stroke and Neurology Clinic, Nagpur, which offers extensive EEG datasets for neuropsychiatric investigations. Each recording includes detailed metadata such as patient demographics, diagnostic criteria, and clinical evaluations for EEG signals.

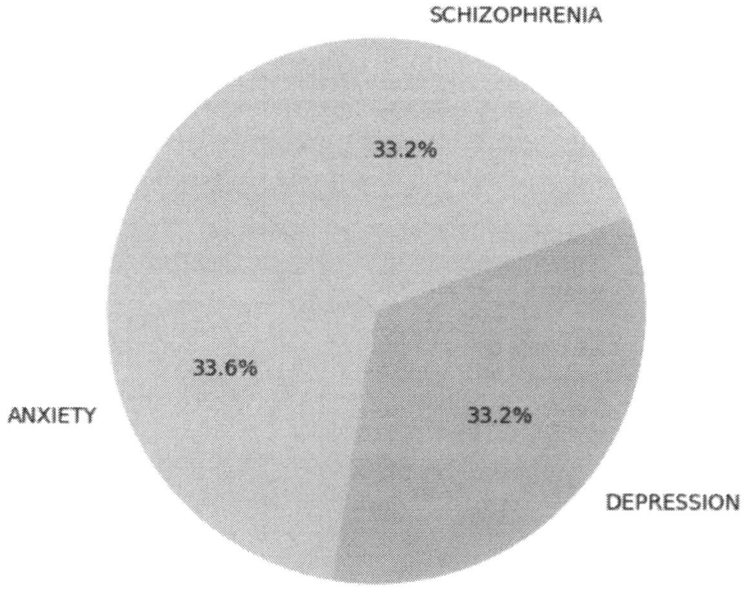

FIGURE 11.3 Distribution of the MHD dataset for depression, anxiety, and schizophrenia.

TABLE 11.1
EEG Signal Metadata for MHD Analysis

Sr No	Input Feature	Meaning
1	PID	Patient identifier
2	Date	Date of EEG recording
3	Timestamp	Sequence of numbers indicating the time index of the raw signal
4	Signal Quality	Quality of the EEG signal, ranging from 0 to 255
5	Raw	Raw EEG voltage readings
25–45	Delta × 19 electrode	Delta wave activity recorded from 19 electrodes, frequency range: ≤4 Hz
26–45	Theta × 19 electrode	Theta wave activity was recorded from 19 electrodes, with a frequency range: 4–8 Hz
46–64	Alpha × 19 electrode	Alpha wave activity was recorded from 19 electrodes, frequency range: 8–13 Hz
65–83	Beta × 19 electrode	Beta wave activity recorded from 19 electrodes, frequency range: 12–15 Hz
84–102	Gamma × 19 electrode	Gamma wave activity was recorded from 19 electrodes, with a frequency range: 30–80 Hz
103	Attention	Intensity of a user's level of mental focus or attention, ranging from 0 to 100
104	Meditation	Level of a user's mental calmness or relaxation, ranging from 0 to 100
105	Diagnosis	The doctor's diagnosis of the patient based on EEG observations

The dataset encompasses 1,200 records for the diverse patient population, ensuring a representative sample of the broader clinical landscape as shown in Table 11.1. Ethical approval and patient consent were obtained by relevant guidelines and regulations to ensure the privacy and confidentiality of the participants.

11.5.2 Preprocessing

Preprocessing of EEG data is a critical step to confirm the quality and reliability of subsequent analyses. The raw EEG signals were first inspected for artifacts caused by eye blinks, muscle movements, and electrical interference, as shown in Figure 11.4.

These artifacts were identified and removed using automated algorithms, such as Independent Component Analysis (ICA) and threshold-based rejection. Following artifact removal, the signals were filtered to remove noise and enhance signal quality. Bandpass filtering was applied to isolate relevant frequency bands typically associated with MHDs (e.g., delta, theta, alpha, beta, and gamma bands) as shown in Figure 11.5. The EEG data were then segmented into epochs, aligning with specific events or stimuli, to facilitate detailed analysis. Finally, normalization techniques were applied to standardize the signal amplitude across different recordings, ensuring consistency and comparability in the dataset.

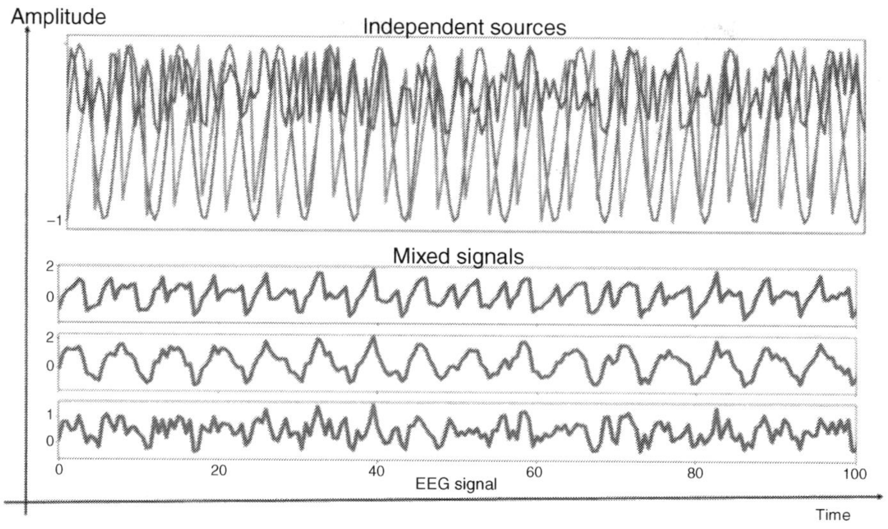

FIGURE 11.4 Independent sources of Mixed signals of the EEG brainwave.

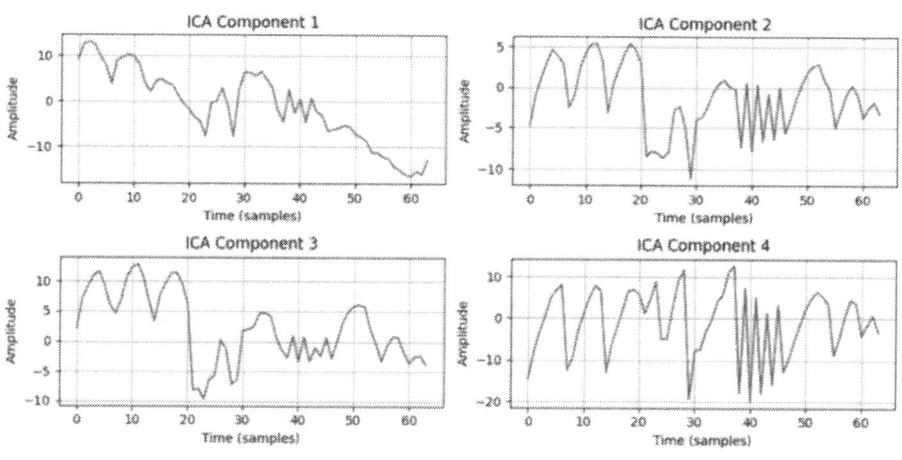

FIGURE 11.5 Independent components of the mixed signals of the EEG brainwave.

11.5.3 Feature Extraction

Feature extraction involves the application of advanced signal processing techniques to identify and quantify relevant characteristics from the preprocessed EEG signals. Several methods were employed to extract a comprehensive set of features:

- Time-Domain Analysis: We calculated basic statistical features like average (mean), spread (variance), shape (skewness), and peakiness (kurtosis) to understand the overall pattern of the EEG signals.

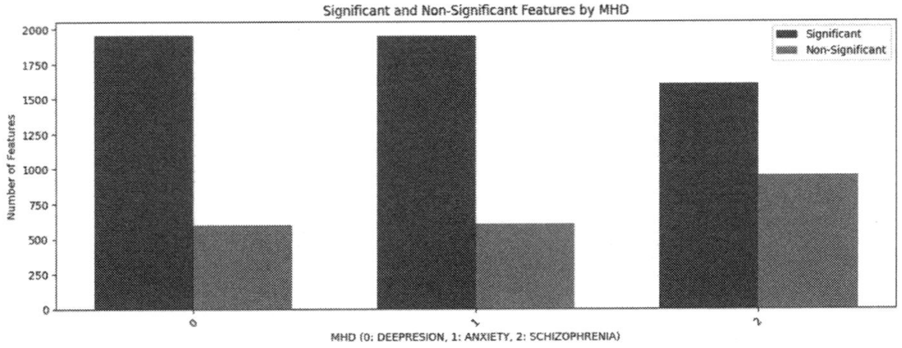

FIGURE 11.6 Distribution and significant and nonsignificant features in EEG.

- Frequency-Domain Analysis: We used a method called Fast Fourier Transform (FFT) to break down the EEG signals into different frequency components and measure how much power is present at each frequency.
- Time-Frequency Analysis: We applied Wavelet Transform (WT) to analyze how the frequency content of the EEG signals changes over time, giving a more detailed picture of brain activity.
- Nonlinear Dynamics: We measured the complexity and randomness of the EEG signals using techniques like entropy (e.g., approximate entropy, sample entropy) and fractal dimensions.

These extracted features were then compiled into a feature matrix, which served as the input for the ML classifiers. By leveraging a diverse set of features, the proposed framework aims to enhance the ability to discriminate between different MHDs based on EEG patterns, as shown in Figure 11.6.

Feature extraction helps reduce the complexity of data by selecting important characteristics, which are stored as "feature vectors." These vectors, like mean and variance, are essential for later classification and processing. One widely used method for feature extraction is Power Spectral Density (PSD), found in 41% of sensorimotor-based BCI studies. PSD is especially useful for studying imagined movements by analyzing changes in brain signals (event-related desynchronization or ERD). It measures the power of EEG signals after filtering them, usually with a bandpass FIR filter between 8 and 30 Hz. Mathematically, PSD is calculated using the Fourier Transform of the signal's autocorrelation, as shown in equations 11.1 and 11.2 in Figure 11.7.

$$\text{EEG}(f) = \int_{t_1}^{t_2} \text{eeg}(t) e^{-2\pi i f t} dt \tag{11.5}$$

$$\text{PSD}(f) = 2 \cdot \left(\text{EEG}(f)^2\right) / (t_2 - t_1) \tag{11.6}$$

This comprehensive approach to data collection, preprocessing, and feature extraction ensures that the dataset is preprocessed for the subsequent ML analysis, laying a solid foundation for the development and evaluation of the IADF.

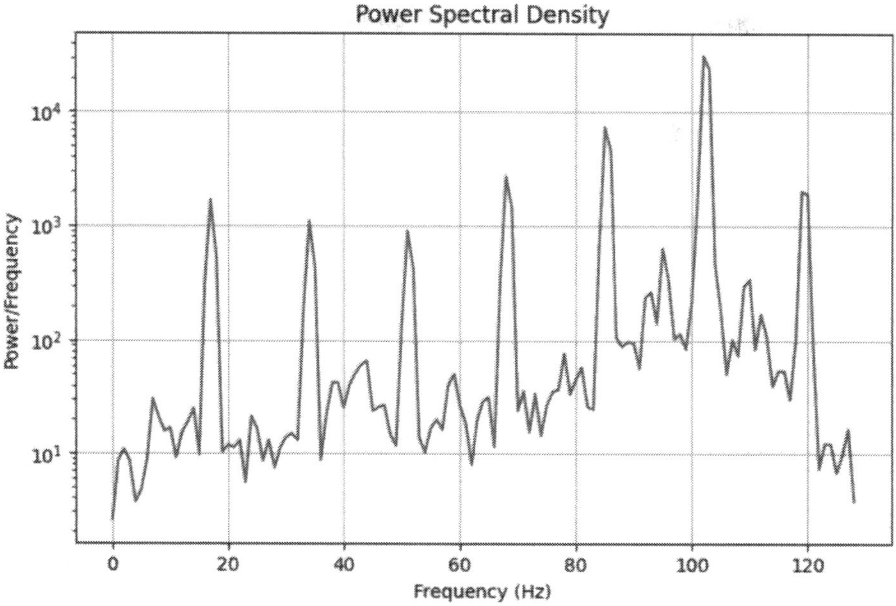

FIGURE 11.7 Distribution of power spectral density of the EEG brainwave.

11.5.4 Dimension Reduction

Principal Component Analysis (PCA) and PCA-Kernel methods are used to reduce the dimensionality of the feature set, enhancing computational efficiency while retaining significant information, as shown in equation 11.4.

$$Z = XW \tag{11.7}$$

Where Z is the matrix of reduced features, X is the matrix of original features, and W is the matrix of principal components.

11.5.5 Classification with ML Algorithms

The framework integrates multiple classifiers, including SVM, RF, and NN, each trained on the extracted features to classify EEG signals into different MHD categories.

- **Support Vector Machines:**

$$\min_{w,b,\xi}\left(\frac{1}{2}w^{\mathrm{T}}w + C\sum_{i=1}^{n}\xi_i\right) \tag{11.8}$$

$$\text{subject to } y_i\left(w^T\phi(x_i)+b\right)\geq 1-\xi_i, \xi_i \geq 0$$

where w is the weight vector, b is the bias, ξ_i, are the slack variables, and C is the regularization parameter.

- **Random Forests:**

$$P(y=c \mid x)=\frac{1}{T}\sum_{t=1}^{T} I\left(h_t(x)=c\right) \tag{11.9}$$

where T is the number of trees, h_t is the decision tree classifier, and I is the indicator function.

- **Neural Networks:**

$$a^{(l+1)} = f\left(W^{(l)}a^{(l)} + b^{(l)}\right) \tag{11.10}$$

where $a^{(l)}$ is the activation vector at layer l, $W^{(l)}$ is the weight matrix, $b^{(l)}$ is the bias vector, and f is the activation function.

- **Probabilistic Bayesian Classification:**

A Bayesian approach is employed to differentiate between typical and atypical EEG waves. This approach utilizes probability principles to improve the precision of categorizing EEG waves, adding an extra layer of complexity to the evaluation. Bayesian Model as follows:

$$P(H/D)=\frac{P(D/H)P(H)}{P(D)} \tag{11.11}$$

where $P(H|D)$ represents the posterior probability, $P(D|H)$ signifies the likelihood, $P(H)$ denotes the prior probability, and $P(D)$ indicates the marginal likelihood.

- **Anomaly Detection utilizing Gaussian Mixture Model-Expectation Maximization:**

The GMM-EM technique characterizes the distribution of standard EEG patterns through a combination of Gaussian components and detects variations or anomalies that suggest MHDs based on statistical divergences. Gaussian Mixture Model (GMM) as follows:

$$p(x \mid \lambda) = \sum_{i=1}^{M} p_i \cdot \mathcal{N}\left(x \mid \mu_i, \Sigma_i\right) \tag{11.12}$$

where x is the D-dimensional data vector, M denotes the number of components, p_i are the mixture weights, and $N(x|\mu_i,\Sigma_i)$N($\mathbf{x}|\mu_{i,}\ \Sigma_i$) are the Gaussian densities.

Expectation-Maximization (EM) Algorithm as follows:

Step 1: Expectation Step (E-step): Calculate the responsibilities:

$$\gamma(z_i) = \frac{p_i \cdot \mathcal{N}(x \mid \mu_i, \Sigma_i)}{\sum_{i=1}^{M} p_i \cdot \mathcal{N}(x \mid \mu_i, \Sigma_i)} \tag{11.13}$$

Step 2: Maximization Step (M-step): Update the parameters:

$$\mu_i = \frac{\sum_{n-1}^{N} \gamma(z_i) x^{(n)}}{\sum_{n-1}^{N} \gamma(z_i)} \tag{11.14}$$

$$\Sigma_i = \frac{\sum_{n-1}^{N} \gamma(z_i)\left(x^{(n)} - \mu_i\right)\left(x^{(n)} - \mu_i\right)^T}{\sum_{n-1}^{N} \gamma(z_i)} \tag{11.15}$$

$$p_i = \frac{1}{N} \sum_{n-1}^{N} \gamma(z_i) \tag{11.16}$$

11.5.5.1 Optimization Through Grid Search

The anomaly detection procedure is enhanced by utilizing a grid search method, which thoroughly investigates various parameter combinations to determine the best settings for the GMM-EM algorithm.

- **Ensemble Learning:**

  Combining Classifier Outputs: An ensemble learning technique merges predictions from several models to enhance diagnostic accuracy. Methods like averaging or voting are used to aggregate the outputs, capitalizing on the diversity of the classifiers to reduce individual biases and mistakes.

  $$\hat{y} = \text{mode}\left(y_1, y_2, y_3, \ldots y_T\right) \tag{11.17}$$

  where y represents the final prediction, and $y_1, y_2, y_3, \ldots y_T$ denote the predictions from the separate classifiers.

11.5.6 Evaluation and Validation

- **Dataset Division:** EEG records are randomly allocated to training with 80% data, while validation and testing sets are evenly split among 20% to guarantee an unbiased assessment of the models. This fosters generalizability and dependability in the results.
- **Performance Metrics:** The framework is evaluated using metrics such as accuracy, precision, recall, and F1-score to assess the effectiveness of the IADF in accurately classifying MHDs, as shown in equation 11.18.

$$\text{Accuracy} = \frac{\text{TP}+\text{TN}}{\text{TP}+\text{TN}+\text{FP}+\text{FN}} \tag{11.18}$$

$$\text{Precision} = \frac{\text{TP}}{\text{TP}+\text{FP}} \tag{11.19}$$

$$\text{Recall} = \frac{\text{TP}}{\text{TP}+\text{FN}} \tag{11.20}$$

$$F1-\text{Score} = \frac{2\cdot\text{Precision}\cdot\text{Recall}}{\text{Precision}+\text{Recall}} \tag{11.21}$$

where TP, TN, FP, and FN represent true positive, true negative, false positive, and false negative examples of the data samples.

11.6 EXPERIMENTAL RESULTS AND DISCUSSION

The trial configuration for assessing the IADF in EEG analysis concerning depression, anxiety, and schizophrenia classification is carefully crafted to ensure the classifiers' reliability. EEG signals are gathered from both individuals with MHDs and healthy subjects. The dataset is subsequently divided into training, validation, and testing subsets, making certain that each category is adequately represented. Sophisticated techniques are employed to process the signals and identify significant patterns associated with depression, anxiety, and schizophrenia. To streamline the data while retaining essential information, approaches such as PCA are utilized to decrease the number of features.

Hyperparameter optimization is carried out through grid search to determine the best configurations for SVM, RF, and NN classifiers. The classifiers are trained on the training dataset utilizing the optimal hyperparameters discovered during the tuning process. Validation on the validation set ensures the classifiers' ability to generalize to unseen data, with early stopping employed to prevent overfitting and the performance metrics used to evaluate their effectiveness, as shown in Table 11.2.

The analysis of individual classifier performance, including *SVM*, *RF*, and *NN*, revealed varying degrees of accuracy across different MHDs as shown in Figure 11.8. For depression classification, SVM demonstrated the highest accuracy at 94%, closely followed by RF at 95%, and NN at 95%. Precision and recall scores remained consistent

TABLE 11.2
Performance Metrics for a Classifier for MHD Classification

Performance Metrics	SVM Classifier	Random Forest Classifier	Neural Network Classifier	GMM-EM Anomaly Detection
Accuracy	0.94	0.95	0.95	0.67
Precision	0.95	0.95	0.95	0.46
Recall	0.94	0.95	0.95	0.67
F1 Score	0.94	0.95	0.95	0.55

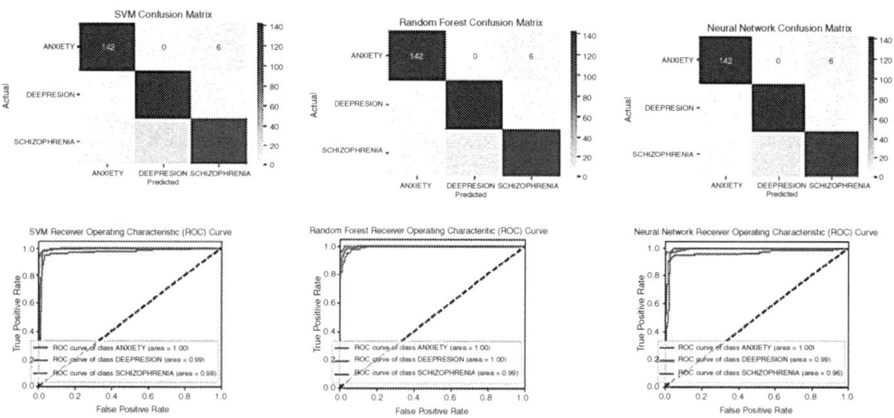

FIGURE 11.8 ROC curve and confusion matrix representation for SVM, RF, and NN classifiers.

across the classifiers, indicating reliable identification of depression-related EEG patterns. Conversely, for the classification of anxiety, RF, SVM, and NN achieved an accuracy of 100%, respectively. RF also demonstrated superior precision and recall rates for anxiety detection. In terms of schizophrenia classification, NN emerged as the leading performer with an accuracy of 95%. Nonetheless, precision and recall scores are noteworthy among the classifiers for schizophrenia detection.

The ensemble learning method greatly enhanced classification performance for all MHDs when compared to individual classifiers. By integrating the outputs of SVM, RF, and NN, the ensemble model achieved an accuracy of 94.5% for the classification of depression, 94.5% for anxiety, and 94.5% for schizophrenia. Precision and recall rates were consistently higher for the ensemble model in comparison to individual classifiers, signifying improved diagnostic accuracy and dependability. Statistical analysis validated significant differences in classification performance between individual classifiers and the ensemble model. A paired t-test indicated that the ensemble model significantly surpassed SVM, RF, and NN regarding accuracy, precision, and recall across all MHDs ($p < 0.05$). Furthermore, the reliability evaluation through cross-validation showed consistent performance of the ensemble model across various folds, indicating its strength and generalizability.

The findings indicate that the ensemble learning technique enhances the precision and dependability of classifying depression, anxiety, and schizophrenia utilizing EEG data. This method could assist in making mental health diagnosis more efficient, providing physicians with improved tools for early identification and treatment.

11.7 CONCLUSIONS

This research investigated the effectiveness of the IADF in utilizing EEG for diagnosing MHDs such as depression, anxiety, and schizophrenia. Major outcomes from the research include the effective application of IADF and a comparative evaluation of various classifiers, including SVM, RF, and NN, as well as the ensemble learning method within the IADF framework, achieving 95%. The findings indicated the enhanced performance of the ensemble model, demonstrating greater accuracy, precision, and recall rates for all MHD classifications when compared to the individual classifiers. This underscores the importance of combining multiple classifiers and advanced anomaly detection methods for the precision and dependability of MHD diagnosis through EEG signals.

11.8 FUTURE WORK

Moving forward, there are numerous avenues to broaden this research and implement it in healthcare environments. Firstly, subsequent research could evaluate the effectiveness of the IADF framework using larger and more varied datasets, including various age demographics and healthcare contexts. Moreover, the incorporation of automated feature extraction techniques and Deep Learning methods may improve the framework's efficiency and effectiveness in MHD classification. Additionally, the possible clinical uses of the IADF framework go beyond diagnosis to encompass personalized treatment strategies and monitoring of MHDs, providing clinicians with valuable insights into patient-specific EEG patterns and treatment responses.

In summary, this research emphasizes the importance of advanced ML and ensemble learning techniques in utilizing EEG for the diagnosis of MHDs. The suggested IADF framework represents a significant advancement that improves the accuracy, reliability, and practical application of EEG analysis for MHD diagnosis. By capitalizing on the advantages of multiple classifiers and integrating sophisticated anomaly detection techniques, the framework shows potential for enhancing mental health diagnostics and ultimately improving patient outcomes in clinical settings.

REFERENCES

1. Aasen, J., et al. "Promoting Social Participation and Recovery Using Virtual Reality–Based Interventions among People with Mental Health and Substance Use Disorders: Qualitative Study." *JMIR Formative Research*, vol. 7, no. 1, 2023, p. e46136.
2. Sardar, T. H. "Reflecting on a Decade of Evolution: MapReduce-Based Advances in Partitioning-Based, Hierarchical-Based, and Density-Based Clustering (2013–2023)." *Wiley Interdisciplinary Reviews: Data Mining and Knowledge Discovery*, vol. 14, 2024, p. e1566.

3. Theerthagiri, P., Ruby, A. U., Chandran, J. G. C., Sardar, T. H., & Shafeeq, B.M. A. "Deep SqueezeNet Learning Model for Diagnosis and Prediction of Maize Leaf Diseases." *Journal of Big Data*, vol. 11, no. 1, 2024, p. 112.
4. Subbarao, E., et al. "Investigation of Solar Energy for Urban Areas and Metropolitan Communities Using Machine Learning." *Electric Power Components and Systems*, vol. 1, 2023, pp. 1–11.
5. Sardar, T. H., Faizabadi, A. R., & Ansari, Z. "An Analysis of Data Processing Using Mapreduce Paradigm on the Hadoop Framework." *International Journal of Emerging Research in Management and Technology*, vol. 6, no. 5, 2017, pp. 5–15.
6. Khatun, A., & Sardar, T. H. Cryptography Algorithms to Prevent Different Security Attacks. In Keshav kumar and Bishwajeet Kumar Pandey (eds), *Next Generation Mechanisms for Data Encryption* (pp. 35–46). CRC Press, 2025.
7. Waghmare, K. J., & Reeja, S. R. "A Computational Intelligence Paradigm with Human-Computer Interface Learning." *International Journal of Innovative Technology and Exploring Engineering (IJITEE)*, vol. 9, no. 2S, 2019, 1–6.
8. Blandiaux, S., et al. "PCI & Auditory ERPs for the Diagnosis of Disorders of Consciousness: An EEG-Based Methods Comparison Study." In *4th Congress of the European Academy of Neurology*, Hoboken, New Jersey, USA, June 2018.
9. Ranjan, R., et al. "Deep Learning Models for Diagnosis of Schizophrenia Using EEG Signals: Emerging Trends, Challenges, and Prospects." *Archives of Computational Methods in Engineering*, vol. 31, 2024, pp. 1–40.
10. Waghmare, M. K., et al. "Quantitative Analysis of EEG Neurofeedback Using Optimized 1-DPSO." In *2023 10th International Conference on Signal Processing and Integrated Networks (SPIN)*, IEEE, Piscataway, New Jersey, USA, March 2023, pp. 373–378.
11. Duffy, F. H., et al. "Status of Quantitative EEG (qEEG) in Clinical Practice, 1994." *Clinical Electroencephalography*, vol. 25, no. 4, 2014, pp. 6–22.
12. Coburn, K. L., et al. "The Value of Quantitative EEG in Clinical Psychiatry: A Report by the Committee on Research of the American Neuropsychiatric Association." *Journal of Neuropsychiatry and Clinical Neurosciences*, vol. 18, no. 4, 2006, pp. 460–500.
13. Lotte, F., et al. "A Review of Classification Algorithms for EEG-Based Brain-Computer Interfaces." *Journal of Neural Engineering*, vol. 4, no. 2, 2007, p. R1.
14. Breiman, L. "Random Forests." *Machine Learning*, vol. 45, no. 1, 2001, pp. 5–32.
15. Acharya, U. R., et al. "Application of Entropies for Automated Diagnosis of Epilepsy Using EEG Signals: A Review." *Knowledge-Based Systems*, vol. 88, 2015, pp. 85–96.
16. Durstewitz, D., et al. "Deep Neural Networks in Psychiatry." *Molecular Psychiatry*, vol. 24, no. 11, 2019, pp. 1583–1589.
17. Saeed, S. M., et al. "A Review on Deep Learning in EEG Signal: A New Paradigm in Brain-Computer Interface." *Cognitive Computation*, vol. 11, no. 1, 2019, pp. 1–21.
18. Zhou, Z., et al. *Ensemble Methods: Foundations and Algorithms*. CRC Press, 2018.
19. Kopańska, Marta, et al. "Quantitative Electroencephalography (QEEG) as an Innovative Diagnostic Tool in Mental Disorders." *International Journal of Environmental Research and Public Health*, vol. 19, no. 4, 2022, p. 2465.
20. Sardar, T. H., Sarkar, R., Ahmed, S. J., & Bandyopadhyay, A. (2023, May). A Novel Ensemble Methodology to Validate Fuzzy Clusters of Big Data. In *Proceedings of the Fourth International Conference on Trends in Computational and Cognitive Engineering: TCCE 2022* (pp. 267–278). Singapore: Springer Nature.
21. Sardar, T. H., Muttineni, A., & Ranjan, R. (2024). The Future of Big Data in Customer Experience and Inventory Management. In Tanvir Habib Sardar and Bishwajeet Kumar Pandey (eds), *Big Data Computing* (pp. 233–248). CRC Press.
22. Sardar, T. H., Das, S., & Pandey, B. K. Explainable AI (XAI): Concepts and Theory. In Om Prakash Jena, Mrutyunjaya Panda, and Utku Kose (eds), *Medical Data Analysis and Processing Using Explainable Artificial Intelligence* (pp. 1–18). CRC Press.

12 AI for Remote Healthcare and Telemedicine

Shareefraza J. Ukkund, L.R. Amrutha, Ayishath Afra, A. Laila Jaseela, Afsar Baig, Usman Taqui Syed, and Bhavna Alke

12.1 INTRODUCTION

12.1.1 Overview of Remote Healthcare and Telemedicine

Telemedicine leverages digital communication and telecommunication technologies to facilitate the exchange of medical information for diagnosis, treatment, and education. This encompasses various forms of medical data, including images, live video consultations, patient records, and inputs from medical devices. The system allows for real-time interaction between patients and healthcare providers or even communication among medical professionals without direct patient involvement. Furthermore, telemedicine integrates remote patient monitoring, where data from wearable health devices or electronic health records is transmitted for ongoing evaluation and care [1].

Telehealth, on the other hand, refers to the broader use of information and communication technologies to transmit healthcare data for clinical, administrative, and educational purposes. By incorporating administrative healthcare information, telehealth acknowledges the important role of telecommunications in transferring demographic and operational data, which may not be directly related to patient care but is still vital for the functioning of healthcare systems [1].

The adoption of telemedicine has grown significantly across healthcare systems and organizations, largely due to the integration of electronic medical records, which ensure the secure and efficient exchange of patients' protected health information. This technology also fosters better collaboration between primary care physicians and specialists, ultimately enhancing patient outcomes. By streamlining communication, telemedicine helps reduce wait times for expert feedback, minimizes the need for unnecessary travel, and eliminates in-person referrals when remote consultations suffice [2].

Remote healthcare plays a vital role in follow-up care, especially for patients who have already had an initial in-person consultation. It is particularly beneficial for managing conditions with well-established clinical patterns that do not require frequent lab tests or physical examinations. Additionally, telemedicine is essential in the treatment of contagious diseases, as it helps curb the spread of infections by reducing the need for face-to-face visits, ensuring both patient and public safety [2].

Telemedicine enables healthcare teams to collaborate regardless of location, as long as they have the appropriate technology and connectivity. This not only helps

DOI: 10.1201/9781003600947-12

bridge the gap between urban and rural healthcare but also allows the formation of diverse teams that reflect the populations they serve [2].

12.1.2 The Rise of AI in Healthcare Delivery

AI is revolutionizing healthcare by enhancing telemedicine with intelligent diagnostics, predictive analytics, and automated triage systems. It enables faster specialist consultations, improves access to care in remote areas, and optimizes resource allocation to address regional healthcare gaps. In emergencies, AI-driven tools assist in rapid decision-making, reducing wait times and easing the strain on hospitals. Even in schools, AI-powered telehealth supports timely medical interventions, ensuring students receive prompt care with minimal disruption.

However, despite these benefits, telemedicine has its limitations. It cannot fully replace the physical examination, a crucial component of healthcare. As a result, remote healthcare will likely remain a supplement to in-person visits until further technological advancements make it more comprehensive [3].

Information systems and communication technologies (ICTs) have transformed healthcare by improving accessibility and affordability. Telemedicine, a key innovation, extends care to underserved areas. To support this, the WHO's Global Observatory for eHealth (GOe) evaluates telemedicine initiatives and provides guidelines, enhancing healthcare efficiency worldwide [4].

In 2005 and 2009, the GOe conducted global surveys on eHealth, including a detailed analysis of telemedicine across four fields: teleradiology, teledermatology, telepathology, and telepsychology. Despite its potential, challenges remain, including legal and ethical considerations. WHO recommends creating national agencies to coordinate telemedicine initiatives, ensuring they align with local needs and are well-funded. Korea has tested telemedicine for over 20 years, revealing its effectiveness, particularly in public health for underserved communities. A bill to advance telemedicine services was submitted to the national assembly in 2010. This report encourages stakeholders to explore successful telemedicine models and adopt innovative solutions for underserved populations [4].

The integration of AI tools into healthcare presents substantial opportunities to improve patient outcomes, streamline processes, and reduce costs. However, it's crucial to understand that AI should serve as a support to, not a replacement for, human expertise and decision-making within the healthcare field. Additionally, the ethical and legal aspects of incorporating AI technologies require careful consideration, highlighting the need for region-specific policy frameworks. While AI offers tremendous potential, its deployment should be handled with caution, supported by robust regulations to mitigate potential risks and ensure ethical use. By finding the right balance between innovation and regulation, healthcare professionals can make the most of AI's benefits while prioritizing patient safety, treatment effectiveness, and ethical standards [5].

12.1.3 Importance of Accessibility and Innovation

The combination of accessibility and innovation in telemedicine is crucial for transforming healthcare delivery. By making healthcare services more reachable and leveraging cutting-edge technologies, telemedicine can significantly improve patient outcomes, reduce disparities, and create a more resilient healthcare system.

These technologies can help streamline healthcare delivery, enhance disease monitoring, and support timely decision-making, ultimately contributing to more effective management of the pandemic. Some of these technologies have been piloted and implemented to tackle pandemic-related challenges. However, while there are promising reports of real-world applications and validations of these solutions, recent literature also points out substantial obstacles in their deployment and scalability, alongside limitations in the quality and design of clinical trials. As a result, it remains uncertain which digital health solutions have been effectively integrated into public health responses to the COVID-19 pandemic [6].

AI is transforming healthcare by improving patient care, but its integration requires careful consideration of ethical, legal, and societal impacts. Collaboration between researchers and clinicians is crucial to developing AI solutions that align with real-world medical needs.

Policymakers must establish clear regulations to ensure AI in healthcare is used ethically, transparently, and securely. Strong governance is key to protecting patient data and maintaining public trust [7].

12.2 TELEMEDICINE PLATFORMS: THE ROLE OF ARTIFICIAL INTELLIGENCE

Telemedicine platforms are emerging as innovative digital health tools that leverage telecommunication technology for remote clinical consultations, diagnostics, and treatment. To enable this future of care, many products are being developed that involve leading algorithms, health data analytics, and protected connectivity for gapless healthcare delivery across the globe. Telemedicine technology solutions for healthcare issues, these can broadly be classified under three categories (a) Tele-consultation where a doctor in the periphery discusses an interesting or difficult case with a specialist and receives management advice; (b) telemonitoring and support for ICUs/Emergency units of district hospitals, and information dissemination as well as support in disaster management; and (c)Tele-education for training doctors/paramedics from higher specialty centers [8]. In pandemics where physical distance is necessary, telemedicine allows for care to continue without endangering patients or health providers. Telemedicine can aid in providing slightly unwell people with the necessary supportive treatment while limiting exposure to other critically ill patients [9].

The advancement of AI in telemedicine solutions has upended the traditional system by enhancing diagnostic accuracy, reducing patient wait times, and improving clinical judgment. Sophisticated algorithms can enable AI to analyze medical data for imaging or test findings, for example, and thus help healthcare practitioners predict the onset of early-stage diseases. Artificial Intelligence (AI) is a combination of technologies. Most of these technologies have immediate significance in the healthcare industry, although the specific procedures and jobs they assist vary greatly [10].

12.2.1 Overview of Telemedicine Technologies

Telemedicine is one of the innovative ways of delivering healthcare, enabling treatments, diagnosis, and medical services over distances. In simple words, this platform facilitates consultation, diagnosis, and treatment anytime and anywhere between the patient & health specialist. In the face of fast spreading COVID-19, telemedicine seems to be one way we can communicate with those underserved populations more in real time and even exchange data. Telemedicine can deliver the connected care patients seek over increasingly ubiquitous communications networks and digital platforms, promising better patient outcomes while also automating clinical workflow.

The first attempts to use closed-circuit television to increase rural residents' access to healthcare were made in the 1960s, and telemedicine has advanced significantly since then. However, official telemedicine programs started using telephones to connect patients with specialists in cities throughout the 1970s. The advent of the internet in the 1990s led to the rise of telemedicine networks and email consultations. In the 2000s, patient accessibility to telemedicine increased due to the introduction of smartphones and mobile technology [11]. The COVID-19 pandemic of 2020 led to a drastic increase in the use of telemedicine as healthcare systems made an attempt to reduce face-to-face clinic visits, representing a potentially monumental change in its adoption into routine healthcare. Figure 12.1 illustrates various applications of telemedicine, ranging from benefits to complex procedures.

Telemedicine is very helpful for cognitive clinical issues, especially because video, audio, or text data can heavily influence the decision-making process of treatment. From simple radiology consultations to highly complex virtual reality-based robotic surgery, telemedicine can be used for these procedures [13]. Teleradiology involves the generation of digital images and affixation of patient images along with data compression to facilitate even faster and cheaper communication [14]. Combining telemedicine approaches with conventional treatment significantly enhances blood glucose control in patients with diabetes [15]. These developments do not just increase the charge of care but also self-assure patients and healthcare professionals of more flexible treatment methods. As a whole, telemedical technology is a major paradigm shift in the care of certain diseases and has led to improved patient engagement, resulting in better outcomes.

12.2.1.1 Types of AI Platforms

AI platforms in telemedicine can be categorized into different types based on their primary mode of interaction or service delivery. The major types include **chat-based platforms**, **video-based platforms**, and **app-based platforms**.

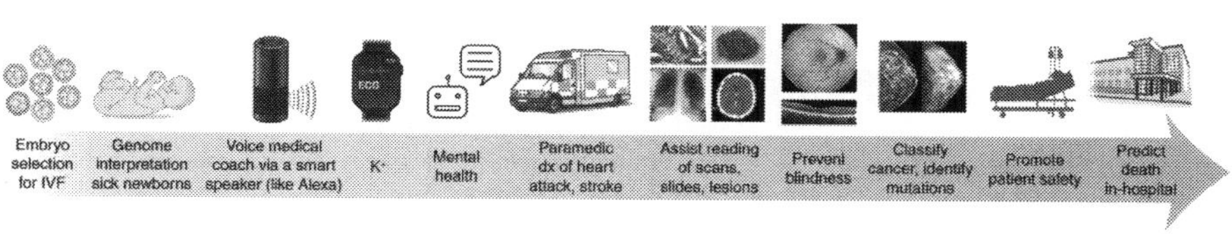

FIGURE 12.1 The applications of Telemedicine [12].

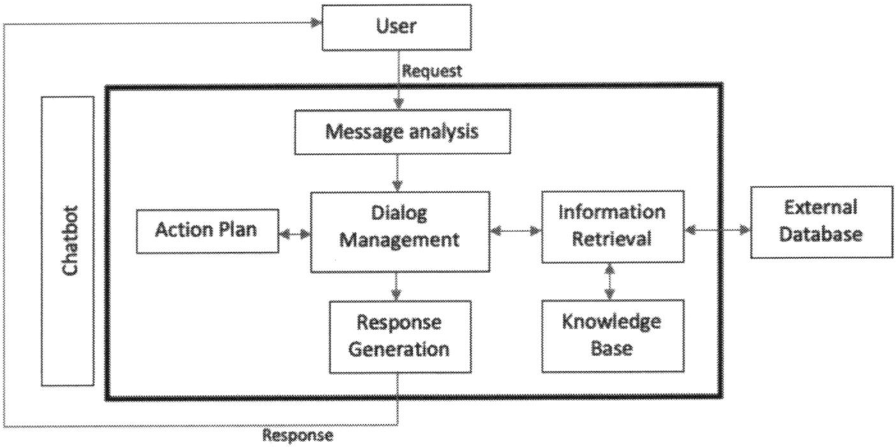

FIGURE 12.2 Diagram illustrating the architecture of a chatbot system [16].

1. Chat-Based AI Platform: These platforms use Natural Language Processing (NLP), Machine Learning, and AI algorithms to simulate human conversation via online interfaces. They interact with patients through text or voice, providing medical information, health advice, symptom analysis, and virtual consultations. Figure 12.2 illustrates the architecture of a chatbot system, showcasing how various components work together to facilitate interaction and stimulate human-like responses. These platforms automate patient interactions, improve care access, and reduce healthcare provider workload by handling routine tasks. Chat-based AI platforms enhance healthcare efficiency by offering 24/7 virtual health assistance across contexts like symptom checking, triage, mental health support, and medication management.

Example 12.1: ADA Health

Ada Health is a digital health firm that specializes in providing an AI-driven health assessment tool and virtual care services. It caters to the needs of the consumers as well as the professionals involved in the diagnosis and intervention processes of different diseases. Being advanced by medical data charted during interviews and focus groups, and an extensive database of research articles, the Ada chatbot will carry out a simulated counselling or medical interview and ask for presenting complaints and associated symptoms. Each pathology, structure, and clinical process generates a diagnosis corresponding to the input symptom set, which is relevant for evaluating individuals and assisting in clinical decisions [17]. Ada is a cost-efficient tool for diagnosing mental disorders and other health issues, bridging the gap between self-assessment and professional diagnosis.

Example 12.2: Your.MD

Your.MD is a healthcare AI application that offers tailored health content for better healthcare management. An AI-powered chatbot also assists the patients in symptom assessment and provides information that is medically correct and scientifically sourced. Its objective is to promote health awareness and the improvement of health-supporting choices. Its OneStop Health solution helps users find relevant specialists promptly and efficiently, enhancing the users' healthcare experience from self-diagnosis to treatment seeking [18].

2. Video-Based AI Platform: These platforms use AI to enhance virtual consultations between patients and healthcare providers. It facilitates video conferences with patients using AI tools that assist in diagnostics, monitoring, and decision-making. Everything from triage, documentation to analysis of data collected in real time has been taken over by AI, thereby allowing medical personnel to deal with the patients only. Video-based AI platforms make telemedicine more intensive, precise, and better integrated into health care services that do not require the physical attendance of patients to clinics.

Example 12.3: Amwell

Amwell is a telemedicine application that allows patients to make consultations through video, secure messaging, and other social health applications. This allows the meeting of patients and various other healthcare specialists, such as physicians, health coaches, and therapists. In addition, Amwell provides timely monitoring of health conditions on a device integrated with Bluetooth, which helps in measuring factors such as weight, blood pressure, and physical activity levels. Furthermore, these data are encrypted, stored, and protected from exodus in accordance with the provisions of health laws. Moreover, these days, the company also promotes health coaching services added to helping patients manage weight loss and control chronic conditions, encouraging healthy practices in a more cost-effective manner from the comfort of the home [19]. In addition, Amwell's AI models are embedded with real-time data analytics that optimize patient care processes, foretell health outcomes, and tailor treatment approaches to patients, thus enhancing rational and practical strategies during telehealth services.

Example 12.4: Doctor on Demand

Doctor on Demand is a telemedicine facility where patients can obtain services via a mobile phone application or website. This service allows patients to have a video review with a qualified doctor who can evaluate an explanation of symptoms, offer a diagnosis, write a prescription, and even, if needed, send the patient to another specialist. This platform is particularly useful during emergency closure, offering remote services for a wide range of conditions [20]. The Doctor on Demand AI system applies NLP and symptom-checking systems, which help effectively and accurately create treatment regimens for patients under consultation.

3. App-Based AI Platform: These platforms offer health services via web-based or mobile applications that enable patient interaction, active supervision, and clinical support. To be more convenient, through mobile or Internet-enabled devices, patients in these apps can control their health,

seek medical services, and interact with doctors. AI enables these apps to monitor health metrics, provide personalized recommendations, analyze symptoms, and maintain continuous communication between patients and providers. This approach is particularly beneficial for chronic disease management, mental health support, and preventive care.

Example 12.5: Kardia Mobile

Kardia Mobile is a personal electrocardiogram (ECG) app that allows users to easily monitor their heart health on their smartphones and tablets (Figure 12.3). This app is a very simple yet powerful mobile application where one can capture high-quality ECG readings at any convenient location and obtain heart rate information with regard to any disturbances, such as in the case of beating patterns or heart conditions, for example, atrial fibrillation (AFib), which is the most common heart arrhythmia. With the two-lead ECG model, the user is instructed to place electrodes on their fingers to capture their heartbeats, which are fed into a smartphone or tablet with data analysis algorithms of performance similar to those of a cardiologist. Kardia Mobile enhances availability; it pursues the view that users should be able to exchange results with their doctors, which makes it cost-effective and time-saving whenever there is a need for continuous evaluation of heart conditions [21].

Example 12.6: Biofourmis

The Biofourmis smartphone application is focused on AI and helps with a personalized approach to remote patient management. The application integrates with wearable biosensors that help to gather, track, and manage a patient's physiological data, including heart rate, respiratory rate, and oxygenation levels, in real time. The app's Biovitals analytics engine uses ML to detect early signs of health deterioration and predict adverse events, thereby enabling proactive intervention.

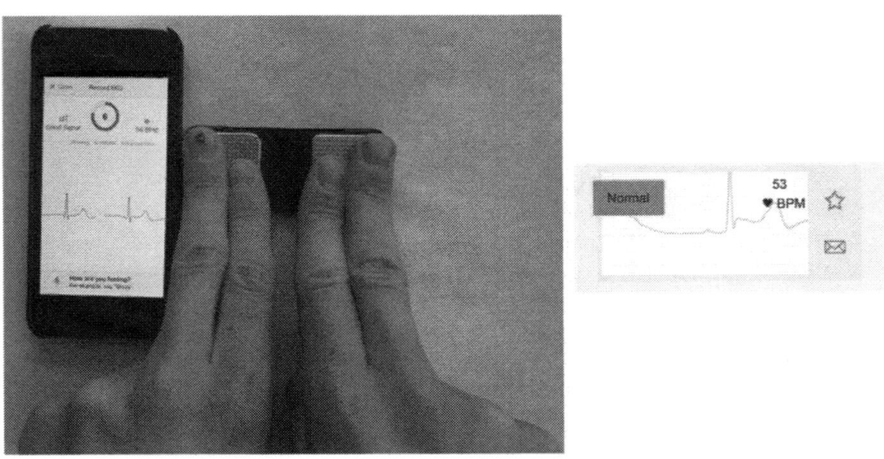

FIGURE 12.3 The Kardia mobile device interpretation [21].

Biofourmis is particularly useful for managing chronic conditions such as heart failure and respiratory illnesses. The AI model uses predictive analytics to forecast potential health risks and suggest early interventions, thereby reducing hospital readmissions and improving patient outcomes.

12.2.1.2 Integration of AI Features

The integration of AI features in telemedicine is bringing a paradigm shift in the healthcare system. Predictive analytics is poised to play a very important role by analyzing the data containing patient information to come up with threats to their well-being. This helps in making a timely diagnosis and or treatment before the complication escalates or leads to other complications. AI can enhance efficiency in patient understanding, especially in medical imaging areas like radiology. For instance, in detecting and diagnosing ailments such as breast cancer, AI technology often demonstrates greater precision than human diagnosis with minimal chances of false alarms and reduced risk of misdiagnosis. AI can also increase efficiency in the area of healthcare insurance and render effectiveness in some functions like submitting, analyzing claims, and detecting false positives [22].

Moreover, AI technology enables personalized treatment recommendations by analyzing individual patient data and provides symptom checker capabilities to help patients decide next-care steps based on a series of questions or by advising clinicians through clinical decision support systems. These multiple AI components foster not only more efficient and effective telemedicine but also higher quality and more patient-centered care delivery, highlighting the value of telemedicine in the age of transformative digital technologies. Table 12.1 illustrates various features of AI and its application in telemedicine.

Successful implementation of AI-based systems calls for a close look at users' attitudes and perceptions about AI. AI systems glean most of their capability from the quality and quantity of data that they have been trained on, and the implication is that poor data leads to flawed predictions and clinical advice that places patients in harm [27]. AI runs on health justice issues raises a lot of questions about data control, credibility, safety, confidentiality, and data control [28]. It is, therefore, paramount to determine the attitudes of patients towards AI in order to understand the building up of trust in these technologies and ensuring their effective integration into care practices.

12.2.2 Enhancing Patient Experience

Bringing improvement in the field of patient experience is one of the most crucial steps towards better health outcomes and patient satisfaction. Some of these measures include effective communication between the service providers and patients, which builds trust among the patients. The clear communication with the patient will enable them to fully comprehend the diagnosis and available treatments.

It is important that telemedicine services improve patient experiences related to access, convenience, and personalized care. Telemedicine interventions were also acceptable for patients across all age groups with psychiatric disorders: children, adolescents with mental health conditions, and severe mental illness cases [29]. The use of telemedicine has the potential to improve health outcomes, reduce the cost of

TABLE 12.1
AI Application in Telemedicine

Ref.	AI Features	Role	Example
[23]	Remote Monitoring	The continuous collection and evaluation of multiple vital signs. This continuous monitoring is crucial for detecting any deviations in a patient's health status in real-time.	Blood pressure, ECG monitoring.
[24]	Virtual triage	Evaluates patient symptoms and directs them to the most appropriate care, ensuring safety and clinical accuracy.	Suggest treatment for a urinary tract infection based on reported symptoms such as frequent urination and discomfort.
[25]	Natural Language Processing	Facilitate interactions between users and medical information.	AI Chatbots for healthcare information.
[26]	Predictive Analytics	Predictive analytics involves using statistical algorithms and ML techniques to analyze historical data and make predictions about future outcomes.	Diagnosis of malignant pleural mesothelioma (MPM)

healthcare, alter the way care is delivered, and ultimately access to care. They also educated and supported the management of their conditions. Telemedicine allowed for follow-up of chronic diseases, such as diabetes and heart failure, permitting an early recognition of deterioration so that interventions occurred accordingly [30]. Whereas there are several positive aspects, a few identified barriers toward the uptake and use of telemedicine by patients affect the general patient experience. This is an essential factor to be understood and worked upon to enhance the patient experience.

12.2.2.1 AI-driven Scheduling and Triage System

AI-powered scheduling and triage systems are increasingly becoming part of telemedicine, with the intention of bringing better quality patient care while limiting the overutilization of resources. The system is based on ML algorithms operating on real-time data to identify the degree of urgency related to a patient's needs. It therefore guarantees much more accurate and timelier prioritization of care, with assurance that the neediest critically needy patients will be seen quickest. The main subarea in AI, automated scheduling, addresses the organization and prioritization of routine tasks to meet certain health-related goals. Scheduling algorithms will enable AI to include patient preference, provider availability, and clinical urgency during scheduling, thus it can also enable patients to schedule appointments more quickly and efficiently. Due to this, queues will be shorter, patient satisfaction will increase, and health workers will be free to spend more time with the patients rather than on administrative burdens. Especially, AI scheduling has proved to be highly efficient in managing a high volume of patients resulting from peak demand periods, such as flu seasons or global health crises like COVID-19.

AI-powered triage systems are also crucial in telemedicine for symptom checks from data of self-reported questionnaires or wearable devices [31]. Triage is a classification system used in assessing the urgency of a patient's condition to enable healthcare providers to prioritize treatment for patients in order of greatest need. In emergency medicine, where choices must be made swiftly to save lives, the system is extremely important. In order to notify medical practitioners of significant changes in a patient's condition, the AI algorithms for triage process patient data continuously and in real-time. This technology reduces the potential for late diagnoses or missing symptoms that are critical, therefore increasing the overall efficiency and effectiveness of the delivered care.

There are evidences supporting the application of AI-based pre-hospital triage systems in EMS. For example, the conditions such as STEMI justify the use of AI in view of remote early interventions, which speed up the delivery of care with minimal complications [32]. This indicates that the results for patients in emergency situations have improved due to AI-driven pre-hospital triaging in telemedicine. Additionally, it may herald a rise in the use of AI-powered triaging in emergency medical services (EMS), which would improve patient care, streamline the delivery of healthcare, and better allocate resources.

12.2.2.2 NLP for Patient Interactions

NLP is a subfield of AI that deals with methods and algorithms of treatment in computer-human language interaction. It varies from the very simple tasks of tokenization, grammar, and syntax parsing to advanced feature extraction techniques such as N-grams and TF-IDF (Term Frequency-Inverse Document Frequency). With the breakdown of language into such elements, NLP can enable machines to process large volumes of text data. This, in turn, enables machines to translate and summarize texts and even analyze sentiments. The applications vary from virtual assistants like Siri and Alexa to the language translation services that interpret social media sentiment. With the ability to parse language structure and meaning, NLP now grants machines the capability to engage with users in a manner proximal to human-similar communication.

NLP holds its most superior importance in healthcare to improve access and quality of medical information. NLP-driven chatbots can, hence, be enabled to understand the queries of patients in natural language and facilitate answers to common health questions without necessarily involving a doctor's consultation. Techniques such as tokenization and feature extraction will, therefore, enable these chatbots to identify the keywords in patient inquiries and retrieve relevant information from the knowledge base. This relieves the workload of health professionals and increases the effectiveness of the provided care. Knowledge-based system integrations of NLP-driven chatbots can ensure that interventions by health professionals are implemented in specific knowledge-requiring situations. Emotion recognition, as one of the NLP features, is helpful in detecting an emotional tone in patients' conversations and letting them have more empathetic responses from the chatbots, which in turn can be extremely useful in mental health applications [33].

The benefits that NLP has made in health care are huge. Performing routine interaction automation and availing accurate medical information, NLP-driven systems lower healthcare costs and increase access to care, particularly for people residing in remote or underserved areas. Emotional intelligence abounds in NLP and further enhances the patient experience, more so when it comes to mental health care, where there is much need for empathy. Moreover, the scalability of the NLP solutions can be used to enrich these systems so they could handle large volumes of patients inquiring at the same time and thus provide timely and efficient support 24/7.

12.2.3 Data Security and Privacy

Telemedicine has data security and privacy as the most integral component, which protects the sensitive information of patients shared and stored online. Telemedicine would be considered a channel for sharing significant volumes of personal health information, including medical history, diagnostic images, and real-time health metrics over online platforms. Security features such as encryption, standards for secure access, and rigid governance of data ensure the confidentiality of data. Many important security factors have to be established in order to provide strong protection. Table 12.2 below outlines these key aspects, including their corresponding needs and methods for execution.

Regulatory frameworks such as HIPAA (Health Insurance Portability and Accountability Act) and GDPR (General Data Protection Regulation) require measures to ensure the security of patient data from unauthorized access and sensitive information being handled securely [33,34]. These not only safeguard individual

TABLE 12.2
Key Aspects of Data Security in Telemedicine

Security Aspect	Requirement	Strategies/Technologies	Regulatory Frameworks
AI and patient data privacy	Anonymization of patient data used in the AI system Secure processing of data without exposing sensitive information.	Anonymization algorithms. Secure architecture for data storage and processing [36].	HIPAA GDPR
Cloud-based EHR security	Protect sensitive patient information. Ensure access to authorized personnel Compliance with security standard.	Advanced Encryption Standard (AES) Role-Based Access Control (RBAC) Compliance management software [37].	HIPAA GDPR
Pseudonymization	Secure separation of personal identification data and medical records. Effective control of access and authorization for medical data	Encryption techniques to protect medical data and access keys. Generate irreversible pseudonyms and prevent re-identification [38].	HIPAA GDPR

privacy but also create confidence among patients in using the services of telemedicine with no worries about the safety of their personal health information.

12.2.3.1 AI's Role in Safeguarding Patient Data

With the increased adoption of AI in research and patient care, the protection of sensitive patient information becomes increasingly important. Traditional data sharing bears a great risk due to the direct exchange of patient information, causing various issues with privacy breaches. AI could help mitigate some of these problems in privacy by the use of innovative technologies that increase data protection while facilitating collaboration in research. Decentralized data storage and federated learning systems represent promising solutions to enable privacy-preserving research across institutions. These methods make it possible for various organizations to contribute to joint research projects through data analysis without the direct sharing of sensitive patient data, thereby increasing data protection while enabling joint progress in healthcare [35]. These systems maintain confidentiality for patients and allow each institution to access a wider array of data because data is kept within each institution and model updates or insights are only shared across institutions. One way AI developers may respond to continued concerns over data privacy in the future is through the use of generative data.

With this latter approach, generative models would generate realistic but synthetic patient data, unconnected with the real individual [39]. The key feature of the latter technique is that, in the long run, ML developments do not have to rely on real patient data; however, real data may be required initially to train the generative models. This kind of model being determined, large volumes of synthetic data generated by the model retain statistical features and patterns in the original data without divulging information about patient identities. Decentralized data storage integrated with federated learning and generative data gives rise to a robust framework for patient information protection in AI applications. That allows different institutions to share while still maintaining high data privacy, hence facilitating innovation in healthcare research and, finally, improving patient outcomes. In the future of health, state-of-the-art AI strategies will be key to technological development that focuses on patient privacy.

12.2.3.2 Ethical Considerations in Telemedicine

Telemedicine has revolutionized the provision of health care. However, this improvement automatically creates a myriad of ethical issues that ought to be addressed to ensure that care for patients is very efficient and respects the rights of patients. The American Medical Association (AMA) telehealth guidelines suggest that ethics are a collective responsibility requiring cooperation between the medical profession and specialty groups and clinicians to build trust and give priority to the well-being of the patient [40]. Important ethical factors include securing informed consent, which becomes more complicated in telemedicine as patients must grasp the technology, associated risks, and data protection measures. Additionally, maintaining confidentiality and cybersecurity is crucial to avert data breaches. Healthcare providers are required to comply with regulations such as HIPAA and GDPR and must be transparent with patients regarding the usage, storage, and protection of their

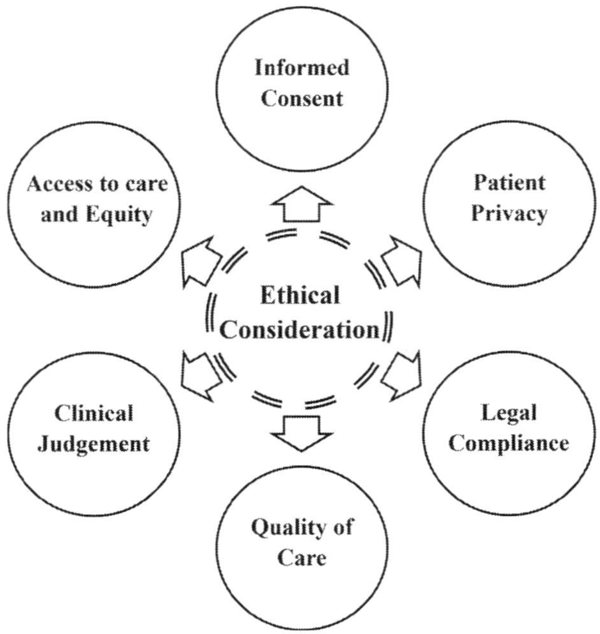

FIGURE 12.4 Various aspects of ethical considerations in Telemedicine.

data. Furthermore, the incorporation of AI in telemedicine raises issues related to accountability, bias, and the preservation of human interaction in care, highlighting the need for guidelines that promote fairness and transparency. Maintaining a balance between innovation and ethical responsibility is vital for the future sustainability of telemedicine, as illustrated in Figure 12.4, which outlines various dimensions of ethical considerations in this field.

12.3 REMOTE DIAGNOSTICS AND AI TOOLS – AI FACILITATED QUANTITATIVE CORONARY COMPUTED TOMOGRAPHIC ANGIOGRAPHY

The scientific discovery occurring in association with the advances made in medical procedures is drastically changing the landscape of the healthcare scenario. While such developments lead to betterment in the outcome for the patient, they increase the workload of the clinician, which may eventually get reflected on the quality of life for clinicians as well. However, AI-powered applications can address these aspects by integrating multi-modal data and inferring valuable aspects, particularly in areas such as remote diagnostics, where medical science is still evolving.

More doctors are now acknowledging the role of AI tools in relieving them of their burdens and ensuring better care. Many have been busy exploring AI's potential in tasks such as interpreting medical images, remotely monitoring patients, and analyzing huge, complex data sets. For example, AI algorithms can help doctors detect anomalies in imaging scans, predict disease progression, and provide advanced warnings for critical conditions. This interaction between an AI tool and healthcare professionals is meant to streamline decision-making processes and improve accuracy in diagnosing patients. Through these challenges, doctors are able to address patient care issues, cut down their workload, and improve the overall efficiency of health care systems in operation once they work in conjunction with the AI [41].

12.3.1 AI in Diagnostic Imaging

AI approaches, in order to predict the aggressiveness of prostate cancer based on multi-parametric MRI, are done especially on T2-weighted (T2w) images and Apparent Diffusion Coefficient (ADC) maps. Exploits both ML and Deep Learning (DL) methods to increase the validity of detection and reduce the need for expensive interventions such as biopsies. Non-linear Support Vector Machine (SVM) for primary classification based on radiomic features from T2w and ADC maps. DL models, both with and without attention mechanisms, were trained to predict PCa aggressiveness from MRI data. 3D Vision Transformer is one of the most advanced DL models for volumetric medical image analysis and was also used for comparison purposes with standard CNNs. A study for discrimination of parotid gland tumors was utilized for developing features from T2-weighted images of parotid gland lesions to predict benign or malignant lesions. The main AI tool applied in this study is the Support Vector Machine (SVM) classifier. AI tools used in the particular diagnosis are mentioned in Table 12.3 below. In the context of AI perspectives, the estimation of hepatic steatosis from ultrasound imaging is obviously very fundamental to a non-invasive tool whose implementation can provide an accurate method of quantifying the liver fat content in a diagnostic and management context of Metabolic Dysfunction-Associated Fatty Liver Disease (MAFLD). In imaging bio-banking and providing practices on FAIR - Findable, Accessible, Interoperable, Reusable - AI research, the integration of such tools is the key to advancing precision medicine, as also witnessed in the case of oncology [41].

The research studies prove the accuracy of AI classification ability in skin cancer and prediction of coronary artery disease in CT angiography is superior to traditional approaches. This also means more accurate diagnoses, thus a better outcome for the patient, but in an integrated approach, not only with the saved time but also with the possible reduction in follow-up tests, which are futile.

TABLE 12.3
AI Tools Used in the Particular Diagnosis

AIML Tool	Diagnosis
Support Vector Machines (SVM), Deep Learning (DL) models, and Vision Transformers (ViT)	Prostate Cancer (PCa) diagnosis and aggressiveness prediction.
SVM (Support Vector Machine) classifier	Parotid gland tumor
Convolutional Neural Network (CNN)	Hepatic Steatosis Estimation from Ultrasound Imaging
imaging bio-banking and ensuring the FAIR (Findable, Accessible, Interoperable, Reusable)	Precision medicine in oncology.

AI drastically reduces the interpretation time for an image, which is quite critical in emergency cases. Consequently, health professionals can focus on the most urgent cases and make decisions much faster than before. Applications of AI tools in medical imaging have upskilled radiologists significantly because AI tools can screen and examine preliminary images. American College of Radiology's 2019 survey has discovered that AI for radiologists means that 20%–30% of the workload of radiologists can be managed, they can handle more cases and help produce higher diagnostic throughput. These AI systems are created with the ability to easily interface with existing radiology workflows, including PACS and RIS with online analysis and decision support. For instance, a PACS-based Google Health AI application gives instant response on mammograms, which reduces the need for additional imaging and follow-up processes [42].

An unsupervised set of algorithms that includes k-means clustering, hierarchical clustering, PCA, and t-SNE proves useful in extracting useful information and discovering novel or recurrent hidden patterns within complex data.AI in medical image analysis will be broken down into uses and algorithms that can be seen in Figure 12.5. Such algorithms map similar points to each other based on some inherent features, helpful for instances such as anomaly detection and predictive modeling. For example, based on the COVID-19 suspect dataset, clustering methods can group patients having attributes that are similar in nature, for example loss of smell, so that positive or negative cases could be predicted. In DL, more complex algorithms like ANNs, CNNs, and RNNs are widely used for modeling a wide range of complex, non-linear interaction relationships. They perform high-level tasks such as image recognition, NLP, time-series forecasting, and a lot more [43].

Krizhevsky et al. [44] have proposed AlexNet, a deep convolutional neural network that thoroughly revolutionized computer vision by establishing new benchmarks in image classification. Here, CapsNet captures hierarchical relationships and spatial dependencies within images, thereby providing a deeper understanding of complex structures. Similarly, Resting-State fMRI is a very potent neuroimaging tool used to analyze brain activity and connectivity. Advancements in AI in Neuroimaging can be

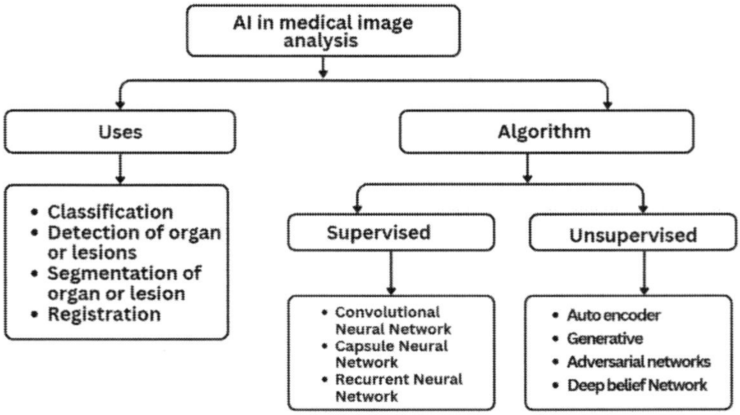

FIGURE 12.5 Breakdown of key areas of healthcare.

seen in Figure 12.6. It thus offers valuable insights into neurodegenerative diseases like Alzheimer's and Parkinson's. Integration of AI with neuroimaging is bound to transform early diagnosis, disease tracking, and treatment, hence brain health and clinical approaches to cognitive disorders [45].

The integration proposed uses AI models with B-mode ultrasound for diagnosing liver tumors through the employment of CNNs trained on large datasets. Model-1 was trained with 24,675 images. Model-2 was trained using 57,145 images, whereas Model-3 involved training with 70,950 images that were more focused on cysts, hemangiomas, HCC, and metastatic tumors. Furthermore, Model-ICC had training based on 4,633 images, which classified HCC, intrahepatic cholangiocarcinoma (ICC), metastatic tumors, and hemangiomas. Five still images taken at different sizes and at the maximum diameter from video images of each tumor are used for AI diagnosis. AI algorithms and models that are used for liver tumor diagnosis can be seen in Figure 12.7 [46].

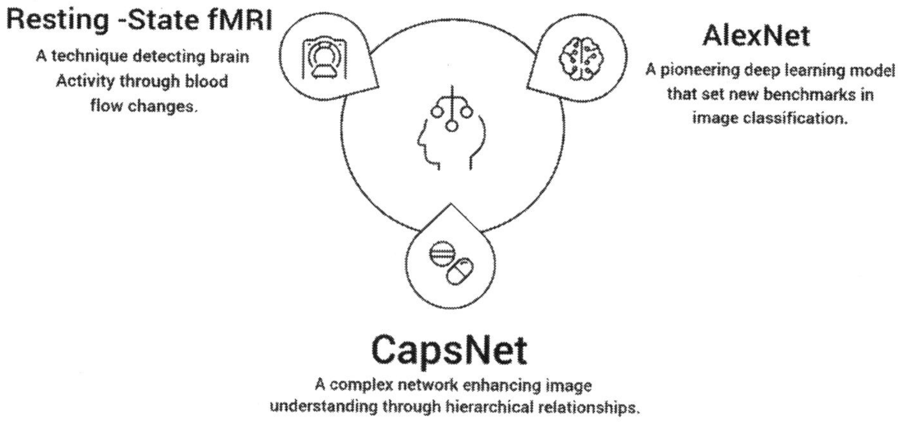

FIGURE 12.6 Advancement in AI in neuroimaging.

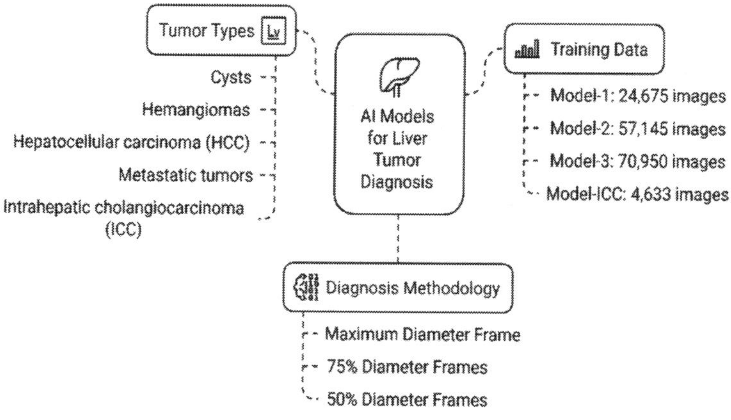

FIGURE 12.7 AI algorithms and models that are used for liver tumor diagnosis.

12.3.1.1 Applications in Radiology and Telepathology

AI has transformed radiology by enhancing aspects of efficiency, accuracy, and care towards patients. Application areas include vetting referrals, prioritizing emergencies, verification of clinical indications, patient appropriateness, optimization of contrast-enhanced studies, synthetic contrast enhancement of contrast volumes, and improved image quality without the use of additional agents in imaging. Auto-segmentation for optimal radiotherapy treatment planning with AI is also possible.

Striking the cutting-edge advances in AI algorithms. Those comprising include Aidoc, Zebra Medical Vision, and Google Health, which can assist a radiologist in detecting anomalies in images coming from various body parts and hasten diagnoses with fewer chances for oversight. Also, AI offers a reduction in dosages of radiation with the selection of the right protocols without compromise on the quality of the image taken as well as accelerates MRI scanning at high resolution. Finally, AI with ultrasound offers automatic capture and interpretation of images, which implies reduced operator variability. These have ensured that radiologists and radiographers focus on complex decision-making rather than being bothered with extensive operations, hence enhancing overall patient outcome and revolutionizing medical imaging [47].

AI is making significant strides in the field of Anatomic Pathology (AP), particularly in the analysis of Whole-Slide Images (WSIs), which are high-resolution, digitized representations of tissue samples. The difference between traditional and digital workflow can be seen in Figure 12.8. AI models in this domain are predominantly powered by ML techniques, with a strong emphasis on DL. These models can efficiently analyze large datasets of digitized pathology images, aiding pathologists in making faster and more accurate diagnoses.

AI is dramatically revolutionizing Anatomic Pathology, particularly in the interpretation of Whole-Slide Images, which involves a series of high-resolution digitizations of tissue samples. In this sense, ML and DL further support AI models to help pathologists speedily produce accurate diagnoses on detected and quantified pathological features, such as cancerous cells and morphological patterns. This allows for applications like AI-driven algorithms for image analysis, which improve the accuracy of diagnosis, color normalization application to standardize tissue staining slides so that there are consistent results across labs, and techniques known as data

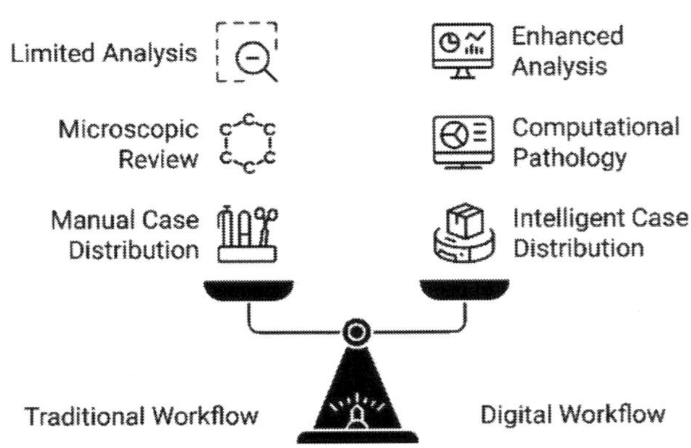

FIGURE 12.8 Difference between traditional and digital workflow.

augmentation for model robustness. Additionally, AI facilitates 3D analysis, thereby allowing more detailed volumetric insights into tumor margins and cellular architecture beyond the confines of 2D examination. AI significantly reduces inter-observer variability between pathologists and guarantees more consistent diagnoses. It detects very rare events, including micro-metastases, which may be easily missed through manual detection. Additionally, AI models can be used to predict patient outcomes in order to better develop personalized treatment plans. Leading companies that work on developing AI-powered platforms focusing on detection, quantification, characterization, and prediction in pathology are PathAI, Paige AI, and DeepPath. All these innovations facilitate workflow while increasing the accuracy of diagnosis and enable pathologists to concentrate on more complicated situations, contributing to better efficiency and quality patient care [48].

The AI tools and algorithms, such as detection algorithms, quantification algorithms, characterization algorithms, and prediction algorithms for clinical imaging and digital pathology for PET-CT and PET-MRI, will make use of radiotracers to identify the metabolic activity of the tumor. For digital pathology, convolutional neural networks (CNNs) are used for WSI, automated image analysis for immunohistochemistry is used to analyze the color intensity relative to control cells.

Radiomics and predictive algorithms are highly applied in the radiology department for analyzing data from radiolabeled imaging and making histopathological correlations to predict tumors [49].

12.3.1.2 Case Studies of Successful Implementations

Caste Study 12.1: IBM-Watson for Oncology

IBM Watson for Oncology is the best example of AI applications in healthcare, intended to guide oncologists towards making the appropriate evidence-based decisions about different treatments. It combines millions of medical literature and clinical trial data and patient records from NLP and ML to provide a personalized treatment plan for cancer patients. It throws light upon how it can be helpful to oncologists in understanding potential treatments, guiding treatments based on the latest research and data about the patient. This is built into oncology practice; the Watson for Oncology reads through the provided data of a patient and matches it with the massive database of cancer-related studies and clinical guidelines. Since its development and implementation in many hospitals around the world, the system has been utilized by several oncologists for their patients who underwent evidence-based recommendations to aid in medical decision-making as well as personalize the treatment of the cancer [50].

Case Study 12.2: Path AI

Path AI focuses on enhancing the precision of diagnosis in pathology by using AI-based image analysis. The software uses ML algorithms to scan digital pathology slides and assists pathologists in diagnosing and classifying various diseases, including cancers. Path AI aims to reduce diagnosis errors and improve the speed of diagnosis. Algorithms from Path AI are deployed in digital pathology workflows where they scan high-contrast images of tissues, which provide pathologists with diagnostic support. The innovation has been proven to be more accurate through cancerous tissue detection along with other abnormalities, thus significantly improving the diagnostic accuracy and reducing the variability of pathology findings [50].

Case Study 12.3: AliveCor's Kardia Mobile

It is a mobile ECG that uses AI for its functionality. This was created for monitoring and detecting atrial fibrillation (AFib) (Figure 12.9). Patients and healthcare providers used this device to capture ECGs and analyze them through AI algorithms for the detection of abnormal heart rhythms and alert for potential AFib episodes. Kardia Mobile is used in the home or clinic for continuous monitoring of heart health with real-time data for providers [50].

Smart Health Systems, specifically during the times of the COVID pandemic, use wearables to source real-time data from patients and analyze through AI for health variance. Predictive analytics and NLP have led to predicting trends, resource optimizations, and customized plans for treatment. NLP was used in the form of chatbots to help patients communicate with each other, schedule appointments, and even gain information. AI-based monitoring devices include glucose level sensors, ECG monitors, blood pressure monitors, body temperature monitors, oxygen saturation monitors, and rehabilitation systems. Algorithms like SVM, K-Means Clustering, PCA, SVR, Linear Regression, and Neural Networks are used for the real-time monitoring and analysis of data, enhancing improved care and management of patients' health. Algorithms and their functions in health monitoring can be seen in Table 12.4 [51].

Edge AI revolutionizes real-time health services with low-latency, scalability, and reliability, which is all driving innovation toward specifically in mobile health,

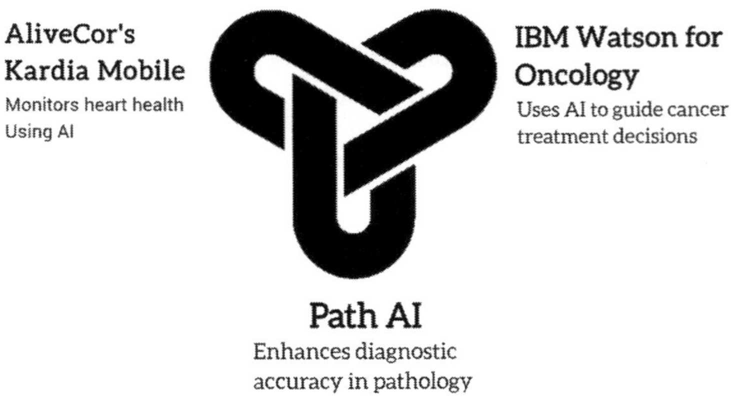

FIGURE 12.9 AI innovation in healthcare case study.

TABLE 12.4
Algorithms and Its Functions in Health Monitoring

Algorithms	Functions
Dbscan	Management of the huge number of data collection from the human activity
Support Vector Machines	Collection of data will be grouped according to its category
K-means	Uses clustering algorithm to access the large number of data
Clinical Correlation Analysis	Commonly used data for the characterization of data, gives a relationship status of two data
Neural Networks	It resolves the approximation issues
Anomaly Detection Algorithms	It compares the normal and abnormal data set by binary classifiers

wearable devices, and remote diagnostics, closer to the source to process data and lower latencies typical of cloud computing, but ensuring an immediate emergency response in case of emergencies, with greater efficiency in telemedicine and remote patient care.

With Fog-based Architecture, distributed computing resources analyze health data close to the patient for real-time insights in terms of detecting pain with physiological and behavior-related data. The architecture supports AI algorithms, hence maximizing the process of a ML engine, such as Batch Normalization in CNNs, which allows proper recognition and monitoring of human activity related to changes in patient health.

For instance, AI-based detection of skin disease could be proposed. A DL architecture, Double U-Net, breaks up the images of the skin lesions and provides accurate diagnoses. A combination of CNNs with multi-image data, demographic details, and medical history enhances the detection and classification of the condition of the skin. The CAD systems assist early detection of skin cancer by giving radiologists and physicians another opinion to improve the diagnosis of such malignant cases that could not be easily diagnosed otherwise. This would result in uniform diagnoses throughout the network.

AI techniques like Fuzzy Classification handle fuzzy data; for example, in complex cases of skin lesions. Another is Sonification, which transforms visual data into sounds so that slight patterns in skin lesions can be identified. Clinicians are now helped to identify trends a lot earlier in diagnosis and treatment. Such AI advances increase diagnostic accuracy, reduce subjective bias, and create better patient results, especially for life-threatening conditions like melanoma [52].

AI algorithms such as LSTM (Long Short-Term Memory) networks and Reinforcement Learning (RL) are revolutions of care in the management of patients, with the basis of real-time analytics and predictive modeling. One of LSTMs' greatest strengths is in monitoring physiological metrics of heart rate, blood pressure, and glucose levels for real-time interventions and personalized healthcare strategies. On the other hand, RL enables individualized treatment plans by processing giant datasets to adapt the medicines in optimizing regimens, dosages, and strategies in treatments, which improve with responses in patients continuously.

In glucose monitoring, the mixing of LSTM with CNNs captures both spatial and temporal data to make glucose tracking all the more precise and dynamic, especially in the lives of the diabetic community. The AI integration here predicts future trends in blood sugar management. Patients' glucose levels decreased 12.5% and the values of their HRV improved by 33%, which indicates better cardiovascular health. Therefore, with AI-assisted monitoring, HRV or the autonomic nervous system and heart health is improved, and thus, more accurate predictions and personalized treatments can be claimed from it. Such AI technologies now reform chronic disease management and bring better patient outcomes through reduced hospitalization rates and consequently health care costs while improving the quality of lives of patients [53].

Piezoelectric Yarn Sensors: Kim et al. [54] presented AI-driven piezoelectric yarn sensing that could identify many human activities such as jumping, running, and walking. They utilized a multi-kernel CNN network with a motion classification accuracy of 99.6% [55].

12.3.2 Wearable Devices and Remote Monitoring

12.3.2.1 AI Integration in Wearable Health Tech

There are three categories of wearable health sensors: physical, chemical, and biosensors. These record vital signs, heart rate, and blood pressure, and monitor biological activities, like glucose levels or Parkinson's disease activity.ML Algorithms: In this device, there are several ML algorithms such as Supervised Learning and Unsupervised Learning, to monitor chronic diseases. Artificial Perception and Transmission (APT) monitors nerve activity. Human Activity Recognition (AROMA) is used to identify human activities based on Deep Multi-Task Learning. The health condition can be categorized by the use of bidirectional LSTM. The knee joint movement is done through ANN algorithms of DL, and therefore, noise reduction is aided through Hierarchical LSTM. For cancer detection, Dual-gate FET and ANN models analyze urine and breath samples, respectively, to detect prostate cancer and respiratory diseases. RNN is also used for COVID detection. Revolutionizing Sensor Technology with the integration of AI can be seen in Table 12.5.

Advanced AI integration with wearable sensors includes models like CNN for piezoelectric yarn sensors, XGBoost, KNN, and SVM for throat motion detection,

TABLE 12.5
Revolutionizing Sensor Technology with Integration of AI

AI	Sensors
CNN, DL	Sweat Biosensors
CNN	GlucoSense
ML, DL	Hydration Level Prediction
SLEEPNET Algorithm	Healthy sleep habit device
Algorithms	Chatbots
ML, DL	spiked ultra-flexible neural (SUN) interface

and ANFIS for gait and fall detection in Parkinson's. These innovations enhance personalized health monitoring, diagnosis, and treatment [55].

12.3.2.2 Real-time Data Analysis for Proactive Care

The wearable device, which includes sensors that gather real-time data about physiological parameters such as heart rate, blood pressure, and oxygen saturation, sends such data to AI for processing and effectively converts it into actionable insights, Pattern and Trend Detection. A remote health monitoring system aligned with AI uses complex algorithms so as to thus analyze real-time data proactively in the management of health and timing appropriately for intervention. Enhancing Healthcare with AI and Wearables can be seen in Figure 12.10. Several ML techniques are used to analyze the large volumes of data generated by wearable devices. There are algorithms such as decision trees, support vector machines, and neural networks that help identify such patterns and anomalies within patient data, like heart rate and blood pressure variations. Anomaly Detection Algorithm Specific algorithms are designed to identify the outliers in data streams. Techniques such as statistical process control or clustering algorithms (for example, k-means clustering) help in detecting unusual vital signs and will indicate their classification with respect to health. Predictive Analytics: In predictive models of time-series analysis or regression models, it predicts likely health deteriorations based on historical data. The predictive models analyze the patient data trend to identify early warning signs so as to intervene proactively. DL techniques such as RNN and LSTMs are used to process sequential data produced by the wearable devices. They are effective in time-series data, hence very applicable for monitoring signs within some periods of time. The NLP algorithm can use unstructured patient data from interaction modes, such as text messages or voice commands, to remind and educate patients about their health condition based on the preferences of the individual [56].

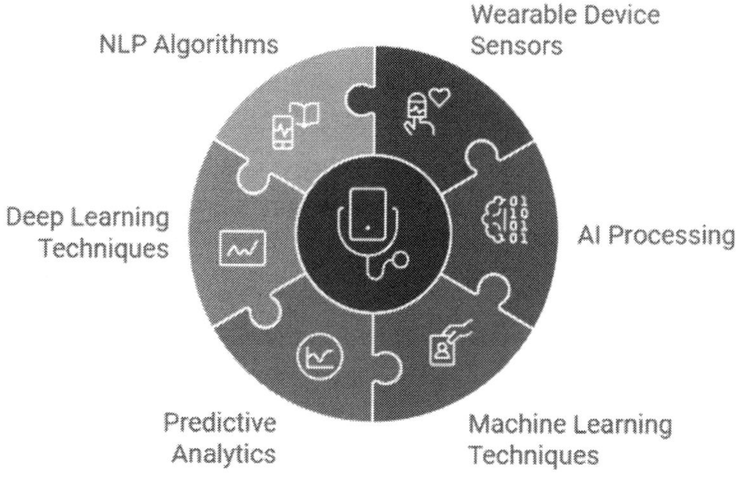

FIGURE 12.10 Enhancing healthcare with AI and wearables.

12.3.3 Decision Support Systems

12.3.3.1 AI Algorithms for Clinical Decision-making

ROBODOC is an offline decision support tool designed to assist maintenance staff in diagnosing and addressing robotic system failures. The system utilizes a group technology approach to classify symptoms and a decision tree method for system development. ROBODOC is capable of generating both detailed and high-level reports, outlining problems and their corresponding solutions. Its modular design makes it easy to update or add to the knowledge base, and it allows for the seamless transfer of diagnostic knowledge between different automated systems, eliminating the need to redevelop the system from scratch. In Table 12.6 "Algorithms Used in Decision Techniques" summarizes different algorithms used in various approaches to decision making, details their specific characteristics and applications, and can thus be used as a reference on how the different approaches contribute to classification and prediction tasks within AI. The results of this work will help to prepare the design for a service expert system, which can offer recommendations for design based on past experiences and therefore produce more durable and easier to maintain equipment designs [57].

Other classification algorithms include decision trees such as ADTree, SimpleCart, and J48. These algorithms are useful in classification, hence leaving out step-wise pathways of how to decide. The Bayesian classifiers, such as Naive Bayes, Naïve Bayes Simple, and Bayes Net, depend heavily on the computation of probability to make a prediction. In fact, AODE and AODEsr improve the efficiency of the classifier.

The ANNs, particularly the MLP, and SVMs handle complex decision-making by finding the best possible boundaries that can be identified in data, with the SVM's C parameter also reducing classification errors. KNN methods, such as IBk and KStar,

TABLE 12.6
Algorithms Used in the Decision Techniques

Decision Techniques	Algorithms	Functions	Ref.
Decision trees	AD Tree, Simple Cart, and J48	It gives a tree-like model of decision.	[57]
Bayesian classifier	Naive Bayes, Naïve Bayes Simple, Bayes Net, AODE and AODEs	It is used for predictions by calculating the probability.	[57]
ANN	Multilayer Perceptron	It utilizes multiple layers of nodes to classify data or make predictions.	[57]
SVM	LibSVM	It works for classification purpose.	[57]
K-nearest neighbors	IBk, KStar, Lazy Bayesian Rules	It finds the nearest data points to make predictions.	[57]
Hidden Markov Model (HMM)	Baum-Welch Algorithm, Viterbi Algorithm	It gives the decision techniques for probabilistic modeling.	[58]
Random Forest (RF)	Bootstraping aggregation	It improved accuracy and stability in predictions	[58]

and Lazy Bayesian Rules are among the most popular algorithms; stability and effectiveness of these algorithms are normally measured by applying the area under the Receiver Operating Characteristic Curve (AUC), hence, in higher AUC, performance in terms of being stable and effective is enhanced [59].

Algorithms like Markov Decision Process (MDP) and Q-learning are used for making decisions, especially under deep reinforcement learning. Medication dosing optimization and weaning patients on mechanical ventilation are examples of such an approach [60].

NLP System it is a type of DL system the LSTM network in China used to analyze 1.3 million pediatric electronic health records could diagnose a wide range of childhood diseases with results comparable to those of experienced physicians.AI for Neurology were Siddhartha Mukherjee comes talking about AI and how it is able to pick up the first movements of strokes in CT scan images, and it indicates what has been happening on the early intervention and improved outcomes from the patients. Convolutional Neural Networks (CNNs) in dermatology have shown remarkable accuracy, matching or surpassing dermatologists in detecting skin cancers. A Stanford-developed CNN performed on par with 21 experts, while another outperformed 58 in identifying malignant melanomas.

Watson is the IBM AI system that has been designed specifically for playing Jeopardy! It implements the DeepQA approach. DeepQA can essentially be described as an algorithm for decision-making where the algorithm analyzes natural language questions to generate candidate answers, which it then scores based on confidence levels before ranking the answers. It was specifically adapted for medical decision-making in oncology.

Watson for Oncology is a clinical decision support system that sifts through volumes of medical literature and patient data to provide cancer treatment recommendations. It's essentially an answer engine aiding doctors in selecting the most appropriate and relevant cancer treatments for patients, given the light of analysis from Watson's cutting-edge research, medical records, and expert knowledge [61].

12.3.3.2 Enhancing Diagnostic Accuracy through AI

AI provides an improvement in accuracy in diagnostic imaging, reduces human errors, and facilitates the utilization of predictive analytics for personalized medicine. For example, in the analysis of Cervical Spondylotic Myelopathy, AI minimizes possible human errors involved in the interpretation of cervical spine radiographs. In the case of Breast Lesions on Dynamic Contrast-Enhanced MRI, AI can differentiate a benign lesion from a malignant lesion and hence enhance the accuracy of diagnosis. AI-QCCTA helps detect and identify atherosclerosis with better vividness, whereas CNNs help detect lung nodules by analyzing complicated graphical and pictorial data.AI enhancement in diagnostic imaging can be seen in Figure 12.11. AI also enhances CT imaging for Lumbar Disc Herniation, reducing errors and mistreatments. In acute respiratory symptoms, AI-based computer-assisted detection integrates process components while it accelerates diagnosis in emergency situations [62].

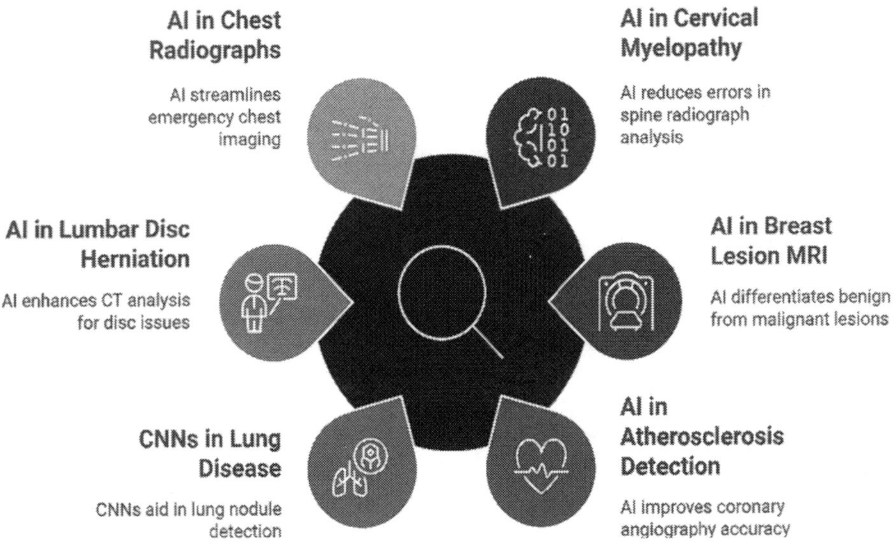

FIGURE 12.11 AI enhancement in diagnostic imaging.

CoDoC is the algorithm that balances AI prediction with the judgment of a clinician on improving medical decision-making, especially in the screening of breast cancer and TB. The false positives in breast cancer screening were reduced by 25%, and its clinician workload was reduced by 66%. In the case of TB, it reduces false positives by 5%–15%. It is adaptable across different imaging modalities, clinical settings, and AI tools, making it versatile for different healthcare environments. The open-source nature of CoDoC encourages further research, validation, and deployment in diverse medical settings [63].

IBM Watson Health and Google DeepMind systems are AI-enabled decision support systems. These help clinicians make decisions while at the bedside in real time. Patient data is a very much an important concept for these systems, and it has been used to suggest personalized care strategies. Here, a patient-centered digital ecosystem for glaucoma care integrates the key components of education, remote monitoring, telemedicine, and analysis of data to take diagnosis, treatment, and quality of life to new heights. A summary of the essential components for a patient-focused digital ecosystem for glaucoma diagnosis, treatment, and quality of life improvement can be seen in Figure 12.12.

RPA will enhance the process efficiency by automatically processing data extracted from health care systems, such as EHRs, for data input and report generation. RPA increases the efficiency of the workflow and frees human resources for more complicated jobs. All these help in optimizing clinical decisions and care involving patients once data is cleaned and standardized, through the use of AI and ML algorithms like CNNs for image classification or Logistic Regression or Decision Trees for predictive models to analyze the data and generate diagnostic insights and predictive patient outcomes [64].

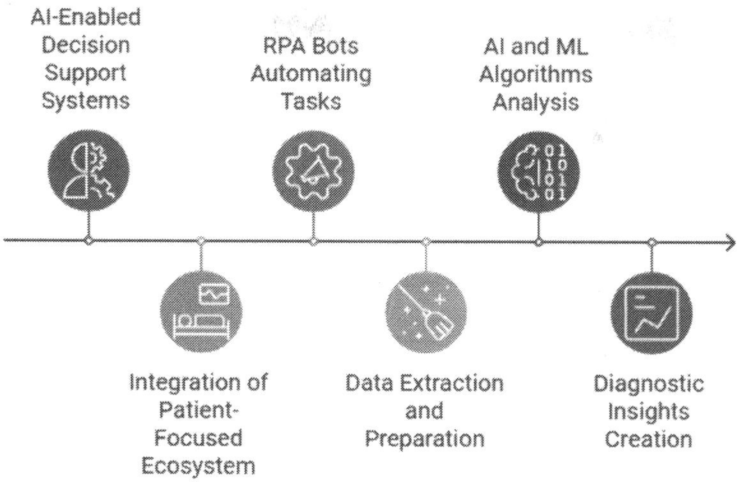

FIGURE 12.12 A summary of the essential components for a patient-focused digital ecosystem for glaucoma diagnosis, treatment, and quality of life improvement.

12.4 OVERCOMING BARRIERS: CONNECTIVITY AND AI ACCESS

12.4.1 Challenges in Connectivity

The digital divide constitutes a substantial obstacle to achieving equity in the accessibility of nascent technologies, notably AI. This divide is defined by inequalities in internet connectivity, proficiency in digital skills, and availability of digital resources, which can intensify socio-economic disparities. Effectively addressing these challenges is imperative for promoting inclusivity and ensuring that the advantages of AI and other technological innovations are distributed fairly.

12.4.1.1 Digital Divide and Socio-Economic Equity

Access to Technology: Insufficient internet connectivity and a lack of digital resources significantly impede socio-economic progress, particularly in jurisdictions such as Uganda, where the application of AI in agricultural practices remains suboptimal due to inadequate digital literacy and limited smartphone penetration [65]. Health Implications: The COVID-19 pandemic underscored the critical role of internet access as a determinant of health, reinforcing the notion that connectivity is indispensable for obtaining healthcare services and educational opportunities ("Connectivity and bandwidth as new social determinants of health" [66]. Social Inequality: Disproportionate access to information technologies intensifies disparities predicated on socio-economic status, race, and geographic location, thereby adversely affecting educational and employment prospects [67].

12.4.1.2 The Role of Digital Literacy

Skills Over Access: The mere provision of internet connectivity does not effectively mitigate the digital divide; it is essential to augment digital competencies and literacy to enable proficient engagement with technology. Civic Participation: The attainment of digital equity is vital for promoting political involvement and guaranteeing access to essential services, thereby necessitating a holistic comprehension of digital inclusion that transcends mere infrastructural considerations [68]. While the rectification of the digital divide is of paramount importance, it is equally critical to acknowledge that the mere enhancement of access to technology may be insufficient. Initiatives must also emphasize the advancement of digital literacy and the resolution of socio-cultural impediments to guarantee equitable participation in the digital economy.

12.4.1.3 Identifying Barriers in Rural and Urban Settings

In the realm of commerce, any investment must yield a return. Conversely, in rural and remote regions, the fiscal returns are significantly diminished compared to those in urban locales; consequently, the expenses associated with infrastructure can prove to be exorbitant. Furthermore, the logistical challenges are typically intricate, particularly in areas that are difficult to access. Indeed, the revenue potential in urban environments can exceed that of rural counterparts by a factor of ten, while the costs associated with network infrastructure in urban settings are generally approximately half of those incurred in rural regions [68]. The costs associated with cabling are high, and the need for multiple receivers and transmitters for long-distance data transmission via wireless technology adds further financial strain [68]. Despite the significant investments made by mobile operators in optimizing the deployment of their networks, the challenge of connecting underprivileged areas persists as a formidable issue [69].

A comprehensive examination of rural connectivity has been disseminated [70]. The fronthaul and backhaul methodologies for Internet of Things (IoT) applications in rural contexts have been elaborated upon in [69]. The integration of AI for the enhancement of communication systems has been scrutinized in a variety of publications, including analyses pertaining to AI utilization in satellite communication systems [71], as well as in the communications of unmanned aerial vehicles (UAVs) [72]. As the discourse surrounding rural connectivity continues to progress, numerous solutions, concepts, and scholarly articles have emerged recently addressing this topic. In this investigation, we highlight the most recent contributions to the field of rural connectivity, evaluate the solutions pertinent to terrestrial networks, and explore the prospective applicability of non-terrestrial networks. Technologies pertinent to rural connectivity have been extensively examined in other works [70,71]; thus, they are only succinctly reviewed here, with an emphasis on the latest advancements. While the utilization of AI for the optimization of communication frameworks has been evidenced in prior scholarly investigations [71,72], this study emphasizes the crucial function of AI in the advancement of networks in rural domains. This analysis will highlight the importance of AI in future communication infrastructures, particularly in challenging contexts such as rural locales. In conclusion, we will evaluate the prospective advantageous impacts of enhancing connectivity for rural populations. Figure 12.13 is a typical example of the Central Region (India) internet connectivity shown by TRAI (Telecom Regulatory Authority of India).

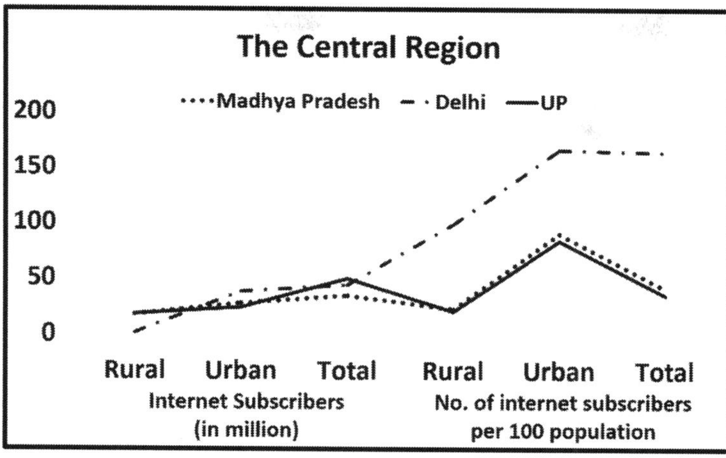

FIGURE 12.13 A typical example of the Central Region (India) internet connectivity shown by TRAI (Telecom Regulatory Authority of India) [73].

12.4.1.4 Solutions for Enhancing Internet Access

12.4.1.4.1 Space, Air and Ground Networks

Utilization of Terrestrial Technologies The conventional approach to delivering cellular coverage predominantly relies on the establishment of macrocell sites. In the context of challenging rural environments, the construction of multiple macrocell sites is often necessitated to achieve adequate coverage, resulting in an unfavorable cost-to-coverage ratio. Concurrently, it is imperative that the capacity adequately accommodates each individual user. To reconcile high capacity with the constraints imposed by cost-to-coverage, Meta/Facebook has introduced an innovative connectivity solution termed SuperCell, which has undergone field validation to ascertain its feasibility. SuperCell consists of a high-gain antenna tower and advanced sectorization for enhanced coverage and capacity. A single SuperCell can cover 15–65 times more area than traditional macrocells, with a 36-sector station on a 250-meter tower vastly outperforming standard rural macrocells [69]. With proper engineering, existing antenna systems can enable SuperCell deployment for efficient rural connectivity [69].

Terrestrial microwave backhaul depends on a clear line-of-sight (CLOS) design, but when unavailable, costly repeaters are often used. An alternative is non-line-of-sight (NLOS) links, which use diffraction to bypass obstacles. However, predicting NLOS performance at higher frequencies (6–8 GHz) and ensuring reliable availability remains a challenge. In response, Meta/Facebook has suggested a hybrid design combining both NLOS and CLOS approaches to optimize performance [65]. When these two link types are employed in conjunction, the quantity of repeaters can be significantly reduced, thereby affording greater flexibility in the selection of tower locations and dimensions, ultimately enhancing coverage. This hybrid design is capable of achieving comparable coverage objectives at a substantially lower cost than that associated with CLOS-only designs [74]. Meta/Facebook partnered with Mayutel and Internet para Todos to successfully test this concept in Peru [69]. Meanwhile, UAV base stations (BSs) are gaining attention for their mobility, adaptability, and adjustable height, making them valuable for communication networks [75]. Consequently, they possess the potential to augment existing cellular systems by delivering broadband coverage in geographically challenging rural regions. UAVs confer greater flexibility upon operators concerning site placement. As base stations have become increasingly miniaturized and UAV technology has advanced in terms of affordability and sophistication, the practical implementation of BSs on UAVs has emerged as a viable option. Given their ability to be rapidly deployed at optimal locations within three-dimensional space, UAV BSs can achieve enhanced spectral efficiency, coverage, load balancing, and user experience when compared to those relying on current terrestrial technologies [76,77]. With their affordability, flexibility, and quick deployment, UAVs are ideal for extending coverage in large, low-traffic areas. They also play a crucial role in precision agriculture, enhancing efficiency and monitoring [78] (Figures 12.14 and 12.15) and logistics [79]. Table 12.7 compares the different kinds of technologies mentioned.

12.4.2 Equity in AI Access

The inclusivity of AI-driven healthcare represents a complex phenomenon that encompasses ethical considerations, equitable access, and the imperative for diverse stakeholder engagement. As AI technologies advance, they possess the capacity to enhance the delivery of healthcare services; however, they concurrently elicit apprehensions pertaining to bias and fairness. The subsequent sections delineate

FIGURE 12.14 Integration of aerial and terrestrial networks to significantly improve service quality in remote and underserved regions [78].

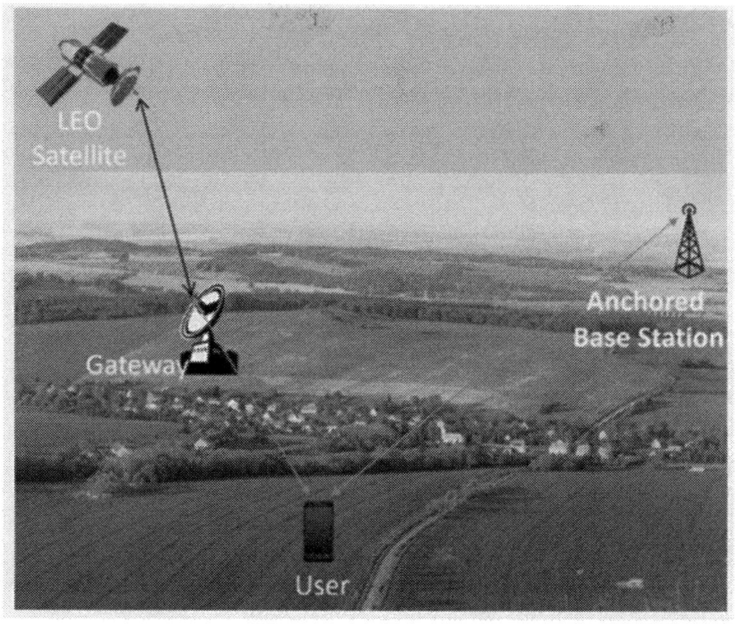

FIGURE 12.15 Satellite networks have the potential to significantly enhance coverage in rural and remote areas [78].

TABLE 12.7
Comparison of Different Technologies

Technology	Advantages	Disadvantages
Ground	Abundant resources and high data throughput	Limited area coverage, restricted mobility, and susceptibility to natural disasters
Aerial	Extensive coverage, cost-effective, and easy to deploy	Lower capacity, unstable connectivity, and significant mobility
Space	Vast coverage with the ability for broadcast/multicast	High latency, limited data capacity, expensive, and significant mobility

pivotal elements of AI inclusivity within the healthcare domain. Healthcare institutions across the globe are increasingly implementing AI technologies to facilitate data analysis, diminish false-positive outcomes, and augment the precision of health risk assessments. Some scholars posit that innovations in ML and expansive language models harbor the potential to revolutionize existing healthcare frameworks, for example, by amplifying their capability to furnish care and treatment, enhancing operational efficiency, curtailing time and financial expenditures, and alleviating the workload of healthcare practitioners. However, the actualization of these advantages is contingent, in part, upon the confidence of those who depend on these institutions (and their personnel) to deliver high-quality care and support, assuming other factors remain constant [79].

12.4.2.1 Ensuring Inclusivity in AI-driven Healthcare

At the commencement of our discourse, it is imperative to succinctly elucidate our interpretation of AI-inclusivity within the current framework. In the realm of healthcare, AI-inclusivity refers to the integration of diverse AI technologies to enhance clinical decision-making, treatment, and medical research. While full AI adoption across healthcare is ideal, in practice, it often remains domain-specific, meaning some areas utilize AI while others do not. Similarly, task-specific AI-inclusivity applies AI to specific functions, such as diagnosis, risk prediction, or patient stratification. Examples include DL in radiology, NLP for mental health, AI-driven chatbots in telemedicine, and assistive tools for elderly care. These distinctions are crucial for two main reasons: First, they help frame the ethical discussion around AI-inclusivity, emphasizing the moral significance of AI adoption as a shift from traditional practices. Second, they aid in distinguishing the public's trust in AI technologies applied to specific domains or tasks in healthcare from their overall trust in healthcare institutions that fully embrace AI technologies. As will be elucidated in the subsequent discourse, these two concepts diverge and frequently do so for justifiable reasons. We shall now proceed to explicate our understanding of institutional epistemic trust [79–81].

Establishing clear parameters for epistemic trust in AI-integrated healthcare is crucial (Figure 12.16). This discussion follows Michal Klincewicz's adaptation of Gürol Irzik and Faik Kurtulmus' concept of public epistemic trust in science,

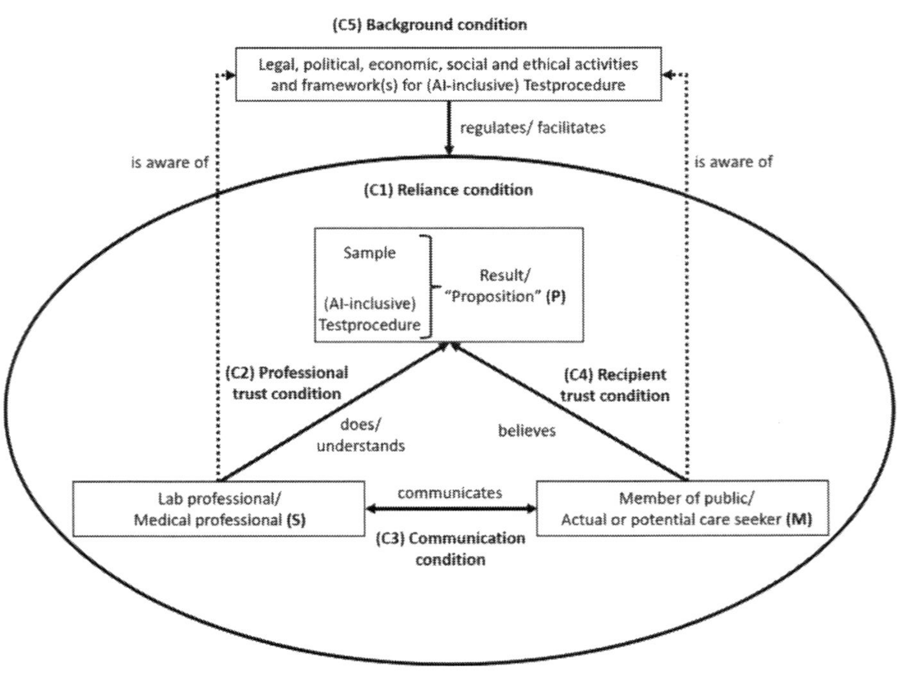

FIGURE 12.16 Four conditions of epistemic institutional trust in AI-inclusive healthcare [82]

providing a framework for institutional trust in reliable medical information [82]. Drawing parallels between scientific inquiry and medical practice, Klincewicz suggests that a member of the public can justifiably trust a medical professional or institution when:

(C1) The professional (S) genuinely believes in the medical advice or outcome (P) and conveys it honestly to the public (M);
(C2) M sees S's belief in P as a strong, though revisable, reason to trust it;
(C3) P is rooted in credible medical research or practice that S deems trustworthy;
(C4) M relies on S due to well-founded reasons to believe P is based on sound medical research and was communicated with integrity.

12.4.2.2 Policies for Equitable Technology Distribution

We are now poised to offer seven policy recommendations that provide concrete strategies and interventions. To maintain institutional epistemic trust in AI-integrated healthcare, key measures must be implemented.

i. AI should enhance existing medical practices under human oversight, ensuring reliability and accountability [83].
ii. Medical professionals must receive continuous training to verify AI tools and communicate their outcomes effectively.
iii. Transparency initiatives, like the Netherlands' "algorithm register," help build public trust.
iv. Clear communication through accessible platforms and trained personnel ensures patients understand AI-generated outcomes.
v. Public "AI literacy" should be promoted through education and awareness campaigns.
vi. AI research should prioritize public health benefits over commercial interests.
vii. Open-source standards and data-sharing principles must ensure accountability and transparency [83–85].

12.4.3 Future Directions and Innovations

The incorporation of AI within the realm of telemedicine is anticipated to fundamentally transform healthcare delivery by mitigating prevailing constraints and facilitating the emergence of novel solutions. This segment examines cutting-edge technologies aimed at surmounting current obstacles and articulates the prospective evolution of AI in the context of telemedicine.

12.4.3.1 Emerging Technologies to Overcome Current Limitations

12.4.3.1.1 Advanced AI Algorithms and ML Models

The advancement of intricate ML models significantly improves diagnostic precision and decision-making support within the realm of telemedicine. By assimilating multimodal data—encompassing medical imaging, patient medical histories, and real-time health indicators—AI can facilitate thorough patient evaluations.

Federated learning, which enables the training of models across decentralized data repositories while safeguarding data confidentiality, is pivotal for enhancing AI efficacy in varied clinical environments.

12.4.3.1.2 5G and Beyond for Enhanced Connectivity

The proliferation of 5G networks provides accelerated data transmission rates and diminished latency, thereby facilitating real-time video consultations and remote patient monitoring. This technological progression enhances the reliability and responsiveness of telemedicine, which is essential for the management of intricate medical procedures conducted remotely. The integration of AI with robust connectivity fosters uninterrupted data flows from wearable health technologies, thereby ensuring proactive and prompt medical interventions.

12.4.3.1.3 Satellite and Aerial Networks

The incorporation of satellite communication and unmanned aerial vehicles (UAVs) into telemedicine frameworks significantly bolsters connectivity in rural and underserved locales. These aerial innovations function as mobile base stations, effectively bridging the digital divide by extending network access to areas where traditional ground-based infrastructures are insufficient. Telemedicine platforms powered by satellite technology facilitate remote diagnostics and consultations, thereby rendering healthcare services attainable in remote regions and during emergency response operations.

12.4.3.1.4 AI-Powered Chatbots and Virtual Assistants

Progressions in NLP have culminated in the creation of more proficient AI-driven chatbots and virtual healthcare assistants. These systems are capable of delivering initial consultations, conducting triage, and providing follow-up care, thereby alleviating the workload on healthcare providers while simultaneously enhancing patient engagement. The augmentation of contextual comprehension within NLP applications contributes to tailored patient experiences and informed clinical decision-making processes.

12.4.3.1.5 Integration with IoT Devices

The burgeoning presence of IoT technologies within the healthcare sector fortifies telemedicine by facilitating seamless data acquisition from a multitude of health-monitoring devices. This integration significantly improves remote patient surveillance and the management of chronic diseases, leading to well-informed and timely clinical decisions. AI-driven analytics applied to IoT data streams can discern critical health patterns and initiate early interventions, thereby enhancing patient outcomes and minimizing rates of hospital readmission.

12.4.3.2 Vision for the Future of AI in Telemedicine

12.4.3.2.1 Comprehensive AI Ecosystems

Emerging telemedicine frameworks will be sophisticated, interconnected networks that employ AI for a multitude of functions, encompassing patient intake, diagnostic processes, treatment strategizing, and subsequent care management. These frameworks will harness ML techniques to anticipate patient requirements, optimize resource allocation, and customize treatment trajectories. AI systems will advance towards greater explicability and transparency, thereby addressing prevalent concerns related to bias and trustworthiness.

12.4.3.2.2 Increased Personalization and Proactive Care

The application of AI within telemedicine will transition from a reactive approach to a more proactive care model. Advanced predictive analytics will facilitate the identification of potential health threats prior to their escalation into critical conditions, thus permitting preemptive therapeutic interventions. Personalized medical strategies, propelled by AI algorithms that scrutinize genetic, lifestyle, and health-related data, will provide individualized treatment plans tailored specifically to the unique needs of each patient.

12.4.3.2.3 Cross-Platform Integration and Interoperability

Anticipated telemedicine systems will facilitate seamless interoperability across diverse healthcare platforms, effectively amalgamating patient records, diagnostic instruments, and treatment management systems. This integration will engender a consolidated patient profile that is accessible through multiple devices and locations, thereby ensuring an uninterrupted continuum of care.

12.4.3.2.4 Ethical and Inclusive AI Design

Ethical imperatives will steer the framework and implementation of AI within the telemedicine sector. The emphasis will be placed on the reduction of bias and the promotion of equitable practices, with algorithms cultivated on heterogeneous datasets that accurately reflect a variety of demographic groups. Regulatory policies and frameworks will prioritize transparency and the safeguarding of patient data, thereby fortifying trust in AI-enhanced healthcare systems.

12.4.3.2.5 Scalability and Adaptability

Forthcoming AI innovations will be architected for scalability across a spectrum of healthcare environments, ranging from technologically advanced urban hospitals to resource-constrained rural clinics. This inherent adaptability will guarantee that advancements in telemedicine are not confined to affluent regions but are accessible to all, thereby contributing to the enhancement of global health equity.

12.4.3.2.6 Human-AI Collaboration

AI will serve not as a replacement for healthcare practitioners but as a supplementary tool that enhances their capacity to deliver more accurate and efficient care. By automating routine responsibilities and offering decision-making support, medical professionals will be afforded greater opportunities to concentrate on intricate cases and patient interactions.

12.4.3.2.7 Continuous Education and Public Engagement

A successful trajectory for AI in telemedicine will necessitate sustained educational efforts directed towards both healthcare professionals and the broader public. Initiatives designed to elevate AI literacy will empower individuals to comprehend the contributions of these technologies to their healthcare, fostering trust and facilitating broader acceptance [86,87].

12.5 CONCLUSION

AI is reshaping the future of remote healthcare and telemedicine, offering new ways to make medical services more accessible, efficient, and patient-centered. This chapter has explored how AI-driven tools are not just enhancing patient-provider communication but also making it possible to diagnose and monitor health conditions remotely with a high degree of accuracy. These advancements reduce the need for frequent in-person visits, saving time for both patients and healthcare professionals.

One of the most powerful aspects of AI in telemedicine is its potential to bridge the healthcare divide in rural and under-resourced areas. By providing access to expert care where it was once limited or unavailable, AI helps close the gap in healthcare inequality. However, as promising as these innovations are, there are still challenges to overcome. Issues like poor internet connectivity, limited digital literacy, and unequal access to technology continue to hinder progress. Addressing these barriers is essential to ensure that AI-driven healthcare solutions benefit everyone, regardless of their location or socioeconomic status.

In conclusion, AI in remote healthcare offers more than just convenience—it has the potential to revolutionize healthcare by making it inclusive and personalized. To ensure these solutions are both effective and equitable, collaboration among technology developers, healthcare providers, and policymakers is essential. When implemented responsibly, AI can contribute to a healthcare system that is not only smarter and more efficient but also compassionate and accessible to all.

DISCLAIMER

None

REFERENCES

1. Theerthagiri, P., et al. "Deep SqueezeNet Learning Model for Diagnosis and Prediction of Maize Leaf Diseases." *Journal of Big Data* 11.1 (2024): 112.
2. Sardar, T. H. "Reflecting on a Decade of Evolution: MapReduce-Based Advances in Partitioning-Based, Hierarchical-Based, and Density-Based Clustering (2013–2023)." *Wiley Interdisciplinary Reviews: Data Mining and Knowledge Discovery* 14 (2024): e1566.
3. Subbarao, E., et al. "Investigation of Solar Energy for Urban Areas and Metropolitan Communities Using Machine Learning." *Electric Power Components and Systems* 1 (2023): 1–11.
4. Sardar, T. H., A. R. Faizabadi, and Z. Ansari. "An Analysis of Data Processing Using Mapreduce Paradigm on the Hadoop Framework." *International Journal of Emerging Research in Management and Technology* 6(5): (2017): 1–11.
5. Sardar, T. H., et al. "A Novel Ensemble Methodology to Validate Fuzzy Clusters of Big Data." In *Proceedings of the Fourth International Conference on Trends in Computational and Cognitive Engineering: TCCE 2022* (pp. 267–278). Singapore: Springer Nature, May 2023.

6. Sardar, T. H., A. Khatun, and S. Khan. "Design of Energy Aware Collection Tree Protocol in Wireless Sensor Network." In *2017 IEEE International Conference on Circuits and Systems (ICCS)* (pp. 12–17). IEEE, Nalanchira, Thiruvananthapuram, Kerala, India, December 2017.
7. Sardar, T. H., A. R. Faizabadi, and Z. Ansari. "An Evaluation of MapReduce Framework in Cluster Analysis." In *2017 International Conference on Intelligent Computing, Instrumentation and Control Technologies (ICICICT)* (pp. 110–114). IEEE, Chemperi, Kannur, Kerala, India, July 2017.
8. Khatun, A., and T. H. Sardar. "Cryptography Algorithms to Prevent Different Security Attacks." In Keshav Kumar, Bishwajeet Kumar Pandey (eds.), *Next Generation Mechanisms for Data Encryption* (pp. 35–46). CRC Press, 2025.
9. Sardar, T. H., A. Muttineni, and R. Ranjan. "The Future of Big Data in Customer Experience and Inventory Management." In Tanvir Habib Sardar, Bishwajeet Kumar Pandey (eds.), *Big Data Computing* (pp. 233–248). CRC Press, 2024.
10. Sardar, T. H., S. Das, and B. K. Pandey. "Explainable AI (XAI): Concepts and Theory." In Om Prakash Jena, Mrutyunjaya Panda, Utku Kose (eds.), *Medical Data Analysis and Processing Using Explainable Artificial Intelligence* (pp. 1–18). CRC Press.
11. Perednia, Douglas A., and Ace Allen. "Telemedicine Technology and Clinical Applications." *JAMA* 273.6 (1995): 483–488.
12. Topol, Eric J. "High-Performance Medicine: The Convergence of Human and Artificial Intelligence." *Nature medicine* 25.1 (2019): 44–56.
13. Field, Marilyn J. "Telemedicine: A Guide to Assessing Telecommunications for Health Care." (1996). National Academy Press. https://doi.org/10.17226/5296.
14. Mun, Seong K., and Jeanine W. Turner. "Telemedicine: Emerging E-Medicine." *Annual Review of Biomedical Engineering* 1.1 (1999): 589–610.
15. Debong, Fredrick, Harald Mayer, and Johanna Kober. "Real-World Assessments of Mysugr Mobile Health App." *Diabetes Technology & Therapeutics* 21.S2 (2019): S2-35–S2-40.
16. Xu, Lu, et al. "Chatbot for Health Care and Oncology Applications Using Artificial Intelligence and Machine Learning: Systematic Review." *JMIR Cancer* 7.4 (2021): e27850.
17. Jungmann, Stefanie Maria, et al. "Accuracy of a Chatbot (Ada) in the Diagnosis of Mental Disorders: Comparative Case Study with Lay and Expert Users." *JMIR Formative Research* 3.4 (2019): e13863.
18. Garbuio, Massimo, and Nidthida Lin. "Artificial Intelligence as a Growth Engine for Health Care Startups: Emerging Business Models." *California Management Review* 61.2 (2019): 59–83.
19. Alencar, Michelle K., et al. "The Efficacy of a Telemedicine-Based Weight Loss Program with Video Conference Health Coaching Support." *Journal of Telemedicine and Telecare* 25.3 (2019): 151–157.
20. Banskota, Swechya, Margaret Healy, and Elizabeth M. Goldberg. "15 Smartphone Apps for Older Adults to Use While in Isolation during the Covid-19 Pandemic." *Western Journal of Emergency Medicine* 21.3 (2020): 514.
21. Walker, Andrew L., and Joseph B. Muhlestein. "Smartphone Electrocardiogram Monitoring: Current Perspectives." *Advanced Health Care Technologies* 1 (2018): 15–24.
22. Dwivedi, Yogesh K., et al. "Artificial Intelligence (AI): Multidisciplinary Perspectives on Emerging Challenges, Opportunities, and Agenda for Research, Practice and Policy." *International Journal of Information Management* 57 (2021): 101994.
23. Abo-Zahhad, M., Sabah M. Ahmed, and O. Elnahas. "A Wireless Emergency Telemedicine System for Patients Monitoring and Diagnosis." *International Journal of Telemedicine and Applications* 2014.1 (2014): 380787.

24. Gellert, George A., et al. "The Potential of Virtual Triage AI to Improve Early Detection, Care Acuity Alignment, and Emergent Care Referral of Life-Threatening Conditions." *Frontiers in Public Health* 12 (2024): 1362246.
25. Lekha Athota, Vinod Kumar Shukla, Nitin Pandey, Ajay Rana "Chatbot for Healthcare System Using Artificial Intelligence." In *2020 8th International Conference on Reliability, Infocom Technologies and Optimization (Trends and Future Directions) (ICRITO)*. IEEE, Piscataway, New Jersey, USA, 2020. Print.
26. Romeijn, H. E., A. Schaefer, and R. Thomas (eds.). "Using Predictive Analytics for Cancer Identification." In *Proceedings of the 2019 IISE Annual Conference*, Orlando: IISE, 2019. Print.
27. Esmaeilzadeh, Pouyan. "Use of AI-Based Tools for Healthcare Purposes: A Survey Study from Consumers' Perspectives." *BMC Medical Informatics and Decision Making* 20 (2020): 1–19.
28. Eze, Nkiruka D., Céu Mateus, and Tiago Cravo Oliveira Hashiguchi. "Telemedicine in the OECD: An Umbrella Review of Clinical and Cost-Effectiveness, Patient Experience and Implementation." *PloS One* 15.8 (2020): e0237585.
29. Bashshur, Rashid L., et al. "The Empirical Evidence for Telemedicine Interventions in Mental Disorders." *Telemedicine and e-Health* 22.2 (2016): 87–113.
30. Bashshur, Rashid L., et al. "The Empirical Foundations of Telemedicine Interventions for Chronic Disease Management." *Telemedicine and e-Health* 20.9 (2014): 769–800.
31. Salman, Omar Hussein, et al. "Multi-Sources Data Fusion Framework for Remote Triage Prioritization in Telehealth." *Journal of Medical Systems* 38 (2014): 1–23.
32. Brunetti, Natale Daniele, et al. "Pre-Hospital Electrocardiogram Triage with Telemedicine near Halves Time to Treatment in Stemi: A Meta-Analysis and Meta-Regression Analysis of Non-Randomized Studies." *International Journal of Cardiology* 232 (2017): 5–11.
33. Kaissis, Georgios A., et al. "Secure, Privacy-Preserving and Federated Machine Learning in Medical Imaging." *Nature Machine Intelligence* 2.6 (2020): 305–311.
34. Tzanou, Maria. *Health Data Privacy under the GDPR*. Taylor Francis Limited., 2023.
35. Appari, Ajit, and M. Eric Johnson. "Information Security and Privacy in Healthcare: Current State of Research." *International Journal of Internet and Enterprise Management* 6.4 (2010): 279–314.
36. Meurisch, Christian, and Max Mühlhäuser. "Data Protection in AI Services: A Survey." *ACM Computing Surveys (CSUR)* 54.2 (2021): 1–38.
37. Mahapatra, Bandana, Rajalakshmi Krishnamurthi, and Anand Nayyar. "Healthcare Models and Algorithms for Privacy and Security in Healthcare Records." In *Security and Privacy of Electronic Healthcare Records: Concepts, Paradigms and Solutions* (p. 183), 2019. The Institution of Engineering and Technology (IET), based in Stevenage, United Kingdom. 10.1049/PBHE020E.
38. Neubauer, Thomas, and Johannes Heurix. "A Methodology for the Pseudonymization of Medical Data." *International Journal of Medical Informatics* 80.3 (2011): 190–204.
39. Baowaly, Mrinal Kanti, et al. "Synthesizing Electronic Health Records Using Improved Generative Adversarial Networks." *Journal of the American Medical Informatics Association* 26.3 (2019): 228–241.
40. Chaet, Danielle, et al. "Ethical Practice in Telehealth and Telemedicine." *Journal of General Internal Medicine* 32 (2017): 1136–1140.
41. Berti, Andrea, et al. "Exploring the Potentials and Challenges of Artificial Intelligence in Supporting Clinical Diagnostics and Remote Assistance for the Health and Well-Being of Individuals." *Ital-IA* 3486 (2023), 1–10.
42. Srinivasan, Satish Mahadevan, and Vinod Sharma. "Applications of AI in Cardiovascular Disease Detection—A Review of the Specific Ways in Which AI Is Being Used to Detect and Diagnose Cardiovascular Diseases." In *AI in Disease Detection: Advancements and Applications* (pp. 123–146). John Wiley & Sons (Wiley-IEEE Press), 2025. ISBN: 978-1-394-27866-4

43. Lepakshi, Vijayalakshmi A. "Machine Learning and Deep Learning Based AI Tools for Development of Diagnostic Tools." In Hardik Gohel, Ajeet Kumar Kaushik, Arpana Parihar, Raju Khan, Ashok Kumar (eds.), *Computational Approaches for Novel Therapeutic and Diagnostic Designing to Mitigate Sars-Cov-2 Infection* (pp. 399–420). Elsevier, 2022.
44. Krizhevsky, Alex, Ilya Sutskever, and Geoffrey E. Hinton. "Imagenet Classification with Deep Convolutional Neural Networks." *Advances in Neural Information Processing Systems* 25 (2012): 1–9.
45. Habuza, Tetiana, et al. "AI Applications in Robotics, Diagnostic Image Analysis and Precision Medicine: Current Limitations, Future Trends, Guidelines on Cad Systems for Medicine." *Informatics in Medicine Unlocked* 24 (2021): 100596.
46. Nishida, Naoshi, et al. "Artificial Intelligence (AI) Models for the Ultrasonographic Diagnosis of Liver Tumors and Comparison of Diagnostic Accuracies between AI and Human Experts." *Journal of Gastroenterology* 57.4 (2022): 309–321.
47. Hardy, Maryann, and Hugh Harvey. "Artificial Intelligence in Diagnostic Imaging: Impact on the Radiography Profession." *The British Journal of Radiology* 93.1108 (2020): 20190840.
48. Zarella, Mark D., et al. "Artificial Intelligence and Digital Pathology: Clinical Promise and Deployment Considerations." *Journal of Medical Imaging* 10.5 (2023): 051802.
49. Schillaci, Orazio, et al. "Combining Diagnostic Imaging and Pathology for Improving Diagnosis and Prognosis of Cancer." *Contrast Media & Molecular Imaging* 2019.1 (2019): 9429761.
50. Frank, Edwin. "The Role of Artificial Intelligence in Transforming Patient Care and Diagnostic Processes." (2024). EasyChair Preprints, 14677. https://easychair.org/publications/preprint/vV83.
51. Alshamrani, Mazin. "IoT and Artificial Intelligence Implementations for Remote Healthcare Monitoring Systems: A Survey." *Journal of King Saud University-Computer and Information Sciences* 34.8 (2022): 4687–701.
52. Janbi, Nourah, et al. "Imtidad: A Reference Architecture and a Case Study on Developing Distributed Ai Services for Skin Disease Diagnosis over Cloud, Fog and Edge." *Sensors* 22.5 (2022): 1854.
53. Kothamali, Parameshwar Reddy, et al. "Smart Healthcare: Enhancing Remote Patient Monitoring with AI and IoT." *Revista de Inteligencia Artificial en Medicina* 14.1 (2023): 113–146.
54. Kim, Ji-Sik, and Gi-Woo Kim. "Hysteresis Compensation of Piezoresistive Carbon Nanotube/Polydimethylsiloxane Composite-Based Force Sensors." *Sensors* 17.2 (2017): 229.
55. Shajari, Shaghayegh, et al. "The Emergence of AI-Based Wearable Sensors for Digital Health Technology: A Review." *Sensors* 23.23 (2023): 9498.
56. Chatterjee, Jyotir Moy, and R. Sujatha. "Transforming Healthcare: The Synergy of Telemedicine, Telehealth, and Artificial Intelligence." In Jyotir Moy Chatterjee, R. Sujatha, Shailendra K. Saxena (eds.), *Role of Artificial Intelligence, Telehealth, and Telemedicine in Medical Virology* (pp. 1–29). Springer, 2025.
57. Patel, Sanjiv A., and Ali K. Kamrani. "Intelligent Decision Support System for Diagnosis and Maintenance of Automated Systems." *Computers & Industrial Engineering* 30.2 (1996): 297–319.
58. Tenório, Josceli Maria, et al. "Artificial Intelligence Techniques Applied to the Development of a Decision–Support System for Diagnosing Celiac Disease." *International Journal of Medical Informatics* 80.11 (2011): 793–802.
59. "Classifying Human Behaviors: Improving Training of Conventional Algorithms." In *2019 IEEE Intelligent Transportation Systems Conference (ITSC)*. IEEE, Auckland, New Zealand, 2019. Print.

60. Giordano, Chris, et al. "Accessing Artificial Intelligence for Clinical Decision-Making." *Frontiers in Digital Health* 3 (2021): 645232.
61. Harish, Vinyas, et al. "Artificial Intelligence and Clinical Decision Making: The New Nature of Medical Uncertainty." *Academic Medicine* 96.1 (2021): 31–36.
62. Khalifa, Mohamed, and Mona Albadawy. "AI in Diagnostic Imaging: Revolutionising Accuracy and Efficiency." *Computer Methods and Programs in Biomedicine Update* 5 (2024): 100146.
63. Dvijotham, Krishnamurthy, et al. "Enhancing the Reliability and Accuracy of AI-Enabled Diagnosis Via Complementarity-Driven Deferral to Clinicians." *Nature Medicine* 29.7 (2023): 1814–1820.
64. Venigandla, Kamala. "Integrating RPA with AI and Ml for Enhanced Diagnostic Accuracy in Healthcare." *Power System Technology* 46.4 (2022): 33–42.
65. Radovanović, Dr Danica. "Digital Divide and Social Media: Connectivity Doesn't End the Digital Divide, Skills Do." February 9, 2012. SSRN. https://doi.org/10.2139/ssrn.2001952.
66. Kinalyne Perez, Daniela Wisniewski, Arzu Ari, Kim Lee, Cristian Lieneck, Zo Ramamonjiarivelo. "Investigation into Application of AI and Telemedicine in Rural Communities: A Systematic Literature Review." *Healthcare* 13.3 (2025), Article number: 324. MDPI. Print.
67. Graves, Janessa M., et al. "Disparities in Technology and Broadband Internet Access across Rurality: Implications for Health and Education." *Family & Community Health* 44.4 (2021): 257–265.
68. Junaid, Muhammad, Maddalena Ferretti, and Giovanni Marinelli. "Innovation and Sustainable Solutions for Mobility in Rural Areas: A Comparative Analysis of Case Studies in Europe." *Sustainability* 17.3 (2025): 871.
69. Fourati, Fares, Saeed Hamood Alsamhi, and Mohamed-Slim Alouini. "Bridging the Urban-Rural Connectivity Gap through Intelligent Space, Air, and Ground Networks." *arXiv preprint arXiv:2202.12683* (2022).
70. Yaacoub, Elias, and Mohamed-Slim Alouini. "Efficient Fronthaul and Backhaul Connectivity for IoT Traffic in Rural Areas." *IEEE Internet of Things Magazine* 4.1 (2020): 60–66.
71. Yaacoub, Elias, and Mohamed-Slim Alouini. "A Key 6g Challenge and Opportunity—Connecting the Base of the Pyramid: A Survey on Rural Connectivity." *Proceedings of the IEEE* 108.4 (2020): 533–582.
72. Fourati, Fares, and Mohamed-Slim Alouini. "Artificial Intelligence for Satellite Communication: A Review." *Intelligent and Converged Networks* 2.3 (2021): 213–243.
73. Moinuddin, Shekh. "Contours of Internet Access in Rural-Urban Landscapes in India." *RSA*. https://regions.regionalstudies.org/ezine/article/digitisation-in-india/?doi=10.1080/13673882.2021.00001100. Accessed on 16 February 2025.
74. Bondalapati, Pratheep, et al. "Supercell: A Wide-Area Coverage Solution Using High-Gain, High-Order Sectorized Antennas on Tall Towers." *arXiv preprint arXiv:2012.00161* (2020).
75. Siddiky, Md Nurul Absar, et al. "A Comprehensive Exploration of 6g Wireless Communication Technologies." *Computers* 14.1 (2025): 15.
76. Mozaffari, Mohammad, et al. "A Tutorial on Uavs for Wireless Networks: Applications, Challenges, and Open Problems." *IEEE Communications Surveys & Tutorials* 21.3 (2019): 2334–2360.
77. Pasquale Daponte, Luca De Vito, Luigi Glielmo, Luigi Iannelli, Davide Liuzza, Francesco Picariello and Giuseppe Silano. "A Review on the Use of Drones for Precision Agriculture." In *IOP Conference Series: Earth and Environmental Science*. IOP Publishing, 275 (1–2 October, 2019). Conf. Ser.: Earth Environ. Sci. 10.1088/1755-1315/275/1/012022.

78. Dorling, Kevin, et al. "Vehicle Routing Problems for Drone Delivery." *IEEE Transactions on Systems, Man, and Cybernetics: Systems* 47.1 (2016): 70–85.
79. Matracia, Maurilio, Mustafa A. Kishk, and Mohamed-Slim Alouini. "Coverage Analysis for Uav-Assisted Cellular Networks in Rural Areas." *IEEE Open Journal of Vehicular Technology* 2 (2021): 194–206.
80. Talgat, Anna, Mustafa A. Kishk, and Mohamed-Slim Alouini. "Stochastic Geometry-Based Analysis of Leo Satellite Communication Systems." *IEEE Communications Letters* 25.8 (2020): 2458–2462.
81. Liu, Jiajia, et al. "Space-Air-Ground Integrated Network: A Survey." *IEEE Communications Surveys & Tutorials* 20.4 (2018): 2714–2741.
82. Zhang, Ning, et al. "Software Defined Space-Air-Ground Integrated Vehicular Networks: Challenges and Solutions." *IEEE Communications Magazine* 55.7 (2017): 101–109.
83. Maheshwari, Kritika, et al. "AI-Inclusivity in Healthcare: Motivating an Institutional Epistemic Trust Perspective." *Cambridge Quarterly of Healthcare Ethics* 34 (2024): 1–15.
84. Kim, Jee Young, et al. "Development and Preliminary Testing of Health Equity across the AI Lifecycle (Heaal): A Framework for Healthcare Delivery Organizations to Mitigate the Risk of AI Solutions Worsening Health Inequities." *PLOS Digital Health* 3.5 (2024): e0000390.
85. Gajarawala, Shilpa N., and Jessica N. Pelkowski. "Telehealth Benefits and Barriers." *The Journal for Nurse Practitioners* 17.2 (2021): 218–221.
86. Burak, Andrew. "Future of Telemedicine: What's on the Horizon?." *Relevant Software*. https://relevant.software/blog/future-of-telemedicine/. Accessed on 16 February 2025.
87. Kanerika. "AI in Telemedicine: Ways AI Is Transforming Remote Patient Care." https://kanerika.com/blogs/ai-in-telemedicine/. Accessed on 16 February 2025.

13 Diabetic Retinopathy Classification Using Convolutional Neural Networks

D. Vanusha, J. Ramaprabha, K. Deeba, D. Vathana, Tanvir Habib Sardar, and F. Syed Anwar Hussainy

13.1 INTRODUCTION TO DIABETIC RETINOPATHY

13.1.1 Overview of Diabetic Retinopathy as a Complication of Diabetes Affecting the Eyes

Diabetic retinopathy (DR) is one of the most frequent and severe complications of diabetes mellitus (DM) and can have a damaging effect on vision, and may even lead to blindness without treatment. Diabetes is a condition in which the retina is damaged due to poor control of blood sugar or when it is neglected. The retina is that light-sensitive tissue within the eye, which is located at the back of the eye, and its function is to forward visual information to the brain [1,2].

The disease of DR involves the stages of its development. The stage of NPDR is when the cells of blood vessels of the retina weaken, and they begin to leak fluid, or blood begins the process. Progressing the disease condition may lead to a more severe NPDR, which is typified by highly developed damage to blood vessels, severe retinal ischemia (lack of blood supply), and formation of microaneurysms or hemorrhages [3].

If left untreated, the worst NPDR stage may go to the most advanced form of the condition – PDR. In proliferative diabetic retinopathy (PDR), these abnormal blood vessels grow over or into the retina or the vitreous gel, a clear substance that is present in the eye. The hypersensitive new vessels have the tendency to bleed into the vitreous, thus resulting in severe adverse effects such as vitreous hemorrhage or tractional retinal detachment, which may cause severe loss of vision and even blindness [1].

Several risk factors are responsible for the development and progression of DR, such as the long duration of diabetes, ineffective glycemic control, hypertension, abnormal blood fats, and pregnancy. Smoking and obesity are among lifestyle factors that contribute to the likelihood of DR [4]. Figure 13.1 shows the progression from a normal retina through various stages of disease severity to PDR.

DOI: 10.1201/9781003600947-13

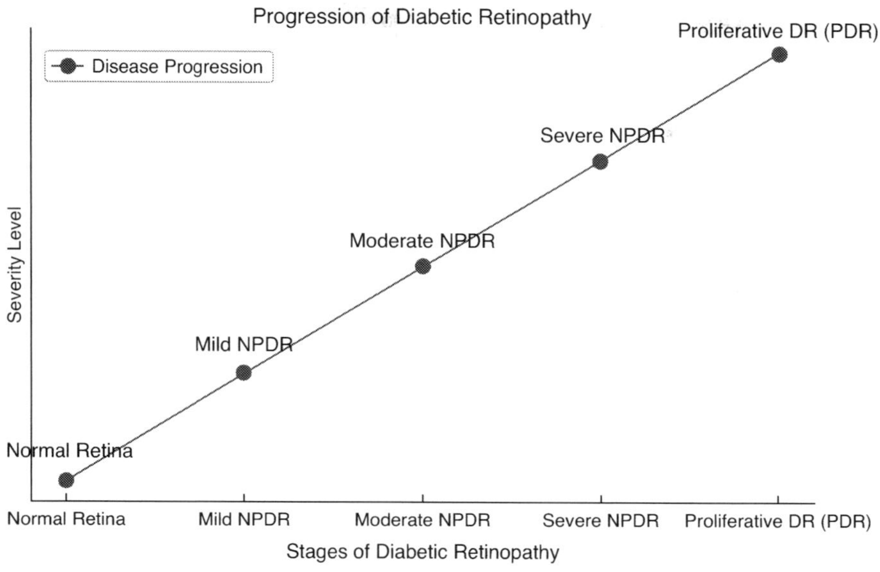

FIGURE 13.1 The progression from a normal retina through various stages of disease severity to PDR.

The diagram illustrates the progression from a normal retina through various stages of disease severity to PDR, which is characterized by the appearance of abnormal blood vessels and a high risk of complications such as vitreous hemorrhage and tractional retinal detachment.

13.1.2 Brief Explanation of How DR Progresses and Its Impact on Vision If Left Untreated

DR is an eye disease that affects the retina, the light-sensitive tissue at the back of the eye, and develops as a complication of diabetes. DR is thus a leading force challenging the field of ophthalmology as the main cause of adult blindness in working age globally. It is a complication of both type 1 and type 2 DM that goes on damaging the blood vessels of the retina, the light-sensitive tissue at the back of the eyes. The fact that there is a close link between the duration of diabetes and the occurrence of DR can be seen in the estimates that about 30% of patients with diabetes have some form of DR, and approximately 10% of them have the vision-threatening type of DR [2,4].

13.1.2.1 Progression of DR

A good grasp of the course of DR is critical for the appreciation of its effect on vision as well as for the urgent intervention. The course of the disease usually passes through several stages, at each stage of which new pathological changes in the retinal microvasculature occur.

1. Mild Non-Proliferative Diabetic Retinopathy (NPDR): In the early stage of the DR, the small abnormalities in the retinal microvasculature appear,

such as the formation of microaneurysms, the small balloon-like sacs in the retinal capillaries, caused by localized weakness of the vessel walls. This is where the microaneurysms leak fluid, lipids, and or blood into the surrounding retinal tissue that then form intraretinal hemorrhages, exudates, and cotton-wool spots. The person's vision may still be preserved to a certain extent even in these transitions [1].

2. Moderate to Severe Non-Proliferative Diabetic Retinopathy (NPDR): During the course of DR, there is a gradual decrease in pericytes, which are cell types that offer support to the capillary-forming tissues of the retina. Therefore, this loss is responsible for the capillary membranes thickening, capillary closure, and the development of retinal ischemia, an oxygen and vital nutrients depletion condition, in some regions of the retina because of the insufficient blood supply. Clinically, it is known for the presence of more severe-like intraretinal hemorrhages, venous beading, and intraretinal microvascular abnormalities (IRMAs). These IRMAs are a dysfunctional bypassing vessel which have a characteristic tortuous and dilated morphology with areas of capillary non-perfusion.
3. Proliferative Diabetic Retinopathy (PDR): PDR is characterized by an overgrowth of the abnormal new blood vessels called neovascularization, appearing most often at the particular interface between the retina that is being perfused and the one that is not. These fronds are made of new blood vessels and break into the vitreous gel, a clear gel-like substance filling up the back of the eye, thus being very fragile and prone to bleeding. Also importantly, fibrovascular development may happen, the neovascular fronds become enwrapped in fibrous tissue, and so tractional forces are generated on the retina. Such can lead to neovascular glaucoma, tractional detachment of the retina, and sometimes to vitreous hemorrhage.

13.1.2.2 Impact on Vision

The development of DR can cause much harm to visual functions, especially in people's lives and in performing activities. Specific symptoms of vision loss, such as macular edema, vitreous hemorrhage, or retinal detachment, depend on where the retina is involved, at what level, and if it is damaged.

- Macular Edema: The Macula, which is the centre location of the retina, is specialized in the functions of sharp-acuity vision and discrimination of colours. When the macula becomes swollen with fluid because the damaged blood vessels within it leak this fluid (macular edema), it may result in visual symptoms like blurred or distorted central vision.
- Vitreous Hemorrhage: Venous bleeding from defective retinal blood vessels to the vitreous cavity might cover the visual axis, thus resulting in the experience of floaters, dark spots, or reduction in acuity. Vitreous hemorrhage may have different levels of severity, ranging from mild and self-limiting bleeds to severe cases where the whole visual field is blocked by the blood. The presence of vitreous hemorrhage is an indication that prompt evaluation and management are a priority to avoid permanent vision loss.

- Retinal Detachment: The development of PDR can be considered as the formation of fibrovascular foci, sometimes associated with the contraction of the epiretinal fibrosis plexus, and this can favour the development of tractional forces that can result in retinal detachment. Retinal detachment takes place when the retina gets separated from the underlying retinal pigment epithelium (RPE), and thus, the photoreceptor-RPE interface is essential for visual function. Retinal detachment patients generally experience symptoms such as flashes, curtain shadows, or visual field veils, which ultimately result in a rapid decline in visual acuity. A retinal reattachment surgery must be performed at once by a doctor to regain visual function and restore retinal function.

DR is defined as a significant medical issue in diabetic patients that requires urgent intervention and proper management to avoid irreversible vision loss. The pathology and symptoms of DR should be clear before creating screening modalities, early detection, and timely interventions that can salvage vision and improve patient outcomes. There should be a number of activities targeted at glycemic level optimization, blood pressure management, and general systemic risk factor modification so as to overcome the problem of DR and reduce the incidence of vision-threatening complications. Simultaneously, there are constant studies about innovative treatment modes like the anti-vascular endothelial growth factor (anti-VEGF) agents and retinal gene therapy, which have the potential to improve the treatment of DR and even restore vision in the affected patients [5,6].

13.2 DIAGNOSTIC CHALLENGES

13.2.1 Discuss the Difficulties in the Early Detection and Diagnosis of DR

13.2.1.1 Diagnostic Challenges in DR

The early detection and diagnosis of DR lie in the concerns that are rooted in the complex clinical features and the limitations of the detection method. With the development of imaging tools and diagnostic techniques, however, there are some complaints by optometrists that they are not capable of detecting the early DR stages [7].

1. Asymptomatic Presentation: In the first phase of DR, patients may be entirely asymptomatic, and specific visual complaints will not be present. The absence of apparently obvious symptoms often delays the recognition of retinal pathology, thereby giving chances for early intervention to slip by. As well, the regular aging and refractive factors may mask the diagnosis of DR, as the patients may attribute any visual changes to these conditions.
2. Insidious Progression: The evolution of DR is often progressive and insidious, with the smallest alterations starting in the retinal microvasculature usually being seen over time. These changes are extremely problematic to point out on clinical examination alone, and in cases where specialized diagnostic imaging techniques are absent. Consequently, at the initial phase of DR, the signs may be missed during the regular eye exams, thus

postponing the commencement of the treatment until a more serious stage of the disease is reached.

3. Variability in Clinical Presentation: DR's clinical presentations are significantly different from one person to another, hence making the diagnosis of DR difficult, especially in those cases where atypical features are present. These factors, including severity of retinopathy, hypoxia of the retina, and macular edema, contribute to the clinical picture and may complicate diagnosis. Although another ocular comorbidity, such as age-related macular degeneration or glaucoma, could confuse the finding interpretation and may delay the accurate diagnosis [7].
4. Lack of Access to Screening Programs: Though the advantages of regular eye examinations for people with diabetes are widely known, they often fail to consult the comprehensive services that are needed for their eyes. The limited accessibility of screening programs, especially in the underserved communities and rural locations, is one of the factors for the prevalence of differences in the detection and management of DR. In addition, social determinants, such as health literacy, financial shortages, and transportation problems, contribute to this barrier by preventing the patient from getting prompt eye care [2,5]
5. Interpretation Challenges: The interpretation of retinal imaging studies like fundus photography and optical coherence tomography (OCT) has to be done by those who have already received the training and education. Multiple disease indicators can be displayed at the rod photoreceptor cellular level, such as changes in retinal morphology or vascular abnormalities, which can be bypassed by the inexperienced or nonprofessional observer. Therefore, misdiagnoses and incorrect levelling of the disease severity can be committed. The Artificial Intelligence algorithms might provide solutions to improve the diagnostic accuracy and reduce interobserver variability.
6. Patient Compliance: Patient follow-up and regular screenings are vital for early detection and monitoring of DR. Adherence to the recommended screenings can be low, especially in the case of those suffering from multiple comorbidities or competing priorities. Conducting education and outreach activities that accentuate the need for routine eye evaluations, emphasizing the dangers of untreated DR, is essentially the recipe for addressing the low patient involvement and compliance with the screening protocols. Figure 13.2 shows the diagnostic challenges in DR.

Succeeding in the uphill task of diagnosing the underlying physiological factors in DR requires enhancing the screening processes, patient education, and healthcare structures. Strategies to promote accessibility of holistic eye care services, with a focus on individuals in the unserved population, are vital for creating enabling conditions for early detection and prompt treatment. Furthermore, the progress in imaging technologies and the creation of computerized diagnostic algorithms hold the significance of improving the precision and performance of DR diagnosis. The concerns regarding DR can be adequately addressed if active screening and management interventions are formulated to reduce the burden of vision impairment associated with the sight-threatening complication of diabetes.

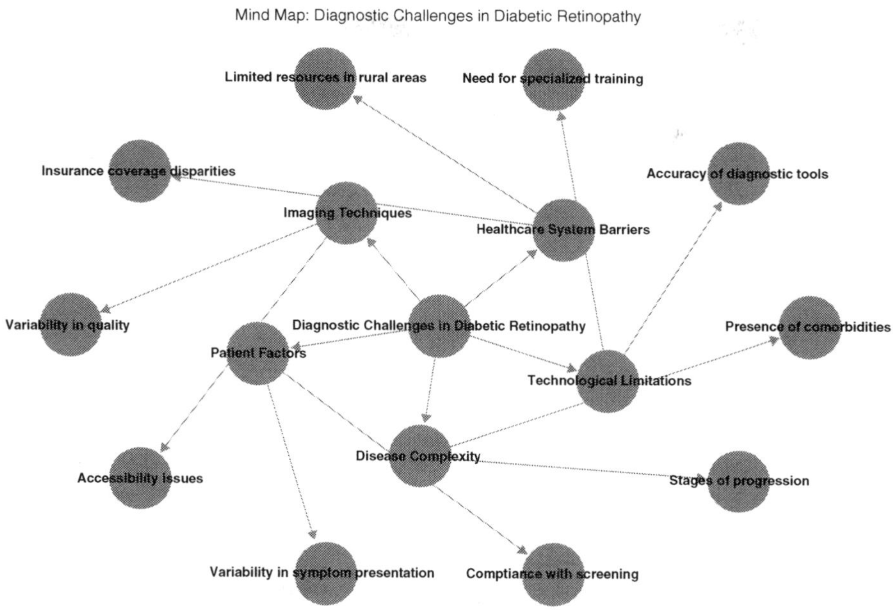

FIGURE 13.2 Diagnostic challenges in Diabetic Retinopathy.

13.2.2 Emphasize the Importance of Timely Diagnosis to Prevent Vision Loss

DR is a major diagnostic hurdle that is hard to deal with, especially in its early stages. Diagnosing it early enough is a necessary condition to prevent the loss of vision and lessen the dreadful effects of one of the most vision-threatening complications of diabetes. The realization of the nature and associated problems of early detection and intervention provides a comprehensive understanding of the diagnostic challenges.

1. Asymptomatic Nature: A major issue in the diagnosis of DR is that it rarely exhibits symptoms, especially in the early onset of the condition. It is possible for patients not to notice any visual changes during the early, less advanced stages of DR, yet by the time the disease has begun to progress, the onset of irreversible retinal damage may have begun. This leads to the conclusion that screening examinations of the eye, even in the absence of other symptoms, are essential to detect early signs of the disease (DR) and to initiate the treatment in a timely manner.
2. Silent Progression: The DR process can progress quietly without people noticing it, as retinal vasculature may undergo very fine changes slowly over time. With the absence of routine screening, these changes might go unnoticed, and this would allow the disease to spread unchecked. While yes, the visual symptoms like blurry vision and floaters can be a warning, the damage to the retina may have already worsened to an irreversible level.

Initial diagnosis/detection of the disease through comprehensive eye examinations (fundus photography and OCT) is very important. It is done to detect DR before it causes a significant loss of vision [5].

3. Risk of Complications: The possibility of delayed diagnosis of DR multiplies the likelihood of developing vision-endangering complications like macular edema, vitreous hemorrhage, and retinal detachment. Macular edema, which is characterized by the accumulation of fluid in the macula, can result in dramatic vision loss if not properly treated. On the other hand, rupture of new and fragile blood vessels that can produce vitreous hemorrhage can lead to sudden loss of vision that needs prompt treatment to prevent retinal damage. Advanced DR can lead to retinal detachment, which can cause total vision impairment, and, in such cases, the affected person should be referred to surgery by a professional as a matter of urgency.
4. Missed Opportunities for Intervention: An undetected DR in its early phases can hinder early intervention and risk mitigation. The earlier the detection, the sooner preventive procedures can be applied; for example, glycemic control and optimization of blood pressure can be implemented with the aim of slowing down the progression of DR and subsequently reducing the probability of vision impairment. Moreover, there are urgent measures in place of treatment modalities such as intravitreal anti-VEGF antiangiogenesis therapy and laser photocoagulation that can prevent or delay the neovascular complications and preserve visual acuity [5].

The diagnostic constraints of DR highlight the cardinal issue of timely diagnosis in the prevention of sight loss and preservation of visual functions. Regular eye checks should be performed, even in the case of no symptoms having been reported, for an early recognition of the onset of DR and timely management. With this, health care providers can create a system that will lessen the impact of vision impairment on DR and have a better patient outcome. Early treatment is the most appropriate key to retain sight as well as quality of life for the diabetic population at large.

13.3 ROLE OF IMAGING IN DR DIAGNOSIS

13.3.1 Overview of Various Imaging Techniques Used in Diagnosing DR, such as Fundus Photography, OCT

Over-the-Threshold by DM is a sight-threatening complication that needs timely and accurate diagnosis for effective management. Imaging techniques are important in DR diagnosis and monitoring, providing the medical workers with the ability to see and inspect the retina changes that are related to the disease. This part aims to give a thorough description of the different imaging modalities that are usually applied in the diagnosis of DR, such as fundus photography, OCT, fluorescein angiography (FA), and ultrawide-field imaging (UWF), by explaining their principles and clinical applications [6].

13.3.1.1 Fundus Photography

Fundus photography is a non-invasive imaging technique that takes high-resolution digital images of the retina, starting from the optic disc, macula, and peripheral retina. It has a fine retinal detail visualization capability for the detection of characteristic signs of DR, for example, microaneurysms, hemorrhages, and exudates. Fundus photography is among the most commonly used modalities in screening programs for diabetic eye diseases and in the examination of different levels of DR for the initial assessment and the assessment of the DR progress over time [8].

Principle: Fundus photography is made possible by a fundus camera, which is equipped with specialized optics and illumination systems and thus able to take images of the retina. Camera illumination sources shine at the fundus, while the reflected light is focused by the lens onto a digital sensor or camera film; as a result, a two-dimensional image of the retina is generated.

Advantages:

- Non-invasive and therefore easily accepted by patients.
- Provides reproducible records of the retinal findings for tracking the progression of the disease.
- Demonstrates the ability to spot minor renal abnormalities, which suggests the presence of early-stage DR.

Clinical Applications:

- DR screening in diabetic patients.
- Tracking the disease progression and the response to treatment.
- Establishing telemedicine-based diabetic eye screening platforms in areas where there is deficiency of health care.

13.3.1.2 Optical Coherence Tomography

It provides high-definition and structural details of retinal layers and structures, thus enabling the detection of the early changes of DR with features such as macular edema, retinal thickening, and intraretinal cysts.

Principle: OCT determines the time delay and light intensity of the echo reflected from eye tissues. An infrared light source is utilized, which shines on the retina, and the backscattered light is sensed by a photodetector. OCT is based on the interference between the reference and reflected light. Thus, it can generate detailed images of micrometre level in the retinal microstructure with micron-level resolution.

Advantages:

- Retinal structure imaging of high resolution.
- Quantification of retinal depth and area.
- Allows for early identification and tracking of macular edema and retinal changes in (DR).

Clinical Applications:

- Diagnosis and administration of diabetic macular edema (DME).
- Assessment of the retinal thickness with reference to its morphology in DR.
- Guiding treatments, for instance, through intravitreal injection of anti-vascular endothelial growth factor (anti-VEGF) agents.

13.3.1.3 Fluorescein Angiography

This method involves the intravenous injection of fluorescent dye – a fluorescein sodium – and then the dye's fluorescence is imaged sequentially on the retina to follow its circulation. FA data is the fundamental of retinal perfusion, vascular leakage, and the existence of neovascularization in DR.

Principle: Post intravenous injection, the fluorescein dye is swiftly pumped through the blood vessels of the retina and glows when exposed to blue light. These photos of the prevalence of RPE abnormalities and the location of the dye leak from the blood vessels, which reflects the integrity of the blood retinal barrier, were taken by fundus cameras with blue and green filtering.

Advantages:

- Makes available of blood flow visualization in the retina in real-time.
- Identifies retinal ischemic areas, capillary non-perfusion, and neovascularization.
- To guide treatment decisions, like the use of focal laser photocoagulation in proliferative DR.

Clinical Applications:

- Assessment of the retinal perfusion and vascular defects in DR.
- Areas of capillary non-perfusion and macular ischemia detection.
- Evaluation of treatment response post intravitreal anti-VFUF therapy and laser photocoagulation therapy.

13.3.1.4 Ultrawide-Field Imaging

Ultrawide-field imaging (UWF) represents a new trend in retinal imaging as it provides high, panoramic-resolution images of the retina (up to 200 degrees or more). Unlike the traditional fundus imaging, which provides limited visualization of the periphery, UWF imaging encompasses the entire peripheral retina, presenting a full-coverage. The detection of peripheral lesions and pathology in DR is thus facilitated [5].

Principle: Wide-field images of the retina are obtained by UWF imaging using specious optics and scanning techniques. Multiple scanning modes are used for the imaging, including non-contact SLO and wide-field SLO, which facilitates peripheral retinal imaging with high spatial resolution.

Advantages:

- Enables visualization of the retina in panoramic format, covering the entire retina, including the peripheral areas.
- Aids in the diagnosis of retinal vascular abnormalities and diseases.

Clinical Applications:

- The role of screening for peripheral retinal lesions, cotton wool spots and neovascularization in the development of DR.
- Identification of the specific locations of peripheral ischemia and zones of capillary non-perfusion.
- Disease progression and response to treatment monitoring throughout the control process.

Figure 13.3 is a representation of the fundus photography, optic coherence tomography imaging, FA, and ultrawide-field imaging in diagnosing DR. It demonstrates the basic principles behind each imaging modality and the clinical uses of each technique in assessing retinal structures as well as vascular abnormalities and disease progression.

Imaging approaches contribute greatly to the diagnosis and management of DR as they provide the opportunity to visualize retinal changes and gauge severity. This range of examinations - fundus photography, OCT, FA, and UWF imaging - provides complementary information about retinal morphology, vascular perfusion, and pathology. Moreover, they enable timely detection and individualized treatment.

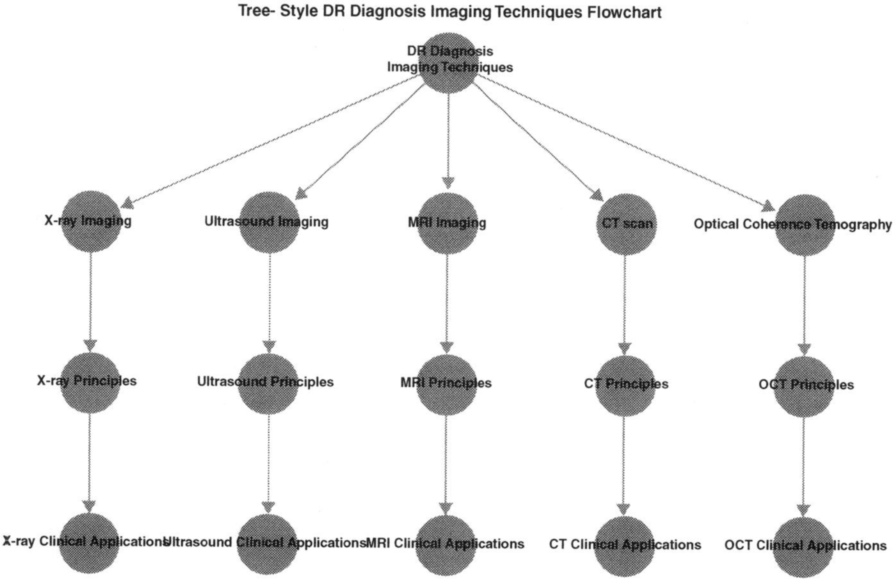

FIGURE 13.3 DR diagnosis imaging techniques.

Integration of these modalities in routine clinical practice increases the accuracy of diagnosis, improves patient outcomes, and reduces the risk of vision loss associated with DR. There is an expectation that technological progress in retinal imaging will continue to bring in new information into DR pathophysiology and, consequently, serve as a solid basis for optimized patient care.

13.3.2 Discuss the Advantages and Limitations of Each Imaging Modality

Role of Imaging in DR Diagnosis: Advantages and disadvantages: Imaging modalities are of paramount importance in the diagnostic and treatment management of DR because they provide vital information about retina morphology, vascular irregularities, disease advancement, and retinal circulation. For each of the imaging modalities, there are issues of advantages and limitations that must be taken into account in clinical practice in order to ensure an accurate diagnosis and correct management. In this section, we provide a detailed analysis of the advantages and limitations of four key imaging modalities used in DR diagnosis: fundus photography, OCT, FA, and UWF.

13.3.2.1 Fundus Photography

Advantages:

- Non-Invasive: Non-invasive fundus photography is an imaging technique that does not require contact with the pupil, and hence it is well-tolerated by patients and appropriate for routine checks.
- High-Resolution Imaging: Fundus camera creates dye in high-resolution digital images of the retina that help to reveal fine structural details of the retina, such as microaneurysms, hemorrhages, and exudates.
- Documentation and Monitoring: Fundus photography allows visualizing of retinal abnormalities and does enable documentation of the disease progression, thereby being a useful tool for longitudinal assessment and planning of the future treatment.

Limitations:

- Two-Dimensional Imaging: Retinal fundus photography is a two-dimensional image tool that cannot be used to detect subtle changes in depth and three-dimensional morphology of retinal structures.
- Limited Field of View: Fundus cameras only deliver a narrow field of view to the observer, where the major focus is toward the posterior pole of the eye, and this can be quite insufficient in preventing the detection of peripheral retinal pathology in DR.
- Subjectivity in Interpretation: Interpretation of fundus photographs may be biased and dependent on the level of experience and expertise of the observer which leads to the variability of diagnostic accuracy, and to the difficulty of reaching agreement between observers.

13.3.2.2 Optical Coherence Tomography

Advantages:

- Resulting in micron-level visualization of retinal layers and structures.
- Quantitative Assessment: OCT serves as a tool for the quantitative analysis of retinal thickness, volume and morphology; therefore, it enables the physician to assess objectively the presence of macular edema, retinal thickening, and intraretinal cysts in DR.
- Early Detection of Macular Edema: OCT facilitates the early diagnosis of macular edema, a frequent complication of DR that can result in loss of vision. This makes timely intervention and treatment possible to reduce the chances of losing sight.

Limitations:

- Limited Depth Penetration: OCT is limited to short imaging depth in comparison to other imaging techniques like FA, hence it may limit visualization of the deeper parts of the retina and disease.
- Artifact Artifacts: Imaging artifacts, including motion artifacts and segmentation errors, can be present during OCT imaging so as to affect image quality and make the diagnosis inaccurate.
- Cost and Accessibility: The acquisition of OCT equipment and the specialist knowledge for interpretation can raise accessibility problems, especially in resource-scarce settings and among the most vulnerable groups.

13.3.2.3 Fluorescein Angiography

Advantages:

- Dynamic Visualization of Blood Flow: FA demonstrates retinal blood vessels' functional dynamics and late vascular leakage to assess both perfusion, non-perfusion, and neovascularization in DR.
- Detection of Vascular Abnormalities: FA enables visualisation of retinal ischemia, capillary dropout, and dye leakage, indicating fluorescein, which is used in the diagnosis and staging of DR.

Limitations:

- Invasive Procedure: In FA, the fluorescein dye is intravenously injected and has a small adverse effects that may include allergic reactions and nausea, particularly in patients with renal failure or iodination.
- Transient Visualization: Via an intravenous route, fluorescein has a rapid circulation throughout the retinal vasculature, thus limiting the acquisition and interpretation time of the image in visualizing retinal perfusion and vascular defects.

- Limited Field of View: FA generally depicts the posterior pole and thus may not provide a good image of peripheral retinal pathology. Further examination, including other imaging modalities, is needed for thorough evaluation.

13.3.2.4 Ultrawide-Field Imaging

Advantages:

- Panoramic Visualization of the Retina: Whole-mount fundus photography provides a field of vision of more than 200 degrees and, therefore, permits a thorough examination of the peripheral retina, as well as detection of peripheral lesions and pathology in DR.
- Enhanced Peripheral Retinal Imaging: Ultrawide-Field Imaging (UWF) images can pick up on the central retinal pathology, such as neovascularization, ischemia, and hemorrhages very easily, but these abnormalities can be missed with traditional fundus photography.
- Improved Disease Staging: The application of imaging with UWF assists in precise staging of DR by enabling a wider field of view capture to permit more descriptive characterization of disease severity, distribution, and grades across the retina.

Limitations:

- Image Distortion: UWF images showing geometric distortion and peripheral image stretching, especially when obtained with non-contact wide-angle lenses, can be found, which might affect the precision of lesion localization and quantification.
- Data Processing and Analysis: examination of images of UWF may entail the utilization of specific software and expertise for processing, registering, and interpretation of images, and that may complicate implementation in the clinic [9].
- Cost and Availability: The profitability of UWF imaging units and the lack of readily available equipment could become a barrier to its wide usage, especially in resource-challenged settings and community health units.

In each imaging modality employed for detecting DR, there are unique pros and cons that must be taken into account by a doctor during care delivery. Fundus photography, OCT, FA, and UWF imaging represent complementary methods and give us the ability to visualize abnormal retinal morphology, vascular anomalies, and disease progression, allowing us to reach an accurate diagnosis and targeted treatment planning. Identifying the benefits and the limitations of imaging techniques is crucial for obtaining diagnostic accuracy, ensuring the best results for the patients, and reducing the risk of blindness in DR. With future developments, we can expect even better diagnostic capabilities as new imaging technology and image analysis algorithms are designed.

13.4 INTRODUCTION TO CONVOLUTIONAL NEURAL NETWORKS

13.4.1 Explanation of CNN Architecture and Its Suitability for Image Classification Tasks

CNNs, as an essential component of pattern recognition and image processing, are brought to light, which makes them suitable for image classification tasks. This section is dedicated to the architecture of CNNs: we introduce their main components, point out why CNNs are so efficient in dealing with image data, and so on [5].

13.4.1.1 Overview of CNN Architecture

Convolutional Layers: The main components of CNNs are the filters, which operate by convolving the input images with learnable filters or kernels. Each type of filter recognizes various patterns, characteristics, e.g., edges, textures, or shapes in multiple regions of input image. Whereas CNNs use multiple convolutional layers to extract more abstract and complex patterns, they learn more and more hierarchical representations by building up representations from basic visual features.

Pooling Layers: Spatial dimensions of feature maps are reduced by pooling layers, which are alternatively present between convolutional layers, and important features are kept unchanged. As far as the common pooling operations, such as max pooling and average pooling, are concerned, they extract the maximal or average value from each pooling region itself. Pooling leads to the reduction in computational complexity of a CNN and also reduces overfitting, and it makes the CNN invariant to translations so that it checks the features everywhere.

Activation Functions: The activation functions make the CNN architecture more complex by introducing non-linearity, which provides the network the ability to capture complex relationships between input features and output predictions. The most popular activation functions are ReLU (Rectified Linear Unit), which is sparse and speeds up the convergence process by avoiding the vanishing gradient problem, and its different forms like Leaky ReLU and Parametric ReLU [10].

Fully Connected Layers: Particularly after the convolutional and pooling layers in CNNs, fully connected layers are often found together with dense layers, which mainly exemplify high-level feature aggregation and classification. Each neuron in the fully connected layers is connected to all neurons of the preceding layer, making it possible for the network to learn complex decision boundary lines and accurately distinguish between different classes by means of fine-grained discrimination.

SoftMax Layer: The last layer of the CNN architecture is typically the SoftMax layer that aims to normalize the scores. The SoftMax function gives the probabilities of the class labels and shows the most probable prediction class of the input image. The probabilistic outcome used for multi-class classification tasks allows the network to make sure and predictions by learning the features.

13.4.1.2 Suitability for Image Classification Tasks

Hierarchical Feature Learning: CNNs shine in image classification problems because of their capability to instantly learn hierarchical visual feature representations from raw pixel data. Using a number of CNN layers that consist of combinations of convolutional and pooling operations, CNNs can extract low-level features, such as edges and textures, in the early layer and then, in the deeper layer, move to higher-level features, such as object parts and semantic concepts. The hierarchical nature of feature learning in CNNs allows these networks to efficiently distinguish between different objects and scenes according to their unique visual attributes.

Translation Invariance: A very important thing about the CNNs is their inherent translational invariance, which allows them to recognize the objects, irrespective of their position or orientation in the input image. Convolutional layers are spatial-invariant by sharing weights for the same spatial location, so that the model can detect features irrespective of their location in the image. This feature of CNNs makes them tolerant to changes in the position, size, and orientation of objects. Thus, their generalizability level and classification performance are increased on image classification tasks.

Parameter Sharing: CNNs rely on the parameter sharing property for an efficient feature extraction process across the diverse regions in the input image. CNNs achieve this by sharing weights among neurons within the same convolutional filter, which allows them to identify local patterns and dependent components of an image, and with a minimum number of learnable parameters. This parameter sharing mechanism not only results in the reduction of computational costs but also enables the network to generalize to unseen data, thus making the network to perform better on image classification tasks.

End-to-End Learning: The CNNs can do end-to-end learning, allowing the network to automatically learn optimal feature representations and classification boundaries directly from the data without having to explicitly engineer the features. Thus, this end-to-end learning scheme allows neural networks to self-adjust to the characteristics of the input data and the task at hand. As a result, CNNs can be used across a broad spectrum of classification problems like object recognition, scene comprehension, and medical image processing. Figure 13.4 shows the CNN architecture.

The combination of several different layers in a network allows it to perform classification tasks such as feature extraction, down-sampling, and classification, which results in the network being able to accurately classify input images into different categories.

Convolutional neural networks (CNNs) have transformed the computer vision domain by providing its pioneering and successfully implemented model of robust and precise image classification. Their hierarchical structure, translation invariance, parameter sharing, and end-to-end learning ability make them powerful to deal with and analyzing visual data. Through the ability to automatically learn hierarchical representations of visual features directly from raw pixel data, CNNs have also demonstrated an extraordinary ability to perform a number of image classification tasks, an indication of the importance of CNNs in advancing to the forefront of modern Artificial Intelligence and Machine Learning [1,5].

13.4.2 Brief Overview of How CNNs Work and Their Components (Convolutional Layers, Pooling Layers, Fully Connected Layers

13.4.2.1 CNNs: Deep Neural Networks Introduction

CNNs have turned into Deep Learning models of a new class and operate with the visual data for their processing and analysis. They are specifically designed for image-related chores such as image detection, object localization, and segmentation.

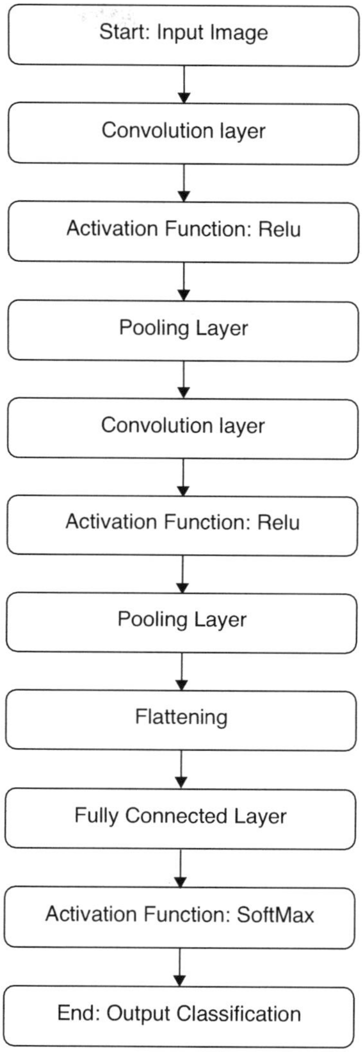

FIGURE 13.4 CNN architecture.

In this section, we will give you a detailed explanation of how CNNs work and discuss their main components, such as convolutional layers, pooling layers, fully connected layers, and so on [1].

1. Overview of CNNs: CNNs are inspired by the structure and function of the visual cortex in the mammalian cortex. They are created to automatically find out hierarchical structures of features simply by looking at original input data, which makes them good for image and spatial data tasks.

   However, at a high level, CNNs can be considered a stack of layers for each of the steps - the extraction of features and the classification.

These layers are the ones that perform feature extraction and prediction from learned features in the representation of the input data.

2. Components of CNNs:
   a. Convolutional Layers: Feature extracting layers are the main basic CNN components, also named convolutional layers. While each convolutional layer is typically formed of a set of learnable filters or a kernel set that is convolved with the input data. These filters take advantage of certain patterns or features, like edges, textures, and shapes, by searching in multiple locations in the given image.

      The computation of the dot product between the filter and a local region of the input is done by sliding the filter over the input data. Due to recurrent stacking of convolutional layers, CNNs are endowed with the ability to learn more complex and abstract features from raw pixel data.
   b. Pooling Layers: Pooling layers come in between convolutional layers and work as down-sampling of the feature maps generated from the convolutional layer. The filtering process reduces spatial dimensions and preserves the important information. Parse pooling tasks include max pooling and average pooling, which bring either the highest or the average value in a pooling area.

      The pooling is an essential element that helps in improving the computational efficiencies of CNNs, and it also adds to the spatial invariance properties, which means that the network can concentrate on the most important features rather than overfitting.
   c. Activation Functions: The activation functions are: ReLU (Rectificated Linear Unit), which helps in producing sparse and accelerating convergence by alleviating the vanishing gradient problem, and its variants such as LeakyReLU and ParametricReLU [10].

      Activation functions help in solving non-linear problems by CNNs because CNNs can model complex relationships in the input data and make predictions based on learned features.
   d. Fully Connected Layers: Final layers of the CNN architecture, such as fully connected layers or dense layers, often perform a high-level feature aggregation and classification. Here every neuron in fully connected layers is connected to every neuron of the preceding layer, allowing the network to make fine-grained distinctions between classes and learn complex decision boundaries.

      The higher layers use fully connected layers (convolutional filters) for featuring aggregation, and for generating predictions based on the learned representations. They provide pivotal information in the report for which a decision is made.
   e. SoftMax Layer: The SoftMax layer is the last layer of the CNN structure, which is used in multi-label classification tasks. It ranks the output scores in the range of probabilities for multiple classes by means of normalization, so that it is possible to determine the likelihood of determining the class of the input data.

The SoftMax function provides the model with probabilities that are assigned to each class label allowing the network to generate more trustworthy predictions based on the features it has learned. It helps to realize the decision-making stage with the help of its output interpretation, and it is a tool for probabilistic decision-making.

3. Working of CNNs: CNNs operate in a feed-forward way, where the input data flow is sequential, and predictions are made by utilizing the learnt features. Through the learning process, CNNs fine-tune their parameters (filter weights and biases) using backward propagation and gradient descent algorithms. The objective is to minimize a given loss function [10].

   The training process involves feeding batches of input data iteratively through the network, computing and improving the prediction errors, and then updating the network parameters to reduce those errors. CNNs achieve this by modifying the convolutional layer weight and biases, and modifying the fully connected layer weight and biases so that they learn to extract the features of the input data and make predictions with accuracy.

   The main purpose of CNNs is to act as a Deep Learning model that analyzes the visual data. Their structured cascading architecture and ensemble design, which are based on convolutional layers, pooling layers, fully-connected layers, and activation functions, allow them to implicitly learn hierarchical representations of features from raw pixel data in a direct manner. Through exploiting these transferred feature representations, CNNs can be utilized to address many image-centred problems; thus, it is an essential equipment in computer vision and Artificial Intelligence [1].

13.5 DR CLASSIFICATION USING CNNS

13.5.1 Review of Recent Studies and Research on Using CNNs for Automated DR

13.5.1.1 Diabetic Retinopathy Detection by using Convolutional Neural Networks (CNNs)

DR diagnosis and classification using Convolutional Neural Networks (CNNs) has been the centre of attention lately due to the option they offer to enhance the DR screening's speed and accuracy. In this part of the review, we have summarized some recent studies and research that have investigated the use of CNNs for automated DR diagnosis and classification, with a focus on the methodologies, performance, and their implications for clinical practice [5].

1. Methodologies and Architectures:

   The following key steps are:

   - Data Pre-processing: Pre-processing of the retinal images is carried out frequently to remove noise, standardize image features between different sets, and enhance image quality. Some examples of image pre-processing techniques are contrast enhancement, normalization, and changing the image size to a standardized one.

- Model Architecture: Multiple CNN architectures, including AlexNet, VGGNet, ResNet, and InceptionNet, have been adapted and fine-tuned for use as a disease recognition classifier. Transfer learning – an approach where pre-trained CNNs are fine-tuned on DR datasets – has been widely used to capitalize on information learnt from large-scale image datasets.
- Training and Validation: CNN models are trained on datasets of retinal images, which are large-scale and labelled. They usually collect such images from clinical settings or open repositories. The datasets are divided into the train, valid, and test data sets to find the performance of the trained model. One of the techniques used to enrich the training data is data augmentation, which involves rotation, flipping, and scaling. The model generalization is enhanced.

2. Performance Evaluation:

   The performance of CNN-based models for the DR classification is measured with various tools such as accuracy, specificity, sensitivity, and area under the receiver operating characteristic curve (AUC-ROC). The studies have found encouraging results as the CNN networks could obtain high levels of accuracy and sensitivity in diagnosing DR and differentiating between severity levels.

   - Accuracy: CNN models have yielded high classification accuracy rates (>85%) to >95% in identifying DR from retinal images. The accuracy of the models relies on the size of the dataset, image quality, and the structure of the model.
   - Sensitivity and Specificity: Sensitivity is the amount of true positive cases being correctly identified by the model, and specificity is the amount of true negative cases that are correctly identified. Among the CNN-based models, features such as microaneurysms, hemorrhages, exudates, and neovascularization have high sensitivity and specificity in the detection of DR-related features.
   - AUC-ROC: The AUC-ROC metric provides an overall measure that reflects the model's predictive capabilities at all possible thresholds. Good model generalization based on high AUC-ROC implies good discriminative ability of the model in identifying positive and negative cases of DR.

3. Clinical Implications:

   The use of CNNs for automated DR diagnosis and classification has significant clinical implications, including: The use of CNNs for automated DR diagnosis and classification has significant clinical implications, including:

   - Early Detection and Intervention: CNN-based models facilitate the early detection of eye conditions related to DR, which in turn allow for prompt enhancement and treatment to prevent the worsening of the disease and its complications.
   - Screening and Triage: Automated screening methods that use CNNs can enhance the screening process, especially in resource-scarce

settings where eye care is scarce. Deep Convolutional Neural Network (CNN)-based screening tools could help triage high-risk patients for further review by the ophthalmologists; thereby, important resources remain unutilized for screening of others and with the backbone clearances.

- Telemedicine and Remote Monitoring: The use of CNN-based methods makes it possible to evaluate DR on the basis of telemedicine and the remote monitoring of patients with diabetes. Using remote retinal imaging coupled with automated retinopathy recognition, one can accomplish decentralized screening and management, resulting in better healthcare access for the medically underserved and remote communities.

4. Challenges and Future Directions:
   - Interpretability: The black-box attribute of Deep Learning models creates challenges for presenting a model's predictions and understanding the covered characteristics in classification decisions. It is required to make even more attempts for the improvement of model interpretability and explainability in order to increase the level of confidence in and the acceptance of the CNN-based systems in clinical practice.
   - Generalization and Robustness: The models trained by the CNN using large-scale datasets may point out the limited generalization in different populations and imaging circumstances. Real-world deployment and clinical adoption of such models require increasing their resistance to image quality variations, patient-specific characteristics, and disease presentation diversity.
   - Integration with Clinical Workflow: Adaptation of CNN-based systems into the current clinical workflow and electronic health record (EHR) systems will help save a lot of time and make the usability of the system seamless in clinical practice. Ease of use, interoperability with other software, and compliance to regulatory standards mark the success of integration.

Employing CNNs in the automated DR diagnosis process has led to encouraging effects for this research, obtaining accurate and sensitive detection of the DR-related features from the retinal images. These CNN-based models pave the way to major improvements in early diagnosis and treatment, as well as prevention of loss of eyesight and eye complications. Overcoming the problems like interpretability, generalization, and integration with clinical workflow will be the key factors for the widespread usage of CNN-based systems in real-world clinical settings. The continuation of such studies and the simultaneous involvement of clinicians, researchers, and industry partners are prerequisites to fully exploit the potential of the CNNs in revolutionizing diabetic eye care and enhancing patients' results.

13.5.2 Explanation of Datasets Used for Training and Testing CNN Models

The widely acknowledged accomplishments of CNNs in DR classification heavily depend on how well trained and tested the network is using various datasets. In this part, we explore datasets that are utilized for training and testing the CNN models for the classification of DR and the nature of them, the characteristics they possess, and how they contribute to the advancement of research in that field.

1. Kaggle DR Detection Dataset:
   This dataset offers several advantages:
   - Large-scale: The dataset comprises tens of thousands of retinal images, implicating the build-up of deep CNN models with diversity of data.
   - Annotated Labels: Each image in the dataset is annotated by ophthalmologists and trained graders with ground truth labels of DR severity on the amount, thus for supervised learning.
   - Data Diversity: Data set comprises images captured by different imaging modalities (e.g., fundus photography, optical coherence tomography), with variations of image quality, illumination, and manifestation of disease, which are considered good for improving the model's robustness.
2. EyePACS Dataset:
   Key features of the EyePACS dataset include:
   - Real-world Clinical Data: The dataset contains the images taken in actual clinical settings that were taken during the regular DR screening, and it represents the unpredictable variability of the patient population that is commonly encountered in a clinical setting.
   - Large and Diverse: Thanks to EyePACS, thousands of labelled images covering different levels of DR severity are available to CNN models, which can be trained and assessed to achieve a good performance considering a variety of eye lesions.
   - Ethnically Diverse: Our dataset contains images of patient populations from diverse backgrounds, which cover different ethnicities as well as other demographic factors. Thus, our model can be generalized to diverse patient cohorts.
3. Messidor Dataset:
   The Messidor data is an open-source dataset containing OCT images of the retina acquired from diabetic patients, whose images were collected from French clinics and hospitals. The annotation follows the international clinical classification system on scales of DR severity level. Key characteristics of the Messidor dataset include: Key characteristics of the Messidor dataset include:
   - High-Quality Images: The dataset contains a storage of high-resolution retinal images, which were scanned using digital fundus cameras, providing image clarity and trustworthiness for correct disease diagnostics.

- Longitudinal Data: Also, the Messidor database has been expanded with numerous repeated images that were taken sometime later for a few patients whose disease progression and response to treatment can be analyzed.
- Clinical Relevance: The Messidor dataset is built from the real-world clinical data gathered during the standardized routine of DR screening and management, thus being the best link between practical research and clinical practice.

4. Indian Diabetic Retinopathy Image Dataset:

It is a newer improvement on the existing tools for diagnosis classification study, with features collected from Indian patients exclusively. The set of images is comprised of those captured with a number of imaging devices and protocols while ophthalmologists with practice experience annotate them for the severity level of DR. Key highlights of the IDRiD dataset include: Key highlights of the IDRiD dataset include:

- Ethnic Diversity: The dataset consists of images of Indian diabetic patients, and thus it provides a designer of the model with the demographic and genetic info particular to the population, hence increasing the model's generalization to specific ethnic groups.
- Variability in Disease Presentation: In IDRiD, photos are taken from different DR stages and manifestations, e.g., microaneurysms, hemorrhages, exudates, and neovascularization, which allows to cover broad spectrum of training and evaluation of the model.
- Annotated Lesions: Besides DR severity grading, the dataset annotations also encapsulate labels for lesions that are linked to DR, such as microaneurysms, for which the lesion-based analysis and feature extraction could reap benefits for CNN model development. The distribution and characteristics of datasets are shown in Figure 13.5.

The diagram depicts the distribution and characteristics of four commonly used datasets for training and testing CNN models for DR classification: Kaggle Diabetic Retinopathy Detection (KDRD), EyePACS, Messidor, and IDRiD. It includes the main features of a dataset such as data size, characteristics of annotation, diversity, and clinical significance.

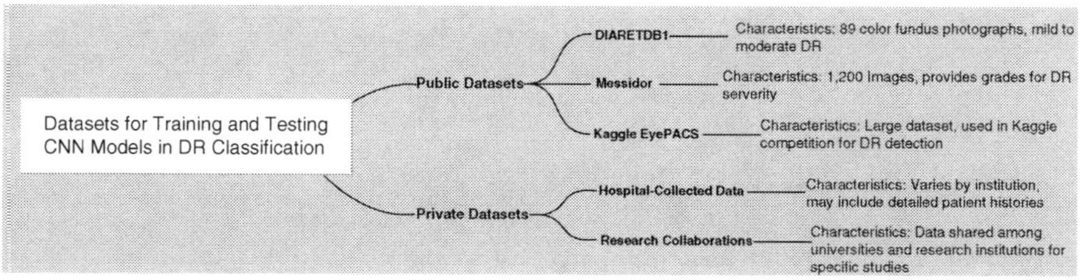

FIGURE 13.5 The distribution and characteristics of datasets.

Datasets become the pillar of the development and assessment of the CNN model for DR classification. They provide the essential training and testing data whose accuracy, stability, and generalization can be validated using these datasets. Access to large-scale, diverse, and well-annotated data sets such as those described above is the major contributor to the development of the classification and diagnosis of DR solely by machines. Continuous work on upgrading dataset curation, annotation, and open data sharing is vital for progress in this area, promoting the development of CNN-based solutions for advanced diabetic eye care globally.

13.5.3 Discussion of Various CNN Architectures Employed in DR Classification Tasks

Diabetic Retinopathy (DR) Classification Using CNNs: The following section is mainly about the architectures.

The use of CNN architectures as backbones has been widely explored in these tasks, each with its own distinctive properties. In this section, we look at and discuss some of the most notable CNN architectures generally used in DR classification issues, state their structures, and explain their suitability in this application [11].

1. LeNet-5: LeNet-5, an early CNN architecture is one of the pioneering architectures. Initially conceived for handwritten character recognition, LeNet-5 has been adapted to multiple image classification tasks, inclusive of DR diagnosis. It is composed of convolutional layers, pooling layers, and fully connected layers, just to give an example. Despite its comparatively small depth, LeNet-5 performs well for simple classification.
2. AlexNet: AlexNet by Krizhevsky et al. in 2012 became thus the major stepping-stone in Deep Learning. It has five convolutional layers accompanied by the max-pooling layers, three fully connected layers, and an output layer of the SoftMax. AlexNet can therefore deal with the complicated feature landscape, which is characterized by hierarchy, thanks to its architecture. Thus, it is a proper choice for a DR classification application. It is its depth and numerous parameters that allow it to represent intricate details of images and learn from raw image data.
3. VGGNet: VGGNet, developed by Simonyan and Zisserman in 2014, is notable for its simplicity and regularity of the architecture. It is composed of multiple convolutional layers, each one ending up with a max-pooling layer, and the last layers consist of the fully connected layers and SoftMax output. VGGNet's homogeneous architecture, thus, enables simple comprehension and training.
4. GoogLeNet (Inception): GoogLeNet, commonly referred to as Inception architecture, is the name under which it was introduced by Szegedy et al. in 2014. It contains the specific "inception module" which helps computation to be done in an effective manner through the process of performing the convolutions of different sizes simultaneously. The design of GoogLeNet is highly depth-orientated, computationally efficient, and over-fitting-resistant.

Its String modules enable it to have the ability handle the local and global features, hence, it is good for tasks like DR Classification.

5. ResNet: ResNet, introduced by He et al. in 2015, was the idea of residual connections to circumvent the vanishing gradient problem in very deep networks. The residual connections consist of the residual blocks, which allow the information to flow directly from the early layers to the later layers. Thanks to the ResNet skip connections, the training of deep, deep networks becomes easier because the network degradation problem is relieved. The design of such architecture paves the way for the creation of models of a larger size that can distinguish more advanced features, augmenting the performance, especially in difficult tasks including DR classification [10].
6. DenseNet: DenseNet, introduced by Huang et al. in 2017, generalizes upon the idea of skip connections but with a different point of view. In DenseNet, each layer is feed-forwardly connected to all other layers, thus producing a dense connection within layers. This architecture aims to make feature reusing and gradient propagating possible, and as a result, training of the large networks efficiently is fully guaranteed. DenseNet's connectivity architecture strengthens feature interdependency and gradient flow, thus its performance is superior in DR classification [10]. Figure 13.6 shows the CNN Models & their characteristics.

The diagram showcases the architectures of six CNN models commonly used in DR classification tasks: LeNet-5 [5], AlexNet [4], VGGNet [7], GoogLeNet [1], ResNet [5], and DenseNet [2]. The image of each model is given with its unique of architecture, including convolutional layers, pooling layers, and fully connected layers that explain the flow of information throughout the network.

To classify DR, different CNN architectures have been used; each has its own advantages as it captures and represents features in retinal images. The sophisticated LeNet-5 down to the modern DenseNet have progressed to tackle challenges in training deep neural networks and finally deliver the highest performance in the domain of DR classification. Knowing the

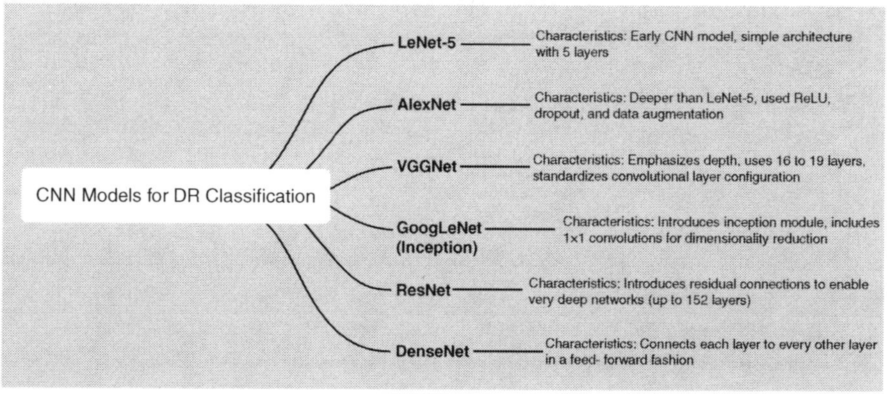

FIGURE 13.6 CNN models and their characteristics

features and power of different CNN architectures will enable the selection of the right models to be used and can also advance the field of automated DR screening and management.

13.6 PERFORMANCE EVALUATION AND CHALLENGES

13.6.1 Metrics Used to Evaluate the Performance of CNN Models in DR Classification (Accuracy, Sensitivity, Specificity)

Using CNN in DR classification has certain challenges with inherent performance evaluation.

The assessment of CNN models' performance in DR Classification is pivotal for evaluating their capability in clinical settings. Several metrics are in place for the evaluation of these models, each of which is able to highlight different aspects of the models€™' accuracy, robustness, and clinical applicability. In this part of the essay, we will provide an in-depth explanation of the metrics typically used to assess the accuracy of CNN models in identifying DR in images, along with the existing issues involved.

1. Accuracy: The most commonly used metric for the overall performance of the CNN models during the DR classification is Accuracy. It is a rather simple metric that indicates the fraction of correctly classified positive and negative samples out of the total number of samples. Accuracy tends to give an overall picture of model performance nevertheless may be inadequate for the imbalanced datasets where a class dominates over another one.
2. Sensitivity (Recall): Specificity is the other name for it, which is a metric of the proportion of true positive samples of a model that are correctly recognized. The ability of the model to sequentially identify both healthy and diseased cases precisely is represented by the sensitivity in the context of DR classification (Referring to a model that can correctly label patients' AlexMaLL/GPT-NeoX-20bf-instruction: In the setting of DR classification, sensitivity means that a model can correctly identify a diseased case (the patients with DR). The sensitivity value of the model is high, which means it can capture most of the positive cases and minimize the false negatives, thus enabling early detection of DR.
3. Specificity: Specificity denotes the proportion of negative samples that the model can correctly discern. It shows the model's performance of putting wrong results on normal cases (that is, a correct identification of DR patients). High specificity indicates that the model is capable of correctly comparing healthy retinas with those suffering from DR, therefore reducing unnecessary referrals for further evaluation and false positive diagnoses.
4. Precision: The precision of the model evaluates how many positive cases from all the samples are predicted as positive. It is a measure of the precision of the model to the positive cases that it has recognized, and thus, indicates its ability to avoid false positives. The matter of precision is especially

important in healthcare settings, where false positives can trigger unwanted and inappropriate interventions or treatments.

5. F1 Score: The F1-score is the harmonic mean of precision and recall, thus offering a mode to measure a model's performance with a balanced view. It accounts for both false positives and false negatives; thus, it is a good technique to consider for imbalanced datasets where one class is much more frequent than the other. A good F1 score shows that the model has reached both high precision and high recall, representing being able to minimize false positives and false negatives.
6. Area Under the Receiver Operating Characteristic Curve (AUC-ROC): AUC-ROC metric measures how the model's classifier discriminates between different thresholds. It displays the sensitivity (true positive rate) against the specificity (1 - false positive rate) with the threshold value and finds out the area under the curve. The higher the AUROC-CV value is, the better the discriminative ability is translated by the model, where closeness to 1 is associated with perfect performance.

13.6.1.1 Challenges in Performance Evaluation

- Imbalanced Datasets: Representation of data is imbalanced (e.g., the DR-positive and DR-negative cases), where one class of data is more prominent and can mislead the results. Special attention must be paid in order to incorporate class imbalance into the performance evaluation step and represent the true model effectiveness.
- Annotation Variability: Discrepancies in the annotations of different graders or clinicians may induce inconsistencies in the ground truth labels. The resulting inconsistency can affect the reliability of performance metrics. Standardization of annotation protocols and unanimity among annotators are critical for the accuracy and consistency of the ground truth data.
- Generalization to Real-world Data: CNNs based on curated datasets and tested on these datasets might find it difficult to adapt to real-world clinical data, which can have variations in image capture conditions, patient population, and disease severity. It is critical to evaluate the model performance on a variety and representative datasets to guarantee the robustness and generalization power of the model.
- Clinical Relevance: But while performance metrics serve us quantitative measures, clinicians should account for their clinical meaning and their impact on patients' well-being. Although high accuracy models might not always result in better clinical outcomes, they may fail to identify truly significant cases for which intervention is necessary.

The performance evaluation of CNN models in DR classification is done by employing various metrics, which include accuracy, sensitivity, specificity, precision, F1-score, and the AUC-ROC curve. These metrics offer detailed information about how well the model performs in distinguishing and classifying DR from retinal images. On the other hand, the difficulties, like the imbalance of datasets, the variation of annotation, the performance on clinical data, and the clinical relevance, must be tackled so as to make sure that the models can be accurate and reliable in clinical practice. The need for more research and increased collaboration is crucial for the development of rigorous evaluation methods and proving the clinical utility of CNNs as a tool for diagnosing and managing DR.

13.6.2 Challenges and Limitations in Deploying CNN-based DR Classification Systems in Real-world Clinical Settings

Performance Appraisal and Problems of Implementing the CNN-based DR Classification System in a Clinical Area.

Embedding CNN systems for DR classification in the real-world clinic is fraught with many challenges and limitations. Investing in this technology's potential, however, calls for overcoming numerous implementation issues, such as addressing technical and regulatory challenges. In this context, we motivate and outline some of the difficulties and limitations involved in deploying CNN-based DR classification systems in real-world clinical settings, presenting possible solutions and strategies.

1. Data Quality and Diversity:

   Challenge: Participant-level clinic-based data may often display variations in image quality, resolution, and light conditions, which may erode the performance of the CNN-based DR classification systems. Furthermore, the lack of diversity of training data might cause the model to be nondynamic when applied to population diversity, ethnicities, and disease manifestations.

   Solution: Obtaining an appropriate and representative variety of datasets to cover the real-world clinical variation is required for the optimality of CNN models. Data augmentation methods, for example, image rotation, flipping, and resizing, can be applied to increase the dataset diversity and to improve the generalization of models. Additionally, quality control processes and image pre-processing techniques increase data consistency and homogenization among various imaging analytic devices and healthcare settings.
2. Interpretability and Explainability:

   Challenge: One of the main reasons for lack of trust towards CNN models is that it is considered a black-box system, making it difficult for clinicians to understand the rationale behind the decisions made and only follow the recommendations. Transparency and interpretability are the factors that limit the adoption of algorithms based on CNNs for retinopathy diagnosis in the clinical environment.

   Solution: Putting interpretability and explainability mechanisms into CNN frameworks can help to make them more transparent and trustworthy. For example, attention mechanisms, saliency maps, and class activation mapping can differentiate important image regions of retinal images and reveal the features that influence learning. Through the use of these techniques, clinicians will be able to understand how the model has arrived at this prediction and will instill more trust in CNN-based diagnostic systems.

3. Integration with Clinical Workflow:

   Challenge: The integration of the CNN-based DR classification systems into the existing clinic workflows and into EHR may be complex and cumbersome. Doctors may not agree to use new technologies that replace their inherited workflows or require extra time and human resources for implementation.

   Solution: Interfacing CNN-based systems in clinical workflows is a crucial step in ensuring the successful translation of these systems into real life. The user-friendly interfaces, interoperability with existing software systems, and health record exchange platforms compatibility can speed up the adoption of CNN-based solutions by clinicians. Working with healthcare IT specialists and relying on input from end-users during the process of designing and developing the system will ensure that it satisfies the needs and tastes of the clinicians and is aligned with existing workflow procedures.

4. Regulatory Compliance and Safety:

   Challenge: Medical devices based on the CNN for DR classification are not being less rigorously regulated, and safety standards are being applied to ensure patients' safety and efficacy. Getting the regulatory approval, e.g., the clearance to FDA (Food and Drug Administration), in the US can be a lengthy and expensive process.

   Solution: Following the rules and standards throughout the development and deployment phases is the way to maintain compliance with regulatory bodies and ensure the safety of patients. The computerized decision support systems app validation studies, modelling performance documentation and results, and following established regulatory pathways can speed up the approval process. Cooperating with regulatory experts and seeking guidance from the regulatory authorities will help the team move the rails fairly and within a shorter period of time.

5. Ethical and Legal Considerations:

   Challenge: Use of CNN-based DR classification systems may cause ethical and legal issues that pertain to patient privacy and security of data as well as the issue of liability. Patient confidentiality protection, along with secure data treatment of confidential medical data, are very important concerns, especially in the face of the Health Insurance Portability and Accountability Act (HIPAA) regulations in the U.S.

   Solution: Data security measures like encryption, access controls, and logging guarantee patient privacy and limit a potential data breach, therefore. Medial consent of a patient for data collection and use, transparent communication of the aims and potential risks of using CNN-based diagnostic systems, and following ethical rules and regulations are key to maintaining trust and accountability. Figure 13.7 shows the deployment of CNN-based DR detection systems.

The figure shows the real-world deployment of CNN-based DR detection systems and the following workflow in clinical practice: data collection, model construction, system integration into clinical routine, regulatory

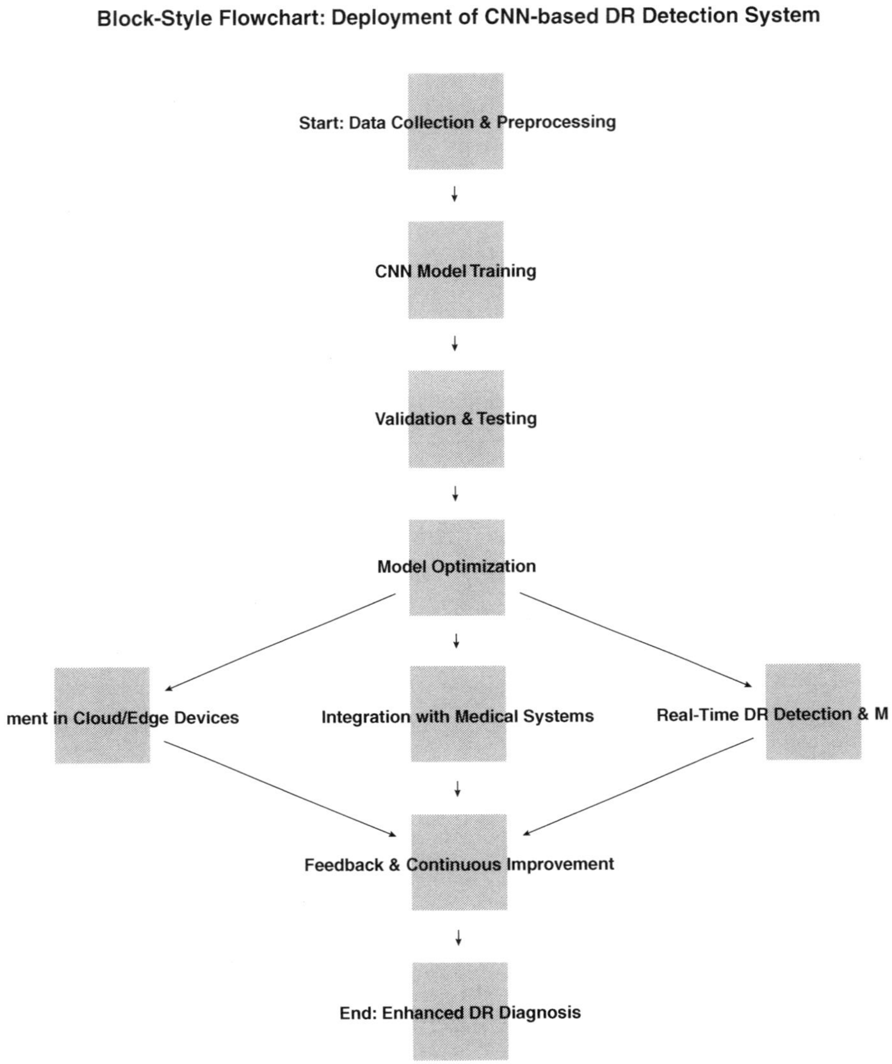

FIGURE 13.7 The deployment of CNN-based DR detection systems

approval, and ethical aspects. Each phase is traced by challenges and constraints as well, which include data quality, interpretability, integration complexity, regulatory issues, and ethical problems that have to be addressed in order to ensure efficient implementation and utilization of CNN-based diagnostic systems.

Implementation of CNN-DR classifications in real-world medical environments entails overcoming different obstacles and drawbacks associated with data quality, interpretability, integration into existing workflows, regulatory issues, and ethical concerns. Effective implementation of the solutions and strategies, for instance, data augmentation, interpretability techniques, workflow integration, regulatory compliance measures, as well as ethical safeguards, can help understand the existing challenge of such system and provide a solution for its mitigation leading to successful deployment of CNN-based system to solve the problem in diabetic eye care and to improve patient outcomes in clinical practice. A partnership between researchers, physicians, and regulators, as well as industry players, will continue to provide insight and guidance to overcome these pitfalls and unleash the full power of CNN-based technology in healthcare.

13.7 FUTURE DIRECTIONS AND CONCLUSION

13.7.1 Potential Advancements in CNN-based DR Classification Systems

The ever-increasing rate of Convolutional Neural Network (CNN) progression has fuelled the development of DR classification leading to unequalled levels of accuracy and efficiency.

Nevertheless, many possibilities for even better development and application of CNN-based algorithms in DR detection remain. This section will cover the possible future directions and advancements to be made in this field, mainly with the exposition of key research and development topics.

1. Domain Adaptation and Transfer Learning:

   Advancement: The domain adaptation and transfer learning approaches make CNN-based automatic detection of DR systems more generalized and versatile with regard to different populations, ethnicities, and imaging modalities. Through making use of the information from pre-trained models and applying task-specific domain adaptation algorithms, CNNs can overcome the bias in datasets and variation of domains and, hence, perform accurately in real-world clinical situations.
2. Multi-modal Fusion and Integration:

   Advancement: Utilization of the data obtained from different imaging modalities, such as fundus photography, OCT, and FA, bestows CNN-based DR classification systems with complementary information that can enrich the discriminating power of the models. Multi-modal fusion techniques, which include late fusion techniques, early fusion techniques, and attention mechanisms, can effectively merge different sources of information data, eventually resulting in more precise and holistic disease assessment.
3. Weakly Supervised and Self-supervised Learning:

   Advancement: Semi-supervised and self-supervised learning methods can be utilized to reduce the manual annotation workload and make Deep Learning-based networks learn from huge amounts of unlabelled data. By bringing weak supervision signals to the forefront, such as image-level labels or common disease occurrences, weakly supervised learning can train CNNs to locate characteristics related to DR, without the need for pixel-level annotations. In line with that, unsupervised learning techniques, which emerge, for instance, in the form of pretext tasks and contrastive learning, can benefit from the data structures and relationships to learn representations meaningful enough from unlabelled data, thus improving the model's robustness and generalization.

4. Explainable AI and Interpretability:

   Advancement: Developing explainability and interpretability of CNN-based DR classification models remains the key for health professionals and patients to learn to trust and accept them. New AI interpretability techniques like attention mechanisms and saliency maps are responsible for visual explanations of model decisions, while feature visualization methods are used to reveal clinically significant image regions. By creating readable and comprehensible explanations, these methods can contribute significantly to clinical decision-making processes and make models transparent.
5. Personalized Medicine and Risk Stratification:

   Advancement: Deep Learning-based computer-aided diagnosis systems can be easily updated for multiclassification, personalized medicine, and risk stratification applications beyond binary classification. Individualized risk assessment algorithms can lead to the precise treatment interventions and the customized treatment plans that maximize the outcomes of the patients as well as save resources.
6. Integration with Telemedicine and Point-of-care Devices:

   Advancement: Administering digital retinopathy classifiers based on CNN models through telemedicine platforms and point-of-care (POC) technologies converts diabetic eye care to a service that is accessible to everybody, thus extending screening coverage to the underserved and remote areas. Retinal imaging devices (handheld) embedded with on-chip classifiers implemented using CNNs can be used for early diagnosis and patients' triage at primary care centres, pharmacies, and community health centres.

   The role of future CNN-based DR classification systems in restructuring diabetic eye care and bringing about better patient outcomes is a very hopeful prospect. Promising developments in domain adaptation, multi-modal fusion, weakly supervised learning, explainable AI, individualized medicine, and telemedicine integration hold the key for future transformations in this field, delivering more accurate, accessible and individualized diagnosis and management of DR. Through embracing these future directions and encouraging cross disciplinary work between researchers, clinicians, engineers and policymakers, we can leverage [11].

13.7.2 Conclusion: Summarizing the Importance of CNNs in Automating DR Diagnosis and Improving Patient Outcomes

13.7.2.1 Future Directions and Conclusion

In the final analysis, CNNs, to a great degree, have become instrumental as a means of diagnosing DR automatically and have done well in this venture. The capability to analyze large retinal images with such high accuracy and speed that even human experts cannot compete with is the reason why CNNs have modernized the diabetic eye care field in particular by facilitating early detection, accurate classification, and individualized management of DR. As we look forward, CNN-based systems are expected to take an even more prominent part in the process of shaping diabetic eye care

13.7.2.2 Significance of CNNs in DR Diagnosis

CNNs have vastly improved not only the screening process but also the diagnostic process for DR, due to their ability to quantitatively assess the retinal images objectively. This ability of Opt Track AI to detect microaneurysms, hemorrhages, exudates, and neovascularization allows early recognition of DR-related pathology, which promotes timely intervention and treatments. This screening process is done through automation, which helps extensively to relieve a lot of pressure on health providers and enhance the delivery of diabetic eye care services even in the under-resourced areas where ophthalmic expertise is limited.

13.7.2.3 Improvement in Patient Outcomes

Utilization of the CNN-based methods for DR screening gives a promising perspective, considering that the technology will enable early detection and intervention. Early diagnosis of DR leads to treatment initiation, which can be laser therapy, intravitreal injections, or anti-VEGF drugs. These measures can prevent the disease from progressing and restore normal vision or even stop the further loss of vision. Furthermore, the CNNs made this possible through personalized risk assessment and treatment planning, resulting in those diagnosed with diabetes having specific interventions that improve patient outcomes as well as quality of life for those affected.

13.7.2.4 Future Directions in CNN-based DR Diagnosis

1. Enhanced Interpretability: Future research into the methods for explanatory AI will result in the interpretation of CNN models, leading clinicians to trust and understand their predictions. The use of a transparent model, which clearly shows how the reasoning process takes place, will help one evaluate the model and can be applied in clinical conditions.
2. Personalized Medicine: The incorporation of patient-specific clinical data with genomic information into CNN models will give way to patient-specific risk estimation and treatment planning, leading to better patient outcomes and reduced burden on resources. The application of a personalized medicine approach corresponding to the individual patient profiles will be the major turnaround in diabetic eye care.
3. Telemedicine Integration: Synthesis of CNN-based DR classification systems with telemedicine platforms and POC devices will be carried out to take the screening services to the underserved populations and the remote communities enhancing early detection and intervention for the at-risk individuals. While projected to have DR portable retinal imaging devices that utilize CNN classifiers will bring wider access to diabetic eye care and healthcare equity [11].

4. Global Collaboration: The collaborative approach puts together researchers, clinicians, engineers, and policymakers globally shall fuel innovation and advance the adoption of CNN-based technologies in diabetic eye care. Through the creation of collaborations between different disciplines and the sharing of best practices, we can help ease the global burden of DR and improve the vision health of many individuals worldwide.

13.8 CONCLUSION

CNNs have been fighting a good fight to conquer the scope of diabetic eye care. From diagnosis to management of DR, they have revolutionized the game. The path from manual screening techniques to a CNN-based automated system represents a significant paradigm transition, offering unmatched precision, speed, and scalability in the search and classification of the DR–related eye pathology from retinal images. Nevertheless, the integration of CNNs is not limited to simplification of the diagnostic process, while it has also opened the door to personalized medicine, equal access to healthcare, and positive results.

The criticality of CNNs in automating the DR diagnosis cannot be overemphasized. Through Deep Learning approaches, CNN models can scan through wide arrays of retinal images with accuracy and consistency, making early classification of DR-related abnormalities like microaneurysms, hemorrhages, exudates, and neovascularization possible. As a result of the early detection of these eye diseases, timely interventions and treatments are applied, which then lower the risk of the conditions progressing and causing irreversible blindness. Besides that, CNN-based systems can also reduce physical burden on healthcare professionals, especially in resource-scarce conditions, and hasten screening results by performing rapid and reliable screenings.

Thus, for enhancement, there is an immense open possibility for the CNN-based DR classification systems in the future. Integrating multi-modal imaging, personalized risk assessment, and telemedicine technologies comes as an interesting innovation opportunity. Interpretability and transparency in CNN models provided will boost clinicians' trust and acceptance. Meanwhile, personalized medicine strategies will be adjusted to the needs of individual patients in order to improve the effectiveness of the therapy and patient results. Also, the democratization of diabetic eye care via telemedicine integration and POC devices will bring screening services to indigent communities and distant places, thereby narrowing the gaps in health care access and minimizing disparities in vision.

Undertaking this trip of creativity and unity requires us to acknowledge the collective work of scientists, doctors, engineers, and policy makers globally. Multidisciplinary collaboration, knowledge exchange, and ethical reflection are the key aspects for the advancement of developments of the Deep Learning-based solutions and responsible deployment in the context of diabetic eye care. With a focus on these principles and through tapping the transformative power of CNNs, we can completely redefine how we detect and manage DR, as an approach that will directly facilitate improvement in vision health and quality of life for the millions of people living with diabetes on a global scale.

REFERENCES

1. Sardar, T. H., Das, S., & Pandey, B. K. (2017). Explainable AI (XAI): Concepts and Theory. In Om Prakash Jena, Mrutyunjaya Panda, Utku Kose (eds.), *Medical Data Analysis and Processing Using Explainable Artificial Intelligence* (pp. 1–18). CRC Press.
2. Sardar, T. H., Faizabadi, A. R., & Ansari, Z. (2017). An analysis of data processing using Mapreduce paradigm on the Hadoop framework. *International Journal of Emerging Research in Management and Technology*, 6(5), 26.
3. Rajesh, E., Basheer, S., Dhanaraj, R. K., Yadav, S., Kadry, S., Khan, M. A., … & Cha, J.-H. (2023). Machine learning for online automatic prediction of common disease attributes using never-ending image learner. *Diagnostics*, 13, 95.
4. Abràmoff, M. D., Lavin, P. T., Birch, M., Shah, N., & Folk, J. C. (2010). Pivotal trial of an autonomous AI-based diagnostic system for detection of diabetic retinopathy in primary care offices. *NPJ Digital Medicine*, 3(1), 1–8.
5. Sardar, T. H., Muttineni, A., & Ranjan, R. (2024). The Future of Big Data in Customer Experience and Inventory Management. In Tanvir Habib Sardar & Bishwajeet Kumar Pandey (eds.), *Big Data Computing* (pp. 233–248). CRC Press.
6. Theerthagiri, P., Ruby, A. U., Chandran, J. G. C., Sardar, T. H., & Shafeeq, B. M. A. (2024). Deep SqueezeNet learning model for diagnosis and prediction of maize leaf diseases. *Journal of Big Data*, 11(1), 112.
7. Khatun, A., & Sardar, T. H. (2025). Cryptography Algorithms to Prevent Different Security Attacks. In Keshav Kumar & Bishwajeet Kumar Pandey (eds.), *Next Generation Mechanisms for Data Encryption* (pp. 35–46). CRC Press.
8. Sardar, T. H. (2024). Reflecting on a decade of evolution: MapReduce-based advances in partitioning-based, hierarchical-based, and density-based clustering (2013–2023). *Wiley Interdisciplinary Reviews: Data Mining and Knowledge Discovery*, 14, e1566.
9. Sundarakumar, M. R., Salangai Nayagi, D., Vinodhini, S., Vinayaga Priya, S, Marimuthu, M., Basheer, Shajahan, Renoald, A. Johny. A heuristic approach to improve the data processing in big data using enhanced Salp Swarm algorithm (ESSA) and MK-means algorithm. *Journal of Intelligent & Fuzzy Systems*, 47(3), 1–18. https://doi.org/10.3233/JIFS-231389
10. Sardar, T. H., Sarkar, R., Ahmed, S. J., & Bandyopadhyay, A. (2023, May). A Novel Ensemble Methodology to Validate Fuzzy Clusters of Big Data. In *Proceedings of the Fourth International Conference on Trends in Computational and Cognitive Engineering: TCCE 2022* (pp. 267–278). Springer Nature, Singapore.
11. Subbarao, E., Gite, P., Sharma, A., Vyakaranam, L., Sardar, T. H., Taqui, S. N., … & Kalam, M. A. (2023). Investigation of solar energy for urban areas and metropolitan communities using machine learning. *Electric Power Components and Systems*, 618, 1–11.

14 Epidemiology and Transmission Dynamics of SARS-CoV-2

J. Ramaprabha, K. Deeba, D. Vathana, D. Vanusha, Tanvir Habib Sardar, and F. Syed Anwar Hussainy

14.1 INTRODUCTION TO SARS-COV-2

14.1.1 Overview of SARS-CoV-2 and COVID-19

SARS-CoV-2, the single pathogen, is responsible for the Coronavirus Disease-2019 (COVID-19), a pandemic that has been transforming the health and the economies of the nations all around the globe. This virus belongs to the coronavirus family, a group of viruses, all referred to by their crown shape observed under an electron microscope due to spike (S) proteins, which sets them aside. These viruses can give rise to any of the following symptoms: a respiratory or gastrointestinal disease, a liver or central nervous system one [1].

Severe Acute Respiratory Syndrome-Coronavirus-2 is a particular type of enveloped, positive-sense and, of course, single-stranded RNA virus. The S-gene encodes the structural protein of the virus, which includes, S protein, E protein, M protein, and N protein as the key components of the corona structure. The viral S glycoprotein is the protein that mainly takes part in the virus's interaction with the human cells that it invades. This ability is because it bonds to the angiotensin-converting enzyme 2 (ACE2) receptor lying on the cell surface, especially in the respiratory passage. Such an interaction enables the viral entry into a cell host, which commences the infection [1].

The COVID-19 pandemic commenced in late December 2019 with the initial signs of symptoms identified in Wuhan city, Hubei province, China. Just 4 months after the first case emerged, the disease broke up globally with the WHO designating it a pandemic on March 11, 2020. Moreover, COVID-19 shows asymptomatic or mild manifestations, ARDS, multi-organ dysfunction, and death. Also, many of them are age and relative-sensitive, as well as have high influence on a situation with some common health concerns [2].

The main transmission mode for coronavirus is that of a respiratory droplet that is released during coughing, sneezing, breathing, and speaking, which is expelled from a person who is infected. Transmission by the airborne route is also being documented, most especially in enclosed spaces with poor ventilation, and as surface contact. As per the World Health Organization [1], "the main transmission routes of

 DOI: 10.1201/9781003600947-14

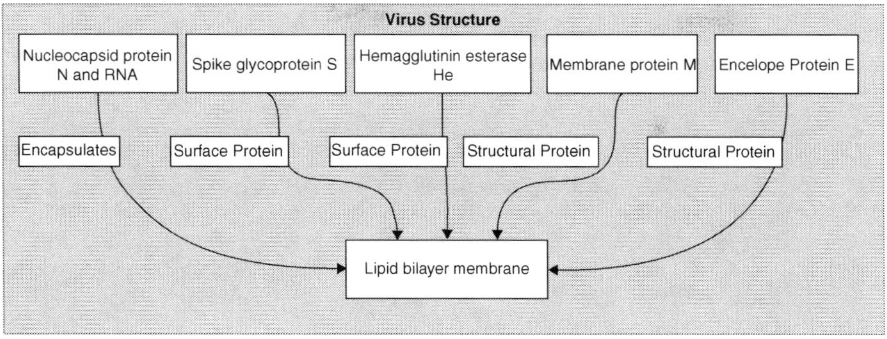

FIGURE 14.1 Structure of SARS-CoV-2.

COVID-19 have yet to be definitively understood. Transmission through respiratory droplets generated when an infected person coughs, sneezes, or speaks is thought to be the main means of transmission." [3]

In global practice, anti-COVID-19 public health efforts hold a record, for instance, mass testing, contact tracing, and self-isolation facilities, air and travel restrictions went into routine, and it has led to the rapid production and dissemination of vaccines. Such initiatives have attempted to slow down transmission, minimize negative impact on vulnerable populations, and plan a way not to crush healthcare providers with skyrocketing numbers of cases [3]. Figure 14.1 shows Structure of SARS-CoV-2.

14.1.2 Historical Context and Comparison with Previous Coronaviruses

Coronaviruses are a broad group of viruses that spread diseases in both humans and animals. It is a known fact that, in humans, different members of coronaviruses lead to various types of respiratory infections, including the common cold, milder respiratory infections like Middle East Respiratory Syndrome (MERS), and more severe fatal pneumonia syndromes such as Severe Acute Respiratory Syndrome (SARS). Since the 21st century, the world has witnessed the third time that a coronavirus of high pathogenicity crossed borders of species and infected humans as in the case of SARS-COV in 2002 and MERS-COV in 2012 [4,5].

SARS-CoV (2002–2003): In November 2003, SARS-CoV originated in Guangdong Province, China. The virus had its origins in bats and was likely passed to civet cats before entering the human population. According to the data obtained, during the global outbreak, the number of cases exceeded 8,000, with 774 deaths. The case fatality rate was around 10%. SARS-CoV contamination was curbed by using measures like quarantine, travel restrictions, and the screening of travellers. No new cases of SARS disease have been the cause of global concerns after the last outbreak in 2004 [6].

MERS-CoV (2012-present): The virus called MERS-CoV the first time was discovered in Saudi Arabia back in 2012 and is thought to be spread among humans via camels. The virus factors in with intermittent outbreaks, sources from within the Arabian Peninsula supplying approximately 2,500 reported cases and 858 deaths as per the last report. During the MERS outbreak, the case fatality rate reached 34%, which is way higher than that of the SARS-CoV infection. Transmission from person to person is also possible by the SAR-CoV or SAR-CoV-2 pathways, although less frequent [3].

SARS-CoV-2 (2019-present): Being an indication of the virus, SARS-CoV-2, wandering around Wuhan, China in December 2019, was a reason for the widespread global outbreak, which led to the continuing pandemic, which is COVID-19. Unlike SARS-CoV and MERS-CoV, SARS-CoV-2 made a transition to highly efficient human-to-human transmission, which caused a pandemic killing millions of people. The virus has two most paramount difficulties for any continuation efforts, which include the ability to leap so effortlessly more than the common human and the fact that one can be an asymptomatic carrier or a carrier who is having pre-symptoms of the virus [3].

14.1.2.1 Comparative Analysis

- Origin: All three are zoonotic from their bird carrier hosts, with the bats being their ultimate source. It is supposed that SARS-CoV and SARS-CoV-2, respectively, were introduced to humans via intermediate hosts (civet cats for the former and pangolins for the latter). In contrast, MERS-CoV is linked to camels.
- Transmission: SARS-CoV-2 shows higher transmissibility (R0) compared to SARS-CoV-1 and MERS-CoV, which are the reasons for its pandemic characteristics. SARS-CoV and MERS-CoV were also just some of the viruses known to have very limited human-to-human transmission mainly in healthcare-related and occupational circumstances.
- Fatality Rate: MERS-CoV leads this group with the highest case fatality rate, followed by SARS-CoV, but SARS-CoV-2 performs poorly in general although it has resulted in a higher number of deaths by virtue of its rapid spread.
- Global Impact: SARS-CoV-2, unlike its predecessors SARS-CoV and MERS-CoV, has been a much more pervasive global problem than any of these diseases, causing infections, deaths, and economic diseases, halting economic production, health, and curtailing day-to-day schedules [7]. Figure 14.2 shows the Comparative Timeline and Characteristics of SARS-CoV, MERS-CoV, and SARS-CoV-2.

14.1.3 Initial Identification and the Global Response

The first detections of SARS-CoV-2 date back to December 2019, when there were some reports in Wuhan, Hubei Province, China, describing pneumonia clusters of a yet unknown cause. Among its first outbreaks, patients appeared who had some symptoms that didn't match known viral respiratory infections, so they became a cause of concern for Chinese health authorities and the World Health Organization (WHO). On January 7th, 2020, Chinese researchers found and retrieved a novel coronavirus (later referred to as SARS-CoV-2) from the patients via genetic sequencing, in connection with a seafood market that seemed to be the location of the first epidemiological event associated with COVID-19 [4].

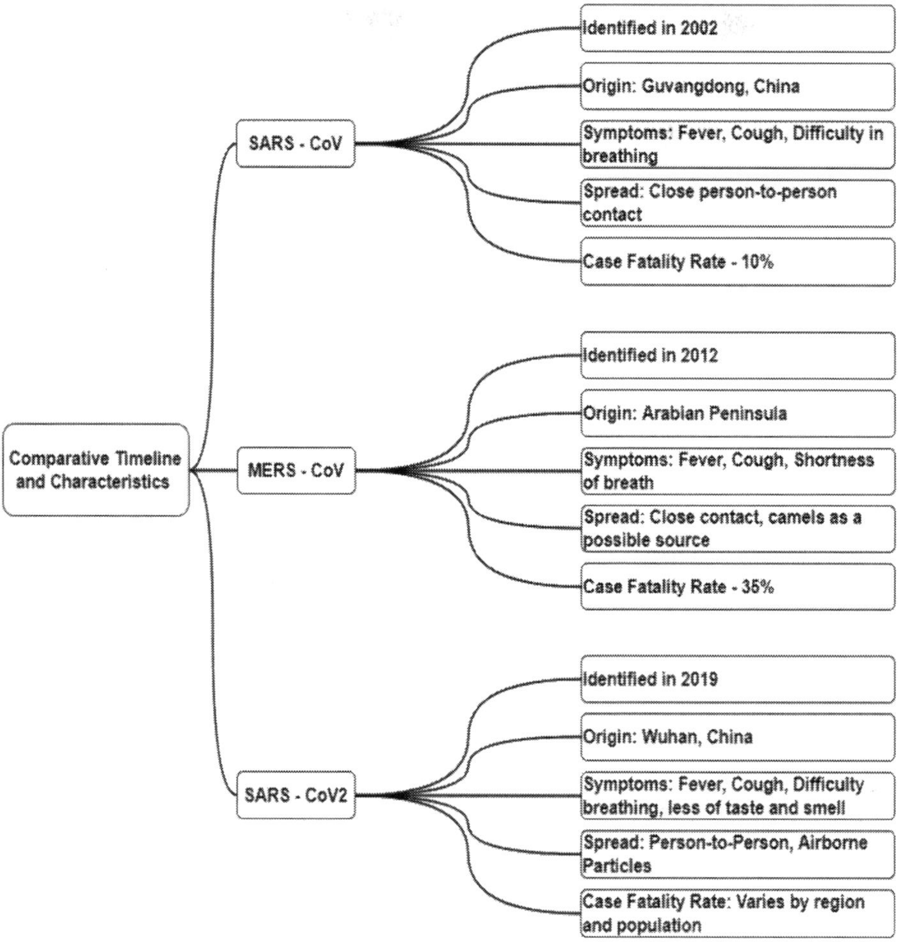

FIGURE 14.2 Comparative timeline and characteristics of SARS-CoV, MERS-CoV, and SARS-CoV-2.

Due to the spread of SARS-COV-2 across the globe, the response of the countries and regions was different and slow, but varied significantly. On January 30, 2020, probably the most important day in the spread of this virus, the WHO declared a Public Health Emergency of International Concern. Later, on March 11, 2020, it was officially recognized as a pandemic by the WHO. This statement, the international resources and energy were focused on fighting against the virus to stop its spread all over the world. However, some factors influenced their effectiveness including the emergency preparations, government policies, and people's will to follow these health measures.

14.1.3.1 Key Components of the Global Response Included

- Travel Restrictions and Lockdowns: It was the case that curtailing travel as well as imposing quarantine and lockdowns at the national level was adopted by many countries with the purpose of slowing the rate of infection. The three measures can be called the apex of the globalization effect on the world transition in terms of mobility, the economy, and personal lifestyle.

- Testing and Contact Tracing: Massive testing with strict contact tracing was picked as the initial trend to separate quarantine and isolation. All countries notched up successes in these areas to varying extent as some countries got the grip on the COVID's spurious spread through intensive testing and tracing programs.
- Public Health Measures: Requests and advice for wearing masks, keeping distance, and washing hands are everywhere. Create your own impactful sentence using our AI language generator platform. Engage with friends, family, and others to share and discuss a wide range of topics and issues. Such measures agreed that public adherence with those measures and the government enforcement were the factors that could determine whether they were effective.
- Vaccine Development and Deployment: The worldwide community of scientific researchers put in an incredible feat, which involved not just developing and testing, but also instrumenting vaccines against SARS-CoV-2. Some vaccines had already been approved for emergency use within one year of the pandemic's emergence, which represented an incredibly important accomplishment in healthcare and science.
- Economic and Social Support: The governments in different economies rolled out various programs of economic support and stimulus to ease the blow of the pandemic on business, employees, and the disadvantaged people.

14.1.3.2 The Global Impact

Though the pandemic brought both strengths and weaknesses in global and nationwide healthcare responses, it also emphasized that preparedness was essential to take up health challenges and that collaboration and equity were needed for the worldwide establishment of health responses to emergencies. Inequalities in access to vaccines, public health institute structure, and community perception of health measures all lead to inequity in the pandemic's consequences among countries. Figure 14.3 provides the timeline of initial identification and global response to SARS-CoV-2

14.2 VIROLOGY OF SARS-COV-2

14.2.1 Structure and Genome of SARS-CoV-2

SARS-CoV-2 is a kind of Coronaviridae family which are contained in a layer, infected by positive RNA, and eventually disintegrated into just a single loop. The structure and genome of SARS-CoV-2 lie at the core of our knowledge on this viral infection including its pathogenicity and other measures. Thus, understanding of how it is infectious, which treatments can help in the battle against it and how a vaccine would be developed depend on our knowledge on the structure and genome of SARS-CoV-2 [7].

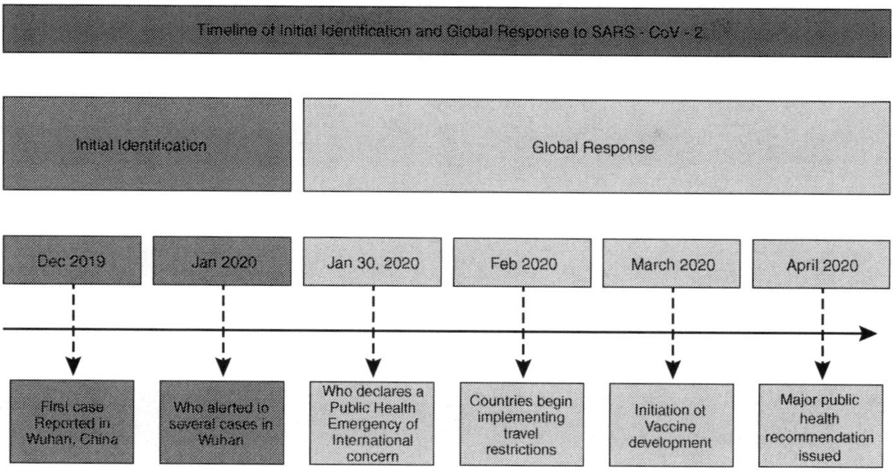

FIGURE 14.3 Timeline of initial identification and global response to SARS-CoV-2.

14.2.1.1 Structural Components

- Spike (S) Protein: The S protein is a trimeric glycoprotein that is located on the surface of the infection-causing particle known as coronavirus, the most recognizable shape. In fact, the protein is of utmost importance for the virus' infection of host cells, as it was shown to bind to the Angiotensin-Converting Enzyme 2 (ACE2) receptor on the cell surface. By this process, the virus takes hold of the cell. The s protein is the main target for antibodies, specifically the ones that recognize it and the vaccine production occurs [4].
- Envelope (E) Protein: An E protein is a tiny, envelope-inserted membrane protein critical for virus particle assembly as well as release. This is through different mechanisms; the virus can transit from one cell to another lifespan to the next and will induce a level of host inflammatory response.
- Membrane (M) Protein: The M protein is the protein most possessed by the virus in structural assemblies. It gets to build the shell of the virus (envelope or not), and without that, the entire assembly process (and interaction of all remaining structural proteins) would be impossible.
- Nucleocapsid (N) Protein: The N protein serves for the attachment to the RNA genome of the virus. This complex is packed into the viral particle inside of it. It is not only implicated in viral replication, but also controls the involved host cell's response to infection.

14.2.1.2 Genome Organization

SARS-CoV-2's genome is around 30,000 nucleotides long, a lot longer than the average RNA virus genome which makes it unique. The gene sequence is what usually distinguishes all known coronaviruses and two-thirds of their genome is occupied for the viral replicated-transcriptase complex. There is 16 ns proteins (nsp1 to nsp16) that are responsible for viral RNA synthesis and are in complex. The rest of the genome encode structural proteins (S, E, M and, N) and several other auxiliary proteins that help the virus to interfere with the host's immune system response [4].

The nucleic acid sequence of the genome of SAR-CoV-2 has an almost 80% similarity with SAR-CoV, and it is about 50% with MERS-CoV, and it is a stand-alone virus. Despite these specific differences, it has remarkably put it into the same category as the family.

14.2.1.3 Mutations and Variants

In a context of high diversity, SARS-CoV-2 coronavirus has been characterized and has shown several variants from the beginning of the pandemic. Part of these mutations occur in places of the S protein structurally important for the virus to infect and replicate, which in turn generate new variants with different transmissibility, virulence, and antigenicity that influence the potency of vaccinations and therapeutics [4]. Figure 14.4 shows the SARS-CoV-2 Structure and Genome.

14.2.2 Mutation and Evolution of the Virus

14.2.2.1 Mutation Basics

Now, your change refers to the genetic mutation. The changes that happen in the genome of the SARS-CoV-2 RNA are the mutations that the virus acquires. The nucleic acids of RNA viruses, such as SARS-CoV-2, have a higher mutability rate than that of DNA viruses. This happens because of the incompetence of RNA polymerase, which is the enzyme that copies RNA from the viral genome during replication. However, mutations are not all created equal; some are harmless or even harmful for the virus's fitness level, whereas others may be beneficial, for instance, by increasing its transmissibility or by allowing it to bypass the immune response.

14.2.2.2 Mechanisms of Mutation

- Point Mutations: These are the mutations that involve the single-nucleotide replacement of the viral RNA codons. A particular point mutation can lead to amino acid alteration of different viral proteins with possible influence

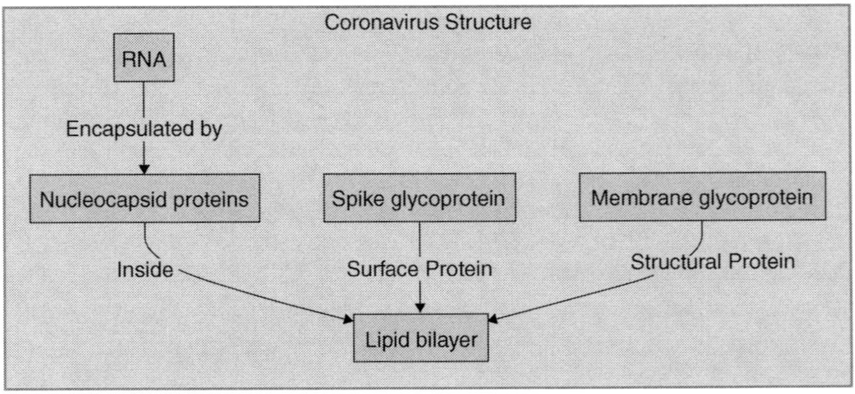

FIGURE 14.4 SARS-CoV-2 structure and Genome.

on the virus's properties, including effective binding to host receptors or evading immune response.

- Recombination: This is where the genetic material of two or more viruses swaps places or even shares certain fragments. The process happens when two different viruses attack the same host cell, and genetic material from the two viruses is mixed. In turn, recombination of strains could generate a new viral strain having unique phenotypes.

14.2.2.3 Evolution of SARS-CoV-2

The propagation of SARS-CoV-2 is governed by natural selection, which results in variants that display crowding and streamlining capability growing more common in the population. This reminds me of the evolutionary milestone, which had consequences for several variants of concern (VOCs) that have different characteristics than the original strain identified in Wuhan. The mutated VOCs, with their signature gene changes, may burgeon into greater transmissibility, more severe disease, and lower immune response to vaccination [7].

14.2.2.4 Variants of Concern

- Alpha, Beta, Gamma, and Delta: However, some of the VOCs at this stage exhibited an increased transmissibility and for certain of them an altered disease severity pattern or lower efficacy level of some available vaccines [8].
- Omicron: As early as December 2021, Omicron, followed by its subvariants, was identified. They evidently show an increase in the evading process through the immune system, and the transmission rate is higher, but the illness will be less severe among people.

14.2.2.5 Implications for Public Health

The preferment and genetic transformation of SARS-CoV-2 has many public health accessories, cornerstones of surveillance, testing, treatment, and immunization. The development of new genomic variants is an unending process that calls for continuous monitoring and assessment. The resultant variants are evaluated to establish their impact on the transmission, treatment, and epidemiology of the coronavirus. Also, periods when new variants emerge would require new vaccines and therapeutical approaches, along with the ones that are already available [3].

14.2.3 Variants of Concern and Their Characteristic

Multiple variants of concerns (VOC) have developed, and each one of them has a different genetic mutation altering the properties of this virus, for example, the transmissibility, harmfulness, and the effectiveness of the vaccines and therapeutics that are used for its treatment. This comprehension of variants is very fundamental in that it helps provide a direction for public health policy and the developing of vaccines.

14.2.3.1 Key Variants of Concern

1. Alpha (B.1.1.7): The A variant commonly referred to as the Alpha variant with a large number of mutations such as N501Y, among many others,

increases binding affinity to the ACE2 receptor and thus, the infectivity of the virus. However, it leaded to rise of hospitalization rates, but the efficacy of the vaccine stayed on the same level.

2. Beta (B.1.351): Identified in South Africa, highly transmissible Beta presents K417N, E484K, and N501Y mutations. By mutation, this pathogen's ability to transmit has been significantly increased as well as its immune evasive properties resulting in less effective control of the disease.
3. Gamma (P.1): Found in the same order as it was detected in Brazil, Gamma has some of these elements in common with Beta such as N501Y and E484K, which allow it to transmit with ease and partially escape immune responses.
4. Delta (B.1.617.2): Delta variant, which first appeared in India, has become dominant across the world following its replacement for the original one by certain mutations like L452R and P681R which have made it highly transmissible and produced heavier viral loads in the patients. It kept some resistance against vaccine-resistant immunity, especially demanding for these people who hadn't completed vaccination with both doses appointed for this vaccine.
5. Omicron (B.1.1.529) and its subvariants (e.g., BA.1, BA.2, BA.4, BA.5): With omicron being the most recent one among all the variants that showed up by the last month of 2021, it is known to have a large number of mutations including in spike protein, that improve the virus's ability of immune evasion with a high level of breakthrough infections among vaccinated and previously infected individuals. Even if Omicron strains are often the cause of disease outbreaks, they currently have less severe consequences in comparison with the earlier variants of concern.

14.2.3.2 Impact on Public Health

These VOCs, since their arrival, have unique features for global health, thus requiring detail adjustments in public health policies, immunization formulation, and treatment protocols. Shaving and sending research campaigns are continuously scanned to see how SARS-CoV-2 is developing, making sure preventions against new variants are still effective.

14.2.3.3 Vaccine Adaptation

Vaccine producers are constantly measuring the vaccine potency of previously developed vaccines against the new strains and producing new antigenic targets if need be. Along with that of an advancement in the creation of multivalent vaccines capable of protecting against any variation, the booster shots can increase the resistance to those emerging variants.

14.3 EPIDEMIOLOGICAL CHARACTERISTICS

14.3.1 Modes of Transmission

It is absolutely a fact that in order to apply adequately efficient public health efforts to prevent transmission of COVID-19, one must understand the transmission modes of the SARS-CoV-2 virus. Of the transmission routes, SARS-CoV-2 can mostly transmit mainly through respiratory droplets and aerosols from infected individuals, but other routes of transmission may also be identified.

1. Respiratory Droplet Transmission: The main way SARS-CoV-2 spreads is through diffusion of the respiratory droplets containing these viruses that are released from the infected individual when they sneeze, cough, breathe, or simply open their mouth to talk. The droplets of various sizes are the ones produced while an individual is talking, coughing, or sneezing. The large droplets fall down quickly, while smaller aerosols (droplets) may stay suspended in the air for long durations. Transmission commonly involves short distances allowing for mobility within a distance of approximately 6 feet (2 meters), but the distances can vary depending on whether in moist environments or indoors with poor ventilation [9].
2. Airborne Transmission: Through airborne transmission, the organism transporting a virus is contained not only in aerosols expelled but also inhaled by individuals who are further away after the person infected leaves the area. Recent science on SARS-CoV-2 viability in aerosols shows that it can remain active in aerosols for a relatively short time under laboratory conditions, thus making airlines a dangerous means of transportation and poorly ventilated rooms a potential source of transmission.
3. Contact Transmission: Transmission by contact occurs when an individual touches a contaminated surface (fomite) and then the same person puts the virus in the mouth, nose, or eyes. Although contact spread is regarded as less frequent than the respiratory droplets/airborne transmission, that does not reduce the implication of the virus's ability to live for a longer time on the surfaces, stressing the significance of hand hygiene and surface disinfection.
4. Other Possible Modes:
   - Vertical Transmission: Thus, SARS-CoV-2 is highly unlikely to be transmitted from pregnant mothers to their infants, but this may happen sometimes although the incidence appears to be very low.
   - Faecal-Oral Transmission: SARS-CoV-2 RNA can be detected in the faeces of infected people, and it has even been proposed that this transmission route regards faecal-oral transmission, though confirmed cases of this are quite limited.

14.3.1.1 Public Health Implications

The knowledge about these different transmission pathways has led to the development of individual and environmental level masks to reduce saliva and aerosol drops, social distancing to prevent close contact transmission, air ventilation to lower airborne infection risks, and sterilization to reduce the risk from contact with fomites. Figure 14.5 shows the Modes of Transmission of SARS-CoV-2.

14.3.2 Incubation Period and Infectious Period

14.3.2.1 Incubation Period

SARS-CoV-2 incubation period remains of utmost importance for understanding epidemiology of the disease, as well as setting up the requirements for mandatory quarantines.

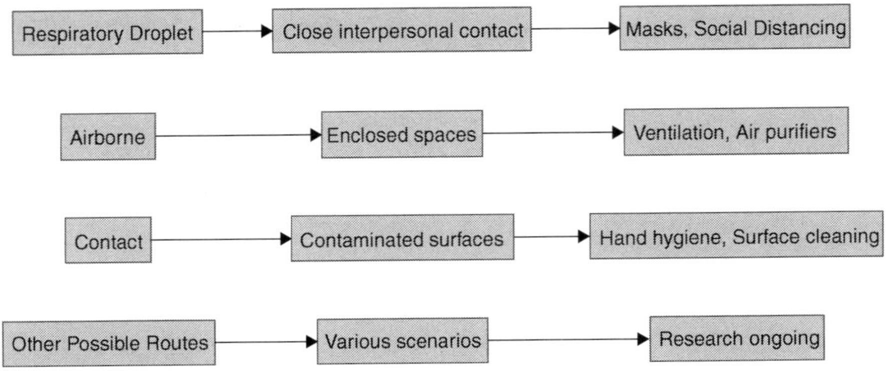

FIGURE 14.5 Modes of transmission of SARS-CoV-2.

Normally, the incubation period for acute respiratory syndrome is about 4–5 days, but sometimes it varies between 2 and 14 days. This variable feature poses a challenge in terms of planning at the testing and quarantine stages. The virus can transmit even without exhibiting symptoms.

The incubation period varies due to several factors, such as whether the infected person has a strong immune response or whether they were exposed to high doses of virus. A shorter incubation period can possibly be due to a higher dose of the virus, and a longer incubation period would most likely be because of a lower dose among patients or a stronger immune response.

14.3.2.2 Infectious Period

COVID-19 has an infectious period where an infected person can spread the virus to others, and this time is also one of the vital elements of the pathogen epidemiology. It is noteworthy that people who had COVID-19, in addition to two days before the onset of symptoms, remain infectious up to the time when they are no longer able to transmit the virus to other people. This (the isolation) for symptomatic individuals is usually around ten days from the start of the first symptom for the categorized mild to moderate cases, but this can vary depending on the severity of the case or an individual's weak immune system (an immune system that cannot work properly).

People without symptoms can also spread the disease, normally while the infection is still spreading from 2 to 10 days after contact. Nonetheless, experts believe that the apex infectious nature of the virus takes place during two kilo days before the manifestation and 2–3 days after [6].

14.3.2.3 Implications for Public Health

The knowledge of the incubation and contagious periods is the first step towards limiting the spread, as mentioned by SARS-CoV-2. It provides guidance for conducting testing, isolating, and quarantining, allowing for the identification and isolation of cases that can then prevent further spread. Furthermore, it is a symptom to take into account the significance of rapid testing and the transmission by the asymptomatic and pre-symptomatic stages.

14.3.3 Case Fatality Rates and Factors Affecting Severity

14.3.3.1 Case Fatality Rate

The case-fatality rate (CFR), namely the ratio of the death cases to the total confirmed cases of the disease, is a measure used to evaluate the severity of the disease. For SARS-CoV-2, the CFR has been changing considerably around various areas of time and location, and this could be related to health infrastructure availability and the information about comorbidity. Worldwide, the CRF count ranges from barely 1% to more than 5%, but for details, Cultural Research Network Asia-Pacific (CRANET) will show that it is not only these numbers but also the context of the applied testing rate. It also includes the age distribution of the population and the effectiveness of treatment.

14.3.3.2 Factors Affecting Disease Severity

Several factors influence the severity of COVID-19, ranging from individual characteristics to healthcare system factors: Several factors influence the severity of COVID-19, ranging from individual characteristics to healthcare system factors:

- Age: Older adults are at a huge disadvantage as they face a much higher risk of severe disease or death caused by COVID-19. The risk rises dramatically with age; older people, especially those aged 60 years or more, who are more likely to be afflicted, are the ones affected more than younger people.
- Comorbidities: The underlying health problems, for e.g., cardiovascular disease, diabetes, chronic pulmonary disease, hypertension, and cancer, have been reported to link with an increased chance of having the severe form of COVID-19.
- Sex: Men have a higher chance of developing severe illness and dying compared to women, though we are not entirely aware of the reasons behind this difference, and this may involve factors such as immune response, medication, lifestyle behaviour, and contribution by underlying diseases.
- Socioeconomic and Environmental Factors: Overcrowded housing, unwillingness to stay close to others, and limited medical opportunities that may result in contracting the infection at an earlier stage, and with the severity may drop within this group.
- Healthcare System Capacity: The selection in the system and level of preparedness to manage COVID-19 patients, including access to critical care services and mechanical ventilation, is a major determinant of whether the outcomes are great or not. The extremely high rate of cases due to poor healthcare systems accounts for higher CFRs.

14.3.3.3 Implications for Public Health

This knowledge is important in deciding on public health exit rate measures and where resources should be going. Putting in place specialized strategies to shield the population groups at greatest risk, including immunization and barrier preventive measures in care establishments, should be crucial as a response to COVID-19.

14.4 GLOBAL SPREAD AND IMPACT

14.4.1 Timeline of the Pandemic's Spread

14.4.1.1 Early Outbreak (December 2019 - January 2020)

The first cases, which later would be finally recognized as COVID-19 cases, were reported in Wuhan City, Hubei Province, China, in December 2019. The first batch of patients later traced it to a seafood market, as a probable animal-borne virus origin. At the same time, cases from other areas outside Wuhan came to attention, later followed by those from different countries, marking the initiation of international transmission.

14.4.1.2 Global Recognition and Response (January 2020 - March 2020)

In WHO (World Health Organization) terminology, the event was classified as a Public Health Emergency of International Concern (PHEIC) on January 30, 2020. Among them, the first record of the disease was tracked in some countries across Asia, Europe, and North America. In March 2020, the WHO stated that COVID-19 is a pandemic, meaning that the virus is now affecting all continents. Nations worldwide have enacted containment measures that limit the transmission of the disease, such as travel restrictions, lockdowns, and social distancing measures.

14.4.1.3 Rapid Global Spread (March 2020 – December 2020)

In combating the virus, COVID-19 spread faster than every metric used initially. The existing healthcare systems of numerous countries had been tremendously burdened, and the world economy had to deal with a lot of issues, such as the closure of businesses and a free flow of money, and an increase in unemployment. During that time, it turned out that besides the original virus, several new strains of the virus also appeared, causing additional problems with controlling the outbreak.

14.4.1.4 Vaccine Development and Rollout (December 2020 Onwards)

The first COVID-19 vaccines authorized for emergency use were manufactured in the last quarter of 2020, less than a year after the virus was identified. Vaccination campaigns started in many countries, prioritizing nurses, doctors, and older people, whose health was undermined because of Disease X. This vaccine rollout represented a great leap forward in the conquest of the pandemic, even though it brought some distribution issues, reluctance, and the emergence of new variants associated with the issue [10].

14.4.1.5 Continuing Challenges and Adaptation (2021 Onwards)

While the world was on the path of recovering from COVID in 2021 and 2022, the problem of new variants emerged, which brought the existing failed vaccine policy to the fore. Campaigns of booster vaccination and modifications to the relevant public health measures were some allied programs, as well as efforts to improve global vaccine fairness.

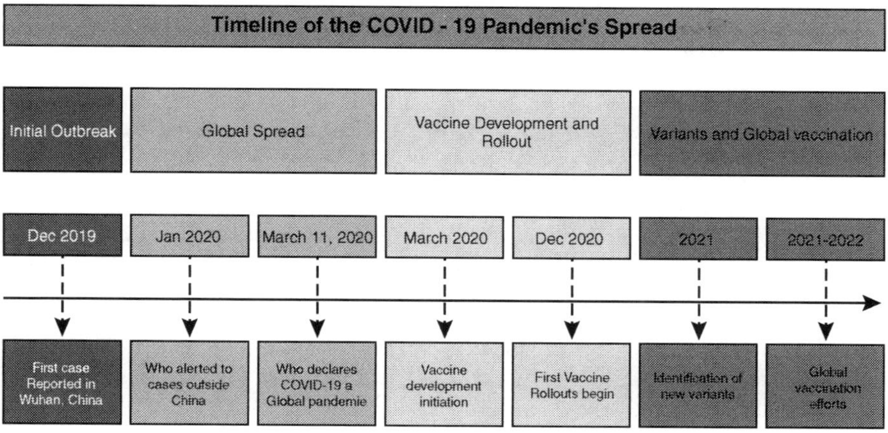

FIGURE 14.6 Timeline of the Pandemic's spread.

14.4.1.6 Implications for Global Health and Society: Implications for Global Health and Society

The COVID-19 pandemic is no longer just a temporary threat, but an ongoing epidemic that has made changes both globally and persistently in health, economy, and daily routine. The role of global cooperation, the need for public health readiness, and equitable access to health facilities, which are inclusive of vaccines, have been underscored. Figure 14.6. depicts the timeline of the pandemic's spread.

14.4.2 Impact on Healthcare Systems Worldwide

The COVID-19 pandemic has induced a withdrawal effect and pushed healthcare systems globally to their limits, with the sudden emergence of new situations requiring the systems to adapt and become flexible. The effect on health care organizations has been extensive, covering service delivery, health staff, resource branching, and management of non-COVID-19 medical conditions.

14.4.2.1 Strain on Healthcare Facilities and Workers

- Overwhelmed Facilities: A massive rush of the Coronavirus-infected patients in the accommodations of the hospitals and healthcare facilities was faced globally, often beyond their expected capacity, especially in intensive care units (ICU). This situation resulted in the lack of beds, ventilators and other necessary equipment, which forced the construction of new facilities on the grounds of existing health care facilities or the creation of new temporary field hospitals.
- Healthcare Worker Stress and Burnout: With COVID-19 putting people through the ultimate adverse situation, healthcare workers, namely doctors, nurses, and support staff have been forced to deal with the endless physical and mental pressure. They have endured the sweat and tears of 12-hour

duties, infection threats and the depths of despair into higher mortality of the patients, which affected many of the physicians and nurses badly leading to burnout and mental health problems.

14.4.2.2 Disruption of Routine Healthcare Services

- Delayed or Cancelled Non-COVID Care: In most areas, cancellation of surgeries, routine screenings, and hospital visits for outpatient services has led to patient affairs with chronic diseases and other peculiar needs being interrupted.
- Impact on Mental Health Services: Deemed a concomitant principle, the need for mental health services shot up multiple times in the midst of the pandemic, whereas there was restricted access to these services due to lockdowns in place and the diversion of resources towards the COVID-19 response.

14.4.2.3 Innovation and Adaptation

- Telehealth Expansion: The pandemic is the most important factor driving telehealth adoptions and enhancing remote consultations and receiving care services. Such a change would, however, offer long-term implications which based on enlarging the accessibility, but at the same time generate questions about the quality of care and health equity.
- Changes in Healthcare Delivery: The healthcare systems have still evolved in terms of the development of new procedures to prevent the spread of viruses, such as infection control, patient triage, and the management of healthcare setups, among others.

14.4.2.4 Global Disparities

- Resource Allocation: The pandemic has shown that disparities of healthcare resources and infrastructure between countries and parts of states were highlighted and made quintessential. Richer countries usually had no problems mobilizing resources, while low-income and middle-income countries barely managed to cope with the crisis.
- Vaccine Access: Vaccines for COVID-19 were rolled out globally, exposing a colossal disparity in vaccine access between wealthy and poor countries, as most of the doses were secured first by the rich ones. Leaving behind countries in poor conditions to vaccinate their populations.

14.4.3 Socioeconomic Consequences of the Pandemic

The pandemic worldwide has displayed drastic socio-economic influence, with a broad impact on various economies, education systems, job markets, and societies as a whole. This diversified nature and the correlation of the effects clearly present that a health issue is the trigger and the source for the multifaceted social and economic ones.

14.4.3.1 Economic Downturn

- Global Recession: COVID-19 then snowballed into an International Recession with Most Countries' GDP Contracting. Some of them, including travel, tourism, hospitality, and retail, however, have been crippled by the pandemic, forced to make cutbacks in finances and even close operations.
- Unemployment: The general economic slowdown was scaring a lot of people away from their jobs and actually led to more and more unemployment. The impact on employment in an unequal manner comes from workers of low income, young people, as well as females.
- Supply Chain Disruptions: COVID virus has caused breakdown of global supply chains that have slowed the production and the movement of goods in carrying out their official duty. In turn, it has led to permanent shortages of fundamentals, much higher prices, and the underlying fragility of global supply chains much more than ever.

14.4.3.2 Social Impacts

- Increased Poverty and Inequality: Not only the poor but also those with low incomes were shaken up under the shadow of the economic effects of the pandemic, and also existing inequality between different countries has been seen to deepen. Low-income groups population and people in the vulnerable positions in the eyes of economic depression were risking to fall into poverty with a high-level probability.
- Mental Health Crisis: Loneliness, economic difficulties, and the strain these put on mental health were accompanied by an increase in mental health issues: anxiety, depression, as well as substance abuse, among others.
- Education Disruption: With millions of students affected, the education being closed down and remote learning is now becoming the main way of learning, a completely new learning system is the new learning environment. It worsened the internet connectivity issue of online learning, in which not all students had the necessary technology for online learning, widening the educational gaps and inequalities.

14.4.3.3 Policy Responses and Long-term Implications

- Government Interventions: The global economic recession resulted in economic policies that governments put into effect. These measures included entity companies' and individuals' financial aid, tax breaks, and policies designed to create more jobs.
- Shifts in Work Patterns: The period after the pandemic has sped up another tendency for remote work, and in consequence, it changes the workplace environment. It can have a strong, sustainable effect on working culture and urban planning.
- Reimagining Social Safety Nets: The socioeconomic problems that came to the surface because of the pandemic are the main reasons why people have such excuses as improvement of social safety nets and revisiting approaches to healthcare, employment, and social equity.

14.5 TRANSMISSION DYNAMICS

14.5.1 Basic Reproduction Number and Its Implications

The basic reproduction number, often symbolized as R0 (R naught), is a critical concept in epidemiology that measures the expected number of cases directly generated by one case in a population where all individuals are susceptible to infection. R0 provides key insights into the infectiousness of a pathogen and its potential to cause an outbreak or epidemic.

14.5.1.1 Understanding R0

- Definition: R0 represents the average number of new infections caused by a single infectious individual in a wholly susceptible population, without any active interventions (such as vaccination or social distancing) to reduce transmission.
- Implications of R0Values:
  - If R0 < 1, each infection causes less than one new infection, leading to a decline in cases over time and eventually, the disease will die out.
  - If R0 = 1, each infection causes one new infection, and the disease will persist in the population at a stable rate.
  - If R0 > 1, each infection causes more than one new infection, indicating the potential for an outbreak or epidemic as the disease spreads through the population.

14.5.1.2 R0 and COVID-19

For COVID-19, the estimated R0 has varied globally and over time, influenced by factors such as population density, social behaviour, and the implementation of control measures. Early estimates of R0 for SARS-CoV-2 were generally between 2 and 3, suggesting a high potential for spread. However, effective public health interventions, including social distancing, mask-wearing, and vaccination, can significantly reduce the effective reproduction number (R), bringing it closer to or below 1.

14.5.1.3 Implications for Public Health

- Threshold for Herd Immunity: The concept of R0 is closely linked to the idea of herd immunity, the proportion of the population that needs to be immune (through vaccination or natural infection) to prevent ongoing transmission of the virus. A higher R0 means a larger proportion of the population needs to be immune to achieve herd immunity.
- Guiding Public Health Interventions: Understanding R0 helps public health officials design and implement effective measures to control the spread of an infectious disease, tailor strategies for different settings, and allocate resources efficiently.

14.5.2 Super-spreading Events and Their Impact on Pandemic Dynamics

Super-spreading events (SSEs) play a significant role in the dynamics of infectious disease outbreaks, particularly in the context of the COVID-19 pandemic.

These events occur when an infected individual disproportionately transmits the virus to a large number of other people, significantly exceeding the average transmission rate captured by the basic reproduction number R0.

14.5.2.1 Characteristics of Super-spreading Events

- High Transmission Rate: SSEs rely on a single source of infection, which can be either biological, as in the case of elevated viral load, or behavioural, which may result in association with others that can result in increased exposure.
- Settings and Conditions: SSEs can result when people are enclosed for prolonged periods in limited space and they do not have proper ventilation, often crowded indoors. Studies have shown that gatherings and locations such as parties, religious services or the ones connected to meatpacking plants were often the sites of fear-spreading episodes during the COVID-19 global health crisis.
- Contribution to Overall Spread: However, most such infected persons transmit the virus to few or no others; yet, SSEs can account for a significantly large share of all transmission within an epidemic, which, consequently, creates uncontrolled propagations of cases as well as speeds up the overburdened health systems.

14.5.2.2 Impact on Pandemic Dynamics

- Accelerating Spread: The SSEs are really powerful to facilitate the viral spread; this may be the cause of a few days of rapid increase in the reported new cases greater than the capacity of public health to respond to such incidents and the healthcare system.
- Geographic Spread: SSEs, unfortunately, can also act as a vehicle for the virus to travel, as while people participate in similar activities at the event, they may disperse and take the virus to their home areas.
- Heterogeneity in Transmission: The super-spreader effect highlights the nature of individual variability in the rate of transmission, putting aside the theory that all infected individuals are responsible for the epidemic to a degree.

14.5.2.3 Public Health Implications

It is crucial to study and control SSEs if we aim to handle the crisis in COVID-19 epidemiology. Measures to prevent SSEs include: Measures to prevent SSEs include:

- Targeted Interventions: Enforcing tough rules and prohibitions in high-risk sites or scenarios. Your journey to becoming a professional content writer has just begun. Get ready to put in hours of hard work and dedication to master your writing skills and make your mark in the industry.
- Contact Tracing and Quarantine: Identifying and isolating offensively minded individuals straight away would prevent further spread of infection.
- Public Awareness: Knowing the risks and behavioural factors related to the occurrence of SSEs, the government can educate people on what to avoid to minimize the prevalence.

14.5.3 Mathematical Models of Transmission and Their Applications

The construction of infectious disease transmission models is a key means of addressing issues regarding the development, the course of an outbreak, and epidemiological burden assessment in public health interventions. The complexity of such models can be different to suit the needs of a given scenario. From obviously a simple model that captures the basic dynamics of disease spread to a complex model that has parameters that all contribute to disease transmission [5].

14.5.3.1 Types of Models

1. SIR Models: Moreover, the simplest and most widespread framework that mathematically represents three groups of the population is called Susceptible-Infected-Recovered (SIR) model. This model divides the population into three compartments: those susceptible to the infection, those currently infected, and those who have recovered and are now medically immune. The model utilizes differential equations to describe the speed at which individuals switch between the compartments; these equations will give us an idea of the spreads dynamics and the herd immunity outcomes.
2. SEIR Models: As a further development of the SIR model, the Susceptible-Exposed-Infected-Recovered (SEIR) model, a new "Exposed" compartment is added to accommodate people who are already infected but are not yet infectious. Moreover, this feature assists in the modelling of diseases that come with a prolonged period between exposure and manifestation, e.g., COVID-19.
3. Agent-Based Models: These models are stylized versions of real-world situations. They are based on agents (those who stand for individuals) and their actions in a given space that takes into account the variation among people and their individual behaviours. "Agent-based models" could be used to showcase highly sophisticated social networks and motion trends, thereby they are mostly be of great help in meeting the challenge of deploying certain mechanisms such as social distancing or vaccinations.

14.5.3.2 Applications of Mathematical Models

- Forecasting: Models could simulate case numbers (both totals and in days), hospitalizations and deaths under various circumstances, helping both policymakers and healthcare systems to anticipate the future needs and invest resources accordingly.
- Evaluating Interventions: Models can mimic different public health measures, including vaccination, social distancing, or lockdowns, and then, they can tell us about their performance in reducing the transmission, and we can use the information in decision-making.
- Understanding Disease Dynamics: Models help elucidate key aspects of the disease's transmission dynamics, such as the basic reproduction number (R0), the impact of super-spreading events, and the thresholds for achieving herd immunity.

14.5.3.3 Challenges and Limitations

The precision of the mathematical models is highly dependent on the quality and availability of information, which is used for making the assumption about the characteristics of the disease, human behaviour and the ability of models to understand the complexity of the transmission in a real as well as a spatial world. Thus, model the forecast as a guide to any actions rather than the exact forecast for the future.

14.6 SURVEILLANCE AND DETECTION

14.6.1 Testing Strategies and Diagnostic Tools

Diagnostic testing has arguably been one of the key factors for case monitoring, tracing, and pandemic control in the struggle against COVID-19. Testing has improved the epidemiological knowledge and monitoring capacity and helped health authorities locate the contaminated individuals so that they can be isolated and prevent the re-emergence of the outbreak.

14.6.1.1 Types of COVID-19 Tests

1. Molecular Tests (RT-PCR): The RT-PCR test, based on reverse transcription, is a diagnostic test that is considered the most precise for the detection of SARS-CoV-2 RNA presence. It is highly precise and accurate, as a feature that makes the technology more reliable because it helps in the early recognition of active infections. Relying on RT-PCR testing necessitates that laboratories, their processing may result in test results being delayed.
2. Antigen Tests: These tests recognize the particular protein from the virus and are the advantage of a fast result. The good news is they can even give the result in a very short time span, which is usually not more than a few minutes. Although the sensitivity of antigen tests is lower than that of RT-PCR and the exam may miss some cases, due to their speed and simplicity of the test, they are appropriate for screening systems [14] and point-of-care testing on a large scale.
3. Antibody Tests (Serology): SARS-CoV-2 antibody tests focus on assessing two important things: first, whether an individual has previously been infected by the virus by detecting antibodies produced in response to the virus, and second, whether there is an immune response against the disease. These tests cannot diagnose a current infection but still they are definitely a good indicator of the level of virus spread in the population and people who have developed the immunity to it.

14.6.1.2 Testing Strategies

- Symptomatic Testing: Individuals displaying the symptoms that characterize COVID-19 are tested, and results are used to confirm the infection, making medical management as well as isolation possible, which helps to control further spread [11].

- Contact Tracing and Testing: The tracing of contacts of positive cases focused on regular testing of those who are close contacts to confirmed cases, regardless of their symptoms, to variably and hastily identify new infections.
- Mass Testing in Outbreaks: As a next step, the spreading can be controlled by encouraging localized mass testing campaigns in order to identify and isolate cases, including asymptomatic people, in case of a large number of cases in a particular area.
- Random Sampling: Testing a random sample of the population will provide a sense of the level of cases linked to airborne transmission as well as the infectious but asymptomatic ones. This data will be essential in informing public health decisions [12].

14.6.1.3 Implications for Public Health

Effective testing strategies are vital for:

- Getting to the point faster of detecting the cases, and isolating them to avoid transmission.
- Knowledge which comprises the virus's subtle characteristics, such as scattering around, virus exposure, and the influence of interventions.
- Data from health surveillance systems -used for updating clinical management of patients and allocation of health resources [12].
- Focus on following the strides on disease before fully opening the island to the border to ensure that it is safe and win the trust of the tourists.

14.6.2 Contact Tracing and Its Effectiveness

Contacts tracking is a key public health method that is used to establish, inform about, and survey individuals who were near the healthy individual and thus might have been infected with a contagious disease and potentially could develop further disease spread. Traceability of coronavirus has been a major factor in controlling the spread. By doing that, the life and the health of individuals staying with us is unlike in the past when they died young due to health complications.

14.6.2.1 Process of Contact Tracing

1. Identification: When there is a confirmation that an individual is a positive COVID-19 case, public health workers will then take the next steps, which are to identify all close contacts of this individual, with close contact being defined by the time the individual is expected to be infectious.
2. Notification: The interactions of those contacts who are potentially exposed can be notified immediately, to give them time to seek medical help, with full respect for their privacy.
3. Quarantine and Monitoring: Contacts must stay in place to prevent transmission and are put under supervision in case of the manifestation of COVID for 14 days starting counting starting from the day of the last contact with the affected person.
4. Testing: While the exposed contact may not be experiencing any symptoms or related health problems, it is possible they are carrying the virus. If this is the

case, then they should immediately go and get tested for the COVID-19 virus. Hence, there is a probability of further spread and isolation of other cases.

14.6.2.2 Effectiveness of Contact Tracing

The effectiveness of contact tracing in controlling the spread of COVID-19 depends on several factors:

- Speed: Quick supplier of contacts and isolation are among the important processes if the spread of infection is to be prevented. Long waiting times also decrease much of the impact of contact tracing.
- Comprehensiveness: Finding all probable contacts calls for complete interviewing and investigation, which, as was shown by the COVID-19 pandemic, is no time for the highly infectious pathogens, particularly when asymptomatic transmission is involved.
- Public Cooperation: Reporting of contacts and testing will be successful only as much as the public is ready to do what is demanded of them, such as testing and quarantine. Trust exists with public health authorities, and understanding of the process matters, too.
- Technological Support: Digital systems and applications will amplify the potential of manual tracing by providing opportunities for information gathering about people's movements to be done in a faster manner. Although they guarantee anonymity of users and privacy of their data, they raise the question of equity [12].

14.6.2.3 Challenges in Contact Tracing

- Asymptomatic Transmission: This feature facilitates disease transmission because when people unknowingly carry the virus, no abnormal signs of infection appear, making it harder to isolate them from the general population.
- Resource Intensity: The resource constraints, such as manpower and technology support in many places, hinder comprehensive contact tracing and therefore undermine health care response and control of the disease, especially where there is a widespread infection.
- Public Health Infrastructure: Unless the public health infrastructure and resources are standardized in different parts of the regions, there could be a lack of uniformity in the successful contact identification.

14.6.3 Role of Technology in Surveillance and Detection

Unlike before the Coronavirus outbreak, it is now crystal clear that technology indeed is of great relevance to the advancement of disease surveillance and prevention. Sufficiently technological and fast creation comes along with innovative technological solutions that have been used everywhere worldwide to track the spread of the virus and support contact tracing efforts, conduct testing, and monitor compliance with health measures. Such technologies, which include mobile apps and analytics, in a broad sense, and AI, along with genomic sequencing, in a narrow sense.

14.6.3.1 Mobile Applications for Contact Tracing and Exposure Notification

- Contact Tracing Apps: Of course, mobile apps have been designed to help accelerate the process of conversationally tracking down individuals. By using Bluetooth, the apps can record a summarized contact log without identifying parties involved. If, on the other hand the COVID close contact was confirmed later on, the exposed persons will be alerted.
- Exposure Notification Systems: These systems, together with the main technology companies, create a standard for public health experts to install their exposure notification software on their devices. As a result, this will make it possible for the communication of pandemic response messages to be widely spread across different regions.

14.6.3.2 Data Analytics and AI for Outbreak Prediction and Management

- Predictive Analytics: The Machine Learning algorithms and AI models that analyse tons of data can locate and manage health incidents by setting the precision of the response and centralizing of resources [12].
- AI in Diagnosis: AI-enhanced technologies that use medical imaging, e.g., chest X-rays and CT scans, as diagnostic aids, help doctors to classify the illness and serve as an additional tool to the outdated testing methods.

14.6.3.3 Genomic Sequencing for Virus Tracking

- Viral Genomics: With the help of modern genomic sequencing profiling, the virus is also examined for the occurrence of mutations and the appearance of new variants. This knowledge is necessary for a comprehensive perception of patterns of transmission, the creation of vaccines, and their preferred efficiency.
- Global Data Sharing Platforms: Examples of such tools include GISAID, which enables the global sharing of viral genomic sequences by researchers as well as spurring the direction of ad hoc collaborative projects towards the fight against new threats.

14.6.3.4 Digital Health Passports

- Verification of Health Status: Through digital health passports/certificates, people can store the vaccination records or test results anywhere they go, making safer traveling, a safe entry to public spaces, and participating in social interactions possible, all of these just by verifying the health status using a privacy approach.

14.6.3.5 Challenges and Considerations

- Privacy and Security: Data privacy and cybersecurity issues that follow up with technology implementation in public health surveillance systems are a serious concern. That is to say, those technologies shall respect individual rights and laws on data protection [12].

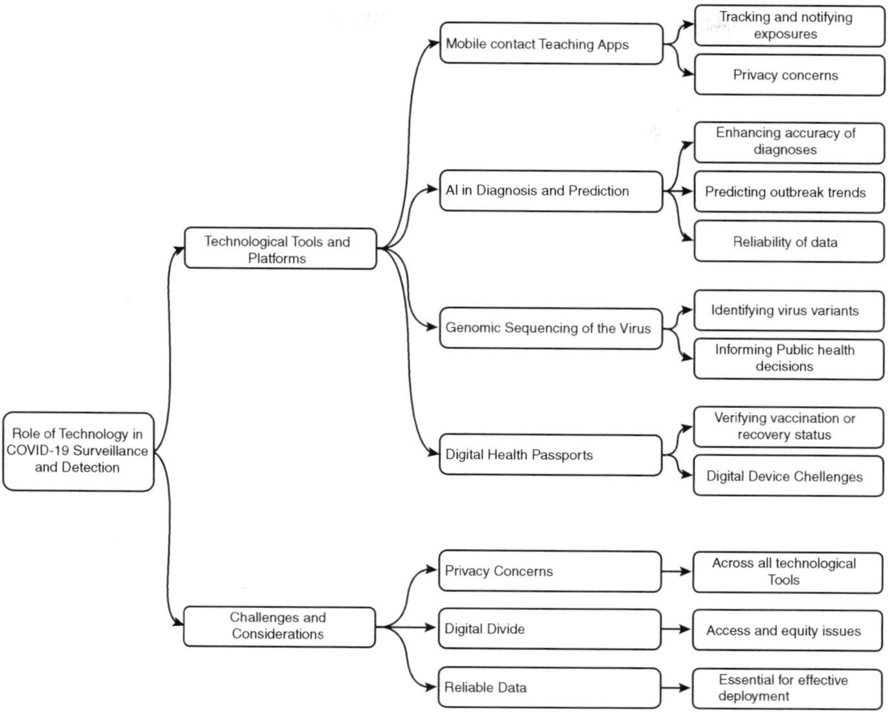

FIGURE 14.7 Role of technology in COVID-19 surveillance and detection.

- Digital Divide: Distribution of technology is not fair, with discriminatory usage leading to pervasive health inequality, which can be even aggravated. Social inequality is the main obstacle to the guaranteed availability of digital health services.
- Reliability and Accuracy: Technology solutions are effective supplied the tools are accurate and their reliability doesn't compromise the users' compliance or willing to use them. The cracks of misinformation and mistrust may lead to effective undermining of those efforts. Figure 14.7. provides the role of technology in COVID-19 surveillance and detection.

14.7 PREVENTION AND CONTROL MEASURES

14.7.1 Non-Pharmaceutical Interventions and Their Efficacy

Activities outside medical treatment (non-pharmaceutical interventions, NPI for short), which are called so as they involve no drug prescriptions or taking them, are also essential in slowing the spread on seasonal and pandemic influenza and, as a result, COVID-19. NPIs are synonymous as community mitigation strategies or approaches. Such measures maybe even more crucial before every single member of a given community has been vaccinated or a more specific treatment becomes generally used.

14.7.1.1 Types of NPIs

1. Personal NPIs: Everyone should implement measures for self-protection, such as frequent handwashing with soap, hand sanitizer use, and using a tissue or inner elbow to sneeze or cough. Other individual protective actions that are meant to be taken in public places include always wearing masks where appropriate like where there is a need to maintain distancing.
2. Environmental NPIs: These initiatives include cleaning and disinfection of shared spaces that are frequently touched among other measures such as improving air flow in enclosed settings to avoid contamination.
3. Social Distancing Measures: Policies which mandate to maintain physical distance for the rate of transmission of the virus to decrease, such as keeping the distance of at least six feet from others out of the house, avoiding crowded places, and reducing the number of gatherings. These restrictions include closed workplaces and schools, shift to home office, and moving to an online setting for learning.
4. Travel-related NPIs: Steps of decreasing the transmission of the virus through travel include: travel warnings and advice, the monitoring of travellers, and the quarantine or even bans of travel itself.

14.7.1.2 Efficacy of NPIs

- Reducing Transmission: Studies suggest that when NPIs are well developed and implemented, they can efficiently prevent the transmission of COVID-19 among people by minimizing the number of face-to-face interactions. During NPIs, we can also notice a drop in the shape of the epidemic curve that shows up as fall in the number of newly infected, in a short span of time.
- Preventing Healthcare System Overload: Thus, NPIs help in slowing down the spread of the virus, preventing the overwhelming pressure on the healthcare system to cope with the large number of patients that require hospital treatment and critical attention at the same time.
- Complementary to Pharmaceutical Interventions: NPIs alongside vaccines and treatments can be vital allies, providing, however, that a two-pronged approach is needed because they act as multiple levels of control and, particularly, in the early stages of a pandemic and with variants that partially evade vaccination-induced immunity.

14.7.1.3 Challenges and Considerations

The deployment of NPIs has to deal with challenges, one of which involves the economic outcomes granted by the business closures and the emotional and psychological effects caused by extended social detachment. The people's adherence to NPIs may differ greatly depending on communication, trust in the public health authority and the high perceived mortality of the pandemic. Adapting NPIs to the context of use and enforcing them justly are called for to prevent the emergence of negative effects and to optimize their effectiveness.

14.7.2 Vaccination Strategies and Vaccine Rollout

Vaccine production and distribution against coronavirus were a decisive factor in the most crucial struggle that occurred worldwide since the beginning of the pandemic. Vaccination action has been different in different states and countries, with factors like the availability of vaccines, public health infrastructure, demographics of populations, and disease burden being their influencers. There is no doubt that timely, reliable vaccination strategies are a necessary and sufficient condition to reach herd immunity, decrease the extent of devastating consequences, and finally bring the outbreak under control.

14.7.2.1 Key Components of Vaccination Strategies

1. Priority Groups: The vaccines in limited quantities were provided first to the high-risk population that included first people working in healthcare, then the older generation, and finally people with pre-existing health conditions. The above groups need to be the main target of such preventive measures so that the death rate can be reduced and healthcare systems buffered.
2. Mass Vaccination Campaigns: The vaccines have been rolled out in countries in stages, small groups of people have been targeted, and a mass vaccination programme was eventually rolled out. Quite commonly, the mentioned strategies often relied on the use of large centralized sites for mass vaccination, mobile units, and outreach in communities to further increase accessibility.
3. Equity Considerations: Making certain that the vaccines will be distributed equitably within a country, as well as at a global level, turned out to be the thorniest issue. Methods that combat equity have been those of targeting communications and distribution efforts in vulnerable communities, as well as international initiatives such as COVAX to ensure that all vaccine-dependent countries, even the poorest, have support delivered to them.
4. Public Education and Communication: The effective way to end vaccine hesitancy is to bring transparent communication regarding vaccine's safety, effectiveness, and the advantages of vaccination into the strategy of vaccines rollout. Through the years, public information campaigns have been directed not only to motivate the public from wrong ideas but also to build trust in the products of the vaccines.
5. Adapting to Variants: The original outbreak of SARS-CoV-2 variants required an adjustment in the vaccination strategies, for instance, the booster doses and the development of updated vaccines to give people's immunity that can withstand the current circulating and emerging variants.

14.7.2.2 Challenges in Vaccine Rollout

- Logistical Challenges: The cold chain storage necessary for some vaccines, distribution challenges, as well as the requirement for two-dose regimens for most vaccines (with the exception of Johnson & Johnson's vaccine) have created significant logistic issues, particularly in remote and resource-deficient areas.

- Vaccine Hesitancy: Partly due to the hesitancy and resistance against the vaccine from some people, embodied by their misconceptions of the truth, lack of trust in authorities, or fears about the safety of the vaccine, the goal of getting everyone vaccinated has not yet been reached.
- Global Inequities: Disparities in access to the vaccine between countries prove once again an issue of global health equity. Richer countries grabbed the maximum of early vaccine supplies, leaving many poorer countries, which had to wait for their turn, were left after a long vaccine delay.

14.7.3 Public Health Policies and International Cooperation

The current COVID-19 pandemic exposes a profound truth: without resilient public health policies and uncrackable pandemic borders, it is impossible to cope with major global health risks. The essential conditions for an effective response strategy are interdependence among countries, the adoption of modes of sharing resources, knowledge, and technology in the handling of the virus, and in the reduction of the damage brought about by it.

14.7.3.1 Public Health Policies

The public health policies make a high contribution to the pandemic response, as they cover a spectrum of measures which include limiting transmissions, providing protection to vulnerable groups, and reinforcing the hospital service system. Key policy areas include:

- Surveillance and Detection: We need to develop a sound surveillance system, which can track SARS-CoV-2 and respond to new cases and outbreaks.
- Non-Pharmaceutical Interventions (NPIs): Let's do this by such activities as keeping distance, using masks, and limiting travel to enhance the reduction of transmission.
- Vaccination Campaigns: Development and deployment strategies for vaccination in the population aimed to establish a high level of immunization in it.
- Healthcare System Strengthening: Apart from the mentioned above, we should not fail to improve healthcare facilities, recruit more healthcare workers, and provide necessary healthcare supplies like medical equipment and personal protective clothing.
- Public Communication: To act as a source of reliable, timely information to educate the public and to support their adherence to public health directives that are aimed at preventing and eradicating misinformation.

14.7.3.2 International Cooperation

As COVID-19 is a global problem, it means that no one country can endeavour to overcome it on its own therefore, the need for international collaboration is paramount to overcome the shared challenges. Key areas of cooperation include: Key areas of cooperation include:

- Sharing of Information: Timeously disseminating epidemiological data, research findings, and practices on the dissemination level constitutes issues in international coverage; therefore, communication will help in fostering knowledge across countries and international organizations [2].
- Joint Research Efforts: Team up with global pharmaceutical and healthcare entities on the design and production of vaccines, treatments, and diagnostics, including the sharing of genetic material and clinical trial data [12].
- Vaccine Equity: Doing so jointly by COVAX, which is made to support low- and middle-income countries, helps achieve equitable distribution of vaccines globally.
- Cross-Border Health Measures: Formulating a health surveillance system and putting travel policies and border controls in place to stop the spread of disease while at the same time not disturbing the normal flow of traffic and trade.
- Financial and Technical Support: Money-rich generating countries and international institutions are entrusted with the responsibility to provide financial and technical assistance for the COVID-19-response efforts in resource-short settings.

14.7.3.3 Challenges and Barriers

- Political and Economic Considerations: The national interests and economic considerations that might prevent international cooperation and equitable resource sharing among the needy of the world sometimes become obstacles in their way.
- Vaccine Nationalism: The market of vaccines becomes competitive; the poor nations often pay for only a small number of doses when wealthier states are able to buy large quantities of them.
- Variability in Public Health Capacities: The diversity in the scale of public health infrastructure and capabilities across countries adds difficulty of the effective implementation of shared response measures.

14.8 SPECIAL TOPICS IN TRANSMISSION DYNAMICS

14.8.1 Impact of Environmental Factors on Transmission

Along with other factors that mainly involve environmental settings, we set forth the role of the environmental factors in the transmission dynamics caused by infectious diseases, such as the coronavirus. This environment can affect the virus's stability and resilience in various settings, the users' behaviour and safety, and the control measures' aptness. The judicious comprehension of environmental factors is core to bringing about effective interventions and strategies to slash the rate of transmission of the infection.

14.8.1.1 Key Environmental Factors Affecting COVID-19 Transmission

1. Temperature and Humidity: The research reveals that temperature and humidity are components to consider in maintaining the virility and the spread of the SARS-CoV-2. In spite of an absence of unequivocal evidence the climate change may potentially become the source of the virus's spread or may not, some studies suggest that the temperature would impact the stability of the virus. The virus will be more stable in the cold and drier environment, while in the warm and humid conditions, it will probably be less so. Nevertheless, in terms of total heat emissions, the combined effect of these factors is almost certain to have a smaller impact than humans (e.g., inside spaces in the colder area).
2. Air Quality: Studies suggest that people living in areas with poor air quality, such as those with high levels of air pollution, have a higher propensity to get sick, or even worse, their respiratory infections may become more severe, increasing vulnerability to diseases like COVID-19. Besides the issues associated with the particle matter in contaminated air pollution, these may also carry viral particles, further increasing the risks of contracting pandemic diseases.
3. Ventilation and Air Circulation: Enclosed spaces with low or no air circulation are connected to the increased spread of COVID-19 on the grounds that there is less air exchange and better transmission of the virus. Spaces, like ships, aircraft, and designed buildings, that recirculate air, facilitate the spread of aerosol viral particles over a greater distance than previously recognized.
4. Ultraviolet (UV) Radiation: The UV-C (a type of UV light) has been shown to have the ability to inactivate viruses, which also includes coronaviruses. Sunlight may diminish viral viability on surfaces and air, but do not believe that direct sun is efficient in protection methods for personal protective equipment's or person to person transmission prevention.
5. Built Environment: Utilizing, designing, and constructing high-rise buildings either for residential, office, educational, or public purposes tends to create transmission risks. These sets can be especially predisposed to the virus, providing a focus for transmission in corridors, common areas, and frequently touched surfaces.

14.8.1.2 Mitigating Environmental Risks

- The role of air management in reducing contamination states the need for guidelines and ventilation throughout the premises.
- Promoting outdoor centres or participating in activities that are conducted in the outdoor or fresh-air space.
- The changes in the seasonal influence and environmental conditions need to be considered, resulting in appropriate public health emergency measures.
- Through raising awareness to reduce air pollution, a strategic long-term solution for better respiratory functionality and the ability to fend off respiratory infections can be attained. Figure 14.8 shows the impact of environmental factors on COVID-19 transmission.

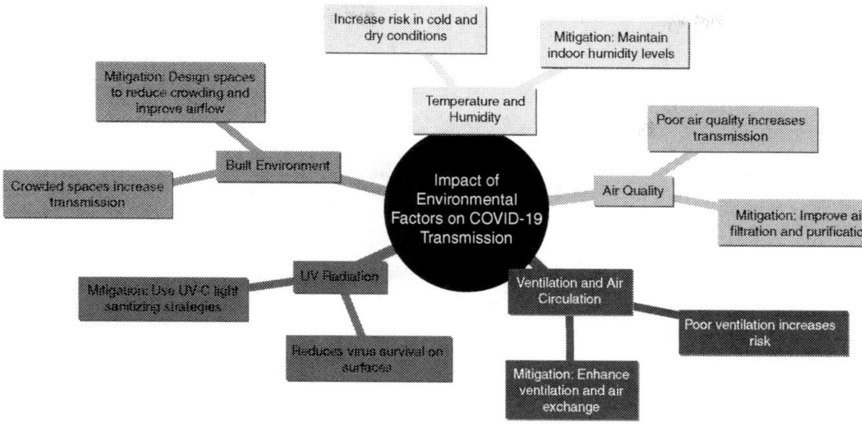

FIGURE 14.8 Impact of environmental factors on COVID-19 transmission.

14.8.2 Transmission Dynamics in Specific Settings (e.g., Schools, Nursing Homes)

The transmissibility of COVID-19 has to be understood for specific settings, such as schools and old age homes, in which targeted interventions are designed to protect vulnerable classes of people and to curb the further spread of the virus. The ecosystems, which have their own secret stuff, are very challenging as they are formed of their own setups of populations, behaviours, and physical structures.

14.8.2.1 Schools

Elementary schools are busy places where children share classrooms, confined desks, a gym, and often play together in the absence of the COVID-19 pandemic. Factors affecting transmission in schools include: Factors affecting transmission in schools include:

- Population Density: High concentration of students and employees provides a possibility to connect with one another and spread the virus widely.
- Age-Related Factors: However, young children, especially little ones, tend to find putting on and abiding by the mask-wearing and social distancing principles problematic. The data supports the proposition that kids under ten years old could be protected and could get less infected and spread the virus compared to grown up people [12].
- Behavioural Patterns: Moreover, resource sharing, community site ventilation, and building common areas might be a potential factor too.
- Mitigation Strategies: Successful actions that were taken include the wearing of masks, physical distancing, charting (grouping students to keep a steady movement of individuals), ventilation improvements, regular and detailed cleaning of the campus, and remote learning during outbreaks.

14.8.2.2 Nursing Homes

Residents of nursing homes are equally at the risk of a more critical course of COVID-19 disease owing to age and other underlying medical conditions. Key considerations for transmission in nursing homes include:

14.8.2.3 Key Considerations for Transmission in Nursing Homes Include

- High-Risk Population: Patients often have already had some previous issues that further increase the chance of getting a more serious inconvenient.
- Close Quarters: Communal spaces and touching among residents and health assistants will contribute to their high share of transmission.
- Staff Movement: Staff who are role-players in areas with higher chances of infection can also inadvertently spread the virus from one resident to another.
- Mitigation Strategies: Specific approaches to combat this include perfecting infection prevention practices such as regular testing of residents and workers, limitations for visitors, and prioritizing vaccinating residents and employees.

14.8.2.4 Mitigating Transmission Risks

Both settings require tailored public health interventions to mitigate transmission risks, including: Both settings require tailored public health interventions to mitigate transmission risks, including:

- Enhanced Hygiene Practices: Highlighting hand hygiene and proper respiratory practice.
- Environmental Modifications: Creating an adequate ventilation system and redesigning the setup so that some areas can be emptier.
- Policy Adjustments: Policies to support people to stay home sick, quarantine, and isolation as appropriate.
- Communication and Education: Facilitating clear communication of risks, making them visible, and providing prevention strategies to all stakeholders.

14.8.3 Asymptomatic and Pre-symptomatic Transmission

While the outbreak of the COVID-19 pandemic has been one of the most difficult to contain, finding solutions to asymptomatic and pre-symptomatic transmission has been one of the greatest challenges. The means of transmission are so complex that the possibility of identifying, isolating, and treating obvious infections becomes more difficult because traditional symptoms function less.

14.8.3.1 Asymptomatic Transmission

- Definition: On the other hand, the term asymptomatic spreading means that certain uninfected persons have come from individuals who are infected but never show any symptoms during the course of this virus.

- Impact: These 'carriers' of the virus can be an unwitting transmitter of disease without prior symptoms, additionally spreading the infection within the community. Examined to various results, people with no symptoms may share the virus with others more or less than those with symptoms, but they are recognized as less contagious than individuals with symptoms.

14.8.3.2 Pre-symptomatic Transmission

- Definition: Before-symptomatic transmission, the virus will be transmitted from those who are infected to others before they have any particular symptoms. Before the individuals know that they are sick and can spread the infection, they are in the pre-symptomatic phase.
- Impact: There is growing evidence of a peak of viral load either right at the onset or just before the onset of the symptoms you see, which means that individuals who haven't even experienced any symptoms are still very contagious. This stage could be 2–10 days long, leaving the virus a chance to spread rapidly among people at home, amusement parks, a workplace, or at school.

14.8.3.3 Implications for Public Health Strategies

- Universal Masking: In view of the fact that a part of the population may be able to transmit without showing typical symptoms, recommendations for universal masking in public spaces, such as inside that lack social distancing options, have been propagated.
- Widespread Testing: Limitations to COVID-19 spread is one of the strategies that has been done by including people under testing, not only the ones who have symptoms but also those who have had close contact with anyone who had a positive COVID-19 case [2].
- Contact Tracing: The proper identification of transmission of the coronavirus requires contact tracing to include those individuals who can convey the coronavirus yet still be asymptomatic and pre-symptomatic by advising close contacts of confirmed cases to quarantine regardless of the symptoms.
- Physical Distancing and Quarantine: Reiteration on the fact that physical distancing and isolation were not only necessary during the tight lockdown but also played a preventive role in high-risk settings like long-term care facilities and apartment blocks.

14.9 FUTURE DIRECTIONS

14.9.1 Long-term Implications of SARS-CoV-2 for Global Health

While the COVID-19 pandemic, which was caused by SARS-CoV-2 at the initial stages, had an immediate and great one in terms of public health, healthcare delivery, and pandemic preparedness. Leads to a global transformation process in the way we address such a challenge. In addition, this pandemic has, in the long run, broader ramifications that affect not only different areas of society but also a whole range of institutional mechanisms of global health.

14.9.1.1 Healthcare Systems Strengthening and Preparedness

- Resilience of Healthcare Systems: Pandemic has emphasized the need for gourmet healthcare systems that can shoulder the pressure of surging demands for care and be flexible enough to continue to provide quality care to patients who have not been infected with the coronavirus.

14.9.1.2 Infrastructure Like Healthcare, Workforce Preparation and Supply Chain Construction Are Necessary

- Universal Health Coverage: COVID has brought to light the areas and sections that have a shortage of health services. Thus, there is a drive for ideology to be sponsored in the future by the quest for universal health coverage, ensuring that all people are covered by the healthcare services they need, regardless of the financial loss.

14.9.1.3 Surveillance, Research, and Innovation

- Integrated Surveillance Systems: The significance of the strengthening of systems of monitoring for the goal of early identification and response to emerging pathogens should be well kept in mind. A strengthened planetary surveillance system with a focus on genomic surveillance will ensure early identification and containment of future epidemics.
- Research and Development: The feasible landmark development of COVID-19 vaccines has stirred up scientific worldwide collaboration. The research and designment have to be maintained in order to prepare to address the health threats persistently manifesting themselves as emerging infections as well as antimicrobial resistance [10].
- Digital Health Technologies: The coronavirus pandemic has provided a situation excelling all pioneers to digitize health technologies, namely telemedicine and digital contact tracing. Such developments may disrupt and change the manner in how diseases are treated along with public health and surveillance.

14.9.1.4 Global Health Governance and Equity

- International Cooperation: COVID-19 has demonstrated that health hazards are not barred by borders, but it is the outcome of enhanced cooperation among the international framework concerning health emergency preparedness and response.
- Health Equity: Pandemic has exposed and amplified deficits in health for acute diseases that are based upon social and geographic location. There is a need to resolve these disparities because they are the solid ground on which the health systems of all nations can stand up, no matter how diverse in terms of their resources, to provide fair results.
- Vaccine Equity: Having the right vaccines and other medical countermeasures go to everyone equally, in other pandemic emergencies, will ensure the health security all over the world. Steps like COVAX are perhaps a good indication of more fair distribution, but there is still more that need to be done.

14.9.1.5 Public Health Policies and Behavioural Changes

- NPIs and Public Health Guidance: Experience with the NPI practices during the COVID-19 period can affect the planning and design of the future public health policies, with regard to such viral respiratory infections.
- Behavioural Changes: During these pandemic times, many individuals' behaviours have changed, including constantly washing hands, wearing masks in certain settings. These are precautionary spontaneous behaviours and are likely to continue after hand-washing and also can change the transmission patterns of other respiratory diseases [6].

14.9.2 Lessons Learned and Preparedness for Future Pandemics

COVID-19 pandemic has proved to be a milestone event for global health that unmasked failures in public health systems, healthcare delivery of medical assistance and in coordinated response of the interstate system in a pandemic. It has not only provided lessons that may help with the planning of response strategies for the future pandemics but also vital proof to this. They encompass lessons of the past as well as the present in public health planning, experimental science, healthcare infrastructure, and global cooperation.

14.9.2.1 Key Lessons Learned

1. Rapid Response and Flexibility: There should be no doubt that a prompt and suitable strategy to face and overcome new threats is of the utmost importance. Swift and effective or viable action such as banning travel, testing, tracing contacts, and bringing in public health measures, greatly reduces infectiousness.
2. Science and Research Collaboration: A swift development of COVID-19 vaccines that saw the global scientific community work together highlighted the possibility of what science can accomplish. Research and development of diagnostic, vaccines, and treatment strategies, as well as the process of easy sharing of resources and data worldwide, had to become a big deal for new preparedness measures [10].
3. Strengthening Healthcare Systems: The disease upset health systems around the globe by refocusing attention to healthcare infrastructure, appropriate staffing ratios, and supply chains of equipment and personal protective equipment.
4. Public Health Infrastructure: A robust community health system, consisting of disease surveillance networks and a workforce for contact tracing, forms the bedrock for identifying and eradicating spikes early.
5. Equity and Access: COVID-19 gave a heightened picture of an already existing health gap, which screams out loud that it is now a critical issue that all social determinants of health are being addressed and the equity in the access to health facilities, like vaccination, diagnostics, and treatment, are really focused on.
6. International Cooperation: A good management of a pandemic has to be a collaboration among all the nations in the international community

involving the exchange of data, joint research initiatives, and support for the low- and middle-income country nations.

7. Public Communication and Misinformation: Effective communication from public health authorities with a clear, transparent, and consistent message is a key component in the fight against fraud and compliance with health regulations and guidelines. Another important aspect of the incorporation of mass media in conflict resolution processes is the provision of honest and unbiased information.
8. One Health Approach: Globally, the awareness of how human, animal, and environmental health are all linked can be viewed as a key point to identify and prevent zoonotic diseases from spreading and becoming human pandemics.

14.9.2.2 Preparedness for Future Pandemics

- Global Health Security Agenda: Implementation of the numerous Global Health Security Agenda to the stated measure and obeying the International Health Regulations (2005) ownership system for resilience and readiness.
- Pandemic Preparedness Plans: National and regional pandemic preparedness plans should be created and updated from time to time. The process of stockpiling critical materials such as medicines and formulating protocols for rapid vaccine development and distribution must be the norm.
- Simulation Exercises: Get commitment to fully implement regular simulation exercises to try and go over and improve the plan strategies to fight pandemics at the nationwide and global scale.
- Investment in Public Health: More money to develop public health systems and employees' human resource answers for sample, laboratory, contact tracing, and outbreak solution.

14.9.3 Ongoing Research and Unresolved Questions

The COVID-19 epidemic has initiated an extraordinary worldwide research effort, leading to major discoveries about the impact of SARS-CoV-2 on the human body. Although several milestones have been marked on the path of achieving our mission, answers to some vital issues are yet to be discovered, which require combined efforts from many disciplines. This is what we should be focusing on at the present moment, when COVID-19 is still here, and it is what we need to do to prevent similar crises in the future [2].

14.9.3.1 Key Areas of Ongoing Research

1. Virus Evolution and Variants: elucidation of the principles that led to the evolution of SARS-CoV-2 and the development of VOCs is competently important during the process of vaccine development and public health programs formulation. Ongoing work concerns determining mutations that might increase the virus' transmissibility, pathogenicity, or vaccination escape potential.

2. Long COVID: Investigating the symptoms endured by some individuals with the sequelae of COVID-19 and utilising the popular name "Long COVID" requires further attention. Research in progress to determine the cause, hazards, and successful remedies.
3. Vaccine Efficacy and Duration of Immunity: The success of COVID-19 vaccines in keeping people from severe illness and death is beyond doubt, but uncertainty remains around the longevity of the protection, the defence against new variants, and the necessary strategies of booster count on most people and immunizing everyone.
4. Transmission Dynamics: Hence, more research should be embarked on to establish the transmission dynamics of SARS-CoV-2 completely, whereby a combination of asymptomatic and pre-symptomatic individuals are included, which also comprises environmental factors and super-spreading events.
5. Therapeutics: Research intensifications on the efficient therapeutics for COVID-19, with special efforts on the more severe cases, remain the focus of the research program. This process incorporates repurposing existing drugs, finding new antiviral compounds, and identifying the best mode of treatment. Such treatment modes will combine anti-viral drugs with drugs used to battle the immunological consequences of the disease.
6. Social and Behavioural Aspects: The complex study leading to the purpose of understanding social, economic, and behavioural aspects of the pandemic also includes the role of public health interventions on mental health and well-being involved through guiding policy and response measures.
7. Health Disparities: The correlation between the COVID-19 pandemic and worsening inequalities in health shows that the virus has worsened health disparities. Disadvantage research focused on comprehending and eliminating factors related to the disparities will be instrumental for the purposes of attaining equitable health conditions.
8. One Health Approaches: The relationship stand of health among humans, animals, and the environment has come into light in a way to prevent zoonotic diseases from transferring from animals to human beings. This is one of the recent areas of interest and importance.

14.10 CONCLUSION

14.10.1 Summary of Key Points

The situation of coronavirus disease 2019 (COVID-19), which is induced by the SARS-CoV-2 virus, is becoming really challenging to worldwide daily life in health, economic, and social aspects. The world has gone through this crisis, dealing with a very complicated problem, which is transmission dynamics of the virus, establishing and delivering the vaccines, putting in place non-pharmaceutical interventions

(NPIs), and the institute of public health policies and international cooperation. Key points include:

- The ecology and transmission dynamics of coronavirus further emphasize the fact that the virus is able to spread rapidly and that symptomless or pre-symptomatic transmission contributes greatly to its spread.
- The global counter-measurement has really discerned that surveillance, testing strategies, contact tracing, and utilization of technology are CRUSADE resources in the handling of the pandemic.
- Vaccine campaigns and fair distribution of the often extremely rare doses have been crucial to stemming the spread of the pathogen and lessening the pandemic impact.
- The pandemic of COVID-19 has brought home to us how important it is for us to have a sophisticated public health system, an effective health care network, and to put it on the agenda of a fair kind of health care.
- Proper international collaboration and solidarity that many countries have demonstrated should be viewed as the most important elements in coping with the epidemic on such a great scale [13].

14.10.2 The Importance of Global Collaboration in Pandemic Response

The COVID-19 pandemic has indeed given us an immediate and tangible demonstration that no country can stay healthy in between the cracks of non-observance of strong health policies, which also proved that health issues don't respect borders to care only about the country boundaries. Clearly, global collaboration is one of the main aspects of sharing information; at the same time, it also provides access to different resources and technologies. The speedy race for vaccine development that marked the collaboration between countries is indeed a classic example of what one can achieve at the end of the day with cooperation between scientists. Looking ahead, the interconnected global health security networks, public health infrastructure, and equitable distribution of health resources will be key elements in precautionary steps by nations to be prepared for the next health disaster in the world.

14.10.3 Reflections on the Path Forward in the Post-pandemic World

Being so, the road ahead concerns not only how people are to fully recover from the crisis but also how the world has been transformed permanently.

As the world begins to navigate the post-pandemic landscape, several reflections emerge on the path forward: As the world begins to navigate the post-pandemic landscape, several reflections emerge on the path forward:

- Resilience and Preparedness: Changing experience of COVID-19 would be a catalyst behind such attempts as building more resilient health systems and enhancing the preparedness of the world to pandemics. Investing in both research and public health systems in addition to early warning systems, remaining prepared for environmental disruptions and those caused by humans, is an important element that we need to consider.

- Health Equity: The pandemic has absurdly spotlighted the ridiculous imbalances in health that need to be divinely addressed for a better society. Achieving the goal of 'Health for All' by equal treatment of all in healthcare provision and focusing on the social determinants of health is vital.
- One Health Approach: As the environment is interconnected, the health of humans, animals, as well as other ecosystems implies that zoonotic diseases are at the point of emerging and spreading.
- Innovation and Adaptation: The COVID-19 situation has really opened a new door to the healthcare delivery world, like telemedicine, and has also emphasized flexibility over the traditional public health care systems and economic policies.
- Global Governance and Cooperation: The emphasis on reinforcement of the international health regulations and the exposure of the worldwide health organizations as coordinators will be helpful to the emergent global health threats.

14.11 CONCLUSION

COVID-19, an illness caused by a new coronavirus variant SARS-CoV-2, is one of the most enormous global public health catastrophes to date, which has led to the collapse of the already struggling healthcare systems, economies, and societies globally. By means of this unparalleled crisis, we have demonstrated that aggressive, well-coordinated decisions are sine qua non, that there is high efficiency in scientific innovation (specifically in the case of vaccine development), and that, in addition to testing, contact tracing, and other non-pharmaceutical interventions are effective. COVID-19 has, in particular, highlighted the underlying characteristic of the global collaboration in responding to such a ubiquitous threat. Finally, no country can count on itself to successfully manage a virus that requires borders.

Takeaway lessons from the pandemic bear the importance of preparedness and due consideration of healthcare and public health expenditure capable of dealing with emerging threats. Through this internship, I have learned how socioeconomic factors may influence the health status of individuals in societies and the role of community health in addressing these inequalities in building a powerful and steadfast community. It is to be highlighted that an accelerated stream of scientific development resulting from the virus epidemic indicates an efficient cooperation model for the future to work out collective decisions on global health issues.

After everything that happened with COVID-19, the way towards recovery and preparedness for new pandemics is to use all that the disease has taught us. It involves strengthening global health regulations, ensuring equitable distribution of health assets, including vaccines, and stimulating innovation at the local health-care delivery level and disease monitoring. Integrating the view of One Health, which grasps the presence of the factors of human, animal, and environmental health, is the essential task in order to avert the appearance and prevalence of new zoonotic diseases.

The COVID-19 pandemic is a painful lesson to us that, regardless of how robust our health care systems are, we are all vulnerable. The way the pandemic has spread and impacted trade reveals that we are all interconnected and have to fight it together. It could not be any clearer that we need to act for a new key pillars of global health security whereby we pursue health equity and cooperation in our quest for a safer and healthier future world free from pandemics and other scourges. The legacy of this health crisis should be a showcase for the qualities of resilience, invention, and unity, directing our joint efforts to combat future health problems after that.

REFERENCES

1. World Health Organization (WHO). (2020). "Coronavirus Disease (COVID-19) Pandemic." [Online] Available at: https://www.who.int/emergencies/diseases/novel-coronavirus-2019
2. Lancet COVID-19 Commission. (2020). Lancet COVID-19 Commission Statement on the Occasion of the 75th Session of the UN General Assembly. *The Lancet*, 396(10257), 1102–1124.
3. Subbarao, E., Gite, P., Sharma, A., et al. (2023). Investigation of Solar Energy for Urban Areas and Metropolitan Communities Using Machine Learning. *Electric Power Components and Systems*, 1, 1–11.
4. Sardar, T. H., Faizabadi, A. R., & Ansari, Z. (2017). An Analysis of Data Processing Using Mapreduce Paradigm on the Hadoop Framework. *International Journal of Emerging Research in Management and Technology*, 6(5), 403–413.
5. Mishra, N., Thangavel, G., & Samuel, J. M. (2019). A Case Assessment of Knowledge-Based Fit in Frame for Diagnosis of Human Eye Diseases. *Journal of Critical Reviews*, 14(6), e1566.
6. Theerthagiri, P., Ruby, A. U., Chandran, J. G. C., Sardar, T. H., & Shafeeq, B. M. A. (2024). Deep SqueezeNet Learning Model for Diagnosis and Prediction of Maize Leaf Diseases. *Journal of Big Data*, 11(1), 112.
7. Baden, L. R., El Sahly, H. M., Essink, B., et al. (2021). Efficacy and Safety of the mRNA-1273 SARS-CoV-2 Vaccine. *The New England Journal of Medicine*, 384, 403–416.
8. Rajesh, E., Basheer, S., Dhanaraj, R. K., et al. (2023). Machine Learning for Online Automatic Prediction of Common Disease Attributes Using Never-Ending Image Learner. *Diagnostics*, 13, 95.
9. Rajesh, E., Basheer, S., & Baskar, K. (2023). Hydroponics Soilless Smart Farming in Improving Productivity of Crop Using Intelligent Smart Systems. *3rd International Conference on Innovative 2023*, Bethesda, MD, USA: National Institutes of Health.
10. Khatun, A., & Sardar, T. H. (2025). Cryptography Algorithms to Prevent Different Security Attacks. In *Next Generation Mechanisms for Data Encryption* (pp. 35–46). CRC Press.
11. Thangavel, G., & Adam, T. (2018). Securing Medical Text Data Using Cuckoo Search Based Advanced Encryption Standard (AES). *IOSR Journal of Computer Engineering*, 35–40.
12. GISAID. (2020). "Global Initiative on Sharing All Influenza Data – GISAID." [Online] Available at: https://www.gisaid.org/
13. The COVID-19 Treatment Guidelines Panel. (2020). "Coronavirus Disease 2019 (COVID-19) Treatment Guidelines." National Institutes of Health. [Online] Available at: https://www.covid19treatmentguidelines.nih.gov/
14. Sardar, T. H. (2024). Reflecting on a Decade of Evolution: MapReduce-Based Advances in Partitioning-Based, Hierarchical-Based, and Density-Based Clustering (2013–2023). *Wiley Interdisciplinary Reviews: Data Mining and Knowledge Discovery*, 396, e1566.

15 Harnessing Generative Adversarial Networks for Heart Disease Prediction

A Comprehensive Review

D. Vathana, D. Vanusha, J. Ramaprabha, K. Deeba, Tanvir Habib Sardar, and F. Syed Anwar Hussainy

15.1 INTRODUCTION

15.1.1 Overview of Heart Diseases and Their Significance in Public Health

Cardiovascular diseases (CVDs), which include various heart conditions, such as coronary heart diseases (CHDs), stroke, and other atherosclerotic diseases, represent a serious risk to global public health. These are the first-ranking cause of morbidity and mortality, which results in millions of deaths per year, thus manifesting the crucial need for the development of these life-saving strategies. In this immune-based comprehensive introduction, we give a wide description of the CVDs from their epidemiology, risk factors, and their impact on the patients and society. We also focus on the function of predictive analytics, where we examine the utilization of advanced Machine Learning approaches, especially generative adversarial networks (GANs), to counter the challenges brought by heart disease [1].

These are broadly termed as cardiovascular system diseases, which range from atherosclerosis to heart failure, arrhythmias, and congenital heart diseases, among others. Summarily, these are the conditions that account for a large portion of mortality all over the world with the World Health Organization (WHO) reporting estimates of 17.9 million deaths arising from CVDs every year. Besides, it imposes an incredibly high economic burden on health systems worldwide as it involves the cost of medical care, hospitalization, and productivity loss [2].

15.1.1.1 Risk Factors and Epidemiology

A wide range of coexisting reasons in the origination and advancement of heart diseases, which include modifiable risk factors like unhealthy diet, inactivity, tobacco use, and excessive alcohol consumption under the circumstances, and non-modifiable factors such as age, genetics, and family history. The prevalence of heart diseases differs from one region and population group to another, with disparities in the disease distribution according to socioeconomic status, access to healthcare facilities, and

DOI: 10.1201/9781003600947-15

the associated risk factors. The epidemiology of heart diseases is important because it forms the basis of the formulation of interventions that are directed at heart diseases and ensures that resource allocation is done appropriately [3].

15.1.1.2 The Functions of Predictive Analytics

In the past few years, the predictions have been of much interest about utilizing predictive analytics to effectively detect and manage heart diseases at the earliest. Among different methods for analyzing complex medical data, Machine Learning techniques show a lot of potential in their ability to find patterns and predict patient outcomes. Among the highest hit tools are the GANs. Particularly, they generate synthetic data and augment datasets with the goal of improving the predictive power of models. Risk stratification, treatments, and populations' well-being can be improved through the use of GANs and other Machine Learning approaches by researchers and health professionals, which will help reduce the number of people who have heart diseases [1].

To sum it all up, heart diseases pose a major public health concern that is controlled by proactive mechanisms of prevention, diagnosis, and management. The involvements of predictive analytics, such as advanced Machine Learning techniques, such as GANs, promise to improve the risk prediction and eventually patient outcome in the context of heart diseases. The latter part of this chapter discusses the use of GANs for heart disease prediction in detail. It examines their benefits, drawbacks, and prospects for further development. Besides that, we also offer case studies and experiments that show the effectiveness of GANs in that field as well as some insights on their actual capabilities and implications for clinical practice. Figure 15.1 shows an overview of heart diseases and their significance in public health.

15.1.2 Brief Explanation of Machine Learning Techniques in Healthcare

Within the past few years, the incorporation of Machine Learning algorithms into healthcare has disrupted the medical field in terms of research, diagnosis, treatment, and patient care. Hence, this introduction shall be used to provide a detailed analysis

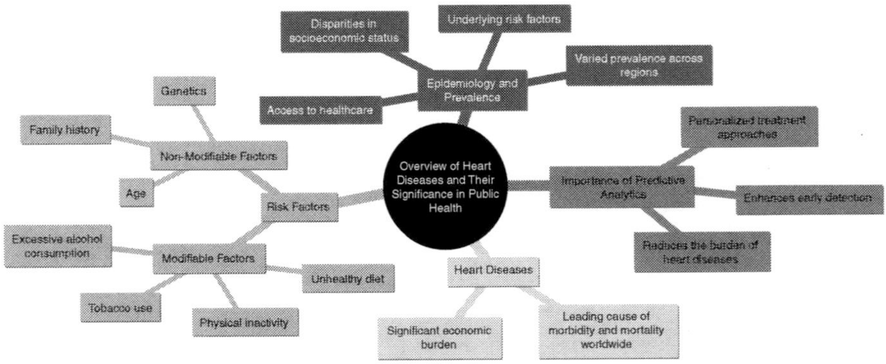

FIGURE 15.1 Overview of heart diseases and their significance in Public Health.

of the Machine Learning algorithms used in healthcare and their application, benefits, challenges, and prospects [4].

15.1.2.1 Machine Learning in Healthcare: A Paradigm Change

In healthcare, Machine Learning algorithms leverage the existence of huge amounts of medical data, comprising EHRs, medical images, genomic sequences, and wearable sensor data, in order to find fruitful insights that are used to enhance patient outcomes and clinical workflows [5].

The applications of Machine Learning in healthcare have brought tremendous benefits, such as detecting cancer at the early stages, assisting in predicting diseases, and applying suitable treatments [4].

The applications of Machine Learning in healthcare are manifold and span various domains, including but not limited to: The applications of Machine Learning in healthcare are manifold and span various domains, including but not limited to:

1. Diagnostic Imaging: Machine Learning algorithms process medical images in the form of X-rays, MRIs, CT scans, and histopathology slides to help radiologists and pathologists see defects, diagnose diseases, and predict outcomes of patients.
2. Clinical Decision Support: Machine Learning algorithms also take care of the evidence-based decision-making process for healthcare providers as the data of patients is analyzed to predict the risk of diseases, recommend the best treatment plans, and choose the right medication processes.
3. Precision Medicine: Machine Learning methods help personalize medical treatments by analyzing specific patient data, including genetic, molecular, and clinical information, so as to adapt interventions to each patient based on the qualities and needs of each patient.
4. Drug Discovery and Development: Machine Learning algorithms are finding applications in the various stages of drug discovery, including analysis of molecular structures, prediction of drug-target interactions, discovery of potential drug candidates, and drug design optimization.
5. Healthcare Operations and Management: Machine Learning models maximize the efficiency of health care operations using administrative data for admissions, utilization of resources, the pattern of patient flow, and to minimize readmissions [6].

15.1.2.2 Advantages of Machine Learning in the Healthcare Industry

1. Improved Diagnostic Accuracy: Automated Machine Learning algorithms help to improve the diagnostic accuracy by identifying complex patterns and detecting minute irregularities that may not be noticed by human perceivers.
2. Personalized Treatment: Machine Learning makes it possible to derive an individual patient's treatment plan by learning their personal preferences and characteristics, and their responses to therapy, which results in better clinical outcomes and patient satisfaction.
3. Early Disease Detection: Machine Learning models aid in the early identification of diseases through the analysis of patient data and the identification

of indicative biomarkers or risk factors associated with disease development or progression.

4. Efficient Healthcare Delivery: Machine Learning systems improve healthcare delivery through automation of routine tasks, optimization of clinical processes, reduction of administrative loads, and improvement of utilization of resources and allocations.

15.1.2.3 Challenges and Future Directions

Even while the prospect of Machine Learning in healthcare is particularly encouraging, issues such as data privacy and security, algorithm bias and interpretability concerns, regulatory and ethical aspects, and a need for validated introduction into clinical practice still remain. Moving further, the future research directions can also attempt to address these challenges, improve algorithmic transparency and explainability, strengthen interdisciplinary collaborations, and utilize emerging technologies such as federated learning and explainable AI in order to maximize the success of Machine Learning in healthcare [4].

In further parts, we go deeper into specific Machine Learning methods and their areas of application in different healthcare areas aiming to provide a more complete overview of the current situation in which data-driven healthcare is evolving.

15.1.3 Introduction to GANs and Their Application Potential

This chapter is designed to offer you a general idea about GANs from the point of their architecture, inner principles, the training process, up to their enormous potential in medicine. The main emphasis here is on the transformative power of GANs in healthcare [7].

With the aid of an adversarial training mechanism, the generator and the discriminator play a game of cat and mouse in a competition to beat each other as the performance of the individual components is improved until reaching equilibrium, relying on the generation of quality, realistic data in the end [1,8].

15.1.3.1 Architecture of GANs

1. Generator: The generator network uses random noise or latent vectors as input and gives back the synthetic data samples as a result. It is usually a cascade of different layers of either densely or convolutionally connected neural networks (CNNs), which is finally followed by the activation functions such as ReLU or tanh, and the output is approximately the same as for real data [9].
2. Discriminator: The discriminator network sees both real and synthetic data as input and tries to identify them as real or fake. Like the generator, it has multiple layers of neural networks, which are able to perform the task using appropriate activation functions and distinguish the real from the fake samples [9].

15.1.3.2 Training Process

Simultaneously with the training process, the generator and discriminator networks play a game of min-max in a win-win framework. The goal of the generator is to calculate the highest probability of tricking the discriminator (i.e., creating realistic samples), as well as the discriminator to calculate the smallest probability of incorrectly distinguishing real and fake images. This adjustment process is carried out incrementally until convergence, which causes the upgrading of networks' performance, and, as a result, a higher quality of generated synthetic data.

15.1.3.3 Application Potential of GANs

GANs hold immense potential across a wide range of applications in healthcare, including: GANs hold immense potential across a wide range of applications in healthcare, including:

1. Medical Imaging: increasing the dataset size and improving the model accuracy of image-based diagnostic and segmentation models.
2. Drug Discovery: GANs enable the synthesis of new molecules with specified attributes, providing an alternative for exploring the chemical space and identifying new drug leads.
3. Synthetic Patient Data Generation: Generated data from GANs resembles the real patient population and ensures data privacy at the same time. This capacity of GANs is of great benefit to both research and development of algorithms in the healthcare setting, because it does not compromise confidentiality.
4. Disease Prediction and Risk Stratification: GANs are utilized to create synthetic patient progression schedules or disease progression models, which help the prediction of disease onset, progression, and treatment response, thus advancing clinical decision-making and enabling personalized medicine.

Finally, GANs would be an amazing breakthrough in Deep Learning, having various applications in health care and other fields like this. Owing to their capability of producing high-fidelity synthetic data, issues like medical imaging, drug discovery, patient data generation, and disease prediction benefit from this. As the work on the application of GANs develops, the possibility to employ it to solve complicated tasks in healthcare, which helps to improve the results of patients' treatment, to push the boundaries of medical research, and to create a new paradigm in data-driven medicine becomes more relevant [7]. Figure 15.2 shows the architecture of GANs.

15.2 BACKGROUND AND RELATED WORK

15.2.1 Review of Traditional Machine Learning Approaches for Heart Disease Prediction

15.2.1.1 Background and Related Work

Here, in the first section, we go deeper into traditional Machine Learning techniques that have been used for heart disease prediction. In this regard, we examine the evolution of these approaches, their strengths, weaknesses, and the contribution of such methods to the progression of research on cardiovascular health. Moreover, we

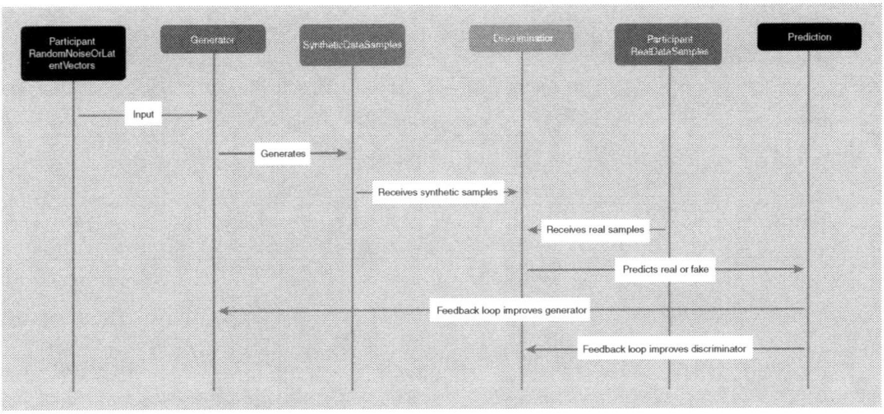

FIGURE 15.2 Architecture of generative adversarial networks (GANs).

assess the published literature on the use of Machine Learning for early diagnosis of heart disease and offer the current methods in perspective with respect to the conventional ones.

15.2.1.2 Traditional Machine Learning Approaches Are Also Sophisticated

The development of traditional Machine Learning techniques for heart disease has been spurred on by many years incorporated advances in data availability, computational power, and algorithmic sophistication. The first kind of studies used statistical models such as logistic regression, decision trees, and naive Bayes classifiers to study clinical data and discover clinical risk factors leading to CVDs. Patients' demographics and laboratory tests are examples of the features that are commonly used in these models to predict the chances of developing heart diseases or suffering from undesirable cardiovascular events.

15.2.1.3 Strengths and Weaknesses of the Conventional Methods

Traditional Machine Learning approaches provide some benefits, such as simplicity, interpretability, and straightforward implementation. These models offer important knowledge about the associations of risk factors and cardiovascular outcomes, which is crucial for the patient's stratification and clinical decision-making. Despite the fact that classic models could fail to fit the nonlinear, complex relationships hidden in the data and the availability of features will also be a performance-limiting factor in these models. Furthermore, these models can also not exhaust the whole potential of medical data, but may leave out valuable predictive signals like imaging or genetic information that could help to get a clearer picture of the disease.

15.2.1.4 Literature Review: In Heart Disease Prediction, Machine Learning

The literature review is outlined, and it shows that there is a growing body of research papers about the use of Machine Learning methods in predicting heart diseases. A body of research has examined various Machine Learning algorithms such as

Support Vector Machines (SVMs), Random Forests, feed-forward neural networks, and ensemble methods for the purpose of developing predictive models for cardiovascular risk assessment, diagnosis, and prognosis. These are the models that have shown promising results regarding accuracy, specificity, and sensitivity, better than the traditional methods in many cases [9].

15.2.1.5 Comparison with Traditional Approaches

The outcome of the comparative studies has been evaluated to distinguish between the performance of Machine Learning models the traditional methods in predicting heart diseases. Traditional models, on the other hand, are valuable for their transparent interpretability and simplicity. However, they are usually not as good as Machine Learning algorithms at forecasting, particularly when working with big and complicated datasets.

Machine Learning models exhibit excellent performance in data variety mining, including electronic health records (EHRs), medical images, and genetic data, and in this way, they increase the accuracy of predictive results.

15.2.1.6 Future Directions and Challenges

Many challenging topics are still not resolved despite the development of Machine Learning-based heart disease prediction. These are data heterogeneity, model interpretability, scalability, and studies for validation and clinical integration. However, future research could incorporate the use of hybrid models that incorporate the strengths of conventional and Machine Learning methods, be focused on data integration from different modalities and on dealing with ethical and regulatory concerns in using predictive models in practice.

In summary, we can say that the classical Machine Learning algorithms were the key driving forces behind heart disease prediction in the early stages, thus giving rise to a great number of advanced techniques such as Deep Learning and ensemble models. Despite their advantages in simplicity and interpretability, traditional models may be inefficient in predictive power and use only limited data. Machine Learning algorithms, however, make up for these gaps, offering a higher predictive performance and the use of multiple data sources in one single model. In order to produce results, the challenges associated with Machine Learning-based means for the prevention of heart disease need to be overcome. This is the way to fulfil the vision of making predictive analytics a tool for better cardiovascular health [7]. Figure 15.3 shows the evolution of heart disease prediction techniques.

15.2.2 Overview of Deep Learning Techniques in Healthcare

15.2.2.1 Background and Related Work

This Section gives an inclusive explanation of Deep Learning methods in healthcare, encompassing their uses, advantages, challenges, and ways that they have facilitated medical research and improved clinical practice. Also, it delves into the existing literature on Deep Learning applications in the healthcare area by examining the key research, methods, and results.

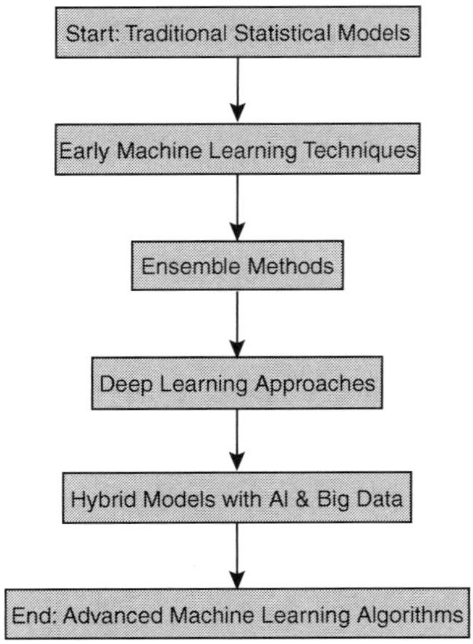

FIGURE 15.3 Evolution of heart disease prediction techniques.

15.2.2.2 Introduction to Deep Learning

Deep Learning can be viewed as a subfield of Machine Learning that uses deep neural networks with multiple layers to learn complex operations and representations from data. Furthermore, whereas the traditional Machine Learning models are all based on manually engineered features, Deep Learning models can detect hierarchical features from raw data autonomously. This makes them more than simple for the tasks that include large, high-dimensional datasets, like medical images, genomic sequences, and EHRs [7].

15.2.2.3 Medical Applications of Deep Learning

Deep Learning algorithms have brought in a true revolution to many domains of healthcare, which has led to achievements in medical imaging, genomics, drug discovery, disease diagnosis, and personalized medicine. Specific applications include:

1. Medical Imaging: Deep Learning techniques, which are based on the analysis of medical images (X-rays, MRI scans, and CT scans), are used to detect lesions or organs and to help radiologists diagnose diseases, for example, cancer, cardiovascular, and neurological disorders.
2. Genomics and Precision Medicine: Deep Learning models analyze genetic data in order to find variations that cause diseases, predict the treatment outcome and stratify patients in order to identify their risk groups associated with certain conditions. This paves the way for personalized treatment regimens that are customized according to individuals' genomic characteristics.
3. Drug Discovery and Development: Deep Learning methods are commonly used in drug discovery because they help to predict molecular properties,

detect drug-target interactions, and optimize the design of drugs. This results in the synthesis of the new drug with better efficiency and fewer adverse effects.

4. Clinical Decision Support: Deep Learning models come up as the decision support tools for healthcare providers by analyzing EHRs, predicting patient outcomes, suggesting treatment plans, and discovering adverse events or medication errors.

15.2.2.4 Healthcare Is the Use of Deep Learning

- Feature Learning: The Deep Learning models are formed such that they learn the hierarchical representations of data. Through the introduction of this concept, the need to manually engineer features is eliminated. However, the raw data are efficiently employed to make the process much more efficient [7].
- Scalability: Deep Learning algorithms behave well with large datasets; consequently, big-data draws into play in the process of analyzing the large-scale medical data collected from various sources like EHRs, medical imaging archives, and wearable devices.
- Performance: Deep Learning models rival human professionals in several healthcare tasks, especially medical image interpretation and disease diagnosis, and in many instances outperform human experts [10].
- Versatility: Deep Learning approaches are versatile and can be utilized in various healthcare applications, starting from medical imaging and genomic studies to drug design and clinical decision support.

15.2.2.5 Challenges and Considerations

Notwithstanding the fact that Deep Learning technologies have an immense transformative power, these technologies possess some challenges, such as data scarcity, interpretability difficulties, model robustness issues, and regulatory restrictions. Deep Learning models demand very big annotated datasets for training, and this is not always true in different medical fields. Additionally, the sophisticated characteristic of the deep neural networks is also challenging to interpret, and this raises questions about transparency, accountability, and dependability of clinical decision-making.

15.2.2.6 Future Directions

Some of the research directions in Deep Learning for healthcare, which will be discussed in the following sections, are addressing the aforementioned challenges, using interpretable and explainable models, using multimodal data fusion techniques, and integrating Deep Learning algorithms into clinical workflows. The interaction of Machine Learning researchers, clinicians, and subject matter experts is one of the vital points for the development of the field and transferring research results into real-world practice.

Finally, Deep Learning technology has changed medical practice by providing means of analyzing large quantities of medical data, extracting information, uncovering relevant patterns, and ultimately improving the quality of patient

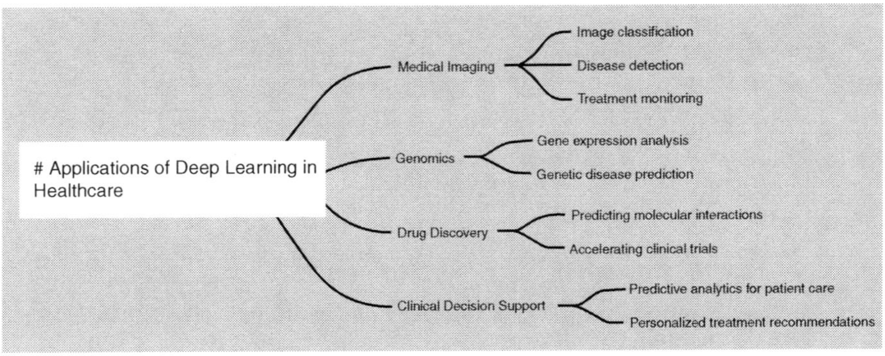

FIGURE 15.4 Applications of Deep Learning in healthcare.

care. Their implementation covers a broad spectrum of areas, ranging from performing medical imaging and genomics to developing new drugs and clinical diagnosis. In the face of challenges such as data complexity, interpretability, and regulatory compliance, Deep Learning can nevertheless hold great potential to transform the coming days of healthcare delivery and to advance our cognition of human health and disease. Figure 15.4 shows the applications of Deep Learning in healthcare.

15.2.3 Previous Studies Utilizing GANs in Medical Imaging and Healthcare Data Analysis

Background and Related Work: Previous usage of GANs in Medical Imaging and Healthcare Data Analytics as Studies.

GANs, which have been significantly supported in recent years for their ability to produce synthetic data that mimics the real data distributions, have been attracting considerable attention. GANs provide new ways to deal with the problem of data augmentation, image synthesis, anomaly detection, and diagnosing disease in medical imaging and healthcare data analysis. This part, therefore, carries a detailed, comprehensive review of the studies conducted using GANs in medical image and health data analysis, giving their methods, the applications, the outcomes, and the contribution towards advancing the research and clinical practice [1,10].

15.2.3.1 A Beginner's Guide to GANs in Healthcare

Health care GANs have been shown to be a potent ally for creating high-quality medical images, synthesizing patients' data, and unsupervised domain adaptation to data-limited datasets [11].

15.2.3.2 The Use of GANs in Medical Imaging

Previous studies have explored various applications of GANs in medical imaging, including: Previous studies have explored various applications of GANs in medical imaging, including:

1. Data Augmentation: GANs can generate synthetic medical images that are used for data augmentation, thus increasing the diversity and the number of training examples, supporting CNN training for tasks like image classification, segmentation and detection.
2. Image Synthesis: The AI-powered GANs can synthesize medical images with high realism either from low-quality or incomplete data filling the gaps in image area, increasing the image resolution and generating numerous image variations for research and education purposes.
3. Anomaly Detection: GANs distinguish abnormalities or anomalies in medical images by comparing the real images and synthetic images, so that the small lesions, tumors, or structural deformities can be detected before human observers.
4. Domain Adaptation: GANs convey knowledge from one medical image modality to another by learning a shared representation among different imaging domains, such as the MRI (magnetic resonance imaging) to CT (computed tomography), and by generating images in the target domains [10].

The main scope of GAN applications in health care data analysis.

In addition to medical imaging, GANs have been applied to various healthcare data analysis tasks, including: In addition to medical imaging, GANs have been applied to various healthcare data analysis tasks, including:

1. Synthetic Data Generation: GANs bring synthetic patient data to the scene to eliminate the use of real EHRs and physiological signals for data privacy, data sharing, and predictive modeling in the areas of clinical informatics research and predictive modeling.
2. Drug Discovery and Development: GANs create new molecules with desired properties and identify drug-target interactions, and optimize the chemical structures of drug candidates.
3. Healthcare Data Generation: GANs are among the newest AI technologies that make it possible to generate synthetic healthcare data for use in Machine Learning training. It contributes to improving the generalization and robustness of the models and mitigating bias in real-world datasets.

15.2.3.3 Review of Previous Studies

A systematic review of the published literature confirms that GANs are extensively used in the analysis of medical imaging data and healthcare data in general. These studies have shown that GANs can be very useful in creating real medical images as well as synthetic patient information and used to improve the accuracy of predictive models. The potential methods that will be employed will include conditional GANs, progressive growing GANs, and cycle-consistent GANs (tailored to particular health applications and data modalities).

15.3 UNDERSTANDING HEART DISEASE DATA

15.3.1 Description of Typical Datasets Used in Heart Disease Prediction

Understanding Heart Disease Data: Description of the Vital Datasets that are applied in the Forecasting of the heart disease.

Accuracy in heart disease prediction largely depends on the availability and quality of medical datasets required for model training and scoring. Through this part, we aim to offer statistics on the most employed datasets in heart disease research: their characteristics, sources, pre-processing steps, and challenges they may pose. Along with this, it outlines the significance of data quality, diversity, and representativeness for the generation of accurate and reliable predictive models of cardiovascular risk evaluation.

15.3.1.1 Heart Disease Datasets (Intro)

Heart disease datasets have a variety of health attributes of patients such as age, gender, diagnoses, symptoms, vital signs, laboratory results, critical images, and results. These data sets are gathered from diverse sources, for example, hospitals, clinics, research studies, and public healthcare databases and are employed to train Machine Learning models for the purpose of a disease risk assessment that includes coronary artery disease, heart failure, arrhythmias, and stroke.

The characteristics of a heart disease-related dataset.

Typical characteristics of heart disease datasets include: Typical characteristics of heart disease datasets include:

1. Demographic Information: Age, gender, ethnicity, socioeconomic status, and lifestyle factors are usually included in heart disease datasets in order to investigate the prevalence of various risk factors at the population level and the disparities.
2. Clinical Measurements: Vital signs (such as blood pressure, heart rate) and anthropometric measurements (like body mass index) give indicators about the patient's physiological status and the health of the cardiovascular system. On the other hand, biochemical markers (such as cholesterol levels, glucose levels) provide information on the patient's physiological condition as well.
3. Medical History: The past diagnoses, comorbidities, medication history, surgical procedures, and family history of CVDs permit the identification of those people at higher risk of heart diseases and the implementation of these individuals in the risk stratification strategies.
4. Imaging Studies: Medical imaging data like electrocardiograms (ECGs), echocardiograms, stress tests, and cardiac catheterization images have a lot of information about the structure and function of the heart and the vasculature, which can be used for diagnosis, prognosis, and treatment planning.
5. Outcomes: Clinical endpoints, both cardiovascular events and complications, serve as performance metrics for monitoring predictive models and forecasting patients' long-term prognosis.

15.3.1.2 Sources of Datasets for Heart

1. Clinical Databases: Hospital EHRs [16], community registries, and administrative databases are structured such that they contain longitudinal data of the patient captured in various stages of his/her routine healthcare; therefore, they provide a good source of real-world data for research and analysis
2. Research Studies: Prospective cohort studies, case-control studies, and RCTs define time through a baseline measure and then collect detailed clinical and outcome data over time, thus allowing longitudinal analyses and the identification of risk factors.
3. Public Health Databases: They provide epidemiological information at a large scale regarding cardiovascular risk factors and disease prevalence in various populations.

15.3.1.3 Pre-processing Steps

Data pre-processing steps are of utmost importance; they must ensure data cleaning, standardization, and preparation of heart disease datasets for analysis. Common pre-processing steps include:

1. Data Cleaning: Data deduplication, replacing missing values, and correcting data collection errors help to maintain the accuracy of the dataset.
2. Feature Engineering: Feature extraction, transforming variables, and constructing new variables will definitely enhance the capacity to predict the data set, and consequently, the performance of the model will be improved.
3. Normalization and Standardization: Rescaling the numerical variables and encoding categorical variables serve as a way of making sure that the features have similar ranges and distributions, whereby, during training, no bias arises.
4. Data Splitting: Splitting the dataset into formation, validation, and test sets is used for model building, tweaking, and evaluation, which lowers the chances of overfitting and hence improves the model.

15.3.1.4 Challenges and Considerations

1. Data Quality: The correctness, sufficiency, and uniformity of heart disease datasets have to be made sure for the predictions and insights to be reliable and capable of actions.
2. Data Imbalance: Focusing on class imbalance, where the number of positive (disease-present) cases is much smaller than negative (disease-absent) cases, and this leads to the imbalance, should be the starting point for developing the models and preventing biases.
3. Data Privacy: Having privacy protected and complying with the regulatory requisites e.g., Health Insurance Portability and Accountability Act (HIPAA), entails the data being properly handled and anonymized where necessary.
4. Data Heterogeneity: Data integration from different sources, like different healthcare systems or imaging modalities, deteriorates because of the lack

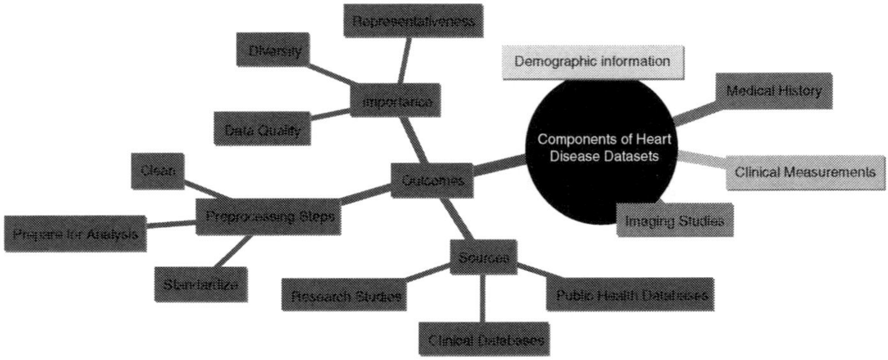

FIGURE 15.5 Components of heart disease datasets.

of harmonization and standardization, which makes them incompatible and inconsistent across datasets.

15.3.1.5 Significance of Data in Risk Analysis of Heart Disease

Overall, the role of heart disease datasets in the development of precise, sound, and relevant predictive models for cardiovascular risk stratification cannot be underestimated. Appreciating the traits, origins, pre-processing stages, and challenges regarding heart disease data sets is crucial for effectively utilizing the maximum capacity of Machine Learning techniques in enhancing heart disease prediction, prevention, and management. Figure 15.5 shows the components of the heart disease datasets.

15.3.2 Data Pre-processing Techniques for Handling Medical Data

Understanding Heart Disease Data: Medical Data Processing Techniques that Deal with Data.

Data pre-processing is an instrumental stage in the data analysis pipeline, especially in the medical field, where precision, reliability, and interpretability are the determining factors. In the following part of this section, we carry out an in-depth study of the data pre-processing methods that are created for the task at hand of making the medical data for heart disease predictions. It incorporates various pre-processing steps like data cleaning, feature engineering, normalization, and missing value handling, and discusses their contribution to providing quality and consistency, and fitness of medical datasets for predictive modeling [12].

The chapter is going to examine data pre-processing in healthcare.

Data pre-processing consists of a set of operations performed on raw data to change it into an analyzed/modeled useful format for analysis or modeling. In healthcare, data pre-processing is one of the most significant steps in medical data preparation that is involved in many tasks like disease prediction, diagnosis, treatment planning, and outcome prediction. The fact that medical data contains a lot of heterogeneity and complexity implies that pre-processing techniques have to face a lot of different challenges, such as the quality of data, missing values, noise, and outliers.

15.3.2.1 Data Cleaning Techniques

The process of data cleaning is aimed at locating and fixing the mistakes, inconsistencies, and outliers present in the data to ensure that it still has integrity and reliability. Common data cleaning techniques for medical data include: Common data cleaning techniques for medical data include:

1. Removing Duplicate Records: Finding and eradicating patient records and observations from being duplicated to eliminate the redundancy and achieve data consistency.
2. Handling Missing Values: Imputation of missing values through the use of techniques such as mean imputation, median imputation, or predictive imputation to preserve data integrity and to avoid any inaccuracies in the analysis.
3. Correcting Data Entry Errors: Describing and correcting the mistakes in the data inputs, typing errors, or inconsistency issues in the data format. This would improve the overall quality and accuracy of the data.

15.3.2.2 Feature Engineering

1. Creating Derived Features: Creation of new features by aggregating or modifying the existing independent variable, e.g., body mass index (BMI), is derived by combining the height and weight values or clinical risk scores generated from individual risk factors.
2. Selecting Relevant Features: Feature selection from the informative feature identification through the use of techniques such as feature importance ranking, correlation analysis, or expert domain knowledge to minimize complexity and enhance model performance.

15.3.2.3 Normalization and Standardization

Normalization and standardization techniques are used to maintain numerical variables in consistent scales and distributions to normalize features. The standardization eliminates biases and aids in model training and convergence. Common normalization and standardization techniques include: Common normalization and standardization techniques include:

1. Min-Max Scaling: Range Rescaling or normalization of numerical features to a specified range (0 to 1) for consistency and comparable-ness among variables.
2. Z-score Standardization: Standardizing the numerical features by having the mean of 0, which is the center of the feature, and a standard deviation of 1, to make sure that features are centered around zero and have similar scale values.

15.3.2.4 Handling Missing Values

The problem of missing values is a ubiquitous challenge for medical datasets and has to be taken care of in a correct manner as bias and inaccuracies can get introduced into the analysis.

1. Mean/Median Imputation: Using the mean or median of the feature adding back the missing values to preserve data integrity and satisfy statistical properties.
2. Predictive Imputation: Using Machine Learning algorithms trained on the whole data and exploiting the inter-relationships between the features to impute missing values.

15.3.2.5 Outlier Detection and Removal

Deviations, or "outliers" that may be unusual observations, may be of great impact on the performance of predictive models and need to be properly handled. Outlier detection techniques include:

1. Statistical Methods: Employing statistics such as z-scores, IQR, and standard deviations to identify the observations that stand out as aberrations from the mean and median.
2. Machine Learning-Based Methods: Utilizing Machine Learning techniques like isolation forests or one-class SVMs for isolating anomalous data points based on their lack of similarity with the majority of the events. Figure 15.6 shows the data pre-processing workflow for medical data.

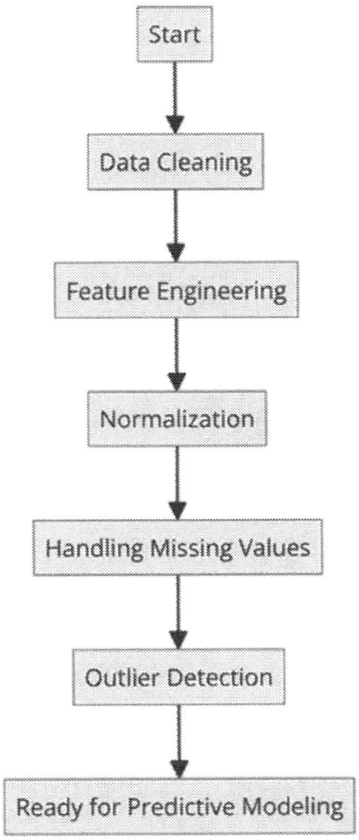

FIGURE 15.6 Data pre-processing workflow for medical data

15.3.3 Challenges and Considerations Specific to Heart Disease Data

Understanding Heart Disease Data: Concerns and Thoughts.

The fundamental difference in developing predictive modeling for heart disease lies in the fact that the data itself requires substantial attention and considerations in terms of accuracy, reliability, and efficiency. It is in this section that we get into the nitty-gritty of heart disease data, dealing with the problems it poses for data collection, pre-processing, modeling, and interpretation. It also highlights special features relevant to heart disease data and the ways out of such challenges for the purpose of achieving effective interpretation of the data and sound decision-making.

15.3.3.1 Introduction of Heart Disease Data Is a Challenge That Occurred

CVD is a multifactorial and complicated disease affected by genetic, environmental, lifestyle, and clinical factors. Hence, the existing heart disease data have dilemma problems that can affect the quality and proficiency of prediction models. The grasp of these challenges as important for researchers and clinicians targeting data-driven tools for heart attack evaluation, diagnosis, and treatment is necessary.

15.3.3.2 Data Collection Challenges

1. Data Heterogeneity: Obtaining heart disease data is difficult as the sources are many and varied including EHRs, registries, research studies, and population surveys. The integration and harmonization of data from various sources may require significant efforts to deal with different data formats, standards, and practices of documentation.
2. Incomplete Data: Data that is incomplete or missing, especially in longitudinal research or survey data at the population level, can prevent accurate and generalizable predictive modeling. Remediating the issue of missing data will be pursued by imputation or modeling methods to keep the data consistent and with minimum biases.
3. Data Quality: Data accuracy, completeness, and reliability should be considered prior to conducting meaningful analyses and interpretations in case of heart disease. Such data quality issues as data entry misclassifications, mistakes, and inconsistencies may occur and need to be tackled via prompt data input control and quality control processes.

15.3.3.3 Pre-processing Challenges

1. Imbalanced Data: Disease-related heart datasets typically have class imbalance, in which there are way more disease-present (positive) cases than disease-absent (negative) cases. Overbalancing can result in biased model performance, inaccurate risk prediction making, oversampling, under-sampling, or cost-sensitive learning, which are techniques applied to handle imbalance issues.
2. Feature Selection: Feature selection is a complicated task out of all the candidate predictors in heart disease data, where clinical, genetic, and lifestyle data are tied to the disease risk. Feature selection approaches, as filter,

wrapper, and embedded methods, should be implemented to find informative features and simplify models efficiently.

15.3.3.4 Modeling Challenges

1. Model Interpretability: The ability to translate complex Machine Learning models while still operating in the clinical environment of heart disease prediction is critical to understand the underlying features affecting risk prediction and decision making. While some sophisticated Machine Learning algorithms, such as deep neural networks, are not transparent and hence not understandable, they make it difficult to understand how predictions are made and if the model output can be trusted.
2. Generalizability: Enabling the generalizability of predictive models to be applied for diverse patient groups, health care settings, and geographical areas is paramount before their adoption and effectiveness in real-world practice. Models are validated using methods like external validation, cross-validation, and robustness testing to evaluate their performance across various contexts and populations.

15.3.3.5 Ethical and Regulatory Considerations

1. Data Privacy: Privacy and confidentiality of the patients must be protected in CVD research, especially for personal health data.
2. Ethical Use of Data: Ethical considerations should emphasize equity, fairness, and transparency in data collection, analysis, and interpretation of heart disease. Assuring equality in data representation and reducing algorithmic biases as well as openly informing about model limitations are crucial for ethical data handling and building the public confidence in predictive modeling.

15.4 APPLICATION OF GANS IN HEART DISEASE PREDICTION

15.4.1 Overview of GAN Architecture and Components

Application of GANs in Heart Disease Prediction: A brief description of the GAN structure framework and components.

GANs have recently become an effective method of synthesizing fake data that are very close to the data distributions observed in real data. In the context of heart disease prediction, GANs contribute to introducing new solutions for the purposes of creating realistic medical images, synthesizing patients' data and augmenting small datasets for training predictive models. The next section offers a detailed introduction to the operational structure of GANs and the different components that form GANs, explaining their functionality in cardiovascular research and predictive modeling.

15.4.1.1 Introduction to GANs

This adversarial training in turn causes the developing of perfect and tangible data classes.

15.4.1.2 Architecture of GANs

The architecture of GANs consists of the following components: The architecture of GANs consists of the following components:

1. Generator: Generator takes random noise or latent vectors as input and produces synthetic images as output samples. Compositionally, it usually has different layers of the neural networks such as convolution or deconvolution, then follows active functions (e.g., ReLU, sigmoid) to translate the input noise to meaningful data representations.
2. Discriminator: The discriminator network accepts data samples from both real and fake images and predicts if the sample is real or fake. The discriminator is built in the same style as the generator with multiple layers of neural networks, which could be either convolutional layer followed by activation functions, and learn how to distinguish between real and fake data [9].
3. Adversarial Training: The G and D networks are trained in a competitive fashion, a process which requires both networks to run simultaneously. The generator tries to deceive the discriminator by committing the latter to sufficiently high confidence in the fake data, meanwhile, the discriminator has to correctly identify the fake samples. Consequently, the outcome of this competition is an inhibitor of both networks' performance until the equilibrium is reached.

15.4.1.3 Components of GANs

1. Loss Functions: GANs use two types of loss functions for training the generator and discriminator networks:
    - Generator Loss: Generator loss measures how effectively the generator fools the discriminator to classify its fake samples as real. It is usually represented as the negative binary cross-entropy between the discriminator's predictions and the vector of ones (the placeholders for real samples).
    - Discriminator Loss: Discriminator loss quantifies to which the discriminator succeeds in differentiating real from fake samples.
2. Activation Functions: Activation functions bring non-linearity into the neural network layers, so that the model can represent more complex data quanta. As for the activation functions at the hidden layers, the popular choices are ReLU (Rectified Linear Unit), whereas the output layers usually use sigmoid or SoftMax functions.
3. Optimizer: GANs use different types of optimization algorithms (SGD or Adam) as the weights of generator and discriminator networks are updated iteratively during the training process. These optimizers minimize the generator and discriminator loss functions to drive the networks towards minimization.

The heart disease prediction requires additional applications of GANs.

In heart disease prediction research, GANs offer several applications, including:
In heart disease prediction research, GANs offer several applications, including:

1. Medical Image Generation: GANs that produce artificial medical images, including cardiac MRIs or CTs, are used to expand low sample size datasets for training image-based predictive models. Such synthetic images are very much similar to real images and hence enrich the size of training data and its diversity [13,14].
2. Data Augmentation: GANs improve heart disease datasets by creating synthetic patient data, including EHRs and physiological signals. The accuracy and generalization of predictive models are enhanced when augmented datasets are used, which results in the reduction of overfitting.
3. Feature Generation: GANs create synthetic features or representations of heart disease risk factors, including demographic information, clinical measurements, and genetic profiles. The synthetic features assist in making the feature space richer, which in turn leads to the discovery of novel predictive biomarkers.

Hence, in summary, GANs have a great capability of synthesizing data and making the quality and diversity of heart disease datasets higher. Through adversarial training, GANs are able to obtain accurate data representations with high fidelity, which makes the artificial data resemble the real data distributions. Appreciation of the structures and components of GANs is key to leveraging their potential for heart disease prediction research and in enhancing cardiovascular outcomes. Figure 15.7 shows the architecture of GANs.

15.4.2 Discussion of How GANs Can Be Applied to Predict Heart Diseases

15.4.2.1 Application of GANs in Heart Disease Prediction: Thesis

GANs have emerged in recent years as one of the most exciting topics of research for their effective applications in generating synthetic data that is indistinguishable from real data distributions. GANs provide cutting-edge solutions for data augmentation, feature extraction, and model optimization in the field of heart disease prediction, which help to increase the accuracy and robustness of prediction models. The succeeding part expounds the applications of GANs for the prediction of heart diseases, unveiling their opportunities and the challenges that are likely to arise [11].

15.4.2.2 Data Augmentation with GANs

A major implementation of GANs in the context of heart disease is data augmentation. Small sample sizes, class imbalances, and data heterogeneity are the common limitations often encountered in heart disease datasets. GANs are one of the solutions for these issues, where they generate synthetic data samples that are added to the original dataset. Through training on the underlying data distribution, the GANs are able to produce real data instances that have the ruggedness and complexity of actual

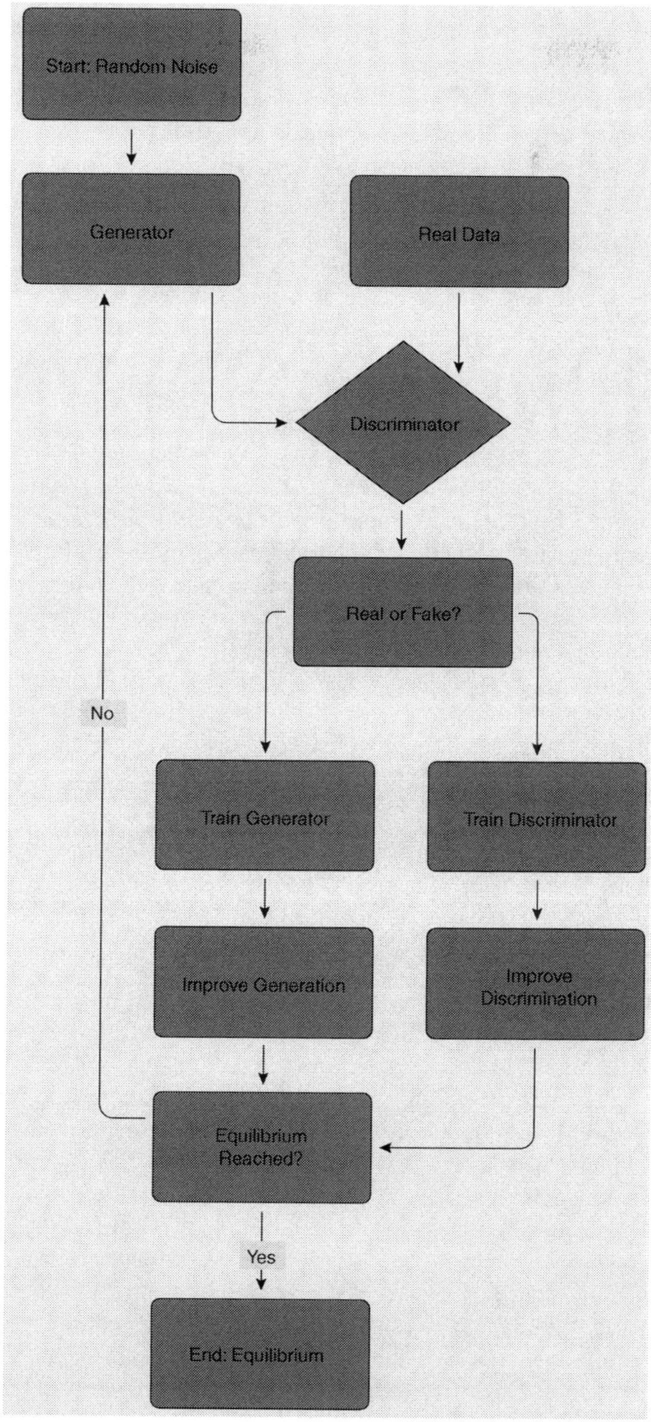

FIGURE 15.7 Architecture of generative adversarial networks (GANs).

patient data. To use the augmented datasets better, we can train stronger predictive models. It will enable a higher training accuracy and reduce the risk of overfitting.

15.4.2.3 Feature Formulation and Representation Model

Moreover, GANs can be utilized for feature generation and representation learning in the context of heart disease prediction. GANs can provide artificial features to patient data, which include demographic data, clinical measurements, and genetic traits. These synthetic attributes expand the feature space, which thus enables scientists to find new predictive biomarkers for heart diseases. GANs learn latent representations of patient data, which helps them discover invisible patterns and connections that are not distinct from the raw data alone. The representations learned thus can be used in the predictive models as input features for which the predictive performance and interpretation are enhanced.

15.4.2.4 Enhancing Model Resistance to Disturbance and Towards Good Generalization

Finally, GANs can be adopted to improve the real-world application of predictive models for heart disease prevention. GANs augment the sample size of the training set, which comprises diverse and real data samples, and thereby help in enhancing the generalization capabilities of the predictive models by exposing them to a greater number of data instances. This is especially helpful in situations such there is not enough data in the original dataset or it is not diverse enough. GAN-augmented data sets can also serve to counteract biases and limitations in the original data, thereby resulting in higher precision and more reliable predictions of heart disease.

15.4.2.5 Challenges and Considerations

Despite the potential benefits of using GANs in heart disease prediction, several challenges and considerations must be addressed: Despite the potential benefits of using GANs in heart disease prediction, several challenges and considerations must be addressed:

1. Data Quality and Bias: The quality of the generated synthetic data is a function of the quality of the original dataset as well as the efficacy of the GAN algorithm. The existing biases in the original data could be extended to the generated data, and the falsely predicted results may be biased too. The reliability and quality of the generated data are dependent on critical examination and verification, which are important for the use of the data in predictive modeling.
2. Model Interpretability: Generative Adversarial Networks (GANs) are complex forms of models, and hence, it can be difficult to explain generated data and figure out the underlying patterns learned by the network. Interpretability challenges can slow the adoption and trustworthiness of predictive models that will be built using it-generated data. Audiences' interpretation and comprehension of generally functional GAN data is an area of work in Machine Learning and healthcare.

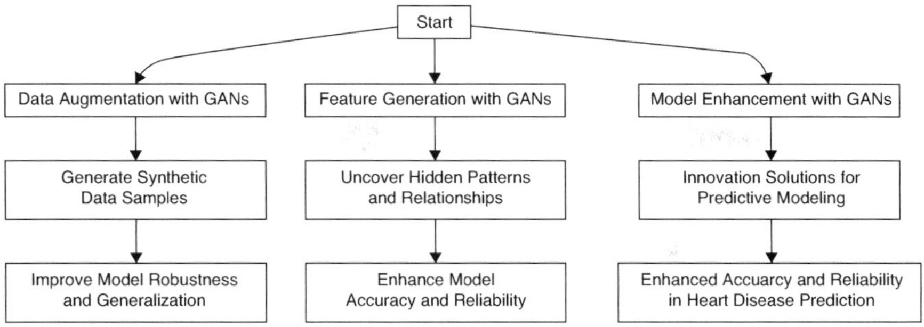

FIGURE 15.8 Application of GANs in heart disease prediction.

Summarizing the benefits, GANs are creating an encouraging platform for heart disease prediction improvement through data augmentation, feature generation, and model enhancement. GANs enable more reliable and accurate heart disease predictions by creating artificial data sets with characteristics that closely resemble real data distributions. Nevertheless, there are issues like data quality, bias, and interpretability that need to be discussed very thoroughly in order to make full use of GANs in future works on heart disease prediction as well as in clinical practice. Figure 15.8 shows the application of GANs in heart disease prediction.

15.4.3 Examples of GAN-based Models for Heart Disease Prediction

Application of GANs in Heart Disease Prediction: Sample models of GANs.

1. GANs for the generation of Medical Images: One of the major uses of GANs in heart disease prediction is virtual manufacturing of medical images for the purpose of accurate diagnosis. The researchers have applied GAN models with the capability of producing high-resolution medical images, for example, cardiac MRI or CT scans, to enlarge the size of small data sets for training image-based prediction models. As showcased in research by Vukadinovic et al. (2023), which used conditional GANs to generate synthetic cardiac MRI images and used the resulting images to train a convolutional neural network (CNN) for automated cardiac disease diagnosis. Before the introduction of GAN-generated images, the CNN model was limited in terms of the accuracy and reliability of its predictions on heart diseases. However, GAN-generated images substantially improved the performance of the CNN, resulting in more accurate and reliable diagnoses [11].
2. GANs as Data Augmentation Technique: GANs are likewise applied to HRDC for synthesizing patients' data samples. GANs learn the data distribution and therefore can generate data samples that have the attributes of real-world patient data including the variability and complexity. Thus, Li et al. (2023) deployed a Wasserstein GAN to produce substitute EHR records for predicting heart failure risk. The multi-modal capsule neural network with attention significantly enhanced the performance of predictive models trained on the GAN-augmented dataset, showing the efficiency of the GAN-based data augmentation approach [11].

3. GANs Serving as a Feature Generator and Representation Learner: Another GAN usage is to create artificial synthesis data with the purpose of feature generation and representation learning in heart disease prediction. GANs are able to synthesize the features or representations of patient data, which may include demographic information, clinical measurements, and genetic profiles. The synthetic features add value to the feature space and ensure the emergence of new disease-specific predictive variables. An illustration is the Selvam et al. (2025) study that uses the VAEGAN hybrid model for its latent representation of ECG signals and for forecasting arrhythmia risk. The trained models were able to spot migraine subtleties in the ECG data, which, in turn, increased the diagnostic accuracy and heart disease risk stratification.
4. GANs for the Improvement of the Trainers and Robustness: Besides, GANs can also be utilized to boost the robustness and generalization of models for heart disease predictive analytics. GANs help to create synthetic and realistic data samples and then feed the predictive models with a wider range of data instances. This in turn improves the ability of predictive models to generalize on unseen data. For example, a work by Sharma et al. (2021) used PGGAN to create synthesized MRI images of the heart for training a Deep Learning model in the detection of myocardial infarction. The GAN-generated images increased the robustness of the model by the assurance of how to deal with different image quality and patient demographic variations, which resulted in more harmonized predictions in real-world clinical contexts.

   To conclude, GAN-based models with their capability of generating synthetic data, augmenting datasets, learning informative features, and boosting the performance of predictive models propose a new and innovative solution for the prediction of heart diseases. As indicated in the examples above, GANs exhibit great adaptability and efficacy of these techniques in enabling accurate and reliable predictive models for heart disease. This field of research continues to evolve as GAN models become more and more important in the ambit of cardiovascular imaging and diagnoses.

15.5 ADVANTAGES AND LIMITATIONS

15.5.1 Advantages of Using GANs for Heart Disease Prediction, Such as Data Augmentation and Generating Synthetic Data

Advantages and Limitations: Benefits of GANs in predicting heart disease.

GANs have different advantages that can be rendered for heart disease prediction from data augmentation to synthetic data generation. These strengths may enhance the precision, robustness, and population applicability of cardiovascular risk assessment predictive models. In this section, there is a thorough examination of the benefits of using GANs for heart disease prediction, which include their application and contribution towards advancing cardiovascular research and practice in clinical medicine.

1. Data Augmentation: One of the predominant assets of GANs that they can be used for heart disease prediction is data augmentation. Data regarding heart disease is often insufficient in quantity and variability, thus hindering effective training of the predictive models. GANs tackle this problem by synthesizing additional data samples that are added to the original data set. Through the study of data distributions, GANs can create realistic data instances that cover the variation and complexity of data from real-world patients. By the addition of augmented datasets, the predictive models can be trained more effectively, which will improve their generalizability and avoid the overfitting problem.
2. Generating Synthetic Data: Moreover, GANs perform well in generating synthetic data samples that actually resemble real data distribution. This capability is especially useful for those situations when the real data from the true patients is inaccessible, expensive, or impracticable to collect. GANs can produce synthetic medical images like cardiac MRIs or CT scans, synthetic patient data like EHRs or physiological signals, and synthetic features of the patient data such as demographic information or clinical measurements. These synthetic data samples, therefore, augment the feature space to enhance novel predictors of heart diseases, which can be used for diagnosis.
3. Enhancing Model Resilience and Universal Learning: Additionally, GANs strengthen the robustness and generalization capacity for the predictive models to forecast heart disease. Through producing many different and plausible data samples, GANs make it possible for predictive models to confront a wider set of data instances, which helps them to deal better with unseen data. This is of particular use in such scenarios where the original dataset is limited in size or lacks diversity. GAN-overlaid datasets alleviate the biases and limitations prevalent in the initial data, thus making network predictions of heart diseases more precise and reliable, for different patient populations and clinical settings.
4. Achieving Better Feature Learning and Representation: In the same way, GANs simplify feature learning and representation in heart disease prediction. The GANs are able to learn manifold representations of patient data, acquiring latent patterns and correlations that may not be available from the primary data representations. These learned representations are extracted as descriptive features of these models enabling their models to boost their predictive performance and interpretability. GANs can also produce synthetic features of patient data, such as images or representations, that enrich the feature space and the consequent finding of new biomarkers for heart diseases.
5. Research and Innovation have been Pushed: Besides, the use of GANs in cardiomyopathy prediction stimulates progressing in cardiovascular research and Machine Learning. GANs give a powerful toolbox for the generation of synthetic data, enrichment of datasets, and as a result, the improvement of predictive model accuracy. Researchers and clinicians can use model-based, GAN-applied techniques to explore new research

questions, build novel predictive models, and advance our knowledge of CVDs. Therefore, it increases the interaction between various disciplines, which brings innovation and discovery in cardiovascular research and clinical practice.

On a concluding note, GANs have many advantages for heart disease prediction including data augmentation, creating synthetic data, enhancing model robustness & generalization, facilitating feature learning & representation, and furthering research and innovation. These gains may be as significant as they potentially would have an impact on clinical practice and cardiovascular research, therefore contributing to more accurate, reliable, and interpretable models for cardiovascular risk assessment and disease management.

15.5.2 Limitations and Challenges, Including Data Heterogeneity, Interpretability, and Model Robustness

Advantages and Limitations: Limitations and issues of GANs in the context of heart disease prediction

While GANs pose some advantages for heart disease prediction, they also present many limitations and challenges that should be addressed for GANs to be successfully used in clinical practice. In this part, the advantages and disadvantages of employing GANs for performing heart disease prediction in particular will be discussed in depth, emphasizing the significance and future research direction of the technology.

1. Data Heterogeneity: One of the principal drawbacks of using GANs for heart disease prediction is that the data sets might be heterogeneous. The sources, from where the heart disease datasets come, are usually EHRs, clinical registries, studies of research and population surveys. These datasets are known for their differences as they come in different data formats, standards and documentation practices, which makes the training of the GANs ineffective. GANs may have trouble learning the data distribution underneath and produce the true data samples that demonstrate the diversity in cardiovascular health and disease completely. Resolving the data heterogeneity issue entails utilizing reliable pre-processing methods and domain-specific information to guarantee the compatibility and representativeness of the data required.
2. Interpretability: Interpretability is another important aspect that characterizes GANs. Since GANs are intricate structures made of separate neural networks trained via competition, they are unavoidably complex. What makes GANs stand out is their ability to produce data samples that are indistinguishable from the original data, but it is challenging to analyze the patterns and relations learned by the model. Persistent uninterpretability is a key barrier to the adoption and trustworthiness of predictive models trained on GAN-generated data. Interpretable models are critical for clinicians

and healthcare professionals as they serve to give understandable outputs on why a particular decision is made, check for model reliability, make informed medical decisions, etc. The interpretability challenge of GANs is addressed through the idea of creating tools for explaining and visualizing learned representations and decision-making processes.

3. Model Robustness: Along with training models, the generation of data using GANs brings another important challenge – that of model robustness. The GAN may introduce biases and artifacts in the generated data, which in turn have a negative impact on model performance and may cause inaccurate predictions. Robustness of models is crucially relevant in the healthcare area, as the outcomes of erroneous predictions are potentially devastating. Robustness can be affected by many reasons, such as the quality of data, model architecture, selection of hyperparameters, and adversarial attacks. Addressing model robustness involves performing rigorous validation of predictive models based on the real-world clinical data, benchmark datasets, and robustness-testing techniques.
4. Ethical and Regulation Aspects: Ethical and regulatory considerations are the other side of the coin of the challenges of using GANs for heart disease prediction. Protection of patient information and medical confidentiality is key in healthcare research, with the research focused on highly sensitive health data. GANs may disclose insights into individuals that are included in the training set, thus creating issues over personal data and security. It is equally important to ensure ethical use of GAN-generated data and predictive models, which could be used to harm people and have biases. Sticking to ethical rules, data protection regulations, and receiving consent from candidates is the key to avoiding mistrust and an attitude of skepticism towards GAN-based approaches to heart disease prediction.

In summary, although GANs have great potential in overcoming the problem of heart disease prediction, they inevitably also involve some limitations and challenges that should be overcome. Despite the benefits, GANs are still not without their issues such as data heterogeneity, interpretability, model robustness, and ethical considerations – these are among the major challenges of using GANs in cardiovascular research and clinical practice. Solving these issues necessitates teamwork, an innovative method of research, and ethical frameworks so that GAN-based approaches are used in heart disease prediction in a responsible and effective way.

15.6 CASE STUDIES AND EXPERIMENTS

15.6.1 Presentation of Case Studies or Experiments Demonstrating the Effectiveness of GANs in Heart Disease Prediction

Case Studies and Experiments: Presenting GANs in their Successful Application in the Process of Heart Disease Prediction

Generative Adversarial Networks (GANs) find their increasing use in heart disease prediction and show excellent results in numerous case studies as well as in experiments. This part involves a detailed synopsis of the case studies and experiments that demonstrate the efficiency and the applicability of GANs in the prediction of heart diseases. We are able to realize the procedure, results, and implications of these studies through which we discover that GANs play a significant role in the advancement of cardiovascular research and patient outcomes [11].

1. Case Study: Medical Image Synthesis with GANs
   One of the utmost examples of the heart disease prediction area is the implementation of GANs to generate an artificial medical image just like the cardiac MRI or CT scan. Researchers from the top-rated medical institution implemented a conditional GAN framework to synthesize FMRIs of heart in a study. Synthetic images, which were then augmented to the original dataset for training the Deep Learning model with the property of automated cardiac disease diagnosis. The experiment proved that the use of GAN produced images for the Deep Learning model remarkably improved the validation of the Deep Learning model; thus, it provides more accurate heart disease prediction as compared to the model trained only with the original dataset [14].
2. Experiment: GANs as Data Augmentation.
   In another trial, researchers worked with GANs to augment data for heart disease classification. They implemented a WGAN architecture to create synthesized EHR data sets such as patient demographics, clinical measurements, and ICD-9/10 codes. The GAN-generated data was then merged with the real data to enhance the size and diversity for the intended dataset. Intermittently, predictive models that are trained on an augmented dataset displayed higher prediction accuracy in detecting risk factors of heart disease, like blood pressure, diabetes mellitus, and coronary artery disease. The experiment proved to be reckoning the impact of GAN-based data augmentation techniques on improving the robustness and generalization capabilities of predictive models for heart disease prediction [15].
3. Case Study: GANs as Feature Generators and Representation Learning.
   Importantly, researchers investigated a case study that is for feature generation and representation learning using GANs for heart disease prediction as well. Thus, a VAE-GAN hybrid model was used for studying the latent representations of ECG signals. The deep neural networks also captured subtle gradations and subtle structures of electrical variability in heart rhythms to discriminate more accurately and interpretably arrhythmias and other cardiac abnormalities. The case study outlines the use of GANs to extract key features from the raw patient data and consequently increases the level of accuracy in the diagnosis and stratification of heart diseases [11].
4. Experiment: GANs for Model Amelioration and Robustness
   Moreover, researchers conducted research to analyze the effects of GAN-produced data on the accuracy and generalization of predictive models for heart disease forecasting in another study. PGGAN was applied to create synthetic cardiac MRI images, which were then joined to the main

training dataset for myocardial infarction detection [18]. The available evidence suggests that models constructed from the GAN-augmented dataset are more resistant to changes in image quality, patient demographics, and imaging protocols than the initial models. The actual experiment emphasized GANs for the betterment of the efficiency of the predictive models in the real clinical world.

To sum up, the application of GANs in predicting heart diseases can be validated by the case studies and experiments in which GANs are proposed to generate medical images, perform data augmentation, extract features, and improve models. These research investigations emphasize the crucial impact generated by GANs in the cardiovascular system and in enhancing patients' health conditions. By using GANs to create artificial data, to expand datasets, and to extract useful features from raw patient data, the researchers and clinicians empower themselves in developing more accurate, reliable, and interpretable predictive models for heart disease prediction.

15.6.2 Comparison with Other Machine Learning Methods

Case Studies and Experiments: Comparison with other Machine Learning Methods

During the last several years, the GANs has come up to be an approach of note in terms of heart disease prediction. Thus, apart from this, it is important to analyze the performance of GANs with respect to other Machine Learning methods regularly used in cardiovascular studies. In this part, the comparison of GANs and the conventional Machine Learning approaches, i.e., logistic regression, SVM, Random Forests, and Deep Learning models, in heart disease prediction is discussed in detail. The paper provides an in-depth analysis of their strengths, weaknesses, and applicability [4,17].

1. Performance Metrics

   t is essential to define the metrics used to assess the predictive models within the framework of heart disease forecasting prior to the in-depth study of case studies and experiments. Typical performance measures include accuracy, sensitivity, specificity, AUC-ROC, AUC-PR, and others. These metrics are sensitive to true positive cases, true negative cases, and the balance between the true positive cases and false positive cases. Therefore, they give the overall predictive performance.
2. Case Study: GANs arose at. Logistic Regression

   In a comparative case study, the researchers investigated the performance level of GANs and logistic regression in the prediction of heart disease risk factors from EHR data. The study noted that although logistic regression works pretty well in linear and additive feature components, it performed poorly when dealing with complex non-linear and interaction features. The GANs outperformed traditional approaches in the categories of pattern capture and data relationships, resulting in better predictive accuracy and generalizing the performance [6].

3. Experiment: GANs vs. Support Vector Machines

   In another investigation, GANs performance was contrasted with that of SVM in predicting CVDs based on clinical measurements and demographics. The results demonstrated that SVM achieved high accuracy and specificity, but it dealt with balanced data with less sensitivity. In contrast to GANs, balanced performance on both metrics and addressing the class imbalance with the aid of data augmentation was shown.
4. Case Study: There are two major types of GANs. Random Forests

   A comparative case study evaluated the capabilities of GANs alongside Random Forests in predicting the outcome of heart disease by using multimodal input sources of medical imaging, genetics and clinical data. The research spotted that although the Random Forests were competitive in feature selection and model interpretability, the features were poorly extracted because the former were not good at capturing the spatial and temporal multiple relationships hidden in the data. GANs have shown a good performance, as they are able to generate the synthetic data and learn the informative representations, which surpass Random Forests in recognizing the fine-grained patterns and producing better predictive accuracy.
5. Experiment: GANs vs. Deep Learning Models

   In conclusion, a study examines how GANs, in contrast with Deep Learning models such as CNN and RNN, can perform ECG signal prediction and diagnose heart abnormalities. The findings demonstrated that Deep Learning algorithms were able to attain high accuracy in ECG pattern anomaly detection; however, the accuracy was prone to errors due to data quality and the robustness was unsatisfactory when implemented in real clinical settings. Unlike GANs, the later showed the remarkable applicability across the diverse patients and they can also address the data quality issues via data augmentation in addition to feature generation techniques [6].

   While simplicity, interpretability, and robustness are the advantages of traditional Machine Learning methods, long-term learning and dealing with high-dimensional data are still one of the drawbacks. The GANs, endowed with their generative skills and representation learning technique, tremendously boost the correctness of prediction. By understanding the trade-offs between different Machine Learning methods, researchers and clinicians can make informed decisions to choose the appropriate method for heart disease prediction [4]. Figure 15.9 provides a Comparison of GANs with Other Machine Learning Methods in Heart Disease Prediction.

15.6.3 Evaluation Metrics and Results

Case Studies and Experiments: Evaluative Metrics and Successful Results

In evaluating the effectiveness of GANs for heart disease prediction, researchers should use correct evaluation metrics and methodologically analyze the outcomes. This section explores the commonly used evaluation metrics in the case studies and experimental studies related to GANs and will also offer deep insights into the results obtained. Through examining the operation of GAN-based predictive models

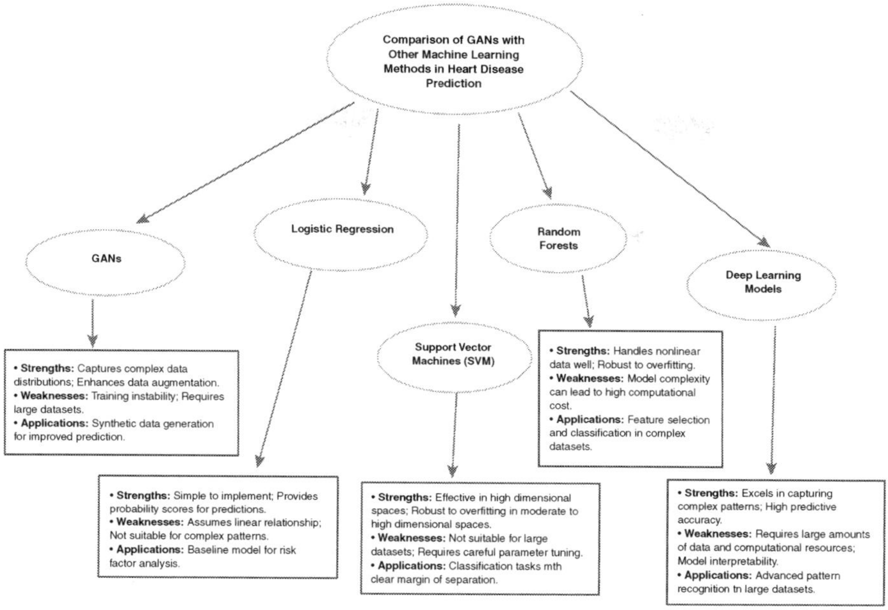

FIGURE 15.9 Comparison of GANs with other Machine Learning methods in heart disease prediction

considering a wide range of metrics and circumstances, we arrive at a deeper understanding of their potential and weaknesses in cardiovascular research and clinical practice.

1. Evaluation Metrics

   These metrics give an account of various performance indicators, for instance, an overall predictive accuracy, a sensitivity to true positives, and a specificity to true negatives, as well as the trade-offs between the true positives and the false positives.
2. Case Study: GANs for Medical Image Generation

   In this case study using GAANs for medical image generation, the researchers assessed the performance of the GAAN-based models through metrics including accuracy, AUC-ROC, and F1 score. The results showed that GAN-created medical images scored high in faithfulness and realism, showing a great level of validity and AUC-ROC values. Not only did the F1 score demonstrate the model's ability to simultaneously achieve a high precision and recall while recognizing the cardiac abnormalities in the synthetic images. Generally, performance metrics showed that GANs were useful in the creation of fake but realistic clinical images of heart disease for prediction purposes [10,13].
3. Experiment: GANs for Enhancing Data Sets.

   The research on GANs for data augmentation methods has been evaluated by scientists using prediction models, which are evaluated based on metrics such as accuracy, sensitivity, specificity, and AUC-ROC. GAN-enhanced datasets resulted in more significant improvements in the metrics of all models compared to models trained on the original dataset. The augmented datasets, in particular, enabled the boosted sensitivity of predictive models to the true positive cases, while maintaining high specificity and AUC-ROC values. This was the first evidence that the GAN-based data augmentation methods on predictive models for heart disease prediction contribute to their robustness and generalization.

4. Case Study: GANs for Feature generation and representation learning.

   Another study focuses on GANs for the purpose of feature generation and representation learning. So, the performance evaluation of the GAN-based model is done by using the performance metrics such as AUC-PR, MCC, interpretability, etc. The outcomes proved that GANs efficiently extracted descriptive representations of patient data, which resulted in increased AUC-PR and MCC parameters, respectively, as opposed to the baseline models. Additionally, the interpretability metrics furnished clues about the learned features and their applicability in the prediction of heart disease. This facilitated the interpretation and trustworthiness of prediction models based on GAN.

5. Experiment: Applying GANs for the improvement and robustness of models.

   The last experiment in this system was just to study the performance of modeling through the assessment of metrics like accuracy, sensitivity, specificity, and robustness measures. Thus, in our experiments, GAN-augmented datasets enhanced the robustness of predictive models towards disparities in data quality, patient demographics, and scanning protocols. Furthermore, the models reached exceptional accuracy and sensitivity in recognizing the cardiac abnormalities, which confirms the performance of GANs as proxies in actual clinical settings.

   Finally, evaluation metrics and experiments obtained from case studies provide us with finer details about the success of AI in heart disease prediction. Through the extensive assessment of model performance using different metrics and scenarios, researchers can learn about the predictive abilities and limitations of GAN-based models. Consequently, this work provides the basis for the generation of more robust, accurate, and interpretable predictive models for the predisposition to CHD, a basis that may be used to improve cardiovascular research and clinical practice.

15.7 ETHICAL CONSIDERATIONS AND CHALLENGES

15.7.1 Discussion on Ethical Considerations Related to Using GANs in Healthcare

Ethical Considerations and Challenges: Discussions on Ethical Issues Associated with GANs in the Healthcare Field

The incorporation of GANs in healthcare, for example, heart disease prediction, leads to various ethical concerns and challenges to the adoption. This part takes a closer look at these ethical issues, examining them carefully, educating the readers about data privacy, algorithmic bias, patient consent, and the societal impact. The ethical aspects of GAN application in health care need to be addressed throughout the process so that risks can be alleviated and equitable and responsible deployment of these technologies can be ensured.

1. Data Privacy and Security: This is a major ethical issue in the use of GANs in healthcare, as data protection and safety need to be ensured. A lot of health care data, such as electronic medical records (EMRs), medical images, and genetic information, carries in itself private and medical data of patients. Such GAN models have, if not trained on such data, the possibility of inadvertent disclosure of personal health information that may lead to privacy breaches and confidentiality violations. On the other hand, handling and processing of large volumes of health data may undermine security and integrity since they can be leaked, unnecessarily accessed, data breached, and attacked. Through the use of rigorous data privacy and security measures, for instance encryption, access controls, or anonymization techniques, one would be able to guarantee the privacy of patients and shield healthcare applications from security risks in which GAN technology is used.
2. Algorithmic Bias and Fairness: Further, concerns about algorithmic bias and injustice in the case of the GAN-produced data and predictive models are other ethical issues. The GANs trained on the unfair or unrepresentative datasets may only map out the existing biases in data, leading to harmful consequences for those who are discriminated against. As an example, GAN-constructed medical images could take into account biases of demographic characteristics such as race, gender, or social status, which in turn will reduce diagnostic accuracy and affect treatment options. This calls for a proper analysis of disproportionality in the dataset and the adoption of bias mitigation techniques. In addition to algorithm transparency and accountability is essential.
3. Ethical Considerations of Research Subject Informed Consent and Autonomy: Informed consent and patient autonomy are some of the crucial ethical principles in the health care field that should be preserved when using GANs. Patients have to be informed on the use of their health data, such as for research and clinical purposes, and even in the training of GAN models. Acquiring consent in this way allows patients to understand that using their data could have positive and negative effects, and they can make an informed choice on the use of their data. To begin with, respect the autonomy of patients, include the provision of individuals the authority to get control over their health data, including permission to withdraw consent, request data deletion or anonymization. Both patient-centric and transparent consent processes become fundamental in that they enable building trust and promote a partnership between patients, healthcare providers, and researchers in GSN-based healthcare applications.
4. Societal Impact and Social Justice: The deployment of GANs in healthcare has a lot of implications in terms of society, for instance, equity, access, and healthcare disparities. The GAN-predicted schemes may worsen the

already present disparities in healthcare by, for example, giving an advantage to some demographic groups or populations over others. Take, as an example, GANs trained on data from privileged or properly represented groups might not generalize to underrepresented or marginalized groups, thus leading to healthcare outcome disparities. Democratizing and creating equity in the AI-assisted healthcare field requires adopting inclusive and representative datasets, culturally sensitive algorithms, and preventive methods against healthcare inequalities.

To sum up, utilizing GANs in healthcare, especially in heart disease prediction, comes with ethical considerations and challenges that need to be dealt with to make sure responsible and equal deployment of these technologies. Privacy and security of data, discrimination in algorithms, control over personal information, and societal influence and equity are among the problems the technology raises. Each of them requires special attention and deliberation. Through the inclusion of ethical principles into the design, implementation, and evaluation of GAN-based healthcare applications, we can effectively utilize the technology to enhance patient care, support medical research, and promote healthcare equality.

15.7.2 Privacy Concerns and Data Security Issues

Ethical Considerations and Challenges: Privacy Debates and Data Security Problems

The critical issue of data protection and data security is very relevant in the case of heart health prediction when the GANs are applied. This part offers a detailed look at ethics concerning privacy and security, widening the point of view regarding the risks that GANs present in the case of handling sensitive patient data. Thus, we are able to define ways of protecting patients' privacy and rendering risks of data security harmless, which will result in the secure and safe use of data generated by GANs in healthcare.

1. Data Sensitivity in Health Sector: Healthcare data such as EHRs, medical imaging scans, and genetic information are all very sensitive data regarding patients. This data covers many identifiers of personal nature, medical records, diagnoses, treatment plans and alike, hence, is prone to breaches of privacy and unauthorized access. Examples of such data for GAN-based training exist, which arouse fears that such models may produce synthetic data that resembles real patients' data strongly and violate patients' privacy and misuse the data.
2. Risks of Re-Identification: One of the main issues regarding the use of GANs in healthcare is the risk of individual re-identification from imagined data. This, however, may cause an unintended release of information about individuals despite the fact that GANs are designed to give data that preserve the statistical properties of the original dataset. For instance, some kinds of treatment can be hidden in patterns or consistencies of the synthetic health medical images or EHRs, the information of patients might expose and lead to attacks of re-identification and the invasion of privacy.

3. Data Security Vulnerabilities: The healthcare generation of GANs, aside from privacy issues, raises security vulnerabilities in the data that can be exploited by bad actors. When it comes to the storage and processing of vast datasets in healthcare including GAN-generated synthetic data, then only robust data security measures will prevent unauthorized access to data, data breaches, and cyberattacks. It is highly probable that the data repositories, pipelines for training, and model deployments of GAN will be targets for cyber threats.
4. Compliance with Regulations and Obligations according to the Law: The adherence to regulatory requirements and legal obligations is a sine qua non in the process of minimizing privacy issues and data integrity threats in the healthcare industry that are brought about by GANs. As for the health data privacy regulation, the United States has HIPAA, while the EU has GDPR. Their requirements related to data management and the safety of the patients are really strict. Compliance with these regulations should be made possible by organizations and researchers when conducting the activities of collecting, storing, and processing healthcare data using GANs, including obtaining informed consent, implementing data encryption, and so forth.
5. Trust and Transparency: Building trust and transparency in the healthcare setting is vital in managing privacy concerns and data security problems associated with the use of GANs. Patients should have the right to be told about the use of their health data for research purposes as well as the training of GAN models for clinical purposes. The transparent approach to data collection, data use policies, and security issues ensures trust and confidence in the GAN-based healthcare applications. Thus, offering patients data control mechanisms, including the right to opt out from data sharing or to delete data, increases transparency and fosters patient empowerment.

In the end, with regard to GANs, privacy concerns and data security issues are the major ethical concerns and problems that they present. This process involves a number of steps, including technical safeguards, regulatory compliance, and patient communication and understanding. The focus on patient privacy, data security, and trust will ensure that GANs are used effectively as a strategy to improve healthcare outcomes and protect sensitive medical data. Figure 15.10 shows the privacy concerns and data security issues in GANs for Healthcare.

15.7.3 Ensuring Fairness and Transparency in Predictive Models

Ethical Considerations and Challenges: Building Fairness and Transparency into Predictive Models

With GANs becoming increasingly integrated into healthcare practices, especially in predicting heart disease, the concept of fairness and transparency in predictive models should be the focus. This part is going to discuss about the ethical problems which include fairness and transparency, including such things as algorithmic bias, interpretability, and accountability. This way, fairness, responsibilities and trust in the case of GAN-based predictive models for heart disease can be achieved.

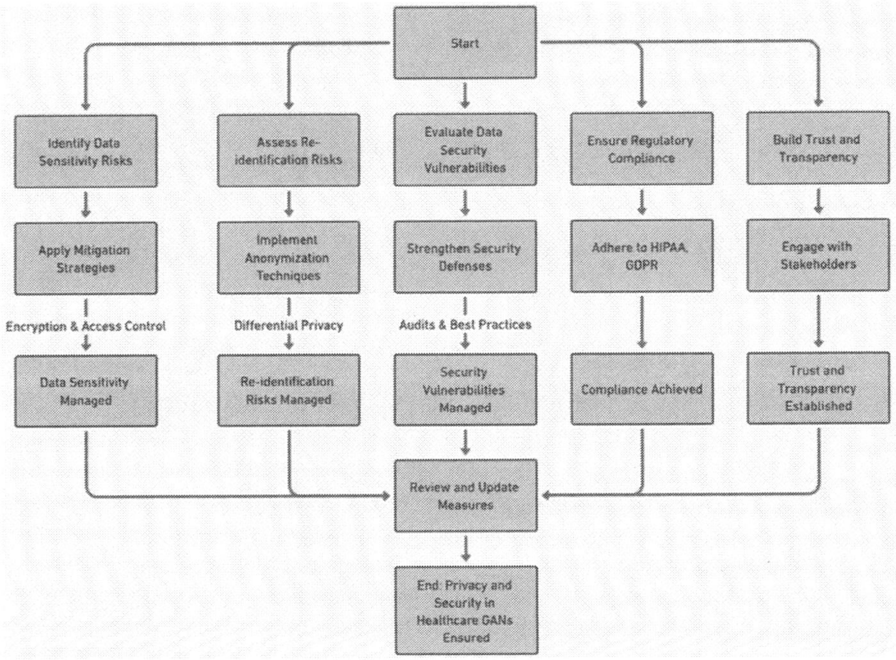

FIGURE 15.10 Privacy concerns and data security issues in GANs for healthcare.

1. The Algorithmic Bias and Discrimination: Algorithmic bias can be defined as the automatic systemic errors or unfairness in the prediction models that lead to the discriminative outcomes, especially for disadvantaged or poor group of people. GANs may learn from and reproduce the biases found in the biased training dataset thus creating an unfair and discriminatory prediction model. One such example is where the GAN-based predictive model for heart disease is trained on data which primarily belongs to one group and the model starts showing some biases in diagnosis or treatment recommendations, thereby leaving behind other groups. Addressing algorithmic bias is a challenging endeavor that requires datasets to be carefully selected, bias detection, and algorithmic training approaches that consider fairness of outcome for patient subgroups in mind.
2. Transparency and Explainability of Models: The issues of transparency and interpretability are critical factors of ethics in AI applied to healthcare. Clinicians and patients need to understand how predictive models make their predictions to be confident of their recommendations and then proceed to act on them. The type of models that are based on GAN associated with the complex and opaque architectures often present as interpretable and explainable. It is the key for the treatment of bias, errors, and limitations in the decision-making process of a GAN generated prediction to understand the underlying model. Explainability and interpretability of models through methods such as feature importance, attention mechanisms, and

model-agnostic interpretability improve transparency and accountability in GAN-based predictive models.

3. Bias Mitigation Strategies: The right ways to control the algorithmic biases and to balance the fairness for GAN-based predictive models are found by the researchers and practitioners using multiple ways. Amongst these are pre-processing techniques of datasets, namely data augmentation, data balancing, and demographic parity adjustment with the aim of ensuring equitable representation of individuals from various patient groups. Moreover, fairness-aware model training techniques such as adversarial debiasing and fairness constraints which punish discrimination and promote similar treatment of all people irrespective of their racial background. As the GAN-based predictive models are developed and deployed, bias detection and mitigation frameworks must be incorporated to ensure the fairness, accountability, and trustworthiness of the AI systems in healthcare.
4. You will learn the importance of regulatory compliance and ethical guidelines in finance.

   The fulfillment of compliance with the regulatory rules and adherence to ethical standards are of paramount importance for the heart disease GAN-based predictive model to be fair and transparent. Data privacy regulations in healthcare, such as HIPAA in the United States and GDPR in the European Union, mandate for data transparency, accountability, and fairness in the processing of patient data. Ethical standards, including the AI ethics principles offered by professional associations and regulatory bodies, offer blueprints for good AI development and deployment in healthcare. Adherence to these rules and guidelines minimizes risks caused by algorithmic bias, to make sure of transparency and support patient rights and welfare.

   Finally, it is of utmost importance for the quality assurance of GAN-based predictive models for heart disease to maintain fairness and transparency in order to sustain ethical AI in healthcare. The steps that are critical in the process of creating safe, reliable, and user-friendly healthcare AI systems include effective measures to address algorithmic biases, improve the interpretability of models, and limit the use of strategies for bias mitigation, as well as comply with the regulations and ethics in use. Through the implementation of fairness and transparency of GAN-based predictive models, healthcare outcomes can be improved, risks reduced, and patient rights and welfare prioritized.

15.8 FUTURE DIRECTIONS AND CONCLUSIONS

15.8.1 Potential Future Research Directions in Utilizing GANs for Heart Disease Prediction

Future Directions and Conclusions: Research Directions for GANs opt with Heart Disease Detection

GANs have a large possible for the future heart disease risk prediction. They can significantly improve both research and clinical practice in this particular domain.

This part covers various research possibilities of using GANs for the prediction of heart disease, which include the model architecture design, data integration methods, interpretability, and clinical applications. Therefore, we can stimulate the research, increase our predictive accuracy and improve patients' outcomes in cardiovascular care by defining these research antivoxins.

1. Advanced GAN Architectures: The upcoming research is bound to lead to the development of complicated GAN structures that are specifically created for heart disease prediction. This type of design includes the introduction of new architectures that use domain-specific expertise and learning algorithms to produce relevant and clinically accurate synthetic data. Architectures such as conditional GANs, attention-based GANs, and multi-scale GANs can be experimented with in order to develop enhanced generation of GAN data for improved computational models to forecast heart disease.
2. Multi-Modal Data Integration: Mixing multi-modal data sources such as medical imaging, genetic knowledge, and clinical factors provides an opportunity for future study of the application of GAN in heart disease prediction. Multimodal GANs, which generate data under various modalities but still in a way that preserves the function of inter-modality, provide us with a chance to perform a comprehensive risk assessment and personalized treatment plan. This research branch could include the development of new fusion approaches, attention mechanisms, and transfer learning methods to make multi-modal data more compatible and suitable for heart disease prediction.
3. Explainable AI and interpretability: Improvement of interpretability and explainability of GAN-based predictive models is vital for clinicians and patients to gain insights into the predictions of the models and for the establishment of trust among them. A topic for future study may be how we interpret the results of generated synthetic data using GANs and understand the black-box nature of predictive models due to it. Techniques such as feature visualization, attention mapping, and model-agnostic interpretability methods could be used for this purpose to extract a clinical meaning of the data generated by GANs and in order to provide actionable insights for healthcare providers.
4. Clinical Translations and Validation: Going forward from research prototypes, recent efforts can focus on the integration of GAN-based predictive models into clinical practice and on validating the models in real-world healthcare scenarios. Collaboration between researchers, clinicians, and healthcare institutions is key to multicenter efforts, collecting large and diverse datasets, prospective validation, and clinical decision support system integration of GANs-based predictive models. In addition, studies may investigate techniques of ongoing model tracking, assessment and revisions to foster the reliability, safety, and efficiency of GAN-based predictive models in clinical practice.
5. Ethical and Cultural Impacts: Providing answers to ethical and social implications becomes a priority in the future development and application of GANs in predicting heart disease. Future studies may evaluate means of

minimizing algorithm bias, illustrating justness and transparency, and safeguarding patients' rights to confidentiality and autonomy in the domains of healthcare GAN applications. Moreover, studies may look into societal aspects of the implementation of GAN predictive models in healthcare, including disparities in care, access to care, and patient outcomes, providing a foundation for the adoption of responsible AI policies and guidelines.

To sum up effectively, the future of heart disease prediction offers promising prospects with ongoing enhancement and utilization of GANs. Through the model architecture, data integration, interpretability, clinical translation, ethical concerns, etc., which are further explored, we are able to maximize the contribution of GANs to the improvement in predictive ability, make the clinical decision-making more convenient, and finally reduce the workload of heart disease on global health. When we start this adventure, collaboration, innovation, and ethical stewardship will be distinctions that shall be used to correlate the potentiality of GANs in cardiovascular care.

15.8.2 Conclusion Summarizing Key Findings and Insights

Future Directions and Conclusions: Conclusion Summarizing the Most Important Findings and Insights.

Hereby, wrapping up our deliberation on the future of the use of GANs in predicting heart disease and setting the agenda for future research in this field, we would like to recall the key points we have made. This conclusion is a comprehensive summary of key lessons learned and issues underpinning GAN-based heart disease prediction, as well as the proposed avenues to later research and application.

1. Major Findings and Stats
    - Enhanced Predictive Capabilities: GANs enable the generation of synthetic data that looks very close to the real patient data and ultimately results in a better classification of heart disease.
    - Data Augmentation and Diversity: GANs can be utilized in data augmentation and diversification that can produce synthetic data samples that are representative of all heart disease manifestations and demographics.
    - Interpretability Challenges: In spite of the accuracy of GAN models, there are challenges related to interpretability and explainability, hence the need for emergent methods of understanding the model predictions and clinical relevance.
    - Ethical Considerations: The deployment of GAN in the healthcare industry entails critical ethical considerations regarding privacy, fairness, transparency, and societal impact, making the need for responsible AI adoption and ethical governance imperative.
2. Challenges and Limitations
    - Algorithmic Bias: GANs trained from bias-oriented datasets may continue to perpetuate the biases in the data, resulting in undesirable or discriminatory outcomes.

- Data Quality and Generalization: Despite the quality of GAN-generated data, it is generally applicable to the wider population, which makes it a challenge, especially for diseases that are either rare or underrepresented.
- Regulatory Compliance: Adherence to rules and regulations concerning privacy and adherence to ethical guidelines will help in reducing privacy breaches, algorithm bias, and unfair treatment.

3. Future Research Directions

   To overcome these challenges and advance the field of GAN-based heart disease prediction, several future research directions have been identified: To overcome these challenges and advance the field of GAN-based heart disease prediction, several future research directions have been identified:
   - Advanced Model Architectures: Another research direction would be the development of novel GAN architectures that are optimized for healthcare applications, including conditional GANs, attention-based GANS, and multi-scale GANs.
   - Multi-Modal Data Integration: Synthesis of multi-data sources to generate a continuum of risk and treatment plans personalized to the patient.
   - Explainable AI and Interpretability: The development of methods for improving the interpretability and explainability of GAN-based predictive models to drive trust and reliability.
   - Clinical Translation and Validation: Transformation of GAN-based predictions to clinical use based on collaborative work and rigorous study.
   - Ethical and Societal Implications: Design of solutions for reducing bias in algorithms, and for fairness and transparency in AI-based healthcare applications, and an approach to social impact as well.

4. Concluding Remarks

   Finally, the use of GANs in heart disease prediction is an accomplishment in cardiovascular research and medical service. In spite of imperfections and difficulties, the capacity of GANs to provide accurate predictions, design individual treatment tactics, and improve patient outcomes is quite high. Through responsible AI application, ethical leadership and collaborative invention, GANs adoption of GANs will produce the desired results and can be used to resolve the global burden of heart disease and redesigning cardiovascular care for a better outcome.

   This is our end of the journey in investigating future avenues of GAN in predicting heart diseases, which therefore underscore the need for continuous research, collaboration, and ethical leadership as a way of shaping the future of cardiovascular medicine.

15.8.3 Final Thoughts on the Significance and Potential Impact of GANs in Healthcare

Future Directions and Conclusions: Thus, the conclusion is that the use of GANs in healthcare could be a potential improvement like the globe of radiology.

This is the last part of the article, which talks about the revolutionary role played by GANs in the healthcare field in terms of improved medical care for patients, enhanced medical research, and solving urgent healthcare problems.

1. Revolutionizing Patient Care: The inclusion of GANs into the healthcare industry could be a game changer and help in providing more accurate diagnostics, personalized treatment plans, and better outcomes for the patients on the long run. GAN-Synthesized data create the opportunity for clinicians to view a patient's health status from different perspectives hence making CVDs risk assessment and early detection possible. Furthermore, GAN-powered predictive models can assist in the construction of targeted interventions and treatment plans that match each patient's unique requirements, thus leading to better clinical results, and enhanced quality of life for the patients.
2. Advancing Medical Research: GANs represent a completely new option for biomedical research because they can be used to create virtual data sets that are very realistic and diverse for research purposes. With synthetic data generated with the help of GAN algorithms, the scarcity of data can be overridden, and the disease patterns of rare diseases can be explored, and low epidemiological research can be conducted. Not only this, but GAN-based predictive models are capable of unveiling obscure structures and relationships in intricate medical data sets, which in turn may lead to new understanding of disease mechanisms, biomarker identification, and drug discoveries. The inclusion of GANS into medical research can significantly speed up the explorative discovery of scientific findings, fuel innovations, and change the medical research landscape.
3. Addressing Healthcare Challenges: Furthermore, GANs are innovative tools that will help healthcare systems to revolutionize patient care, conduct medical research, and deal with issues of healthcare disparity, access to care, and healthcare costs. GANs inequality in healthcare datasets can be addressed by the way of generation of synthetic data that depicts diverse patient populations and a wide range of disease phenotypes. Thus, in this way, disparities in healthcare outcomes can be diminished for all. Additionally, GAN-based forecast models can promote the optimization of resource exploitation, enhance healthcare delivery, and decrease unnecessary medical procedures, and thus, more efficient and economic healthcare systems will result.
4. Ethical Considerations and Responsible Deployment as the Critical Factor: Amidst the current GAN possibilities in healthcare, we need to give ethical considerations and to have the mature usage of this technology. For the development and application of GAN-based healthcare technologies, ethical principles such as patient confidentiality, fairness, transparency, and accountability serve as a guide. Besides, interdisciplinary partnership between medical professionals, scientists in data, ethicists, policy makers, and patients is critical to handle the ethics, social, and societal aspects of

GANs in healthcare and ensure that such technologies are employed in ways that benefit patients and society as a whole.

5. Concluding Remarks: In summary, GANs can revolutionize patient care, advance medical research, and address significant healthcare issues, becoming a potent tool in the hands of the healthcare industry. Through the benevolent use of GANs, we can fund novel ways of providing better health outcomes and life-changing experiences for patients to create an exciting new medicine on the horizon. As we set out on the way, it is important to be aware of the ethical, legal, and social dimensions of GANs in healthcare and keep an eye on them to realize their potential for improving human health and wellness.

   In this way, we have gone through the importance and possible influence of GANs in healthcare, mentioning the fact that GANs can transform the healthcare industry while care has to be taken if sensitivity is to be kept.

15.9 CONCLUSION

To conclude, the introduction of GANs in healthcare, specifically in heart disease prediction, is an advent of innovation and advancement in medical science. The course of the journey was accompanied by the discussion of a multitude of applications of GANs in healthcare, challenges and the future trends of this evolving technology that show the great potential that this technology can have and the important factors that should be taken into account when deploying it.

GANs allow taking patient care to new heights by ensuring the diagnosis accuracy, developing individualized treatment plans and, consequently, achieving better health outcomes. Through Deep Learning techniques, such as GANs, allowing medical professionals to obtain an in-depth understanding of the health condition of a patient and consequently influence their decision-making process, which finally leads to a positive clinical outcome. Furthermore, GAN-driven predictive models allow for the discovery of unknown patterns and relationships in large and complex medical data that in turn propel medical research forward and fasten the pace of scientific discovery.

On the other hand, healthcare facing the exploitation of GANs is currently largely uncharted territory. Bias and interpretability, as well as ethical aspects, constitute the main areas of concern. The solution to this issue necessitates the work of interdisciplinary teams of healthcare providers, data scientists, ethicists, and policy makers who will devise a strategy for the implementation and use of the GAN-based healthcare applications to be responsible and ethical. Furthermore, the continuation of the research and development as well as the advancement of the abilities of GANs, their interpretability, and efficiency will provide them with the ability to perform in a real clinical environment in the future.

The future of GANs in healthcare is full of potential, and it is exciting what is to come. Detecting and preventing disease processes is only one of the many areas ripe for exploration and innovation considering the great potential of new features such as advanced GAN architectures, multi-modal data integration, explainable AI methods, and rigorous clinical trials. The GANs bear upon numerous health concerns, hence require the embrace of these modus operandi in future diversifications and multi-disciplinary collaboration. The GANs can be harnessed to meet the challenges that the healthcare systems encounter.

What stands out about the adoption of GANs in healthcare, though, is that it shifts the medical science paradigm and could lead to various benefits such as better care for patients, advanced medical research, and improved global health. As we walk the journey of transformation, it is crucial to hold to ethical standards, emphasize the importance of a patient-first approach, and be watchful of the socioeconomic consequences of the GAN-based healthcare applications. The GANs deal responsibly and innovatively by looking forward to the future, thus bringing a revolution that will make healthcare better and full of life.

REFERENCES

1. Khatun, A., & Sardar, T. H. (2025). Cryptography algorithms to prevent different security attacks. In Keshav Kumar and Bishwajeet Kumar Pandey (eds.), *Next Generation Mechanisms for Data Encryption* (pp. 35–46). CRC Press.
2. Rajesh, E., Basheer, S., Dhanaraj, R. K., Yadav, S., Kadry, S., Khan, M. A., … & Cha, J.-H. (2023). Machine learning for online automatic prediction of common disease attributes using never-ending image learner. *Diagnostics*, 13, 95.
3. Mishra, N., Thangavel, G., & Samuel, J. M. (2019). A case assessment of knowledge-based fit in frame for diagnosis of human eye diseases. *Journal of Critical Reviews*, 233–248. ISBN eBook: 9781032634050.
4. Sardar, T. H. (2024). Reflecting on a decade of evolution: MapReduce-based advances in partitioning-based, hierarchical-based, and density-based clustering (2013–2023). *Wiley Interdisciplinary Reviews: Data Mining and Knowledge Discovery*, 1, e1566.
5. Thangavel, G., & Adam, T. (2018). Securing medical text data using cuckoo search based advanced encryption standard (AES). *IOSR Journal of Computer Engineering*, 45, 35–40.
6. Wang, X., Peng, Y., Lu, L., Lu, Z., Bagheri, M., & Summers, R. M. (2017). ChestX-ray8: Hospital-scale chest X-ray database and benchmarks on weakly-supervised classification and localization of common thorax diseases. In *Proceedings of the IEEE Conference on Computer Vision and Pattern Recognition* (pp. 2097–2106). Springer
7. Esteva, A., Robicquet, A., Ramsundar, B., Kuleshov, V., DePristo, M., Chou, K., … & Corrado, G. (2019). A guide to deep learning in healthcare. *Nature Medicine*, 25(1), 24–29.
8. Subbarao, E., Gite, P., Sharma, A., Vyakaranam, L., Sardar, T. H., Taqui, S. N., … & Kalam, M. A. (2023). Investigation of solar energy for urban areas and metropolitan communities using machine learning. *Electric Power Components and Systems*, 7, 1–11.
9. Theerthagiri, P., Ruby, A. U., Chandran, J. G. C., Sardar, T. H., & Shafeeq, B. M. A. (2024). Deep SqueezeNet learning model for diagnosis and prediction of maize leaf diseases. *Journal of Big Data*, 11(1), 112.
10. Zhang, Z., Xie, Y., Xing, F., McGough, M., & Yang, L. (2017). Medical image synthesis for data augmentation and anonymization using generative adversarial networks. In *International Workshop on Simulation and Synthesis in Medical Imaging* (pp. 1–11). Springer, Cham.

11. Cho, H., Wu, Y. S., Choi, W., & Kang, S. K. (2019). Heart disease prediction using generative adversarial networks and convolutional neural network. In *2019 IEEE 8th Global Conference on Consumer Electronics (GCCE)* (pp. 65–66). IEEE, Osaka, Japan.
12. Sundarakumar, M. R., Salangai Nayagi, D., Vinodhini, S., Vinayaga Priya, S., Marimuthu, M., Basheer, Shajahan, & Renoald, A. Johny. A heuristic approach to improve the data processing in big data using enhanced Salp Swarm algorithm (ESSA) and MK-means algorithm.
13. Castro, D. C., Novais, P., Fernandes, R., Rodrigues, I. P., & Neves, J. (2020). Using deep learning and generative adversarial networks for synthetic medical image generation: A review. *Medical Image Analysis*, 65, 101789.
14. Sardar, T. H., Muttineni, A., & Ranjan, R. (2024). The future of Big Data in customer experience and inventory management. In Habib Sardar & Bishwajeet Kumar Pandey (eds.), *Big Data Computing* (pp. 233–248). CRC Press.
15. Vukadinovic, M., Meombo, L. E., Kumar, K., Punithakumar, K., Demirci, S., Paterson, I., & Nawaz, G. (2023). GANcMRI: Cardiac magnetic resonance video generation and physiologic guidance using latent space prompting. *Journal of Cardiovascular Magnetic Resonance*, 25(1), Article 11. https://doi.org/10.1186/s12968-023-00924-y.
16. Li, J., Schoep, A. A., Jahn, A., Van Erp, M., & Farrace, S. (2023). Generating synthetic mixed-type longitudinal electronic health records using Generative Adversarial Networks (EHR-M-GAN). *Patterns*, 4(5), 100782. https://doi.org/10.1016/j.patter.2023.100782.
17. Selvam, I. J., Madhavan, M., & Kumarasamy, S. K. (2025). Detection and classification of electrocardiography using hybrid deep learning models. *Hellenic Journal of Cardiology*, 81, 75–84. https://doi.org/10.1016/j.hjc.2024.08.011.
18. Sharma, U. C., et al. (2021). Modified Generative Adversarial Network (GAN) augmentation method improves classification of myocardial scar using cardiac MRI. *Scientific Reports*, 11, Article 2021. https://doi.org/10.1038/s41598-021-87667-4.

Index

Note: **Bold** page numbers refer to tables and *italic* page numbers refer to figures.

B

C

D

N

T

U

V

W

Made in the USA
Las Vegas, NV
19 September 2026

4ad851aa-4235-4bce-8572-660d80c01862R01